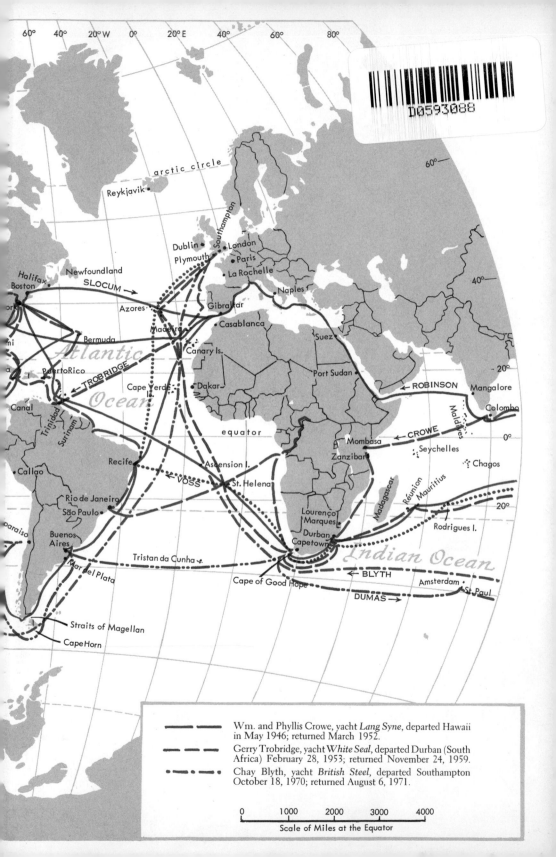

60° **40°** **20°W** **0°** **20°E** **40°** **60°** **80°**

arctic circle

Reykjavik

60°

Dublin • Southampton
Plymouth • London
• Paris
La Rochelle

40°

Halifax
Boston
Newfoundland
SLOCUM →
Naples

Azores •
Gibraltar
Madeira
Casablanca
Suez

Bermuda
Canary Is.

Atlantic
Puerto Rico
TROBRIDGE
Cape Verde
Dakar •
Port Sudan
ROBINSON →
Mangalore

20°

Canal
Trinidad
Surinam
Ocean
equator
Colombo
Maldives
CROWE ←
0°

Callao
Recife
Ascension I.
VOSS ←
St. Helena
Mombasa
Zanzibar
Seychelles
Chagos

Rio de Janeiro
São Paulo •
Réunion
Mauritius
20°

araiso
Buenos
Aires
Tristan da Cunha ↙
Lourenço
Marques
Durban
Capetown
Madagascar
Rodrigues I.

Indian Ocean

Mar del Plata
Cape of Good Hope
← BLYTH
Amsterdam
St. Paul
DUMAS →

Straits of Magellan
Cape Horn

0   1000   2000   3000   4000
Scale of Miles at the Equator

Wm. and Phyllis Crowe, yacht *Lang Syne*, departed Hawaii in May 1946; returned March 1952.

Gerry Trobridge, yacht *White Seal*, departed Durban (South Africa) February 28, 1953; returned November 24, 1959.

Chay Blyth, yacht *British Steel*, departed Southampton October 18, 1970; returned August 6, 1971.

D0593088

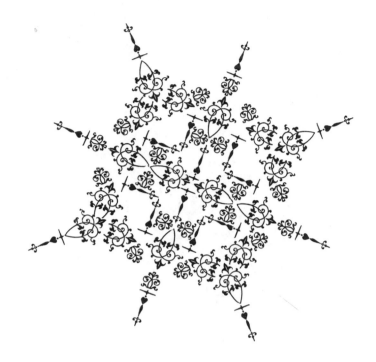

THE CIR

Small Boat Voyagers of Modern Times

PRENTICE-HALL, INC.

CIRCUMNAVIGATORS

BY DONALD HOLM

Englewood Cliffs, New Jersey

The Circumnavigators: Small Boat Voyagers of Modern Times
by Donald Holm

Copyright © 1974 by Donald R. Holm

Printed in the United States of America

Prentice-Hall International, Inc., London
Prentice-Hall of Australia, Pty. Ltd., Sydney
Prentice-Hall of Canada, Ltd., Toronto
Prentice-Hall of India Private Ltd., New Delhi
Prentice-Hall of Japan, Inc., Tokyo

10 9 8 7 6 5 4 3 2 1

Library of Congress Cataloging in Publication Data
Holm, Don.
The circumnavigators.
Bibliography: p.
1. Voyages around the world. 2. Sailing.
I. Title.
G440.A2H64   910'.453   74–13607
ISBN 0–13–134452–8

Design by Janet Anderson

About Sources

A book such as this is not put together by one person, in spite of the byline. In this case, the persons involved and the sources of information were scattered around the world—and in some instances, were on the high seas, days and even weeks from the nearest communications.

Tracking down individuals under the circumstances, at times became a frustrating chore, involving hundreds of letters to all parts of the globe to check facts or obtain additional information; many letters required the inclusion of International Reply Coupons for encouragement. Since these are negotiable in many exotic hideaways, and since smallboat voyagers as a rule dislike writing letters when wine is cheap and companionship warm, some of the replies no doubt got lost between the anchorage and the local *poste marque* office. If this is the case, they have my heartiest good wishes and no hard feelings.

But the replies that did come in, and the enthusiastic and spontaneous co-operation encountered among real bluewater sailors, was astonishing, and I am deeply indebted to all these individuals and organizations. Among these, I would especially like to thank:

Neal T. Walker, secretary of The Slocum Society, Hilo, Hawaii, which is a gold mine of unpublished information in a most idyllic place for research, and which Neal put completely at my disposal. Similarly of great help was The Slocum Society Sailing Club, of which Jean-Charles Taupin is commodore.

Thanks go, in addition, to Marjorie Petersen of *Stornoway*, somewhere in the Mediterranean; Dr. Hamish Campbell at Durban, South Africa; Miles Smeeton, Cockrane, Alberta; Dr. Robert Griffith of *Awahnee*; Tim Campbell of Gray's Publishing Ltd., Sidney, B.C.; Eleanor Borden, Spindrift Point, Sausalito, California; Kenneth E. Slack, Toongabbie, N.S.W., Australia; Warwick M. Tomkins, Sausalito, California; the late L. Francis Herreshoff, Marblehead, Massachusetts; Howard I. Chapelle, Smithsonian Institution; Thomas E. Colvin, Miles Post Office, Virginia; Steve Doherty, Seven Seas Press; Peter H. Comstock, secretary, The Cruising Club of America; William A. Robinson, Papeete, Tahiti; Louis and Annie Van de Wiele, Château de Madaillan, France; Commander Erroll Bruce RN (Ret.); Eric Hiscock aboard *Wanderer IV* somewhere in New Zealand; John Guzzwell on *Treasure* at Honolulu; Ray Kauffman of *Hurricane* fame; Dwight Long of *Idle Hour*, and his brother, Philip; and Richard Zantzinger, Jr. of the *Molly Brown*; and Marcel Bardiaux, Algarve, Portugal.

Without the enthusiasm and leadership of Dennis Fawcett of Prentice-Hall, this book certainly would not have been created; and without the meticulous and conscientious copy editing by Barbara Palumbo, I doubt if I could have coped with the high standards of production at Prentice-Hall. After twenty-five years of professional writing, I was astonished at how much I had to learn.

Thanks also go to Charles E. Mason III of *Sail* magazine; James E. Liston of

Popular Mechanics magazine; Maury Gwynne, editor of *The Victorian*, Victoria, British Columbia; Albert F. Smith, Jr., Allied Boat Company, Inc.; H. B. Fowler, Ocean Cruising Club, Burnham-On-Crouch, Essex, England; Vern Griffin, San Diego *Union-Tribune*; Miles Ottenheimer, *American Boating*; David Pardon, *Sea Spray* magazine, Auckland, New Zealand; John G. de Graff, Tuckahoe, New York; Frank Bowers, Editor-in-Chief, Fawcett Publications, special interest books and magazines; Peter R. Smyth, *Motor Boating & Sailing* magazine; David R. Getchell, *The National Fisherman*; artist E. Bruce Dauner, Lake Oswego, Oregon; the John G. Alden Co., Greenwich, Connecticut; Robert Hitchman, Seattle, Washington.

I would also like to acknowledge such invaluable sources as *Rudder* magazine, *Boating* magazine, *Yachting* magazine, all in New York; *Pacific Yachting*, Vancouver, British Columbia; *Financial Times, London Daily Express*, the *Sunday Times, London Daily Telegraph, Manchester Guardian, Yachts & Yachting, Sunday Mirror, English Yachting Monthly, Daily Observer, Sunday Express, Yachting & Boating*, all in England; *South African Yachting*, Cape Town; *Neptune Nautique, Neptune Nautisme, Voiles et Voiliers, L'Aurore, Le Yacht*, Paris *Match* in France; *Nichi Bei Times*, San Francisco; *Examiner-Express*, Tasmania; *Seacraft Magazine*, Australia; Honolulu *Star-Bulletin & Advertiser*; Hawaii *Tribune-Herald*; *Cork Examiner*, Ireland; *Los Angeles Times*; *Washington Post*; *The New York Times*; Vancouver, B.C. *Sun*; *Miami Herald*; *Chicago Daily News*; *The Oregonian*, Portland; *Seattle Times*; Seattle *Post-Intelligencer*; the *Cruising Club News*; *National Geographic* magazine; *Nor'Westing* magazine, Edmonds, Washington; San Francisco *Chronicle*; Chicago *Tribune*; Minneapolis *Tribune*; *Sea* magazine; *Die Yacht*; *Oceans*; and *Sea Frontiers*.

Special thanks also go to the following publishers for permissions:

Rutgers University Press; Westover Publishing Company; W. W. Norton & Company, Inc.; Oxford University Press; William Morrow & Co., Inc.; E. P. Dutton & Co., Inc.; Harper & Row, Publishers, Inc.; Macmillan Publishing Co., Inc.; Rupert Hart-Davis; Harcourt Brace Jovanovich; William Heinemann, Ltd.; Edward Arnold & Co.; Adlard Coles, Ltd.; Van Nostrand (Litton Educational Publications); Flammarion, Paris; Stein and Day; David McKay Co., Inc., Coward McCann, Inc.; Nautical Publishing Co., Ltd.; William Morrow & Co.; Samson Marine Designs Enterprises; Victor Gollancz, Ltd., Grenada Publishing Ltd.; A. M. Heath & Co.; and the clip files of the old *Seattle Star* newspaper.

Finally, I should also credit my bride, Myrtle, for channeling my time and energies into the path of voluntary servitude, to get the job done, even when the midsummer temperatures soared to 100° F., and our 42-foot sloop *Wild Rose* rocked invitingly at her moorage.

Introduction

Within a few miles of my home in suburban Portland, Oregon, there are perhaps two dozen small ships—all sailing vessels of thirty to forty feet in length—in various stages of construction, with the ultimate purpose of carrying their owners and builders on world voyages.

The shipyards are old barns, backyards, temporary sheds of wood framing and plastic sheeting. Even at the small moorage on Multnomah Channel where I keep my sloop, there are four such vessels being built in a corner of the parking lot, and there is a waiting list for the space.

I am sure that similar activity can be found at every seaport of every maritime country in the Free World where the political, social, and economic status is sophisticated enough to stimulate the natural human urge to escape to a more simple life, or to indulge one's curiosity and restlessness by travel to faraway places.

And for every ship abuilding there are perhaps a thousand or more secret dreamers (many of whom live hundreds of miles from the nearest salt water) who spend their leisure hours marking ads in the classified sections of metropolitan newspapers and boating periodicals, or prowling the marinas, yacht clubs, and small boat harbors searching for a ship in which to make their escape at a price within their dreams.

Most of them, of course, will never get beyond the ad-marking stage; or if they do, most of their ardor will have been dissipated by the actual physical activity and the reality of inquiry. There is nothing new or unusual about this. Civilized man has endeavored to escape to sea at least since the time of the Minoans, circa 1500 b.c. Daydreams like this are what help many over the small daily crises, the frustrations of the job, and that state of mental rebellion that Henry David Thoreau was trying to define when he wrote that most men lead lives of quiet desperation.

Some of these owners, builders, and searchers have announced their intentions in advance, and are already savoring the heady stimulation of publicity and small notoriety which they hope to earn later.

Others hold it as a secret ambition and will not talk about it, or if they do, they are vague about future ports of call and even departure dates. A few are building only what they refer to as "retirement boats," for which they have no conscious plans other than living aboard when the ship is finished and launched. These are the cagey ones. They not only have the dream, but they have the means, the time, and the personal discipline it takes to accomplish it. One has a feeling that they are waiting to see what the situation looks like when they are ready for sea, and chances are pretty good that one will learn at some future date that they are on their way around the world after all.

Among these dreamers is a bachelor and college professor who is completing his 32-foot Atkins ketch at precisely the same rate as his academic career draws to a close. When his boat is finished and his retirement checks are coming in regularly, he plans to sail the one hundred miles down the Willamette River of Oregon to the Columbia, and then down the ninety miles or so to the Pacific Ocean.

"When I get there," he told me, "*then* I will decide whether to turn right or left."

Like many other unfortunates, I am incited by and envious of all these dreams and ships abuilding, for I lost my chance years ago. I, too, once planned a solo circumnavigation, only to become one of the thousands who were thwarted by fate and circumstances. Born and raised on the bleak prairies of North Dakota, in almost the exact center of the North American continent and as far as you can get from any ocean, the sea fascinated me since my earliest remembrance. Perhaps it was some latent manifestation of my Viking ancestry; more likely it was merely the result of my early reading of Robert Louis Stevenson or Herman Melville or John Masefield. I had never even set eyes on an ocean until I was nineteen years old.

But my first conscious urge to build my own ship and travel to faraway places (although I had built rowboats and canoes when I was not more than ten years old for use on the local Mouse River) was fired by John Hanna's wonderful little *Tahiti* ketch, hundreds of which have been built by dreamers like me, and dozens of which have made long voyages, even around the world. Created on his drawing board as *Orca* at Dunedin, Florida, in about 1923, this famous 30-foot double-ender was released to an eager audience through a series of articles in the old *Modern Mechanix* that were subsequently collected for reprint in the 1935 edition of *How To Build 20 Boats*.

Today, almost forty years later, I still get the same thrill and feel the same yearnings as I did when I first devoured Hanna's own explanation:

> *The Tahiti design has been built, tested, put up against real deep water and dirty weather, and proved good. Not one boat, but five of them. Not by one man, but by many skilled sailors and competent judges. Not in just one place of favorable conditions, but in the Atlantic, Gulf, Chesapeake Bay, the Great Lakes, and the North Sea, off England's coast. Not in one pleasant summer, but in all weather as it comes for six years. I put the first one through her paces myself, sometimes with one man, sometimes handling her alone. Everything the owners of others have reported to me has simply confirmed my own observations, or gone farther.*
>
> *She is dry; that means she stays on top of the waves, and does not tend to stick her nose under them. She is easy in her motion; she is remarkably easy to handle, and obedient to her helm; the rig, known as the ketch rig, is extraordinarily well balanced, not only under full sail, which all boats are, but under any combination of sails, which few boats are; and she has that much-desired but seldom-attained merit of a good cruiser, the ability to sail herself and hold her course for hours with the tiller lashed.*
>
> *She has laughed at the worst storm she has ever met—wind estimated at 75 to 90 miles an hour by the Boston papers.*
>
> *In short, whatever it takes to get to Tahiti and back, this ship has.*

What daydreamer, be he a young kid on a Midwest farm, or a middle-aged Walter Mitty on New York's Madison Avenue, could resist that kind of romance!

Moreover, this was one enthusiastic project that withstood a half century of actual experience, and there are probably more people building *Tahiti* types today than ever before—proving the wisdom and soundness of the late John Hanna's siren call. (Incidentally, I still have the original articles and plans for *Tahiti*, almost disintegrated by time and handling.)

I was only sixteen and chafing under the social and economic restraints of a small town in mid-America when exposed to the *Modern Mechanix* articles. I spent hours reading and rereading them, and teaching myself how to understand blueprints, to loft lines, and to set up molds. This was during the Depression and the Great Drought of the mid-1930s—before the dogs of World War II had been unleashed. Though life was a great deal less complex and the future less uncertain than now, this seemed to have no bearing on the ageless urge to escape to sea.

As Melville had written almost a century before, "I thought I would sail about a little and see the watery part of the world. It is a way I have of driving off the spleen and regulating the circulation."

Leaving home immediately after graduation from high school, I spent several years roaming about, finding work where I could. At last, in 1939, I was established in Juneau, Alaska, with a steady job and a small savings account. My magic carpet was getting closer to reality.

By this time, another wonderful thing had happened: A boat-building firm in Michigan, Bay City Boats, was manufacturing prefabricated kits for a line of boats that could easily be assembled at one-third the cost by diligent amateurs. Among the models in Bay City's line were a 45-foot schooner, Hanna's *Gulfweed* and *Carol—* and right after the war, L. Francis Herreshoff's famed *Marco Polo— and the Tahiti* ketch!

For about $600, you could purchase the complete frame for *Tahiti*, all ready to set up and bolt together. For another $250, you could purchase the planking, cut, drilled, and ready to bend on. Other kits for the engine, tankage, rigging, and sails were available at equally reasonable prices, even for 1939.

At last, I had the means and the facilities to make the dream come true, and off went my order for the frame kit. Meanwhile, I found space in town for a temporary shipyard. But like the dreams of thousands of others of military age, my plans were thwarted by the outbreak of war in Europe and subsequently Pearl Harbor. Wartime restrictions and long years of military service (ironically often served in those very same exotic South Pacific areas that had once fired their imaginations) killed the dream for most. The luckier ones, like Dwight Long of Seattle, who departed in his *Idle Hour* just in time to avoid the opening of hostilities, got their dreams fulfilled before it was too late. For others, the passage of too many years and the subsequent readjustment to peacetime and a cold war had caused the magic moment to be lost forever. For them, things were never quite the same, and never would be again.

But for many, the dream did continue, and each upcoming generation had its usual quota of dreamers. In the mid-1950s and again in the late 1960s, there was a boom in the number of small boats setting out on world cruises. The trend today toward bluewater voyaging is even greater. In fact, the present-day boom in sailing and boat building is unprecedented. If it continues, future escapists may find the ocean lanes of the world regulated by traffic signals. Today there are literally thousands of yachts en route to exotic places, while there were hundreds in the 1950s and 1960s. The urge to go has even taken on a sort of frantic overtone, fed by the affluence of this decade and the availability of improved designs and new maintenance-free materials such as fiber glass, aluminum, and even ferro-cement.

Perhaps some of this frantic feeling today is due to the underlying insecurity of the times, the realization that the world is not only becoming overcrowded and polluted as it shrinks, but that the old personal freedoms and individual enterprises are being eroded by the emergence of monolithic political systems, of totalitarian communist aggressions that, once imposed, are never again thrown off, and of new welfare states that sap the initiative and dull the imagination.

The oceans of the world are now all that remain for those who seek personal freedom and challenge. The quiet desperation of many who still cherish individualism has become a crushing anxiety to embark before it is too late.

As for myself, I have learned to indulge my inner yearnings with coastwise cruising, sailing among the islands of the north, and in offshore fishing trips to Alaskan and Mexican waters. Time spent in the Navy during the war and on commercial fishing boats in the North Pacific has helped compensate for the feeling that something has been missed. The writing of books and articles and a daily column in a metropolitan newspaper on related subjects has been an effective outlet for repressed impulses. And, as a frustrated world voyager, over the years I have been an avid follower of the sea adventures of others, getting a vicarious pleasure this way. As a hobby, I have studied and analyzed the voyages of nearly a hundred circumnavigators—those who succeeded and those who failed and those who were never heard from again.

This book is my attempt to pull together the best and most representative of these voyagers, and to try and define for my own personal satisfaction and curiosity, if nothing else, many of the underlying reasons that motivate a man to leave the comforts of an established society and bounce around the world at an average rate of five miles an hour in cramped, damp, and often extremely uncomfortable quarters.

Who are these people? What are they really seeking? What motivates them to undertake the risks involved in crossing vast oceans in tiny ships, frequently alone, always dependent upon the prevailing winds and currents, subject to all the raw hazards of the open sea, the possibility of accident and sickness, fearful uncertainties of the unknown, and the inevitable and exasperating red tape of many petty customs and port officials in foreign lands? Certainly, there is nothing easy or simple about a bluewater voyage.

Are these people seeking adventure? Romance? Escape? Or are they really searching for meaning in their lives? Do they desire fame and fortune? Or is it just an impulse for achievement against overwhelming odds?

Are they anachronisms in a world that no longer has use for explorers and pioneers? Are they bums, dropouts, copouts, or just plain nuts? Do they have something that you and I do not, besides money? Or, as one psychologist opined, are they just people with suicidal compulsions, their voyages being spectacular manifestations of it?

Of enduring interest to all erstwhile voyagers, of course, be they daydreamers or actual doers, are the technical details of these voyages. How did they do it? How did they get the money and the years of time it takes to go on a world voyage? What kind of boats did they find most seaworthy and comfortable? How did they cope with heavy weather? How about medical supplies, stores, fuel, water, food, spare parts? How did they cope with port and customs authorities? What about landfalls and uncharted reefs, or celestial navigation? How did they manage on passages of a month or more without sight of land or another ship? And when they did make a landfall, which natives were friendly, and which were not?

Thwarted dreamers or serious planners all eagerly lap up such fascinating bits of business, for this is the stuff of which dream ships are derived, even if vicariously.

Here then are the most notable men and women who have circumnavigated the world, and especially those who have solo navigated. World voyagers are the elite of modern travelers, and circumnavigators in small ships are the nobility of the elite.

The solo circumnavigation is the epitome of all personal odysseys.

CONTENTS

✎§ V ß✎ THE GOLDEN GLOBES

✎§ VI ß✎   THE MULTI-HULLS

✎§ VII ß✎   THE PERMANENT ITCH

✎§ APPENDICES ß✎

✎§ INDEX ß✎

For My Wild Irish Rose

*In an age when mass society has rendered obsolete the
qualities of individual courage and independent thought,
the oceans of the world still remain,
vast and uncluttered, beautiful but unforgiving,
awaiting those who will not submit.
Their voyages are not an escape,
but a fulfillment.*

❧ THE SLOCUM SOCIETY ☙

THE
PATHFINDERS

CHAPTER

1

The Pilot of the Pinta

I had resolved on a voyage around the world, and as the wind on the morning of April 24, 1895, was fair, at noon I weighed anchor, set sail, and filled away from Boston, where the Spray *had been moored snugly all winter. The twelve o'clock whistles were blowing just as the sloop shot ahead under full sail. A short board was made up the harbor on the port tack, then coming about she stood to seaward, with her boom well off to port, and swung past the ferries with lively heels. A photographer on the outer pier at East Boston got a picture of her as she swept by, her flag at the peak throwing its folds clear. A thrilling pulse beat high in me. My step was light on deck in the crisp air. I felt there could be no turning back, and that I was engaging in an adventure the meaning of which I thoroughly understood.*

SAILING ALONE AROUND THE WORLD,
BY JOSHUA SLOCUM

THUS BEGAN THE FIRST AND MOST FAMOUS SOLO CIRCUM-navigation in maritime history, a voyage of adventure and escape, and a feat of seamanship that remains unsurpassed in all the annals of men who go down to the sea in ships.

The author of these charming lines, and the skipper of the 37-foot

Spray[1] on that crisp April morning, was Captain Joshua Slocum, and he had just marked his fifty-first birthday. Behind him were a 20-year career as master of some of the finest merchant ships afloat; a supremely happy life with his sea wife, Virginia, which produced four surviving children all born at sea or in exotic ports; and high adventure—most of which crumbled around him in ruins, tragedy, and personal despair in middle age, the most critical time in any man's life.

The *Spray* was all that he had left, and it was a century-old oysterman that had been hauled out on the beach unused for many years. Given to Slocum by a friend, Captain Eben Pierce, as a joke, he set about characteristically and rebuilt her from the keel up, at a cost of $553.62 and thirteen months' labor.

Slocum's description of his departure from Boston on his solo circumnavigation, written several years later, did not fail to recapture his exhilaration and exuberance of once again walking the slanting deck of his own sailing ship, escaping to the wonderful sea that had charmed him since his childhood.

Left behind were agonizing memories of Virginia, who had died suddenly in Buenos Aires aboard their beautiful bark *Aquidneck* some years before, the confusion and hopelessness of an old sailor cast up on the beach, a second wife whom he regarded as little more than a babysitter for his children, and the great social and economic disorders that were changing his world as he knew it, and to which he was unable to adapt.

He had $1.80 in cash, agreements with several newspapers to file stories along the way at space rates, and a number of copies of a book he had written previously and printed at his own expense, *The Voyage of the Liberdade*.[2] He did not, however, have any timetable, nor even any clear-cut idea of what route he would take. His first landfall was Gloucester, only twenty miles away. There he spent two weeks enjoying a visit, and acquiring a dinghy by the simple expedient of sawing a Cape dory in half and boarding up the open end so that it would fit athwartships on the deck between the trunk cabins.

Leaving Gloucester, he sailed east instead of south as everyone expected—including his irritated editors. He sailed through the tide race in the Bay of Fundy and to Brier Island, where he had been born and raised. A month passed, then another, and he was still in Nova Scotia. Finally, on July 2, his gamming with relatives and old boyhood friends done, and the *Spray* made ready for sea with stores of fresh butter, potatoes, water in casks, and a dollar-and-a-half tin clock with broken hands that he had acquired as a chronometer,[3] he let go his grasp on the North American continent. Eighteen days later, after a magnificent sail, he reached the Azores.

After a short visit there, Slocum left for Gibraltar with a supply of fresh white cheese and ripe plums. Gorging on these as he sailed into a storm area, he was soon immobilized by cramps and passed out on the floor of the cabin. It was during this wild night, as his ship raced through the storm unattended, that Slocum recalled the pilot of the *Pinta* coming aboard to assist him in the crisis.[4]

At Gibraltar, Slocum was welcomed heartily by the British Navy, wined and dined, and even taken on an excursion to North Africa aboard a newfangled motor torpedo boat at a speed of 20 knots. Naval officers warned him not to attempt an east-to-west passage through the Mediterranean because of pirates, so he then altered his plans to follow the trade route south through the Atlantic and around Cape Horn to the Pacific. Forty days later, after a few hours of thrilling suspense when a pirate felucca put out from Africa to intercept him, he arrived at Pernambuco (Recife), on the bulge of Brazil. Here he tried to collect some money due him from the Brazilian government, and failing this, continued on along the coast to Rio de Janeiro, some 1,200 miles in 12 days, stopping for mail, selling books, and renewing old acquaintances among seafaring people.

Leaving Rio, Slocum ran aground just south of the Brazilian border, and after refloating he continued on to Montevideo, where he met an old friend and Río de la Plata pilot, Captain Howard of Cape Cod. Together they sailed across to Buenos Aires, where Virginia had been buried in English Cemetery.[5] Then, overcome by his old grief, Slocum departed suddenly for the challenge ahead. On the way south, he encountered a monster wave, a frighteningly common occurrence in the southern latitudes, but *Spray* came through the ordeal easily, which gave Slocum the final confidence he needed that his ship would take him anywhere.[6]

In early February, he rounded Cape Virgins, deciding to make the passage through the Strait of Magellan. It was the wrong time of the year to attempt the outside passage around the Horn. At the small frontier city of Punta Arenas, Slocum stopped for rest and recreation, and here was warned about the murderous savages who preyed on ships and stranded seamen in the Tierra del Fuego labyrinth—and especially one Black Pedro, the most wicked, murderous, and cunning of them all. He was given a box of carpet tacks and told how to use them to prevent being surprised at night while at anchor. For the

next two months he battled the fierce williwaws and tidal races of the
Strait, outguessed and outfought fleets of fire canoes, and even survived an encounter with Black Pedro himself. On his first attempt to
break out the western entrance, Slocum was caught in a storm and
swept southward around the Horn for days, during which he decided
he would change his plans and sail east-about after all.[7] Then, spot-
ting an opportunity, he turned in through the frightening Milky Way
reefs that Charles Darwin had first described in awe, and safely made
his way back into the Strait again.

On his second attempt, on April 13, *Spray* succeeded in making an
offing, and Slocum joyously steered northwest for the Robinson
Crusoe island of San Fernández. Here he was welcomed by the
islanders, and for nearly a month enjoyed their hospitality, especially
that of the children, whom he liked to be around.

Sailing on May 5, 1896, he ran down the trades for seventy-three
days in one of his most enjoyable passages, most of which was spent
in the cabin reading, with no one at the wheel. Passing up the
Marquesas, a popular stop for all sailing ships, he made his landfall at
Samoa. Here he paid his respects to Fanny Stevenson, widow of his
favorite author, and spent the rest of the summer. In October, after a
boisterous passage, he arrived in Newcastle, New South Wales, now a
year and a half out of Boston.

Slocum had friends and relatives here, for this was where he had
met and married Virginia and carried her off on his ship as a young
bride. His voyage had now become famous all over the world, and
much publicity was generated by his appearance and stay in Australia.
He made the most of it. Then, restless again, he departed. At first, he
planned to sail south of Australia, around Cape Leeuwin, but because
of the season of the year he decided to cross over to Tasmania instead. At Hobart, he beached the *Spray* for maintenance, and gave
lectures to raise funds. In May, he was sailing inside the Great Barrier
Reef the other way around Australia, through Torres Strait. By June,
he had left the Coral Sea and was en route across the Indian Ocean
to the tiny atoll islands of Keeling-Cocos. It was on this leg that he
made his classic passage down the trades from Christmas Island—
2,700 miles in 23 days with the helm untouched—to arrive at this
tiny flyspeck in the center of the entrance channel!

Slocum records a delightful stay on the islands, which were owned
by the Clunies-Ross family,[8] but it was the children whom he most
enjoyed, especially a ten-year-old named Ophelia, who wrote a poem

in his logbook about the great *kpeting* (giant crab) that kept ships there by holding onto the keel.

Admiral Fitzroy of the *Beagle* had written of these tiny isolated islands "where crabs eat coconuts, fish eat coral, dogs catch fish, men ride on turtles, and shells are dangerous mantraps."

Slocum refitted the *Spray,* then threw overboard his ballast and loaded the hold with giant tridacna shells which he planned to sell or trade later in the voyage.

On August 22, the *kpeting* let go his keel and Slocum departed for Rodriguez. His stay there was also pleasant, as a guest of the governor, but after only eight days he departed for Mauritius, loaded down again with fresh fruits and vegetables.

It was still winter off the great Cape of Good Hope, so he tarried on this pleasant island until October 26, and then set sail via Cape St. Mary on the southern tip of Madagascar, weathering the stormy Mozambique Channel, and arriving in Durban, South Africa, on November 17. News of his arrival was already in print and on the street in the morning newspaper before he arrived, and a copy was handed to him by port officials. Port Natal was then, as now, a favorite stop for world voyagers because of the hospitality of the local yachtsmen, and because it afforded a safe haven in which to wait for favorable weather to double the Cape.

Slocum was again wined and dined, introduced to all the important people, sought out by President Paul Krüger and the famed explorer, Stanley, of Stanley and Livingstone legend, colonels and colonels' ladies. He took trips into the back country, visited schools where he had the pleasure of meeting many bright children, and like almost all other visitors clucked sadly over the rigid social and economic barriers of the South African society.

On December 14, Slocum reluctantly departed, managed the frightful seas off the great bight of the continent, rounded Cape Agulhas (the actual southernmost tip of Africa), Cape of Good Hope, Table Mountain, and came to anchor off the city of Cape Town. Again he settled down for weeks of socializing with admirals, colonels, high-placed politicians, local yachtsmen, and hospitable citizens of all rank. As many other voyagers, he was tempted to end his journey and settle down in this pleasant and dynamic country, but on March 26, 1898, he was on his way again with a nice light morning breeze giving him an offing for the next leg to the island of St. Helena, with the *Spray* running sprightly under a single-reefed mainsail, whole jib, and flying jib, leaping along among the marching white sea horses, with porpoises playing off the bow. On April 11, he caught sight of the island where Napoleon spent his last days, opened a locker, and with a bottle of port wine toasted the health of his invisible helmsman, the pilot of the *Pinta*.

As usual, Slocum was given the freedom of the port and was hosted by the governor. He paused to visit with the local families, and was given a goat by the American consul there, a Mr. R. A. Clark.[9] Slocum, who did not like pets, had nothing but trouble with his goat and managed to put it ashore in Ascension, but not until it had eaten his only chart of his next landfall, the West Indies. He had the *Spray* fumigated here and the ship's papers put in order by the British officer in charge of the "Stone Frigate."

On May 8, 1898, the *Spray* crossed her outbound track, thus completing a technical circumnavigation to a point on his track of October 2, 1895. Slocum sailed south of Fernando de Noronha, passing it at night. On May 10, there was a change in the condition of the sea, and to Slocum, an old hand in these waters, this meant that he was off St. Roque and was in the north-moving current. He had been in the trade winds for some time, and now also had the benefit of a forty-mile-a-day current.

Somewhere in this region, he encountered the U.S.S. *Oregon*. The battleship hoisted the signal "C B T," meaning, "Are there any men-of-war about?"

Slocum replied in the negative and then added his own signal: "Let us travel together for mutual protection."

Thus, Slocum learned that the United States was at war with Spain. On May 18, he saw the north star or Polaris for the first time in nearly three years, and he was logging better than 140 miles a day. His first stop was at Grenada, to which he carried letters from Mauritius, and he came into the roads off the island on May 22. On June 1, he arrived at St. John, Antigua, where he was welcomed by the governor and his lady, and was invited to lecture on his exploits. On June 4, he cleared with the United States consulate, and his yacht license was returned to him for the last time, with a personal note written on it by the consul.[10]

On June 8, the *Spray* passed under the sun and bounded joyously for home waters. For three days, Slocum was becalmed in the Sargasso Sea, then entering the Gulf Stream, he encountered a fierce gale which broke some of the weary rigging. Fighting his way through squalls and cobble seas northward to Fire Island, there he was caught in the tornado of June 25, which had wrecked buildings a few minutes earlier in New York City.

With a sea anchor out, he weathered the storm, and when it was over and the *Spray* was safe once more, Slocum recorded that he never saw the pilot of the *Pinta* again.

The *Spray* rounded Montauk Point, carried Point Judith abeam at dark, and fetched in at Beavertail. Sailing on, Slocum hugged the shore going into Newport Harbor, which was mined, and at last, reached safe anchorage at one A.M., June 27, 1898, after a voyage of 46,000 miles and an absence of three years and two months—a voyage that carried him into immortality.

Later, the *Spray* waltzed cockily around the coast and up the Acushnet River to Fairhaven, where Slocum secured to the same stake driven into the bank to tether her when she was launched.

"I could bring her no nearer home," Slocum wrote.

The world was now ready for Captain Joshua Slocum, and like a true Yankee shipmaster, he was quick to take full measure of it.

When Slocum had departed on his voyage three years before, one of the last well-wishers to see him off was the girl to whom he dedicated his book, twenty-four-year-old Mabel Wagnalls, daughter of an old friend, Adam Wagnalls, the publisher. First to come aboard to write a welcome in his logbook was Miss Wagnalls—"the one who said the *Spray* would come back."

Slocum's original motive for making the voyage around was, ostensibly at least, to write stories about it for publication, including possibly a book. Although his initial arrangements to file stories to newspapers had collapsed along the way because of the time element and lack of editorial interest, he still wanted very much to write up his accounts in the same vein as the popular travel books of Mark Twain and Robert Louis Stevenson. So, while still at the Keeling-Cocos Islands, he wrote to Joseph Benson Gilder, editor of *The Critic*, the literary magazine of the day, and younger brother of Richard Watson Gilder, the great editor of *Century Magazine*. Young Gilder had previously written a favorable review of Slocum's book, *The Voyage of the Liberdade*, and can now be considered the first to "discover" Slocum's literary potential. The letter, written seven years afterward while the *Spray* was tied to a palm tree on remote Keeling-Cocos, can be considered the genesis of *Sailing Alone Around the World*, one of the all-time great maritime classics, which Van Wyck Brooks described in *The Confident Years* as the "nautical equivalent of Thoreau's account of his life in the hut at Walden."

"Do you think," Slocum concluded in his letter to Gilder, "our people will care for a story of the voyage around?"

Now, immediately after arriving home, Slocum received a telegram requesting his story from Richard Watson Gilder. It was the beginning of Slocum's happiest association since the death of Virginia, and the culmination of a lifetime ambition to be an author. At first, however, because he was still restless, it was hard to settle down to the actual chore of putting together his story. The Spanish-American War was still occupying the front pages and Slocum thought of volunteering to skipper a gunboat in the Philippines, still remembering the perfidy of petty Spanish officialdom from the days when he was a shipmaster and shipbuilder in the China trade. He talked of fitting out a college ship to accommodate three hundred student-passengers on a voyage around the world, during which they could learn seamanship as well as study liberal arts and engineering courses.

At last, he got down to work on the series, first while living with his wife, Hettie, whom he had rejoined, and later in the winter aboard the *Spray* tied up at the Erie Basin Drydocks in Brooklyn. He delivered the manuscript in the summer of 1899 and immediately celebrated with a cruise in New England waters, correcting galley proofs as he sailed. The story was published in monthly installments, from September 1899 through March 1900. The book was published by the Century Company on March 24, 1900, illustrated with pen drawings by Thomas Fogarty and George Varian. A second edition was published the same year in England. There were sixteen reprintings by Century through 1941, three printings by Blue Ribbon Books in the 1930s, and additional printings by Sheridan House, Inc., and Grosset & Dunlap, Inc. Charles Scribner's Sons brought out an abridged edition for schools in 1903. French, Polish, German, and Dutch editions appeared over the years. The book entered the public domain in 1956, and since then numerous reprints have appeared in various forms with seemingly a steady increase in reader interest rather than a decline.

Sailing Alone Around the World was an immediate critical and financial success. With the proceeds of its sales, plus Slocum's lucrative lecture and lantern slide appearances, he was able to pay off his debts and buy a farm for Hettie on Martha's Vineyard. In addition, he was able to capitalize on his new fame by selling copies left over from his previous publishing efforts, *The Voyage of the Liberdade* and *The Voyage of the Destroyer*.

He wrote and published pamphlets to advertise his wares, such as the *Sloop Spray Souvenir*, which he sold at the Pan American Exposition at Buffalo, where he exhibited the globe-circling *Spray*, charged admission, and sold books and souvenirs.

He planned also to exhibit an expedition to Iceland and the Arctic at the Universal Exposition in Paris. He toyed with underwater experiments and with the newfangled flying machine; he became a frequent visitor and confidant of President Teddy Roosevelt and often took the President's son sailing on the *Spray*; he made short cruises in New England waters, and in 1905 made the first of several annual winter sojourns to Jamaica, Grand Cayman, and other ports in the West Indies.

Returning from one cruise, and while on a lecture tour in New Jersey, he was arrested on a charge of molesting a twelve-year-old girl. After spending two months in jail, he then pleaded *nolo contendere* to a reduced charge and was released by the judge after a lecture on morals. It is unlikely that Slocum was actually guilty of molesting the child; more likely, his flinty pride refused to take the charge seriously. His biographer, Walter Magnes Teller, draws a perceptive parallel in Melville's *Mardi*, "the heart-loneliness which overtakes most seamen as they grow aged, impelling them to fasten on some chance object of regard."[11]

In any case, Slocum did not let it trouble him. He went from the jail in New Jersey to Sagamore Hill, where he was welcomed cordially by President Roosevelt and took young Archibald Roosevelt for a week's cruise.

Each winter thereafter, Slocum sailed south to the Caribbean, increasingly restless and unable to settle down in Martha's Vineyard with Hettie. In 1909, at age sixty-five, he set off on another expedition, this time to explore the Orinoco up to the Río Negro, then sail down the Amazon to the Atlantic Ocean. He was never seen nor heard from again, and was declared legally dead as of November 14, 1909.

There have been many theories about his disappearance including suicide, fire at sea, storms, and even disintegration of the aged *Spray*. The most logical is the one suggested by Slocum's eldest son, Victor, also an experienced sea captain. Victor believed that his father was run down at night in the crowded ship lanes off Cape Hatteras. Collision at sea between large, fast vessels and small craft, particularly in such congested areas, remains a major hazard today.[12]

In spite of his simplistic, dead-center Yankee manner and appearance, Joshua Slocum was a complex man, a personality of paradoxes. Born February 20, 1844, on Brier Island, Nova Scotia, he was descended from a seafaring English family that had settled in New England in the early eighteenth century, but removed to Nova Scotia during the War of Independence. Later, the family drifted back to Massachusetts and Joshua became a naturalized American.

His father was a large, muscular, somewhat frustrated and embittered man, stern and unrelenting in views, a church deacon, farmer, and bootmaker. His mother was a daughter of a lighthouse keeper on Brier Island, small, delicate, gentle, and fine-featured. Joshua took after her in physical appearance and appreciation of finer things and after his father in grit, determination, and aggressiveness.[13]

His mother was young Joshua's whole world, and as long as she lived, he endured his father's brutality and the harsh life. When she died at forty-six, he left home for good to follow the sea. His first voyage was at sixteen on a British ship. Quick, intelligent, loyal, and handy with his fists, he learned fast and rose quickly, obtaining his first command as captain of an American coastal schooner out of San Francisco when he was only twenty-five. During this period, he also engaged in various adventures on the northwest coast, including commercial fishing, trapping, and boat building. His son Victor credited his father with the design of the famed Columbia River gillnet boats, although this is unlikely.

His second command was the bark *Washington*, which sailed from San Francisco to Sydney with a mixed cargo. There he met Virginia Walker, daughter of an American immigrant, and after a two-week courtship, they were married and spent their honeymoon on a voyage to Cook Inlet in Alaska to take on a cargo of salmon. Virginia was a perfect soul mate, witty, intelligent, cultured, yet courageous and adventurous—and a dead shot with a pistol, which came in handy during several attempted mutinies in later years.

Though the *Washington* was wrecked in Alaskan waters, most of the cargo was saved by the efforts of her captain, and the owners responded by giving Slocum the command of another ship, the bark *Constitution*. Victor was born aboard this vessel in 1872. The next residence of the little family was aboard the square-rigger *B. Aymar*. Then followed a shipbuilding period in the Philippines in which he acquired a beautiful little 45-ton schooner *Pato*, Spanish for "duck." The *Pato* was first employed in salvage operations, and then, with his family that now included two boys and a girl, Slocum picked up gear, dories, and a crew in Hong Kong and sailed through the Sea of Japan to waters off Kamchatka on a cod-fishing venture. Thousands of miles from the nearest medical help, Virginia gave birth to twins. They

died four days later, and the following day Virginia joined the rest
of the crew at the rail, bringing aboard a cargo of cod which was
salted down and taken to Portland, Oregon, and peddled from door
to door. With the proceeds of this operation, during which the
family lived ashore on the east bank of the Willamette River, and the
sale of the *Pato* in Honolulu for $5,000 in gold, the Slocums next
acquired the 350-ton *Amethyst* and fitted it out for the China lumber
trade. Another daughter was born, but she died soon after. In Hong
Kong, March 3, 1881, Virginia gave birth to her seventh child, James
Garfield Slocum.

Now Slocum moved up to captain and part owner of the beautiful
1,800-ton clipper, the *Northern Light,* one of the tallest and fastest
ships of the day.

On a bright June day in 1882, Slocum sailed her up the East River
under the new Brooklyn Bridge, her rig so tall that the upper section
had to be struck to pass under, a proud ship with a proud captain at
the pinnacle of his career. Later, there was a mutiny aboard the
Northern Light during which Virginia backed up her husband with a
loaded pistol and in which the ringleader was stabbed to death.
Continuing on to Yokohama to discharge cargo, on the return trip
the *Northern Light* passed the island of Krakatoa a few days before it
blew up, suffered damage off the Cape of Good Hope and lost most
of her cargo, and again endured an attempted mutiny led by an ex-
convict who came aboard at Cape Town.

The next ship was the little bark *Aquidneck,* which Slocum described as the "nearest to perfection of beauty" any man could ask
for. This was operated in the South American trade and was a happy
but brief interlude in the captain's career.

On one trip to Buenos Aires, Virginia took ill suddenly, and on the
evening of July 25, 1884, she died with her husband and the children
at her bedside, not yet thirty-five years old.

Slocum, who had lost his mother when he was sixteen, now lost the
second woman in his life when he was thirty-nine. When Virginia
died, Slocum died with her spiritually. In his grief, he ran the *Aquidneck* aground once, then two years later, with his second wife, his
cousin, twenty-four-year-old Henrietta Elliott, and two of the brood,
Victor, age fourteen, and Garfield, age five, sailed for South America
on a wedding trip. The *Aquidneck* was wrecked on this voyage
through a series of unfortunate incidents including a cholera epi-
demic and a mutiny during which Slocum killed two men, and
everything was lost.

Salvaging what he could from the wreckage, Slocum set about building a 35-foot sailing dory, which he called the *Liberdade*, because it was launched the day the Brazilian slaves were freed. In this craft, with his family for a crew, Slocum sailed 5,000 miles from Paranaguá Bay to Washington, D.C., one of the most remarkable small-boat voyages of all times.

He wrote a book about this, which he published himself and tried to sell for $1 a copy. In the winter of 1892, his friend Captain Eben Pierce gave him the ancient *Spray*, which was on the beach at Fairhaven. Slocum, who had been five times around the world, and spent a lifetime at sea, had little use for a yacht, but he set about rebuilding the sloop for want of something better to do, and also as a cozy seagoing home in which he could retreat.

He fished in the *Spray* one season, with little success, chartered an occasional party, and then, in December 1893, he undertook a commission to deliver the Ericsson iron-clad gunboat *Destroyer* to the Brazilian government during the insurrection. After another incredible voyage and masterpiece of seamanship, he was cheated out of his pay and returned home broke again to write a book about this hazardous voyage, which did not sell well either.

Returning to the waiting *Spray*, which he had recreated with his own hands and now seemed his last refuge, he conceived the idea of a singlehanded voyage around the world.

Although his life had crumbled around him, he still had his charts, sextant, compass, his favorite rifles, and books, and he knew the way, oh so well. For him, the sea was a friend, a haven, a world he understood and which understood him.

He was about to discover the one thing that almost all men seek and which few ever find in their lifetimes—meaning.

And, as Slocum exclaimed to his eldest son on seeing him again, "You could have done it, Vic—but you would not have been first!"

CHAPTER

2

The Venturesome Viking

It was during the Spring of 1901, in Victoria, B.C., that Mr. Luxton, a Canadian journalist, asked me if I thought I could accomplish a voyage around the world in a smaller vessel than the American yawl Spray, *in which Captain Slocum, an American citizen, had successfully circumnavigated the globe.*[1]

THE MORNING OF MAY 20, 1901, CAME ON CLEAR AND mild, and except for a low bank of haze over the Strait of Juan de Fuca, above which the snowy Olympic Mountains to the south seemed to float, it looked like the beginning of a fine spring day in Victoria. Just pulling away from the rickety dock at Oak Bay was one of the oddest vessels ever to set out on a circumnavigation before or since. It looked like a Haida war canoe, carved from the trunk of a giant cedar, which in fact it was, although now it had a cabin amidships and three small masts of a miniature schooner.

On board this bizarre vessel was perhaps the most unlikely pair ever to embark on such an adventure: Norman Kenny Luxton, in his twenties, but already with a colorful career behind him, a sometime newspaperman and promoter, slight of build, with brown hair and pale blue eyes; and Captain John (Jack) Claus Voss, a short chesty German in his middle forties, with handlebar moustache and sharp gray eyes, thin brown hair, and imperious manner, a Victoria, British Columbia, hotel keeper, sea captain, soldier of fortune, smuggler, treasure hunter, and family man.

On the wharf, waving to them as they drifted slowly away with the tide and morning offshore breeze, were friends and family members of both men—no doubt wondering if they would ever see either of them again.

The name on the bow of this new-painted vessel was *Tilikum*, which was an Indian word for "friend." The name was appropriate to the tenor of the times, with the world beginning a new century bright with optimism, hope, peace, prosperity, and universal friendship. It was a time of great and lively interest in adventuring and exploration. The Klondike and Alaskan gold rush had reached a peak of public interest. Great fortunes were being made everywhere, it seemed, in lumbering, mining, shipping, fish packing, railroad and townsite speculation, oil, and mercantilism. The panic and depression of the late 1890s had finally been broken. It was time for daring and gambling for big stakes. Great economical and social changes were afoot. It was great to be alive and a participant and challenger in life.

The *Tilikum* was only one of numerous vessels in various countries of the world that was launched, proposed, or already afloat for the purpose of imitating or outdoing Captain Joshua Slocum and his *Spray*, the fame of which had by now become worldwide, to say nothing of profitable. *Tilikum* was 38 feet overall including the native figurehead, 30 feet on the waterline, with a maximum beam of 5 feet 6 inches at the rail, 4 feet 6 inches at the chine and only 3 feet 6 inches wide on the bottom. She had been purchased for $80 from an old Indian who had been softened up, Voss claimed, with a "drap of ol' Rye." The original red cedar dugout was rebuilt with a stout keelson, oak frames, and a keel of 300 pounds of lead. The sides were built up 7 inches, and a 5 foot by 8 foot cabin was erected with a cockpit for steering. Three masts were stepped to handle four small fore and aft sails, totalling 230 square feet of canvas. Inside went a half ton of ballast, between the floor timbers, and 400 pounds of sand in 4 bags to be used for trimming ballast. About a hundred gallons of fresh water were carried in two galvanized iron tanks under the cockpit. Provisions included three months' supply of tinned goods and other staples; equipment included a camera, two rifles, a double-barrel shotgun, chronometer, water, barometer, and sextant. Loaded and with crew aboard, the *Tilikum* drew 24 inches aft and 22 inches forward.

Despite outward indications, *Tilikum* was surprisingly seaworthy and handy, although her windward ability left room for doubt. The modifications and outfitting had been the work of Voss himself, and were the result of years of experience. Born probably in Germany in the 1850s,[2] he went to sea when he was nineteen, sailing the oceans on the tough square-riggers, did some sealing in the Bering, prospected for gold in Nicaragua, did a little smuggling of Chinamen into the United States, showed up at the gold-rush centers of Colorado and British Columbia, was master of several vessels, and mate of tall lumber clippers out of Puget Sound ports. He had more recently engaged in a fascinating and adventuresome expedition on the *Xora*, a pretty little 10-ton sloop, to the Cocos Islands and South America in search of buried treasure. From about 1895 until meeting up with Luxton in a bar, he had been a hotel owner and operator.[3]

Co-owner and mate Norman Luxton had been born on November 2, 1876, at Upper Fort Garry, now Winnipeg, Manitoba, Canada, son of the founder of the *Winnipeg Free Press*, and at age sixteen became a clerk at the Rat Portage Indian Agency. Later he went to the Cariboo gold fields, worked on the *Calgary Herald* as reporter and typesetter, and migrated to Vancouver where he founded, with Frank Burd, who later owned the *Province*, a weekly gossip sheet. When this folded, Luxton went to work for the *Vancouver Sun*, and it was probably during this period when he met Jack Voss in a bar and they began to talk of ships and sea adventures and Captain Slocum's feat.

Voss was a man who thoroughly enjoyed his *schnapps*, and bragging of his past exploits and personal prowess was a favorite indoor pastime. This talkativeness when in his cups seems to have been a Voss characteristic. When sober, he was virtually inarticulate, and so unconvincing that he had a reputation for being a monumental liar.[4]

Voss was described by young Norman Luxton as a hardened seaman, egotistical, subject to black and violent moods when drinking, full of braggadocio, aggressive, and provocative. In a posthumously published biography edited by his daughter, Luxton actually accused Voss of murder and of accepting Luxton's financing on condition that all rights to subsequent literary endeavors would be given in return, then double-crossing him.[5]

An analysis of Voss's book, *The Venturesome Voyages of Captain Voss*, Luxton's posthumous journal, and independent research, however, indicates that the only difference in the degree of prevarication and personal egotism between the two was their ages. Of the two, Voss's written account is by far the most lucid, informative, and

genuinely interesting, in spite of the fact that Luxton was supposed
to be the professional writer, and Voss the inarticulate sea captain.

In any case, meet they did in a bar, and they became attracted to
each other for different reasons, no doubt (Luxton, with an eye on a
spectacular story, and Voss with a sense of adventure rekindled by
the enthusiasm of his new-found 25-year-old friend). The dugout
canoe was purchased, rebuilt, and then for several weeks sailed on
shakedown cruises among the beautiful wooded islands of the British
Columbia coastal waters. According to Luxton, who was interested in
artifacts and native customs stemming from his early years as an
agency clerk, the two of them raided sacred burial grounds for
souvenirs with bullets zinging around them, and on one beach dug up
an old brass cannon left by an early Spanish ship.[6]

On the morning they left on their circumnavigation, Luxton wrote,
he learned that Voss had registered the *Tilikum* as the *Pelican* in
order to confuse the U.S. Coast Guard revenue cutter that was supposed to be waiting to intercept Voss, who was wanted for alleged
smuggling of dope and illegal Chinese labor. Luxton related how
smugglers like Voss, when caught by the fuzz, would drop the
Chinamen over the side in gunny sacks.[7]

Seeing them off were Captain Voss's family—his wife, daughter,
and youngest son; Luxton's brother, George, and O. B. Ormond,
proprietor of Ormond's Biscuits in Victoria. After attending an all-
night dance at the Dallas Hotel, Luxton was in no shape to navigate,
and as soon as they were off, went below and hit the sack. He didn't
wake up until the *Tilikum* entered the violent rips at Race Rocks,
about ten miles from Victoria.

From here on, they hit head winds and had difficulty making their
way out the strait, so they pulled in at Sooke Harbour and beached
the boat to check on several leaks which had developed through open
seams. Departing again, they attempted to double Cape Flattery but
the weather again forced them to run back to shelter on the west
coast of Vancouver Island. There they spent several weeks visiting
with white families and the Indian villagers. At one point, Luxton
related how he joined a native whaling foray offshore. At another
time, he told how a friend had tried to shanghai him aboard a sealing
schooner bound for the Bering. (Luxton claimed to have made
several such trips and to hold a mate's ticket, a claim that cannot be
substantiated by any records now extant.) In any case, they spent a
leisurely few weeks exploring the west coast of the island and getting
Tilikum ready again.[8]

On July 6, they departed at last, bound for Pitcairn Island and the Marquesas. They had not gone more than twenty-five miles when they were surrounded by a large migration of gray whales, then common on this coast, and were in danger of being struck and crushed by the cavorting cetaceans.

Down along the west coast of North America they sailed, experiencing fine weather and frequent gales, learning to handle the *Tilikum* and settling into a daily routine of sixty to seventy miles. On this leg, Captain Voss gave Luxton some of the best on board training in small-boat handling under bluewater conditions ever related, and the techniques Voss described were little-known then and decades ahead of the current crop of heavy weather sailing manuals. Down through the northeast trades they went, then into the doldrums and across the equator into the South Pacific. Instead of Pitcairn or the Marquesas, they made their first landfall at Penrhyn Island on September 1. The two men had a violent argument here about landing, Voss wanting to continue on to Samoa because he feared the natives on Penrhyn would be hostile. But land here they did and found anchored the two-masted schooner *Tamarii Tahiti*, the French trading vessel, commanded by Captain George Dexter, a half-caste Tahitian-American, and his partner, the legendary Captain Joe Winchester, "an English gentleman and sailor," who was the father-in-law of James Norman Hall of later *Mutiny on the Bounty* fame.

Their stay on Penrhyn was apparently an eventful one, at least for Luxton, who related that he was trapped into a marriage by the mother of a local "princess," from which he escaped only by quick thinking and a glib tongue; and on their final departure, they were attended, Voss said, by two young "princesses," who came aboard to wish them *bon voyage*. To nineteenth-century searovers, apparently any dusky native belle was a "princess," a bit of harmless Anglo-Saxon chauvinism which went over big with the folks back home, but which any World War II G.I. in the South Pacific Theater forty years later had another name for.

The *Tilikum* stayed in the Cook Islands until September 25, when Voss and Luxton departed for Samoa by way of Danger Island.[9]

They paused briefly here, and on the passage to Samoa trouble erupted between the two with Luxton claiming that Voss threatened to "throw him overboard." The younger man then armed himself with a .22 caliber Stevens target pistol and locked Voss in the cabin until they reached Apia. There they appeared to have patched up their differences and enjoyed a short stay and the hospitality of the local white colony and natives alike. Luxton here became involved with a Sadie Thompson with "legs like mutton and breasts like huge cabbages," who wanted him to manage her store.[10]

Luxton visited the sights, including Robert Louis Stevenson's *Vailima*, and his tomb, wherein the famed author had inscribed his own epitaph, quoted by every voyager to visit here, ". . . Home is the sailor, home from the sea,/And the hunter home from the hill."

The first week in October, Luxton said he hunted up Voss, and they got underway for Fiji. Before they left, however, Luxton took Voss to Mr. Swan's store and read to him an account of their differences with a statement of Voss's threat. The paper also stated that, if Luxton went missing between Samoa and Australia, Mr. Swan was to take such action as necessary to make Voss prove he had not killed Luxton. In his journal, Luxton claimed that Voss signed the statement as correct, although Voss makes no mention of this, and the paper which Luxton alleges Voss signed no longer exists.

On the third day out of Samoa, they sighted Niuafoo, where they were met by an island lass who swam out to beg for a plug of T and B chewing tobacco. Two days later they came to one of the Fiji islands where Luxton went ashore to explore with gun and camera while Voss tended to the ship's needs. The next day they sailed for Suva. Luxton related that while ashore he had been met by a white official on horseback who told him a permit was needed from the Tonga government to land on the island, and that the natives were inclined to find "long pig" tempting as a dietary supplement. While in these waters, the two men were threatened by natives sailing their fast catamarans, who were dissuaded from attacking when Voss fired the old Spanish cannon which they still had aboard along with the Siwash skulls they had robbed from the British Columbia Indian burial ground. Luxton had neglected to tell Voss, however, that the cannon had been unshipped at Apia, and never made fast again. The black powder recoil tore it from its block and sent it over the side, lost forever. The natives, meanwhile, had abandoned their canoes and swam ashore. The two men collected the canoes, tied them together, and sent them sailing off by themselves, an episode that sounds like it came straight out of a Grade B western, with canoes instead of Indian horses.

Voss never mentioned anything about this, which Luxton explained in his narrative by saying that "Jack was afraid he might go to jail for shooting at them," and because they had also stolen some of the native paddles and weapons from the canoes.[11]

It was here that Luxton (without credit)used the old "tack" trick to warn against hostile natives coming aboard at night. He claimed a George Ellis had insisted on his taking a supply of carpet tacks along to the Fijis to sprinkle on deck at night (just as Captain Slocum's friend Samblich, in Punta Arenas, had cautioned him to do when he set out to sail through Magellan Strait).

Unlike Slocum, Luxton heard a noise in the night, rushed out on deck, and stepped on the business ends of his burglar alarm.

It was during the passage from here to Suva that Luxton claimed they were shipwrecked on a reef, and that Luxton was left for dead on the beach—until he came back to life again with a body full of contusions and abrasions. They stayed here several days patching the *Tilikum*, and then, on October 17, sighted Suva Harbor lights and were taken in tow by the port captain's launch.[12]

The stay in Suva was pleasant, and Luxton, who said the shipwreck on Duff Reef had taken his last reserve of strength, here parted company with his partner. Voss, who did not even mention the shipwreck, claimed Luxton approached him with the proposal to engage another seaman in his place, and to continue on to Sydney by steamship himself.

Luxton's version was that Voss had approached him with the news that the doctor had told him that Luxton was in no condition to continue on the *Tilikum* and should go to Australia by steamship. Also, Voss warned, it was either that or write to Mr. Swan in Samoa, that Luxton had decided to commit suicide.

Luxton did leave the *Tilikum* and took passage to Sydney, leaving Voss to recruit a man named Louis Begent in a Suva bar. Luxton said he tried to get Begent to throw away the *Tilikum*'s liquor supply before they departed, and warned him about Voss, to no avail. During the passage, Voss claimed Begent was washed overboard in a storm. In his private correspondence, Luxton later said he felt sure that Voss killed Begent in a drunken fight and threw him overboard. He also claimed that Voss did not deny this when Luxton accused him of it. While he was convalescing in Sydney, Luxton primed the newspapers to expect Voss and the *Tilikum* (and no doubt share the publicity with him). When Voss finally landed, days overdue and Begent missing, the papers had an even better story. Luxton said Voss was in the hospital for weeks suffering from exposure and "sickness he contracted through the women on the islands" (those "princesses," no doubt).

After making numerous appearances together in Australia, the two erstwhile adventurers parted company in Melbourne. Luxton had an extended stay in Australia, and fortunately being a fair photographer even in that day and with the equipment he carried with him, he left a remarkable record of their ports of call and life aboard the *Tilikum* which did not come to light until his journal was published in 1971. Although he claimed he still owned two-thirds of one-half of the *Tilikum*, and all the rights to subsequent published works, he never pressed his claims, and was even enthusiastic about Voss's later book, which he recommended highly for its value as a sailing manual for small vessels.

Luxton never saw Voss again, and returning to Canada, married, and founded a tourist haberdashery, trading post, and taxidermist shop in Banff, which he called "The Sign of the Goat Trading Post." He also bought and published Banff's first newspaper, the *Crag and Canyon*, and as early as 1906 established himself as a publicist and promoter of Banff as a Canadian Switzerland. For the next half-century, until he died October 26, 1962, Norman Kenny Luxton was a familiar sight in the growing little tourist center of Banff, usually dressed gaily in his buckskin clothes and wearing a ten-gallon hat. He received many civic honors in his active life, including the title of Chief White Eagle from the Blackfeet Indians for his support of the Indian Association and his efforts in founding the Banff Indian Days annual celebration. He married his "princess," daughter of David McDougall, a pioneer rancher and trader, who was the first white child born in what is now Alberta.

As far as is known, Luxton never even saw the ocean again and never discussed in public his adventure with Captain Voss. In his journal, written for his daughter, Eleanor Georgina, he claimed that a spiritualist, whom he consulted before he left Australia, described to him exactly what happened that night when Voss allegedly had a drunken fight with Louis Begent and threw him overboard. Until his death, Luxton also firmly believed that Voss was lost at sea during his Japanese adventures.

Meanwhile, however, Captain John Claus Voss, whom we left alive and well in Australia, had a different story to tell. He said that upon arrival he looked up Luxton, who had given him up for lost. Luxton was distraught about the loss of Begent and blamed himself for leaving the *Tilikum*. Voss called Luxton a good shipmate and a careful sailor. "I am quite sure that had he remained on the vessel in Suva and made the trip with me to Sydney, the accident would not have happened. I therefore urged him to continue the voyage to

Europe, but in spite of all my pleadings he refused to go on, and so I became the sole owner of the *Tilikum* and all her fittings."[13]

Voss's version of the spiritualist was that Luxton had engaged her and she had warned him the *Tilikum* would be damaged before he left Australia. The vessel was placed on display by Voss, along with the British Columbia Indian artifacts which were still with them, and taken on tour of various cities to earn money for the voyage. At one point, *Tilikum* was dropped by a carrier while being moved and Voss sued the company for damages.[14] He also recruited another mate for the next leg of the voyage, one of many male and female applicants, and the first of several before the voyaging was done with. After numerous adventures, Voss sailed to Hobart, Tasmania (as Slocum had), where one of his greeters was the sister of Louis Begent, whom he reported, bore him no ill will.

New Zealand was the next stop of the *Tilikum*, and a fine welcome was had. There he participated with the vessel in local celebrations which included an exhibition of running the surf to the delight of spectators, and for which he was paid £50.

After a lecture tour and many fetes, the captain departed New Zealand August 17, 1902, with MacMillan, a well-educated man of refined manners, for the New Hebrides and the Great Barrier Reef. They explored through Torres Strait and into the Indian Ocean, sailed to the Keeling-Cocos Islands, Rodriguez, and Durban with many adventures.[15]

A long stay was made in South Africa, and in Johannesburg he ran into an old fortune-hunting buddy from *Xora* days, now married and with a beautiful home, a wife, and two sweet young children. "Mac" was still chasing rainbows, and in Africa he was on the trail of gold and diamonds. Captain Voss found Johannesburg, at six hundred miles from the ocean, too far from salt water, and soon departed.

In Pretoria, *Tilikum* was damaged,[16] several old friends from Victoria showed up, and a new mate was signed on. The next stop was St. Helena, and then course was shaped for Pernambuco on the Brazilian bulge, which Voss had not visited since 1877 when he was on his first voyage to sea in a 300-ton sailing ship out of Hamburg, Germany, bound for Guayaquil, Ecuador. They remained two weeks in Pernambuco, and on June 4, at 3 P.M., they were towed to sea and the long sail uphill to London by way of the Azores began.[17]

On August 29, *Tilikum* was tacking off the Cape Lizard light. On September 2, at 4 P.M., the jetty at Margate was rounded, and thousands of people lined up to watch.

From the distance came a voice: "Where are you from?"

"Victoria, British Columbia."

"How long have you been on this voyage?"

"Three years, three months, and twelve days."

Then a great cheer went up from the crowd.

In England, Captain Voss was lionized and idolized. Twice he was nominated for a Fellowship in the Royal Geographical Society, although for unknown reasons he was never elected nor ever officially became a member.[18]

Other adventures followed, including a spell on the Japanese sealing schooner *Chichishima Maru*, and a subsequent voyage on the *Sea Queen*, a Thomas Fleming Day *Sea Bird*-type, built by two young men, F. Stone and S. A. Vincent of the Yokohama Yacht Club. On July 27, 1912, they put to sea in the *Sea Queen*, on a planned world cruise which terminated in a typhoon and a limp back to port a month later under jury rig.[19]

Nothing much was known about Voss after his Japanese episode[20] until his surviving daughter, Mrs. Caroline Kuhn, was located in Portland, Oregon, in 1972. Luxton was convinced that Voss had died in the typhoon. Others think the John C. Voss "of Germany," who died of pneumonia in Tracy, California, on February 27, 1922, was the same man who sailed out of Victoria in the *Tilikum* on May 20, 1901, with Luxton. On his death certificate, he was listed as "Captain, Sea Boat."

The *Tilikum?* After she arrived in England on September 2, 1904, she was exhibited for a time, and then left to rot on the Thames mud flats for twenty years or so. In 1928, a group of British naval officers found the derelict ship with the help of the National Museum at Greenwich, the Victoria Publicity Bureau, and various yachting magazines. The canoe was then in the possession of two brothers, E. W. and A. Bydord, who agreed to give it to Victoria on the condition that *Tilikum* never be exhibited for financial gain. She was transported to British Columbia and restored by the Thermopylae Club and public donations. Since June 8, 1965, *Tilikum* has been on display at the Maritime Museum in Victoria. The figurehead, which had been damaged by a kick from a horse in Pretoria, has been restored, as have other parts, exactly the way it was when Voss and Luxton sailed her.

While researching the Voss legend in 1972, which turned up sources in Canada, Australia, New Zealand, South Africa, Japan, and England, I discovered that Captain Voss's only surviving family member, Mrs. Caroline Kuhn, then about eighty-four, was living less than two miles from my office in Portland, Oregon. She had lived in her neat and aging little home in the Albina district for forty years, there raising two daughters of her own after divorce from her husband, and educating them on a small income as a pianist. Alert, rather dainty, but with unmistakable Voss features, she idolized her father.

"The last time I saw him before he died in Tracy, California, we talked a lot. He was always laughing."

Her father, she said, loved the sea and always believed he would never drown. He was a restless man, always on the go, and he had made a lot of money in the hotel business. Caroline, the oldest of three children, could not remember how she came to be born inland at Denver, Colorado, but at this period Voss had been following the gold fever and no doubt it was for business reasons.

Caroline grew up in Victoria, where her father owned and operated at least two hotels, the Queen's and the Victoria. "It was during the gold rush and father did very well." She thinks her father financed the *Tilikum* venture, not Luxton.

Before he left, her father told her that, if she had been a boy, he would have taken her along. He did not, however, indicate that he wanted to take either of his two sons. From Australia, he sent for his wife. Caroline remembers her mother "dropped her off in Portland" on the way, where she has made her home ever since.

After Voss returned from his sea adventures, he bought another hotel in Victoria and brought Caroline up from Portland for the grand opening. This was before she married, and her father gave her a lot of money, she said, "to buy all the clothes I needed."

Later Voss moved to Tracy, California, where he had relatives. Caroline believed it was because of a pending divorce. Her mother followed him to California, but later returned and divorced him. Her father, Caroline said, was very bitter about this.

Voss never went back to the Pacific Northwest. He bought a Ford and started a jitney service—a sort of mini-bus type of operation, common to West Coast cities in those days. He was in his eighties, she thinks, when he died.[21]

She had not read Luxton's journal, but defended her father vigorously. "Anyone who knew him would never believe those things about him. He was very kind to us, and everyone liked him. He was a good man who could not get over his love for the sea."

And so Captain John Claus Voss passes into a kind of immortality, along with the man he tried to surpass, Captain Joshua Slocum. A man inclined to braggadocio perhaps, and even to prevarication, but he was a master of the sea and its moods and of small vessels that challenge it—perhaps one of the greatest seamen of all time. For half a century, he has been a mysterious, controversial character, and his techniques have been belittled and disparaged by some of the best-known bluewater sailors. But they invariably were given to superficial conclusions.

An innovator and experimenter, a resourceful and courageous man, his greatest fault seems to have been the inability to sell himself convincingly. He was a man of action, not of words.

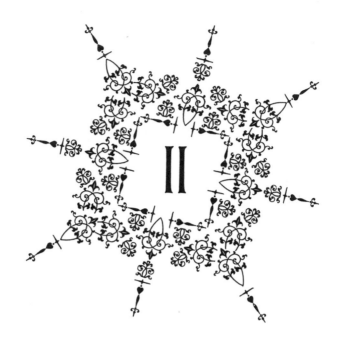

II

BETWEEN
TWO
WARS

⁓ 3 ⁑

Three on a Dream Ship

*We all have our dreams. Without them we
should be clods. It is in our dreams that we accomplish the impossible; the rich man dumps
his load of responsibility and lives in a log shack
on a mountaintop, the poor man becomes rich,
the stay-at-home travels, the wanderer finds an
abiding-place.*[1]

WORLD WAR I STILL GRIPPED THE EXHAUSTED COMBATANTS
on the battlegrounds of Europe, in the air over France, and on the
North Sea and English Channel. In the mud-slung trenches, foul
with the stench of the dead and the garbage of the living, weary foot
soldiers of all nations dreamed impossible dreams—of home, of girls
left behind, of escape to the tranquillity and unreality of some South
Seas paradise.

In the hospitals, the lucky ones who knew they would never have
to fight again anticipated the cessation of fighting and the postwar
world, and made their plans.

One of these patients was a slight, sandy-haired Englishman named
Ralph Stock, a professional writer of popular fiction who, for all his
youthfulness, had accumulated a colorful background even before the
war. He had tramped around the world on rusty freighters, worked as
a cowhand and woodsman in Canada, and now, having survived the
ultimate commitment of the young, he was alive and well in a British
field hospital awaiting transportation home.

Hope, optimism, and reprieve welled up great lumps in his throat, as in a man who has just been told he does not have cancer after all. The world, he reflected from his hospital bed, was his for the plucking, and he knew exactly what he wanted.

Discharged before the Armistice, Stock immediately began his search. He found her six months later in a backwater creek at Devon, in almost-new condition under the layers of wartime neglect. The moment he set eyes on her he knew that this was his dream ship. She was a North Sea pilot cutter, designed by the late Colin Archer and built at Porsgrund, Norway, in 1908. Slightly more than 47 feet overall, she was 41 feet on the waterline, 15 feet of beam, and drew 6 feet 6 inches of water. She was built solidly of Norway pine and Italian oak, and registered 23 tons. According to her papers, she had been in service as a lifeboat for the North Sea fishing fleet. Gaff-rigged, she could also set a large leg-of-mutton topsail, a staysail, and headsails.

There in "glorious Devon" she had been waiting for him, he wrote, but like most dreamers he had no money. "I have never had any money, but that is a detail that should never be allowed to stand in the way of a really desirable dream."[2]

With his discharge from the medical board, Stock pestered the army until he got his mustering out pay. He hermitized himself in a dingy flat and cranked out short stories which he sold easily in a wartime market. He hunted up maiden aunts upon whom he could put the bite. He did anything to make a shilling, and all of it went into the sock. In the end, the Colin Archer dream ship became his, and he named her, of course, the *Dream Ship*.

"To sail a dream," he wrote, "is an easier thing than to climb out of the rut you are probably in." But you have to be ready and willing to take the chance. "There may be excellent reasons for staying in the rut—marriage, family ties, or ill health—but those are the only insurmountable obstacles in the path of any dream merchant worth his salt."

Moreover, one must work for dream fulfillment just as one must work for anything else worthwhile. But if you have enough money to buy a car, why not get a tight little cruiser in which you can sail where you will? If you don't have the money now, you could soon make it. Even a plumber could make it, wrote Stock (in those days before plumbers became the elite of the wage earners), for their trade is "less precarious than mine."

A dream ship as large as his was not one that could be handled alone at sea—not with those huge gaff sails, even after they had been cut down to manageable size. He needed a crew, and he had one ready-made. There was his sister, a petite tomboy he called "Peter," an impish bundle of energy and enthusiasm who weighed in at ninety-eight pounds; and an officer friend, Steve, recently demobbed, who, "on hearing that these (South Sea) islands were not less than three thousand miles from the nearest early-morning parade, offered his services with unbecoming alacrity."

But owning a dream ship (which had taken all his money) and enlisting a crew were not enough. It still cost money to outfit a yacht for a voyage around the world—which was what Stock had in mind, beyond visiting the South Seas. And they were all broke. At the fish market one day, Ralph was struck by the unreasonable high cost of fresh fillets. Why the high price for fish? Because they had to be harvested by hand at sea, under wartime conditions, and as for price, don't you know there's a war on, matey? This gave him a plan. He spent some time at the waterfront pubs, there making friends with fishermen and learning to his astonishment that trawling for plaice, turbot, and sole was more profitable than writing fiction stories.

So, while Peter and Steve attended to preparations on the beach, Ralph enlisted a crew of two fishermen and spent months, until the war was over, trawling. He quickly learned that the most profitable fishing was inside the prohibited zones established by the navy, wherein numerous mines had been set for enemy submarines, and where anything that moved was considered a target. This not only appealed to his sense of adventure, but was exceedingly profitable poaching. After many close calls and misadventures, he retired from the fishing business with the necessary funds for a protracted voyage around the world.

Now it was time to clean up the *Dream Ship*, do the necessary outfitting, and load supplies aboard—among the stores were a clarinet, a half ton of "trade goods for the natives," and a piano. None of the crew knew anything about bluewater voyaging, and even less about celestial navigation, but they practiced lunar calculations and collected charts and pilot books.

On the other side of the creek, the owner of a pretty little six-tonner was also fitting out for a voyage, but his wife would not let him go, so he took out his frustrations with paint brush and scraper. Naturally, he was interested in the *Dream Ship*, and he volunteered to teach them navigation.

Peter came down from London for the last time with a load of "barter goods" that included print goods, looking glasses, imitation tortoiseshell combs, brown paper belts, and Jew's harps.

The Skipper, as their friend from the permanent moorage across the creek was called, had by now become an unpaid tutor, confidant, and watchman during their absence on foraging trips. In fact, the Skipper had become so involved with them that he could not see them go off alone this way. He volunteered to accompany them as far as Spain, until they "should get the hang of longitude."

It had been twenty years since the Skipper had last sailed. All his voyaging, for all his talk, had been only in his dreams, nurtured by his puttering around on his little six-tonner. By now, he had thought he was too old, and that maybe he had missed his dream—but by heck, in spite of his missus's objections, he was going with them at least to Spain.

So, one day in 1919, with a combined capital of one hundred pounds sterling and a clearance for Brisbane, Australia, they set sail from Devon under a dismal early-morning overcast.

No sooner was the anchor up and the sails drawing, but Steve sat on a skylight which crashed shut on one of his fingers. While the dinghy was being stowed, it crashed on the Skipper's toe. The moorings had been cast off prematurely and they found themselves on the wrong tack and sailed into a nearby fishing smack, breaking the bowsprit. Fouling most of the other hundred or so vessels moored in the harbor, they somehow managed to round the breakwater without the help of the engine, which would not start. The port navigation light was in splinters, the Skipper was steering with one hand on the tiller and the other holding his toe, and Peter was administering first aid to Steve's finger.

Then somehow they were clear and bowling along before a nor'-wester, with Ushant light showing intermittently ahead. The wind increased to a gale and flung them into the Bay of Biscay on long rolling swells, increasing until everyone including the Skipper was seasick. It was a typical rough Biscay passage, during which the kerosene tank came loose, followed by the piano, and a two-hundred pound drum of Scotch oatmeal that broke and mingled with the brine from a barrel of salt horse. Then the boom snapped off clear about five feet from the end, followed by a number of lesser episodes. Somehow, days later the sweet smell of land came to them, and under double-reefed mainsail they made the mouth of the Vigo River in Spain. The engine performed for the first time, and they came to anchor amid skyrockets, star shells, and firecrackers. The welcome was not for them, however; a Spanish fiesta was in progress. But the *Dream Ship* had made its first foreign port.

A pleasant stay was spent in Vigo, sightseeing, attending fiestas, dancing, and entertaining aboard the *Dream Ship*, which vibrated at times with songs on deck accompanied by Peter's piano below. The boom was repaired with the help of the Skipper, who reluctantly at last had to give up his dream, and with a sorrowful shake of the head limped down to the steamer dock carrying his suitcase.

The remaining crew dropped down the Vigo River and set course for Las Palmas in the Canary Islands—and somehow made it without the help of the Skipper, although they did not then, nor at any other time during the entire voyage, know where they were within a hundred miles of their estimated position.

Landfall was made somehow on the peak of Tenerife, and soon after they entered Las Palmas and were mobbed by bumboats. After several near misses, they rammed the dock of the Club Nàutico, and ashore came the 140-pound Ralph, his 98-pound sister, Peter, and their 145-pound mate, Steve.

They spent six weeks in this dirty, dreary port where the only recreation was club dances and roulette at the yacht-club tables. They made friends with the hard-bitten skipper of an American schooner, whose entire crew was absent without leave in the local jail. Steve and Peter returned his kindness with entertainment on the *Dream Ship*, featuring clarinet and piano duets. When the West Indies hurricane season was over,[3] they sailed for Trinidad on their first ocean passage, a rather boring crossing punctuated by recitations of poetry, piano and clarinet concerts under the stars, and practice in shipboard cookery and navigation, which they never seemed quite up to.

While becalmed during one dull watch, Steve and Ralph devised a game to test their sense of direction. They would throw a life ring out a few yards and then dive off to see if they could come up inside it on the first try. Once, while both of them were in the water and Peter was asleep below, a breeze sprang up, the sails filled, and *Dream Ship* began to move off without them. They yelled and swam frantically after the boat, and at the last moment up from the cabin came the petite pajamaed figure of Peter. She started a sleepy yawn and stretch, heard voices from astern, and then screamed in horror. Quickly, she unlashed the tiller and came up into the wind. A few minutes later, with Steve and Ralph aboard, the *Dream Ship* was boiling along at seven knots.

Although they had aimed for Trinidad, Barbados turned up first, so they settled for that and soon came to anchor in Bridgetown.

There they spent two weeks "swizzling" with the local smart set, and Stock noted in his log that the American consulate was swamped with black refugees from the new self-governing dominion trying to get visas into the United States.[4]

From the West Indies, they made the rough passage to Colón, a distance of 1,200 miles in seven days. They were measured for the canal passage and paid the $15 toll, reducing their capital to $78. They took on the pilot and after the usual harrowing experience in the locks,[5] passed out into Gatun Lake. There the engine refused to work, and not being allowed to sail through the canal, they were forced to hire a tug at $6 an hour. They arrived finally at San Miguel, after a somewhat nightmarish trip for them, and tied up at the "Onion Club" in Panama city.[6] Soon they were participating in the waterfront life, sipping beer in the bistros and listening to painted damsels rasping painful ballads amid the tinkling ice and tobacco smoke.

To refit for the next leg, they anchored off the busy sea lane into Balboa, a key point on the route that was already becoming an oceanic freeway for yachts escaping to the South Pacific. Following Stock in *Dream Ship* later would come Harry Pidgeon in *Islander*, Alain Gerbault in *Firecrest*, Robinson (twice) in *Svaap*, Dwight Long, Muhlhauser, and a hundred other well-knowns, plus thousands of anonymous sea wanderers.[7]

By now they were broke, but by that great good fortune that follows those who carry on with good heart in spite of such minor distractions, Ralph received word from his agent in New York that one of his books had been purchased by a Hollywood movie producer. It was an unexpected windfall of breathtaking amounts. When Ralph cashed the check at the bank, he exchanged it for $20 gold pieces which he brought down to the *Dream Ship* and rained on the salon table to the stunned pleasure of his companions. They now had plenty of funds for an extended voyage, at least as far as Australia.

Setting out for the Galápagos, they made an easy passage and a perfect landfall on Tower Island by sheer good luck. In fact, they almost sailed right up on the rocks before they rushed on deck to find that they were within jumping distance of shore. Their destination was Cristobal—which they never did find—finally bypassing it with the intention of sailing on to the Society Islands. By accident, they came upon Wreck Bay, just missing the outlying reef, and came to anchor. Here they heard about the current treasure-hunting excitement, but decided not to join the rush.[8]

After an enjoyable visit ashore, they filled their water tanks with doubtful fluid by means of empty kerosene cans,[9] and filled away for the Marquesas. On board, they had a new crew mate, the local Ecuadorian *comisario*, who was tired of the long hours and low pay, a handsome lad who wore silk socks, a passionate tie, and a loudly striped shirt.

For the next twenty-two days, they carried a southeast trade wind, during which the *comisario* suffered alternately from seasickness, homesickness, and chronic laziness. The water tanks became aquariums for all manner of bug life and the biscuit supply crumbled under an army of red ants. Otherwise, it was a fine passage and soon Nuku Hiva appeared across a sparkling blue bay. Here they encountered their first South Sea paradise island.

With the war over, they found on Melville's *Typee* a collection of war veterans, dropouts, and copouts from the world of reality—English and French ex-soldiers with whom they drank, compared war stories, and raised toasts to the Royal Field Artillery, the Mitrailleurs, and the incomparable French infantry. After goat hunting and sailing along the coast and commenting on the new wave of missionaries infesting the South Seas,[10] they sailed on.

Seven days after leaving the Marquesas, they were becalmed in that frightening maze of atolls and coral reefs called the Tuamotus or Dangerous Archipelago. After some time with the pearl fleet, they finally made it to Papeete, Tahiti, tying up stern first to the quay and going ashore to enjoy iced *vin rouge*, and to dine on *poulet rôti* with fresh *salade* and *omelette à la maître d'hôtel*.

The *Dream Ship* crew found Tahiti to be all they had hoped and Papeete an exotic crossroads for the romantic South Seas, with planters and schooner traders, remittance men and adventurers, and a Sadie Thompson or two, all mingled in that unique type of society for which the French colonies are known. At Papeete, they lost their Galápagos *comisario*, who turned out to be a fair cook after all, but who never got over his seasickness, homesickness, or laziness. The last they saw of "Bill," as they called him, he was selling underwear and perfume in a French store, and escorting admiring Tahitian beauties to the movies every night.[11]

With some regret, the *Dream Ship* crew escaped the euphoria of Papeete and continued their adventure at Mooréa, fifteen miles away.

Ralph was able to repair the recalcitrant engine with one of Peter's hairpins, cleaning out the carburetor air vent which had been the source of all the trouble. From there, they sailed to Palmerston Island during the tail end of the hurricane season, visiting William Masters, the charming old seadog who had come to this place in 1862, leased it, married three wives, by each of whom he had a large family, and all of whom now lived a simple but happy and wholesome life.

Next they called at Savage Island, or Niue, the former haunt of the terrible blackbirder, Bully Hayes. The Friendly Islands came next, now the kingdom of Tonga, where the crew of the *Dream Ship* were warmly entertained.

It was here, at the island capital city of Nuku Alofa, in a local social club, that Ralph met a genial gentleman who much admired the Colin Archer cutter and wanted to buy her. Stock said he did not want to sell. The man asked him how much the vessel was worth to him. Stock replied with such an outrageous figure that he expected the genial gentleman to be off. Instead, the genial gentleman said, "I'll take her," and whipped out his checkbook.

In a daze, Ralph Stock left the club with a small fortune, but no *Dream Ship*. The voyage had come to an end. Now one problem remained: how to break the news to Peter and Steve. This proved to be painful and embarrassing, and Peter would not speak to Ralph for days.

Flushed with new wealth, Ralph tried to salve the situation with a new plan. They would continue their journey around the world, but by steamer, stopping at various places to explore at their leisure. No more seasickness, faulty celestial navigation, bad water, and harbor thieves. They would do their circumnavigation in style.

But his companions were not buying this. Steve went to Samoa and obtained a government job in Apia. Peter took herself off to New Guinea alone. Ralph went to New Zealand and Australia, visiting until he became bored with it all. Hearing about the pearl luggers of Torres Strait, he hurried to Thursday Island in hopes of finding another *Dream Ship*. But his stay on "T.I.," or "Thirsty Island," was spent socializing with the local military and government families and the owners of the pearling fleet. The population numbered only five hundred, and most of them remembered very well the visit of Captain Joshua Slocum. Ralph went skin diving with the Japanese divers, made several side trips, and tried to put together a dictionary of pidgin English. Then one day a steamer from New Guinea tied up to the wharf and off stepped Peter, this time in a more forgiving mood.

Together they made their way home via the Indian Ocean, the Suez Canal, and the Mediterranean, never having found another *Dream Ship*.

Back in England, Stock restarted his sporadic literary career, spent his spare time looking for another yacht, lived in France for a while where he became acquainted with another ex-soldier, now a famous tennis star and restless young socialite named Alain Gerbault.

Once more returning to England, Stock wrote a couple of books and several stories and finally found *Dream Ship II*, an English Bristol Channel pilot cutter, for which he paid £1,450. Immediately he notified Peter to come a-running and sent a cable off to Steve in Samoa.

Then one day, while he was working on deck, a thin, lithe, sharp-faced young man appeared alongside. It was his friend Alain Gerbault from France, in England for the tennis matches. He came aboard, and Ralph got out his best wine. Gerbault seemed somewhat preoccupied, but he expressed much admiration for Stock's new boat. He had read Ralph's book on the South Pacific cruise. They talked of ships and bluewater sailing, and of anchorages in faraway tropical ports. Life had become a bore, unreal, Gerbault confided. There must be some meaning to it all, somewhere.

While they talked, Gerbault's eyes wandered to a nearby yacht, a sleek, lean Dixon Kemp six-meter racing machine with the plumb stem and the extreme overhanging counter popular in that day. The name on the transom was *Firecrest*.

Gerbault inquired of the yacht. Was she for sale? Probably. Would Ralph introduce him to the owner? But, of course. In the end, *Firecrest* became Alain Gerbault's dream ship and magic carpet to immortality.

As for Ralph Stock and his *Dream Ship II*, the new voyage to romance and exotic places never materialized. Somehow the zest had gone out of it. As with the novelty and thrill of a first love affair, everything else was anticlimactic.

Once dreams are gone, Stock came to understand, they cannot be rekindled. When he sold his boat in Nuku Alofa, he had peddled his dreams for coin. Such fragile, nebulous things cannot be tinkered with. You must grab them while you can, for usually you do not get a second chance.

CHAPTER

4

Amaryllis Shows the Flag

At first sight it may seem a remarkable feat to take a small vessel of twenty-eight tons gross around the world via New Zealand, and a relatively short time ago it would have been so regarded, but it is now recognized that quite small, well-found vessels are safe even in bad weather. They are not comfortable under such conditions, indeed they are acutely, almost intolerably, uncomfortable, but most of them are safe if properly handled.[1]

THE AUTUMN SUN HUNG LOW AND BLINDING TO THE EYES when facing it. The harbor at Plymouth, England, lay still and not a ruffle of wind disturbed its oily sheen. Presently chugging along, raking a deep furrow and rolling smooth twin waves from her plumb bow, comes a yawl-rigged Brixham-type yacht, starchly white under a new coat of paint, her gaffs swaying gently as her two-cylinder American kerosene engine pushes her at four knots toward the open sea.

At the dockhead stands the deputy assistant harbormaster in his new blue uniform with gold lace. Across the water comes his voice:

"Hallo! What ship is that?"

"The *Amaryllis*."

"Where bound?"

"Auckland, New Zealand."

There is a pause, then: "Well, good luck."

The time was September 6, 1920. The long and exhausting world war had been over for almost two years. England and the world had begun to recover. War wounds were healing. Adventure again had begun to appeal to restless men. Ex-sailors, with four to six years of hellish sea duty behind them during the war, either never wanted to see salt water again, or were drawn back by incurable sea fever.

One of the latter was the ex-Lieutenant George H. P. Muhlhauser, who had served brilliantly as navigator and commander of Q-ships, patrol craft, hydrophone trawlers, and minesweepers. One day, while waiting in an Admiralty office, Muhlhauser glanced idly through a set of *Sailing Directions* for various parts of the world. The descriptions of exotic ports, courses recommended through intriguing straits, winds and currents in the high southern latitudes, struck a vague response. He could not get this out of his mind, and when demobilized soon after and a free man and his own master once again, he determined to find himself a suitable vessel and sail her around.

He found his dream fulfilled in the *Amaryllis*, which a well-known yachtsman had been outfitting for a West Indies voyage before changing his mind. Muhlhauser paid an exorbitant price for her, although she was not the ideal vessel in his opinion,[2] and then suffered through long months of shipyard strikes and shortages before he was ready to sail.

Amaryllis[3] had been built in 1882 by A. E. Payne—later Summers and Payne—and her hull was still as sound as the day she was launched. Of 36 tons Thames and 28 tons gross, she was 62 feet overall, 52 feet on the waterline, 13 feet beam, and drew 10 feet of water. There was 3½ tons of lead on the keel and the rest inside was iron ballast.

She was flush decked with skylights and hatches, but had no cabin trunk. Below in the fo'c's'le were cots for three men and a coal stove; behind this were the pantry and lavatory, with an alleyway to the saloon. Then came a cabin on the starboard side, the small engine on the port side, and finally the owner's cabin with two bunks.

Muhlhauser, a bachelor, was already in his middle forties, and in his pragmatic, rather starch-collared way, he was working off a middle-aged itch. Born in Surrey, England, he was educated at Merchant Taylor's School and immediately went into business. But since childhood he had had a deep affection for the sea and ships. During school holidays, he would ship out with the North Sea trawling fleet. Once in business in Essex, he was able to save up enough to buy an interest in a three-ton sloop in 1901. Four years later, he and two friends purchased the *Vivid*, and in 1910 Muhlhauser became sole owner of the *Wilful*.

Muhlhauser's idea of yachting was to put to sea and stay out of sight of land until he had to come back. He became an expert in the ways of the sea and especially in navigation. A few weeks before the guns of World War I thundered, he sailed *Wilful* to Norway and back with a companion who was sick all the time and stayed in his bunk. Muhlhauser gloried in the boisterous passage, and turned around without going ashore to make the return trip, much to the disgust of his companion.

Just after his return, England went on a wartime footing. He laid up his yacht and volunteered for the Royal Naval Reserve, obtaining a commission and later transferring with a fellow yachtsman, Stuart Garnett, to active sea duty on the former steam yacht *Zarefah*, which was manned by Cambridge rowing blues.

A superb seaman and a natural and instinctive navigator, his most astonishing exploit was taking the captured German oreship *Dusseldorf* of 1,200 tons from Norway to Scotland without a sextant and a compass made erratic by the ore. Traveling in a North Sea storm and with a rebellious German crew, Muhlhauser made a perfect landfall after weaving through the minefields.

So now, on September 6, 1920, he stood at the tiller of his own ship again, his piercing blue eyes conning the channel with the easy attention of the professional.[4] Graying hair showed around the band of his yachting cap with the RCC emblem. He was a reserved man, not easily approached except by close friends, inclined to be frank and direct in his remarks. His lips formed a close straight line, and he had prominent clefts in his cheeks, a bold bulldog chin, pug nose, and dark heavy eyebrows. He spoke in crisp tones and was inclined to be somewhat lofty with those not considered his equals. He was a martinet aboard a vessel, but with close friends he was a warm, sensitive person. He was, in every way, a professional yachtsman. He had already published one book on the subject,[5] and in the back of his mind he planned another based on his journals of this voyage around the world.

Aboard the *Amaryllis*, Muhlhauser carried 240 charts, which would take him as far as Australia. Before he returned, the number would grow to 500, and he would have sailed a total of 31,159 miles, ending at Dartmouth.

His circumnavigation took him to Vigo, Spain; thence to Las Palmas, Funchal, Santa Cruz, Barbados, Trinidad, and the Caribbean islands, the Panama Canal, Marquesas, Tahiti, Fiji, Australia, New Zealand, the East Indies, the Indian Ocean, the Red Sea, the Suez Canal, and the Mediterranean.

Amaryllis was believed to be the third small vessel to circumnavigate, and the first English yacht.[6]

Typical of Muhlhauser, although he did not like the *Amaryllis* and the voyage began to bore him by the time he reached the South Pacific, he took time to thoroughly cruise New Zealand and Southwest Pacific waters, which had seldom been done, and he was the first to cruise extensively through the East Indies. His seamanship, flawless passages—that included plotting great circle courses even near the equator—and boldness of decision make him one of the greatest of all small-boat voyagers.

As the *Amaryllis* made for the sea, the burgee of the Royal Cruising Club flew from her masthead. Guests and crew aboard included Charles L. Prowse, a RCC member, his brother, John M. Prowse, and A. D. (David) Craig, a young Irishman who had responded to an advertisement from Italy. Muhlhauser had also signed on a young fisherman to go as far as New Zealand, who turned out to be a dud and had to be bought off with a month's pay in order to get rid of him even before they left England. Charles Prowse was an experienced yachtsman; his brother, John, who was not, volunteered to be cook.

Off Ushant, they were becalmed, but the passage to Spain took only five days, and gave them an opportunity to shake down their gear and routine. They left Vigo on September 17 for Funchal, Madeira, and on this leg experienced a violent series of squalls, easily weathered, which proved to be the last bad weather experienced before *Amaryllis* reached Tahiti, 8,500 miles away.

In Funchal, they took on fresh fruits, dined at the Palace Hotel, and made the hair-raising toboggan ride down the cobbled street on a sled piloted by two elderly men.

From there, they sailed to Las Palmas, where they obtained Greenwich time from a British warship and loaded aboard more fresh fruits. Leaving Las Palmas, David Craig came down with a virus, and unable to beat it back they put into Santa Cruz, Tenerife, to see a doctor. After a short visit, they departed for the West Indies. A few miles out, John Prowse came down with the same virus. Muhlhauser consulted the Ship Medical Guide, and the only thing he could find with the same symptoms was beriberi. They decided it was the same mild virus that David had caught.

Landfall was made on Barbados, and twenty days out of Tenerife they put into Carlisle Bay off Bridgetown. After the formalities of customs, health, and harbor fees, they settled down for a short stay. John left the yacht here, finding work on a vessel going to the United States. Muhlhauser tried to recruit a crewman to take his place, including a convict the prison warden wanted to get rid of, but in the end found a bright lad from a Venezuelan schooner, named Stèphane, whom Muhlhauser described as "90 per cent white, but for his woolly hair would pass anywhere, except perhaps in America."[7]

Stèphane could write but not speak English, although he could speak both French and Spanish, which Muhlhauser attributed to the fact that the lad was *"un peu catholique, un peu protestant."* He was quick to learn and became a faithful if somewhat erratic member of the crew.

They stayed a month in Trinidad, where they were entertained by the local society and diplomatic corps. Muhlhauser had to discharge James, a native boy he had also signed on, who turned out to be a trouble-maker who had the cunning to know something of his "rights." Muhlhauser had to buy him off, too, and send him home first-class on a steamer.

The *Amaryllis* continued a leisurely cruise of the West Indies, during which time David joined his wife in Jamaica and left the ship. Charles Prowse had already taken his departure. So now Muhlhauser had only Stèphane to help him with the big yacht. A broken boom caused by a gybe, and a fouled propeller delayed them in Kingston. A San Blas Indian named Sam was taken on here upon the recommendation of the local sailmaker. Sam could speak no English and only enough Spanish to quarrel incessantly with Stèphane.

On March 4, they departed for Colón, went through the usual formalities, and made the canal transit. Muhlhauser reported a delightful visit here with the consular corps and the American colony. Several days were spent at Balboa, taking on stores and getting clearances for the Galápagos and Marquesas. The well-known Ecuadorian red tape was frustrating, but Muhlhauser was determined to visit the "Darwin" islands (made famous by Charles Darwin of the *Beagle*), influenced by Ralph Stock's fascinating account of his visit the year before. On April 9, they crossed the equator and celebrated with a Christmas pudding sent by Muhlhauser's sister, and an extra issue of jam, which the boys ate like candy.

They spent a short time in the Galápagos, just long enough to take on water, and then departed on the 3,057-mile leg to the Marquesas.

The time passed quickly, but as Muhlhauser wrote: "A small sailing ship wants as much looking after as a harem, and there was always something to do about the decks." The only break in the routine otherwise was the constant bickering of Sam and Stèphane.

On May 10, they came to anchor under the lee of Ua Huka and the next day sailed into Nuku Hiva. Here Muhlhauser was greeted by the legendary Bob McKittrick, and made the acquaintance of the famous Nuku Hiva *no-no* fly. A pleasant time was had with the local colony, which included beachcombers, American botanists, and French officials. In Tahiti, Muhlhauser met a broad-gauge American named Frank N. Abercrombie, whom he took a liking to, and who joined the ship at various times in the South Pacific. Muhlhauser was also astounded and somewhat disturbed that the British consul in Papeete was an American. "Why this should be so, when there are plenty of suitable British about, seems strange," he wrote.

Considerable time was spent in Mooréa with friends, including Captain Gilmour, an RAF ace who had thirty-four German airplanes to his record, and who had escaped after the war to the South Seas to live in seclusion with a Chinese servant.

Muhlhauser did not enjoy his stay at Rarotonga, mostly because of the noisy natives who pestered him. In Nuku Alofa, he came upon a piano which he said had once been aboard the *Amaryllis* before he owned her.[8]

At Suva, he met another local personality often mentioned by voyagers in the 1920s, the obliging harbormaster, Mr. Twentymen. Here Muhlhauser also encountered his first newspaper reporters, whom he despised. One, a Mr. Able, rowed out to interview him, and although Muhlhauser told him nothing, "he had made quite a long article out of it."

He goes into great detail about the famed German raider, Count Von Lucknow, who ended his career in these parts. On September 9, his friend Abercrombie showed up on the steamer and joined the *Amaryllis* as cook. They stopped for a visit at New Caledonia, where they were "depressed" by Nouméa. At Sydney, after a rough passage, Abercrombie told George he wouldn't take a million dollars for the experience, and wouldn't do it again for another million. Both the men fell in readily with the social whirl of Sydney, and received much attention from the press and newsreels. Stèphane and Sam saw themselves on the screen for the first time—to their delight and Muhlhauser's disgust. Here Muhlhauser met an old Q-ship comrade and suffered an attack of homesickness.

He was now fed up with his ship and the voyage and tried to sell *Amaryllis*. Failing this, he sailed for New Zealand and spent two pleasant months cruising the coast. The Tasman Sea crossing was a nasty one, and Christmas Day was spent hove-to. Again he advertised *Amaryllis* for sale, and finding no takers for a forty-year-old ship, he had no alternative but to sail her home. There were three possible routes: westward and north of Australia, via the islands of the East Indies, and around Cape Horn. He chose the exotic East Indies, waters that were not well-charted and through which few yachts had ever gone.

Sam left the ship in New Zealand, and in his place came aboard a Niue islander named Pinimake or "Joe" for short. Joe did not get along with Stèphane even as well as Sam, so Muhlhauser took on a man named C. R. Tadgell of Melbourne, who wanted passage home to England. He was a man of twenty-five and experienced on sailing dinghies—and as it turned out, he was an agreeable companion. Moreover, Tadgell brought along some eighty admiralty charts.

After four months in New Zealand, the *Amaryllis* departed, stopping again at New Caledonia, on her way to New Guinea, New Britain, the Solomons, Java Sea, Timor, Singapore, and Penang. This intricate leg of thousands of miles was made in typical flawless fashion. It was especially enjoyable to Muhlhauser, who was fascinated by the region and the people. Tadgell and the boys fell ill several times with various diseases, but if Muhlhauser was distressed, he never hinted at it in his journals. In some backwater areas, formerly under German control, he found people who did not even know the war was over. Frequent stops were made for sightseeing, and Muhlhauser proved to be a fair-to-good photographer.

From Bali, they went to Batavia, then across to Sumatra, sailed up Banka Strait to Singapore, then through the Malacca Strait past the tip of Sumatra at Sabang, and stopped at the Nicobar Islands.

From here, Muhlhauser felt at last they were on the homeward leg. He began worrying about his business, and how to sell the ship. The crew now included a Lascar, Abdul Rahman, hired for $25 a month and homeward passage; and a man named Enden, who soon resigned in a huff over one of Muhlhauser's candid remarks.

A ketch or schooner, Muhlhauser noted in his journals, would be more suited to the tropics. The gaff yawl, he conceded, was the worst type for a voyage of this kind.

At Sabang, he checked his chronometer with the captain of a Dutch ship, and found an error of only two seconds. At Colombo,

Ceylon, they took on provisions, and Muhlhauser met another Q-ship comrade, now the pilot of a tug. The hull was scrubbed and routine repairs made. Muhlhauser found Aden, on the coast of South Arabia, to be a fascinating combination of Moorish and Oriental culture. The passage up the Red Sea was a difficult one, with head winds and uncharted reefs. At Port Sudan, they restocked and enjoyed the local hospitality. On March 29, they left Suez and proceeded up the canal, stopping at the midway point of Ismailia, where Muhlhauser and Tadgell left the ship for a visit to Cairo and the pyramids, and spent some time at the yacht club in Alexandria. Returning to the ship, they went on through into the Mediterranean after pausing again at Alexandria for more party-going. The thirty-day passage through the Red Sea is considered, even today, as a most remarkable one, and by now Muhlhauser was considered a celebrity in yachting circles.

Before leaving Alexandria, he had the ship's bottom coppered, and accepted a life membership in the Royal Yacht Club of Egypt. He inspected the Boy Scouts and Girl Guides at ceremonies as the band played "God Save the King."

On April 22, he departed with a large escort, including the Scouts who raised their oars in salute. He had taken on another crew member, a man named Horowitz, who was soon discharged. Following a quarrel with Stèphane at Malta, Hashim, a new recruit, also wanted to leave, but was reconciled. Stèphane then tried to resign and even left the ship, but returned later. Another new man named Galea came aboard.

"Galea," Muhlhauser wrote in his rock-ribbed Empire Tory style, "is shaping up very well. It is a great thing to have a white man forward; natives are all very well in their way, but a white man is best."

He stopped at Cagliari Harbor, Italy, for sail repairs. It was now 750 miles to Gibraltar, and 1,070 miles to Dartmouth. He was getting anxious. A stop was made at Minorca. Then came Gibraltar and lunch with the Admiral and members of the RCC and a visit to a Moorish castle. At Vigo, Spain, a stop was made after a rough passage past Portugal. At 7 A.M., on July 6, land appeared out of the mist. The next day, the *Amaryllis* entered Dartmouth harbor and moored at the yacht club, ending the long voyage around the world. Muhlhauser's arrival was met with quiet British reserve. Not a single reporter was there to interview him. He was immensely relieved.

The last entry in his journals was:

"Here not a soul has taken the slightest notice. It is delightful. I smile when I think of the ruses I planned to avoid reporters. This is a real homecoming to dear old casual England."

He did not live to finish his book. It ends in the East Indies. There were some knotty business affairs to take care of. For many weeks, he had the feeling that all was not well, that his time was running out. Once home was reached, he began to go downhill rapidly. A friend, E. Keble Chatterton, saw him on the *Amaryllis* in August and reported that Muhlhauser had aged ten years in three. Then he had to enter a hospital for an operation.[9] Not long after he died. He was buried, as he would have wished it, with the White Ensign, under which he had served so well, and the Blue Ensign, which he had flown from the *Amaryllis*'s mizzen around the world. These two flags, Chatterton said later, symbolized Muhlhauser's life.

His book was finished by his sister, who edited down the voluminous journals to fit the publication limits.

Always aloof and uncompromising, with rather Blimpish views of social and political matters and a somewhat condescending manner toward those below his station, he was, however, a man who all his life had one overwhelming passion, and that was for the sea.[10]

CHAPTER

5

Hi Jinks on the Speejacks

Man was never meant to dwell for a year and a half in a world measuring 98 feet by 16 feet, and if he sets out to do so he must be prepared to pay a price for the happy memories which will be his reward for the foolhardiness.[1]

As the decade of the 1920s began, the world was still adjusting to the post-Armistice economy and social upheaval, if not to peace. In the United States, Red anarchists were being deported by the shipload from Ellis Island. Troops were deployed along the Mexican border as Americans were being killed by *Villistas*. President Wilson had come home from Versailles broken in health and in spirit by double-dealing and with less to show for his efforts than the defeated but truculent enemy.

Elsewhere, violence continued in Germany and Switzerland, where Reds were fomenting riot and revolution, and a permanent League of Nations had been empowered to maintain liberty and justice forever. Insulin, discovered by Canadian doctors, made possible the treatment of diabetes for the first time. Captain John Alcock and Lieutenant Arthur W. Brown flew nonstop across the Atlantic in a Vickers-Vimy from Newfoundland to Ireland, most of the time "upside down" in a heavy fog, making the 1,980 miles in 16 hours and 12 minutes.

It was the decade of the Flappers, rum-runners in the dry United States, bow ties and Bearcats, Hemingway and Fitzgerald, speakeasies and short skirts, Charleston and runaway inflation, shortages of everything but bathtub gin, barnstorming thrill-seekers in war-surplus Jennies—and of circumnavigators in small ships.

Joshua Slocum and John Voss had already done their thing. Jack and Charmian London had already abandoned their *Snark* in the South Pacific and gone back to their own paradise in Mill Valley. Ralph and Mabel Stock and their friend, Steve, were on their way in the piano-equipped *Dream Ship*. The quiet martinet, G. H. P. Muhlhauser, was about to embark in his *Amaryllis*. Puckish Conor O'Brien was having his *Saoirse* finished at Baltimore in Ireland, even as the Civil War was ending. Captain Harry Pidgeon had completed *Islander* on a Los Angeles harbor tide flat and was getting ready for his world trip by making a shakedown cruise to Hawaii and back.

In New York City, the summer heat wave of 1921 continued fiercely into August, breaking all records, drying up reservoirs. The first automatic telephones were being installed. Herbert Hoover made a speech in Washington that was heard and *seen* in New York on an experimental A.T.&T. apparatus called "television," but commercial use of it was doubted by many experts in the industry.

On August 21 a vessel named the *Speejacks* departed New York with a crew of eleven men and one woman, outbound on what was one of the most astonishing and unusual, if not entirely arduous circumnavigations.

Speejacks had been built by Consolidated Shipbuilding Company of Morris Heights for a wealthy Cleveland and Chicago industrialist and sportsman named Albert Y. Gowen and his wife, Jean, a charming and outgoing Texas beauty. *Speejacks*[2] was the fifth yacht of this name built for Gowen, each one a little larger and more elaborate. She was built of wood, with teak decks and coppered bottom, 98 feet overall by 17 feet wide and drawing only 6 feet of water. A typical J. P. Morgan type of yacht, she had a straight stem, rounded fantail, single dummy stack coming out of the deckhouse, a full-length awning, and a mast on which a steadying sail could be set. *Speejacks* was powered by two 250 horsepower Winton gasoline engines, consumed about 2 gallons a mile at cruising speed of 8 knots, although she had a top speed of 14 knots. Her fuel capacity was 5,000 gallons and Gowen had arranged for fuel dumps at strategic points around the world. The problem was that *Speejacks* had a safe cruising range of only about 2,000 miles and some of the ocean passages were nearly 4,000 miles long. But for a man like Gowen, this was just another little challenge to be accepted.

The yacht reflected Gowen's nature. Virtually a mini-ocean liner, she was a self-contained little world, equipped not only with the most modern internal combustion engines, but with intercabin telephones, an elaborate wireless communications system, electric heating, lighting, refrigeration, cooking, and ship-handling machinery. In addition to the usual life-saving equipment, there was a large raft mounted on the deckhouse top, and two small boats including a New England dory.

Provisions for months at sea were stored aboard, including fresh meat, fish, and vegetables in the freezers and coolers. Every possible item of luxury, convenience, and emergency was aboard—including two World War I machine guns in case they were attacked by pirates.

The Gowens occupied one of the two luxurious cabins aft; the other was taken by a party of guests that included Ira (Jay) J. Ingraham and Bernard (Burney) F. Rogers, Jr., both of Chicago. Ingraham was a professional motion-picture photographer who recorded the voyage on 100,000 feet of film. Rogers was an accomplished amateur photographer and a friend of the Gowens. In Australia, another guest came aboard, Dale Collins, a friend of a friend of the Gowens who became the expedition's official chronicler, equipped with endless enthusiasm and admiration for the Gowens, if not with much writing talent.

The crew included Cal, the Australian wireless operator; Oscar, assistant to the chief engineer, Jack, who had also supervised construction of *Speejacks*; the navigator, Cap, also an Australian; Bert, the moon-faced Belgian cook, who was afflicted most of the time with seasickness; and Louis, a French sailor gone native on the beach in Tahiti where they picked him up as a deckhand. For the first half of the voyage, the captain was Jack Lewis, who even performed a marriage ceremony (of doubtful legality) aboard ship.

The sea tracks of *Speejacks*, as Collins called them, took the yacht from New York to Panama via Jamaica; from Balboa to Tahiti, Fiji, Samoa, Nouméa, Australia, New Guinea, the Solomons, New Britain, the Admiralty and Hermit Islands, Spice Islands, Celebes, Java, Singapore, Seychelles, the Red Sea, Cairo, and Spain; thence across the Atlantic by the southern route to the West Indies, Miami, and home to New York.

Flying the burgee of the Cleveland Yacht Club, *Speejacks* motored 34,000 miles and consumed 73,000 gallons of gasoline costing from 31 cents to $1.24 a gallon to become the first motorboat in history to circumnavigate.

The run to Jamaica was uneventful, although they just missed a hurricane. At Panama, they encountered another and larger yacht, the *Aloha*, owned by Commodore Arthur Curtis James of New York, also making a famous circumnavigation. Alongside the *Aloha*, *Speejacks* looked like a tender. The canal transit was made without difficulty. In Panama, a Peruvian oil magnate tried to court Jean, whom he thought was Gowen's daughter. Once through the canal and tied up at the Balboa Yacht Club, their first problem faced them—the 4,000-mile passage to Tahiti with no refueling stops. How was this to be accomplished? By obtaining a tow, of course. Gowen arranged to have the U.S. steamship *Eastern Queen* take them in tow so they would not have to burn any gasoline until they got within range of a supply.

Speejacks thus could also claim the longest tow of its kind in history. A 10-inch manila hauser, forming a sling or cradle around the entire ship, was used. This was attached to a 6-inch towing cable. Although *Speejacks* was a superbly designed and built yacht, she was tender and quick in a seaway. Under tow, she was even worse. The 3,400 mile tow was a nightmare from the start. Everyone was seasick almost continuously, and no one became accustomed to the awful motion. Cooking was virtually impossible. Meals became mere snacks grabbed with one hand while hanging on with the other, eaten merely to keep alive. At one point during some rough weather, the *Eastern Queen* sent over a crew to adjust the rope cradle. They were overcome by seasickness and the *Speejacks* crew had to finish the job.

They crossed the equator on October 3, during cold, squally weather. A week later, a wireless message was intercepted with the news that *Speejacks* had been lost at sea. The news made headlines all over the world and caused much consternation at home. The *Eastern Queen* dispatched a signal that all was well.

About eighteen days out, the water supply ran low and the crew was limited to a gallon a day.[3] On the twenty-first day, the *Eastern Queen* notified *Speejacks* on the wireless that she was about to release the tow rope and make for Takaroa. The Winton engines were started, and the *Speejacks* got underway on her own, hoping for an easy hundred-mile run to replenish water tanks. Only twenty gallons of distilled battery water remained on the yacht. But, at midnight, the rudder cable broke and an emergency tiller was rigged. In the morning, Takaroa appeared on the horizon. The party found much hospitality here, but no water. They were entertained with dancing, singing, and a roast pig. Among the visitors was the famous schooner *Roberta* and Captain Winnie Brander. Burney Rogers and Jean demonstrated the latest Broadway dance steps on the beach under *Speejacks*'s electric lights, to the tune of the latest music on the gramophone records.

The 250 miles to Tahiti were made without water. There the captain took time to marry a couple. The bridegroom was the father of a well-known American baseball player, and the bride the divorced wife of a local gentleman who also was the best man at the wedding and gave the bride away. The reason for the shipboard wedding was French law, which prohibited remarriage within six months. After the wedding, a huge party was given for everyone at the home of the ex-husband.

Speejacks left Tahiti for Pago Pago on the same day that 200 townspeople gathered to watch a Chinese being beheaded, which rounded out the entertainment during their stay there. The 1,300-mile passage to Samoa was a rough one, during which green water was taken over the ship and the electric system drowned out temporarily.

The next leg took them to Fiji and past Good Hope Island, otherwise known as the Tin Can Island.[4] In Fiji, everyone went sightseeing in earnest. During the eleven days there, they spent ten days on a canoe trip up the Wainibuka River, each night stopping at a native village and eating native food. They witnessed the fire walkers of Bequa, dined on turtle flippers, drank *kava*, and were entertained by native chiefs who had been educated in Europe.

Nouméa, the capital of New Caledonia, came next, after an 800-mile rough passage, with the crew landing on New Year's Day. Here they found Jack London's *Snark*, now a dirty and neglected island trader.[5] The party noted that the island was overrun with deer, which were hunted wholesale. The government even paid a bounty on them.

The next stop was Australia, where Dale Collins joined the cruise. From Sydney, the yacht meandered along the coast of Queensland for a thousand miles. Many stops were made to explore ashore where they met hermits and aborigines, and beachcombers on the famous Dunk Island. On March 12, they turned through Cook Passage and headed for New Guinea, making Port Moresby their first landfall.

Here they all joined in adventures among the pearl divers, and visited savages living among the mangroves, missionary stations, and sticky Australian plantations. Up the coastline of Papua, they cruised, stopping to fish and explore. Leaving New Guinea waters, they sailed for the Trobriands through unmarked and uncharted reefs. After two days, they reached these "isles of pearls," a romantic, lovely, and mystical paradise guarded by reefs and great sharks. They reached Rabaul in New Britain at Easter. At Maron, north of the Admiralty Islands, they celebrated the twenty-fifth anniversary of the Anzacs at Gallipoli with four ex-soldiers aboard to help them. The party was held in the tropical palace, built by the German Pacific millionaire, Rudolph Wahlen, in prewar days.

Next came Hollandia, the cosmopolitan city in the Dutch New Guineas of the Southwest Pacific.[6] During their visit, the Bird of Paradise boom was on, and these gorgeous birds were being hunted down and exploited. Two pounds each was the going price for these beautiful golden-brown and rare creatures. Many of the Dutch colonials they met had not seen Europe or their homes for more than thirty years, but still held on rigidly to their "civilized" old country customs.

For the trip to Ambon on the island of Ceram, they had a fuel supply of only 2,080 gallons—the exact amount calculated to reach their destination without refueling. They tried to get a tow from a Dutch ship, but were quoted a price of £500. Running on one engine to save fuel, they started out. On the eighth day, they reached Ambon with a margin of only 100 gallons of fuel left.

Here, for the first time, they entered a different world—one of spices; Malays in bright sarongs; Arabs in gold-topped, round white hatchs; bearded Indians; Chinese riding bicycles in their "pajamas"; bullock carts, and a river of humanity with all the smells of the ancient Orient. Among these odors, Collins commented, were those of spices, drying fish and smoke, and the "distinctive smell of coloured peoples."

Here they found the Dutch masters, living in the colonial splendor of three hundred years of rule—the social routine of afternoon siestas, evening drives in the country, whist clubs, drinking beer and gin at the clubs, dances and concerts, entertaining on the wide verandas of their baronial cottages, dining late at nine or ten o'clock. They found the Dutch colonials to be great eaters, starting at six A.M. with a breakfast of sausage, snacks of cold meat, spiced tidbits; later, *riz tafel* or rice table was served at midday, with dozens of native boys waiting upon them carrying plates of stewed meats, curry, salted and smoked fish, boiled fowl, chutneys, bread made from prawns and batter, spices that burned like hot coals. In the evening came another *riz tafel*, and then the main banquet.

Next came the Celebes, the great whirlpools of the Malay Straits, and a visit to the sultan of the fairy kingdom of Bouton, the Portuguese colony of Makassar where the richest man was a Malay who lived in native fashion—although he owned a fine home—and the greatest landowner was a Chinese whose father had arrived there as a coolie.

The Dutch, they found, were the merchants, importers, and exporters, and the Chinese were the middlemen and the gamblers. The natives were the producers.

Next came Bali, with its lovely bare-breasted women, where much time was spent ashore exploring and enjoying the local scene. Then they headed for Java and at Surabaja they missed their mail because of the Dutch law which did not permit holding mail more than thirty days. They did find a few registered packets waiting which had just arrived, however. The crew and guests of the *Speejacks* were glad to leave this noisy, greedy, raucous commercial port, but first the yacht had to be drydocked, recoppered, fumigated and the engine overhauled. In spite of frustrations with incompetent workers and broken promises, they accomplished this—but only with the influence, financial resources, and energies of the owner. While the work was going on, they visited the health resorts in the mountains and made train trips to inland cities. Gowen, the financier, marveled at the huge profits of the sugar barons. Some plantations made three hundred percent a year; an average profit return was fifty percent.

The party also took in Singapore in the Straits Settlements, and a motor trip was made to Batavia. When *Speejacks* sailed again, she was spotless in gleaming white, her cockroaches were gone, a bent propeller shaft had been straightened, and the valves ground on the Wintons.

"You leave Java behind," Collins wrote, "with a feeling that, in company with the rest of the Orient, there is a growing unrest here. Gandhi's preachers from India have made their appearance, and there is much talk of Java for the Javanese. It is the same problem that Britain is facing, but the Dutch have neither the power nor the prestige of Britain with which to stem the tide. They have no easy task in the management of this small island with a population of 35 million, but they seem to be fair and far-sighted rulers."[7]

The Gowens had hoped to go from Colombo to the romantic Seychelles, where the Vacuum Oil Company had agreed to dump fuel supplies, but at the last minute no ships were available. After weeks of uncertainty, a sailing schooner was dispatched from Mauritius with fuel supplies,[8] and they were able to cross the Indian Ocean before the monsoon season. They sailed out through the Banka Straits into the China Sea without Bert, the Belgian cook, who could not take the seasickness any longer and left in Singapore. That night they crossed the equator for the second time, played a concert on the gramaphone over their wireless to the shore stations listening, and entered the crowded shipping lanes filled with lumbering junks, fleets of sampans, and ships of all flags. Much as they disliked some of the colonial ports, they spent much time visiting and being entertained by the Chinese millionaires of Singapore.

They called at Sumatra, the port of Belawan Deli, again finding the Dutch colonials to be a strange bunch—just as have other voyagers in small vessels since then. But Sumatra was clean, orderly, and prosperous for the Dutch, if not the natives. From here, *Speejacks* returned to Singapore and Batavia for supplies and fuel. They took aboard 3,200 gallons of gasoline and carried 300 cases on deck, making a total of 6,200 gallons for the 3,100 miles of ocean they must cross. Five tons of water went into the tanks and the pantries were jammed with food.

A large crowd saw them off, and on board were three new passengers: Fleurette Finnigan, Peggy O'Neill, and Michael—three monkeys given them by friends. Also aboard was Charlie, a Chinese cook who replaced Bert.

Starting out running on one engine to conserve fuel, they found that they could make six knots this way. A strong southeast trade wind helped them on the way, but the seas were on their quarter and at times the wind and waves were boisterous. Then they rigged a steadying sail. Chasing the sun, they headed across the Indian Ocean. The new pets aboard became increasingly annoying, and after much debate the monkeys were chloroformed and their bodies committed to the sea.

The days and weeks passed. They averaged about 175 miles a day.[9] In the Seychelles, they found their shipment of fuel waiting. After a short stay here, they continued to the Red Sea, stopping at Aden to explore ashore. At Port Sudan, they stopped to refuel again, and then spent eleven days making the 1,400-mile passage, burning 4,700 gallons of fuel. With a pilot, they passed through the Suez Canal to Port Said; then it was on to Alexandria, where the party made a fast visit to Cairo and visited the pyramids.

In the Mediterranean, they visited Greece, where Gowen threw a party for seven that cost only $3.86. In the Corinth Canal, that ancient slot built in A.D. 67, they went aground and nearly met with disaster. But they found the Adriatic blue and beautiful, and passed Scylla and Charybdis without seeing any monsters. At Naples, A. Y. bought a Fiat at a bargain price, and while the yacht proceeded to Marseilles, he, Jean, and Jay motored via Rome, Genoa, and the Riviera. At Monte Carlo, A. Y., the high-roller, began losing. He was implored to stop, but he kept betting on 35 and 26, the latter because it was the Broadway address of the Standard Oil Company. Finally, number 26 began winning. A. Y. doubled his bets. The bank notes on the number began to pile up. Next he played 35 again, and again the bank notes began to pile up. At that moment, when spectators who had crowded around to watch the action thought he would go on to break the bank, the Yankee millionaire exercised his unique instincts and quit. He had won enough to pay for the car and the entire European portion of the voyage.

A call was made at Barcelona, where A. Y. and Jean were horrified at the killing of bulls in the bullfights, although the matadors, including Del Monte, the idol of the period, were personally presented to the Gowens.

From Spain, they went to Gibraltar, stopping to entertain the men of the U.S.S. *Pittsburgh*, which was in port. Then the course was joyously set for home, with a rough run to the Canaries, during which the *Speejacks* was again reported lost at sea. The 1,500-mile run to the Cape Verde Islands was made in the worst gale of the entire voyage. There 6,000 gallons of fuel were put aboard. Fortunately, the crossing was a mild one, what with the huge deckload they carried. The 2,600-mile run to Puerto Rico proved to be easy. At San Juan, the yacht tied up to American docks for the first time since Pago Pago. They picked up hundreds of letters and telegrams from friends and family, and then continued on to Miami, which they had not seen for sixteen months.

As far back as New Guinea it had been decided that Thanksgiving would be spent in America, and the timetable had that in mind. At Gibraltar, A. Y. had cabled a friend, Carl G. Fisher, offering to bet that *Speejacks* would arrive within an hour of 10 A.M. on Thanksgiving Day. Fisher declined to wager. The yacht actually arrived at 11:15 A.M.

A large fleet turned out to welcome *Speejacks* to the Flamingo Dock. Sirens, whistles, and flags flying greeted the voyagers. The thousand-mile run uphill to New York was made in heavy and bitter cold weather, but they arrived on December 11, again receiving a tumultuous welcome.

A. Y. was heard to remark: "I wouldn't have missed it for anything, but I wouldn't do it again for a king's ransom!"

Jay had taken 93,000 feet of film, all but 300 of which was considered good footage. Total mileage was 34,000; total fuel, 73,000 gallons. The Winton engines performed flawlessly, requiring only valve grinding. Replacement parts included only one leather washer, costing 15 cents.

As *Speejacks* lay at the New York Yacht Club dock, her guest book was full of names from more than a hundred exotic ports, and her bright work showed the effects of sun and sea from three oceans.

How much did the voyage cost? A. Y. remained close-mouthed about this. All he would say was that it cost a great deal more than he expected. But he could afford it. Taking a vessel of this sort around the world in those times, in spite of his resources, was a remarkable feat, and it was surprising that so little difficulty was encountered. The voyage of the *Speejacks* was important, not only because of this, but for the era she represented, which was coming to an end in the aftermath of World War I.

Moreover, she proved that you don't have to be a penniless dreamer or a dropout from conventional society to sail around the world in your personal dream boat. Even millionaires can do it, and have fun, too.

CHAPTER

6

The Farmer
Who Went to Sea

The Islander was my first attempt at building a sailboat, but I don't suppose there ever was an amateur-built craft that so nearly fulfilled the dream of her owner, or that a landsman ever came to weaving a magic carpet of the sea.[1]

WITH THE COMING IN OF THE NEW YEAR 1917, THE QUIET harbor of Los Angeles lay peacefully in the early morning fog; the delicate scents of the land and of the fresh orange crop and of the eucalyptus groves mingled with the more pungent smells of the tide flats now momentarily bare. The sound of a church bell came faintly across from the direction of Long Beach. A tuna clipper moved out of San Pedro. A couple of yachts drifted out with the tide, heading for Catalina Island. Although a terrible war gripped Europe and much of the world, America was not yet in it; even so, a number of defense industries, including new shipyards, were already operating in the Los Angeles area in anticipation of United States participation.

On this particular Sunday, however, peace lay over the land and waterfront so heavy that it almost seemed tangible. Most industries and the docks were shut down. The only sound was a steady ring of an adze striking its cutting blows on a huge Douglas fir timber.[2]

The man working so industriously this Sunday morning was a Quaker, although not an outwardly practicing one, and he did not consider what he was doing as working on Sunday. He was building his dream ship. A small, wiry man with thin sandy hair and blue eyes, he had come down to Los Angeles harbor from the Sequoia country, where he had been operating a photo business for the tourist trade, to find work in the defense effort. The tourist trade was bad enough in summer, but in winter, with war clouds hovering, there was no money in it. So he sold out the business, and with the proceeds of a small farm he had inherited, he packed up and came down out of the High Sierras to the big city. He was forty-five years old, a bachelor without family ties, and behind him lay a colorful and even adventurous life that belied his modest and unassuming manners. Essentially, Harry Pidgeon was always his own man who all his life had done just about everything he felt like—except sail to the romantic islands of the world in his own ship. A few days before, he had rented a lot on the beach and set about to fulfill that oversight.

At the moment, a casual visitor even from Pidgeon's home state of Iowa—where most of southern California at that time came from—would have considered him just another nut on the beach. Nearby, across the channel on the Terminal Island side, a "colored Moses," as the locals called him, was building an ark in which to transport his followers to Liberia, the size of the ark being regulated by the amount of donations that came in. As funds continue to come, the ark continued to increase in size until it was now two stories high, covered with windows through one of which a stovepipe emitted smoke from a cooking fire on this Sunday morn.

A beachcomber in a nearby shack was working on a vessel which would use an electric motor to generate power, run by a windmill on deck.

The harbor was an interesting place with fascinating people and projects going on, and there was no lack of friendly visitors and onlookers, many of whom volunteered advice gratuitously. It was a happy place to live and carry out one's dreams, but Harry Pidgeon, the individualist, needed neither advice nor help. He was accustomed to being alone and doing things his own way.

Born in 1874 on a farm in Iowa, he did not see salt water until he went to California at age eighteen. None of his ancestors had ever been seafaring people, and as far as he knew they had always been dirt farmers. After several dull years on a ranch, during which he had built a canoe but had no place to use it, he headed for Alaska with another young farmer named Dan Williamson. Alaska was still a place of mystery and adventure, and the famed Gold Rush had not yet started. All he knew about the territory he learned from Lieutenant Schwatka's expedition in *Along the Great River of Alaska.*

With Dan, Pidgeon shipped out to the landing below Chilkoot Pass, joined a party of prospectors going over, and on the shores of Marsh Lake, a source of the Yukon River, he and Dan whipsawed some planks from a spruce tree and built a boat. With no experience on water at all, they paddled out of the lake and shot the rapids in Miles Canyon, where they found others portaging. Next came Five Finger Rapids, where one of the party they joined, an ex-sailor named Peter Lorentzen, drowned. Harry and Dan rescued the others and took Peter's partner, Henry, to Circle City, the new mining town.[3]

That fall, after many adventures on the Yukon River, the two young farmers reached the mouth at St. Michael's Island and took passage on a freighter, the *Bertha*, for California.

Back on the farm in Iowa, Harry found he could not settle down again. He went back to Alaska and spent several years exploring and hunting, and taking pictures with his camera, which was a hobby that he turned into a business. He built several boats, one of which was a sailboat in which he explored the islands of the Panhandle section. Later, he made a trip to the old homestead in Iowa, became interested in the Mississippi's possibilities, went to Minneapolis and built a houseboat below St. Anthony Falls, and spent a year floating down to New Orleans. Abandoning the flatboat at Port Eads, he returned to California and spent the next few years farming and operating a photo business in the Sierras.

In his mind, he could not forget his dream to sail to faraway islands. When Thomas Fleming Day, the legendary editor of *Rudder*, and his staff developed the *Sea Bird*, and its variations the *Naiad* and *Seagoer*, Pidgeon recognized his dream ship immediately. He sent for the plans, which were in a booklet called *How To Build a Cruising Yawl.*[4] The lines and offsets for all three yawls were included, so he borrowed ideas from each of them and added a few of his own. The finished result, which he named *Islander*, was outwardly the *Seagoer*, with the deep keel containing 1,250 pounds of cast iron attached to heavy timbers that formed an enormously strong backbone. She was yawl-rigged, 34 feet overall, 10 feet 9 inches beam, and drew 5 feet of water with no load. She was rigged with 630 square feet of canvas and had no motor, which Pidgeon did not want and could not afford. Completed, the *Islander* had cost $1,000 and 18 months of hard labor.

For the wartime years, Pidgeon lived aboard his yawl and made short coastwise cruises, meanwhile studying celestial navigation from a textbook, *Navigation* by Harold Jacoby. After the war, a yachtsman friend invited him to sail to Hawaii, which seemed like an ideal way to get some practical ocean experience. Leaving *Islander* with a friend, Pidgeon joined the other yacht. Like Slocum, the men took aboard a box of ripe plums which they ate as they sailed out. When clear of land, they encountered a strong gale and heavy seas—and the effects of the ripe plums. Unlike Slocum, who had the pilot of the *Pinta* aboard, the owner and crew quickly lost enthusiasm for Hawaii. The owner turned around and sailed back. This experience convinced Pidgeon that the singlehanded sailor was better off.

Sometime later, he decided to sail *Islander* to Hawaii, and did so in twenty-five days, during which he experienced the exhilaration of running down the trades, and the beauty of the open sea in all its moods. It gave him the needed experience in manning the ship singlehandedly and put to use his studies in navigation. But he was sea weary when he got to Honolulu and thought twice about beating back against the trade winds. After an extended stay, he departed via the northern circle route with a friend, an undertaker's son named Earl Brooks, also from California. They made the passage in forty-three days, during which Pidgeon became thoroughly familiar with handling his yawl in all conditions of sea and weather.

At noon on November 18, 1921, Pidgeon departed Los Angeles harbor alone in *Islander*, bound for the Marquesas. He had laid aboard enough staples to last a year, with plenty of space left over. Aboard were beans, peas, rice, dried fruits, sugar, and bacon. For bread, Pidgeon carried wheat and corn which he ground into flour with a handmill. All these were kept in air-tight containers to exclude moisture and insects. He also had a large supply of canned salmon and milk, as well as fresh potatoes, onions, and garden vegetables and other foods.

On the first leg, Pidgeon ran before a mountainous sea and a gale, but then reached the trade winds belt and enjoyed fine sailing. On December 21, he crossed the equator, and at 3:30 P.M. on December 30, he sighted Ua Huka Island, and soon after dropped the hook at Nuku Hiva, forty-two days from Los Angeles.

A student of Melville and Porter, Pidgeon was fascinated with the Marquesas and spent considerable time here. Ashore he met André Alexander, the French commissioner, and Bob McKittrick, the storekeeper and greeter of hundreds of yachts.[5] McKittrick told Pidgeon about the two English yachts that had recently called there, *Amaryllis* and *Dream Ship*. Sightseeing in Melville's *Typee* and taking pictures for later lectures, the time passed easily for Pidgeon. Also among the callers to the Marquesas was Captain Joe Winchester on the *Tahitian Maiden*, about whom both John Voss and Kenny Luxton had written earlier. And the colony included the usual botanists and naturalists from American museums.

While here, Pidgeon had an abscessed tooth removed by a Mr. Sterling of the American colony, suffered an injury to both arms, and an infected foot from stepping on a sea urchin. He managed, however, to haul the yawl and clean the bottom.

At noon on May 3, 1922, he sailed from Nuku Hiva to Tahiti via the Tuamotus, where he visited the Mormon missionary on Takaroa, who related to him the visit of the *Speejacks* some time before.

Pidgeon was delighted with Tahiti, and especially the quiet peaceful town of Papeete, hidden among the trees, and the picturesque harbor. The climate was balmy and restful, and the people friendly. Here a party of Americans took him for a motor ride around the island, during which the driver, a Californian, showed the passengers how they drove at home, rolling the vehicle over on a curve. No one was hurt, however.

While he was there, the American yacht *Invader* from Santa Barbara came in with her owner, J. P. Jefferson. When the cruise ship arrived from San Francisco, a man who had earlier tried to join Pidgeon on his voyage came up and shook hands. After celebrating Bastille Day, Pidgeon departed for Mooréa, Bora Bora, and Samoa. He was unable to obtain a chart of Fiji, but found a small map on a steamship folder which he used. In Suva, he was welcomed by the ubiquitous harbormaster Mr. Twentymen, enjoyed a lengthy stay, and then sailed to the New Hebrides on April 25, 1923. New Guinea came next, and then Torres Strait and Thursday Island, where Pidgeon expected to pick up his mail.

He suffered a bad infection in his thumb during this period, which was treated by friends. At Thursday Island, he had to endure the Australian red tape, but this was a crossroads point where he could go south behind the Great Barrier Reef, or pass through the East Indies to the Orient and the Philippines, or he could return to California via Captain Slocum's track across the Indian and Atlantic oceans.

Islander needed some repairs. She had encountered a reef, suffered several groundings, had once pulled the anchor and sailed off by herself, and in general needed attention. For this Pidgeon moved over to the lee of Prince of Wales Island. While here, the American yacht *Ohio*, with the newspaper tycoon E. W. Scripps aboard, arrived. Pidgeon was invited aboard with the mayor of Thursday Island. The *Ohio* had been cruising Southeast Asia, and there were political discussions about Japanese-American relations, but Mr. Scripps was most interested in Captain Harry Pidgeon and his little *Islander*, especially when Scripps learned that it cost only fifty cents a day to operate.

Also while here, the Americans learned of the death of President Harding. Mayor Corwin put the flag at half-mast on the town hall and declared a holiday.

Pidgeon sailed on August 7, 1923, stopping at Koepang in Dutch Timor, then at Christmas Island, where he had an enjoyable visit.

At the Keeling-Cocos Islands, he was welcomed by a descendant of the founder, John Clunies-Ross, and spent a weekend on Home Island.[6] On October 13, Pidgeon made Rodriguez, learning that the famous yacht *Shanghai* had been there just ahead of him. He visited the caverns, enjoyed the local hospitality, and was robbed of his money and photographs, which were later recovered.

In Mauritius, Pidgeon was also welcomed and enjoyed the stay. He sailed on December 4 for South Africa, passed Madagascar, and encountered a storm in the Mozambique Channel. He came into Durban on the tail end of the northeaster and was towed to a berth in the creek.

Christmas was spent here with new friends and several lectures were made with his lantern slides. Then, on February 27, 1924, he put to sea again. The worst weather and biggest seas were encountered on the sail around the Cape of Good Hope, but the little *Islander* was up to it. With sheets close-hauled and sprays flying, Pidgeon beat up to Green Point where he was met by a launch and towed to a berth at the docks in Cape Town. Among the delegation awaiting his arrival was the commodore of the Royal Yacht Club, who extended the club's courtesies to him.

Pidgeon very nearly abandoned his circumnavigation to settle here permanently. Of all the places he visited, he liked South Africa, its people and climate, best of all, but in the end his restlessness moved him on.

Soon after leaving Cape Town on the Atlantic leg, *Islander* was driven ashore—embayed—on a sandy beach. Some nearby farmers took Pidgeon into their home and helped him get his yawl afloat again. Like Slocum, Pidgeon's hosts could not understand how he could be sailing home by going west all the time. The world was flat, the old folks said. Their children, however, scoffed at the elders. "Oh, mother," said one, "don't you know the world is round?"

On September 22, Pidgeon sailed from Cape Town for the second time, and called at St. Helena, where the islanders still recalled Slocum's visit in 1898. The American consul, R. A. Clark, who had given Slocum the troublesome goat, was still there.

The next stop was Ascension. Leaving there, Pidgeon had an accident in which the water cask sprang a leak and filled the bilge. Fernando de Noronha was sighted on December 26. On January 10, *Islander* was damaged and nearly run down by a passing ship whose captain thought Pidgeon was in trouble.

Pidgeon reached Trinidad on January 20, delivering some mail from friends back on Mauritius. He enjoyed the carnival in Port of Spain, and then repaired the battered *Islander*. After that, he visited the pitch lake from which Sir Walter Raleigh got the tar to caulk his ships in 1595, visited among the West Indies, and then departed for Panama, arriving at Cristobal on May 2.

At the post office, Pidgeon received mail and newspaper clippings from California containing an interview with Captain Johnson of the S. S. *San Quirino*, an oil tanker which had nearly run him down in the South Atlantic. Later he visited the ship in Los Angeles and had a good laugh with the crew over the incident.

Pidgeon tried to visit the San Blas islands, but could not get permission. He did visit Portobelo with a local photographer named Lewis. He also encountered the yacht *Los Amigos* from Los Angeles on which his friend from Hawaii days, the undertaker's son, Earl Brooks, had helped organize a treasure-hunting expedition.

For the Panama Canal Passage, *Islander* was rated at five tons. The charge was $3.75 for the toll and $5 for measuring. Instead of hiring a launch, Pidgeon used the outboard motor which he borrowed, run by his friend from the *Los Amigos*, Captain Goldberg. The outboard failed them, so Pidgeon spread his sails and ghosted through into Gatun Lake where he anchored for a few days. Among the ships that passed was the old *Tusitala*, one of America's last square-rigged windjammers.

At Balboa, Pidgeon encountered Alain Gerbault, the famed French tennis player and war veteran, who was now on his way around in *Firecrest*. Harry did not like *Firecrest*, which was a racing cutter; and *Islander* did not appeal to the Frenchman's esthetic senses. Here, Pidgeon also met again Mr. Scripps on the *Ohio*, which was on its way to Africa, where later the newspaper magnate died at sea. In Balboa, Dr. William Beebe arrived on *Arcturus*, en route to the Galápagos Islands. Then came a party of British scientists on the yacht *St. George*, en route to Easter Island to solve the riddle of the stone faces planted on the hillsides by ancient peoples.

Pidgeon enjoyed most the visit from the sailors on the U.S.S. *Wyoming*, which was in port, and his visits on the warship. Many of the sailors were fascinated by his life and vowed they would do the same when they got out.

At Farfan Point, Pidgeon beached the *Islander* and repainted. He also replaced the cookstove and made other repairs. On August 7, he stood out to sea again for the final run to Los Angeles. This proved to be the longest and most tedious leg, taking him west of Clipperton, and up the long pull to the California coast, eighty-five days during which *Islander* grew a garden on her bottom and drifted for weeks in the doldrums.

Still in good health and uncomplaining as usual, Pidgeon hauled down the sails in Los Angeles harbor on October 31, 1925.

For his circumnavigation, Pidgeon was awarded the third Blue Water Medal in the history of the Cruising Club of America. Charter member Clifford Mallory arranged to have both Pidgeon and his yawl transported from California to the East Coast free of charge on one of his American-Hawaiian Line steamers to attend the April CCA meeting in 1926, and to speak to the members of his experiences.

The club took to Pidgeon warmly and he was induced to stay in the East, which he did until 1932. For four years, while he was writing his book, Pidgeon moored the yawl at a dock at George Bonnell's island at Byram Shore, Greenwich, and took his meals ashore with George.

John Parkinson, Jr.,[7] the late secretary of the CCA, recalled that his father, a famous yachtsman, had invited Pidgeon to spend a week at their home. He remembered him as a small man, retiring to the point of shyness, but a man of charm and humor when speaking on subjects which interested him.

In 1928, Pidgeon took part in the Bermuda Race, winning over two other boats in his class, one of which was *Svaap*, with William A. Robinson, who started his circumnavigation with this race and also won a Blue Water Medal later.

In 1932, Pidgeon set off on another circumnavigation also taking five years. During World War II, he married, and in 1947, with his bride, at the age of seventy-three, he departed Hawaii for his third circumnavigation on the aging *Islander*. A typhoon caught him in

Hog Harbor in the New Hebrides, and the venerable old yawl was driven up on the rocks and destroyed.

Subsequently, he began building another yawl, this time a *Sea Bird*, somewhat smaller than *Islander*, but before he could sail again, death took him at age eighty-one.[8]

A friendly, unassuming man who charmed people wherever he sailed in the world, from natives to millionaires, Pidgeon never really asked much of life, except the privilege of going his own way alone. He never sought fame and never accumulated wealth. He was a man, however, gifted with that illusive knack of getting the most out of life with the least amount of fuss.

"Ulysses," he wrote, "is fabled to have had a very adventurous voyage while returning from the sack of Troy, but for sufficient reasons I avoided adventure as much as possible. Just the same, any landsman who builds his own vessel and sails alone around the world will certainly meet with some adventures, so I shall offer no apology for my voyage. Those days were the freest and happiest of my life."

7

The Irish Rebel

I was invited to join a mountaineering party in the New Zealand Alps at Christmas, 1923, and having a nearly new yacht I regarded this as an excellent opportunity of finding out the merits or demerits of her design, which was of my own making.[1]

As the gentle martinet and quiet briton george muhl-hauser closed the last sea miles toward Dartmouth, England, on *Amaryllis* to end his circumnavigation—and his life—over in Dublin, Ireland, now free from English rule, a haughty little Irishman named Conor O'Brien, whose attitude toward the English was patronizing at best, was setting out on the first yacht voyage around the world south of the three stormy capes.[2]

O'Brien, a prickly intellectual, was a product of the Irish Rebellion or Civil War, depending upon whose side you were on, and with his sister had been a militant underground fighter and gun-runner. The escapades, however, which gave him more puckish pleasure, had been those smuggling runs in disguised fishing smacks under the noses of the British contraband patrols.[3]

After the war, O'Brien completed *Saoirse*—Gaelic for "freedom" —at the Fishery School shops in Baltimore, County Cork. He had designed her himself, after the lines of an Arklow fishing smack, one of which he had served on as a gun-runner and for which he had more than a sentimental attachment. She was 42 feet overall, 37 feet on the waterline, had 12 feet of beam, and drew almost 7 feet of water when loaded. She was planked with pitch pine over oak frames with iron fastenings. Eight tons of scrap iron were carried inside. About 200 gallons of water was stored in galvanized tanks, and replenished from whatever source available on the voyage.[4] Fresh foods, staples, and potatoes for three months made up the ship's stores.

Potatoes, O'Brien commented en route, were the seaman's curse. "There are only three places in the world where they are worth taking on board: Ireland, Argentina, and Tristan da Cunha."

Although O'Brien had never been off soundings before, he had considerable experience in sailing boats in coastal waters. And, contrary to his little bit of fancy, the purpose of his circumnavigation was not primarily to go mountain climbing in New Zealand. He was also stricken by sea fever, as were many postwar men and women, and a circumnavigation around the world in the high southern latitudes was a challenge that appealed to him. He does not explain why he did not take his sister, who had shared many of his adventures, as had Ralph Stock, but the reason probably was because by now she had become a settled housewife. In any case, in the early 1920s, interest in bluewater sailing yachts had begun to boom in many maritime countries. Yachtsmen had begun to haunt used book shops scrounging for logs and old accounts of colonial passages, whaling voyages, and explorations for vicarious research or actual planning of proposed voyages.[5]

O'Brien was especially interested in the logs of the *Lightning* and *Oweenee*, whose routes had been down the Atlantic, across the Indian Ocean in the high latitudes, and back again via Cape Horn. Always curious and an experimenter, O'Brien was not only charmed by these old voyages, but wanted to see for himself what it was like, especially with a modern fore-and-aft rigged ship, taking advantage of the normal wind and currents of the world.

His route took him south from Dublin to Madeira, the Canary Islands, Cape Verde; thence to Pernambuco in Brazil, southeast to Trinidad, across to Tristan da Cunha and Cape Town and Durban; eastward across the Indian Ocean via St. Paul's and Amsterdam islands, south of Cape Leeuwin to Melbourne; thence to Auckland, New Zealand, east around Cape Horn, stopping for an extended visit in the Falklands and a side trip on a support ship to the whaling grounds in the Antarctic; and home again via Trinidad, Pernambuco, and Fayal in the Azores.

So, on June 20, 1923, the Irish yacht *Saoirse*, of 20 tons Thames measure, left Dublin bound for the Cape, with the owner and an untried crew of two on board. O'Brien, who was an impatient man, had conducted a shakedown cruise from Shannon to Dunleary prior to leaving, during which the green crew somewhat got the hang of things. But throughout the voyage, he constantly complained about his crew—which varied from two to four, and included waterfront hangers-on, stranded yachties, rumpots, green kids, old men, and natives picked up along the way. Like many a voyager before and after him, including Robinson, Long, and even Muhlhauser, O'Brien found the native islanders to be the most dependable companions on long passages.

"I have not described life on board," he wrote in his log, "for I do not suffer fools gladly and cannot trust the discretion of my pen."

From the first, O'Brien was forced to admit that *Saoirse* was not ideal for ocean cruising, being more suited for the short choppy seas around the British Isles. But he knew what he wanted and had designed her for living aboard—which helped to take the sting out of his constant crew problems. She had a raised poop deck aft with a small cockpit and a charthouse with a bunk. One could sit in the shelter of the chartroom hatch and steer in bad weather. The fore-peak included a large sail locker, aft of which came a generous crew cabin, then a huge galley and saloon with a swinging table to accommodate many for meals and card playing or letter writing, then the captain's stateroom on the starboard side aft of this, convenient to the chartroom and steering cockpit. *Saoirse* had no engine, and it was for this reason, O'Brien said, that he decided not to use the Panama Canal and the traditional trade winds route.

With her eight tons of inside ballast, *Saoirse* proved to be very stiff, which contributed to her first accident—a broken mast. O'Brien quickly concluded that the ketch rig at sea was "an infernal nuisance," and he experimented constantly with variations that included staysails, squaresails, foretopsails, and even stunsails. With all sails flying, *Saoirse* at times carried an enormous cloud of canvas—almost 1,600 square feet![6]

O'Brien was nothing if not a perfectionist and a martinet at sea. They fortunately encountered fair winds as far as Cape Verde Islands. In about latitude 4° S and longitude 24° W, just after picking up the southeast trades, they discovered that the masthead was sprung and split. O'Brien decided to go into Pernambuco for repairs, and at the same time scrub the bottom, as the yacht was not coppered.

Pernambuco was O'Brien's first foreign port, and it took three weeks to find the right tides for the bottom scraping, the mast repairs, and to have the chronometer rated. Leaving on September 1, a fast passage of thirty-five days was made to Cape Town, at an average of 111 miles a day. News of his coming had reached South Africa before his arrival, and even as Table Mountain appeared with the "table cloth set"[7] he was met by yachts and trawlers that signaled a welcome. With a mast still needing repairs or replacing, he hurried to beat the southeaster into the port.

A complete refitting was carried out in Cape Town, including a new and heavier mast, while O'Brien was entertained by local yachtsmen and taken on sightseeing side trips. On the third Sunday after his arrival, he left again and it seemed the whole town turned out to witness the departure. The famous Danish yacht *Shanghai* was also sailing at the same time, which probably accounted for the crowds. Refusing an offer of government tugs to tow *Saoirse* out of the harbor, O'Brien prevailed upon the *Shanghai*, which had an engine, to snake him out of the crowded port. Once at sea and with a new crew, O'Brien discovered he should have stayed around and supervised the repairs and the outfitting. There were more than a dozen defects of workmanship and parts, and not only were there serious defects in masts and rigging, but the main water supply had been broken and then covered up by workmen to hide the mistake, which resulted in losing a third of his water. The steering gear now jammed because the wrong size chains had been installed. The American salt beef which he had ordered turned out to be spoiled. On top of that, *Saoirse* had a close call when it rammed a huge finback whale, and the passage around proved to be a cranky one, during which O'Brien was often unsure of his position. Finally and prudently, he decided to put into Durban to correct the defects and re-outfit. Here two of the crew, known only in the log as "H" and "P," left the ship. After a month's visit, O'Brien shipped two experienced seamen from a bark that was stranded in port over unpaid debts, and at the last minute took aboard a teen-ager who, O'Brien wrote, was "shanghaied on board by his father, who said, quite untruthfully, that the boy wanted to run away to sea, and that he, the father, wanted to make sure he ran away in a well-managed ship."

The lad, who was as anxious to get away from his father as the latter was to be rid of him, turned out to be the best helmsman O'Brien ever had. Later, the boy found a good job in Melbourne and was grateful ever after that O'Brien had "made a man of him."

O'Brien left Port Natal on December 11 bound for Melbourne. The route took him within sight of Amsterdam and St. Paul's, but at the last moment he decided not to stop even though he had a special chart of the remote islands given him by the ship chandler at Durban, who encouraged him to check them for shipwrecked mariners. The passage was made mostly along 38°, but good winds were found here. It took 51 days to sail the 5,700 miles. On January 29, they made land on the beam and saw the first vessel in 50 days. They drifted slowly up the coast and came to anchor at Port Phillip, Australia.

O'Brien divided up the cash on board, about £17, and they set out to see the town. A near mishap occurred when *Saoirse* dragged her anchor and scraped several other yachts. When O'Brien rushed up to save her, he discovered that the crew had deserted the ship, taking the skiff with them.

At the time, Melbourne was in the grip of a crime wave, and it was unsafe to be alone on the streets in some sections. He had been given much publicity on his arrival, of course, and had numerous applications for prospective crew members. One of his first recruits was murdered on his way down to join the yacht. Three Tasmanians were finally shipped aboard and the departure was made in a seven-knot tide rip off Port Phillip Heads. Two of the new hands became so seasick, and the third so frightened, that O'Brien returned and dumped them off at the Shipping Office. While in port, he met the skipper of the *Seaweed*, a yacht of about the same size as *Saoirse*, which had left Southampton a fortnight before and arrived at Melbourne a month earlier, with the skipper, his wife, and one other crew member.

Finally getting away from Melbourne, which he despised, O'Brien now had a new crew—a Swede-American, a slow man with an engaging smile and easy-going nature, and another who claimed to have shipped in large schooners, but who became a trial upon O'Brien's patience. The third crewman was a wiry man, full of complexes and nervous energies, who had come from a good family and had been a British naval officer. In spite of O'Brien's natural dislike for this Britisher, the man was well-educated, and for the first time O'Brien felt he had an intellectual equal aboard.

It was already too late for mountain climbing when they reached New Zealand, but not too late for passing around Cape Horn. Unable to sell his yacht either in Australia or New Zealand, O'Brien got a clearance for Dublin and departed. About 150 miles out, it was discovered that a line dragging astern had fouled and killed a molly-hawk or albatross. From then on, it was bad luck. One of the crew injured his elbow, which became worse and needed medical attention. Weather and adverse winds portended a bad passage. Soon after, another crewman injured a leg which became septic. Water had gotten into the cabin and ruined the supply of matches. A sack of coal had been washed overboard. It was too much. By May 10, they were back in New Zealand. Leaving the injured crewman in Napier, O'Brien sailed on to Auckland, paid off the rest, and changed his route to visit the Cook, Fiji, and Samoan islands.

O'Brien, like Muhlhauser, spent much time carping about New Zealand, which he considered over-organized and badly "Americanized." O'Brien, forgetting his own rebellious nationalism, complained that in New Zealand, "nationalism ran mad in the streets, accounting for a good deal of jealousy of strangers and intolerance of foreign ideas."

He also commented on the widespread use of ferro-cement in New Zealand for construction purposes, which anticipated the ferro-cement boatbuilding boom by half a century.

By now, O'Brien had lost his patience in finding crewmen. "I am now resigned to looking for two more or less competent slaves." He found a crew of native Tonga boys who wanted to go home, and a couple of Irishmen who had sailing ship discharges, "and that was the end of my stay in New Zealand."

From Auckland, he sailed for Nuku Alofa. Word of his departure got him pressed into service as a mail and cargo vessel, for which he was paid a small fee. It was a rough passage, but Tonga proved to be one of the few exotic places he saw on the entire circumnavigation. Still bothered by his foul bottom and corroding iron fastenings, which he had been unable to repair in New Zealand, O'Brien tried to sell *Saoirse* in Tonga. But unlike Ralph Stock, who had no trouble peddling his *Dream Ship* in a Tonga clubhouse, O'Brien found no buyer. Here he paid off one of his Irishmen, found a clockmaker who was also a sailmaker, and had a new jib made. He found no slipways here, and moreover the tides were so small that it was impossible to beach the vessel. But the Tongans impressed him more than any of the other "foreigners" he met on his voyage, and here he picked up Kioa, a local boy who worked in a garage and wanted to escape from an uncle who dominated him. Remembering his success with the lad from Durban, and being naturally sympathetic toward a rebel, O'Brien took him aboard. Kioa proved to be a superb sailor, a good cook, and a dependable and willing hand at all times. It was the best thing that happened to O'Brien on the entire voyage around.

It now became imperative to return to Auckland to stop the destruction by worms in the hull. There he lost all his crew again except Kioa. After repairs were made and preparations for the Horn passage completed, he shipped aboard "W," who was escaping from a wife; "C," who was beyond redemption by anyone but the Devil; and "B," a bricklayer's laborer, who was trying to escape from having to work and thought a voyage on a yacht would be an ideal vacation.

On October 22, 1924, *Saoirse* left Auckland, homeward bound via Cape Horn. Sailing in the forties and fifties, the long passage was relatively uneventful, save for the constant aggravation of O'Brien's lazy crew. The westerlies carried them well up toward the Falklands, and, on December 6, they arrived at Stanley Harbour, 46 days out and having sailed 5,800 miles nonstop.

"K" (Kioa), who had sworn to go to the ends of the earth with O'Brien, proved his value from the beginning, and took much of the worry off the skipper, especially during the dreaded encounters with ice and some heavy seas when the rudder chain broke and had to be repaired. The actual rounding of the bleak and dark Horn Island, however, was made with true Irish luck on a mild day in clear weather. Even dragging a foul garden along on the bottom, O'Brien was making 140 miles a day. And, by chance, when they arrived at Stanley Harbour, the Christmas festivities were underway.

Several weeks were spent sightseeing on the local mail boats, hiking over the tundra, and enjoying the local hospitality. *Saoirse* was taken to a cove and beached for cleaning and repairs. During the stay here, O'Brien shipped as a passenger on a mail and supply trawler to the whaling settlements in Antarctica and the Palmer Peninsula. Although fascinated by the excursion, he was somewhat appalled by the whaling industry. "When I tasted whale meat, I admitted it was necessary to kill whales for the sake of the kitchen, though the other aspects of the industry rather disgusted me."

The South Shetlands, he noted, looked rather like the Outer Hebrides at home, with "little excuse for existing."

During the stay in Stanley, one of the crew became enamored of a lady and married her. O'Brien paid him off, loaded fresh meat and water aboard, and, on February 28, departed. Because of "M's" defection, he was now shorthanded. The first part of the trip was rough. Not until St. Patrick's Day, he noted, did the weather moderate. On the passage, he traveled over uncharted shoals which he named "Saoirse Rock." Another crewman became ill, so he decided to put into Pernambuco again. The work was now left to him and Kioa.

In Pernambuco, O'Brien enjoyed another fine visit and discharged the ill man. The vessel was again hauled and scrubbed, and repainted. On April 6, he was cleared for Dublin. During this passage, he had trouble with his eyes, and for a time was almost blind, not being able to shoot the sun. He was forced to depend entirely on Kioa, to whom he gave lessons in navigation.

A landfall was made on Pico, the 7,500-foot mountain on Fayal. By letter, O'Brien had arranged for his sister to come out to meet him. There was a reunion and a visit. The last 1,300 miles to Dublin was made quickly. Making Fastnet Light on the nose on June 15, soon they were at Wicklow where a reception committee awaited to take them in tow. In the Roads, his other sister came off to "give him his sailing orders" with the customs officer.

Then, at last, met by cheering crowds, bands playing, and many speeches, he was towed to Dunleary and the long procession formed to carry him up to Dublin.

Somewhat embarrassed by all the attention, but nevertheless relishing it, O'Brien was pleased to be the first Irishman to circumnavigate in a yacht. "It is good to have sailed around the world in order to be home again," he wrote.

Soon after, he published his book, *Across Three Oceans,* based on his logs, which became a best-seller. Written with puckish humor and filled with fascinating details of yacht management on long passages, it is so well-written that most readers have been misled by the easy, off-hand narrative into thinking the circumnavigation was easy. As Claud Worth wrote in his introduction to O'Brien's book, "Mr. O'Brien's seamanlike account is so modestly written that a casual reader might miss its full significance. But anyone who knows anything of the sea, following the course of the vessel day by day on the chart, will realize the good seamanship, vigilance and endurance required to drive this little bluff-bowed vessel, with her foul uncoppered bottom, at speeds of from 150 to 170 miles a day as well as the weight of the wind and sea which must sometimes have been encountered."

O'Brien subsequently wrote several other books on yachting, which became standard references. In *Deep Water Yacht Rig,* he ruefully admits that many of the conclusions he had reached on his circumnavigation about rigs and yachts were wrong in light of subsequent voyages on the North Atlantic. Many yacht designers and owners who read *Across Three Oceans*, but not the subsequent works, accepted these early conclusions, however, as gospel.

After his famous circumnavigation, the years between wars were spent writing and sailing, and enjoying his notoriety as an Irish patriot as well as a world voyager.

In World War II, too old to fight—and anyway, O'Brien was more of a writer than a fighter—he enlisted in the Small Vessels Pool as a lieutenant in the reserve, ferrying ships from the United States to England. Now sixty-three, he was spare of build and somewhat stooped, with graying hair and a shaggy moustache. As an officer with one of the "runner crews," he seemed to be fulfilling a need. Besides, under wartime conditions, paper was scarce and he couldn't get his books published. "I thought I'd better go back to sea," he told a reporter, his blue eyes twinkling.[8]

During one of his trips to New York, O'Brien was invited to Ipswich, Connecticut, by another famous circumnavigator, William A. Robinson, now land-bound for the duration as a successful shipyard operator. O'Brien went up and stayed for a weekend, during which he and Robbie talked of many things—of ships and the southern seas, the remote islands in the sun, the wild and stormy forties and fifties, and of bluewater rigs and ideal ships. Even then, Robinson was living aboard the unfinished ultimate dream ship, *Varua*, designed for him by Starling Burgess and L. Francis Herreshoff to his specifications, especially for escaping to the islands again, and built in his own yard.

They talked of times when a man with a ship like *Saoirse* or *Svaap* could once again cast loose the bonds that held them to humdrum moorings.

For Robbie, it was a dream that would come true within a few years. For O'Brien, who did not share the same type dreams as Robinson except those of freedom and spirit, it was the ending, for not long afterward he died.

He had thrice won the Challenge Cup of the prestigious Royal Cruising Club, and assured himself of a measure of immortality among dreamers and lovers of the sea everywhere, and his many innovations of rig and sailing had become standard. In spite of her lumbering appearance, *Saoirse* logged 31,000 miles in 280 sailing days, averaging 5¼ knots, a record that is seldom beaten with today's modern yachts and rigs.

During his entire circumnavigation, O'Brien called only at twelve ports. He was not a gregarious man, and many things about the world and about people he had difficulty accepting. He was an intellectual, and like most intellectuals, he was forever dissatisfied and disappointed in what he found around him. He was imperious, and even cocky and arrogant at times, but he remained essentially a Gaelic spirit, comfortably provincial in ideals and outlook.

But, for all this, he probably would be most pleased and delighted to know that his *Saoirse*, at this writing, is still sailing the waters around the British Isles, virtually unchanged in rig or appointments since she carried him across three oceans and around the three stormy capes.

8

The Magnificent Schizoid

After the war I could neither work in a city nor lead the dull life of a businessman. I wanted freedom, open air, adventure. I found it on the sea.[1]

FIRECREST WAS A TYPICAL ENGLISH RACING-CRUISER OF THE middle 1800s. Designed by the famous Dixon Kemp, she was built by P. T. Harris at Rowhedge, Essex, in 1892. She was 39 feet overall, 31 feet 6 inches on the waterline, with a beam of 8 feet 6 inches, and displaced 12 tons. Long and narrow, with a deep keel and three and a half tons of lead for ballast, she was a rule cheater of that day, but for all that a good sea boat and fairly comfortable. The original rig was a cumbersome gaff-headed sloop with many variations of headsails and topsails, but with the newfangled roller-reefing boom, 27 feet long.

She was exactly the type of vessel that would appeal to the popular French war hero and tennis champion, Alain Gerbault. In 1921, while visiting England during the tennis matches, he was a guest aboard Ralph Stock's new yacht at Southampton.[2] Nearby at her moorage lay *Firecrest*. Although she was older than Gerbault himself, he recognized in her some vague affinity that, perhaps, rooted far back in his restless subconscious. Ever since the war ended he had been searching for something, and he knew it could not be in civil engineering or in business like his father. Here was his friend Ralph Stock, who had made his *wanderjahr* already on *Dream Ship*, returning to write books about it and enjoy the acclaim of the public and the admiration of his generation.

The marriage of Alain Gerbault, the young intellectual war hero, social rebel, iconoclast, middle-class man-of-the-world, self-appointed member of the new Lost Generation,[3] and the dowdy matronly *Firecrest* fulfilled a sort of mother-image (his own mother had just died) and provided him with a perfect *modus operandi*.

Born in 1893, Gerbault spent an idyllic youth at Dinard, France, near the ancient city of St. Malo, home of the legendary corsairs who led France to glory on the seas 350 years ago. Of an upper middle-class family, Alain and his brother spent much of their summers on their father's yacht, played tennis and football, went hunting and fishing, and slummed around with the sons of the Breton fishermen. Once the brothers had saved up money to buy a boat of their own, but it was sold before they could acquire it. In the winter, they attended the proper schools, learned the social graces, and the indoor sports such as bridge and whist, and devoured books of adventure on land and sea, particularly those of the gold hunters in the Yukon and Alaska, and of explorers in Africa and the New World.

It was a happy youth, but then came the time for college and Alain was sent to Paris to study for the civil engineering profession at Stanislaus College. He did not like the confinement and discipline of boarding school, and he always considered this the unhappiest period of his life. But he had a good mind and was able to carry the curriculum easily, and at the same time withdraw when needed into a world of books and adventure and dreams.

At twenty-one, Alain enlisted in the Flying Corps, and served as an officer in the 31st French squadron, which also had some young American volunteers. One of these gave Gerbault Jack London's *Cruise of the Snark*, in which he realized perhaps for the first time that it was possible to cross an ocean in a small boat.[4]

"I decided at once that it was going to be my life, if I was lucky enough to get through the war," he wrote. "Later I was able to include two of my friends in my schemes, and to decide to buy a boat, and sail round the world after adventure. But these two friends were killed fighting in the air, and I was left alone at the armistice."[5]

In 1919, Alain came out of the Flying Corps as a decorated hero and instead of becoming the World War I version of the hippie dropout, he immediately set about becoming tennis champion of France, and a bridge player of international rating. He was a leader of the smart-set social structure, a charming, articulate quick-witted man of small but lithe stature in superb physical condition. While he professed a social conscience, like most intellectuals, he concealed a typical middle-class snobbery toward those of more humble standing—a trait that remained with him even during his Noble Savage wanderings among the natives in the remote Pacific islands.

During this period, Gerbault was said to have had an affair with Suzanne Lenglen, the famous Wimbledon champion, and almost married her.[6] But women apparently did not have the same attraction for him as they did for most red-blooded males, especially those with Rousseauean proclivities. He searched for "something to do." At one point, he thought of trying to fly the Atlantic—an impossible feat against prevailing winds at that time. He later dwelled at length in his writings about his affliction with sea fever, but as Jean Merrien wrote in *Lonely Voyagers*, his was not so much a longing for the sea as it was the spirit of the record-breaker, the writer, the artist, the apostle, and always the disturbed intellectual.

He was neither basically nor temperamentally a sailor; but in the end, perhaps he did become one.

After purchasing *Firecrest*, his life style did not change radically. With an English boy, Alain said he spent a year or so sailing the vessel on the Atlantic and Mediterranean, "preparing himself" for his future sea adventures. Actually, he took the vessel to the south of France via the Canal du Midi, and most of his sailing was in and out of Cannes, while he socialized ashore, played tennis and bridge, and acted out the part of the lone sea adventurer getting ready for the next epic voyage.

On June 6, 1923, after a rough and almost disastrous passage to Gibraltar (where he was lionized by the British naval colony), he departed for New York via the southern route, not telling anyone his destination, but characteristically hinting at it to foster curiosity. Actually, his was a bold venture for that time. Although the southern route is a common yacht passage these days, until Gerbault few had attempted it.[7] Indeed, a transatlantic crossing in a small vessel in either direction was considered a daredevil stunt in spite of Slocum, Voss, J. A. Buckley, Captain Hudson, Alfred Johnson *et al.*

On board, Gerbault had supplies of salt beef, ship's biscuit, bacon, potatoes, jam, butter, and fresh water for several months. He also had about two hundred books by his favorite authors—Conrad, London, François Villon, Shelley, Plato, Kipling, Poe, Tennyson, Verhaeren, Loti, Farrère, Masefield—to say nothing of voyagers' accounts such as those by Slocum, Voss, his friend Stock, and of course books on navigation, natural history, and geography.

Although he speaks of vast preparations for the adventure, it is evident that Gerbault departed haphazardly without even a good suit of sails and adequate rigging. He had not even had enough experience with *Firecrest* to learn her characteristics, and especially how to balance her sails. Not long out of Gibraltar, Alain discovered that he had been cheated by the ship chandlers, who had sold him spoiled salt beef (disguised by a layer of good meat on top), an inferior grade of tea instead of the well-known brand he had ordered, and new water kegs that soon polluted his supply with tannic acid. But Gerbault, if nothing else, was a brave man with a noble spirit. He passed close to Madeira, but did not put in. Weeks later, during the hurricane season, his water supply almost gone, his vessel in need of repairs, and he himself sick, Alain passed close to Bermuda, but elected to go on to New York without stopping.

Beset by calms and by squalls that ripped his rotting sails, Gerbault once was swept overboard, and only by a miracle did he get back on.

Down to a glass of tainted water a day, he became ill with a sore throat and a high fever. When he wasn't trying to survive the storms, pump out the bilge, and make repairs to the deck and hatches, he was forever trying to keep ahead of his tattered sails with needle and palm.

This was a typical day:

> At nine a.m. the reef lacing of my staysail breaks. The motion of the boat is now so violent . . . that I cannot repair it. All my cups and glasses are broken into small pieces. At noon a huge wave breaks aboard and carries away my sail locker. A big hole appears in my staysail, and my mainsail rips down the centre seam, leaving a three-yard-long slit. I can hardly stand on the slippery deck. It is raining hard. In the saloon the water is at floor level. I have made the annoying discovery that my pump is out of order. I am soaked to the skin. There is not a single dry place in the boat, and I cannot find a way to prevent the rain water from leaking through many places around the skylight and hatchways.[8]

In the Gulf Stream, Gerbault was caught up in the heavy shipping traffic. A Greek ship came alongside one day and took the wind out of his sails so that he could not maneuver. It annoyed him and he told the Greek captain so. Comparing positions, he had the satisfaction of knowing his own calculations were exact, while those of the Greek were erroneous.

Then he encountered fog, but spoke a French fishing boat from St. Pierre. At 2 A.M. on September 15, after 101 days at sea, he anchored off Fort Totten, having made a landfall on Nantucket, and having sailed through the United States fleet maneuvering off Newport. Thereupon he was boarded by newspaper reporters, newsreel cameramen, and given a hero's welcome by yacht clubs and the public alike. William Nutting, the ubiquitous founder of the Cruising Club of America, took him in tow and opened the doors of the influential and the mighty. He spent months as a guest of new friends while his boat was cared for nearby. He began to write his book, *The Fight of the Firecrest*, a somewhat lurid account of his transatlantic crossing in which he reveals to experienced seamen, if not the panting public, his lack of sea sense and sailing ability.

But Alain Gerbault was one of those rare individuals who had the charisma of which heroes and the famous are made. Everything he did made news—even if he did nothing it made news. In the U.S., where public heroes are a social necessity, he became the darling of the press and the cult of the Lost Generation, as well as the staid old yachting society. He lectured and wrote articles for money; he fended off erstwhile adventurers who wanted to join his next voyage; he was honored at the Explorers Club. And he loved every minute of it, while at the same time professing annoyance at the intrusion into his private life.

He left *Firecrest* in New York and returned to France to finish his book, to be decorated with the Legion of Honor, and to accept a 10,000-franc prize from the Academy of Sports.[9] Then he returned to New York amid much advance publicity and prepared for his voyage to the South Pacific via Bermuda and Panama. Numerous repairs were made to *Firecrest*, including modification of the gaff-headed rig to the Bermudian style which was easier for one man to handle.

Refitted and loaded down with supplies, fresh water, food for months, gifts from friends, rifles and ammo, bows and arrows, charts and instruments, and a movie camera with a mile and a half of film in air-tight containers, *Firecrest* left Fire Island for Bermuda in early September, 1924. This time, Alain had a send-off by members of the

CCA and the Explorers Club, the widow of Bill Nutting, who was lost meantime in Greenland waters, by the yachting press and many officials, accompanied by three-gun salutes and a dipping of the French flag.

A typical rough passage was made to St. George's harbor, and three months were spent in Bermuda once again making repairs. He complained that the money he spent in New York on outfitting would have bought a new yacht in France. But he was placated by receiving the CCA's coveted Blue Water Medal for 1923, presented aboard a British vessel.[10] He took on a native boy for a cook here, but during a galley fire the lad was burned so badly that he died. After that, Gerbault never attempted to take a companion or crew member on his voyages.

On April 1, at 8 P.M., *Firecrest* reached Colón. Gerbault's fame, of course, had preceded him, and he was made welcome by the French, British, and American officials. By extraordinary courtesy, the lock operators had been ordered to regulate the valves so that *Firecrest* was gently carried upward instead of being subjected to the usual turbulence and often dangerous locking that every other yacht before and since has been subjected to.

At the Pacific end, he hobnobbed with the captains and admirals of the American and British ships at Balboa, met Dr. William Beebe again who was there with the *Arcturus*, took time out to win the tennis championship of Panama, and prepared for the long Pacific passage. Typically, although he detailed at great length his social activities, he never so much as mentioned Captain Harry Pidgeon, who was there with *Islander*, and with whom he exchanged visits. During the two months spent here, he received from home a new movie camera, a gift from his friend Pierre Albarran, and a Gramophone sent over by the French tennis champion, Jean Borotra. With local customs officials, his every wish was their command. The American admiral donated a tender to tow him around and men and materials for work on *Firecrest*. A new sail arrived from New York and was bent on. The officers of the *Rochester* feted him at a send-off luncheon, and on May 31, 1924, Alain Gerbault, the iconoclast, the escapist, the railer against society, and the dropout, sailed for the South Pacific.

He only got as far as Toboga Island where he paused to make notes, and then on June 11 sailed for the Galápagos Islands. His stay there was short, and was highlighted by a visit to the Progreso *hacienda* of Señor Don Manuel Augusto Cobos, son of the island's owner who had been murdered by his employees, and a young man who had been educated in Paris.[11]

After a short visit and study of local flora and fauna, Alain exchanged ceremonies with Cobos and departed for Mangareva, which he reached after forty-nine days at sea. After leaving the Galápagos and entering the Pacific island world, Gerbault became increasingly introspective and egocentric, and devoted his writings to long discourses on the social, economic, and historical aspects of the islands and their inhabitants. In fact, his endless variations of this theme detract greatly from his undeniably perceptive and intelligent analysis of conditions.

He visited the Marquesas, which he explored and analyzed at great length and in great detail, and then—as he boasts—he ventured into the dreaded Tuamotus where such people as Muhlhauser, Stock, London, and Stevenson did not dare to sail.[12]

At last came Tahiti, the mecca of every South Pacific voyager. He was not disappointed with this paradise, but the French officialdom and the commercialization of Papeete bothered him, as did the "exploitation" of the natives on all the islands. While there, he often visited with Marau Taaroa a Tati, the widow of the former King Pomare V. He played tennis and football, but was disappointed in the lack of interest in such sports.

After refitting again, *Firecrest* sailed on May 21, 1926. During his stay at Bora Bora, one of Gerbault's favorite places, an English sloop and a French warship put into the harbor about the same time and entertained the lone voyager. Next came Samoa, where Gerbault was hosted at the American July 4 celebration, watched a baseball game, and played tennis.

On Friday, August 13,[13] he sailed out of Apia for his unluckiest encounter at Uvea, one of the Wallis Islands, where years before a French warship, *Lermite*, had been wrecked. After a rough passage, he entered the fringing reef and anchored off the jetty at Matautu. During the night, the wind veered and a gale arose, and *Firecrest* was driven up on the reef. The next day, Alain discovered that the four-ton lead ballast had broken off the keel after the beating on the coral.

With the help of the natives and two Chinese artisans, Gerbault removed the rigging, emptied the ballast from inside, and took off his personal belongings, which were stored with the French trader. *Fire-*

crest was righted and shored up. The lead keel was salvaged. He managed to get a wireless message off, relayed to his influential friend Pierre Albarran in Paris, and orders went out. The French warship *Cassiopée* was dispatched with bronze keel bolts and other materials. Meanwhile, help also came from the Burns, Philips Company ship *Pervenche*, and the rescue and repair of *Firecrest* became the most imperative undertaking in the South Pacific that year.

At last, on Thursday, December 9, after four months at the Wallis Islands, he weighed anchor and sailed again, to the Ringgold Islands where Jack London had nearly lost *Snark* and where Lord Pembroke had piled up his luxurious *Albatross*.

Alain spent several months at Suva, hosted by the local society, playing tennis, and writing about the native people and customs. Next came the New Hebrides, where he found the *Snark*, Jack London's ill-fated vessel, in the service of a trader at Port-Vila. He sailed for New Guinea on April 12, where his vessel was attacked by a giant swordfish.

He called at Port Moresby, played tennis ashore with local officials and their families, then wandered through the Coral Sea to Thursday Island, and across the Arafura Sea to the Indian Ocean. His route followed Slocum's from here on, out to the Keeling-Cocos, where he paused briefly and then went on to Rodriguez and Mauritius, playing tennis ashore as usual for relaxation. He finally tore himself away from the social routine and left Réunion for Madagascar.

On December 4, Gerbault sighted a whale and the next day a comet in the sky. On December 8, he witnessed a total eclipse, which gave him an opportunity to check his chronometers.

Instead of stopping at Madagascar, he sailed on to Durban, South Africa, where he received a tumultuous welcome and celebrated Christmas, while commenting in his journals that he was an enemy of civilization.

On January 4, he left Durban, and after three weeks of calms varied with rough weather arrived at Cape Town and put up at the Royal Yacht Club.

He refitted again here, and was soon ready to sail after turning down a cabled invitation from Jean Borotra to wait for the French touring tennis team and join them.

He called at St. Helena where he stayed for some time and took part in a football match between the English garrison and the "natives" of the island. Next came Ascension, His Majesty's "Stone

Frigate," where he was welcomed by the Cable Company employees, and with whom he played tennis and climbed to the top of the mountain.

On May 26, Gerbault began the long passage up the Atlantic to the Cape Verdes, crossing the equator on June 5, after three years in southern latitudes. On July 9, he narrowly escaped disaster on St. Vincent when he went aground through a blunder. Rescued again, he put the *Firecrest* into a yard for repairs, had new sails made, left once more, had to return again for more repairs, and finally decided to stay there and complete another book that winter.

The months passed easily at Porto-Grande. He enjoyed time ashore and visiting other ships, played tennis and football, and worked on the book.

In October, the French warship *Edgar Quinet* arrived. On board was Captain Darland, who with Pierre Albarran and the Minister of Marine had sent the *Cassiopée* to his aid in the Wallis Islands. Then came the U.S.S. *Raleigh*, with Admiral Dayton aboard, along with Captain Jacobs who had been port captain in Cristobal, when Gerbault passed through the canal. Next came the *Antares*, French sister ship to the *Cassiopée*, just in time for Gerbault to take the officers to the New Year's Eve dance given by the Cable Company. At midnight, when 1928 gave way to 1929, the Swedish training ship *Fylgia* arrived and accidentally damaged *Firecrest*'s bowsprit, but the Swedish carpenters later replaced it with American spruce.

Before sailing, Gerbault played on the football team as center-forward against the English team from the cruiser *Durban*. Then he offered a cup to be given to the winner of the best team on the island, a cup that had been his first tennis trophy, won when a boy at Dinard. By happy coincidence, Gerbault was on the team that won, and it was he who kicked the winning goal.

On May 6, he weighed anchor and sailed for home. Eleven days later, he discovered that he suffered from catarrhal conjunctivitis to his great discomfort. On May 26, at 10 A.M., he crossed his outbound track and thus completed a circumnavigation begun some six years before.

Now the Southern Cross, which he had come to regard as his symbol of freedom, was put down behind him and ahead lay a return to "civilized life."

The trade winds became feeble, then he entered a zone of calms, variables, and squalls. He decided to put into the Azores, where he again received a warm welcome—and took on the best tennis players on the island. Once again he left. On Tuesday, July 16, the steamer *Michigan* of the French Line spoke him, and Gerbault sent a message to his friend Pierre de Pacquier. He refused proffered food, but accepted some newspapers in order to catch up on tennis matches.

On July 20, he entered the English Channel, and a fog. Early in the morning, when he encountered the *Mistinguette,* the ship's crew recognized him and some came aboard with bottles of Spanish cider.

He gave in to a little homesickness at this time and accepted a tow which, he said, would enable him to watch Jean Borotra play for the Davis Cup, which was to start the following morning.

At 11 A.M. the next day, he sailed into Cherbourg harbor. He hoisted the *Firecrest*'s code number— O Z Y U. The following morning, he left for Le Havre. Then, at last, after ninety-six hours without sleep, there was the welcoming committee of harbor boats, officials, reporters, friends like Pierre de Pacquier and Coco Gentien, and his best friend of all, Pierre Albarran, in the crowd at the quay at Brest.

His voyage had taken, in total, seven hundred days spent at sea, and covered more than forty thousand sea miles. Home again was the sailor, malcontent, tennis champion, iconoclast, war hero, intellectual, dropout, and social reformer, home from the sea. *Firecrest,* his vehicle, his *modus operandi* for his vague and restless dreams, was now old, worn, and battered beyond redemption.

Now he was an even greater hero. Now more than ever he had demonstrated France's historic mastery of the seas in a way that inspired and excited the public. He was sought after, quoted, honored, interviewed, lionized, and virtually worshipped. But now this left a curious distaste for it all that he had not felt before. He began to realize that he had left what he had sought back there in the remote Pacific islands. He gave *Firecrest* to the French government as a training vessel, and she was reported sunk in a squall on her first trip with cadets aboard.

He then built another vessel to his own specifications, a smaller ship, only 34 feet overall but more comfortable, which was painted a glistening black and named with the supreme egoism that Gerbault could not disguise, the *Alain Gerbault,* honoring himself. Now, with plenty of money and the world his own special oyster, he sailed for the South Pacific and disappeared from public scrutiny for years. These were, at last, the happy years for Alain Gerbault, spent wandering from island to island, living and working with the natives, campaigning on their behalf against colonial bureaucracy, writing, thinking, trying to understand the meaning of things. Infrequently, he put into Papeete, where he visited with friends, such as William Robinson, who now lived there permanently, posed for photographs taken by visiting yachtsmen like Dwight Long, and then disappeared again among the islands.

On August 22, 1944, wire service stories appeared around the world that Alain Gerbault was dead. His beloved *Alain Gerbault* had taken a direct bomb hit in the East Indies, and he had died of a tropical fever as early as December 1941 on Portuguese Timor.[14]

Not until 1947 was his body recovered by the French Navy and returned to his favorite island, Bora Bora, where he was buried with full military honors beside the lagoon he loved best, his grave marked with a monument.

A unique person, Gerbault became, in maturity, a true man of the world, one who at last found peace and meaning. Outstanding physically, with a superb sense of timing and almost limitless endurance, he was also a man of keen mind. Like Robinson, he could have risen to the top of any profession in "civilized" society, but chose to go his own way. Fortunately, also like Robinson, he was a gifted writer, one of the few who could finance his dreams while living them.

He was also one of the immortals among those with wandering sea fever. Like Slocum, he will not be forgotten. As he himself once cabled to his friends and admirers back home:

> *You must not be sad, for one day I shall come back.*
> ALAIN GERBAULT

9

The Connecticut Tahitian

*When I am old I will have my past, and if
that measures up at all to the future I dream of
now, my life will have been complete.*[1]

AT THE MOUTH OF A VALLEY CALLED OFAIPAPA, OPENING
on a lagoon into which murmurs a clear mountain stream with a
series of little waterfalls and pools fringed with luxurious ferns, there
is a home, Polynesian style, with terraces and pandanus roof, open
at both ends for the wild pigeons and doves to fly through, the
grounds lush with a curious combination of native and exotic plant-
ings—tropical cherry (for the birds), hotu and frangipani, ironwood,
tamanu from Panama, Barro Colorado jungle trees from Chile and
Peru, hybrid hibiscus and exotic fruits, all botanical experiments by
the owner.

In this lyrical scene, too, there is a disguised and soundproofed
diesel generator that makes electricity for hot water and cooking, and
stereophonic renditions of Tchaikovsky, incongruous in the evenings
as the changing colors of the setting sun outline the magic island of
Mooréa some twelve miles to the west.

On the steps of the terrace sits a man with snowy white hair and
deep-lined skin, chatting happily with his beautiful daughters, typical
Tahitian girls of mixed bloodlines, who call him "Poppy"—which
never fails to arch the eyebrows of the tourists just off the Quantas jet
when he and the girls go down to Papeete to shop at the early-
morning market.

Onlookers are apt to think that here is another wastrel or remittance man, descended to a life of beachcombing and native wenching on this tropical South Pacific isle now somewhat tainted by crass commercialism and an international jet airport. But Poppy is no ordinary South Seas derelict. He is a supremely happy man with a life of fulfillment behind him that began in the late 1930s when he purchased *Svaap*, which means "dream" in Sanskrit, for $1,000, and sailed her around the world—at that time, the smallest vessel ever to have circumnavigated.

He is still a handsome man, but now the stern lines of his rather long face and thin tight lips that were outward marks of his inner drive and great self-discipline have softened almost in repose.

And why not? His life had almost been programmed as a living dream. Many people have sailed around the world in small vessels. Many have escaped to what they believe at first is a personal paradise. Others have spent their lives doing pretty much what impulse or whim suggested. Few of them have ever found the real happiness they said they were seeking, for they who actually do achieve such goals are usually the unhappiest. Oddly enough, it was this man himself who said it is more important to have good dreams than to attain them, the ultimate happiness being not in the accomplishment but in the seeking.

The man, of course, is the almost legendary William Albert Robinson, who, now in his seventies, is able to look back on a life that not even Hollywood would dare suggest. He not only sailed the smallest vessel around the world, but also wrote several best-selling books and countless articles that made him famous and well-heeled; and he founded a shipyard that started out to build Baltimore clippers and other beautiful sailing ships, including his own personal dream ship, the 70-foot brigantine *Varua*, but ended up building minesweepers and patrol boats for the Navy in World War II—which earned him millions. He owned trading ships and private tropical islands. He bought a piece of Tahiti in 1929, when it was still unspoiled (and cheap), and built a home there for himself and the three marriages he found time for, one to a wholesome New England girl, another to a sophisticated and famous lady artist, and the third to a mystically beautiful and exotic Siamese-Tahitian girl called Ah You.

Romance, adventure, fame, fortune—these should have been enough. But Robbie, as his friends knew him, believed there was more. He used his trained and disciplined mind and physical energies to build lasting things, and his money and scientific curiosity to create medical institutes and foundations for research and treatment of tropical diseases. While his contemporary, Alain Gerbault, wrote about the plight of the native islander, Robinson invested his time, money, influence, and ingenuity into positive efforts to do something for them.

For all this, he was a superb, courageous, and resourceful sailor, and a gifted writer whose command of words and imagery at times come off the pages dripping with salt spume and tropical perfumes. Robbie, a Renaissance man in the ultimate sense rather than a follower of Henri Rousseau or an imitator of Somerset Maugham, would have excelled in any field he chose. To have done so in several nonconventional ones, for a Yankee with a stern and straitlaced beginning, perhaps makes him all the more unique.

On the warm and humid evening of June 23, 1928, a 25-year-old ex-engineer who had spent the last three years working in a textile factory on the lower East Side while preparing for his personal dream, left New York in the 32-foot Alden ketch *Svaap* as an entry in the Bermuda Race of that year.[2] With him as crew were several college chums, none of whom realized that Robbie had plans to continue on from Bermuda around the world in the smallest yacht ever to attempt it.

Svaap had cost Robinson a thousand dollars and he had found her in almost-new condition, only three years old, a product of the genius of Boston's John Alden and the craftsmen of Shelbourne, Nova Scotia. Although she was a work of art in every way, with the lines of the famed Gloucester fishing schooners, she was not Robinson's ideal—she was just all the boat he could buy at the time. Ketch-rigged, she was 32 feet 6 inches overall, 27 feet 6 inches on the waterline, 9 feet 6 inches of beam, and drew 5 feet 6 inches of water. The original sail plan was 660 square feet, which was reduced to 550 for deepwater voyaging. Moderate in all her dimensions, *Svaap* was easily driven, handy on the helm, and supremely seaworthy. With three tons of ballast outside, she could stand up to her canvas and some passages were astonishingly fast, close to the 200-mile noon-to-noon goal of all small boat voyagers. For ease of getting in and out of harbors and clawing off reefs and lee shores, *Svaap* also had a dependable 10-horsepower Kermath that at times on the circumnavigation was made to burn a wide range of exotic fuels.

The Bermuda Race proved to be *Svaap*'s ultimate test. It was a stormy and at times harrowing passage, with an amateur and seasick crew, an inexperienced skipper, and an untried boat. The little ship stood up to the test supremely well, and instead of suffering the trauma of such a desperate experience, this was just what Robbie needed to gain confidence in himself and his vessel.

By the time he reached Bermuda, Robbie was firmly convinced that *Svaap* was his dream ship. She was also the culmination of a boyhood enterprise. As a youth, he had sailed a 16-foot canoe on Lake Michigan, which he parlayed into a 28-foot sloop and now into a world-ranging Alden ketch.

In Bermuda, after his college friends left to return to New York, Robbie enlisted the first of his paid hands, a Bermuda boy, Willoughby Wright, who stayed with him until they reached Tahiti. Refitted and provisioned, *Svaap* cruised the West Indies with stops at Haiti and Jamaica, and, on August 12, anchored at Cristobal. A month or more was spent exploring the San Blas Islands, where a native *cayuca* was purchased for a tender.

Robbie was one of the first to describe the ordeal of taking a small sailing vessel through the locks, and typically he devised a way to thwart the destructive impulses of the lock tender by rigging four lines to hold the vessel in the middle of the lock as the water enters.[3] At the Pacific end, he took on more provisions and obtained with some difficulty a visa for the Galápagos Islands and a French visa for Oceania. Here Robbie made a square sail for running down the trades, and re-rigged the ketch to his own specifications.

On October 25, *Svaap* departed Balboa with a pet honey bear aboard as a pet. The 1,100-mile sail included squalls, calms, adverse currents, and head winds, as usual, until they made a landfall on Tower Island. Robbie was fascinated by the Galápagos Islands, and after a romantic and carefree interlude that included a love affair with Karin, the beautiful, dark-haired, half-wild daughter of a Norwegian colonist, he tore himself away to pursue his greater dream.[4]

Before leaving, Robbie stopped at Post Office Bay to drop off some mail for home, just to test how long it would take. By coincidence, Cornelius Crane's *Illyria*, on a scientific cruise, picked it up soon after and posted it at *Svaap*'s next port!

Departure was made in hopes of making the next landfall, 4,000 miles away, on New Year's Day. Slowly Floreana dropped from sight behind them. There was no turning back against the winds and currents. They were alone on the longest, loneliest ocean passage on the globe. Only then did Robbie suffer his first shock of realization. "I felt a sudden panic," he wrote. "I felt as a bird might feel, starting out to wing a lonely way to the moon."[5] Gradually he adjusted to the long-passage frame of mind he was to adopt many times. Then came the exhilaration and exultation of sailing down the trades. It was his first experience with the Pacific Ocean, which ever after would be "his ocean," where he felt most at home.

At noon, on December 31, they were ninety-four miles from Fangahina in the Marquesas. On January 1, 1929, at dawn, little *Svaap* rolled up on the crest of a swell and just ahead stood the bulge of a mountain. The landfall had been made precisely to the minute he had estimated at the beginning of the passage.[6]

They sailed through the Tuamotus and on to Tahiti, entered the pass, and tied up to a buoy along the Papeete waterfront. The air was heavy with the scent of flowers, and filled with strange land noises—a milkman making his rounds, dogs barking. Robbie raised the yellow Q flag and waited for the authorities.

"I gave myself over to the ecstasy of it all—a feeling of utter relaxation and peace, and of accomplishment."[7]

This first impression of Tahiti turned out to be a lifelong love affair, but there were still worlds to see and conquer. Here Wright left the ship, and Robbie engaged a Tahitian man of all trades, Etera, and made the first contacts with people who were to influence him in later life, such as Dr. Lambert of the Rockefeller Foundation, who was doing medical research in the Western Pacific, and Henri Grand, a local entrepreneur, who later became a business partner.

For six months, Robbie stayed at Te Anuanua, making short trips to Mooréa and other islands while he was a house guest of friends. By then, he had gotten over his yearning for Karin and found compelling reasons for going on. He departed Wednesday, August 28, 1929, with Etera, a character who became to Robinson a constant source of frustration, disappointment, admiration, and comradeship. A small craggy man, Etera was a mixture of Gilbertese, Fijian, and Tahitian, and already had a colorful background as a blackbirder, pearl diver, and cook on trading schooners. He was about forty-one years old with a bushy head of coal black hair and a broad flat nose. Aside from adventuring, Etera best liked women and wine, in that order. For the rest of the circumnavigation, Robbie was bailing him out of jail at every port, picking up forged markers at strange waterfront bars, and trying to separate him from his latest harem. When Etera had applied for a job the night before Robbie sailed, he was asked how much time he would need to wind up his affairs before leaving on a world cruise. "Five minutes," Etera told Robbie. This consisted only of getting his possessions out of hock at the Chinese laundry for forty francs.

Together they sailed and explored the waters of Polynesia, Micronesia, and Melanesia, poking into remote places, living off the land and sea when they ran out of food and fuel, weathering hurricanes, making notes on native customs and taboos, compiling a dictionary of pidgin English, and even dining with cannibals—all in that dim period prior to World War II, before the Southwest Pacific became a vast wartime theater of operations. When Robbie visited the area, much of it was not even charted, and he found countless colonial pestholes dating back to the eighteenth century, cesspools of World War I intrigue, lonely missionaries, feudal planters, and Sadie Thompson dives on sultry waterfronts.

They visited Hollandia, once a teeming colonial city when Muhlhauser was there, now almost deserted of Europeans, and later to become a military staging base. They called at the uninhabited Komodo Island of the giant monitor lizards, long before the television travelogs had heard of it.

Sailing through the exotic Java Sea, they called at Batavia, went on through Banka Strait to Singapore, and entered the South China Sea.

They had now sailed as far east as they could go, in spite of having been pointed west all the time. From here on, they would be homeward bound.

Like most travelers then, they received a hospitable welcome at Singapore, and survived the Christmas festivities of 1930. Sailing on Sunday, December 28, they cruised for three weeks in the Strait of Malacca, stopping to go ashore frequently, with Robbie often trudging miles into the jungle while Etera stayed behind to guard the boat. On the last day of the year, they left Malacca and went to Penang, a most fascinating and exotic port filled with junks and sampans that looked clumsy until Robbie tried to race them. Here *Svaap* was hauled out and reconditioned. Next came a glorious sail to Sabang, the little island off the north end of Sumatra, with the next port Colombo, Ceylon, where they stayed a week. The wettest passage was along the Malabar Coast where the anchorages were open roadsteads. He wanted to stop to explore the maze of canals and lagoons, the ancient walled cities, temples, and old palaces, but for this he needed an outboard motor and small boat, and, besides, the season was now becoming advanced for the passage to the Red Sea.

They left Mangalore on February 20, 1931, for Makalla, down to a ration of six small potatoes, half a tin of sardines, an onion, and a tin of evaporated milk for the 1,000-mile passage. They found no Europeans at Makalla, but an Arabian Nights atmosphere of fierce Arabs, bearded Bedouins, religious fanatics, sultans, and exotic drums. Ashore, Robbie was caught in a mob scene and in danger of being killed. He was saved by a tall stranger and later given the protection of the sultan, as well as a farewell gift of 150 rupees for "the brave American who sailed for the first time an American boat to Makalla."

The next stop was Aden, followed by two months of fighting their way against hot head winds and through uncharted waters, reef crawling most of the way. There was a brief spell in a local jail, a melodramatic escape from captors who held him for ransom, and the elusion of a pirate dhow. Graciously, King Ign Saud himself extended his personal protection to Robbie for the rest of his stay in Arabia. Entering the Gulf of Suez and fighting all the way, the *Svaap* inched up to Suez after three months of heat, sand wastes, hostile natives, adverse winds, and dangerous reefs.

After passing through the Canal, *Svaap* was overhauled at Port Said with the help of the Canal Company. Course was set for the Greek Islands, which Robinson wanted to explore. The winds and seas were violent most of the time in the Mediterranean. They went through the Corinth Canal, built by Nero 1,900 years before. They visited Ithaca, sailed through Charybdis and past Scylla, paused at Capri, weathered more gales, and then went on to the Italian Riviera. On July 23, they rounded the cape and came upon Villefranche and entered the small basin.

There a man dashed out on the pier shouting, "Robinson? For God's sake don't leave yet. I've got your grandmother in tow!"

Months before, Robbie had made a date to meet his grandmother, who would be traveling in Europe, on a certain day. This was the day, and it was twelve minutes before noon, the time appointed for the meeting.[8]

Remembering his Bermuda Race experience, Robbie was in no mood to cross the Atlantic between July and October. He decided to wait until November. This would give him six weeks in France. Etera had been in so many jams that Robinson had lost count. He had nursed Etera back to health on one occasion. Often he had taken the mate back after firing him or after Etera had quit numerous times.

In Paris, Etera lived up to his old tricks. He forged checks on "Captaine de Yak *Svaap*, Robinson" at bars and brothels. Finally, on September 11, they left for Gibraltar, and sailed for home via the southern route. Robinson wrote:

When two people have faced death, adventure, and romance of all sorts together in close association for more than two years, the combination is not easily broken. At sea he (Etera) was a splendid little sailor, afraid of nothing. Never once did he fail to produce regular meals. His originality in port brought on some difficult situations, and some amusing ones. The pathetic letters he wrote from various jails he got into were themselves worth his keep.[9]

In Tenerife, Robbie had to shanghai Etera away after more shore trouble, just ahead of the police, slipping out of port at dawn. Boiling down the trades, they made the long passage skirting a hurricane cell. On November 1, staggering before an easterly gale, with a falling glass, they crossed Robbie's outbound track and thus completed the circumnavigation in an elapsed time of three years and nine days to the hour.

There were eight hundred miles to go. They entered smoke from a forest fire. Looking for Frying Pan Lightship, they thought the chronometer was off and later learned that the ship had been moved. Soundings showed them the shoal. For ninety miles, they groped northward in the gray blanket of smoke. When they were where Robbie thought they would hear the surf on Cape Lookout Shoals, he started the engine and said to Etera, "In a half hour we will stop the engine and listen again. I think we will hear the bell buoy that marks the entrance to Morehead City." Within minutes after stopping the engine, they heard the harsh clang of the bell. Once again, Robinson's uncanny sense of timing had proved accurate.

"Capitaine! Capitaine! It's the bell! C'est fini la guerre!" Etera cried.

Svaap had come home.

They continued on up to New York and tied to the mooring at the Battery. Robinson was given a hero's welcome. He wrote a best-selling book of adventure and escape with the same exquisite timing he showed in his navigation. He wrote magazine articles and went on a lecture tour. He got married. He was famous.

Two years later, with his bride, Florence, a New England girl who had learned to sail in dinghies, and a cousin, Daniel T. West, Robbie sailed again in *Svaap*. After more adventures in the West Indies, and a grounding in a river on the Central American coast, they went through the canal again and headed for the Galápagos Islands. The purpose of this voyage was mainly to do some scientific research, and to make a movie of penguins on one of the islands. For props, they had brought doll-house furniture, purchased at Macy's, and on the island they built a small "penguin city" of lava rock.

Just as they began filming, Robbie, who had never been sick a day in his life, came down with appendicitis, which ruptured on the second day and peritonitis set in. A thousand miles from help, on a lonely island, and with a maximum of three days estimated time before death would come, there appeared miraculously in the cove an American tuna clipper, the *Santa Cruz*, with a long-range radio.

Next followed a race with death in which the U.S. Navy at Panama dispatched a destroyer with complete operating facilities and a flight of Army planes to assist in the rescue. The dramatic, almost melodramatic episode caught the attention of the world at a time when the public needed something to shake the routine boredom. Newspapers and radio stations all over the world followed the rescue effort minute by minute as the dispatches came in. If Robbie had been famous before, now he was a superstar.

His luck still holding, he was taken aboard the destroyer for an emergency operation, then taken to Gorgas Hospital in Balboa for further treatment and two more operations by Dr. Troy W. Earhart, one of the world's finest surgeons. While he was recuperating, President Franklin Delano Roosevelt passed through the Canal Zone bound for Hawaii. Robinson was invited to meet with the President and had an opportunity to thank him for the assistance of the Army and Navy.

Robbie then decided to give *Svaap* to the Naval Academy at Annapolis. Before salvage operations could be organized, it was learned that the local military commander at Wreck Bay had commandeered *Svaap* for his own use and wrecked it on a reef.[10]

He and Florence later sailed to Tahiti on a steamship and built their home there. In 1937, restless, his New England conscience telling him that he should not be living such an idyllic life, they returned to Ipswich, on the Connecticut River, where Robbie indulged his second great love, after Tahiti—that of designing and building sailing ships. In his small yard, which he founded, he rounded up old-time New England craftsmen and they began turning out beautiful vessels such as Baltimore clippers, as well as trawlers for the fishing fleet.

Then came World War II, and his yard was taken over and expanded for Navy vessels. At the peak, more than six hundred men were employed and some two hundred ships were built. Just prior to the defense effort, Robbie had purchased in Ceylon a beautiful full-rigged ship and had it brought to Gloucester as a model for designing and restoring classic old vessels. Later he sent this vessel to Tahiti to be operated in partnership with Henri Grand. During the same period, he designed and built with W. Starling Burgess and L. Francis Herreshoff his idea of an ultimate yacht, the 70-foot *Varua*.

He lived on *Varua*, tied up in the river, during those hectic war-time years, dreaming of returning to Tahiti some day. Meanwhile, he had been divorced and married again, this time to Sarah Lancashire, an artist whose professional name was Sallie White.

At last, on July 7, 1945, after winning the Navy E, completing the ship contracts, and disbanding the business, he departed on the unfinished *Varua*. In his papers was a letter of authorization from Admiral Chester Nimitz himself to enter the South Pacific war zone. On board were Sarah, or SLR, as he called her, and two of his closest wartime assistants. They made a stormy passage via the old sailing route to Port of Spain and Panama, where the two old friends left the ship.

With a hired Haitian as crew, and SLR as mate, he sailed to the Galápagos for a visit, calling upon his old romance, Karin, now burdened with children and living in semi-poverty. Then *Varua* sailed down the long passage to the Tuamotus and Tahiti and home for Robbie.

Life in Tahiti was not one of idleness. Robbie kept busy with a project of building a native community on an atoll he had purchased at auction from the government with Henri Grand as partner and there engaged in medical research. He sailed *Varua* on exploring missions among the islands, and even up to Hawaii. He wrote books and articles. He lived his dream at last.

Ultimately, SLR could not take the island life any more, and yearning for the world of art, patrons, and more intellectual outlets, she left for Italy. They parted on good terms and with mutual respect. In Italy, Sarah reached full development as an artist and achieved worldwide acclaim.

Next we find Robbie married to Ah You, an exquisitely beautiful half-caste. On *Varua*, with Ah You and a native crew, Robbie sailed on a year-long voyage along the clipper route in the forties and fifties, during which he encountered the ultimate storm, described in great detail in a later book.[11] They visited Chile and Peru, pausing for long periods for inland excursions, went up past the Guano Islands to the Galápagos for his fourth visit to the Enchanted Islands, and put in at Balboa where Ah You gave birth to their first child, a girl.

When the baby was only two months old, they departed again for home on Tahiti. More voyages followed, usually combined with scientific research, more intense work on his favorite project—finding a cure for elephantiasis—and trying to trace the migrations of the Polynesians. More children also followed. As they prepared for a long cruise to Southeast Asia and Siam, Ah You became ill. She stayed behind, planning to join Robbie and the children later by air. But that was the last they saw of her, for she died soon after.

Back in Tahiti again, Robinson now found his roots deeper than ever in his beloved Ofaipapa, and his long years of work to bring about Franco-American cooperation in medical research reaching a point where it no longer needed his drive, ability, and financing.

What else would a man want?

> *The sea is strange and alien to man. It is cruel. It is beautiful. I could never understand the recent vogue for drifting on rafts, trailing barnacles and seaweed while growing biblical beards. The sea is for action: cresting white foam at the bow, racing wake astern. You long for port, although at the very end you are never quite sure whether it is the delight of the landfall or regret that the voyage is done . . . but underneath it all you know that what is troubling you is that your goal has been achieved and is gone.*[12]

Gone are that sturdy little ketch, *Svaap*, and Etera and a thousand strange and exotic islands. Gone are Karin and those wild moonlight rides over the ridges of San Cristóbal. Gone the shipyard and six hundred loyal workers. Gone are Florence and the full-rigged Malabar ship he named for her. Gone the exhilaration and exultation of riding the foaming crests of a storm on a long Pacific passage. Gone is SLR, whose mind and artistic talent were keen enough to collide with his own. Gone is Ah You, the half-caste girl of mystical beauty, almost too unreal to be mortal, but who lives on in their daughters. Gone are the Arabian Nights adventures, the stimulation of goals and projects, the heady essence of fame and success. He has had them all.

Yet, he still has the memories, and on a cool evening from the veranda at Ofaipapa he can see *Varua* in the harbor, resting sleekly at her moorings, her unique foremast yard harbor-braced and cocked, eager and able to take her owner anywhere in the world. There, with the sunset colors playing in the last light, he can see the fairy island of Mooréa some twelve miles away to the west.

All is peace at last.[13]

Together, Virginia and Joshua Slocum lived one of the great love stories of maritime history. They are shown here at ages 33 and 39 respectively. (Photo from B. Aymar Slocum; first published in *The Voyages of Joshua Slocum*, edited by Walter Magnes Teller, Rutgers University Press, 1958)

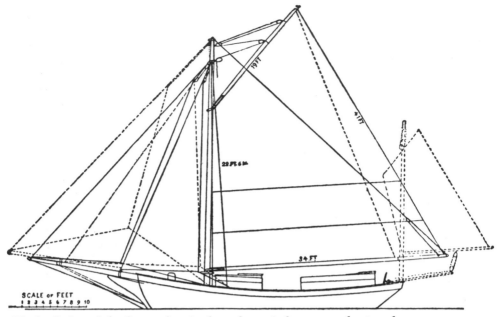

Final sail plan of the *Spray*, showing how the main boom was shortened at Buenos Aires, and a jigger mast installed. The bowsprit was also shortened at this time. (*Sailing Alone Around the World*, by Joshua Slocum)

The burgee of The Slocum Society Sailing Club. This red-and-white checked flag was the house flag of the last merchant shipping line Captain Joshua Slocum worked for before he acquired ownership in vessels he commanded, The Ben Aymar & Co. Line. (The Slocum Society)

Captain Joshua Slocum. (Don Holm)

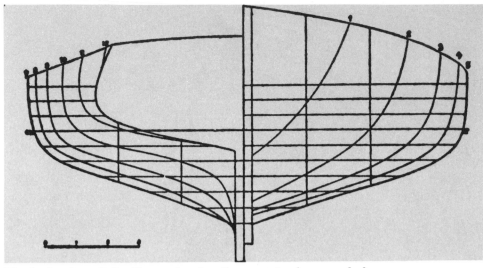

The body plan of the *Spray*, showing the excessive beam and sharp bilges and shallow draft. Originally the *Spray*, an oysterman, had a centerboard, which was removed when Slocum rebuilt her. (*Sailing Alone Around the World*, by Joshua Slocum)

News of Captain Slocum and the *Spray* was carried in this item from *The Standard*, a weekly English language newspaper in Buenos Aires, on Monday, December 30, 1895. Note it indicates the captain had already decided to go through Magellan Strait instead of around the Horn. It also perpetrates the hoax about Slocum's old dollar-and-a-half watch. Other newspapers, especially the Spanish editions in Montivedeo, apparently did not have any complimentary remarks for Slocum. (The Slocum Society)

WEEKLY EDITION

BUENOS AIRES, MONDAY, DECEMBER 30, 1895

We have received a nice letter from Captain Slocum, of the famous little craft "Spray," who expresses his great regret that he will not be able to visit Buenos Ayres, as he is anxious to resume his long voyage to Australia, via the Straits of Magellan. We wish him safe through his perilous undertaking. Capt. S. has sent us a letter of introduction from our old friend Chevalier Hairby of the Wordsworth, who informs us that the plucky Captains only chronometer while going round the earth is an old watch that cost him one dollar and fifty cents! We much regret to note that one of our Montevideo contemporaries printed in Spanish has had this bad taste to publish some remarks insulting to Capt. Slocum,

The *Spray* during Slocum's stay in Australia. (*Sailing Alone Around the World*, by Joshua Slocum)

The *Pato*, one of Captain Slocum's least-known commands, was a small, fast schooner built to the lines of the famous yacht *Sappho*, and owned by Slocum briefly in the 1870s. In it, with his family, Slocum made one of his most interesting voyages, from Hong Kong to Portland, Oregon, via the Bering Sea, and thence to Honolulu. While in Portland, Slocum sold at fancy prices a load of salt cod taken aboard in the Bering. (Slocum family records and *The Oregonian*, Portland; original art by E. Bruce Dauner)

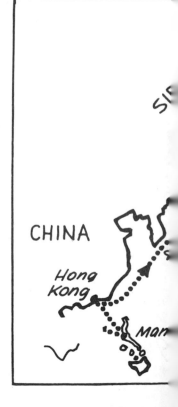

Route of the *Pato*, one of Captain Slocum's little-known adventures with his family. (Slocum family records and *The Oregonian*, Portland; original art by E. Bruce Dauner)

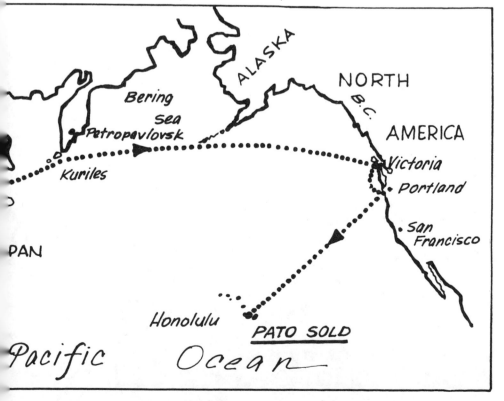

Mrs. Caroline Kuhn, only surviving child of Captain John Voss, as
she appeared in 1971 at her home
in Portland, Oregon. (Maury
Gwynne, the *Victorian Weekly*)

The Voss family, circa 1900 in Victoria, B.C. Oldest daughter, Caroline, is on the right. Note the boy has the name of one of Voss's yachts on his jacket. (Maury Gwynne, the *Victorian Weekly*)

Captain John Voss, as a first mate on merchant vessels, circa 1890. (Copy of a photo by Maury Gwynne; from collection of Voss's daughter, Caroline)

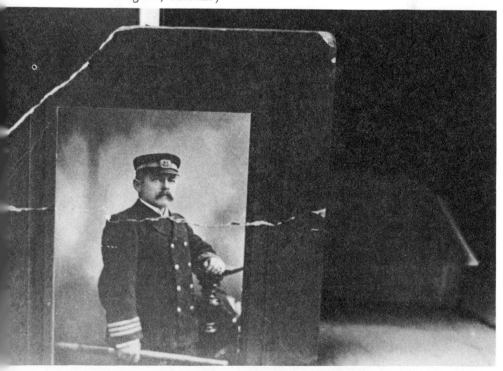

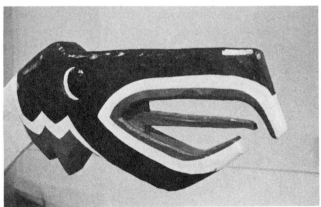

The figurehead of the *Tilikum*, as restored at the Victoria Maritime Museum. The original was broken by the kick of a horse in South Africa, according to Voss. It represents a typical Northwest coast Indian totem. (Photo taken at Maritime Museum, Victoria, British Columbia)

The *Tilikum* shown at Oak Bay near Victoria before Voss and Luxton departed on their voyage. Taken about 1901. (Courtesy of the Provincial Archives of British Columbia; furnished by Maury Gwynne)

The *Tilikum* as she looked restored in 1973 at the Victoria Maritime Museum. The vessel obviously is basically a seaworthy craft and not a simple "dugout canoe." (Photo taken at Maritime Museum, Victoria, British Columbia)

The *Tilikum* hauled out at Cape Town. Voss usually beached the vessel at major ports and put her on exhibition. Sometimes he hauled her inland on railroad flat cars to display her for a fee. (Photo taken at Maritime Museum, Victoria, British Columbia)

Norman Kenny Luxton at the time of the *Tilikum* adventure. Photo taken in Australia after he had left Voss. (Courtesy of Gray's Publishing Ltd., Sidney, B.C.)

Norman Kenny Luxton in later life as a popular civic leader and promoter at Banff. (Courtesy of Gray's Publishing Ltd., Sidney, B.C.)

The *Amaryllis* at Alexandria, during festivities honoring Muhlhauser.
(*The Cruise of the Amaryllis*, by G. H. P. Muhlhauser)

G. H. P. Muhlhauser, Lt., R.N.R., prior to his voyage around the world. (*The Cruise of the Amaryllis*, by G. H. P. Muhlhauser)

Ralph Stock's *Dream Ship*, as she looked ready for her circumnavigation, which ended on a whimsical note in the South Pacific. (*The Cruise of the Dream Ship*, by Ralph Stock)

☙ 10 ☚

The Young and
Innocent Rotarian

*After figuring and refiguring my dead reckon-
ing, I decided the island was Mehetia and not
Tapuaemanu, about 60 miles east of Tahiti,
and on that assumption changed our course. If
I was wrong we would be heading for the
Antarctic.[1]*

THE 32-FOOT IDLE HOUR LEAKED LIKE A SIEVE. MOST OF
the time the floorboards were awash. It was necessary to man the
pumps every four hours. On board, the 22-year-old skipper, Dwight
Long, had just recently learned the rudiments of celestial navigation,
but could not afford a chronometer—so he had to depend on a cheap
pocket watch for longitude. Now, forty-four days south of Hawaii,
after blundering through the maze of reefs and atolls that make up
the Tuamotus or Dangerous Archipelago, they were lost.

On board also were Mr. Loy, a retired postal worker who had never
seen an ocean before much less a small sailing vessel and whose eyes
were so bad that he could not see the binnacle at night; Bill Weld, a
young man of Long's age from Maine, who had no previous sailing
experience, and Hugo, Long's scrub dog.

If the island on which they had made a landfall was Mehetia
instead of Tapuaemanu, then they were only sixty miles east of
Tahiti. If not, then they were in real trouble. Dwight decided to sail

west for twenty-four hours, running with the southeast trade. It was a gamble, for if he were wrong they would never be able to beat back against the winds. Their food and water were nearly exhausted, and Long suffered from a badly injured hand which had swelled up to double its normal size.

Twenty-four hours pass. Nothing is sighted. Had they really left Mehetia, or had it been Tapuaemanu, which was sixty miles to leeward? Dwight decided to run one more hour before attempting to regain all those miles to windward.

Then, on the horizon ahead, rose the dark peaks of Tahiti. For the first time in forty-four days, Long knew exactly where he was. Mooréa loomed up to starboard. Soon they were abeam of Venus Point, running in enormous seas. The mizzen gaff lashing parted. The wind failed in the lee of the island near the pass. Just then, the pilot launch came to meet the ship, and they were towed into Papeete's calm, smooth lagoon.

At last in Tahiti, the waystation of all circumnavigators, Dwight Long felt seriously for the first time that he would become the youngest person ever to sail around the world. Moreover, his *Idle Hour* was slightly smaller than Robinson's *Svaap*, which had been the smallest vessel to sail around.[2]

Long had bought his first boat at age seven with money earned "peddling bills"—that is, advertising circulars door to door in Seattle. His craft was a tiny rowboat, scarred and leaky, but he loved her. He painted her up nicely and sold her for a profit. Then he bought another, fixed this one up, and sold it for a profit. For the next ten years, Long traded up through fourteen boats, each one a little larger, until owning boats became more than a hobby—it became an obsession. All during grade and high school, he worked at part-time jobs, investing his earnings into boat projects. In his spare time, he used them on the bays, inlets, and waterways of the Pacific Northwest, once or twice venturing as far north as British Columbia.

Ultimately, of course, Dwight would arrive at an age when he must make some decisions. He was energetic, thoroughly happy and well-adjusted, with few hang-ups, the son of a well-off Seattle businessman and civic leader who was especially active in clubs like International Rotarians. He had to halt his boat-trading ventures and begin thinking of college. With the University of Washington near at hand (actually the campus is right on the waterfront, with its own docks and sailing and rowing clubs), it was the practical thing to do.

Then, one Sunday in the local newspaper magazine section,

Dwight read an article by Alain Gerbault, the noted French tennis champion and circumnavigator, propounding his reasons for escaping to the South Seas and the uncomplicated life. That article was the genesis of Dwight Long, the young circumnavigator.

The Great Depression was still on. Millions of people were out of work. In Seattle, the powerful Teamsters Union had a stranglehold on all employment. It was said they even controlled the watchmakers, because their products had wheels. Even news butchers on the street corners, who did not knuckle under, might look forward to having an arm broken across a curb by a goon squad.

Would there be any opportunities open in the professions if Long did get a college degree? Were there not doctors, dentists, and engineers now in the bread lines or working at manual labor? Dwight decided to try it for two years, and if the prospects did not then look better, he would get himself a ship like Alain Gerbault, and sail around the world.

He confided this to an adventurous pal who was enthusiastic about joining him—provided they could leave immediately. When it turned out to be a project that would require months of planning and preparation, the friend lost interest and Dwight enrolled at the university. Typically, he organized a landscaping business on the side which prospered as he acquired two trucks and six employees. At the same time, he studied hard and got good grades. Like all good, conservative sons of Rotarians, he was doing what was expected of him, and doing it better than most.

But world economic conditions did not seem to improve. There was no assurance that once he had his college degree, he would not still be running a landscaping service. Why not look around a little for a suitable ship, one in which he could sail to any place on earth if he wanted and live aboard if times got tough? He would then be completely independent no matter what happened to the world. Besides, looking for one's dream ship is a fascinating and universal hobby, something to add spice to a tough grind of study and work.

In the beginning, Dwight was only half-serious, but as the search went on, he became obsessed to the point where he neglected his landscaping business. Oh, well, there was no future in that anyway. He concentrated on finding a boat. For six months, he searched every port from San Francisco to Juneau—and then found *Idle Hour* right there under his nose at a Lake Washington yacht club.

Eleven years before, a professional shipbuilder, Carl Rathfin, had built *Idle Hour* for his own use. Carefully constructed of selected two-inch thick, full-length fir planks over oak ribs, she was heavily built for any use, including voyaging to the ice fields of the north. Completed in November 1922, the owner set sail with a companion for Hawaii. Twelve days out, his companion came down with infantile paralysis. Putting about, they encountered the worse storm in forty years and narrowly escaped the ordeal. Then Rathfin sold the ketch to a couple of trappers, who took her to the Arctic for several seasons, on the last trip wrecking her upon a lonely beach. Patching the hull with tin cut from cans and with rags, they made it back to Seattle. *Idle Hour* was sold again, this time to a yachtsman who replanked her.

Long paid $1,600 for her, all the money he had. Then he began learning to sail and to save for a world cruise. For two years, he hired her out as a charter boat among the San Juan Islands, learning how to handle her between clients. He found a new partner for his circumnavigation, a fellow student who had studied trig at the university, and who boned up on navigation in his spare time.

Setting September 20, 1934, as departure date, he neglected to tell his parents, who learned about the voyage from a newspaper feature story. When they recovered from shock, his father gave him introductions to Rotarian leaders around the world. The mayor of Seattle also gave him a letter of introduction. The president of the Foss Tug and Barge Company volunteered to tow *Idle Hour* out to Cape Flattery, 120 miles to the open sea.

With supplies aboard, *Idle Hour* was six inches below her marks. Family and friends showed up to see them off. They entered the Hiram Chittenden Locks, passing out into Puget Sound. There a Foss tug gave them a wild ride, almost sinking the boat as the water poured in through scuppers and hawse pipe. In the Strait of Juan de Fuca, another Foss tug, with a log boom in tow, picked them up and took them to the open Pacific. Off Neah Bay, the tug slipped the cable and they were on their own.

At first, the run south, about fifty miles offshore, was fair sailing. They even caught a number of albacore tuna off Oregon. In San Francisco, they tied up to the St. Francis Yacht Club moorings. Then Dwight and Jack, his partner, went sightseeing. At Palo Alto, they called on former President Herbert Hoover, who entertained them and gave them a box of fishing gear. Dwight also noted that Public Enemy Number One, Al Capone, had just taken up residence on Alcatraz Island.[3]

One day they climbed to the top of Telegraph Hill and saw the giant rollers of a tidal wave beginning to break upon the coast. They visited Amundsen's famed sloop at Golden Gate Park.[4] Then, with a newspaper send-off, they departed, sailing out of the Golden Gate past the huge caissons for the new bridge and the 600-foot high towers, yet to receive the suspension cables.

At Los Angeles harbor, Dwight found a man from his home town in charge of the movie ships, one of which was the *Bounty*, just refitted for use in the motion picture with Clark Gable and Charles Laughton. The crews of these old ships were veteran sailing-ship sailors. They helped Dwight refit *Idle Hour* for the Pacific passage, replacing the rigging and making baggy wrinkles to prevent sail chaff.

Long thought it would be a good idea to get Hollywood backing for a movie he would make of his cruise and called on Will Rogers at his Santa Monica ranch. "Dwight," Will told him, "you could die outside one of the studios and be dead for two weeks before anyone would smell the body."

Rogers gave Dwight a letter to Mack Sennett. The latter, however, had just got stung on an expensive South Seas expedition. The famous producer of comedies did not think it funny.

At Los Angeles, the *Idle Hour* took on a paying passenger, the son of a wealthy Chicago family, then another guest, a German who had spent three years building a boat to sail to the South Seas and then lost it to creditors during the Depression. Just outside the harbor, Dwight discovered that the compass was defective. They anchored in a cove at Catalina, went goat hunting the next day, and then sailed down the coast to San Diego. There *Idle Hour* was hauled on a slipway and painted, after the compass had been repaired. On the slipway, because of a worker's error, the hull was damaged, the dinghy crushed, and the oars broken. The owner of the yard repaired the damage, and finally they sailed for Hawaii, on November 30.

Nearly run down by a destroyer on the second day out, they finally reached the trade winds belt. Hugo, Dwight's dog, became seasick; all their wood for the stove washed overboard; the boat began to leak through planks that had opened during the exposure to California sun; the bilge pump failed; they encountered heavy weather and frequent squalls; in a moment of exuberance, Hugo jumped up on Dwight and a clawnail pierced his lip; they were becalmed; Jack's navigation proved faulty; the German came down with an attack of appendicitis—but, somehow, on the twenty-eighth day out, they came in sight of the volcanic cone of Haleakala.

In the harbor, they passed the famed Royal Hawaiian Hotel,

Waikiki Beach, and were assigned a berth just ahead of none other than sixty-year-old Captain Harry Pidgeon, who was on his second circumnavigation in *Islander*.[5]

In Hawaii, all three of *Idle Hour*'s crew and guest list departed. The four weeks on the passage overkilled any desire the German had for tropical cruising. The wealthy lad from Chicago who had spent years trying to elude his parents, rushed to a cable office and let them know where he was. Jack had to return to his studies. All three left on the next steamship for the mainland.

Dwight spent his twenty-second birthday on a tour of the islands with the local Rotarian leader. Hugo had to go into quarantine. Dwight tried to charter his vessel for trips among the islands, but bad luck coupled with bad publicity in the local press drove away all his potential business. He locked up *Idle Hour* and shipped out on the S.S. *Lurline* for several trips back and forth to California to earn some money. He re-outfitted *Idle Hour*, with the advice and help of his new friend, Harry Pidgeon, who also taught him some navigation. Long accepted an invitation from the owner of Hawaiian Tuna Packers to haul *Idle Hour* for bottom repairs. A young man from Maine named Bill Weld, who had necessary funds for the passage, including the landing bond in Oceania, joined Dwight. On May 12, Hugo was finally returned from quarantine. On departure date, friends came to see them off. Harold Dillingham, well-known commodore of the TransPac, came alongside in his *Manuiwa* to give them a final *aloha*.

At Hilo, a Mr. Loy joined the voyage. Dwight was taken on a tour of Hawaii by the local Rotary Club leader. Then, with charts given him by none other than Rear Admiral Yarnell, Dwight set sail on the same course Jack London had taken in the *Snark*.

It was more of an ordeal than a cruise. The boat leaked so badly that they had to man the pumps every four hours. Everyone on board was seasick except Dwight. Bill developed sores on his wrist. Dwight had a sore heel from an abscess that had been lanced in Hilo. The elderly Mr. Loy, who could not see very well, was of little use as a relief helmsman.

Heading for the Southern Cross, they passed through the doldrums, and suffered squalls and calms. In the middle of a rain squall, Mr. Loy stood on the deck holding a mast and spoke: "The Lord surely wastes a lot of water on the ocean. Arizona and New Mexico could certainly use it." Then he added, "But who am I to advise the Lord what to do?"

The ordeal continued through the Tuamotus, with a number of close calls, until finally they found Tahiti after forty-four days at sea.

In Tahiti, Mr. Loy and Bill Weld left the ship. Dwight had an introduction to Governor Soutot, who commended him to the commander of the French frigate *Zelee*, who invited Dwight for a four-day cruise to Tau Island. He had his hand treated, which turned out to be broken. It was there, also, that he encountered Etera, Robinson's man Friday, on the quay and introduced himself. Dwight eventually met Robinson and also Alain Gerbault in person, and took a rare photograph of these two voyagers together. Gerbault could not resist the artless naïveté of the young Rotarian, and they became good friends. Gerbault showed him about his new yacht, the sleek *Alain Gerbault*, and introduced Dwight to Charles Nordhoff and James Norman Hall, two former Lafayette Escadrille veterans whom Gerbault had known during the war in France, who were working on their new epic, *Hurricane*.

He discovered Zane Grey in residence at the time and called upon this famous author and big-game fisherman.[6] He dined with Robinson at Ofaipapa, and greeted the irrepressible Fahnestocks as they arrived in *Director*. Also in the area were Ray Kauffman and Gerry Mefferd on *Hurricane*.

Etera, seeing in Long another chance for a berth, tried to hire aboard, but Long had been warned about this from Robinson. Instead, on Bora Bora, he found a fifteen-year-old Tahitian lad named Timi who became his companion and trusted friend until they reached Ceylon.[7]

Bidding good-bye to Alain Gerbault, who was also in Bora Bora, Dwight sailed with Timi (after getting permission of the lad's parents and the authorities), and a passenger named Sam, for Penrhyn.[8] After a visit, during which Dwight went pearl diving with the natives, they sailed for Samoa—one year to the day after he had left Seattle. They paused at Palmerston to visit the famous Masters family, and then reached Pago Pago for a long stay. Dwight got his hair cut in a shop at the Sadie Thompson Hotel where Somerset Maugham wrote *Rain*.

When the cruise ship S.S. *Lurline* arrived, Dwight signed on as a wiper, leaving Timi in charge of *Idle Hour*. Long visited New Zealand and Australia, and while in both countries he took time to go ashore to arrange to write articles of his adventures for the local newspapers, and to make future contacts with influential people. On the return cruise, he went aboard *Cimba*, Richard Maury's ill-fated 35-foot schooner which had piled up on a Suva reef.[9]

Back in Samoa, Dwight found Timi and *Idle Hour* waiting for him. He also entertained a new friend, Wilbur Thomas, who was to join the cruise twenty-one months later in France. During Dwight's absence, he had dreamed that *Idle Hour* had caught fire. On his return, he learned that a nearby vessel had burned to the water, but Timi had been able to move *Idle Hour* to a safe place. Leaving Samoa, they passed close to Tin Can Island, then in a storm *Idle Hour* was dismasted, and Hugo was lost overboard.

Under jury rig, they made New Zealand. Christmas was spent here, and the crew of the *Idle Hour* were warmly welcomed. Timi had a broken tooth repaired by Dr. Batten, father of a famous New Zealand aviatrix. Dwight addressed meetings of the local Rotary clubs and accepted offers from various sources for repair and outfitting of his yacht. He earned some money writing for the newspapers. He had an audience with New Zealand's Prime Minister, James Savage, and met the mayor of Auckland, Mr. Davis, who took Dwight and Timi on a cruise aboard the luxurious 85-foot schooner *Marewa*.

One day, a short moustachioed character came down and introduced himself. It was Captain Tommy Drake, who claimed to be a descendant of Sir Francis Drake, and who had lived some time in the Seattle area, built three or four vessels named *Pilgrim* and *Progress*, wrote the *Log of the Lone Sea Wanderer*, and finally went missing on his last voyage. Drake was then seventy-four, and at the time was touring the Southwest Pacific by steamship.[10]

Timi was injured in a bike accident; Dwight met Alan Villiers who was there with the training ship *Joseph Conrad* on a world cruise; and the *Idle Hour* took part in regattas and other festivities, then sailed for Australia.

In Sydney, there was more publicity, more Rotary lectures, more guided tours, and more interviews with people in high places. A paying guest joined *Idle Hour*, who turned out to be a bumbler who was mostly bad luck. Sailing up inside the Barrier Reef, they called at Hayman Island, where Zane Grey was making a motion picture called *White Death*, and were hosted by the famous author. After many adventures and fascinating detours, they called at New Guinea. In Port Moresby, Dwight dined with Beatrice Grimshaw, the famous authoress, made side trips inland with native guides, sailed on to Timor, visited the island of the giant lizards, Komodo, went through the Java Sea, had the same bad experience in Surabaja with the haughty and uncooperative American consul that Robinson had written about, out-bluffed some arrogant Dutch officials, and then reached Singapore.

It was Generalissimo Chiang Kai-shek's birthday, and the city was jumping with celebrations. With his usual talent for seeking out people in influential places, Long enjoyed an eventful stay here, while preparing for the homeward voyage. He also received a letter from Robinson in Tahiti, with advice on the route through the Indian Ocean and Red Sea.

"Remember," Robinson wrote, "you can do anything you want to hard enough, if you never slip up on the eternal vigilance."

Timi, still homesick, was cheered up by letters from Dwight's sister, but he began to come down with periodic attacks of malaria, and refused to take his medicine as directed by the doctor. Before departing, Dwight received a radio message from the chief officer of the *President Adams*, a Dollar liner en route to Ceylon, advising on weather and sea conditions. A visit was made to Great Nicobar Island, as Zane Grey had suggested. In Singapore, Dwight had also met Martin and Osa Johnson, and had been given the benefit of their experience.[11]

One day, in Colombo, who should come aboard but William A. Robinson. Robbie was there outfitting a 70-ton square-rigger that he had seen on his circumnavigation and fallen in love with. With a native crew and his wife, he sailed the beautiful ship back to Gloucester, visiting many out-of-the-way places en route. The vessel, which he named the *Florence C. Robinson*, was a teak replica of the old China tea clippers.[12]

Next, Timi and Dwight visited Kandy, Ceylon. Before they sailed, Timi took sick again. Instead of improving, he got worse. With that instinct which all islanders seem to have, Timi knew he was dying and resigned himself to it. After a dismaying period with Dwight at his bedside constantly, the lad expired as a Catholic priest gave him his last rites. It was a severe blow for Long since he had regarded Timi as a younger brother with whom he was sharing a great adventure.

When Long finally sailed again, he had with him Raymond Milton, a tea planter returning to England, who weighed 280 pounds and turned out to be a delightful companion. Also aboard was Peter Collins, the son of an English mother and a Cingalese physician.

The departure date was December 27, Dwight's birthday, the same day he had landed in Hawaii with a guest suffering with appendicitis, the same day he had reached harbor under jury rig in New Zealand after a dismasting and the loss of Hugo, and now the same day he was leaving Timi behind in a Ceylon graveyard.

The *Idle Hour* crossed the Indian Ocean and went up the Red Sea to Suez with frequent stops for adventures among the Arabs, and, as usual, Dwight displayed his knack for seeking out people of influence, including Adbul Mijib, finance minister of Saudi Arabia, and the local managers of American and British firms. *Idle Hour* was dry-docked in Port Said. Dwight visited the pyramids. At Jidda, where Long went to photograph the pilgrimage, he was almost shot by the Khan's men, but the American local manager, Mr. Twichell, interceded with the potentate.

On one side trip, Dwight took a train to Palestine along with Elizabeth Bergner, the famous actress who had recently played in *The Boy David*, and her husband.

Idle Hour zigzagged across the Mediterranean. Near Gibraltar, two of Il Duce's bombers passed low overhead. The Rock was crowded with refugees. At the American consulate, Dwight got his mail, including a letter from Wilbur Thomas, who was coming to join him, and one from his father, who was in Europe to attend an International Rotarian conference.

In Cherbourg, France, he tried to telephone his dad in Paris, but missed him by an hour. With the help of the *New York Herald* Paris staff, he made contact with his father in Zurich, where the elder Long had been elected member of the board.

After a reunion in Zurich, Dwight took *Idle Hour* to Cowes, England, for the winter, where he wrote his book, visited the yacht clubs, and did his usual sightseeing. War clouds were already forming in Europe. Long remained aboard *Idle Hour*, tied up in the Thames, almost on the prime meridian, thirty thousand miles from Seattle, until spring; then he sailed for New York.

In the United States again, Dwight got the usual hero's welcome. Invited to appear on an N.B.C. radio broadcast, he was at the studio when a hurricane struck the area. Learning that *Idle Hour* had broken loose, he tried to leave the studio, but the broadcast was already in progress. When he was interviewed, he departed from the script to appeal to listeners to be on the lookout for his boat, but most of the power in the area was already out and few were listening.

After the broadcast, he hurried out to Long Island and began searching himself. He finally found *Idle Hour* wrecked among hundreds of others on a long stretch of beach.

With the nationwide publicity of the radio broadcast and later newspaper stories, aid came from many sources. Back in his home town, folks got together and raised a fund for rebuilding the now-famous yacht. Then Long continued on through the Caribbean to Panama, and sailed the long passage uphill to Seattle at last.

The youngest to circumnavigate in a small boat, Long also was one of the last before World War II. During the war, he served as a Navy officer, attached to headquarters in Honolulu on special assignment, and *Idle Hour*[13] finished out her career as a charter boat among the San Juan Islands, where she had started.[14]

❧ 11 ❧

The Spray Comes Back to Life

When I determined to try the glare of the sun on dancing waves, instead of on chromium plate along our dusty highways, I was totally devoid of those rabid prejudices one usually encounters among yachtsmen in favor of their local designs, for I had never owned or sailed anything larger than a canoe.[1]

ALTHOUGH ROGER S. STROUT HAD NEVER SAILED ANYTHING larger than a canoe, he had been born and raised on the coast of Maine and had acquired a sense of proper seagoing craft by osmosis, if nothing else. His wife, Edith, however, was a Colorado gal from the Rocky Mountain country, and about as far removed from the sea as one can get.

So it was with astonishment that friends and associates at the Georgia School of Technology in Atlanta learned that Roger and Edith were going to build a boat for ocean cruising, perhaps one that would even take them to New Zealand and beyond. They were especially astonished that Strout would give up a good-paying post as assistant professor, as this was 1933 and the country in the depths of the Great Depression, even though Franklin Delano Roosevelt had just been elected and a New Deal had taken over.

Times were indeed uncertain and unsettled. In Europe, Hitler took over as Chancellor of Germany. In France, M. Deladier was having trouble with the socialists in his cabinet. President Machado of Cuba was accused of killing hundreds of political prisoners, and was opposed to any intervention by the United States to straighten out the tangled affairs of his country. The Japanese invading forces in China pushed on with fierce fighting. Mayor Anton Cermak was shot by an assassin named Zangara in Miami, Florida, who had been aiming for F.D.R. A mob in Russia attacked Stalin's home and was driven off by troops after four hundred people were killed, according to a Tokyo report. President Roosevelt declared a bank holiday, called Congress into special session, and declared an embargo on gold. Kidnappers had grabbed St. Paul millionaire brewer William Hamm, and held him for $100,000 ransom. And Roosevelt took a few days off in June for a vacation voyage with his son James, and some friends on the *Amberjack II.*

Clearly, these were times enough to try men's souls and to escape if possible to happier places where one could try the glare of tropical sun on dancing blue waves.

Professor Strout chose for his escape machine the famous sloop *Spray* of Captain Joshua Slocum—both the subjects of a current resurgence of interest and controversy in the yachting magazines. Slocum and *Spray*, of course, were gone, posted as missing on their last voyage more than twenty years before, but the *Spray*'s lines had been published, first in *Rudder* by the well-known designer Charles Mower who had taken them from a hand-carved model done by Slocum himself.[2]

Dozens, perhaps hundreds of copies of the *Spray* had been or were being built around the world. One, the *Pandora*, built in Australia, had sailed around the Horn and up to New York, but as it departed for Europe, it too went missing in approximately the same part of the Atlantic as the *Spray* had disappeared. Another, the *Basilisk*, built by Gilbert C. Klingel for a scientific expedition to the West Indies, had been shipwrecked on Great Inagua.[3]

The controversy over the merits of the *Spray*, begun before Slocum disappeared, had been revived from time to time, and continues even to this day. Such famous designers as John Hanna, who even produced a copy of the *Spray*, and Cipriano Andrade, Jr., to say nothing of Thomas Fleming Day, Charles Mower, and Howard I. Chapelle, have cursed or praised the design, according to each one's personal opinion.[4]

Neither Roger nor Edith Strout knew about any of this, and so were not infected by bias. They simply wanted a small but roomy boat with a simple rig, one they could handle as amateurs to take them anywhere in the world.[5] Strout had grown up in a seafaring environment where work boats were the common type, and he naturally turned to a work-boat model when it came to choosing a design. The *Spray*, as every reader of sea stories knows, had been an oyster smack for nearly a century before she was given to Slocum, who rebuilt her in a Fairhaven pasture. Moreover, the Strouts had no particular desire to sail around the world. In fact, Roger was dead set against such nonsense. In his view, Magellan had already chalked up a first in that department, and everyone who came after was merely an imitator. No, the Strouts had read a lot about the wonderful scenery of coastal New Zealand and wanted to visit there, but the only practical way to do so was in one's own boat.[6]

The work went well, and although he had never built a boat before, Professor Strout was handy with tools, a careful and meticulous worker, and was a trained engineer. Edith helped where possible, including the job of puttying 10,000 nail holes. The result was a sound and solid copy of the *Spray* (perhaps even sounder and more solid than the original), with enormous carrying capacity for a 37-foot craft, spacious deck, and good seakeeping qualities.

They named her *Igdrasil*, after the Tree of Life in Norse mythology, which has roots running down into Hell while the branches reach up to Heaven. The end of the world comes, the myth has it, when the tree Igdrasil dies or falls.

In June 1934, the Strouts departed from Jacksonville, Florida, for the West Indies, learning how to sail and handle the ship on this leg of their journey with the first destination to be Jamaica.

This was the season of hot, humid weather and squalls, but they soon adapted to the routine, keeping watch on watch, marveling at the sea life—the sargasso weed, the chattering terns, the jellyfish, the blowing porpoises close aboard, the shining ribbons of phosphorescence at night, the screaming long-tailed boatswain birds hovering over the sloop, the gorgeous blood-red sunrises and sunsets.

It was hot in Jamaica, being July, so they did not stay long. The passage to the Canal Zone was made without incident. They had heard much about the terrifying canal passage, but in their case, in contrast to the experiences of other voyagers, the water came into the locks so gently that they hardly noticed it.

It was the rainy season here, so they pressed on to the Galápagos

Islands, across the Gulf of Panama and its squalls, finally emerging from the rain and mist to see the Enchanted Islands basking in the sun. They called at Marchena, found some tracks of high-heeled women's shoes, but no humans here. They visited Santa Cruz and the Seymour Islands, Barrington, and Santa Maria where Post Office Bay was located. They spent Christmas on Santa Cruz with the settlers at Academy Bay and climbed to the top of Indefatigable. They visited Elizabeth Bay in Penguin Cove and found no evidence of anyone having been there.[7] They visited with Mrs. Witmer on Santa Maria.[8]

Unable to get drinking water and having only 30 gallons left, the Strouts set sail for the Marquesas, 3,300 miles away. As usual, this was a glorious sail, during which both of them were able to get a full night's sleep for 25 out of 30 days. There were some tense moments, however, when whales were encountered. Two finbacks accompanied them for hours, playing around and under the boat, blowing their nauseous breath on them. Once, when the *Igdrasil* touched one of them, the brute nudged back, shoving the boat several yards sideways. Another time, a small whale struck the rudder so hard that it jerked the steering wheel out of Edith's hands.[9]

They enjoyed a stay in the Marquesas, visiting the remains Melville had written about in *Typee*. At Nuku Hiva they called on Haka Hau, the last of the Taipis and collected some *tiki* souvenirs. Stopping at Hikeu Bay, they found an American living there, an ex-navy enlisted man, who welcomed them and pumped them for news of home.

The next call was Manihi in the Tuamotus, and then Tahiti, where they stopped only long enough to collect their mail. Next came Mooréa and the Leeward Islands, including Raïatéa, then Bora Bora and Samoa.[10] The Fijis delighted them and considerable time was spent there. Then they headed for New Zealand, their original destination. The season was now advanced, so they sailed directly from the Bay of Islands around North Cape to the Sounds. On the way, they passed the cadet cruise ship *Joseph Conrad* under full sail, skippered by Alan J. Villiers. Finally, they got their first glimpse of the Southern Alps, sighting Mount Aspiring and Pembroke Peak.

For nearly two years, the New Zealand Sounds had been a goal. Now they cruised and explored extensively but leisurely at will. As winter came on, they hurried north, stopping briefly at Dunedin, Lyttleton, and Wellington on their way up from Bluff. Now, it was time to leave for home. Which way to go? Back across the Pacific, or around the Cape of Good Hope and up the Atlantic? They figured the latter route would be easier, more pleasant, and interesting, and thus they decided on a circumnavigation.

After a boisterous crossing of the Tasman Sea, they called at Brisbane, then headed north for warmer weather inside the Great Barrier Reef along the Queensland coast. At Thursday Island, they visited the pearling operations, and then went on to Darwin. As the wet season approached, they sailed on to Christmas Island, where they were hosted warmly by the British colony engaged in phosphate mining.

Next came the long sail down the trades along Slocum's track to the Keeling-Cocos Islands, where they enjoyed a visit with the Cable Company team on Direction and the Clunies-Ross colony on Home Island, where the natives still remembered the visit of Captain Harry Pidgeon. Governor John S. Clunies-Ross himself welcomed them.[11]

The *Igdrasil* left Keeling-Cocos for a fine sail of 16 days and 2,300 miles to Rodriguez. There they visited the caves, as all the previous voyagers had done, and enjoyed the hospitality. The next call was Mauritius, as usual, and more visiting and sightseeing.

The worst weather of the entire trip was encountered in the Mozambique Channel between Madagascar and the African main-land, at one time being hove-to for thirty hours in a cyclone. While Edith passed the time by scanning the African coast for native signs, the first recognizable object was a golf course—in Darkest Africa. Durban was entered at night before a brisk gale, and soon they were moored and ashore.[12]

The passage around to Cape Town was uneventful, except for several routine gales. After taking in the sights of South Africa, they sailed in late February 1937 for St. Helena, the usual stop for circum-navigators homeward bound. They found St. Helena a fascinating place with many evidences remaining of Napoleon's exile here.[13] Ascension came next, where they visited the lonely colony. The long run to the Barbados brought them within sight of the Brazilian penal colony island of Fernando de Noronha. Crossing their outbound track in the West Indies, they again experienced the hot, humid, and rainy summer weather. They called at the Bahamas and then rode the Gulf Stream northward to New York, their final destination.

In three years, they had sailed 38,000 miles around the world to become the first copy of the *Spray* to make it.

The following year, the Strouts became the first of a series of man-wife teams of voyagers to receive the coveted Blue Water Medal of the Cruising Club of America, given them without date.

This was not the end of their sailing days, however. They soon departed on another long voyage, this time through the Caribbean to the Panama Canal, then over to the Hawaiian Islands, northward to the Aleutian Islands and Alaska, and down the Pacific Northwest coast to California.

In 1939, *Igdrasil* was sold to D. Grant and L. Smith, who changed her name to *Tané* and intended to sail her to the South Pacific. The next owner was probably Edwin L. King of Newport Beach, California. She was remodeled and refitted during 1957 and 1958, and a new Gray engine was installed. In 1959, she was advertised in Los Angeles newspapers for $20,000. The last-known owners were Mr. and Mrs. Paul Lewis, Jr., of Los Angeles, who apparently restored the original name. Among the visitors who came to see the venerable old *Spray* copy were Professor and Edith Strout, who spent a night aboard for old time's sake. They had not seen the *Igdrasil* since they sold her in 1939.[14]

Much to the delight of *Spray* and Slocum *aficionados*, the Strouts had successfully completed a leisurely and extended circumnavigation with no misadventures or disasters, using the original lines for their copy, and having had no previous experience either at boat building or voyaging.

The Strouts had not intended to make a circumnavigation, and there was little publicity generated. They did not write a book about their adventures, although both Roger and Edith did articles for various periodicals such as *Yachting* and *National Geographic*. They found *Igdrasil*, as Slocum reported *Spray*, to be sea-kindly, docile under heavy weather conditions, easy to handle even for amateurs (many detractors have claimed it was Slocum's skill that kept him out of trouble), and capable of surprising speeds, averaging at times 170 miles a day. They proved also, using sails that were duplicates of *Spray*'s, that the vessel was indeed self-steering on many points of sailing. Like Slocum, they changed their rig midway during their voyage. Slocum added a jigger mast and a small sail aft, making *Spray* technically a yawl. Strout added a mizzen mast in New Zealand, shortening the mainsail and converting *Igdrasil* into a ketch (not a yawl as most published accounts have it).

Igdrasil, like *Spray*, was roomy and comfortable to live aboard, and capable of carrying an enormous load. Slocum filled his hold with tallow and other salvage while on his voyage; the Strouts used their large tankage to buy fuel at 10 cents a gallon in the Canal Zone. Before leaving home, they loaded aboard scraps from the construction of the boat for stovewood. When they sold the boat, more than half of this supply was still aboard.

Years later, in a letter, Roger wrote: "I honestly believe that *Igdrasil* was the safest and most comfortable vessel of her length that was ever built."[15]

In her, he said, they had voyaged in safety, eaten well, and slept in peace.

Not even old Joshua Slocum could have claimed more.

⊷§ 12 §⊷

Hurricane Leaves
a Ribald Wake

*It would be as natural, I thought, as eating
breadfruit, to drift into the easy logical life of
Polynesia, and I said, "Gerry, it would be too
bad if those girls fell into the hands of the
Chinese."[1]*

IN THE FISHING VILLAGE OF PASCAGOULA AT THE MOUTH
of the Pascagoula River, just west of the Alabama-Mississippi bound-
ary, on a seven-acre site subdivided over the generations since it was
first homesteaded, lived Sidoine Krebs and his family—sort of a
bayou version of Ma and Pa Kettle, except that the Krebses had
been master shipbuilders since the first one cleared the ground and
built the ways on the banks of this tidal slough. Now it stood idle,
in the depths of the Great Depression, a seventy-foot fishing smack
built on speculation still on the stocks, the boiler tubes rusting in the
sawmill.

It was the autumn of 1934, and for months two young and easy-
going buddies from Des Moines, Iowa, named Ray F. Kauffman and
Gerry Mefferd, had searched the Gulf Coast from New Orleans to
Tampa looking for a dream ship to take them around the world.
Prior to that, they had planned, saved, and prepared for years—even
to the point of practicing celestial navigation in nearby cornfields
where they could see the horizon.[2]

From a previous trip to the Gulf, Kauffman remembered the Krebses. In fact, he recalled, who could forget them?

"Sidoine Krebs was an honest man, building ships today as his grandfather had done a hundred years ago, but slowly conforming to the demands of the present-day owners and skippers."[3]

The dream ship that Kauffman and Mefferd had in mind was largely the work of Kauffman, who had some technical knowledge. When they gave the specs to Sidoine, the boat builder filled his jaw with Beech Nut and allowed as how blueprints sure made pretty pictures, but he'd left his glasses up at the house and couldn't read them figgers nohow. Jest tell me how long you wants her, an' how wide an' deep, and I'll model her out.

The boys decided to take a chance. After all, Sidoine had thirty-five fishing boats working on the Campeche Banks, all of them sound and successful. The price Sidoine gave them for the complete hull, launched, was $2,000. When Kauffman offered to pay half down, Krebs said he didn't want to get paid until the work was done—all he needed was a few dollars to replace those boiler tubes. And, no, he didn't reckon they needed to draw up no contract. There was no getting Mr. Krebs down on paper, Kauffman observed.

The two buddies then moved in with the Krebses, paying Ma Krebs $3.50 for room and board. In a few days, the model was ready, neatly laminated of red cedar and cypress in alternate layers, 21 inches long and to the scale of a half inch per foot. It was a thing of beauty, and the boys fell in love with it right off. Then, while the boiler was being repaired, Sidoine took them inland into the piney woods where trees for the masts, keel, and planking were selected, cut down and towed downriver to the mill.

The mill ready, they finally got to work in earnest on the project. Chips, smelling of turpentine, began to fly in the crisp fall air. Smoke belched from the tall stack as the Negro fireman shoveled in wood and the pressure came up on the gauge and live steam hissed from the many leaks. The bandsaw began its whining crescendo and soon the frames were cut. Meanwhile, large timbers had been dragged to an open patch and the men went to work with adze and chisel. The Krebs shipyard had come to life again.

Into the winter the work progressed, interrupted at times by chilling blue northers, as Kauffman and Mefferd grew progressively more impatient. But the Krebs compound was a continual source of wonderment and merriment. There were Ma and Sidoine; the unmarried offspring, Bertie, Leo, Marietta, and Rosie; eldest son, Roy, next door, with his wife and three small children; Hilda, the eldest daughter, married to a northerner, an ex-Coast Guard sailor named Stanley, better known as Hacksaw, and their two mischievous small boys; Sylvester, Sidoine's brother, known as Uncle, who lived back of the mill; the black dog, Nigger; various chickens, pigs, calves, and neighbors and hangers-on. The shipyard also boasted a pecan grove, a stand of satsuma trees, a few yellow pines for shade, and a garden.

The round-the-world adventures of Ray Kauffman and Gerry Mefferd actually began the day they moved in. The building of the boat and the launching was the first adventure.

When the cold northers blew, Sidoine would stamp in from the shipyard, his visored cap with the paint company trademark on it, his mackinaw collar pulled up around his neck, blowing his big red nose into a big blue handkerchief, and work would stop for a few days until either the weather moderated or the customers went to town for some bootleg moonshine.

At last came the day when the shutter planks were scheduled to be installed. It seemed that the custom in the Krebs shipyard called for a celebration on this occasion, and canny Sidoine approached the subject obliquely saying he was having trouble getting good ship carpenters to work these days without some incentive. Ray and Gerry got the message. Besides, they were always ready for a party anyway. On a trip to New Orleans, Ray found a supply of good-quality booze, and to further enhance the celebration, promised that when the shutter planks were in they would knock off for a day's fishing on the Bayou Battre.

But the cold rains continued and they couldn't work, and cooped up inside, there was nothing to do but sit around while the women-folk boiled chicory coffee and baked corn sticks, and everyone got on everyone else's nerves. So they had the celebration anyway, which was a strategic mistake.

> *That evening, as ambassadors of goodwill, we made the four corners of Krebsville with disastrous results. Hacksaw went into town and never showed up for two days. Uncle's wife chased poor Uncle off the front porch with a broom. Sidoine fell over the dinner table and stuck his nose into the hot grits. He then staggered off to bed. . . .*[4]

After that episode, Ray and Gerry determined never again to speed the wheels of progress with corn likker.

Finally, all was ready for the launching. The customs man came to measure the boat for documentation and was told that the vessel, now named *Hurricane*, was 43 feet long by 13 feet wide. Instead, the official measurement turned out to be 45 feet long by 14 feet wide. No wonder, Ray said, he could make nothing fit in the cabin.

Sidoine, it seemed, had measured everything with a two-foot rule, marking each measure with a squirt of tobacco juice. Confronted, Krebs feigned surprise. But Roy chuckled: "Papa always builds 'em a little bigga than the model." Then Sidoine owned up to it. It seems that years before a man had ordered a fishing smack which when it was launched turned out to be nine inches shorter than the contract called for. Sidoine had been penalized $100 for those nine inches. Ever since then, he had been building all his boats "bigga than the model" to make sure there were no complaints.

During the construction that winter, Ray and Gerry continued their planning, and advertised for paying guests to accompany them. The only place they could find privacy in the Krebs shipyard to discuss their plans was in Sidoine's two-holer backhouse, which was equipped with last season's Sears Roebuck catalog. For weeks, the Krebses shook their heads over the funny habits of these northerners who had simultaneous bowel movements. Then there arrived one day a freelance herpetologist named J. Morrow Allen, who had been selected from many applicants to join them. Allen, a tall, blond, handsome young scientist, had contracts for collecting snakes, frogs, turtles, and jaguars from various museums, which he would share with Ray and Gerry. When Allen arrived, however, it broke up the backhouse conferences, because there were only two holes.

The construction took six months, and when ready for launching, the Krebs family, the man who had rebuilt the old Cleveland tractor engine found in a cotton field, the plumber who installed the tanks, the sparmaker, the caulker with the long, flowing moustache, friends, onlookers, neighbors, in-laws, and all the local hands who regularly attended funerals and lynchings, showed up to watch and to circulate around the stone jugs of likker cooling at the pump under the live oak festooned with gray moss. Even Nigger, the dog, was there to lick the tallow from the ways. An ancient tug showed up, moored its bow to a tree, and raced its propellor to churn up a hole in the mud of the bayou to make it deeper. As the tide reached the high point, the wedges were knocked out and the vessel swayed gently; then it began to move backward, sailing out on the water and across the bayou to come up in the saw grass on the other side, floating high like a swan.

Baptized with corn likker and anointed with tobacco juice, *Hurricane* became twenty tons of beautiful ketch—although when Sidoine saw the sail plan, he called it a "backwards schooner." He had never heard of a "sketch."

The outfitting and supplying was done at the village wharf among the fishing boats. Then, in the late afternoon as the local people crowded the dock to watch, *Hurricane*, with the three young adventurers aboard and with Sidoine and his son Roy as guests, moved out through the pass under power. Outside Horn Island Pass, they hoisted the sails. The easy swell of the gulf met them. A light breeze came up and *Hurricane* heeled sweetly and hurried along toward Florida. Three days later, they were hit by a black northwesterly, with rain and gale winds. They hove-to comfortably, with only one man on watch.

At Cedar Keys, Sidoine and Roy left for home. Ray's relatives came down to see them off including his father, various nephews, and friends. His father gave Ray a letter of credit to use in an emergency, and then they sailed to Key West where they cleared for Cozumel in Yucatán, via the Dry Tortugas. On the fifth day, they entered their first foreign port.

For the two young Iowa lads, it was the culmination of two years of planning and six months of hard work. And a more compatible crew could hardly be found. Kauffman and Mefferd never at any time took themselves seriously, yet never acted irresponsibly. Kauffman (known as "Coppy"), the financier of the expedition and its leader, combined a high degree of intelligence with mature judgment, and a knack for seeking out interesting people and getting along with everyone. He was a handsome young man with a superb physical build, but in a rugged way that pleased both men and women. Gerry Mefferd, young, curly-headed, somewhat slighter in physical build, was unfailingly bright and happy of mood, had complete confidence in Ray's judgment, and was always game for anything. He had taught himself to be a skilled navigator in that Iowa cornfield, and was writing a book.[5]

Allen, although young, was an experienced scientist and collector of tropical specimens, a determined man who was not easily thwarted by jungle obstacles or petty officialdom. In Cozumel, where they stopped to do their first collecting in the coastal jungles, they also hired a crewman, a young Mayan named Hector Emanuel Gonzales Brito, who was five feet tall and had a profile like Buster Keaton. Hector was a true character in the Kauffman-Mefferd manner. He spoke almost no English, was a terrible cook and an indifferent deck-hand with a violent temper at times, but a loyal and usually enter-taining companion who stuck with *Hurricane* all around the world.[6]

Before their departure, Kauffman's father had told Ray and Gerry: "Each of you try to do more than your share of the work and you'll avoid a lot of problems."[7] There was little need for the advice. The two lifelong friends experienced not the slightest friction during the voyage.

At Belize, British Honduras, Allen shipped home the Cozumel collection; then in torrential rains, they sailed on to Nicaragua, where they were met at the customs wharf by an angry crowd and a larcenous squad of *aduaneros* in sloppy uniforms who arrested them for not having a Nicaraguan flag and slapped an excessive fine against the boat. On the way to the governor's office to straighten things out, they stopped at the United Fruit office where Ray sent a cable to the State Department. The governor treated them as criminals, and there was a standoff for two days until a cable arrived from the State Department. Then the governor sent for them, gave them permits and a letter of safe conduct for the Gardia Nacional, and they were free to continue.

They sailed up the Escondido River into the dense jungle, to the Rama River and its pestholes, and finally into the Mico River, where they stopped at a village below impassable rapids. Here, they left the boat in charge of Hector, and went on up into the jungle by canoe for two weeks of collecting. When they returned, half-starved, insect-bitten, and exhausted, they found *Hurricane* in danger of coming loose in a flash flood, with Hector loyally doing all he could alone. They departed downriver then, trying to beat the falling water, at one point going aground and having to hack their way back to the channel with machetes.[8]

Before they left Nicaragua, a large fat black woman came running down to the dock swearing at Hector. It seemed he had promised her some money in return for her charms and Ray had to pay her off.

Allen went back to the States with the collection of live boas, pickled jaguars, turtles, frogs, and lizards. Ray, Gerry, and Hector sailed on to Panama, where they stopped long enough to overhaul the rigging and continue work on the boat while they spent the nights visiting the hot spots in town.[9]

They made the canal transit without incident, in spite of the engine which had no clutch or reverse and required continual starting and stopping. At Balboa, they completed their outfitting, obtained more charts, and put another coat of copper on the bottom. On the morning of September 23, they sailed out of Balboa for the Galápagos Islands. Landfall was made on Pinta Island, but they visited Santa Cruz, Albamarle, Tagus Cove (of *Svaap*'s adventures), Post Office Bay on Floreana, spent some time pig hunting with the Witmer family, and then left for the Marquesas, hoping to get to Tahiti by Christmas.[10]

The last day before sailing, Ray posted a handlettered menu on the galley bulkhead:

BREAKFAST—
Fresh orange juice, pancakes, fried strips of fish, coffee.

LUNCH—
Fresh vegetable soup stewed with pork, barbecued ham with baked potatoes, radishes, cinnamon rolls, and hot chocolate.

DINNER—
Fresh lobster cocktail, broiled Galápagos Islands duck, hot corn bread, orange marmalade.

They had learned, Ray said, that a successful voyage depends upon a satisfied stomach.

At Ua Huka in the Marquesas, they got their first taste of a South Pacific island and liked it. Ashore, they met Ray Meliza, a retired navy man from California and, Michel, also an ex-navy man, who had retired to the islands and married a fat *vahine*. Mike had been in the Veracruz action and professed a hatred of Mexicans, which made him a mortal enemy of Hector. Vulgar, profane, lascivious, Mike, however, was good company for Ray and Gerry, who liked characters. Mike deserted his wife and sailed to Tahiti with them, proving valuable as a navigator and a man who knew the natives well. They stopped at Takaroa in the Tuamotus, where they were met by friendly natives and Hooty Park, another beachcomber who was married to a native. The boys became heroes when Gerry—Dr. Mefferd, that is—cured the chief's constipation with an oversized dose of Sal Hepatica. The latrine was built out over the water, and every time the chief had a bowel movement, watching native boys carried the news to the *Hurricane* where the beginnings of a wild party was making up, with the help of Hooty, the chief's son-in-law.

Hooty, when asked to get girls for them, wanted to know if they wanted Mormons or Catholics. What was the difference? Well, it was simply a matter of taste. The atoll's natives were divided between converts left over from missionary days. The Mormon girls would eat dog meat; the Catholics would not.

At Papeete, *Hurricane* joined the company of several other yachts, including *Director* from Manhasset, L.I., with the irrepressible Fahnestock brothers and their equally fun-loving crew.[11] Others were *Four Winds* from Pittsburgh, *Viva* from the West Coast, and later the *Yankee* arrived with the Johnsons and their crew of amateurs, followed by Dwight Long in *Idle Hour*, and Alain Gerbault on *Alain Gerbault*.

Mike had given the boys good advice about Tahiti: Don't trust the Chinese storekeeper, buy drinks only at Quinn's Bar, don't criticize the French, and don't even spit without permission from the gendarmes. The Christmas season on Tahiti was a round of merrymaking, during which Ray and Gerry spent the last of their money. They, as usual, fell in easily with people, regardless of rank or station, even being invited to lunch by James Norman Hall and his wife. Then came time to find a place to "winter" while waiting for the trade winds to start. This meant some remote island or village to leeward. There were farewell celebrations and all of Papeete came down to see them off.

They tried several places, finding them pestholes or populated by thieving natives, or not good anchorages, until at last they came upon the village of Vaitape on Bora Bora. Here they were taken in by Marii and his young wife, Pepe. The flaw in this paradise was the Chinese storekeeper, to whom everyone on the island was indebted, which gave him the pick of all the choice young girls. On a voyage to a nearby island to get bamboo for Marii's house, they were taken by the flirtations of Marii's two young nieces. When they got back, they asked Marii to have the girls move in with them. Thence followed months in which Ray and Gerry went completely native in an idyllic existence of the kind Melville must have had in *Typee*.

The voyage would have ended right there, had not the fancy cruise ship *Stella Polaris* showed up with a load of tourists who were anxious to see the South Pacific islander in his native haunts. The villagers, however, put on their best Mother Hubbards before they paddled out to the ship to trade. The only two "natives" who were dressed like natives were Ray Kauffman and Gerry Mefferd. Then from the deck came a woman's voice: "Have any of you seen Ray Kauffman?"

It was a girl from Des Moines, Iowa, who had been asked by Ray's parents to look him up in Tahiti!

The two erstwhile voyagers were invited aboard for dinner.

Ray, dancing with well-dressed white women, smelling of perfume, realized how much he had longed for intimate contact with his own race. Soon after the *Stella Polaris* departed, they readied *Hurricane* for the next leg of their circumnavigation. But their departure was a tearful and even poignant one, for Marii's family had by now adopted them as their own. During their idyllic months in the village, the domestic life had seemed as complete as anything in paradise. Food was plentiful, no one worked seriously, everyone drifted along in the warm lazy air. Ray and Gerry had become Polynesians in habit, color, and taste, permeated with the scent of coconut oil, frangipani, and fish. They had lost track of time, and their upbringing faded away in Gauguinian euphoria. Others had done the cooking. The girls took care of their clothes and their sex life. A food surplus meant more pigs, and more pigs meant more feasts.

They had, in those months, come to an understanding of the Polynesian concept of life, perhaps more so than any of the other circumnavigators before or after them. But, inevitably, their Anglo-Saxon roots had proved stronger, when the *Stella Polaris* had sailed in one day, and they had once more held in their arms a woman of their own race and cultural background.

But farewells were not easy. As departure drew near, the girls turned sad and lapsed into periods of staring out toward the barrier reef. *"When the moon is full we dance, sing and laugh. You leave, we will be in darkness and shame. Why do you go?"*[12] There was no answer.

It was now April and the winds were fresh. Kauffman, plagued by infections from coral cuts and boils, had to go to Papeete for medical attention on the trading schooner while Gerry stayed with *Hurricane* at Uturoa. Returning to *Hurricane*, Ray brought with him some recruits, including Michel, and Bob Burrell, an American living in Tahiti who wanted to see Singapore. They were reunited with *Director*, and for months after they raced the other yacht from island to island and adventure to adventure. Penrhyn came first, where they traded for pearls with the natives, went diving and fishing, and made love. In Samoa, they looked up a buddy of Mike's named Milton J.

Cruze, otherwise known as Johnny, finding him as predicted in a Pago Pago bar, going home with him to his huge native wife and large family of happy kids.

Repairs and alterations were made to *Hurricane* here with the help of the navy shops. Also in Samoa, they encountered one of the few instances of native thievery and perfidy, which left the two Iowa lads with a rare feeling of disillusionment. Here also they met Sam Elbert, a friend from Des Moines, who had been in the islands for years and spoke the dialects. He sailed with them to the Fijis, on the way stopping at a remote village never before visited by white men. They were received coldly at first, but Ray and Gerry's unfailing manner along with Sam's knowledge of the language brought an invitation to spend the night, followed by exchanges of gifts, feasting, entertainment, dancing, and later a platoon of native girls to rub them caressingly with oil when they retired for the night. On the run out across the reef the next day, Ray's canoe capsized in the surf and he nearly lost his life. The coral cuts he suffered later brought on infection and more boils.

In Fiji, there were parties ashore with *Director*'s crew, explorations, races to the next group of islands, stops at remote plantations to visit traders and their wives, as they lived mostly on gin and tonics. During calms on the high seas, they would rendezvous with *Director* for gams.

In the New Hebrides, Ray's boils and carbuncles had become so bad that he needed hospital attention. Brisbane was 1,200 miles away, so they parted with *Director* and headed for Australia. They had now been in the South Pacific for eleven months. In Australia, they found many friends, liked the country and the people, and before they knew it, had put down roots. Here they rebuilt *Hurricane*, removing the centerboard and case, tearing out the darkroom to enlarge the main cabin; they added a thick ironwood outer keel, changed the sail plan, raised the cockpit sides and replaced the tiller with a wheel. Here, also, they painted the hull black, which horrified Hector. It was bad luck, he said. *Malo*.

After nearly a half a year in Australia, they departed for Lord Howe Island. Hector's warning proved accurate—from here on, they were plagued by bad luck and misadventures. At Lord Howe, they were delayed two months instead of the two weeks they had planned on. Their former shipmates had already left them and returned to Tahiti's charms. Leaving Lord Howe to sail through the reef-strewn western Pacific, they learned that their compass was in error and that they had sailed one hundred fifty miles off course. In Papua, they visited ashore with Harry Morley, a seventy-year-old prospector who had been looking for a gold vein for thirty years. Months later, they learned he had finally found the vein and had become immensely wealthy—and miserable, now that his quest was over.

One night, chugging along on a glassy sea with the engine running, with Ray at the wheel, the yacht suddenly lurched gently, then stopped and leaned over sickeningly. The others rushed up on deck in alarm. They were fast on Uluma Reef. In the morning, they loaded what they could, including the instruments and ship's papers, into the ten-foot dinghy, and rowed the twelve miles across to Wari Island, praying that the wind did not come up. Crossing the fringing reef, they got ashore and enlisted the help of the villagers led by the chief whose name was William Street, after a place in Sydney where he had spent some time.

They went back to the wreck in the morning with the native launches, removed everything that could be taken off, and stacked it on the beach at Wari, where Hector was stationed to guard against pilferage. Then they went to Samarai, a small island and Papua's second largest port where about fifty Europeans lived. They secured boats and help from the mission station, went back and patched the *Hurricane*'s hull before she broke up on the coral, got her off in an almost super-human effort, and limped back to Samarai. Here, with continued Yankee luck, they were able to hire carpenters to haul her out and repair the damage.

Meanwhile, they visited local plantation managers, and some on the other islands, and prepared for the next leg. At Port Kennedy in Torres Strait, they encountered the Johnsons on *Yankee* again, and obtained much information on Singapore and the East Indies. The next day, they slipped out the pass into the Arafura Sea.[13]

During the next few months, they adventured and romanced in an entirely different world, visiting Timor, the Dutch and Portuguese settlements, where they joined in drinking matches with colonial planters. In Bali, they found the true romance of the Indies, and waxed ecstatic about the island life and especially the delicate and beautiful women. They also fell under the spell of spices, the Oriental atmosphere, the crowded harbors, and shallow straits filled with picturesque *praus*. They reached Singapore and met a yacht they had accompanied off and on, the *Kewarra*, with its Australian owners, and another American yacht, the *So Fong*.

In the Indies, Ray and Gerry suffered frequent attacks of malaria and dengue fever, and Ray's boils recurred from time to time. Their food supplies became low, their flour and rice filled with weevils, and the ship's hull encrusted with barnacles.

In Singapore, at the Yacht Club, they hired a Chinese cook who soon ruled the galley with an iron hand, but who turned out fantastic meals for only $25 a month. They hired native craftsmen, including Ah Gin, the carpenter, a real artisan but also an opium addict. Soon *Hurricane,* born in a Mississippi bayou shipyard, was transformed into Oriental splendor with teak decks, exquisite carvings, new sails, skylights, trim, and colorful paint (the hateful black had been scraped off and replaced).

Ashore, the adventurers made friends, went exploring, attended parties on estates, danced at bistros with beautiful Eurasian girls with sloe eyes, jet black hair, soft creamy skins, and slender bodies sheathed in satin dresses with split skirts.

Leaving Singapore finally, they visited an outlying plantation at the invitation of the owner, a character named V. W. Ryves, who kept a pet tiger around for kicks. At Penang, they shipped aboard the vice-consul, John Peabody Palmer, who was on leave and wanted to go to Ceylon. They sailed to Colombo via the Nicobars, where Palmer left. In his place, they took on Bill Cross, a merchant seaman who wanted a ride home. While on Ceylon, Ray and Palmer took the train to the six thousand elevation station where they shivered in the unusual cold.

On New Year's Day, they sailed for Africa, after first shanghaiing Cross from the bar where they had celebrated all night. When they were seventy miles at sea, Cross woke up to find that they had not been kidding when they offered him passage home. The next stop was Zanzibar and more adventures ashore. On the way, they had encountered some bad storms, and at least one close call with whales.[14] But now they felt the pull of home, and the subtle beginnings of channel fever. By this time, they were out of the steaming East, where they had spent so many months enduring the weevils in the flour and rice, the cockroaches, and the rats that were so bold that they would come out and eat the calluses off Hector's feet at night. The bouts with malaria had eased up. And the ship herself was in better conditon than even at the start of the voyage.[15]

In the Mozambique Channel, they encountered gales, calms, and contrary winds after leaving Zanzibar. During a Force 6 blow one night, both main shrouds parted and looped around the mast. They put into Mozambique, about sixty miles away, where the local Portuguese government offered their shops free for repairs and sent two riggers to help. Leaving again, they thrashed about for a few days, then on an excuse to get some eggs, put into Lourenço-Marques. They stayed five days and returned to the ship with hangovers. A carnival had been in progress ashore. By the time they reached Durban, Hector was seriously ill, with a fever of 104°. The harbor was closed due to a rough bar, and so they heaved-to all night outside. Just after daylight, they followed the pilot boat in. The port doctor came aboard, and they carried Hector to the hospital with malignant malaria, dysentery, and hemorrhoids. It would be two weeks before he would be well.

Repairs were made to the rigging, and the ship was fumigated again. As usual, Gerry and Ray were warmly welcomed to the local yacht club, and many new friends were acquired. When they sailed from Durban, they had aboard two members of the yacht club. Bill Cross left here to take a job in Johannesburg. A farewell banquet was held for them at the Royal Natal Yacht Club, complete with speeches and endless toasts.

The tough leg around the bight of South Africa put most of the crew in the bunk for days at a time. Much of it was beating to windward in bitterly cold weather. They put into Simon Town where Ray was forced to accept an invitation to dine aboard a navy ship, while the others took the trolley to Cape Town. Returning at a late hour, Ray saw *Hurricane* anchored in a different place. She had dragged her anchor, and not being able to start the engine, Gerry had to take her out and sail back in, tacking back and forth for an hour trying to pick up the dinghy which had come loose.

In Cape Town, the two Durban crew members left, and after a week or more of idleness ashore, they left for St. Helena with a passenger, George Mason, one of the survivors of the yacht club's anniversary dinner in Durban. At Jamestown harbor, they fell in with the officers and crew of an Argentine freighter, and for five days feasted and celebrated Empire Day, Argentine Independence Day, and Napoleon's banishment.[16]

They then sailed for Barbados, one last ocean to cross to complete the world cruise. The passage was uneventful. They passed Fernando de Noronha, then the brownish water off the Amazon River, picked up the South American coastline, and, on June 28, arrived off Bridge-town, having sailed 3,800 miles in thirty days.

The next major stop was Mujeres Island, Yucatán, where Hector tearfully departed, having circumnavigated the world on *Hurricane*.

They anchored in the same spot they had three years before on reaching their first foreign port. The same customs officer in the same boat and uniform came out to meet them. Out came the rum bottle, and before long the officer had forgiven them for Hector, who had no papers or identification of any kind to prove he was Mexican.

They said good-bye, and then departed in a series of rain squalls. Shorthanded, they could not take in sails fast, so they fairly flew homeward. On the last day of July 1938, off Mobile Bay, they made the final entry in a 1,215-page logbook. The pilot boat and customs officer came alongside. The pilot handed them a letter of invitation from the yacht club. They then moved into the harbor, finding their families waiting for them. Also waiting was Sidoine Krebs.

"I knowed it was the *Hurricane* as soon as I saw that backwards rig," he said.

Later, they brought the ship into the Pascagoula River and into the bayou at the Krebs shipyard where *Hurricane* had been born. There, under the huge moss-bearded live oak where the launching whiskey had been kept in cool jugs, she floated motionless as if at peace with the world she had circled.

But this child of the cypress swamps and saw grass was not quite the same. Her decks now had come from the jungles of Siam; her keel, from the hardwood forests of Queensland; and her sails, from the hands of Chinese artisans in Singapore.

Ray wrote:

> I wonder if her crew has changed beyond the deep teak tan which would fade in an Iowa winter like the decks of a ship in the sun. Would we retain the lessons we had learned? For the long night watch under the mystery of space had given us a quieter mind, the long hot calms had taught us patience, and from the close association in confined quarters we had learned a great tolerance. If we should forget, then three and a half years would have gone from our lives in utter futility.[17]

Who knows what the future brings? For the two Iowa cornfield circumnavigators, just around the corner waited World War II, and after that nothing would ever be the same again. *Hurricane* had been the last of her kind.[18]

13

Tall Ship
and High Adventure

*In contrast to the momentous happenings of
the day, our light hearted adventure in the
Cap Pilar seemed a disappointing trivial affair.
Two years ago we had looked upon our voyage
as a gesture of defiance in a gloomy world. Now
the gesture had assumed more the appearance
of a facetious grimace.*[1]

IT WAS OCTOBER 1932, AND THE FINNISH FOUR-MASTED
bark *Olivebank* boiled along at fifteen knots in the South Atlantic
bound for Australia. Out of the half gale in the distance, a cloud
bank thickened and then became the lonely pile of Tristan da Cunha.
At the rail, standing in the rain, stood two off-watch seamen and
good friends, Lars Paersch of Finland and Adrian Seligman of Wimbledon, England.

Someday, Lars said, we will fit out a ship and visit Tristan da
Cunha, instead of sailing by.

That, Adrian said, caught up in the idle romance of the moment,
we will do, Lars—someday.

On December 8, 1935, the last day of another voyage on another
ship, the *Ramsay*, one of those young sailors, Seligman, was coming
home, this period of his life over, another about to begin. Standing at
the rail as the *Ramsay* shouldered her way up the drizzly Irish coast,

he felt the warm fires of anticipation and new adventures in the pit of his guts. He did not know what form the next period of his life would take, but felt certain it would be brighter than the past six years as a merchant seaman. And there was also Jane to come home to.

Born in Wimbledon in 1910, Adrian recalled his first trip abroad, to St. Jacut on a rocky island in the Gulf of St. Malo, with his parents when he was four. The family stayed all summer. After the war, in 1925, they rented a stone cottage near the fishing harbor at St. Jacut which became a second home.[2]

At age nine, Adrian went to prep school in Wimbledon. There he became close friends with George, the headmaster's son, and with George's sister, Jane. At fourteen, he was sent away to public school, but, in 1929, again was reunited with his friends for a couple of years. Then, suddenly, Seligman dropped out of school and went to sea. For six years, he sailed on various ships, rose to get his second mate's ticket, but still the future was not bright—by this time, he was too old in rank to make it in the merchant marines. His last ship was the British tramp *Ramsay*, and at Vancouver, British Columbia, where one of the officers had taken sick, he had paced the bridge as second mate.

Now, on this bitterly cold winter day, the northerly tore at his ears and made his eyes water. But into view came Tuskar, Cahore, and Wicklow Head, then Slieve Donard and the mountains of Mourne.

Picking up his glasses, Seligman looked through the lenses at the gorse-covered hillsides, and a great longing again welled up inside him. He had left Cambridge six years before to gain experience to become a writer. By George, now was the time to make the break.

But, ashore again and reunited with his family, friends, and sweetheart, Jane, he found that Fleet Street would have none of him. There was a depression on, jobs were scarce, money was tight, and on the horizon the dark clouds of war had made everybody's future uncertain.

Then, unexpectedly, when he had given up hope of getting a shore job, he fell heir to a legacy of £3,500 left by his grandfather.[3] At the end of a long, weary day of tramping the city in search of a job, the idea came to him. With £3,500 you can buy and outfit a small ship for a voyage around the world!

Adrian rushed to Essex, where his friend George was teaching. With him was his fiancée, Jane. They talked over the idea, the three of them. Caught up in the excitement of the adventure, George quit his teaching job. Meanwhile, Adrian had written to Lars in Helsing-förs, where the Finn was sitting for his mate's examination. Then they all went over to St. Malo and tramped the waterfront in the rain, looking over the derelicts for sale. One of them was the *Cap Pilar*, a barkentine with green moss covering the rotting decks, smelling horribly of bilge water, with fraying pieces of canvas hanging from the yards.[4] They went elsewhere, searching the Brittany coast, rented an old Citröen, and covered all the yachting centers, looking at ketches and yachts.

Meanwhile, they had placed an ad in the London *Times* for a crew to sail to the South Seas, leaving in August. Six young men were wanted, each required to have £100 to contribute toward expenses. They were deluged with mail from erstwhile adventurers among the youthful generation who saw nothing in the future but depression and war. News reporters spotted the ad and sensed a story. The newsreels picked up the story, too. The publicity made them celebrities before they even had a ship to sail away on.

This reaction was common in the 1930s. The Irving Johnsons were on their first series of circumnavigation. The Martin Johnsons were adventuring in exotic places. Dwight Long, Gerbault, Robinson, the fun-loving Fahnestocks, Kauffman and Mefferd on *Hurricane*, Maury on *Cimba*, Al Hansen, Vito Dumas, and a hundred or more anonymous adventurers were doing their thing. This was also the period when John Hanna's famous *Tahiti* ketch appeared first on the oceans of the world, the first truly practical and economical round-the-world yacht.

They advertised in *Lloyd's List*. Adrian and Jane, married now, went to Helsingförs and rented a cutter. For Jane's first boat trip, they sailed to Stockholm to look for a schooner. In June, they returned to England after weeks of furious activity. Still without a ship, they had three hundred applicants for berths.

They went back to Europe and searched every harbor north of Brest. They tried Dieppe, Le Havre, Fécamp, Cherbourg. And, finally, they went back to St. Malo and looked again at the *Cap Pilar*. This time, she looked better. It was summer and the leaves and flowers were out. Everything looked better. Two days later, they had the surveyor's report and went to the ship broker.

Nous l'acceptons! Down upon the ship swarmed shipwrights, ship chandlers, riggers, sailmakers. They promised to have the ship ready in a month. Lars arrived from Finland. A family friend, the famous seadog Commander J. R. Stenhouse, RNR, who had been master of

Shackleton's *Discovery*, came over to help with a crew of volunteers.

Finally, the great day came. A tug warped the *Cap Pilar* out from the dock, and the first voyage, to England, began. It took five days. Aboard were Jane's father, some volunteers, and many guests. In London, the first nine crewmen were signed on. They included Francis Newell, Willie March, John Donnelly, Alan Burgess, Pete Roach, Alexander Drummond Sanson, Dr. Edmund Atkinson, Kurt Romm, Alan Roper, in addition to Jane's brother, George Batterbury. They included a doctor, a biologist, an eighteen-year-old teacher, a student, a laborer, and a gardener. The crew eventually included a ventilating engineer, a solicitor, and an ex-paymaster in the Royal Navy.

A *News Chronicle* reporter named Gelder was assigned to cover the story full-time. He not only kept the story alive, but helped with the outfitting and preparations. During the two weeks in London, the publicity attracted the attention of the Tristan da Cunha Society, which asked Seligman to carry a cargo of supplies to the islanders.

On Tuesday, September 29, 1936, they were ready to leave and took aboard the last recruit, Duncan McDonald, who had heard about the voyage only that morning. He quit his job as a clerk in a shipping office on a moment's notice.

The following morning, at 11 A.M., the *Cap Pilar* departed. On board as guests were Commander Stenhouse, Adrian's father, plus the nineteen, including Gelder, the reporter. Off Plymouth, the pilot boat came out and Adrian's father and Commander Stenhouse went ashore. After an exchange of hearty cheers, the *Cap Pilar* filed away for the open sea.

Before they left London, the German army had marched into the Rhineland. A passing German liner ignored their salute. In an atmosphere of uncertain future but high hopes for adventure while it was still possible, the crew of the *Cap Pilar* stood out to sea on one of the most unusual voyages ever undertaken by amateurs.

The route would take them down the Atlantic via the Azores and Cape Verde, across to Brazil, back to Cape Town, down the Indian Ocean slant to Australia, then to the Marquesas and to the west coast of South America, up through the Panama Canal, to the West Indies, then to New York, and finally home to England, arriving in September 1938, two years after their departure.

But it was not to be that simple. Few of the crew had any bluewater experience. The *Cap Pilar*, in spite of the rebuilding, was in pitiful condition, and leaked badly. It was too much ship for the experience of the crew to handle. Only three knew anything about navigation. The youngest was eighteen; the oldest, twenty-eight. There was neither a radio nor engine aboard. The ship had been too stiffly ballasted, and in the boisterous Bay of Biscay, she rolled and plunged sickeningly.

No sooner had they passed Eddystone Light when the first of a series of gales struck. Great seas broke over the decks. Water poured into the hold. The bilge pumps had to be manned constantly. Everyone aboard was sick. At one point, the *Cap Pilar* went tearing along at ten knots in the wrong direction.

Somehow, everything held together and they sighted Porto Santo. Ashore, they went sightseeing and forgot the miseries of the crossing. They worked on the ship's ballast, tried out the waterfront bistros, and took care of ship's business in the first foreign port. Then, in better spirits, they sailed for Salvage Island.

They visited Tenerife and Santa Cruz as the Spanish Revolution started. Ashore, vigilantes were hunting down and executing communists. Even children were dressed up as soldiers.

On October 27, they departed for Rio via Cape Verde, leaving behind for a time all manifestations of impending war. By now, the crew had acquired some experience and had gotten to know one another. There were fourteen days of calms, then the ship began to move. After forty-one days at sea, they rounded Cape Frio and came in for a boisterous welcome to Brazil. It was now summer here.

Life in Rio became frenetic. There was sightseeing, dancing, and cheap food and drink. The German warship *Schlesien* was there at anchor. The Rio Sailing Club, the English colony, and the Brazilians took the crew to their hearts. Christmas came and went. Romm left here, as did Payne, another crewman. Then, with a new crewman, José, they departed for Tristan da Cunha, bringing news and supplies to the lonely islanders.

From there it was twelve days to Cape Town, where they arrived on Monday, February 15. The crew took a week's holiday while Adrian tried to figure out how to finance the rest of the voyage. There was a crisis aboard. Jane was expecting their first child. There was no more money. All £3,500 had been spent on the ship, plus another £1,400 had been borrowed for stores and supplies. There was dissension in the crew. The ship needed new sails to go on.

To save harbor fees, it was decided to move the ship to Saldanah Bay up the coast. It was a very rough passage that took five days (the train trip took only one hour). In Simon Town, there was more trouble. Jane might have to go home as soon as the baby arrived, but plans changed week by week. Four South Africans joined the crew, and contributed £75 each. Roper disappeared to find a job on a farm. They were kicked out of the hotel where they were staying for rowdyism. Some of the crew took up with local girls and left. There were garden parties and a wagon trek to the desert. Then suddenly came an unexpected letter from England with money from home.

The ship was readied for sea. The crew now included a 34-year-old English photographer; a cadet from the Alan Villiers training ship *Joseph Conrad*; an accountant; the son of the mayor of Cape Town; a musician; and George Smith, fifty-eight, a pensioned chief petty officer from the Royal Navy and instructor from the South African training ship *General Botha*. Another recruit was Jack Ovenstone, a seventeen-year-old boy, who came to the ship each morning in a chauffeur-driven limousine.

The *Cap Pilar* left two weeks before Jane, who remained with friends. She would follow later by steamship.

On the passage across the Indian Ocean, they made 220 miles a day frequently, with gale after gale. Many of the new recruits suffered chronic seasickness, but the rough passage made sailors out of them. They now had a piano aboard, and, on May 12, they celebrated the coronation. During the stay in Cape Town, the planks had parted and now much water got into the hold and ruined supplies. On May 28, after forty days at sea, they sighted Eddystone Rock off Hobart.

They got a boisterous welcome at Sydney, where Jane met them at the dock. There were newspaper headlines and much publicity. In Sydney, Adrian and Jane enjoyed the happiest three weeks of their marriage so far. The baby had not yet arrived. They decided to go on to New Zealand. Ovenstone, the seasick lad, left to go home. José also left ship here. Three new hands were taken on.

On Monday, June 28, *Cap Pilar* picked up anchor and sailed out of Sydney Heads for the passage to Auckland, nine days of close-hauled beating. Jessica was born in Auckland, Jane having followed the *Cap Pilar* aboard the American liner *Monterey*. The blessed event, on the night of Friday, July 16, 1937, became a long-awaited celebration. Adrian, Jane, and the baby moved into a little cottage in Mount Eden. A friend loaned them a Ford V-8. On weekends, they took trips into the country for picnics.

But another crisis arose. They needed money again. New contributing crew members were recruited. The crew, fed up with mountain climbing, skiing, and sightseeing, became restless. A meeting was called aboard to air grievances and complaints. With Jane and Jessica aboard, a doctor was needed. A Dr. Stenhouse volunteered. He brought not only money, but a small radio and 1,200 of the best New Zealand eggs packed in waterglass.

On Friday, September 17, they departed. The crew now numbered twenty-eight, including Jessica, who was signed on as stewardess. They now had a ship's newspaper, *The Caterpillar.*

They sailed north to the Gambier Islands, Rapa, and the Marquesas, reef crawling, beachcombing. At Nuku Hiva, they were met by Bob McKittrick, the trader.[5] Jessica thrived on the life, but most of the crew broke out with sores from the festering bites of the *nonos.* Dr. Stenhouse became depressed, and infected the entire ship's company with the same mood. There were frequent quarrels. "The curse of the Marquesas is upon us,"[6] wrote Adrian.

Detouring past the Tuamotus, they nearly lost the ship in the tide rips off a reef while trying to get into a pass. They made friends with an American Mormon missionary from Inspiration, Arizona, and spent Christmas at Hao with the natives, dining on roast corn beef, potatoes, and a pudding from a recipe in an American magazine. Jessica was happy and everyone aboard adored her. On Boxing Day, 1937, they left Hao for the long passage to Callao, Peru. On February 6, 1938, they sighted the Andes rising in the east, forty-four days out of Hao.

At Lima, they made many friends and went sightseeing over the Andes by train. The ship was infected with harbor fleas and harbor thieves. Just before sailing for the Galápagos, Jane was stricken with appendicitis and was taken ashore to an American hospital in agony for an emergency operation.[7]

George stayed behind with Jane and Jessica. The ship sailed on to the islands. On the radio, they heard the news of the Russians at war with Finland. There was trouble between Poland and Lithuania. America was concerned. Japan regrets.

At Wreck Bay, they were parted with £20 by the port officials. They met the Cobos family at Progreso.[8] They explored some of the islands. On April 5, they left. Crossing the equator called for a ceremony. Then, on May 1, they reached Panama, went sightseeing, and made the passage through the locks. Jane, Jessica, and George arrived by steamer. During the two and a half months, Jessica had grown surprisingly.

From Panama, they had a stormy passage to Jamaica. There they found much unrest among the blacks. On June 11, they left Montego

Bay and stopped at Grand Cayman to attend a ball in Georgetown, where the Big Apple was the popular dance. Then came the skyline of Miami. Jessica was now 11 months old, and the ship had traveled 32,500 miles at an average speed of 4 knots in 345 days at sea.

In New York, they all got a warm welcome, but were upstaged by Howard Hughes, who had just flown around the world nonstop and was being given a ticker-tape reception up Broadway. There were exciting times in the big city—visits to Greenwich Village, to night-clubs where they paid to see South Sea island girls dancing, Wall Street, the zoo, night spots in Harlem. They liked the friendly open-handed casual way of American life.

Jane's sister, Mary, arrived from Canada. With the baby, Jane went back to Canada for a visit. On July 25, the *Cap Pilar* went down the Hudson, through the Narrows, and sailed to Halifax where they picked up Jane and Jessica again. On August 14, they sailed from Halifax with the magic words, "Falmouth for orders," on their clearance.

The homeward voyage was through heavy traffic—first fishing boats, then military craft. On September 11, they sighted the Lizard and at last gazed upon homeland after completely circumnavigating the world.

The headlines on September 24, when they arrived at London at the East India Docks, blazed WAR AND DISASTER. Everyone was caught up in the war fever. In contrast to their departure two years before, their arrival was almost completely ignored by the press.

But they were home again with twelve of the original crew still aboard. The *Cap Pilar* laid up in London for the winter. Jane and Jessica went to Wimbledon by car. In January, the ship was sold to the Nautical College of Haifa and sailed there by Adrian's old friend, Commander Stenhouse.

Before they had left London in 1936, the Germans had started their moves. On the day of their return, off Brighton, they heard of the Czech acceptance of compromises. Off Beachy Head, they listened to hourly news bulletins. Londoners were digging trenches in the parks. Mr. Chamberlain was flying to Godesberg.

The voyage of the *Cap Pilar* in the end became a sort of casualty of World War II. Seligman's book, which he had planned to be his bid for a journalistic career, was lost in the confusion of the times. Again, his timing was unfortunate. Next he joined the brigantine *Research*, then stationed at Dartmouth. On the same day, nine of the old crew of the *Cap Pilar* also joined as Lars went back to Finland.

In September 1939, Seligman was commissioned a sub-lieutenant in the Royal Navy Reserve. He had a good war record, rose rapidly, and when demobilized was a commander in rank on the Admiralty staff. After leaving the service in October 1946, he published another book, *No Stars to Guide*. By then, he and his wife had four daughters, the oldest of whom was Jessica, now a young lady of ten, born during her parents' greatest adventure, grasping at the last shreds of youth and freedom before the world plunged into the darkness of the war years, after which nothing would ever be quite the same again.

ᴈᏐ 14 Ꮠᴅ

The Yankees Go Around and Around

*Each new sailor has to make his own terms
with the sea. He will inevitably learn to accommodate to the motion, he will learn to box
the compass and steer a course, he will learn to
sleep when watch is over—regardless of the
clock, he will learn the lines, the sails and what
they do.*[1]

ELECTA SEARCH HAD BEEN A COLLEGE CHUM OF GWEN
Tompkins of the famous bluewater sailing family, and after a weekend aboard *Wander Bird*, a converted German pilot schooner, she
took the train back to Rochester to explain to her family why she
was quitting her job to go cruising in European waters.

The scene shifts next to a rough autumn day in 1931 off Le Havre
in the English Channel. Electa had purchased a Siamese kitten in
Paris because she had always wanted one and there they were cheap;
but the kitten, unlike Electa, did not take to the sea and died. To
console herself, Electa decided she needed a haircut—especially since
there was a young crewman aboard from Boston who liked to cut
girls' hair, if it were the right girl.

While young Irving Johnson wielded the clippers, taking what
seemed like an unusually long time about it, Electa studied him

surreptitiously in the mirror. They talked of many things, and became better acquainted.

At twenty-six, Irving McClure Johnson was what we would call today a dropout, but he had already acquired an astonishing background in seamanship and bluewater sailing. Born July 4, 1905, to Clifton and Anna Johnson, farmers, he was graduated from Hopkins Academy in 1923. He and his brother owned a sloop when he was eighteen, and he crewed on local yachts frequently. To gain more experience, however, he went to sea for ten years in as many types of craft as he could.

In 1929 and 1930, he signed on for a 93-day voyage around Cape Horn to Chile in the German four-masted bark *Peking,* bound from Hamburg to Talcahuana for nitrate. On this voyage, he took some remarkable 16-mm motion pictures for later lecture tours, and also wrote *Round the Horn in a Square-Rigger.*

The following year, Johnson signed on as mate aboard *Shamrock V,* Sir Thomas Lipton's America's Cup contender, for the return trip to England. The voyage included a severe encounter with a hurricane, during which the racing craft proved to be not intended for such voyaging.[2]

In 1931, Johnson sailed as mate with Captain Warwick Tompkins on the *Wander Bird,* sailing from Newport on European excursions, returning via the West Indies. The same year he also sailed on George Roosevelt's *Mistress* in the Fastnet Race. In 1932, he was skipper and navigator aboard the 43-foot schooner *Twilight* in the Bermuda Race, coming in second in Class B.

On September 15, 1932, Irving and Electa were married and thus began one of the most remarkable family enterprises—one that was to culminate in *seven* virtually flawless and accident-free circumnavigations.

During the winter following their honeymoon, they spent days with charts spread out on the living-room floor, in correspondence with yacht brokers, and in planning the ship they wanted, the ports they wished to visit. They had this idea: to sail around the world with a crew of young people selected for skills and compatibility, with Irving as skipper-owner, and a paid hand or two—but everyone else would be amateurs sharing expenses. Everyone would have regular duties aboard and would stand regular watches. The first and second mates would always be experienced men, but aside from that, sailing experience would not be a prerequisite. The plan was an adaptation from Tompkins and the *Wander Bird,* and they both agreed that the ship would have to be one of those superbly seaworthy and comfortable North Sea pilot boats.

Most of these pilot boats were in the 90- to 100-foot overall class, built heavily to last, with 7 by 7 oak frames, and 3-inch-thick oak planks. The pilot boats had to spend two weeks at sea in all kinds of weather on station, and their crews had to be smart sailors, for the competition for jobs on incoming ships was fierce. With the passing of the tall clipper ships, the old pilot boats were replaced by steam and motor launches. A few wound up as yachts, such as *Wander Bird* and the former Dutch *Loodschooner 4*, which was owned by Captain Claude Monson of Ipswich, England.

The Johnsons went to Germany as a result of negotiations with a broker named Erdmann, who claimed to be sole agent for the *Glückauf*. This proved to be a long and frustrating experience, during which Erdmann flipped his lid and accused Johnson of trying to kill him; and the lady dentist who owned the vessel, with her lawyer, gave the Johnsons an expensive runaround. Regarding the young Americans as a couple of patsies, they baited the Johnsons on, and then tried to double the price. But the Johnsons were not that naïve. They had already sent an inquiry to Captain Monson, who was rumored to be in a mood for selling his pet, the *Loodschooner 4*, now named the *Texel*.

During the low point in the negotiations with the conniving lady dentist and her lawyer, the Johnsons received a cable from Monson accepting their offer. Within minutes, they had tickets and were off for England. Captain Monson, it turned out, who had met Irving before, liked the Johnsons and felt his ship would be well taken care of and sailed as she should be.

It was spring in England and beautiful. The Johnsons went directly to Ipswich and got ready to sail. Included in the first crew was a German professional sailor named Franzen, who had worked for the movies in Hollywood and who knew how to rig a ship. Also coming aboard were some crew members from home—Arthur Murphy, Bill Yeomans, and Douglas Hancock. After changing the name of the ship to *Yankee*, and the registry from British to American, they then sailed for Hamburg and the small yard of Herr Porath on the Elbe at Finkenwarder for the final rigging and outfitting.

The sail plan was changed somewhat, and a new foretopmast was obtained from the *Bremen*, which was being dismantled nearby. Other crew members began to show up, until the little inn at Finkenwarder began to look like a college dormitory. Here the

Johnsons acquired one of their greatest assets, a German cook named Fritz, who was a confirmed Nazi, but otherwise a loyal and dependable hand.

On July 5, they were ready to sail. *Yankee* had a new rig, a new coat of white paint, and a rearranged interior. The owner's cabin was aft, with two small cabins to starboard, one double and one single cabin, engine room, and bathroom to port. Forward of these were the main cabin with an upper and lower tier of bunks, six to port and eight to starboard. There were benches and boxes for provisions under the bunks. Along one side of the cabin was what would become a Johnson trademark on all their vessels—an enormous swinging teakwood table that always remained level no matter how the ship heeled. Forward of the main cabin was the galley, then a companionway to the teak deckhouse, with bunks, chart table, and storage for several thousand charts.

As outfitted, the *Yankee* was 92 feet overall, 76 feet on the waterline, 21 feet wide, and drew 11 feet of water. She had four water tanks holding 2,000 gallons, and oil tanks with a capacity of 350 gallons.

First they sailed back to England, anchoring at Cowes at the Isle of Wight for the Fastnet Races and then went to Falmouth, in Cornwall, looking for the *Wander Bird*. There she was, just as the Johnsons had arranged with the Tompkinses on a cold March day in Boston, when they had said good-bye; and nearby was the old *Cutty Sark*, the last clipper afloat, tied up across the harbor, a symbol of an era that was not yet dead, not while there were Johnsons and Tompkinses to sail the seas.

From Falmouth, they sailed to Ireland, then across the North Atlantic in the steamer lanes to Newfoundland, St. Pierre, the Bras d'Or Lakes, and finally to the home port of Gloucester. *Yankee's* maiden voyage had been a boisterous but delightful one.

The next two months were spent collecting a ship's company for an eighteen-month cruise around the world. Times were tough. It was the early years of the Depression. Millions were out of work. Breadlines and riots characterized the streets of the large cities. Never had the compulsion to escape been stronger, and from a mountain of mail, much of which bordered on the crackpot, they settled upon a crew of seventeen. The first mate was Frederick Jackson of Providence, a Dartmouth grad who had been second mate on the Atlantic voyage; Douglas Hancock, as second mate, had also been with them during the summer; Arthur Murphy of West Newton, and Theodore

Hixon of Springfield, two other veterans of the maiden voyage. Unfortunately, six days before sailing, Arthur was involved in a bad auto accident, but he arranged to meet them later in Tahiti.

Robert Murray of Waban, a friend of Arthur's, signed on as "engineer." Dr. Rufus Southworth of Cincinnati became ship's surgeon—he was the oldest member of the crew, at fifty, but had a hardy constitution and much experience in foreign places. He was signed on in spite of Irving's conviction that men more than forty had no place aboard a sailing vessel, unless they had done a lot of sailing in the past. Southworth also brought along the youngest member of the crew, Edward Danson of Cincinnati.

Others included Peer Johnson of Beverly, Massachusetts, Charles Tifft of Boston, Dr. Walter Garrey of Massachusetts General Hospital who was going as far as Panama, and Roland Wentzel, a young German-American commercial artist from New York, as cook's helper.

Most welcome aboard were two girls, Betty Schuler of Rochester, New York, and Dorothy Brandon of Toronto. Dorothy planned to leave at Singapore. Peer Johnson's sister was to meet them in Tahiti. All of the girls were between twenty-four and thirty, including Electa, and had the same general interests. Betty was signed on as blacksmith, Dorothy as lamptrimmer—two old windjammer jobs— Deborah and Electa as stewardess and hairdresser. None planned to be overworked in their official capacities, the titles of which caused considerable confusion among petty and often ignorant port officials around the world.

On November 5, 1933, the new-born *Yankee* sailed from Gloucester on its first circumnavigation. As soon as the harbor was cleared and the crowds gone, the sails were hauled up and the shipboard routine began. That night it snowed. Through the bitter winter night, they pressed out to sea toward the Gulf Stream. Those who had never been on a sailing ship before were obliged to go aloft and work sails—and they learned quickly. South of Hatteras, they encountered a proper gale, but soon passed out of the bad weather and the days became sunny and warm with moderate winds. By this time, the new crew was thoroughly initiated and began to enjoy the voyage.

At Colón, the crew went ashore for the first of many celebrations. They then passed through the locks, where *Yankee* was given a thorough threshing and crashed into one wall. With power and sail, they went through Gatun Lake, and late in the afternoon tied up at the dock in Balboa.

Here they stayed a while and the crew scattered on various adventures, shopping and exploring. Electa bought a Thanksgiving turkey in a local market. Charlie and Doug went into the hospital with an infected ear and an appendectomy respectively.[3] The crew was joined by Frank Longshore of New Orleans, who had signed on for Tahiti.

The fourth day at sea, Charlie's appendix began acting up. The skipper and Dr. Southworth decided to go on. The next day, Charlie had another attack, so Irving changed course for Buenaventura, Colombia, which had air service to Panama. Using the diesel engine, Irving made port the day before the scheduled flight. The town was eight miles upriver, and the channel was filled with unmarked shoals. When almost to the town, they went aground in the mud—the rainy season had started. Charlie's appendix was worse, and now the *Yankee* buzzed with angry officials who had not been informed of their coming, and who were insulted because the *Yankee* did not fly the Colombian flag.

After a series of misadventures during which they nearly lost the ship, they got Charlie ashore and to his airplane. The next day they got a telegram from Gorgas Hospital saying that the appendix had been duly removed and that Charlie was doing well.

At last, the *Yankee* escaped from the miseries of squalid Buenaventura and its officials, and headed for the Galápagos Islands. The next day they crossed the equator with appropriate ceremonies.

Their stay in the Galápagos was delightful. Christmas was celebrated at Chatham. They visited the colony which included the beautiful Norwegian girl of Robinson's voyage, Karin, now married to Señor Cobos.[4] They left letters at Post Office Bay. Electa and the others also made the acquaintance of the Ritters, the Baroness and her lovers, and most of the other eccentrics on Floreana.[5] Electa's account of the settlers and what happened to them was probably the last reliable one to be published.

One day at San Salvador, a shore party came upon a tin box containing a message from William Robinson who had been there in *Svaap* in 1928. The original, which was still in good condition, was replaced with a copy of their own.

Just before leaving, a ship hove into sight. It was the *Blue Dolphin* of Gloucester, which had been fitting out near them, and which was now under charter to Alfred Chandler and family of Wilmington, Delaware. Then the *Yankee*'s bowsprit was pointed toward Pitcairn, more than three thousand miles away.

Pitcairn was seldom visited by any ships, much less yachts, which was typical of the pattern the Johnsons followed in all their voyages. They had no idea of what they would find there, but it turned out to be the first of many visits with the descendants of the *Bounty* mutineers, and the beginning of a close relationship.[6]

It was hard to break away from the Pitcairn hospitality, but as it turned out, they would return sooner than they thought. At Mangareva, they found seven Pitcairn islanders who had been stranded for five months after their trading schooner from Tahiti, the *Patria*, piled up on a reef,[7] and who had managed to get to Mangareva in the lifeboat. Now they were homesick and wanted the *Yankee* to take them back to Pitcairn, which the Johnsons reluctantly did.[8] On the way, Captain Johnson married one of the islanders to a sixteen-year-old Mangareva girl who came along. At Pitcairn, their arrival caused no surprise. The Johnsons were told that they had been expected.

In 1934, Tahiti was far different than the island today, with its jet airport and booming tourism. The *Yankee*'s crew thoroughly enjoyed this tropical paradise. When the steamer from San Francisco arrived, aboard was Arthur Murphy, recovered from his accident. Charlie appeared in a native dugout. He had been waiting in Tahiti for two weeks. Newspapers from the States carried strange stories about the New Deal and something called "N.R.A.," bank holidays, and social and economic experiments. But life in Tahiti was one round of parties. The only link with home was that most of the merchandise and furnishings of the villagers outside Papeete came from the Sears Roebuck and Montgomery Ward catalogs.

They visited Mooréa, across the way, then Bora Bora, the Cook Islands, Tonga, Fiji, the New Hebrides, the Solomons, Borneo, poking into out-of-the-way places. Captain Johnson did not realize it, but he was covering water with which, as a wartime captain of a navy survey ship, he would become intimately acquainted.

Arriving at the mouth of the Bangkok River in Indochina, they went up that chocolate waterway to Bangkok to become the first American yacht to visit that city. Here the Johnsons celebrated their second wedding anniversary, and reflected on all that had happened during those two years. A train trip was made inland to the Angkor Wat, the ruins of the ancient city in the jungle, built by a vanished race of Khmers and lost to the world for centuries.

Next came Singapore, crossroads of the Pacific. Here, where labor and teak was cheap, the *Yankee* acquired new floors and other improvements. Then they were off for Sumatra, Bali, Java, passing by

Krakatoa, which had erupted in 1883, killing 36,000 people and sending tidal waves around the world.

Then came the Indian Ocean, Keeling-Cocos Islands, and Mauritius. On Cocos, Electa found members of the Clunies-Ross family who remembered Captain Slocum's visit nearly a half century before.

Christmas was spent at sea. On December 31, they sighted Africa, then came into the harbor of Durban and tied up to a berth only ten minutes' walk from the center of town. They appeared on a South African radio broadcast and then departed for Cape Town. Expecting the worse, they had a pleasant run around the Cape, logging one record noon-to-noon passage of 234 miles.

They enjoyed a visit to Cape Town, then pushed on to St. Helena, Ascension, Fernando de Noronha, and Devil's Island. Coming to anchor off the French prison colony, they were refused permission to land. But it was well that they hurried on, for near Georgetown, Ned's appendix flared up, and he was taken to a tropical hospital ashore for an emergency operation—the *third* appendectomy of the voyage.

Here they encountered Art Williams, an American bush pilot, who flew Johnson and several others on a spectacular run into the jungle where one waterfall, 840 feet high, was discovered and named Yankee Falls.

Next came the West Indies, which they had missed on the outbound trip. They stopped at Trinidad, Antigua, Saba, and the Virgin Islands.

On May 5, they sailed into Gloucester harbor, accompanied by a fleet of boats sent out to meet them with flags flying and whistles blowing. Their first circumnavigation had been completed.

During the pre-World War II days, *Yankee* made two more voyages around the world with amateur crews. The Johnsons' two sons were born and learned to walk on heaving decks. In the spring of 1941, they sailed *Yankee* back for the last time. Two months later, Irving was an officer in the Navy, and the family was on its way to Honolulu. *Yankee* was sold to the Admiral Billard Academy. Irving was assigned to the War Plans Office because of his intimate knowledge of the Pacific islands.

Then came the Pearl Harbor sneak attack. Irving went to sea on the survey ship, U.S.S. *Sumner*, charting the islands and passages where the fighting became hot and desperate—Guadalcanal, Tarawa, Kwajalein, and Iwo Jima. In early 1942, he was with the marines in the landing on Wallis Island, where he had once taken *Yankee*. Ultimately, he became skipper of the *Sumner*, on which he served three years. During the Iwo Jima operation, the *Sumner* was under continuous attack by air and shore batteries for eleven days. Johnson retired with the rank of Captain, U.S.N.R., after the war.

Coming home to Gloucester, he sailed in the 1946 Bermuda Race on the *Brilliant*. Meanwhile, he and Electa searched for another *Yankee*. They found her, with the help of a friend, the movie actor Sterling Hayden, who had been mate on the second world cruise, in the *Duhnen*, the last schooner the Germans built before steam took over. During the war, the schooner had been a Luftwaffe recreation ship. The British took her over as a prize, and she ended up as an RAF recreation ship.

After some convincing, the Air Marshall agreed to sell. The ship was refitted and renamed *Yankee* at the Brixham yards. The new *Yankee* was 96 feet overall, with a waterline of 81 feet, a maximum draft of 11 feet. She was a smart sailor with a top speed of 12 knots, had a pair of diesels with plenty of tankage, and electric power for lights, refrigeration, and hot water. She even carried an electric welder, a handy thing to have on a steel ship. The rig was changed to that of a brigantine with 7,775 square feet of canvas.

The first crew included the wife of General William (Wild Bill) Donovan of OSS fame, who had sailed around in the old *Yankee*. The Johnsons' two sons, Arthur and Robert, eleven and eight, also came aboard as veterans. Arthur had been given the middle name of "Cook" and Robert that of "Parkin," in honor of the great English explorer and of Parkin Christian, one of the Pitcairn islanders.

The first voyage of the new *Yankee* included Irving's nephew, Stephen, a merchant marine veteran; Jack Braidwood, a former Canadian navy commander; Frank Power of Santa Monica, California; a North Hollywood doctor, Charles T. Bothamley, forty-five; Peter Sutton and Hazard Campbell of Buffalo, New York; Alan Pierce of Fairhaven (where Slocum's *Spray* was born in a pasture); Jack Trevett of Evanston, Illinois; Eric Wolman, the youngest member at sixteen; Larry Bard; Neil Chase from Deerfield; John Wright of Sharon, Massachusetts; Ray Moeller, an engineer; Ed Douglas, an actor who had toured in *Kiss and Tell*; Jim Wells; and Don Crawford, a professional cook.

This time, the girls included Louise Stewart of Philadelphia, Wellesley grad and columnist for *Ladies' Home Journal*, and a former captain in the Marines; Mary Booth of Larchmont,[9] who had sailed with the Johnsons one summer, a Smith grad and aeronautical engineer; Terry Glenn of Chicago, also an aeronautical engineer and a pilot; and Meg Young of Muskegon, Michigan, a former secretary and saleslady.

Between 1947 and 1958, the Johnsons made four circumnavigations with amateur crews. On one trip, Irving discovered and raised the anchor of the *Bounty* at Pitcairn. Between voyages, the Johnsons published several books and lectured extensively. They also chartered on short trips up and down the coast, one summer carrying 2,200 Girl Scout mariners from New York to the Bras d'Or Lakes.

Irving was a member of the prestigious Cruising Club of America and always flew the CCA pennant. Surprisingly, the Johnsons were never cited with the Blue Water Medal, although they had the respect and admiration of the club members.

In the CCA book, *Nowhere Is Too Far*, the late John Parkinson, Jr., wrote: "It is almost appalling when we consider that Irving Johnson skippered the two *Yankees* seven times around the world. Certainly he is worthy to take his place in history with Magellan and Sir Francis Drake as one of the world's greatest sailors in sail."

Then, at last, after a quarter century of voyaging around the world, the Johnsons sold the brigantine *Yankee*. The old North Sea pilot boat was soon after wrecked on a reef in the South Pacific by the new owner. Irving and Electa had Sparkman and Stephens design for them a third *Yankee*, this one a 50-foot steel centerboard ketch with shallow draft, masts stepped in tabernacles so they could be folded for passage under low bridges, and began a retirement period cruising the vast canals of Europe. On one trip up the Nile, Irving suffered a bad fall while climbing on the ruins, but recovered.

The Johnsons were among the most unusual and competent of all the voyagers who have undertaken a circumnavigation, and certainly hold the record for the number of times around. More important, all these voyages have been made with consummate skill, with unending attention to detail and vigilance, and good old-fashioned judgment. Because of the Johnsons, hundreds of amateurs from all walks of life who had dreamed of the sea were able to make a voyage of a lifetime in complete safety and without the burden of yacht ownership and years of preparation necessary to make it on their own.

There was always unfailing discipline aboard the *Yankees*, but this never intruded on the easy comradeship and the informal life the Johnsons tried to maintain. With few exceptions, those amateurs who signed on were able to adjust easily to shipboard life and the inevitable togetherness on long passages. Perhaps the secret of the success of these voyages was the fact that the Johnsons themselves never lost that feeling of excitement and curiosity that comes with visiting exotic places and meeting different peoples. They were essentially inveterate tourists, with insatiable enthusiasm and curiosity.

For those hundreds of amateurs, no matter how humdrum or frustrating was the rest of their lives, they would always be able to look back on the great adventure, when for one brief period the world and its romance spread out before them on a magic carpet called the *Yankee*.

⊸§ 15 §⊷

The Lonely One
in the Roaring Forties

I do not know how long it was; but at about 2 o'clock in the night of the 12th of July I awoke. The bunk was damp. Could a wave breaking on deck have got in through the port-holes? But I knew that they were shut tight. As I moved my arm felt lighter. Thank God! There was a gaping hole about three inches wide in my forearm; pus was flowing from it.[1]

UNTIL 1934, NO YACHTSMAN HAD EVER SUCCEEDED IN doubling Cape Horn the impossible way, from east to west. In that year, Al Hansen, a Norwegian, on *Mary Jane*, a double-ender Colin Archer type, succeeded alone—only to be wrecked on the coast of Chiloé, and never to be seen again.[2]

While at the yacht club in Buenos Aires before starting his voyage, Hansen met and became good friends with Vito Dumas, a well-known Argentinian yachtsman with considerable ocean experience. Dumas had under construction at the time a "Norwegian-type" ketch, designed by Manuel Campos on lines modified from the Colin Archer principle and the Platte River whaleboats. Dumas, too, had ambitions to sail around the Horn from 50° S to 50° S. In fact, he wanted to sail around the world alone like Slocum had done.

In 1933, Dumas was a man of some substance. Born in Buenos

Aires on September 26, 1900, of Italian immigrants and a family background of artists, engineers, and politicians, he was a strong, chesty, vigorous, and robust boy, an accomplished swimmer who at 23 had crossed the Platte estuary from Colonia, Uruguay, to the Argentine coast in 25½ hours. Brought up in poverty, he left school to work at an early age. He prospered, went into the cattle business, joined the yacht club, and indulged his hobbies during the 1920s. As a yachtsman, Dumas was noted for his skill and daring in those often boisterous southern waters off Brazil and Argentina. In 1931, he purchased an ancient International 8-meter class racing boat in France and sailed it alone from Arcachon to Buenos Aires, a distance of 6,270 nautical miles in 76 days. This boat was *Legh I*.

In 1933, Dumas commissioned Campos, who was famous for his double-ender types influenced by Colin Archer, Atkins, and local native craft which had originated in the Mediterranean, to design and build a 32-footer expressly for ocean voyaging.[3] *Legh II* was 32 feet 2 inches overall, 10 feet 9 inches wide, and had a maximum draft of 5 feet 7 inches—the ultimate refinement of its type and very nearly a perfect model. She was ketch-rigged and had 9 tons of iron ballast outside.

It was at first the similarity of their boats that brought together Hansen and Dumas, but in each other they saw kindred spirits—a strange, deep loneliness and restlessness, in spite of outgoing manners, and an unusually strong tie to their mothers even when grown men that perhaps psychologists would relate to their inexorable passion for the mother sea. Each, too, was a man somewhat larger than life who could never be content unless struggling to climb above the ordinary.

In any case, Dumas saw Hansen off and went back to the task of completing *Legh II*. Dumas later wrote of Hansen:

> *What a joy it was, that sunny morning in 1934, when he came to see me, signed his name on a panel of* Legh II, *then building, and expressed his approval. He talked of the mother he had left far away in his Norwegian fjord and discussed his plans. It seemed unthinkable that he, with all his determination and optimism, should have finished as he did.*[4]

For reasons not clear, Dumas's projected world voyage never came off. Perhaps he was discouraged and shaken by the death of his friend Al Hansen—more likely it was for financial reasons. His business began to deteriorate. The Depression was on. In some parts of the world, such as Europe, the traditional market for South American products, there was political upheaval. Herr Hitler had come on the scene, as had Mussolini, in Dumas's own Italy. In Spain, often considered the Mother Country by Latin Americans, there was strife and revolution. At home, the government was unstable, with much heated dissension among various factions. And Dumas was having family as well as financial problems.

For the next several years, *Legh II* was sailed locally and raced in the Rio offshore competition. Returning from Rio after one series of races, Dumas encountered an unexpected *pampero* and a freak wave which capsized and rolled *Legh II* over with apparently little damage. From that moment on, Dumas had sublime faith in his little Norwegian.

But soon he had to sell *Legh II* to buy some cattle, and with it went his dream of a solo circumnavigation. But as his finances and family problems worsened, he found he could still dream of escape. On rainy days, he could bend over his charts and let his soul sail away on "the impossible route"—around the world in the Roaring Forties.

World War II came to engulf the world. Dumas was now forty-two years old and a failure. Worse yet, he felt a vast void of unfulfillment in his life that had begun as a child when he had given up school to go to work to help support his mother and father. He had the Argentine version of the seven-year itch, and now, with the breath of war reaching into every ocean and every country, time was running out. How long would it last? How old would he be then? Maybe there was still time.

He hunted around for *Legh II*, and found that she was still in the hands of the original purchaser. But now, he was to learn, the owner would not sell for anything except cash. All Dumas had for collateral was a herd of cattle which had been driven from farm to farm and fair to fair so often that they were too weak and skinny to hold up their own weight. The beef market was down. No one wanted them. It was ironic that Dumas had sold *Legh II* in order to buy cattle; now he could not sell his cattle to buy his boat back.

At last, an old friend came forward and gave him the cash. As news got around of Dumas's plans, old friends appeared out of nowhere. They loaned him money, gave him supplies and equipment, clothing, medicines, books, encouragement. Friends and club members showed up with tools, lunch baskets, and maté to help him refurbish and outfit *Legh II*. If nothing else, his decision to beat the war around the world evoked an outpouring of respect, friendship, and admiration from old friends, family members, and even hundreds of strangers.

After all this, it was difficult to tear himself away from it all, but finally, on Friday, June 26, 1942, he made his last rounds of port and customs, got together with an inner circle of close friends for a last party, and the following morning, before crowds of thousands of well-wishers and press representatives, Dumas had a tearful and emotional good-bye scene with his mother, brother, and son.

Adios, my country. Tears rolled down his cheeks. Slowly he moved down the channel. Several yachts escorted him. On one was his son, Vito Diego. "Keep well, Vito," he called to him. "Be good!"

Then he was off through the congested river traffic for Montevideo. There he waited out a blow at the yacht club, went through another gay and emotional departure, and headed at last for the Atlantic into the teeth of a sou'wester.

He could not have picked a worse time. *Pamperos* were frequent. The wind and seas were vicious. The nights were black, without sign of life. *Legh II* ran on, her sails not yet balanced, not having got her sea legs. On July 3, exhausted, Dumas heard running water inside. Inspection showed a bad leak. Enormous seas battered the boat. Somehow he cleared away five hundred bottles and other gear and discovered a crack in a plank. Quickly, he made emergency repairs with canvas and red lead. During this, he injured his arm in the violent motion, but he had saved the ship. He went to bed and slept, only to awaken with an infected right arm. For several days, he fought the infection with injections of antibiotics to no effect.

The seas continued violent. The leaking plank opened up again. A jar of honey broke and its contents ran into the bilge. Dumas was now running a high fever—every movement sent streamers of pain through his body; he became delirious. The putrid odor of decaying flesh filled the close cabin. Hundreds of miles from land, there seemed no alternative but to amputate his own arm at the elbow with an ax or a seaman's knife—but before he could do this he passed out. When he awoke, he was lying in a puddle. The wound had opened and pus was draining out. There was a three-inch hole in his arm. With his knife, he pried out the core of the abscess; then he dressed the wound and gave himself another injection.

As if to celebrate his recovery, the sun came out and the wind veered to the south. He put the ship in order, cleaned the cabin, had something to eat, and then went on deck and took the tiller which he had not touched in days.

Cape Town is on approximately the same latitude as Buenos Aires. On this long passage, Dumas ran before gale winds, with seas often 50 feet high, when steering became an ordeal of endurance. On August 5, he sighted the cloud bank over Tristan da Cunha. On the thirteenth, he crossed the prime meridian into East Longitude.

One day, he heard a siren and rushed up on deck to find a Brazilian ship hailing him. It being wartime, they were all on edge until identification was made. By now, German and Japanese raiders roamed all the oceans of the world. The United States was still reeling from the sneak attack on Pearl Harbor and the loss of half the Pacific fleet. Tankers were being sunk off the U.S. east coast by the dozen. The Doolittle Raid on Tokyo with B-25s launched from the deck of the *Hornet* would have little effect except to bolster morale among the Allies.

On August 31, *Legh II* was spoken by a British warship, which had a submarine lurking close by. Then, fifty-five days after leaving the River Plate, he sighted Table Mountain. At dusk, he came into the harbor where he was met by officials, the press, and well-wishers. It was 3 A.M. before he was alone again and able to lie down for his first real rest without motion. Even for wartime, he was given a most cordial welcome. The ten pounds which made up his total finances at the time, went unspent. All fees were waived. Parties and receptions were held for him. His fame had preceded him—a senior naval officer there had read his first book about his voyage in *Legh I*.[5] His public image was not only that of an intrepid solo bluewater sailor, but of a literary personage, too.

He received many letters and telegrams from people who wanted to meet him. One was an invitation from a lady of means, a thirty-year-old widow who was also lonely and had artistic tastes (Dumas, among his other talents, was also a painter). He moved in with her at her villa for several idyllic weeks. For a Latin in his troublesome forties in need of emotional and spiritual feasting, he was tempted to accept her offer of a permanent residence in this South African love nest; but he remembered the old Argentinian *modismo:* Never let a friend's hand get warm in yours.[6]

Finally, he had to say *à demain.* Again, his departure was hectic. Preparations were endless. People donated time and money to him. He acquired charts that would take him past the remote St. Paul and

Amsterdam, where it was said that Alain Gerbault had once planned a get-rich fur-trapping scheme. On Monday, September 14, Dumas took aboard the last supplies, made his tearful farewells with emotional embraces and handshakes, and made his way out of the harbor.

Soon he moved into the region of constant storms, at times surrounded by gigantic waterspouts, averaging 120 to 150 miles a day, with waves often 50 feet high and 900 feet long—he was in the Roaring Forties, those legendary latitudes which, until Dumas, had never been experienced by yachtsmen. He passed out of the Atlantic into the Indian Ocean. For weeks on end, he sailed alone through the region of phantom ships such as the *Flying Dutchman*, the ghosts of ancient ships of the old East India trade. He thought of the *Marie Celeste* found with all sails set, a meal in the galley, and no one aboard. Once he heard voices coming from the forward locker, which he never used, voices in Spanish, talking about how they could steal food without Dumas knowing. Once a voice asked him for cigarettes. Because he was in a storm, he could not leave the helm. At the end of three days, he was able to go forward armed with a gaff; but by then the voices had disappeared.[7]

He also had many encounters and close calls with whales. He grew a beard. He marveled at the sea life between gales, and experimented with rigs and techniques. What else does one do on a voyage of 104 days?

> *It is said that solitude is best shared with another. These seas offer joys to anyone who is capable of loving and understanding nature. Are there not people who can spend hours watching the rain as it falls? I once read somewhere that three things could never be boring: passing clouds, dancing flames, and running water. They are not the only ones. I should add in the first place, work. The self-sufficient man acquires a peculiar state of mind.*[8]

Once he saw ten albatrosses sitting on the water examining an object, which turned out to be a small jar, and the birds seemed to be having a conference to decide what this foreign object was. On October 28, Dumas passed Amsterdam Island, with St. Paul to the north—and he avoided them. "All I could possibly find would be some shipwrecked mariner waiting for his death."[9]

Daily runs became about one hundred miles. He recorded a new kind of porpoise with white belly and tail and brown back, as have other sailors in these latitudes. He also discovered a fly aboard. (Slocum had his spiders; Caldwell his cockroaches and rats for companions.)

The whales became a menace, sometimes charging at him, only to swerve away at the last moment. He found that at night he could scare the whales away with a flashlight. On November 6, a gigantic wave broke aboard with a crash.[10]

As he sailed into a cyclone on his approach to Australia, he battened ship and offered a prayer to St. Teresa. Tempted to run for land, only 130 miles away, he instead changed course to pass Cape Leeuwin and make New Zealand in one stage from Cape Town. His fresh water had dwindled to mud, and in spite of massive doses of vitamin C, he had the first symptoms of scurvy. There were yet 1,440 miles to go to reach Tasmania.

Riding enormous seas, his clothes in rags, weak from malnutrition, with an injured leg, he sailed on across the Tasman Sea. On December 16, he was 160 miles from Cape Providence, 800 miles from Wellington. After 101 days at sea, he was only a quarter mile out from his reckoning. On December 27, he neared the coast with lovely white houses on shore. Off Worser, he luffed up and came alongside a harbor launch.

"Where have you come from?"

"From the Cape of Good Hope."

Behind him were 104 days of solitude, struggle, sickness, and the will to survive. For the first time in history, a lone sailor had accomplished the formidable nonstop route from Cape Town to New Zealand. "*I will never, never sail again!*"

Wellington, now on full wartime footing with large numbers of British and American military forces there, extended all its warm hospitality to the lonely Argentinian. The British and American sailors adopted him. A local family, the Meadows, took him home to stay.

But, finally, on January 30, he broke away again, and embarked on the old clipper route toward Cape Horn with his next stop, Santiago, Chile, 5,000 miles away. Again he was alone on the loneliest ocean on earth. Again he encountered menacing whales, once climbing up on the back of one *cacholot*. He fell down a hatch and broke a rib. He read and slept a lot, and made from 100 to 130 miles a day. Once, halfway there, he saw something floating on the water. It was a woman's pink slipper with a pompom of silk. Where had it come from? What lady once daintily slipped it off her foot, perhaps for the benefit of a man in the first suggestive courtship ritual? It must have been an elegant lady—it was size 4.

On March 4, he saw a westbound ship. Two days later, some birds from Pitcairn joined him. He tried to build a binnacle for the compass, but had lost his only tool, a screwdriver, overboard. He had more close calls with whales. On Sunday, April 11, at 2000 hours, 71 days out, he came on deck to see the lights of Point Curaumillas flashing to starboard. Valparaiso was ahead. His landfall had been perfect. Just across the bay, he could see the lights and hear the sounds of the barbor. A voice came out of the darkness. "Muchacho," he called. "Be a good chap and tell the harbormaster."

He planned to attempt Cape Hcrn between the middle of June and the middle of July. Dumas knew what he was doing. He had studied the impossible route for ten years. He calculated daily runs, time traveled, winds and currents. He thought he knew the secret of the Horn.

Not until the end of May did he sail. Meanwhile he was feted as usual as a hero and celebrity by his fellow South Americans. The Chilean navy, famous for its hospitality, took Dumas to their hearts and overhauled *Legh II*. His chronometer was repaired and rated. He was given a set of charts. From his home across the Andes, where news of his arrival had reached, came messages and gifts from friends.

On Sunday, May 25, he went to Mass, then to the hotel room for his luggage, and while the city slept, boarded *Legh II*. Loaded down with wine, spirits, food, and supplies for six months, he embarked on the shortest and most dangerous leg of his voyage. Soon Juan Fernández, the Robinson Crusoe island, showed ahead, and was left behind. The seas became boisterous, with waves breaking in frightening sounds. After six days of gales, he was 600 miles from Cape Horn. On June 18, he was abreast of Cape Pillar, the entrance to Magellan Strait, 180 miles to the east. On June 22, he sighted Tierra del Fuego to the northeast. He lay in his bunk and read the records of Cook and Bougainville, and recalled the joy of hearing that Al Hansen had succeeded, and the sorrow later. Could he escape the curse that broods between 50° S and 50°S?

One dark stormy night, he estimated that the Horn was abeam. It was about midnight, and the wind and seas were high—he could not go outside. All he could do was hang on with both hands. There was a violent shock. He was thrown forward and struck his face on a panel. His nose spouted blood. It was broken.

Cape Horn makes everyone pay tribute.

The twenty-fifth came and went. He forged on under mizzen, storm trysail, staysail, and jib. He had left the Horn behind. Beside him stood the ghost of a dead sailor, Al Hansen. Dumas wept.

His course then led northward past Staten Island, the coast of Patagonia over shallow areas where the depth was eighty fathoms or less. Here, seas could not get up enough to harm him.[11]

On July 5, he saw a Chilean steamer with a four-master in tow. He was five miles off the coast. His chronometer had been in error. The low hills behind the dunes loomed up. The water was green. At night, he came to the *Mala Cara Buoy*—the ugly one. Mar del Plata, eighteen miles away, was sighted on July 7. He came upon some fishing boats in the bright morning and asked them to notify authorities. They opened a bottle and sang sea chanties. A towline was passed and *Legh II* entered port sedately.

He was given a hero's welcome. Greetings arrived from everyone in Argentina, it seemed. There were receptions at the Rotary Club, the yacht and sailing clubs, and in private homes. Reporters and photographers hounded him. There was a ceremony at sunrise on July 19. All the crews of all the ships stood at attention, as the sun climbed rose red in the pale sky, and a bugle broke the silence as the flag went up.

"For this I would go around the world a hundred times."[12]

For Dumas, it was fulfillment at last. This he could savor and contemplate over and over again from a remote hideaway in the Sierra de Córdoba, where he could look down as the lights came on in the evening in the valley, blinking like falling stars, each of them a boat on land with its own particular problems. He contemplated the scene and the peace he had at last achieved.

"*Lord, be lavish of Thy Peace and guide to all the ports of the world, those sailors who are orphaned in the immensity of the sea.*"

Later, Dumas would be honored by the Royal Cruising Club of London, awarded the first Slocum Prize of the Slocum Society. He would settle on a country estate near Buenos Aires, but his sailing days were not over. In 1946, after the war, he took *Legh II* on a voyage to New York, the Azores, the Canary Islands, and back. In 1955, he again set sail, this time in a new vessel, the *Sirio*, making New York in one landfall, 7,100 miles in 117 days.

Dumas was a true Renaissance man. Not only was he a superb sailor, farmer, and cattle raiser, but a musician, an artist with an original and innovative style, a lover, a family man, and an eccentric. His solo sailing techniques have been copied by others, such as his bold running before the waves of the high southern latitudes instead of heaving to or lying to a sea anchor, which he abhorred; and his relying on his patron saints instead of bilge pumps or tools (he carried only one screwdriver). He suffered from malnutrition because he would not catch and kill a fish. He was determined that if he died it would be with his boots on.

Legh II would become a derelict at Mar del Plata, the Argentine summer resort. Toward the end of August 1971, she was sailing from Buenos Aires with students from the National Nautical School. When the weather turned bad, *Legh II* was driven ashore. Later she would be salvaged and placed in a maritime museum.[13] She had died with her boots on.

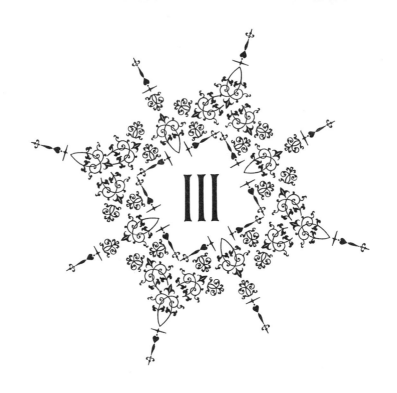

III

AROUND THE BEAUTIFUL NEW WORLD

CHAPTER

⋖ 16 ⋗

For Auld Lang Syne

The day was Easter Sunday, 1948. A fine Hawaiian day with fresh trade winds chasing broken white clouds across a blue sky. Outside the harbor, as sails were hoisted, the strong wind, taut sheets and a ship come to life wiped away all nostalgia. Lang Syne heeled under full sail, took a bone in her teeth and raced as though rejoicing to be in her elements again.[1]

AND NOW IT IS JUNE 1972. IN A NARROW, DEEP, AND QUIET cleft rent from barren, uninhabited Todos Santos Island on the lonely coast of Baja, Mexico, there lies quietly at anchor a rugged, hefty Block Island schooner. Although almost forty years old, she looks not more than ten. Her cosmetics are fresh, her rigging taut, her superstructure well-kept. The same might be said for her crew, Bill and Phyllis Crowe, who a quarter century before had been the second couple in history to have made a circumnavigation in a dream ship built with their own hands. Time has been kind to both ship and crew. . . .

Lang Syne's story began, like many of her kind, in the depression-ridden 1930s in balmy Southern California, long before the smog, the freeways, the crowded suburbs, the race riots, and the frantic millions all getting into each other's way; when a Sunday drive in a Model A roadster from L.A. to Long Beach took you down orange and palm-lined roads with cozy little five-acre *haciendas*, and occasional oil derricks and pumps, and open-air fruit and grocery stalls run by Japanese-American families, to the enormous harbor protected from the open sea, where about the only activity at times appeared to be the Catalina ferry landing, and the friendly people building dream boats on rented waterfront lots.

Like most Californians of that genre, the Crowes originated somewhere else. Phyllis had been born in Iowa (where in those days all good Californians were said to be from), birthplace of many a sailor, such as Harry Pidgeon; while William was an authentic "prune picker," since he was second generation—his parents having reached the promised land via prairie schooner across Death Valley before he was born.

Bill ran a refrigeration business, which in those depression years was more of a migraine headache than a business, and after their marriage, Bill and Billie (as he called Phyllis) escaped from their problems as often as possible in an ancient 34-foot cruiser which they had patched together. Selling this, they acquired a sailing canoe, then a 19-foot skipjack, and finally built their first real dream ship, a 25-foot *Sea Bird* type, the original and smaller version of Harry Pidgeon's *Islander*, which had also been built right here at Los Angeles harbor.

They named her *Corvus* (which means "crow," naturally), and for two years sailed the yawl on coastal waters and back and forth to Catalina and other channel islands. These short voyages, as is usually the case, rather than satisfying their restlessness, only increased it. They sold the business, their car and house, and all other unneeded possessions, and shoved off for Hawaii a week ahead of that year's TransPac Race fleet. They would have entered, but their ship was too small to qualify. As it was, they arrived, after a 20-day passage spent "laughing all the way," days before the fleet, including the 85-foot scratch boat.[2]

Once in prewar Hawaii, all thought of returning to the mainland disappeared. They had found the life they wanted. They made new friends, went for short cruises among the islands, and took up permanent residence. In those days, Hawaii was a semitropical paradise, a world crossroads for sea wanderers. In port at the time were such vessels as *Viator*, a little schooner en route from Tahiti; the 32-foot ketch *Te Rapunga*, in from Amsterdam via Australia with George Dibbern, the eccentric who renounced all citizenship ties and created his own flag (and who had dominion over his own cell when World War II broke out); the catamaran *Kaimiloa*, bound for France; the

34-foot ketch *Hula Gal*, headed for Seattle—and none other than the *Islander* with Captain Harry Pidgeon himself living aboard.

But the winds of change were already blowing, even in languid Hawaii, where Waikiki was still a tropical beach with palm trees and beachcombers and bare-breasted native girls doing laundry. The Japanese attack on December 7, 1941, was perhaps in the planning stage when Bill and Phyllis decided that their *Corvus* was too small. With a set of borrowed blueprints of Howard I. Chapelle's updated version of the Block Island schooner, they set about building their ultimate dream ship on the beach at Waikiki on a lot they rented for $5 a month.

At no time in history was there a better opportunity to build one's dream ship than in Hawaii in the late 1930s. Labor was cheap and plentiful, and top-quality materials such as Philippine mahogany were abundant. Even in Hawaii, they were able to obtain prime vertical-grained Douglas fir planks from the Pacific Northwest for one-piece full-length strakes. With the help of friends, they set up the keel, steamed the frames, and planked the hull, taking about two years for the project. At one point, not having received a bill from suppliers for months, Crowe went to the Honolulu office to inquire why not. The office manager seemed surprised. It was customary, he said, to send statements only on January 1, unless there was some pressing reason to do otherwise.[3]

Before the hull was completed, they moved aboard and "lived with" each arrangement before making it permanent. The ship was launched during an earthquake, and christened with a bottle of beer. For a name, they thought of *Auld Lang Syne*, in memory of all the good times they had had so far and expected to have in the future, but because this was too long to go on the nameboard, they shortened it to *Lang Syne*.

Lang Syne was a luxury cruise ship compared to *Corvus*. She was 39 feet overall, 34 feet on the waterline, with a beam of 14 feet and a draft of 6 feet. She was double-ended with a salty sheer line, and rigged with a gaff-head main and jib-headed foremast. The first engine was a small Scripps gasoline mill.

In July 1938, the shakedown cruise was made to California via the northern circle to avoid the trades. *Lang Syne* proved to be a real seagoing home—fast, seaworthy, and comfortable. They made a landfall on familiar San Nicolas Island within minutes of their E.T.A. Later they cruised back to Hawaii, where *Lang Syne* was moored at the yacht club in Honolulu when the sneak attack came on the morning of Sunday, December 7, 1941. The war years were spent on the beach, working in the defense facilities, saving up for the bright new postwar world everyone hoped they were fighting for.

In May 1946, the Crowes set off on their first long voyage in more than four years. Now *Lang Syne* was 10 years old, but as good as new and her Scripps had been replaced with a new 37-horsepower Hercules-Kermath diesel. In nine days, they sailed half the distance to California, and then were becalmed. During the calm, they noticed a large black buoy with spikes on it nearby—a loose mine—but were able to motor out of the way. The crossing took 33 days, compared to their first crossing of 47 days on the *Lang Syne*'s maiden voyage. It was the first yacht crossing in five years.

In Los Angeles, they bought a car and spent two months sightseeing, camping, hiking, and visiting relatives. Then they went back to their schooner home, intending to return directly to Hawaii and build a home on land they had purchased during the war. But because a shipping strike was on and there were shortages of everything, the Crowes decided to return via the Marquesas and Tahiti. Before leaving, they installed a clutch arrangement on the engine shaft which was linked with a generator to keep batteries charged while under sail, and would hopefully reduce propeller drag.[4]

In April 1947, they departed Los Angeles harbor for Guadalupe Island, the remote rock owned by Mexico some two hundred miles south of Catalina. They spent several days beachcombing and photographing the sea elephants, although the island was a refuge and off-limits. Just as they were departing, they were boarded by a government boat, but allowed to continue.[5]

In the Marquesas, they were met by trader Bob McKittrick, still the unofficial greeter of yachts and sea wanderers since the days of Muhlhauser and Stock. They were given a sack of mail to deliver to Tahiti by the administrator, and reached Papeete via the Tuamotus on June 3. At dawn, the pilot boat appeared outside the pass. Bill refused its services, but was told it was compulsory. In the harbor, they tied up to the quay where the port doctor, police, and other officials crowded aboard to find out why they were without visas or passports. Crowe told them he did not want to come in, but the pilot had told him it was required. The pilot, a Captain Bailly, who was also the harbormaster, and obviously a man with a sense of humor, confirmed this.

There were already two American yachts in Papeete, the *Island Girl* and *Tere*. The Crowes spent two months here and at Mooréa, where a Belgian couple managed the small hotel.[6] On the way north to Hawaii, they called at several island ports in the Tuamotus where they were welcomed with much hospitality.[7] They stopped again in the Marquesas to drop off some supplies, much to McKittrick's surprise, who thought that, like most yachts that made promises that were not kept, they would never return. At the Marquesas, they learned that the *Kon Tiki* raft was nearing the area, but declined to cover the event for the waiting world press. The passage to Hawaii was made in the record time of 14 days, beating the previous record of 16 days set by the 48-foot ketch *Altair* for the 2,100-mile run.

Home again and recapping their odyssey with friends, it occurred to them that they had already gone a third of the way around the world.

"Let's go the rest of the way," Phyllis blurted.

The only other couple to have made a circumnavigation alone was Roger and Edith Strout in *Igdrasil*, a *Spray* copy, back in the 1930s. So it was decided. They found a secondhand sailmaking machine, rented the armory for a loft, and made a new set of sails. After acquiring another dinghy, they made a cockpit shelter, and installed extra butane tanks.[8] Diving gear, a brazing outfit, a war surplus radio transmitter, pilot books, light lists, charts, and sailing directions went aboard.

Among their friends in Hawaii were the Irving Johnsons, who were in port with the new *Yankee* and crew of amateurs on their fourth circumnavigation. The Johnsons prevailed on them to meet in Pago Pago for the annual Samoan festival. The Crowes still had their car to dispose of and no buyers, but, at the last moment, a friend came along and offered to trade a beach lot for it. The deal was made on the spot, sight unseen. A beach lot in most parts of Hawaii in the 1970s would be worth enough to make one independently wealthy, which indicates that sea wanderers don't necessarily have to be poor businessmen.

They departed on Easter Sunday, 1948, for Samoa. The passage was a rough one with towering seas and gale winds. Billie was seasick for the first few days. On this passage, they encountered the phenomenon of tidal overfalls marking the meeting of equatorial currents near Fannings Island, which appeared like a line of breaking surf. The last few days to Samoa were spent motoring in a calm. They crossed the equator on April 6, and on the afternoon of the seventeenth, anchored at Tutuila, one day before their rendezvous with the *Yankee*.

The stay in Samoa included a round of parties and sightseeing, mostly with the *Yankee*'s crew. The visit was marred, the Crowes complained mildly, by bothersome natives—the usual complaint of visitors ignorant of Samoan customs. Here, also, the Johnsons confided to the Crowes that the responsibility of managing a big 98-foot brigantine sometimes left them wishing they could get back to the simple life.

Leaving Pago Pago, the Crowes encountered a violent gale which snapped the gaff boom, and Bill was nearly lost overboard getting in the headsails, which would have been more than disastrous, since Billie had not yet learned celestial navigation. But once safely hove-to, *Lang Syne* rode the gale easily.

On the way to the Fijis, calls were made at several out-of-the-way places, such as Niuafoo, the Tin Can Island in the Tongan group. At Suva, they were made honorary members of the yacht club. One evening at anchor, a beautiful little half-caste girl swam out to *Lang Syne* and pulled herself up on the rail. She wanted to sign on as a crew member. Bill told her there was already one woman aboard. "Wouldn't two be better?" he was asked.

In Suva, Bill also had a molar extracted by an Indian dentist who spoke fluent English and was surprised to find that Crowe still had all his teeth at age fifty. The extraction was made without novacaine and without Bill knowing it until the dentist showed him the molar. Apparently the dentist had hypnotized him. The next stop was for a haircut by an Indian barber. The extraction had cost $1.25; the haircut, 20 cents.

On the way to Australia, they passed remote Walpole and Kunie islands near New Caledonia, and received news on the radio that Captain Harry Pidgeon was shipwrecked only four hundred miles away on his third circumnavigation aboard *Islander*. Before leaving Hawaii, Crowe had asked Pidgeon if he were not leaving too early to avoid the hurricane season, and was told, "Those things always happen somewhere else. They don't worry me."

With his wife, Pidgeon had anchored in Hog Harbor, Espiritu Santo, in the New Hebrides, a harbor normally well protected, and had been blown up on the beach.

They called at Brisbane, covering the 1,600 miles in only 13 days, on the way nearly colliding with a large pod of whales. After a wild tow up the river by the pilot boat, they were invited to use the private mooring of Eric Dalby at his waterfront estate. They were given an honorary membership in the Royal Queensland Yacht Club and Billie became the third woman in the history of the club to be invited to the commodore's luncheon.

The long trip around behind the Great Barrier Reef was one of their most enjoyable and fascinating passages. Nights were spent anchored in remote creeks, days with visiting people ashore in isolated settlements, skindiving, fishing, and hunting on shore. They prowled the reefs from late June until September, and came very near to remaining in this region permanently. They stopped at Cairns before this port became world-famous as a game-fishing center, and traveled inland on a switchbacking railroad to the town of Lareeba at 3,000-foot elevation. At one stop, in Cook's Passage, Bill was skindiving when a large octopus grabbed his leg. He managed to get loose with a tire iron. They passed Sunday Island in Torres Strait, went around Cape York, and picked up their mail at Thursday Island.

The local agent, who was holding their mail, grinned as he handed them a notice from Uncle Sam's Collector of Internal Revenue.

Next came the New Guinea coast. They enjoyed a brief stay in Dili, the capital of Portuguese Timor. The East Indies were then in the early stages of postwar political turmoil. Worse yet, the uncharted waters and misplaced navigational aids were complicated by bands of armed natives with itchy trigger fingers. But they kept another appointment with *Yankee* at Bali, and then went on to Batavia, Singapore, and Ceylon. They had one tense period in the Java Sea, when boarded by a band of armed natives, whom Crowe met with a calm and bold front and just the proper degree of indignation. It was a close call.

Before leaving Singapore, Bill bought a Christmas tree marked "Made in England" to have aboard when the day came. After Billie had gone to sleep on Christmas Eve, Bill got out the tree and fixed it to the cabin table. When Billie awoke, she gasped with delight.

They made heavy weather on the passage to Ceylon. After a short stay there, they went on to Mombasa by way of the Maldives. One evening, clipping along at eight knots, they collided with or were attacked by a whale, one of several sleeping on the surface. The encounter broke their bobstay.

At 3 A.M. on the morning of January 25, they smelled the burning sugar cane on the mainland of Africa. The American consul at Mombasa presented them with a new national ensign, replacing the one they had won in a 1940 race and carried to four continents.

There was quite a lively American colony here, including a vivacious young girl named Margery Passmore who managed the Ritz Hotel. The *Lang Syne* was the first American yacht here after the war.

At Zanzibar, 120 miles down the coast, they were directed to an unprotected anchorage, and in a blow *Lang Syne* went aground. This nearly ended the voyage, but the Crowes, in their usual competent way, kedged off while the port authorities stood by, wringing their hands but not helping. They beached the vessel for repairs among the fleet of Arab dhows, and became guests of the governor for the rest of their stay.

On the 1,700-mile passage to Durban, South Africa, Billie caught a kingfish on "Alfonso," the battered feather jig they had dragged halfway around the world. On March 4, after reef crawling the African coast, they arrived at Durban. Here, of course, they found a warm welcome from local yacht clubs and were invited to lecture. They showed movies of Hawaii, and during one presentation in the crowded hall, someone suddenly shouted, "With all that at home, what in the world are you doing in Durban?"

Leaving on St. Patrick's Day, they hugged the coast and had a fair passage around to Cape Town, where the Royal Cape Yacht Club had the welcome flag up for them. Some of the yachts that came out to meet them beat the harbor officials, somewhat to the Crowes' embarrassment.

Picking up their first mail since Singapore, the Crowes made a few minor repairs including a new photocell for "Pete," the automatic pilot, and, on July 10, departed with an escort of dozens of yachts and press boats.

Instead of the usual route, they followed the coast up to the mouth of the Congo, crossing the bar to the old town of St. Paul de Luanda. Gracious local officials made arrangements for a native pilot to take them upriver. They met a local doctor who told them he had treated Alain Gerbault years before, at Dili, while they had been prisoners of the Japanese.[9]

Lang Syne was taken about twenty-five miles upriver to Zenze Creek, where the Crowes anchored in front of the Katala village. They spent several days here, bartering with the natives, listening to the jungle sounds at night, and watching the crocodiles play. Bill made the downriver run himself without a pilot, a tense but masterful piece of small-boat handling.

From the Congo, the Crowes wandered the Atlantic, putting in at Rio de Janeiro, where some difficulty was experienced with local officials who seldom saw an American yacht. They quickly made friends and fell in with the local social whirl. Here they found a letter from Herbert Stone, publisher of *Yachting*, waiting at the yacht club. He extended an invitation to come to New York and also asked for a series of articles on the voyage. They also received another notice from I.R.S. saying their payment made from Cape Town was $14 short, and please remit with interest.

The long, hard uphill beat was made to Recife, capital of Pernambuco. After some difficulties over papers, they managed to escape and had six days of easy sailing to the mouth of the Amazon. Then came Port of Spain, the Antilles up to Puerto Rico, the Virgin Islands, Bermuda, and through the Sargasso Sea to the United States, arriving off Sandy Hook, New Jersey, in late May. They sailed up the Hudson, past the Statue of Liberty, and put in at the Seventy-ninth Street Landing, where a buoy was assigned to them. From the deck of *Lang Syne*, the Crowes looked up at the solid rows of apartment buildings and the traffic on the parkway, and then looked at each other, reached across the boom, and shook hands.

They spent the summer cruising Long Island Sound, visiting with the Johnsons, who had beaten them home by a year, and with their son, Steve, who had married one of the crew, Mary Booth, and now lived in Larchmont.

The Crowes had never seen television. Yacht-club friends arranged for them to see a replay of their arrival in New York, which had been covered by a battery of cameras. New York fascinated them mainly because it proved to be the yachting capital of the world. They also enjoyed a stay in New England waters. In August, they set sail for the south via the Intercoastal Waterways, traveling with other snowbirds heading for Florida. Along the way, they received word that they had been awarded the coveted Blue Water Medal of the Cruising Club of America.

From Florida, they made a leisurely visit to the Bahamas, then sailed for Jamaica, and on to Panama. Like many others before them, they complained of the rough treatment in the locks. They stopped at the Balboa Yacht Club, beached the vessel for a bottom painting, loaded supplies aboard for the last leg of the cruise. They got clearance for Los Angeles, visited ports in Central America and Mexico, Las Perlas Island, and Cocos. At the latter place, they anchored in Chatham Bay alongside a large diesel yacht from Gulfport, and loafed for several days. At Acapulco, where they put in for fuel, they encountered difficulties with authorities, but with the assistance of

Enrique, their friend who had sailed the *Barco de Oro* around the world—the first Mexican yacht to do so—they overcame.

On June 5, they saw their first North Pacific albatross. On June 12, they passed Santa Catalina and ran into the San Pedro Channel. They did not want to be "in" yet, until they could clean up the ship and get organized. An enterprising *Examiner* reporter, however, discovered *Lang Syne* anchored by using one of those pay telescopes at Point Fermin Park, and came out in a water taxi.

The next few months were spent in the Los Angeles area with family members, and cruising their old waters around Catalina. Finally, on March 15, 1952, they cut loose again and headed home to Honolulu. After a rough passage, they put in at Hilo for a few days, then went on again to *Lang Syne*'s birthplace on the beach at Waikiki.

In the lee of Diamond Head, sails were furled, a string of flags of all countries visited was run up, and the schooner was escorted into the basin by a parade of yachts with horns and whistles blowing, and leis of orchids, ginger blossoms, and fragrant carnations draped on the rigging.

The story of the Crowes' circumnavigation in *Lang Syne* is one of quiet competence by friendly, outgoing people, who planned and prepared thoroughly, had few untoward incidents, never took unnecessary chances, but never passed up an interesting port or anchorage.

As the cca put it in the Blue Water Medal citation:

"They cruised the waters of the world with no heroics and a minimum of misadventures. In its preparation and execution, the Crowes' voyage has exemplified outstandingly the meritorious seamanship to which the Blue Water Medal is dedicated."

⊷ 17 ⊶

Stornoway and the Good Samaritan

*All Wanderers on the sea are brothers, but this
one is a born gentleman, and a rare sailor.*[1]

THE 1952 COMPETITION FOR THE COVETED BLUE WATER
Medal of the Cruising Club of America included an unusually large
number of outstanding candidates, not the least of whom were
Carleton Mitchell of *Caribbee* and *Finistere* fame, who had won the
Transoceanic Pennant for his passage to England in 1952; Patrick
Ellam, who with Colin Mudie sailed the tiny *Sopranino* from Eng-
land to the United States in a remarkable passage; and a Dr. Davis,
who sailed the ketch *Miru* on a stormy voyage from Australia to
Boston.

When the winner was announced at the January club meeting, few
people had even heard of Alfred Petersen of Brooklyn, New York,
whose circumnavigation on the 40-year-old, 33-foot gaff cutter *Stornoway* had begun in New York in June 1948—one of the first postwar
voyages—and ended at the same place on August 18, 1952.

In fact, no one could even find him to present the award. He had
just married a Metropolitan Life secretary and taken a job as a crewman on another yacht. His *Stornoway*, in fact, was better known and
easier to find than the modest ex-machinist and lone sea wanderer
who sailed her.

Stornoway was a Colin Archer cutter scaled down to 33 feet overall by designer Albert Strange. She was built in 1926 by Dauntless Shipyard, Essex, Connecticut, of oak frames, longleaf yellow pine planking, and fir decks. The vessel was named for the main town of the Isle of Lewis in the Outer Hebrides west of Scotland. The original owner had been CCA member Lloyd Nichols.

The sail plan included a main of 350 square feet, jib, trysails, and twin staysails. The engine was a two-cylinder Palmer gasoline mill. For ballast, she carried 5,000 pounds of iron outside and 1,000 pounds of lead inside.

In 1948, World War II was still a recent memory among millions of G.I.s who had been rotated home on the point system, before the Cold War had really started and with Korea still two years away. The weary and already aging warriors who came home to get married, go to college, start businesses, and build dream homes in the suburbs mostly were in a rush to catch up and get back to normalcy. For a few, the dream home was a dream ship. One of these was Alfred Petersen, to whom the end of the war meant freedom to roam the seas, to visit exotic places, to come and go as he chose. A quiet and competent man, friendly and easy with company, but used to being alone, Petersen was Harry Pidgeon all over again.[2]

It was June, and now that he had *Stornoway* all spruced up and outfitted to his ideas—including headsails and twin staysails which made her self-steering much of the time—it was time to go. He sailed south to Oxford, Maryland, to complete final preparations, then continued on down the Intercoastal Waterway to Miami. In November, he sailed via the Windward Passage and Jamaica to Panama. There, *Stornoway* was measured, the canal dues paid, and a pilot was taken aboard for the passage.[3] From Balboa, Petersen sailed down to the Galápagos, then on the long downhill run to the Marquesas. From this popular yacht stop, he navigated through the dangerous Tuamotus to Tahiti, then on to New Zealand and Sydney, Australia.

Taking the classic route of the singlehanded circumnavigators, Petersen sailed north behind the Great Barrier Reef in the wake of Slocum and others and just ahead of the Crowes. He followed Robinson's route through Torres Strait and up through Indonesia.

Navigating the treacherous East India waters in the postwar period while dodging marauding gangs of pirates and guerillas left over from the wartime period was a challenge even to such voyagers as the Irving Johnsons, with large crews. For a singlehander like Petersen, it was a bold and hair-raising feat—ordinarily. But Petersen, whose skill as a navigator was even more precise than that of Gerbault (whose life had ended in a Japanese prison camp at Dili), shrugged it off. His route took him from Port Moresby to Timor, Kupang, Bali, Surabaja, Dakarta, Singapore, and across the Indian Ocean to Ceylon, then to the Red Sea, still following Robinson's track.

At Aden, Petersen entered the Red Sea, notorious for its adverse winds and currents, and uncharted reefs. He managed to reef crawl upward with no serious mishaps, until one night he ran aground while catnapping at the tiller. Going ashore to find help, he left *Stornoway* alone. When he returned, he found her stripped of everything movable by thieves.

The Red Sea passage had long been a dream of Petersen's. He had looked forward to it in spite of its hazards and blistering heat, rather than the Cape of Good Hope route usually taken by yachts. Now it seemed to have come to a disastrous end on a lonely reef in the Strait of Bag-el-Mandeb, along the desolate Yemen coast, and seven miles from the old town of Al Mukha where he had sought help while the thieves made off with compass, sextant, spare sails, food, supplies, and bedding.

Returning to Al Mukha, Petersen appealed to local officials, and not being able to speak a language they understood, he tried to draw pictures of a boat on a reef. He was then seized and thrown in jail for four days, as a suspicious character. Released from jail, he was able to hire a fishing vessel to help him. The ballast was taken off, the fuel and water tanks emptied. He then hired twenty Arab policemen, including some of the pirates who had robbed him, and *Stornoway* was pulled free and anchored in deep water eleven days after she went aground.[4]

Patching up the vessel, he made his way slowly across the Strait of Eritrea to the town of Assab and anchored while he settled up his bills and refitted. Final repairs and outfitting were made further up the coast at Massawa, where better facilities were available. By the time this had all been accomplished, Petersen was nearly a physical and nervous wreck, suffering from the strain and anxiety, from the crushing heat and dysentery, with running sores over his entire body. But rather than stay around longer, he started out on the 900-mile run to Suez.

Going through the canal, he stopped briefly at Port Said, and then sailed on to Cyprus, in company with the English voyager, Edward Poett, who was having trouble with his 13-ton cutter, *Kefaya*. Petersen left *Stornoway* at Cyprus, and sailed with his friend to Nice on the cumbersome *Kefaya*. Returning to Cyprus, he picked up *Storno-*

way, and then made a difficult 34-day passage to Gibraltar against head winds and short steep seas. From there, he sailed to Dakar, already delayed about five months due to his Good Samaritan deeds.

At Dakar, he found his friend Poett again, seriously ill. Again, he tied up *Stornoway* and helped Poett sail *Kefaya* from Nice, where the hard-to-manage cutter had been left, down to Dakar.[5]

Petersen said good-bye to Poett in French West Africa finally, and sailed to New York in fifty days nonstop, completing his circumnavigation in four years and four months, and then sank into anonymity again.

Had not his friend Poett become worried, Petersen may not even have come to the attention of the Cruising Club awards committee. The Englishman wrote in a letter to *Yachting* magazine:

". . . by helping me, Petersen was seriously handicapped in his own voyage with respect to seasonal hurricanes. But that was Al Petersen, a gentleman by heart and by instinct. Your readers are too experienced not to fully realize that what has gone into the handling of his small boat is real first-class seamanship. Good sailors are usually fine men. Don't you find it so?"

When located by cca, Petersen was now married to Marjorie, a New York secretary, a former dinghy sailor who had won many trophies, and one of the few women at that time to have earned the rating of Navigator of the U.S. Power Squadron.

Although experienced in small boats, Marjorie had never been out of sight of land. In 1955, after two years of marriage, during which Al had seen enough of life on the beach, he said to her one day:

"Let's go for a sail on the ocean."

"Oh, no," she replied, "I couldn't."

Why not? Because she had never done so. All the more reason why she should.[6]

So they departed on *Stornoway* for a long cruise to Bermuda, which Al had missed on his circumnavigation, followed by a leisurely visit to many out-of-the-way places. During this voyage, Marjorie discovered that she was incurably susceptible to *mal de mer*, but did not let it conquer her. Back in New York, they worked ashore again. Al, a machinist, and Marjorie, a secretary, had no difficulty finding ready employment wherever they went.

Thinking of all the places Al had missed on his solo voyage, they prepared for another long trip, refitting *Stornoway* and putting aboard supplies for a year. Finally they departed Sheepshead Bay for the short run to the Atlantic Highlands on June 10. The weather was foggy and unsettled. Two friends, Jean Lacombe, and John Pflieger of the Slocum Society, came down to see them off in a motorboat loaded with champagne and food for a final banquet. At last they got away, motoring out of the fog to the Ambrose Lightship where sails were set for the 3,000-mile passage to Lisbon, with *Stornoway* self-steering most of the way, and the voyage without incident, except for a near collision with a large metal pontoon.

From Lisbon, they went on to Marseilles, Monaco, and the Côte d'Azur or Blue Coast. In December, they sailed to Bonifacio, Malta, Tunisia, and back to Gibraltar.

The return trip was made across the Atlantic from the Canaries to Barbados, and home via Antigua and Savannah. They had sailed thirteen thousand miles in safety and reasonable comfort, and visited 85 ports and anchorages in nine European and African countries, taking almost two years to the day.

On this, as on all the *Stornoway*'s voyages, planning was thorough and meticulous. Marjorie and Al were able to reduce living aboard a small vessel, not as big as some of the modern motor homes on the U.S. freeways, to an art—regardless of where they anchored. Marjorie proved to be a perfect balance wheel for the somewhat shy and retiring Al. Enthusiastic and outgoing, her personality complemented his. Wherever they went, they fitted in easily with the local yachts people and townfolk, seldom had difficulties with port officials, and always were self-sufficient.

In 1966, they left again on another long cruise, this time down through the Panama Canal and up to San Francisco. In the summer of 1970, *Stornoway* tied up at the small-boat harbor in Sausalito, California, after having completed a long and leisurely circumnavigation of the Pacific, taking three years to reach Japan via the Marquesas, Tuamotus, Tahiti, and the East Indies.

Of the last stormy leg to San Francisco, Marjorie wrote:

> *Well, we finally made it—but it took 70 awfully long days, about 45 of them very unpleasant indeed. Gale force winds, tremendous curling seas, fog, cold—that was our lot. A breaking wave smashed in Lewis,[7] the dinghy, a total loss, we fear. Another big one hurled me across the cabin breaking my upper left arm. This was only three weeks out, so I had seven more of jouncing (although we did have five days of calm and some moderate going toward the finish). The battens and sail ties we used as*

*a splint did a good job, though. X rays, nine weeks later,
showed that the break did not quite come together, but
I grew a bridge of bone right across, more bone than I
needed actually which accounts for a bump in my arm,
but this will absorb in about four months. Therapy—
only six sessions, although I still have to keep exercising
—has done wonders—wish it would fix up Lewis, too.*[8]

In 1972, they again said good-bye to friends and headed south, along
the west coast of Mexico and Central America, through the Panama
Canal, like true wanderers of the sea, heading once more for the
Mediterranean.

In a letter from Panama, Marjorie wrote:

> *We arrived at Cristobal . . . and are headed for the
> Mediterranean, eastern part this time, and hope to reach
> there by late summer, cruise for a short time and then
> find a winter haven. We have another book at the pub-
> lishers,* Trade Winds and Monsoons, *and tells of our tour
> of the Pacific—the islands, New Zealand, Australia, In-
> donesia, Singapore, Manila, Hong Kong, and Japan,
> thence return to San Francisco. We also did many articles
> for the American magazine* Motorboating *and the Aus-
> tralian* Modern Boating, *during this time. We will soon
> be leaving for Port au Prince, having some chores to do,
> stores to collect, and securing five-day stays from customs
> and immigration. . . .*[9]

Thus *Stornoway*, modest, beamy, but comfortable, graceful, and
salty, sails on, the world-wandering home for the Petersens, just as
Lang Syne has been for the Crowes, on the oceans of the world. It is
all they have ever asked for.

⤳ 18 ⤶

The Proper Wanderers

Yesterday afternoon, Mr. and Mrs. Eric Hiscock left Yarmouth, Isle of Wight, on the first stage of a voyage round the world in their 30-foot yacht Wanderer III. *The voyage is expected to take three years.*[1]

To LIVE ON THE ISLE OF WIGHT AND NOT TO BE A FARMER or make one's living from the sea is unthinkable. It is even more unthinkable to live on Wight and not own or sail a yacht. This oyster-shaped island lies just off Southampton Water, separated from the mainland by the famous yachting grounds, the Solent, and provides a buffer between the mainland harbors and the English Channel. Directly south and about sixty miles away is Cherbourg and the Normandy peninsula. About the same distance to the east is the prime meridian of Greenwich, which separates the globe into east and west longitude. From here, it is said, you are already halfway to anywhere.

At Cowes, on the inner side, on the Medina River, is one of the most famous yachting centers in the world, and the home of the Royal Yacht Squadron, and the scene of the historic race in 1851 between the *America* and 14 British vessels around the Isle of Wight for the 100-guinea prize now known as America's Cup.[2] On the western tip lies Yarmouth, at the mouth of the narrow inlet.

Eric and Susan Hiscock lived on the island at Yarmouth, and like everyone else were close to the sea. Eric's first boat was an 18-foot sloop, built in the 1890s and named *Wanderer*. She was lean of bow and fat in the haunches and was a bitch to sail in any kind of a breeze. But she was all Eric could afford when he bought her for $125, and before he got rid of her for another, she very nearly drowned him.

The internationally famous Jack Laurent Giles was just getting started as a yacht designer when Eric approached him to build *Wanderer II*. Giles had under construction then the first of his famous *Vertue* line of fast, seaworthy 25-footers which have since sailed all the oceans of the world in safety. Hiscock could not afford a boat this big, so Giles reduced the model to fit his pocketbook. The result was a fast and handy little sloop of 21-foot waterline and 7-foot beam. In her, Hiscock cruised extensively in channel and European waters. Then, when he and Susan were married, they made a honeymoon cruise to the Azores and back along the coast of Spain and France. *Wanderer II*, even though it did not have an engine, was a proper yacht, and gave the couple some of their most nostalgic sailing experiences. It also taught them to be expert sailors under all conditions.

As is usually the case, the Azores voyage did not satisfy their craving for wandering—it only stimulated it. Now they wanted to see more of the world, but in a larger yacht so they could carry more stores and water. So they went back to Jack Giles and he drew up *Wanderer III*, an enlarged *Vertue*, 30 feet overall, with a waterline of 26 feet 6 inches and a beam of 8 feet 6 inches. Like all Giles boats, she was narrow, but not tender as was *Wanderer II*. She was built of iroko and steambent oak frames, copper-sheathed and rigged as a Bermudian sloop instead of a gaff cutter. She also had a 4-horsepower engine, and a fuel capacity of 50 miles.[3]

For the next 17 years, *Wanderer III* roamed the oceans of the world, the Hiscocks becoming the first couple to make two circumnavigations. Early in his sailing career, Hiscock had begun to write accounts of his cruises for the yachting magazines, illustrating them with his own photographs. The honeymoon cruise to the Azores provided material that helped pay for the trip. On the first circumnavigation, the Hiscocks also helped defray expenses with articles and photography. *Wanderer III*, and later *Wanderer IV*, was equipped with a darkroom. The several books that resulted from these voyages became best-sellers among yachting and cruising folk.[4] The income from these, plus fees for lectures upon their return to England, prompted them to sell their home and cut their ties permanently with land-living. On the second circumnavigation, they filmed the voyage for a television documentary, which earned them enough to build *Wanderer IV*, a large and commodious 49-foot steel ketch.[5]

At the time they began their first circumnavigation, the Hiscocks were only allowed to take £25 of foreign currency a year out of England, so it was necessary to stock up as much as possible before leaving. *Wanderer III* was launched one lovely spring day in 1952, with Susan breaking the bottle of wine over her bows. Shakedown cruises were made from Yarmouth, and around Ireland, seeking out the worst weather and sea conditions to test the new vessel. Then the fitting out began. When all the books, photographic supplies, canned foods, and materials for a year were aboard, *Wanderer III* rode six inches lower in the water than Jack Giles had designed her.

Departure was made from Yarmouth on July 24, 1952, and after a lumpy voyage that included stops in many out-of-the-way places in France, Spain, and Portugal, they arrived on October 2 at La Palma, a distance sailed of 1,857 miles. At Cascais, near Lisbon, they mingled for the first time with that elite society of yachting people, the ocean vagabonds and their little ship-homes. Waiting at Cascais for the proper season were Peter and Anne Pye in *Moonraker*, and the Dutch yacht *Harry*, both bound for British Columbia on the Northwest coast of America, and the *Viking*, with the charming Swedish couple, Sten and Brita Holmdahl, who like the Hiscocks were embarked on their first circumnavigation, and who would be encountered frequently in exotic places during the next few years.

At Cascais, too, the Hiscocks got their first taste of official arrogance and harassment by police, which came as a shock to these gentle people.

From Cascais to Madeira, they enjoyed a near-perfect sail—long days of bright sun in a clear blue sky, at night a sky brilliant with stars and a wake full of blazing phosphorescence. It was almost lyrical.

In Madeira, they caught up on their writing and photography, maintenance on the boat, and enjoyed the local yachting society. On October 11, they departed for their first long ocean passage, to the West Indies, timed to avoid the hurricane season. The voyage took twenty-five days, and for the most part was a delightful cruise in spite of the heat and the often violent rolling under twin headsails. In the cool of evening, they would spend their twilight hour together in the cockpit over a drink, talking of many things, watching for that elusive moment when the sun suddenly goes down in the west with a green flash, then the first view of Venus between the luffs of the twins while Mars rose astern, and everything in the world was at peace.

The only thing to disturb this tranquillity, Hiscock observed wryly, was the motion of a narrow boat running under twins in a seaway. The human body can adjust to almost any inconvenience or discomfort but this.

They cruised among the West Indies until December 28, when they sailed from Antigua to Cristobal, Panama. On January 15, they made their first canal transit. Their first encounter with American officialdom was pleasant. The brisk and efficient officer filling out the form asked Hiscock's age. It was forty-four, he answered. The official then wrote down thirty-nine for Mrs. Hiscock. "How did you know?" Eric asked. "Well," said the official, "no dame is over thirty-nine."

The passage through the notorious locks cost them $3.75, including the services of the pilot. But even with the help of Sten and Brita Holmdahl, the transit was somewhat of an ordeal. Once in the Pacific, they tied up at the Balboa Yacht Club, and joined the crowd of sea wanderers that included Buzz and June Champion on their Hanna ketch, *Little Bear*. With the help of new American friends, they spent a busy ten days making preparations, and were invited to a "brawl" at the American Legion Club, where, to get in, they had to climb a ladder and slide down a wooden chute.

They had intended to visit the Galápagos for water and fresh provisions, but Ecuadorean red tape and the large fees demanded changed their minds. They confided to a friendly canal pilot that they might stop there anyway, but the pilot warned them not to do so as many fishing vessels and yachts had been seized even on minor technicalities. The Hiscocks then decided to go directly to the Marquesas, 4,000 miles down the trades and the longest passage of their career. Leaving January 26, they arrived at Nuku Hiva on March 4 in a flawless passage.

At 10:30 P.M. on the thirty-sixth day at sea, when they saw Ua Huka rising under a new moon, they thrilled at their introduction at last to the enchanted South Pacific islands. The track up to this point was fairly standard for voyagers. From here on, they went directly to Tahiti, and after a long stay in the Society Islands, sailed to Pago Pago, then to Fiji, cruising among these islands for a month or more, and then went on to spend the winter (summer there) cruising the delightful waters of New Zealand.

On January 12, they crossed from Whangaroa to Sydney, where they spent several months. On June 9, they departed up the coast of Queensland inside the Barrier Reef, went through Torres Strait, and continued on to Thursday Island.

They crossed their third ocean, the Indian, without the usual gales. Christmas Island came up on July 4. From here, following Slocum's classic route, they made Keeling-Cocos on July 17. After a month here, they sailed on to Rodriguez, arriving September 7. After a short stay, they went on to Mauritius, where they waited until October 2 before departing for Durban. They rounded the bight of South Africa from December 31 to January 17, with a stop at Port Elizabeth. Three months were spent in Cape Town. On March 15, they sailed for Robben Island, and then on to St. Helena and Ascension. From Ascension, they made their longest passage, fifty-one days and eleven hours, to Horta, Azores. On June 22, they departed Horta, and arrived off England on July 6. From July 10 to 13, they sailed around to Yarmouth and home.

The short passage from Horta to the Lizard, only 1,200 miles, would normally be no problem for these new world travelers, except that now they experienced their first taste of "channel fever." Anxious to get home, they were becalmed off St. Mawes. Finally, they made an anchorage where customs cleared them and old friends welcomed them to home waters. After a short rest, they started around to the Isle of Wight, passing the familiar landmarks of Start, Portland, Anvil, and the Needles, and then *Wanderer III*—now a true and tested sea wanderer, her brown sails faded by tropical suns, her ropes bleached white by the spray of three oceans, and flying the ensigns of all the countries she had visited from the starboard yard—slipped quietly into Yarmouth harbor, concluding a delightful 32,000-mile circumnavigation.

The next voyage of *Wanderer III* was by truck at Christmas, 1955, to the Second National Boat Show at Olympia, at the request of the designers and builders, and in collaboration with the Beaverbrook newspapers, for an exhibition of British boat-building skill.

There, for ten days, Eric and Susan, with the gentleness, patience, and good feeling they have for their fellow man, stood eleven hours a day as the crowds filed by to have a look at this famous little ship and talk to the owners. They answered each question, no matter how silly, for they understood how it is with people who have secret dreams. . . .

In order to escape from the pressures of lectures and writing assignments, and from their new notoriety, the Hiscocks sailed once more in July 1959 for their second circumnavigation, going east-about via Panama and the Suez Canal. In 1965, they crossed the Atlantic and cruised around the United States for a couple of years.

Now, with royalties coming in steadily, lecture offers plentiful, and a new source of income from television—to say nothing of worldwide prestige and a Blue Water Medal from the Cruising Club of America—they felt that they had outgrown their faithful *Wanderer III*. They sold her reluctantly and acquired *Wanderer IV*, designed by S. M. Van der Meer and built of steel in Holland in 1968. She was 49 feet overall, ketch-rigged, and had a 61-horsepower Ford diesel. She was first exhibited in an English boat show, then sailed to the West Coast of North America via the West Indies and Panama.[6]

From there, the Hiscocks sailed to New Zealand to cruise those delightful waters at their leisure. At this writing, they were still there, living aboard *Wanderer IV*, which they found too large for them, a bit of a maintenance problem, and a sluggish sailor under light winds, in spite of all her modern conveniences and appointments. Much of this, no doubt, was pure nostalgia for their home of seventeen years, the handy little *Wanderer III*.

The Hiscocks did not go to sea to experience hair-raising adventures. All of their voyages were carefully planned and flawlessly executed, with few surprises, and in the proper way for a middle-aged British couple seeking only personal tranquillity and the freedom of long ocean passages. In their quiet and competent way, without the fanfare of a Chichester or a Blyth, they came to epitomize, perhaps more than any yachtsmen in British history, the proper seagoing citizen.

CHAPTER

❧ 19 ❧

Because It Was There

*It has been left to Miles and Beryl to tell us
just where the limits of safety lie. At the risk of
offending them, however, I must stress the fact
that these are most unusual people, lest ordinary yachtsmen should be tempted to follow
them down towards Cape Horn.*[1]

YOKOHAMA AND TWENTY YEARS LATER, THE TALL, ERECT,
craggy man with the mass of bushy graying hair, and his tall and
energetic wife, left their yacht, *Tzu Hang*, and motored up to the
Defense Force Headquarters in Tokyo. They found that the colonel,
who was writing the history of the war in Burma, was a small, precise, and meticulously dressed man who spoke English well.

The couple told him of their mission: to return the sword of surrender to a general whose name they could not remember, but who
was chief of staff of the Japanese Thirty-third Corps and later of the
Japanese army in Burma.

"Ah," said the colonel, "that would be General Sawamoto. You
have good fortune, for he has only come up to Tokyo today. He is at
the officers' club now. I will ring up the club and tell him you have
brought his sword."

The sword had been a prize of war, taken by Brigadier Miles
Smeeton, whose brigade was in contact with the enemy in Burma at
the time of the surrender. Smeeton had been ordered to give the
surrendering forces their preliminary instructions, which were handed
to General Sawamoto, and hostilities formally ceased.

Later, Smeeton was in charge of the large number of Japanese prisoners in the area, and when the generals officially surrendered their swords, he was given that of General Sawamoto. When Smeeton left Burma, the sword went along with him, rolled up in his bedding, and was left with his other military and war memorabilia with his sister in Yorkshire, where it remained for the next eighteen years. The sword had been brought out to the Orient again with Miles and Beryl Smeeton on *Tzu Hang*, their only weapon on this leg of their circumnavigation. War and the military life had been left in the far distant past. The Smeetons wanted nothing left around to remind them.

Arrangements were made over the telephone to meet the General and his wife at the Hong Kong and Shanghai Bank in Yokohama and then go down to the yacht for the presentation. The meeting was held on schedule aboard *Tzu Hang*, the General's wife dressed in *obi* and *gaetas*, accompanied by a merry, roguish interpreter who had been a senior intelligence officer in the India-Burma area, and the man behind the Indian politician and defector, Subhas Chandra Bhose.

There was some small talk and tea, then came the formalities. The General read a long letter of gratitude, interpreted by "the rogue." They both bowed. Smeeton then got the sword out of the forward cabin and presented it formally, with more bowing, and a great deal of emotion. The General recognized it as the sword given him by the Emperor, and of greater personal value than his other sword, a Samarai.

Before the guests left, the General gave Miles a silver cigarette case, and Miles thought that he was a good man and now was glad he had gone to all the trouble to return the sword. A few months later, back in Canada, Smeeton had word that the General had died.

Born in Yorkshire in 1906, Miles Smeeton went to Wellington and Sandhurst, then joined the army, first serving in the Green Howards and later in Hodson's Horse in the Indian army. His army career in the halcyon pre–World War II days took him to many parts of the world. When war broke out in the east, with the Japanese attacks of early December 1941, Smeeton had already served with distinction in the Western Desert where he won the M.C. Sent to the Burma Theater, he rose to brigadier and was awarded the D.S.O.

His wife, Beryl, grew up an army brat—her father and brothers were soldiers. She was one of those indomitable English ladies who are completely unflappable and manage to find themselves at home in Tibet or Patagonia. She had traveled widely in Russia, Persia, China, and South America, and had written extensively about her travels. Married in 1938, for the next few years she and Miles lived the colonial soldier's life, mostly in India. They were active people, both keen for mountain climbing, as are many bluewater yachtsmen. Together they climbed Tirich Mir, one of the Himalayans, where Beryl went higher than any other woman had previously climbed.

The war over, the Smeetons, like many other British colonials, were wearied by the long conflict and the tensions, and retired in Canada, where they bought a farm on Salt Spring Island, British Columbia. By 1950, the damp and unexciting life on a British Columbia stump farm had begun to pall. The Smeetons took a year's absence, went home to England for a visit, and there discovered for sale the graceful Bermudian ketch with the fascinating name of *Tzu Hang*.

Tzu Hang, they learned years later in Japan, meant "the wooden ship of Kwan Yin" or "under the protection of Kwan Yin"or "Kannon Sama." (Kwan Yin and Kannon Sama were the Chinese and Japanese names for the same goddess.)

Here was a dream ship to lure the most unromantic. In a ship like this, one could go anywhere in the world, and in the 1950s there was a great awakening among yachtsmen to the romance of bluewater voyages. Many people, restless with the letdown of the postwar period, and still nursing childhood dreams of sailing around the world, had begun to haunt the boatshops and moorages. It doesn't hurt to look, does it?

Neither Miles nor Beryl had ever sailed a boat before, but they fell in love with *Tzu Hang* immediately, perhaps because of the fetching name. So they bought her, and with Clio, their only daughter, then only eleven and still in school, they packed up and sailed *Tzu Hang* back to British Columbia via the Azores and West Indies, and Panama and the west coast of North America. They learned their seamanship, navigation, and meteorology en route, and at the same time gave Clio her regular daily classroom lessons.

Back in Canada (they regarded themselves now as Canadians, but were about as much Canadian as Jean Gau was American), they settled into a life divided between the farm, the local social whirl of Victoria, and sailing the coastal waters.[2]

In 1955, the Smeetons could not resist the call any longer. *Tzu Hang* was a ship made for sailing to exotic places, not to be moored to a British Columbia stump farm. They sold the farm, loaded Clio and their belongings aboard, and sailed to Australia via the United States west coat and Hawaii. There they spent the remainder of the year fitting out the vessel for a passage to England via the old clipper route along the Roaring Forties and around Cape Horn.[3] Not many small boats had attempted this up until then, and of those that had, few had survived. There had been *Pandora*, the *Spray* copy, which had been rolled over and dismasted; and Conor O'Brien on *Saoirse*, who made it look so easy; and, of course, Vito Dumas, who had circumnavigated around all three capes while Miles had been fighting in the desert war.[4]

Back in San Francisco, before crossing the Pacific, they had encountered a fellow Yorkshireman, John Guzzwell, who had also migrated to Canada where he built the tiny *Trekka* and was single-handing around the world. *Trekka* and *Tzu Hang* sailed to Hawaii together, cruised there among the islands, and then headed for Australia and New Zealand. For the Cape Horn passage, the Smeetons sent Clio to England by air, and enlisted Guzzwell as a crew member. *Trekka* was hauled out and stored in New Zealand.

On December 22, 1956, *Tzu Hang* cast off from the moorage in the Yarra River at Melbourne. The course took them southeast past Tasmania to about 170° longitude, then around the south side of New Zealand, along the fiftieth parallel, which they followed closely during most of the war.

Weeks later, nearing the region of the Horn, they encountered a survival storm. While Beryl was at the tiller, a giant wave pitchpoled *Tzu Hang*, throwing Beryl into the sea and dismasting the vessel. The doghouse top was gone, the interior a shambles. Somehow Smeeton and Guzzwell managed to rescue Beryl, who was badly injured. Then, with great skill and courage, drawing from their enormous reserves of discipline, the three made repairs, rigged a jury sail, and limped into a Chilean port for repairs.[5]

With the help of the English colony, the Chilean navy, and Guzzwell, who was a first-rate cabinetmaker, the Smeetons rebuilt *Tzu Hang*. When the work was nearly done, Guzzwell left to continue his own adventures on *Trekka*. Had it not been for him, they might not have survived the dismasting, but they could not ask him to stay on any longer.

On Christmas Eve, 1957, Miles and Beryl were again alone in *Tzu Hang*, boiling along under twin jibs and reefed mizzen in the boisterous Southern Ocean, about three hundred miles off the Chil-

ean coast and five hundred miles off the entrance to the Strait of
Magellan. It had been a lonely day, and they were somewhat depressed. They had their evening cocktail and settled down for the
night.

The next morning, they set the twins early and opened Christmas
presents at breakfast, finding bottles of Vermouth and Pisco, cigarettes, and cookies. The barometer was still falling, and soon the
wind was up to Force 7. By midday, it was Force 8. They drank to
Clio's health and to friends. They ate lunch in the doghouse below
the half-open hatch. In the afternoon, *Tzu Hang* was leaping from
crest to valley. First they had to shorten sail, and finally hand them
entirely. They secured for the night and went below while their ship,
unattended under her little storm jib, reeled off the miles south
through the dark night, the mugs shaking on the hooks and the stove
rocking in its gimbals.

They could not sleep. They lay in the bunks, reading and now and
then getting up to check. At daylight, Beryl took the helm. The
barometer was down to 28.8. By 10 A.M., the gale was full-blown, and
the glass was at 28.6.

Back at Talcahuano, navy men had told them, "Don't let the tigres
get you." The sea now took on a whitish look, streaked and furrowed
with foam, with wide white tops roaring down in a mass of spume.
They lashed the helm and went below to lie in the bunks and read,
or watch the seas through the doghouse windows. Miles suggested
they put out a sea anchor. Beryl thought a moment and then said it
was a bit late, was it not? Besides, they had never tried a sea anchor
under such conditions. They did not think of using oil, although they
had some spare engine oil handy. As they settled back again, the cat
Pwe went from one to the other to be petted. They clutched the
sides of their bunks anxiously as each spiller roared down on them
and struck the hull. The cat was unaware of the danger, and her calm
and unconcern served to calm the Smeetons.

At 4 P.M., Miles thought of making tea. The storm had been
raging for ten hours but now the glass seemed steadier. There was
relief with the thought that it might soon be over. Just then, *Tzu
Hang* heeled over sharply as everything went dark again. Instead of
panic, Miles found himself cursing.

Not again! Not again!

Then there was total darkness. He was struggling under water. He
found Beryl in the water and together they struggled up. The dog-

house was still there, but the hatch was gone, along with the mainmast. On deck, everything was a jumble of broken spars and rigging. Below, everything was a mess, too.

"It's the same again," said Miles.

"I'll see to the jib," said Beryl.

This second capsizing and dismasting occurred at about 48°30'S and almost due west of the Strait of Magellan, in the same general area as the first one, a year previously.

Once again they set about, first to save the ship, then to make repairs, and finally to rig a jury sail and limp back to Valparaiso. This time, they simply loaded *Tzu Hang* aboard an English freighter and sailed back as passengers via the Panama Canal. Home in England, they hurried off to see Clio. The first words she said were: "Are you going to try again?"

"Once was enough," said Miles. "Twice is too many," said Beryl.

At least for the time being.

After a winter tied up in Paris, writing a book, they returned to England to ship a new diesel engine.[6] With the help of designer H. S. Rouse, they added a new doghouse, bow and stern pulpits, an improved rig with slightly larger sail area, and made other changes. At Falmouth, Clio rejoined them and they sailed August 2, 1960, from the Helford River on the first leg of their next long journey.

They had no particular itinerary, except to go east-about. They stopped at Spain and Portugal, visiting and exploring ashore. From Gibraltar, they called in frequently along the south coast to Cartagena and Ibiza, where they spent the winter. From Minorca, they called at African ports, then went to Malta, through the canal with some difficulty from officials, then down through the Red Sea to sweltering Aden. Reef crawling, they sailed the north shore of the Gulf of Aden to Ras, then picked up the northeast monsoon and ran down to Socotra. From there, they cruised down the east coast of Africa to Mombasa, headed east to the Seychelles, then to Diégo Garcia, and reached down across the southeast trades to Rodriguez, Mauritius, and Réunion. From here, they sailed to Durban, stopping at exotic places along the way. After some time in South Africa, they went up to Mozambique, crossed to Madagascar and went north again to the Seychelles. At various times, they shipped friends aboard as crew members.

From the Seychelles, they beat to Addu Atoll, north of Chagos, then to Ceylon and from Colombo to the Nicobars. Their unusual route took them on to Penang, Singapore, Malaya—places long familiar to the couple—which they now experienced in the context of postwar politics. They were in Sarawak when the news came of the assassination of President Kennedy.

Taking the ship route to Sibu, they found the Ghurkas fighting the guerillas, and met a famous lady war correspondent who was doing a story on them. Since Miles had fought with the Ghurkas, and Beryl had been with them on her mobile canteen in the Burma war, they were allowed to go along in the helicopter back into the bush to the encampment.

From Malaysia, they sailed across the Sulu Sea to the Philippines, winding through that archipelago to Okinawa. Wintering in Hokkaido, Japan, they hauled *Tzu Hang* out and refitted her. On May 15, they sailed from Kushiro, bound for the Kurils, the Aleutians, and British Columbia. On board were Clio; Henry Combe, a friend; Kochi, the dog, and Pwe, the cat. They put in at Attu to the astonishment of the lonely U.S. Coast Guard post there. They landed opposite the loran station and hiked across on foot. The first voice they heard was a sailor yelling, "Hey, you guys, there are two broads and a man in a red coat coming over the hill!"

They were entertained here and at numerous other outlying posts along the chain, becoming one of the first yachts to explore these fascinating waters. They had written the U.S. Defense Department for permission to enter Dutch Harbor, but had not had a reply. As they arrived, they saw a truck coming down to the pier. It was a man named George Wright and a couple of helpers. He shouted across to them that he had just finished reading Annie Van de Wiele's book, and looked up to see *Tzu Hang* entering the harbor.[7]

At Cold Bay, they encountered an unfriendly and aggressively combative female postmaster, who was also part-time customs official, who told them that *Tzu Hang* had entered U.S. waters illegally. They were advised by friendly fishermen, however, to go to Sand Point in the Shumagins which had a port of entry for Canadians.[8] There they were warmly welcomed and helped through the red tape, but received orders to report to the customs officer in Juneau. The trip across the Gulf of Alaska was marred by a feeling of impending doom. At Ketchikan, however, they reported by radio. By now, the news of their plight had become widely known. Although they were technically liable for a fine of up to $3,000, they were let off the hook for only the price of a telephone call. From Ketchikan, they entered Canada again at Prince Rupert.

The next year was spent trying to decide what to do next, and in the end, the call of the wild goose flying south got to them. They packed up and headed out the Strait of Juan de Fuca, past Cape Flattery, and down the west coast, stopping at San Francisco, Los Angeles, San Diego, the Mexican islands, and Acajutla in San Salvador, where they were arrested and taken to port by two trigger-happy gendarmes and had to buy their way out of another customs mess. They stopped once more at Punta Arenas in Costa Rica, went on to Balboa, through the Canal and on to Portobelo and Jamaica, where Miles had once served some time.

From Jamaica, they went to the Grand Caymans, through the Florida Straits and up the U.S. coast to Charleston. By now, through their books and articles, they were world-famous among yachtsmen. The Smeetons were lionized at every stop. They were guests ashore at the lovely tidewater Delaware mansion of Henry Du Pont. They were invited by the prestigious Cruising Club of America to join their annual summer cruise to the Bras d'Or Lakes and Newfoundland, and were nearly overwhelmed by the yachting communities of New York and New England.[9]

From Nantucket, they sailed with a loose fleet of yachts to Nova Scotia, then to St. Peter's and Bras d'Or Lakes on Cape Breton Island. From Sydney, they crossed Cabot Strait to Newfoundland, then continued on to Belle Isle and across the Atlantic via Iceland and the Hebrides to England.

They had, at last, completed a long, unplanned circumnavigation east-about.

Now it was 1968, and Clio was married and had a nine-year-old daughter. With her husband, Alex, and the new grandchild of the Smeetons, they came down to Yarmouth to visit. Somehow, Miles and Beryl felt cast adrift after almost two decades of wandering the oceans of the world. They had been thinking for some time of returning to Canada. They were also remembering their two unsuccessful attempts at Cape Horn. *Tzu Hang* was ready to go. They did not want to try it alone, however, so they enlisted Bob Nance, brother of Bill Nance, who had sailed *Cardinal Vertue* around the three capes alone. They had met him two years before as a crew member on Andy Whall's thirty-foot Australian sloop *Carronade*. He was twenty-six then, tall, broad-shouldered, and robust, a typical Aussie ready to try anything.

Soon Bob arrived with a large roll of charts. *Tzu Hang* had been given a new coat of red paint. Sailing on August 19 from Yarmouth, they went to Spain, then to the Cape Verdes, and across the South

Atlantic to Montevideo. From here, they started the rugged loop of 50°S to 50°S as had Al Hansen on *Mary Jane* years before. They remembered that Al Hansen had been lost, wrecked on the Chiloé coast.

On December 11, they were off the entrance to the Strait. On the thirteenth, they passed Staten Island. On December 15, they were on the latitude of Cape Horn, and on the eighteenth they passed close to that misty rock just as the weather cleared enough to see it and take pictures. On December 17, they were south of Diego Ramírez, and on the twenty-first in approximately the same location as they had been on their second dismasting years before. By the end of December, they were well up toward Juan Fernández. After stopping at Talcahuano again, their old refitting port, they sailed to Nuka Hiva. They had an easy passage to Hilo and spent several weeks cruising the islands.

Suddenly Beryl came down with a severe intestinal attack, requiring an emergency operation. Had this occurred only a few weeks earlier, it would have been fatal. It was something to think about.

Leaving Oahu on June 5, they made an easy passage to Victoria, arriving June 29. In British Columbia again, they sold their beloved *Tzu Hang* to Bob Nance, who went to work in Canada to pay for it.[10] Then the Smeetons disappeared for a time, showing up in the mountains of Alberta, far from the sea. This time, they had swallowed the anchor.[11]

20

The Saga of the White Seal

*Once upon a time, there was a white seal who
lived with all the other seals among the icebergs
of the South Atlantic, happily and without fear.
Then one day a ship appeared among the ice
flows and all the seals swam out to greet it—and
all but this one, who escaped the eyes of the
hunters, were slaughtered. And forever after,
the white seal roamed the oceans of the world,
looking for a safe place to live.[1]*

GERRY TROBRIDGE GREW UP IN JOHANNESBURG, SOUTH
Africa, in the 1930s, with a restless curiosity about the world, and a
hope of someday building his own dream ship. As a child, he had
listened enthralled as his father read bedtime stories to him. One of
his favorites was Kipling's tale of the white seal.

Mechanically talented, Gerry served an apprenticeship as a metalworker as the uncertainties of war grew stronger each day. Finally, he
enlisted in a South African infantry battalion and found himself
heading north for the battlefields.

In the 1930s, like many other lads, he had been exposed to the
wonderful little ocean-roaming ketches from the board of John G.
Hanna, the Dunedin, Florida, genius, and had followed the exploits
of many a *Tahiti* or *Carol* across the pages of the leading yachting
publications. While still in the army, in 1943, he purchased a set of
plans for the 30-foot *Tahiti*,[2] and carried them with him everywhere

the battalion was sent in North Africa and Europe. At every opportunity, he would haul them out and dream over the lines.[3]

By the time he was demobbed after the war, he had already decided to build *Tahiti*'s larger sister, *Carol*.[4] Being a metalworker, he also decided it would have to be of steel and not wood, which meant redesigning the vessel. He first wrote to Hanna, who understood such things as few naval architects do, and exchanged a new set of *Carol* drawings for the old battered up *Tahiti* plans. Gerry then bought the lot next door to his parents' house, poured a 15 by 40 concrete slab to work on, and enrolled in a correspondence course to learn the basics of yacht design for the sole purpose of converting Hanna's original lines into a chine hull so that a metal skin could be developed on them.

Again, with straightforward audacity, he sent *his* drawings to Hanna for checking. Hanna gave his approval, but not much encouragement for the use of steel instead of wood. Gerry then sent the plans to J. Murray Watts, one of the leading U.S. designers of steel vessels, and got his favorable opinion.

By August 1946, Trobridge was making up a new table of offsets and laying down full-size lines. By January 1947, he had the keel and frames set up. About two years later, the hull and deck were plated. Two more years, in August 1951, and he had the cabin on, the spars made, the interior roughed in, and the boat ready to launch. It had not been easy. Boat building is a tedious job, especially when you have to do it in your spare time while holding down a regular job to earn a living. He suffered the inevitable delays, the long weeks of doubt, depression, and discouragement when he could not stand the sight of that skeleton out in the yard that never ceased to demand attention and energy.

But gradually all the interminable details were sorted out, the dream ship took final form, and his spirits and enthusiasm rose along with it. Once during the construction, he fell and injured his back. While confined to bed, he studied celestial navigation. When he broke his arm, he used his convalescence to take care of light chores he could handle with one wing. Trobridge had not only grown up with his dream, but with the single-minded purpose and indomitable nature needed for a project of this kind.

Then came time for launching and christening. The family and the neighbors gathered one Sunday morning after church. His mother christened the dream ship *White Seal* after Gerry's favorite childhood tale. There was a short invocation, a wish for a long, happy, and safe life in an often hostile world. Someone cut the birthday cake, with its little white seal in a cradle, and then everyone pitched in for the celebration.

At christening, *White Seal* weighed 15 tons and was 500 miles from salt water. After the party, Gerry and friends jacked up the 37-foot hull onto a lowboy trailer, and the next day the journey overland to Durban began. After launching, *White Seal* was outfitted, and, by April 1952, she was ready for a shakedown cruise.[5]

Gerry, with three young and inexperienced friends, made the shakedown voyage to Lourenço Marques in southern Mozambique, about 300 miles up the east coast of Africa. The trip took three and a half days going and six and a half days returning, treating them to flat calms and roaring gales that shook the kinks out of boat and man. The voyage taught them many things about the sea and small-boat handling they had not thought of. One of the lessons learned early was the technique of heaving-to, a necessity for any ocean voyager in any size craft. Gerry also got a chance to practice his celestial navigation, and worked out at least one perfect fix. Defects in the rigging were noted and later corrected.

Gerry also learned to master the use of the ancient 28-horsepower American-made Le Roi stationary engine that a friend had given him. Characteristically, he had rebuilt the engine and refitted the carburetor to burn kerosene. At 1800 r.p.m., it burned 1.5 gallons an hour and propelled *White Seal* at 5 knots.[6]

About a year later, Gerry was ready to begin his world wandering with *White Seal*. On February 28, with four companions, he departed Durban for England, and for the next 6 years, 9 months, and 63,000 miles, *White Seal* roamed the world looking for a better place to live. Her route was one of the most unusual, and possibly one of the most interesting of all circumnavigations. Whereas most voyagers head immediately for the tropical South Seas and hopefully an idyllic life with broadminded native girls, Trobridge and his intrepid companions sailed northward to England. From there, the track led to Spain, Portugal, the Canary Islands, Trinidad and the West Indies, Florida, New York, Toronto, the Great Lakes, down the Mississippi River, and through the Yucatán Channel to Panama; then to the Galápagos Islands, the Marquesas, Raïatéa, Tahiti, Bora Bora, Samoa, Fiji, Brisbane, up behind the Great Barrier Reef, through Torres Strait to Darwin, the Keeling-Cocos Islands, Mauritius, and back to Durban.

Thus, Gerry Trobridge in his dream boat, White Seal, became the first South African to circumnavigate in a small yacht, and the first to leave Durban and go around.[7]

White Seal proved to be a superb sea boat, easy to handle, dry and comfortable of motion, roomy and able to carry astonishing stores of food and supplies—as much as six months' supply for four people. She was fairly fast—up to seven or eight knots under the best of conditions (but carried an enormous cloud of sail, almost 1,200 square feet with everything flying). She was a gentle lady in a following sea, or hove-to, or even lying at anchor in a breeze. The mild steel used in the hull was of South African manufacture and proved to be completely practical and immensely strong in the face of sometimes crashing seas and occasional groundings. There was little difficulty with rust and corrosion, the only protection ever given the hull being paint and zinc sacrifice plates.

White Seal's accident-free, 63,000-mile circumnavigation, of course, was due not only to ordinary good luck, but also to the ingenuity and skill with mechanical things, and the inherent good judgment of the skipper. His philosophy was: Keep it simple, and you won't have to fix it.

At the start of the world cruise, Gerry had with him as crew Colin Greenaire (as far as Cape Town), Gene Greathead, Bill Riggs, and Bunny Lagerwey—all bachelors, full of adventure and high spirits, but with little practical sea experience. Lagerwey, an airline pilot, was a skilled navigator, however. Clearing for Cape Town, they left in the wake of a Mozambique hurricane while the sea was still boisterous, and soon all were seasick. Gerry moved off soundings to get away from the chop and found enormous swells running, which scared them back inside the 100-fathom line. On shore, they had to buck southwest winds and adverse current, making less than ten miles a day. With a sick and demoralized crew, Gerry ran back out again during the night (in the dark, he would not have to look at the enormous seas)—discovering, as others have, that outside there is usually a helping current instead of a hindering one, and often better time can be made in spite of the large seas.[8]

At Cape Town, where they were assisted in mooring by a tipsy crew of club members, followed by a night-long celebration, they learned another lesson. They woke up and found White Seal had snapped her lines and lay alongside the dock untied. By happy coincidence, it was a flat calm period in a notoriously windy harbor.

Sailing on the thirteenth of the month, they made the nine hundred miles to St. Helena in thirty-one days. Next came Ascension, St. Vincent Island, Horta, and the long run uphill to England.

Gerry and *White Seal* spent a year in England, he working as a marine diesel mechanic and lecturing. Two of the crew left the ship here, but on May 9, 1954, with Gene Greathead, Gerry departed London, called at several ports, and then cleared from Falmouth on August 20 for Vigo, Spain. Next came Portugal, then Tenerife, and directly across to Georgetown, British Guiana. From here, *White Seal* and her crew cruised and chartered up and down the West Indies for a year of so, living off the land and sea, without any definite plans.

Finally, it was time to move. Leaving Charlotte Amalie on June 20, 1955, *White Seal* sailed to Port Everglades, Florida, via the Bahamas, then up the coast to New York through the Hudson waterway to Toronto, arriving on August 6. Greathead had now left the ship, too. Gerry continued on up the Hudson, through the Erie Canal to Buffalo, Lake Erie, working along the way as a machinist and steamfitter. During 1957, *White Seal* cruised the Great Lakes, visiting thirty-seven ports. From Toronto to Detroit, Gerry had Ron Shettel as crew member. In the Detroit area, Gerry met and married Marie, and she joined *White Seal* for the rest of of the circumnavigation.

On August 22, they left Chicago via the linkage to the Mississippi, with Shettel still aboard, and went down the river to New Orleans. On October 30, Marie and Gerry alone departed New Orleans for Biloxi, and then sailed directly for Panama.

On this leg, while Marie was still new to *White Seal* and to the ocean, they were caught in one of the worst storms of the year—which battered them mercilessly for three days. Finally making Grand Cayman, they rested for nine days until the weather improved. The six hundred miles to Panama was made in six days, in time to spend Christmas with Marie's parents who flew down from the States.

It was three months before Marie got over the encounter with the storm and was ready to move on. By this time, she was also pregnant, so when they left Balboa it was with a strong urgency to reach Australia in time for the baby to be born. During the three months in Panama, Gerry worked at odd jobs and made some alterations to *White Seal*'s rigging. At this point, Gerry and Marie also came to an understanding: A Caribbean storm is a traumatic experience the first time you go to sea in a small boat. It is also superfluous to get married and go to sea, if the only social contact you will have is while passing in the hatchway while changing watches.

From then on, the watch-and-watch routine was out. *White Seal* was made to steer herself. Electricity was put aboard so a masthead light could be rigged. From then on, in good weather, they let the ship tend herself at night, or they lay ahull and went to bed.

The leg from Balboa to Galápagos was an idyllic sail, which continued all the way to the Marquesas. In fact, reaching the Marquesas after thirty-nine days, they were almost reluctant to stop and share their world with anyone.

In Tahiti, they took on a paying guest, Kevin Ardill, an Australian looking for a way home. After visiting Bora Bora, Samoa, and the Fijis—where Gerry got work as a machinist—they arrived in Brisbane on October 1, 1958.

During the stay here, a baby girl was born, and Gerry obtained work for nine months or so. When the baby was six months old, plans were made to continue the voyage.[9]

On May 27, 1959, *White Seal* departed at last, with a crew that now included the baby, Tracy ("the most demanding and useless crew member we ever shipped"), three enormous cartons of disposable diapers; Dave Benedict, a young, competent, and good-natured (but always broke) Californian; and Alan Moulton, an Australian who went as far as Townsville. Another, Keith Buchanan, joined the ship at Cairns for the trip to Darwin.

The cruise up inside the Great Barrier Reef was a Sunday sail that lasted three months. They arrived at Thursday Island on August 7, 1959, after visiting 38 ports and anchorages. After a few days, they departed for the Keeling-Cocos Islands on September 6. From here on, easy-going Gerry became impatient to reach Durban and complete a circumnavigation. The voyage across the Indian Ocean was agonizingly slow. For the first 10 days, they made only 378 miles, until they came under the influence of the trades, then they began to make 1,000-mile weeks.

After a short stay at Cocos, they had good sailing for several days, then a period of violent squalls, followed by high winds. They arrived at Mauritius seven days ahead of estimates, and here took a good rest while anchored in the Black River.

Leaving on November 8, they had a violent passage on the final leg, marked by squalls, boisterous seas, and changing winds. At midnight, on November 24, 1959, Gerry and *White Seal* entered Durban harbor to fulfill his goal.

Home again, the young man who had built his dream boat and sailed the world looking for a better place, moved ashore with his family and got a job. They tried to sell their beloved *White Seal*, but life ashore began to pall. Disillusioned with local politics and the problems of society, they left Durban on February 12, 1963, this time with a second child. When they moved aboard, everything had seemed to shrink in size from what they remembered. The first month aboard, prior to departing, it rained constantly, trapping them in close confinement. The kids got into everything, broke things, ran thirty gallons of kerosene into the bilge, and hurt themselves. Once underway, with Hamish Campbell and David Cox as crew members, they sailed to Cape Town via Port Elizabeth.[10]

At Port Elizabeth, Tracy got the mumps. Before they arrived in Cape Town, all the crew had come down with them, and they were quarantined for two weeks.

Here, a painter, George Enslin, came on the scene with a deposit for the purchase of *White Seal*. Gerry agreed to the price and also to sailing with Enslin to the West Indies to teach him seamanship and navigation. The family moved off the boat and took passage to the States on a freighter. Three weeks later, the deal fell through, and Gerry was stranded with no family and no money.

He raised a crew of three in two days and couldn't have done better if he had screened candidates for a lifetime. With Mike Smith (son of Bill Smith, who was on the original shakedown), Roger Williams, and John Scott, *White Seal* departed on April 9, 1963, arriving at St. Helena on April 26; Ascension, May 5; and Trinidad, B.W.I., on June 5. From Trinidad, the voyagers loafed through twenty ports and anchorages to Port Everglades, arriving July 10. On July 20, they reached Patchoque, New York, and the end of the trail for *White Seal*.

Now more than twenty years old, *White Seal*, the backyard-built Hanna ketch, is owned by Mr. and Mrs. Steve Doherty of New York, and with some modifications, mainly of engine and accommodations, she sails on as spry and as lively as ever.

The Trobridges? The family found a home at last on shore in Maryland.

White Seal, like the restless creature of Kipling's tale, sails on and on.

One of the few photographs, if not the only one, extant of the legendary beachcomber and unofficial greeter at Nuku Hiva in the Marquesas, Bob McKittrick. (William Crowe in *Heaven, Hell and Salt Water*)

Mrs. Gowen at the helm during the voyage of the *Speejacks*, on which she was the only woman. (*Sea Tracks of the Speejacks*, by Dale Collins)

Speejacks was the first motorboat to sail around the world, although actually she was towed partway. She was 98 feet overall, by 17 feet wide by 6 feet draft. (*Sea Tracks of the Speejacks*, by Dale Collins)

A. Y. Gowen, owner of *Speejacks*, who conceived the unusual voyage. (*Sea Tracks of the Speejacks*, by Dale Collins)

The *Islander* tied up to the seawall at Takaroa in the Tuamotus on Pidgeon's first circumnavigation. (Harry Pidgeon in *Around the World Singlehanded*)

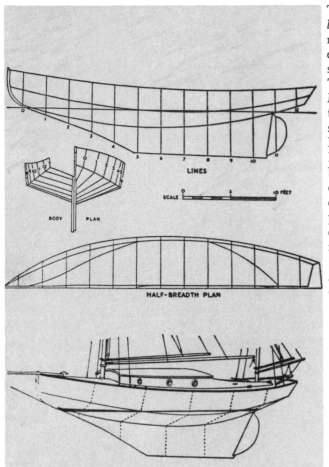

LINES

BODY PLAN

SCALE |———|———| 10 FEET

HALF-BREADTH PLAN

The lines and perspectives of *Islander*, in which Harry Pidgeon made two circumnavigations. Dozens of copies have been built and sailed on the oceans of the world. The hull model is an enlarged *Sea Bird*, which Thomas Fleming Day, the great editor of *Rudder*, designed with the help of Thomas Mower, and in which he sailed to Rome. Hundreds of *Sea Birds* have been built and sailed on the oceans of the world. Voss's *Sea Queen* was one of these copies. It was the first practical ocean-going yacht de-designed for home-building and using the V-bottom or hard-chine. (Reprinted with permission of *Rudder* magazine, copyright, Fawcett Publications, 1946)

Harry Pidgeon aboard *Islander* after his second circumnavigation. (George Bonnell)

Captain Conor O'Brien with his faithful mate, Kioa, the only hand he signed on during the entire trip whom he could trust. (*Across Three Oceans*, by Conor O'Brien)

Sail plan of *Svaap*, showing the straight-forward ketch rig. (Courtesy of John G. Alden, Inc.)

William Albert Robinson at the helm of *Svaap* during his first circumnavigation. (W. A. Robinson in *20,000 Leagues Over the Sea*)

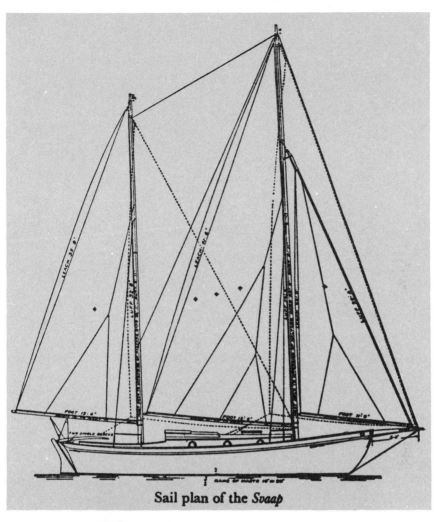

Sail plan of the *Svaap*

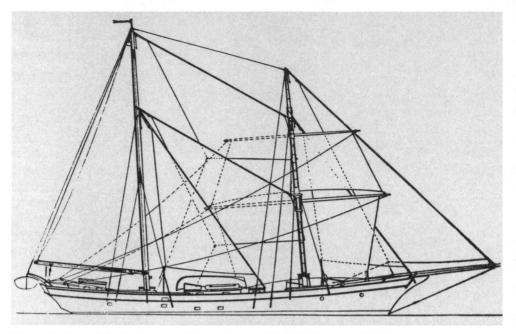

The sail plan of the brigantine *Varua*, designed by Robinson with the help of such prestigious designers as Starling Burgess and L. Francis Herreshoff. (W. A. Robinson in *To the Great Southern Sea*)

W. A. Robinson's beautiful brigantine, *Varua*, off Tahiti. (W. A. Robinson in *To the Great Southern Sea*)

Idle Hour, tied up at the quay in Ismaili, Suez Canal. (Dwight Long)

Portrait of Timi, Dwight Long's mate, cook, companion, and man Friday, a young Tahitian who accompanied him on *Idle Hour* as far as Ceylon, where he died of pneumonia. Like O'Brien, Muhlhauser, and Robinson, Long found his most dependable crew members in the islands. (Dwight Long in *Seven Seas On a Shoestring*)

The *Idle Hour* under sail. (Dwight Long)

A most unusual photo taken of two legendary circumnavigators together, William A. Robinson (left) and Alain Gerbault, in Tahiti. (Dwight Long in *Seven Seas On a Shoestring*)

Dwight Long with the famed author and big-game fisherman, Zane Grey, in Queensland, Australia. (Dwight Long in *Seven Seas On a Shoestring*)

The skipper, Ray Kauffman, at the helm of *Hurricane* in the South Pacific. (Ray Kauffman in *Hurricane's Wake*)

Gerry Mefferd, taking a sun sight somewhere in the South Pacific near Tahiti. (Ray Kauffman in *Hurricane's Wake*)

Ray Kauffman (left) and Gerry Mefferd (right) greeted by Sidoine Krebs, builder of *Hurricane*, on their return from circumnavigation. (Ray Kauffman in *Hurricane's Wake*)

CHAPTER

⋰⋰ 21 ⋱⋱

Awahnee Means Peace

> *The circumference of the earth at 60° south
> latitude is half what it is at the equator; our
> projected course from New Zealand to New
> Zealand was 12,000 miles. We hoped to sail it
> in 100 days. We took aboard enough stores to
> winter over in Antarctica, 16 months supply, in
> case some accident or failure befell* Awahnee.[1]

AT 0400 HOURS ON DECEMBER 22, 1970, A LONG SLEEK,
seawise cutter moved out from Bluff on the southern tip of South
Island, New Zealand, with the wind west by south, and ran across
Foveaux Strait under storm jib and double-reefed main. A call was
made at Stewart Island, then after final preparations and last-minute
letter writing and a good dinner ashore, the yacht put to sea again at
2020 hours, just as darkness fell.

The yacht was the world-girdling *Awahnee*, the first ferro-cement
vessel to circumnavigate, now carrying her owners, Dr. Robert Lyle
Griffith, his wife, Nancy, and son, Reid, on their third circumnavigation of the world, this time on a track never before attempted by a
pleasure craft.[2]

Aboard on this voyage, as usual, the Griffiths had several crew
members, all stout New Zealanders who had volunteered—Pat
Treston, an Auckland lawyer; Ash Loudon, a student at Otago; and
John O'Brien, an Auckland businessman.[3]

The yacht was actually *Awahnee II*—the first one of that name,

designed by the famed Uffa Fox, and in which the Griffiths made
their first circumnavigation, was lost on a voyage in the French
Oceania area. *Awahnee II* was built by the Griffiths in New Zealand
from the original plans but in the then experimental ferro-cement
mode, in which New Zealand has become a world leader. *Awahnee
II*, like the original, was 53 feet overall, with a 42-foot waterline, a
beam of 12 feet, and a draft of 7 feet 6 inches. Loaded, she displaced
25 tons. A 22-horsepower Yanmar three-cylinder diesel provided
auxiliary power.

For the Antarctic circumnavigation, the ship had been completely
reconditioned and modified. The hull and decks had been sandblasted to bare concrete and then fiberglassed with cloth and resin.
The interior was lined with Styrofoam to insulate and prevent
condensation. A sixty-foot exhaust pipe was fitted from the engine
forward through the two cabins on the port side under the berths,
then aft again to come out behind the cockpit. This dry exhaust, the
first ever installed that was longer than the boat it was installed in,
provided heat in the cold latitudes. In addition, a closed-circuit
engine-cooling system was devised from two drums that didn't work
—which became apparent before they left Whangarei harbor.

Aboard the double-ender was a year's supply of groceries in case
they became ice-bound or otherwise incapacitated and had to wait
out an Antarctic winter, as had many explorers of old when they
found themselves frozen in the ice pack for a year.

Departing Bluff, the Griffiths and their crew of New Zealanders
headed southeast in the general direction of the Ross Sea, roughly
following the course of Captain James Cook, the first to circumnavigate the Antarctic and whose 205-year-old journal was kept aboard
and read aloud by Nancy as they followed his track. Passing Auckland
Island, the first port of call was the remote and lonely station on
Campbell Island, a New Zealand weather-reporting installation,
where they celebrated Christmas with the crews at the station and
from the U.S. icebreaker *Staten Island.*

Heading south through the Furious Fifties and into the Shrieking
Sixties, they encountered monstrous waves and gale winds, and their
first sign of ice, which required a constant lookout day and night. On
New Year's Day—midsummer there—the temperature was 32°. Four
days out of Campbell Island, they lost a headstay and repairs were
made by agile Reid. At 63°S, they were trapped by ice and had to
backtrack for 40 miles. On the tenth day, at 61°S and 159°W, they
sighted three islands where no land was shown on the charts.[4]

Sailing among tall icebergs, some 200 feet in height, they got their first look at the Antarctic continent at 66°S as they passed about 600 miles south of Cape Horn. At Palmer Station,[5] they were received with astonishment by the U.S. and British scientists. They were now a third of the way around the world at this latitude.[6]

From here on, they visited nine scientific stations—U.S., Argentine, British, Russian, and Chilean—and two whaling stations, now defunct. On Deception Island, they anchored in a submerged crater, where there is now a 900-foot-high island.

At the U.S.S.R.'s Bellinghausen Base, they learned from the doctor there that Nancy was pregnant. They tried to land a plaque from the New Zealand Shacketon Sea Scouts on Elephant Island, but could not get ashore. This was the survival camp of the ship *Endurance*, which was crushed in the ice in 1914. At Signey Island in the South Orkneys, they survived the British conviviality. From the Argentine base Orcades, they departed for New Zealand with a drum of fuel and a generous food supply given them by the men, who were already short since the annual supply ship had not arrived.

Fearing a disastrous holing of the hull by growlers and floating chunks of ice, they sailed usually with a drogue out on rough nights to steady the yacht, sometimes making 6 knots under a 48-foot storm staysail alone. They came into the Indian Ocean about 1,600 miles from Africa, and three days later crossed the Antarctic Circle. Fresh water was obtained by melting ice from the last berg encountered on a calm day. As they crossed under Australia, they were struck by a staggering blow which sent green water over *Awahnee* again and again. The final run to Stewart Island and Bluff was made in brilliant sunshine and light winds.

The circumnavigation had taken 111 days (the fastest on record), 84 of which were sailing days and 27 of which were in port or partial sailing days. Nancy left to rejoin their baby son, Tenoi'i, in Whangarei, a thousand miles north. Bob and the crew sailed *Awahnee* up the coast, on the way being struck by lightning and dismasted only 60 miles from home port. It was a climactic end to their third voyage around the world.

Born in January 1917, Griffith grew up to be a prosperous and successful veterinarian and cattle rancher in Tomales Bay, California, about sixty miles north of San Francisco. In middle age, he found himself on a treadmill, headed for a cardiac or ulcers, and decided it was time to broaden life a little. Searching the waterfront brokerages and yacht clubs, he found the original *Awahnee*, which had been built by an Englishman for use as a family yacht. Griffith and his wife made a shakedown cruise up the California coast, and then they set out on the first voyage, a scientific expedition to the Marquesas. After this came other charter trips around the Pacific, then they settled down in New Zealand.

After some time ashore, the Griffiths took off again, on their first circumnavigation, west-about across the Indian Ocean, with a crew of five in a fast passage until the Red Sea was reached. There they ran up on a reef and were impaled. At least 250 ships passed by refusing to answer their distress signals. Going ashore, Griffith beame embroiled in local politics and red tape. He went back to the vessel with some dynamite and literally blew *Awahnee* free, immediately running the yacht ashore before she filled with water. They beached safely and made repairs, then went on into the Mediterranean, where they cruised for months. Passing out through the Strait of Gibraltar, they encountered the worst gale of the voyage, with winds recorded to 138 knots.

Their first Atlantic crossing, however, was made in the fast time of eleven days in perfect sailing weather. Then they went down through the Panama Canal and into the Pacific to complete their first circumnavigation.

After a few months of leisurely cruising, they went in search of a missing American yacht—after first being arrested as gun-runners and forced to clear their record of the charge by the French police. They did not find the missing yacht, but did find three others that were wrecked and unreported. Then *Awahnee* was carried onto a reef and wrecked. The Griffiths spent a week salvaging everything they could, including rigging, masts, machinery, and food before she broke up. The family had then been to sea for four years.

At first, they thought the island was uninhabited, but then found two natives gathering copra. One of them, Teka, later became a long-time member of their crew. After sixty-seven days, they got word to French authorities and were rescued. The rescue was typically Gallic. A gendarme waded ashore, decked out in his finest uniform, and was met by Dr. Griffith in tattered clothes and beard. The gendarme extended his hand.

"Dr. Griffith, I presume?"

They were taken to Tahiti under guard and accused of being atomic spies. Later cleared, they bought another boat, an ancient English ketch, and sailed to New Zealand. There they found the ferro-cement business going strong. Redesigning *Awahnee*, they traveled over the country looking at boats under construction. Some were so bad that the owners merely dug a hole and bulldozed the hulls into it. But the Griffiths decided this was it. They spent five months building, and another in outfitting *Awahnee II*. The work was done at Auckland and attracted much attention. The ribs were ¾-inch water pipe welded in place. Two miles of steel wire was stretched between the ribs, and eight layers of chicken wire stretched over the whole frame (the entire supply available in the city). This was then plastered with a cement mixture in a continuous operation. The shell had an average thickness of ⅞ inch. After launching, she weighed fourteen tons, which went down to twenty-three tons when fully loaded, about ten percent lighter than the original wooden vessel.

After a shakedown, the Griffiths departed on their second circumnavigation. Five days out of Russell, *Awahnee* was punching through 40-foot seas and hurricane winds, and twice was knocked down. In subfreezing weather, they rounded Cape Horn where the anchor froze to the deck and ice hung from the rigging.

On a passage from Peru to the Marquesas, a 4,000-mile run, they took only 25 days from the fuel barge at Callao on September 1966 to Taa Huku Bay on the evening of October 13. Fast passages were a trademark with the Griffiths. Usually, they carried a crew of volunteers and, as Dr. Griffith remarked later, out of two hundred extra crew members shipped, all but three would be welcome back.

Reid, the Griffith son who began sailing at age five, grew up at sea where he learned to cook, to work a noon sight, to hand, reef, and steer with the best bluewater sailors. Nancy Griffith, also, became an expert sailor and navigator, and on at least one voyage (to Hawaii) skippered the ship with a crew of amateurs while her husband was away on business. On one passage, Nancy was almost lost. Thrown overboard by a freak jibe of the mainsail, she was in the shark-infested waters of the Indian Ocean for a half hour before she could be spotted, the vessel turned around, and a rescue made.[7]

During the second circumnavigation, *Awahnee* sailed up for Japan and clockwise down around the Aleutians, the Gulf of Alaska, and back to California. At this time, the Griffiths had been at sea for eight years and covered 150,000 sea miles. In San Francisco, the family found the freeway traffic and the crowds more terrifying than anything encountered at sea.

After further adventures in the Pacific, the Griffiths came back to

California, settling for a time at Inverness, where Bob became
involved with a nonprofit enterprise to turn the 100-foot schooner
Westwind into a training ship for boys.

At the annual dinner of the Cruising Club of America in New
York, January 25, 1973, Griffith was the featured speaker. Since 1959,
with his family, he had sailed 170,000 miles and made three circumnavigations in two yachts. His was a most remarkable record, and for
it, he was awarded the prestigious Blue Water Medal for 1972. The
late John Parkinson, Jr., awards chairman, commented, "In all my
years of serving on this committee, in my opinion we have never had
a recipient so deserving of this honor."

The last passage *Awahnee* made prior to the award, was one of 19
days to Tahiti, then 19 days to Honolulu and 18½ days to San
Francisco, arriving there in time for their daughter, Fiona Nikola
Antares, to be born in the United States. Reid attended summer
school, and later finished high school, while Dr. Bob holed up to
write a book on a farm in New England. When the book was done,
the babies were older, and Reid graduated from high school, the plan
was to cast off moorings at Tomales Bay and set sail again for whatever adventures remained.[8]

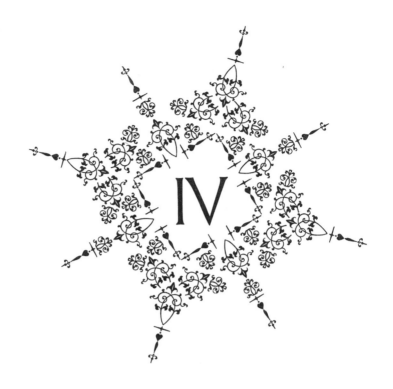

IV

LES

QUATRE

FRENCHMEN

❧ 22 ❧

Thunder Out of Brittany

*I was a stubborn lad, a fighter, eager to redress
wrongs, touchy, shy, idealistic, a whole-hogger.
I recoiled from telling lies and hated liars. At
the age of fourteen, my education had provided
me with a number of over-simplified principles
which I accepted as absolute.*[1]

IN 1940, WHEN THE GERMAN BLITZKRIEG BROKE THROUGH
the Maginot Line and rolled across France, the invaders interrupted
the entrance examinations at the Naval School for a young man
named Jacques-Yves Le Toumelin, who was more annoyed possibly
at the Germans for this distraction than for the invasion. Like most
Bretons, he was a practical man first and a patriot second, and
Brittany had seen invaders come and go for centuries. No, young
Toumelin had set his mind upon sailing around the world in his
own ship, and the war was merely a minor annoyance, something to
get over, like the German measles. He had crammed hard for the
Naval School exams, because of his plan, which was to get into the
navy, save enough to buy his own boat, while at the same time discharge his military obligations and learn something of ocean navigation. For a twenty-year-old Breton, this was a practical and well-
organized plan.

When the Germans came, he had no intention of falling into their
hands, so after helping refugees for several days, he became one
himself. He and his best friend pitched a tent in one of the shooting
preserves, fishing and hunting to feed themselves.[2] Soon they decided
to try for Arcachon and there to steal a boat and escape to England.

They set out on foot, but were overtaken by the Germans and separated. Alone, Le Toumelin made his way back to Brittany.

Unable to get to the Free Zone, he did the next best thing to entering naval school; he transferred to the School of Hydrography at Nantes, where he completed his theoretical work in 1941. He needed then only a ship to qualify for his mate's certificate. Meanwhile, he had purchased a copy of *Sailing Alone Around the World* by Joshua Slocum, and like Alain Gerbault, after reading Jack London's *Cruise of the Snark*, he now had a sense of direction as well as a purpose. He needed only money, opportunity, and a ship of his own—three prerequisites that seldom deter a dedicated circumnavigator.

Jacques-Yves Le Toumelin came from a long line of Bretons who had been seamen for centuries. His father was a sea captain before the war, had made long voyages in square-rigged ships, and was a reserve navy commander. His mother came from St. Malo, home of the ancient granite fortress from where Cartier, Duguay-Trouin, Surcouf, and other famous courtiers and corsairs had come. Centuries before, the Gauls had massacred the Legions of Julius Caesar in this coastal area and wiped out the Druidic wisdom. The original name of Brittany, in fact, was Armorica, which means *ar mor*, the seas.[3]

The sea is an inseparable part of life in Brittany, and life itself is regulated by the ebb and flow of the tides. There is a saying that every Breton, no matter where he is or how far removed, has this call of the sea in his blood.

Le Toumelin had missed being born there, the event having happened while the family sojourned in Paris. He passed some of his boyhood in the city, but he hated the place and lived for the summer period when he could go back to Brittany by the sea. He had no memory of learning to tie a square knot, scull an oar, or reef a sail. These came instinctively. By the time he was fourteen, his schooling had managed to oversimplify the principles by which he had been taught to live—his belief in his God, his country, and himself were unshakable.

As a Breton, he was also stubborn, single-minded, and idealistic. He hated the sophistication of society and politics and set out to do something about it. He joined radical groups and demonstrated against authority. By the time he was fifteen, he had been thrown in jail and been the object of much publicity. A lenient court, taking his age into consideration, acquitted him as "having acted without discernment," one of those delightful and practical applications of logic for which the French are known. But the episode turned the lad against the sordid trappings of politics and he became a dropout, spending the next months sailing, fishing, and hunting before he had to return once more to the gloomy boarding school. On the wall of his cubicle at Le Croisic, he had copied from José de Espronceda's *Canción del Pirata*:

> *My ship is my all, my only wealth*
> *My God, my liberty. . . .*

He became ill and missed his October exams. The next school year he was sent back to Paris to the Lycée Louis le Grand, but that spring he became ill again, and returned to the seacoast to recuperate. It was during the 1937 school year that he heard about Captain Bernicot and his exploits in *Anahita*, and determined he would obtain a ship of his own and sail around the world and "never return to Europe."

After the invasion, when he had completed his theoretical work at the School of Hydrography, he went out with the fishing fleet off Mauretania in the trawler *Alfred*. From 1942 to 1945, he fished the coastal waters of Le Croisic in sailing smacks. He acquired a two-ton cutter, *Crabe*, for fishing. One day, returning to port, he encountered a neat new fishing vessel named *Marie*. In his diary, he wrote, "I shall set out alone in a craft like *Marie*."

That fall, Le Toumelin sold *Crabe* and delivered her to the buyer in Nantes. Then he returned to Le Croisic to begin construction of a vessel, and to pass the time while waiting for materials, he shipped out to the West African Coast on a trawler. It was a hard life, but he managed to save some money. He next made a brief trip to Senegal, and returned to France with a tidy stake.

Now he bought a half-decked cutter named *Marilou* for fishing. In the spring of 1943, he obtained permission at last to build his dream ship. Because of shortages, he had to get the keel cast in Quimperlé and shipped to Le Croisic, where he dragged it by hand to the shipyard. Other materials were just as difficult to get. He obtained the anchor in Paris, and when he tried to board the train with it, the conductor stopped him.

Finally, on May 20, the start was made. On October 28, 1943, she was launched. After rigorous inspection by the Germans, he was allowed to enter in the fishing trade. He called his ship the *Tonnerre*, which is French for "thunder." Now he was relatively happy, sailing and earning a little and laying in stores and arms for the time when he could escape. At last, with only a few hours to go before he planned to set out, with only some boxes of food and arms to bring aboard, he learned that the Allies had launched the invasion of Normandy.

France immediately became a wild, disorganized country, swept by waves of hatred, of vengeance, of guerilla bands looting and raping, of refugees again. Le Toumelin could not leave now. He had to find out what happened to his family, so he set off on a rented bicycle for Paris, with a few hundred francs, a knife, and a revolver. He was appalled by what he encountered. It seemed to him that his country was in the grip of murder, theft, petty vengeance, and savage exultation.

When Paris was liberated, he returned to Le Croisic to find the Germans still occupying the St. Nazaire pocket. They had searched his attic room and found his hidden store of guns and ammo and had seized his cutter. As soon as the Germans were gone, he began to search for his ship, and finally, on May 29 he found two drawers from a locker which he recognized. Then he met a sailor who told him that the boat had been wrecked, that the remains were in a shed at St. Marc.

Back at Le Croisic, he began planning again. All he had left was his sextant, which one of the Germans, through some mystic understand-ing, had rescued and given to a friend to keep. The instrument was valued because it had belonged to his father.

Le Toumelin applied for compensation for the loss, meanwhile consulted with a naval architect, and was called up to serve on active duty with the navy. On his short sea duty, he was able to get ashore in England and obtain some much-needed parts. On Feburary 2, 1946, he was demobilized and free to work on his second dream ship, which he had named *Kurun*, meaning "thunder" in Breton. By this time his ideas of a deep-water yacht had been refined.

Kurun was built entirely of fine, close-grained oak. The top sides were 1⅛ inch thick, the hull double-planked on steam bent acacia ribs. There were massive cross-timbers and the bulwarks were a foot high and double-planked also. *Kurun* had no engine, a device which Le Toumelin despised. She was launched on a cold winter morning with a northeast wind blowing. Le Toumelin was on crutches, for he had broken a bone in his foot. At first, *Kurun* refused to be launched. Then she shot away out of control. The cradle broke with Le Toumelin on board, and the keel plowed a furrow in the mud. At high tide, *Kurun* rose gently, and at 4:30 P.M. he broke a bottle of champagne on the stem—a bottle he had brought from St. Marc, the place where *Tonnerre* was wrecked.[4]

Le Toumelin moved aboard. He was now twenty-nine years old and his boyhood dream was coming true. "I had disciplined myself and learned to think straight, to know myself, to judge the modern world. I was ready to depart."

Sailing around the world, although it had been a dream, was one he had shared with thousands through articles written for the yachting publications. As a result, he was inundated with applicants. His worried parents wanted him to take someone, so he shipped along a family friend, Gaston Dufour, a young man who had just returned from fighting in Indochina. On September 4, they said good-bye to friends and family in Paris and returned to Le Croisic for supplies of books, food, stores, and clothes. Loaded, *Kurun* rode low in the water.

On September 19, Le Toumelin paid off the last of his debts and had lunch ashore with his father. Some friends came to see them off. At 4 P.M., with the tide, lines were slipped and the jib set. *Kurun* sprang to life. They moved away from the quay where he had played as a child. The escort vessels fell behind. At 5:40 P.M., they passed the familiar buoy of Bonen de Four, and as darkness fell the sky took on an ugly look and the weather deteriorated.

Behind Le Toumelin were his childhood, the German occupation, the long, hard years of saving and planning, the reconstruction days, the setbacks. Now at twenty-nine, he thought bitterly, he had wasted most of his life. *Mais je suis libre!*

Because of the weather, *Kurun* put in at Vigo, Spain. At Morocco, his friend Dufour left him. Le Toumelin shipped another mate, 25-year-old Paul Farge, a Parisian, a scout, and one of 14 children, out to see the world. They sailed to Las Palmas on an easy run, then departed for the West Indies, with the first 17 days being plain sailing, after which came squalls and calms. On June 2, they sailed into Martinique, a grand entrance with all sails set.

"Never," he wrote in *Le Yacht*, "have I driven the boat so hard. *Kurun* went like a race horse, sailing upwind. At exactly 5 o'clock the anchor went down 50 yards from the quay at the Yacht Club."

Next came Colon via the Venezuela coast. In the passage through the Panama Canal, Le Toumelin, unlike Gerbault who had pulled strings and made an easy transit, antagonized officials with his imperious way. As usual, he did not find the manners and mores of

Americans equal to his own, and his writings reflected this in frequent snide remarks and *non sequiturs*. At Balboa, he beached *Kurun* and found her sound. After cleaning and painting, he departed for the Galápagos Islands and anchored at San Cristóbal on October 20. He did not spend much time in the Enchanted Islands, only six weeks during which he traced the visit of Melville who was there in the *Acusnet*; of Gerbault, whom he envied for his reputation and despised for his inaccuracies, and of Robinson, who had been there in *Svaap*. He called on Señora Cobos, the Karin of Robinson's romantic stay, who now had a daughter, a beautiful blonde of sixteen. Le Toumelin went for moonlight rides with her, just as Robbie had done with her mother. He called on the other settlers, and he went hunting with his .22 revolver.

During his visit, he encountered the French ketch *Fleur d'Océan* from St. Malo on a cruise to Tahiti.[5] On November 5, late in the afternoon, he departed for Tahiti—a departure delayed somewhat by Farge's sudden illness, which appeared to be malaria. The Marquesas had been part of Le Toumelin's dream, and he recalled Robert Louis Stevenson's words, written in 1888, after he had visited there on the *Casco*:

> *Few who come to the islands leave them; they grow grey where they alighted.*

Here Le Toumelin shyly met his first native girls, about whom he commented in great naïveté. He spent much time in the Marquesas exploring, then sailed through the Tuamotus to Tahiti and came to anchor near the famed American circumnavigator *Yankee*. Also in port were the three-masted schooner *California*, with a crew of four going around the world, and the ketch *Kariachi*, with a young couple and a little boy of seven, finishing a cruise of three years. When the *Yankee* departed, her place was taken by the ketch *Ho-Ho II* of the Royal Norwegian Yacht Club, a Colin Archer of 39 feet overall. Then came the *Manzanita*, with the singlehanded navigator, Lee, whom Le Toumelin liked because he had been a commercial fisherman. Lee was unschooled, kept no log, knew no celestial navigation, and used only crude charts of the Pacific. He had been a commercial fisherman in the Pacific Northwest of North America, and he had saved enough to buy a crude boat.[6]

Le Toumelin had hoped to meet Robinson, but was disappointed, although he admired the beautiful *Varua* anchored in the roads. Then, meeting Robbie one day on the street, he boldly asked the legendary circumnavigator if he could visit the ship. The Yankee replied that he had no time to spare.[7]

Farge left *Kurun* at Tahiti. Le Toumelin turned down all other applicants, wanting to continue alone. Before leaving, he made a triangular sail for the masthead, which he called "paimpolaise"—"my little Tahitian."[8]

The hot sun of the tropics had opened *Kurun's* seams, and she had to be recaulked. Le Toumelin made a new gaff from a piece of Oregon pine and also bought a supply of those "amazing American batteries" for his radio, which performed faultlessly during the rest of the voyage. On October 15, he weighed anchor. The harbor was now deserted. Only Farge came down to see him off. From Tahiti, he sailed to Uturoa and Bora Bora.

"To be on Bora Bora without thinking of Alain Gerbault is impossible." He visited the tomb and monument erected by the Yacht Club du France in the square at Waitape. Now his feelings toward his dead rival softened.

Next came New Guinea, where he encountered heavy weather and survived a knockdown. He could obtain no fresh food at Port Moresby, so went on to the Keeling-Cocos Islands via Torres Strait. From the cable company crew and the Clunies-Ross family, he received a warm welcome, staying in a bungalow where he found a photograph of Captain Bernicot on the wall. In his provincial way, Le Toumelin called Ross the "King" of the Cocos, and referred to the natives as half-caste slaves (possibly one reason why later voyagers have not been welcomed so cordially). Oddly enough, his description of the life on the atolls is the best of all the circumnavigators.

From here, he sailed to Réunion via Rodriguez, collected his mail and enjoyed a stay in the house of Commander Fournage, a former submarine commander and commercial manager of the port. From Réunion, he went to Durban, through heavy weather, and on December 4 hoisted the Q flag off the jetty. He was welcomed as all voyagers have been, and also as most Frenchmen have, he commented on the curious relationship of the whites to blacks in South Africa. In Natal, he found immigrants from Mauritius who had known Slocum, one an old lady who, as a young girl, had been a visitor aboard the *Spray.*[9]

Kurun needed repairs. The mast had to be replaced, being eaten by worms which Le Toumelin identified as Capricorn beetles. Once more, as soon as his firearms had been returned to him, he departed. From the pier came a booming voice. It was Gerry Trobridge, who was preparing *White Seal* for a circumnavigation. On February 14, he reached Cape Town, where he had a long pleasant stay. Among the vessels in port were the *Sandefjord*, the 47-foot Colin Archer; the *Stella Maris* of the famed voyager, Georges de Leon; and the reconstructed *Dromedaris*, the ship in which Van Riebeeck, founder of the Cape Colony, had arrived in 300 years before.

On March 16, he departed with a green frog for a stowaway, which he named Josephine. On April 7, he came into Jamestown on St. Helena, and was met by the French consul, M. Peugeot. On April 19, he departed for a long, tedious, nonstop voyage to Le Croisic. On the way, he almost ran into a derelict. On June 25, at 10:35 P.M., he saw the lights and about 1:10 A.M., hailed *Le Brix*, a frigate, and got a position report. He was 68 days out of St. Helena. To his amazement, all aboard the frigate knew about him. He kept in company with the vessel and even had lunch aboard with the captain. The next day, they parted company. Then he began to encounter tunny boats. From one of them came the voice, "There's the lad from Le Croisic who's sailing around the world!" Jacques Yves Le Toumelin was no longer a nobody, an obscure Breton.

Slowly he passed familiar places . . . Houat, Hoedick, Les Cardins . . . the lighthouse at Le Four . . . then, at 12:55, came the peninsula of Le Croisic.

A launch came out. It was the fisheries' patrol vessel. Aboard was the Maritime Registrar, as well as the editor of *Col Bleu*, and various officials with messages from the Minister of Merchant Marine and the announcement that he had won the Knight's Cross of the Order of Maritime Merit. Then came a little launch with his friend, Jano Quilgars, with his mother and father aboard. At 3:25, he entered the channel, seventy-nine days out of St. Helena. The voyage was at an end. *Kurun* was scarred and worm-eaten, but victorious and sound of heart.

"*I felt, as I moored* Kurun, *that I had not come back to the harbor to stay. I was merely at a port of call.*"

But the young Breton rebel who had "wasted" most of his life because of society and politics and war had now left all his troubles "aft of *Kurun*'s sternpost."

CHAPTER

23

The Chef's Special

There was no mistaking that this boat had come a long way. One can tell at a glance whether it is an offshore pleasure boat or an ocean racer. And there was no doubt that this was the latter. It was a ketch, called Atom. *I felt a little pang in my heart, however, when I saw that it was the American flag this single-hander flew—for in spite of her American nationalization, she was very French.*[1]

THE TIME WAS ONE A.M., OCTOBER 25, 1971. THE PLACE, 14 miles off Assateague, the long barrier island on the Maryland-Virginia border, some 25 miles south of Ocean City, Maryland. The vessel, *Atom*, a 30-foot *Tahiti* ketch, on her tenth crossing of the Atlantic and third circumnavigation of the world. Her skipper, 69-year-old Jean Gau, erstwhile New York chef, dishwasher, sailor-adventurer, painter, was now nearing the end of an arduous 108-day passage from Spain.

Jean did not know why this passage should have been so difficult. *Mon Dieu!* Had he not made it easily nine times before? He had hoped to pass the time in serene isolation, as usual, working on his latest painting, reading, and contemplating life. But, no. He had experienced contrary winds, calms, extreme temperatures, then had taken a battering from Hurricane Edith. Now, caught for five days in the tail end of Hurricane Ginger, he was tired. Oh, he was tired. Perhaps, like *Atom*, he was finally getting old.

217

On the night of October 24, he had gone below to listen to radio reports. He had wanted to stop at Puerto Rico, but Edith would not let him. He had come near Bermuda, and wanted to stop, but Ginger had kept him off. For five days, he had been awake most of the time, coming up toward New York, pumping almost constantly, while Ginger raged.

"This time," Gau said, "I think she is finished, but I make it just the same."[2]

As he went below, thoughts crossed his mind of Dumas, the Argentinian singlehander who had gone up on the beach on the Patagonia coast through fatigue, almost at the end of his circumnavigation in the Roaring Forties; and of even the old master, Joshua Slocum, who ran his *Spray* up on a Uruguay beach; and Pidgeon, whose *Islander* had been embayed and grounded on a South African beach.

While below, he dozed in a stupor, as if drugged, not alert enough to sense the shift of wind, until at one A.M., something aroused him. He sat up, listening for the sounds of the ship and the rigging to tell him what was wrong. Then he heard the hiss of breakers. He rushed up on deck, but it was too late. *Atom* was already on top of the beach.

Fortunately, he had grounded on an extremely high tide, which carried *Atom* above the surf line before she became battered. When daylight came, Gau packed a bag with food and clothes and started walking, dragging the sack in the sand wearily and despondent.

He did not know it, but he had beached on one of the most uninhabited and desolate stretches of coast on the entire Atlantic seaboard. Moreover, it was a National Seashore and National Wildlife Refuge, not a place for humans, kept as primitive as possible by federal law. He only knew that *Atom* had been his home for twenty-six of her thirty-three years. He knew her as well as he knew himself. He had weathered many storms in her over the past twenty years at sea, including hurricanes that had wrecked larger ships. Now she was gone.

When he began walking, by sheer chance he headed north. Had he walked south, he would have had to go nine miles without hope of finding anyone. As it was, he walked only a mile and a half and came to the Maryland border, where he encountered the only two private homes on thirty-five miles of lonely beach. One of them belonged to Robert Clements, a Washington, D.C., resident, who was there with his family, on this Monday morning, only because it was a school holiday.

"I heard a dog barking and that voice of the dog was the sweetest music to me," Gau later said.[3]

Until this moment, life had seemed to come to an end for Jean Gau. Born February 17, 1902, at Valras-Plage, France, as a young man between the wars, penniless but with a dual love for sea and painting, he had gone to America for the freedom and opportunity to pursue both mistresses. In New York, he obtained work as a dishwasher, then became a fry cook, assistant chef, and then chef in a large hotel. With French frugality, he lived simply, spending his spare time painting or haunting the waterfronts. He became a naturalized American, in fact, if not entirely in spirit, for his residence was confined to the New York area. For Jean Gau, the heart would always be in France, no matter where the body was.

In 1936, as the Great Depression was easing off, he bought the forty-foot schooner, *Onda II*, and, on June 15, left New York on a long voyage, with a stop at his home in Valras-Plage. Near Cádiz, Spain, he ran aground and *Onda II* was lost, along with many of his best paintings, some of which were regarded by experts as too valuable to be taken to sea.

Back in New York again, he went to work in the hotel until he had saved up another stake, enough to buy *Atom*, one of the first ot the famed *Tahiti* ketches, designed by John Hanna, the Dunedin, Florida, genius.[4] *Atom* had been built in 1938 from the plans which had been released by John Hanna and published in *Modern Mechanix*. She was seven years old when Gau found her, as World War II was ending, and moved aboard. She was perfectly suited to his temperament, personal habits, and needs.

When hostilities had ended formally, he made ready, and on May 28, 1947, departed New York bound again for Valras-Plage via the Azores on his first circumnavigation. In the next twenty years, he was to circle the globe twice, cross the Atlantic ten times, survive hurricanes, and become a legend among bluewater voyagers.

On his first circumnavigation, returning to New York, he was caught by Hurricane Carrie, six hundred miles southwest of the Azores, which on the afternoon of September 21, 1957, sunk the four-masted bark *Pamir*, bound for Hamburg with thirty-five seamen and fifty-one cadets. Gau, in tiny *Atom*, weathered the hurricane hove-to. Later in New York, his interview in the *New York Times* went thus:

"How was it?"

"The world? Oh, very nice."

"Any trouble?"

"No trouble, no accidents, no sickness, a few gales."

Before Carrie struck, he had furled sails, lashed the helm, rigged a can of oil to drip over the side, and gone below to read, paint, and sleep.

On his second circumnavigation, Gau left New York in the summer of 1962 bound for Cartagena. His log records departure from that port in the autumn of 1963, bound for San Juan, Puerto Rico. From there, he sailed to Panama in the summer of 1964. Next came Papeete via the usual route from Balboa. In the summer of 1965, he sailed to Auckland, then later went on to Port Moresby, and the long passage across the Indian Ocean to Durban, South Africa, where he sojourned for some time with three famous countrymen and voyagers, Bernard Moitessier, Marcel Bardiaux, and Joseph Merlot, on *Marie-Thérèse II*, *Les Quatre Vents*, and *Korrigan*, respectively.[5]

In February 1966, he left Durban, and on this passage he was capsized and dismasted. During this encounter, he lost his wire cutters overboard, but was able to cut loose the wreckage with a hacksaw blade held in his hands.[6] Putting into Mossel Bay, he made repairs, and then, in the late autumn, he departed for Puerto Rico and New York, arriving on June 10 after a five-year absence.

His second circumnavigation had been most interesting. It had taken him, among other places, to the Galápagos, to Pitcairn Island (where he could not land as the Johnsons in the well-manned *Yankee* could), and to many places off the usual track of world voyagers. In Torres Strait, he ran onto a coral reef and thought the end had come.

> *I was high and dry and got out of my boat to walk around the reef at 5 a.m. I found parts of masts and spars and a rusted cable and blocks, tangled crazily in seaweed. It was an old wreck imbedded in the coral with human skeletons aboard. To think that my fate would be practically the same, made it more depressing. Luckily, at 1900 hours, at high tide, I was able to get my boat off. Then I sailed across the Arafura and Timor Sea.*[7]

After his capsizing and repairs, he did not stop at Cape Town, but sailed directly to Grenada, a distance of 5,463 miles. On December 7, he passed St. Helena, on December 29 was rolling off Fernando de

Noronha, and on February 4, 1967, was 35 miles off Puerto Rico in the middle of the American fleet on maneuvers. He signaled that he needed help, having lost the mainsail and the engine being inoperative.

"Don't worry, *Atom,*" came the reply, "we are sending a tug."

Then a sub surfaced and asked if he needed food and water. He said he was thirsty but needed no food. Over came 20 bottles of ice-cold beer. Then the big tug came and towed him at 8 knots into the naval base, where a delegation of officials, reporters, and photographers waited. He was taken to a hospital, examined, then hosted at the base. The passage from Mossel Bay had turned into his longest— 6,000 miles in 123 days.

He stayed in Puerto Rico for sixty-nine days, waiting for weather, meanwhile selling a few paintings and articles to the local papers. He was often a guest of local residents. And the publicity had got for him a set of new parts for the engine from the Palmer Company.

On April 27, he departed for New York, 1,380 miles away. On June 9, he saw the flash of the Ambrose Lightship, forty-five days out, during which time he had seldom left the tiller. He entered a dense fog, with much ship traffic. On June 10, he entered the quarantine station, and at 4 A.M. the next day picked up his mooring at the Sheepshead Bay Yacht Club.

He was home again after 40,000 miles and five years.

He had already planned for his ninth crossing of the Atlantic to visit his mother in France, but meanwhile he again picked up his chef's cap at the New American Hotel to replenish his bankroll. He worked nights and returned to the yacht club at 4 A.M. each morning. It was a bad winter, with much ice, and since *Atom* was moored a hundred yards out, he had to cross in a dinghy. In January, Sheepshead Bay froze over and he could not get aboard. He stayed onshore with friends. Then the ice broke up under a gale and *Atom* went up against a dock, damaging the bowsprit and part of a rail.

But spring came, and again *Atom* was ready. Loaded down with gifts from friends at the club, he departed. The weather was variable, and on the radio he heard that a French warship had picked up Edith Bauman, the German woman participating in the Single-handed Transatlantic Race, from her life raft after she had encountered Hurricane Brenda.

On July 31, at 8:30 A.M., a U.S. Navy plane came over and signaled with a flare that he was approaching danger. It turned out to be a white buoy marking the spot where the submarine *Scorpion* had been lost. He put in at Fayal, where he was given a hero's welcome by the Club Nàutico. He had a pleasant stay, attended the bull fights, talked to yachting groups. On August 18, he departed for Gibraltar, reached the south coast of Spain on September 19, was received with great hospitality at the Real Club de Regata, as usual. He arrived at Valras on October 8, after 106 days sea time, completing his ninth crossing.

In the spring of 1970, he tried to return to New York, but twenty days out he had to put in for repairs. In the spring of 1971, he started out again on his tenth crossing, which was to be the start also of his third circumnavigation. But by the time he had piled up on the beach on October 25, he had already given up the idea, and was returning to New York to work in the Taft Hotel in order to make enough money to return to France. There, in Marseilles, a yacht harbor had been built and dedicated to him, Jean Gau, and also it had been decreed that Jean Gau could moor his *Atom* there for the rest of his life.

But now, on the lonely coast of Maryland, his home for twenty-six years was high and dry. What would happen to him? When he stumbled to the beach cottage of Robert Clements, one of only two houses on thirty-five miles of sandy seashore, Jean Gau could not believe his good fortune. But there was more to come. Clements was an insurance man, and knew what to do. He called his colleagues in Washington, as well as the Coast Guard, the Coast Guard Auxiliary, and the Boat Owners Association of America. Soon Jean Gau was almost overwhelmed with Good Samaritans.

A guard was posted immediately to prevent anyone from making a salvage claim. The National Park Service rushed in to help. The navy and the Coast Guard dispatched men and equipment. On November 6, just 13 days after *Atom* went aground, a Park Service crew dug a 30-foot trench, 8 feet wide and 4 feet deep. A six-man navy salvage crew brought in a 44-foot utility boat and sand-moving equipment. The sand and water were pumped out of *Atom*, the hull patched with fast-setting cement. With the private cruiser *Janet L* offshore pulling on a hauser, *Atom* was brought free of the beach at 8:22 A.M. and towed to Ocean City to be hauled out by crane for permanent repairs.[8]

The order for the navy salvage assistance had come direct from the Pentagon, from Commander Robert Moss, deputy director of ocean engineering, who said his decision was made because "of the old gentleman's history with his boat." It was not, he added, a normal navy-type duty, but they did try to help out now and then and show human compassion.

As for Jean Gau, he was more than ever confused. He had lived as he wished all his life, accepting the best his two countries could offer, although he had asked nothing but freedom and opportunity. In *la belle* France, there awaited a new yacht harbor dedicated to his honor. In his adopted country, he had been able to finance his every wish. And now, such an outpouring of compassion, completely unsolicited, when his beloved *Atom* came to grief on this lonely seashore—it was too much.

Eh bien? Tout est bien qui finit bien!

24

Four Winds and a Bachelor

When you get near the Strait of Magellan, you will find that the test of human endurance has been sufficient, and you will stow your chart of the cape. Let me give you my charts of the strait, which will then come in useful.[1]

DURING THE DARK DAYS OF THE GERMAN OCCUPATION OF France, in a first-floor home workshop, about twenty yards from a bridge over the Marne at Nogent-sur-Marne, a young man laboriously worked with hand tools, cutting and forming ribs for a boat with lumber scrounged from dumps, and assembling them into frames on paper patterns. The boat was a nine-meter sloop, designed by the well-known naval architect Henri Dervin for coastwise cruising and racing, but radically modified by this young man whose name was Marcel Bardiaux.[2]

It was not a time for yacht building—or perhaps it was. Anything to keep one's mind off the war and the morale uplooking. At the time, England still reeled from the air assault. The Americans were bogged down in the Pacific, slowly beginning the island-hopping comeback toward Japan. Vito Dumas was home again after his strange circumnavigation in the Roaring Forties. During the next three years, the world would descend into the desperate abysses of total war. There would be no personal freedom, and in much of the world, not even hope.

The young man, Marcel Bardiaux, however, had other plans. A

seaman, discharged by the navy after the fall of France, he yearned for the freedom of the oceans, like Gerbault some twenty years before. The dream ship taking shape on the floor of the workshop was, indeed, similar in lines to *Firecrest*, Gerbault's Dixon Kemp racer; and, like Gerbault, Bardiaux had been a national champion in a popular sport. He had everything but money. Living in occupied France was an extreme hardship for him and his mother, who was a war widow from World War I.

Life had always been hard for Madame Bardiaux. During the 1920s, even with her small widow's pension, she had been forced to work to raise her son, Marcel, an only child with delicate health (and to tell the truth, somewhat overprotected from life). When Marcel was only eleven, in spite of his fragile physique, he went to work to help support the family. Frugality is a French national trait, and out of his small earnings he managed to save enough to build his first boat. At fourteen, he left home and went to Le Havre to find a ship to sail on, but instead the police found him and returned him to his mother.

Next, Marcel turned to the outdoors—camping, canoeing, fishing. He designed a lightweight tent for hiking, and a kayak that was so successful that soon he was selling all he could produce. He became a founding member of the Kayak Club of France, a restless group of youths who spent long weekends on the Marne. During this period, he had his first real adventures. He paddled down the Danube to the Black Sea and Istanbul. He crossed the Aegean, went on to Marseilles, and returned to Paris via the inland canals. By the time he was nineteen, Marcel was the canoe and kayak champion of France.

He also took up skiing, motorcycle and car racing, and studied river navigation. He entered the navy as the war clouds gathered in the halcyon 1930s. Instead of a delicate child, he had grown into a wiry, robust, rugged young man, with a collection of many skills, and a keen mind sharpened by competition. The delicate wings of the child had grown tough and powerful.

Out of the service after the Occupation, there was little to look forward to but long years of war. In a bookshop one day, he came across the plans for Henri Dervin's little sloop in a yachting publication.

She was a Bermudian, 30 feet overall, without bowsprit, with a beam of 8 feet 10 inches and a displacement of 4 tons. Not designed for ocean travel, yet her lines showed a good seaworthy model. With his experience with small craft, he set to work with wrapping paper and pencil and soon modified the hull to suit his needs. He knew from reading *Le Yacht,* and the books of Slocum, Pidgeon, Gerbault, and O'Brien, what was required. He made almost a clean sweep of the deck, leaving only a small trunk cabin which he faired in like an airplane wing. This still gave him 5 feet 8 inches of headroom and yet gave the boat a configuration similar to a submarine.

He had already named her: *Les Quatre Vents* ("The Four Winds"). And she would become the smallest yacht yet to circumnavigate. *Qui sait?*

But first she must be launched; and before that she must be built—in wartime occupied France.

He began collecting materials, including 1,274 kgs. of scrap lead, old battery plates, with which he built the keel himself in his shop, melting down each batch and casting the last of it during a midnight air raid. By 1945, when the Germans were retreating, he had the frames and other parts ready to set up. Then the Germans blew up the bridge only 20 yards from his shop, and nearly ended everything. He salvaged the parts and found a shed in a safer location. Finally, at 12:30 naval time, July 29, 1949, the war over, with the help of friends he hauled *Les Quatre Vents* through the cobbled streets of Perreux on two truck axles and launched her.

The next months were spent outfitting his dream ship, and writing articles for *Le Yacht.* His project received wide publicity, and, in some cases, newspaper stories not to his liking. Then on Sunday morning, January 1, 1950, the time had come. With typical Bardiaux zest and flare for center stage, the erstwhile circumnavigator welcomed at first the flotilla of kayaks and motor launches on the Seine, the banks crowded with spectators, the newspaper and television cameras. It was a jolly crowd that became more boisterous, until it turned into a jeering mob as he tried to start his tiny gasoline engine. But one figure in the crowd everyone recognized and respected. It was Marin-Marie, the famous painter and bluewater sailor.

Marin-Marie called down to Bardiaux, "Let them chatter, my lad; it's the only thing they know how to do."

It was now past time to go. Behind him was the send-off party of the Touring Club of France, and that of the Federation of Ex-Sailors of the Merchant Marine and Navy. But it had been one of those days. On his way to the quay that morning, he had been arrested for speeding. Now the pesky engine would not start. In anger, he threw down the crank and took up a sculling oar.

"Bravo!" came a voice from the audience. "But if you are planning to go around the world like that, you will have sore wrists!"

Out of sight of the crowd, he accepted a tow, and after many false starts, encumbered by friends and well-wishers and a female companion or two, he made it to the coast. Because it was cold that winter and Bardiaux had little heat aboard, his linen got moldy, the photographic equipment sprouted fungus, and everything was covered with beads of condensation. In the middle of January, at Tancarville, he tied up to complete the outfitting. A trial run was made with friends on January 22. They were caught by a falling tide and grounded for seven hours. On February 3, he reloaded and headed for the customs office, which was closed for the weekend. He had to wait until Monday to get his seaworthiness inspection, before he could get his papers.[3]

When he was finally cleared, a raging gale swept over the region, accompanied by neap tides. Not until February 14 did he get away, departing in a nasty sea—then going aground near the lighthouse. Later, at Ouistreham, he was welcomed by the local canoeing society. Additional repairs were made.

Not until late June did he reach the pleasant little port of La Rochelle, as he made it a practice to stop and visit at every opportunity and to enjoy the hospitality of yacht clubs. He learned that the fabled lone navigator, Commander Louis Bernicot, was here on *Anahita*. Marcel sought him out and was welcomed aboard the veteran cutter. The two talked for hours, and Marcel got Bernicot's autograph on his copy of the navigator's book, *The Cruise of the Anahita*.[4]

Before they parted, Bernicot told him, "I will sail as long as I can climb the masthead."

The words were prophetic. Sometime later, Commander Bernicot was killed in a fall from the mast.

From La Rochelle, Bardiaux sailed to Arcachon for more repairs and alterations, then on Saturday, October 21, at 0600, he said goodbye for the last time and sailed from France for Vigo, Spain, in what was probably the longest good-bye in maritime history.

He arrived at the popular yachting stop in Portugal on November 7. It was December before he could extract himself from the festivities and formalities. *Les Quatre Vents* took a beating on the crossing to Casablanca, but there Marcel found the port full of vagabond yachtsmen waiting for weather to follow their whims. He enjoyed himself among other sea wanderers, such as Edward Allcard, and managed to wreck a friend's car and suffer a twisted knee that required a doctor and a month's bedrest.

On March 24, Bardiaux planned to leave but inspection showed the hull copper corroded from the harbor pollution. He was delayed until May 11. He had been tempted to take aboard the beautiful stowaway from Allcard's yacht, but "saw a dangerous reef ahead." He later wrote: "This act of courage (in resisting temptation) was not accomplished without lingering regrets."

He arrived at Las Palmas on June 6, 1951, to spend some time in languid loafing amid the harbor thieves and pollution. He stocked up on fresh fruits and vegetables, enjoyed some local female companionship, and, on June 18, cleared for Dakar.

Les Quatre Vents had already proved to be a wet boat. Most of his equipment became encrusted with mildew or rusty. At Dakar, he was warmly greeted by the navy club, his coming announced in advance by his articles in *Le Yacht*. The time passed. He beached the boat for repairs. He cut his foot and got infection from jiggers that burrowed into his flesh. He injured his jaw, got an infection in his left hand. Air France pilots advised him to wait for a better season.

Because he always carried a kayak on deck, local canoe enthusiasts sought him out. Dakar was no exception. He made many friends, stayed in private homes, and made side trips into the country. A local navy officer taught him navigation and the use of the sextant and tables. He refitted with nylon rigging. Then, on September 23, 1951, he weighed anchor and set out for South America.

It was a boisterous passage, for twenty-eight days it was like living inside a cement mixer. Finally reaching Rio, he was made a guest member of the Rio Yacht Club and entered upon a long, exhausting round of social activity. The French warship *Jeanne d'Arc* was also in port, but he found himself snubbed by the officer corps aboard, although the local consular community had adopted him. His plans for leaving were nearly upset by a girl named Leni, and by running out of funds that sent him back to the typewriter for *Le Yacht*.

During this period, he found among his mail a haughty letter from the French consul informing him that his reserve unit had transferred him from the navy to the army.

Je n'y comprends rien. The French, he thought, have a genius for utilizing skills. Having been conscripted into the navy, he had worn out many broomsticks on the flagstones of the fleet depot at Brest. Then, having earned an A.B., he was given a telephone switchboard to man during the war, on a lookout post. After all this training, when he had finally learned navigation, now he was to be transferred to the infantry.[5]

So now the new private of infantry put to sea, bound south, with a send-off flotilla of yachts from the club. He stopped at Ilha Grande, the Brazilian "Polynesia," and managed to injure his arm again. Further down the coast, he stopped at the outstation of the Yacht Club de Guaruja, amid a cloud of mosquitoes. He visited São Paulo, "the only city in Brazil where people work." Here he found Americans owned much of the business, but French, Italian, and German firms were not far behind. They were producing chemicals, coffee, and pharmaceuticals, for Brazil and all South America took pills for every possible ailment and change of the weather.[6]

After sampling the wine and women of São Paulo, he sailed on to Buenos Aires. He had now become a celebrity in South America, and at each stop it became more difficult to leave. But on March 8, 1952, he sailed from the Argentine Yacht Club moorage, stopping at Mar del Plata to careen, and spent two happy weeks at the naval base at Puerto Belgranco, where he had access to the shops and marine ways. Most Argentine towns have cultural centers called Alliance Française for teaching French. He was always welcomed at these centers.

Getting away again, Bardiaux gave wide berth to the Gulf of St. George. Soon he began to encounter the mirages of which Slocum had written. He stopped in at Puerto Deseado, and was welcomed by people who had expected him. An Argentine training ship was in port along with French wool buyers.

On April 23, he headed south, called at San Julian where Magellan had wintered, and found a friendly family ashore to visit. He spent weeks on this coast, visiting out-of-the-way ranches owned by Englishmen, Americans, French, and Argentines. He made side trips to immense sheep ranches and magnificent villas in the outback.

The austral winter was approaching. On May 7, Bardiaux was close to San Diego Cape, the southeast corner of Tierra del Fuego. The weather was terrible, the currents running nine knots, the barometer falling. He recalled that the *Bounty* had not been able to get around the Horn at this time of year, and was forced to go east-about. He went into Thetis Bay for shelter, but the violent currents and swells broke his anchor chain. A swirling snowstorm struck, and he suffered a sixty-hour sleepless vigil. Finally, he got through the channel with the keel touching occasionally. In calm water, he sept soundly for ten hours.

Cape Horn was less than 100 miles away. He rounded Cape San Diego in weather so frigid that he had to dip his sails frequently to unfreeze them. There was a heavy current and frequent breakers. He could not heave-to or put out a sea anchor. Then, suddenly, cooped up in the cabin trying to hang on, he felt the boat begin to turn over. He leaped out of the cabin and was almost taken overboard. Finally, *Les Quatre Vents* recovered, and sluggishly returned upright. The bottom was filled with water, the deck swept clean, the bilge filled with broken glass, and the cabin filled with the odor of carbon tetra-chloride from the fire extinguisher. He got everything secured at last, changed into dry clothing, and lay down for a rest.

On Sunday, May 11, 1952, he was off again. Soon he sighted Deceit Island and let down twenty-five fathoms of anchor chain to reach bottom. He spent two nights here but did not rest. Many times he told himself, "If I get away with it this time, I will never set foot in a boat again."

He wanted to pass Cape Horn in daylight so he could take photos. The swell was enormous. There was drifting ice about him. At 0600, on May 12, four hours after leaving Deceit Island, he figured he was five miles off Horn Island. At 1230, the sky opened for a few minutes and the pyramid of Cape Horn was abeam. There was no chance of landing there, but he saw St. Martin's Cove on Hermit Island, twelve miles to the west. He made it and anchored in thirty fathoms, with waves breaking and violent williwaws lashing at him.

Anyway, he had conquered Cape Horn. *Tenez bon!*

The Argentine navy was expecting him at their base at Ushuaia, so he set off again and worked his way through the strait between Lennox and Navrin islands and into Beagle Channel. He stopped briefly at the little cosmopolitan settlement of Port Haberton, populated by Yugoslavians and Portuguese. This was the route of Al Hansen, who had been first to round the Horn from east to west.[7]

On May 16, breaking ice off the sloop with a hammer, he left for Ushuaia where he was given the V.I.P. treatment with a suite of his own at the base. Through June, he worked his way among the Patagonian channels, not seeing another person for two months. He passed the Milky Way of Slocum's experience, and then went north-ward to Chiloé where Al Hansen had disappeared. In Chilean waters, he was adopted by the navy and air force. He took many photos and wrote many articles. Often encountering wretched specimens in native camps, he would give them food in return for pelts, until his vessel began to look like a Hudson's Bay trading post. He was welcome, of course, wherever he called.

At Valdivia, where Robinson had lingered with *Varua*, he was hosted by the Yacht Club and the Aero Club. He thought the city looked much like Rouen, which was known as the Sink of Normandy. The roads were impassable for nine months of the year. Some French ranchers sent a private plane to pick him up for a visit at their estate. Leaving, he partied his way up the coast to Valparaiso, whose harbor he found even more polluted than Casablanca. He stayed at the naval base in Quintero for six months, living at the officers' mess and using the facilities to refit. An airplane and a car were placed at his disposal, and he was taken to Santiago to see a specialist about his partially paralyzed leg.

On Saturday, April 4, he departed Coquimbo for Tahiti via the Marquesas, 4,880 miles away, which kept him at sea for 43 days. Arriving finally at Papeete, he received his worst reception of the entire voyage from a countryman, a pompous harbormaster, who did not regard Bardiaux as a conquering hero, but only another penniless yachtsman.

From Tahiti, his voyage took him to Bora Bora, New Caledonia, New Guinea, New Zealand, and to Indonesia, during the monsoons with experiences among pirates; to Bali, and then to Keeling-Cocos, Réunion, Mauritius, and to Durban for a long visit with the other well-known French voyagers in port, to Cape Town; across the Atlantic again to the West Indies, up to Bermuda and New York, and then finally home to France.

He had exceeded Gerbault's long voyage, having made 543 landfalls in eight years, and by his own count, attended 5,000 parties. He had kept his word not to return to Paris until he had circumnavigated the world.

But it was good to be home again. *C'est bon!*

❧ 25 ❧

Moitessier:
The Logical Sea Tramp

*I have no desire to return to Europe with all
its false gods. They eat your liver out and suck
your marrow and brutalize you. I am going
where you can tie up a boat where you want
and the sun is free, and so is the air you breathe
and the sea where you swim and you can roast
yourself on a coral reef. . . .*[1]

IN EARLY MARCH 1969, THE FRENCH-COLONIAL SINGLE-
handed circumnavigator Bernard Moitessier, aboard his unique 39-
foot steel ketch *Joshua*, rounded Cape Horn and stood to the north
"outside" the Falkland Islands for the long run uphill to England to
finish first and fastest in the *Sunday Times* Golden Globe Race
around the world.[2]

Joshua was so far ahead of the other entrants that winning was
almost a certainty, barring any unforeseen emergency–and there were
few exigencies that the capable and versatile Frenchman could not
handle, including Cape Horn, which Moitessier had now doubled
twice in his long sailing career. Waiting for Moitessier would be the
cash prize of $25,000, the trophy, and the inevitable storm of noto-
riety, adulation, and perhaps a million dollars in books, endorse-
ments, public appearances, emoluments of all kinds—to say nothing

of the nationalistic pride of beating the English at their own game, and winning the *Légion d'honneur*.

Joshua at the moment was a shoo-in. Then something happened. Moitessier changed course, headed eastward along the Roaring Forties (after having already crossed his outbound track) on a *second* nonstop circumnavigation, automatically dropping out of the *Times* race.

In his log, and in a long letter composed for his publisher, which he hoped to give to a passing ship, Moitessier's reasons were—although he professed to be of sound mind—weird in the extreme, incomprehensible at best. He was in a region noted for phenomena and hallucinations, which had affected many lone voyagers such as Captain Slocum (for whom *Joshua* was named), Al Hansen, and Vito Dumas. Had he succumbed to some strange mental unbalance? Had he just plain gone nuts?

> *Why am I doing this? Imagine yourself in the forest of the Amazon. Suddenly you come upon a small temple of an ancient, lost civilization. You are not simply going back and say, "I have found a temple, a civilization nobody knows." You are going to stay there, try to decipher it . . . and then you discover that 100 kilometers on is another temple, only the main temple. Would you return?*[3]

But no. How could anyone understand? It is this thing, this strange cosmic dimension, which time takes. You feel as if you could sail on for a thousand years. . . .

Yet, to have not done what he did, Moitessier would have been out of character. His actions were completely logical for a man whose kinship with the sea was as nearly complete as is possible for a land mammal.

As his friend Jean-Michel Barrault wrote of him in *Match*:

> *For five months alone at sea, a man had dealt with a multiplicity of technical problems, had shown his physical stamina, had run risks which most would not have faced but above all had sought his own truth, had silenced the sounds of the world and talked with the waves, with the flying spume, with the torn clouds, with the albatross and the petrels. He had lived in the roaring forties, not as a stranger but deep in the beauty of the*

*ocean of which he said, "I shall always cherish the
memory of these gigantic waves, of this incredibly beautiful sea." What was waiting for him in Plymouth was
also the other side of glory, the tumultuous crowds, the
lack of respect for the individual, prying indiscretions.
The rape of his realized dream—he could not accept this.*[4]

Bernard Moitessier was born in Saigon in 1925 of a well-to-do
colonial family, and grew up in the colonial pattern of aloofness from
the native, conservative in politics and religion, set in ways, rigidly
conforming to social convention, narrow and bureaucratic of mind,
dedicated to proper physical activity and to evening soirees on the
veranda cooled by swaying fans manned by servants. In this atmosphere, he had an easy and delightful childhood, learned well the arts
of social intercourse, and became an accomplished swimmer and
tennis player, drinker, and flirt.[5] Because of the accident of birth, he
was too young for World War II, and anyway the Japanese quickly
ran over all of Southeast Asia in the beginning. In the political
upheavals following the war, when France tried unsuccessfully to
cling to its colonial empire in this region, young Bernard was prepared to find another world, one more suited to his imaginative and
romantic instincts. He was one of the early dropouts of his generation, to whom nothing made any sense, except one's own free spirit.

Thus, on September 4, 1952, Bernard Moitessier, bachelor, French
colonialist, free spirit, found himself alone on the Siamese junk
Marie-Thérèse, eighty-five days out of Singapore on the Indian
Ocean, somewhere near the Chagos Reefs, bound for he knew not
where. He was not even sure of where he was at the moment, as he
did not have aboard even a chronometer or a transistor radio with
which to determine his longitude. But he was happy. Behind him was
a life of crumbling estates with vast lawns, a procession of tutors,
pink teas and delicate women in lace and floppy hats, and politics
which he detested. He was young, a robust and wiry athlete who had
just won the 100-meter freestyle of all Southeast Asia. He spoke
several languages and dialects including French, English, German,
Dutch, Vietnamese, and Siamese. He was well-read, and particularly
conversant in the classics, and had a talent for writing, although he
had not published anything of importance as yet. He had long been
fond of sea classics, and especially the accounts of voyages in small
boats, such as those of Slocum, Pidgeon, Bernicot, Gerbault, and
Dumas.

Although he did not know where he was, he was not concerned. His ship had already become a part of him, and he felt himself to be more of a sea creature than a land animal, partly mesmerized by the continual oozing of fragrant tropical oils from the ancient timbers of his graceful Siamese junk.

Now it was night. The moon had just begun to dip to the west when a sudden lurch threw him against a bulkhead. He rushed up on deck in time to grab the mast as the sea swept over the deck. To his horror, he found *Marie-Thérèse* locked on a reef in three feet of water, some distance off Diego Garcia, with the tide falling and the sea making up.

Getting ashore with some of his belongings, he hiked down the beach for help. Coming to a shack, he hammered on the door and was greeted by a glowering, half-drunk black. Bernard spoke to him in English, Spanish, Vietnamese, and Malayan without success. Then he tried French, with was understood. He had happened upon the land of the Mauritian copra company on Diego Garcia.

At daybreak, with a large crew of natives, he and the manager of the company went out to rescue *Marie-Thérèse*, but the junk had disappeared into the sea without a trace. To Bernard, it was like losing a loved one by drowning.

After six weeks on Diego Garcia, Moitessier got to Mauritius via a British corvette. There began a happy interlude on this friendly island, with many friends, working at various jobs, first with the idea of working a passage to France on a ship, then persuaded to stay to earn money to build a boat. He began writing at the suggestion of the local newspaper editor, lectured to groups with slides, became a charcoal burner, then a commercial fisherman with scuba gear. He found the underwater world full of fish which he could sell for good money at the local market. In three days, his equipment was paid for. In one month, he was able to buy a secondhand Renault 4CV. He brought in from 80 to 150 pounds of fish a day, all of which sold readily.

On January 22, 1953, according to local newspaper stories, he was attacked by a shark, which tore off part of his foot. He escaped and was operated on at the clinic, and recovered nicely. A month later, he could walk normally and wear flippers. Next he was engaged to manage the local fishing and guano business. His bank account grew, and finally he was able to start work on *Marie-Thérèse II*, a double-ender of his own design, 28 feet overall, with a 10 foot 9 inch beam, and ketch-rigged. She was launched nine months later, and on November 2, 1955, Moitessier was ready to sail to more adventures.

Durban, South Africa, was as far as Bernard got. There he entered another happy interlude during which there gathered one of the most unique groups of sea wanderers ever assembled. Three of the most famous French singlehanders were in the yacht club harbor at the same time: Jean Gau (a naturalized American, but still essentially French), Marcel Bardiaux, and Joseph Merlot of *Atom*, *Les Quatre Vents*, and *Korrigan* respectively. And now another, the erstwhile colonial, Bernard Moitessier on *Marie-Thérèse II*. The bull sessions these four were to hold that winter, usually aboard *Korrigan*, would become legend.[6]

In Durban, Moitessier also met Henry Wakelam of *Wanda* fame, and hit it off immediately with the energetic Britisher. Together they went to Cape Town when they had exhausted Durban's resources, spending a year or more in balmy South Africa. From Wakelam, Moitessier seems to have learned much about scrounging and living off the land, including cormorants and penguins killed by slingshot in the harbor. The two young men made alliances with a couple of local belles and a delightful foursome emerged. They salvaged nylon warps discarded by whalers, untwisted them strand by strand, and rewound them into halyards.

From Cape Town, the two yachts sailed and raced across the Atlantic, stopping for several weeks on St. Helena, visiting Ascension and Fernando de Noronha, and making a landfall at Trinidad. On Martinique, Bernard lectured before the Alliance Française meetings, scraped the bottom and repainted, corresponded with his girl friend, Joyce, who was trying to join him by ship. On March 26, 1958, he sailed for Santa Lucía with a young Argentinian named Adolfo. Having no word from Henry Wakelam or Joyce, and feeling alone and depressed, he decided to go to Grenada and wait. On the way, tired and exhausted from standing watch for hours, he fell asleep at the tiller one warm tropical night. At two o'clock, he was wakened by a violent crash. *Marie-Thérèse II* had sailed up on the rocks. He managed to escape again.

Once more he was stranded and penniless, this time in the West Indies, half a world from the scene of his first disaster. Now he descended into the depths of mental depression, spending much of his time in saloons, begging drinks. In this state, he conceived the idea of building a paper boat and sailing it to France. The editor of the local newspaper offered to supply the paper, and volunteered a stake of $100 as soon as the boat was launched. Bernard actually began building this vessel. Fortunately, the Norwegian consul called him in and offered a job aboard a freighter bound for Europe. Within minutes, Bernard had rushed back to get his sea chest.

The tanker was sailing for Stockholm via Hamburg, where the ship was scheduled to go into drydock for repairs. Moitessier left here and took the train to Paris. Back in his homeland, Bernard now felt out of place, but he found a job as a medical "detail man," calling on doctors. Next he became a boat salesman, and at the same time completed his first book, *Un Vagabond des mers du sud*.[7]

The book was a best-seller, appealing not only to the reading public of the time, but also to a large and eager audience of would-be bluewater sailors for its intimate details of life at sea and practical information on small-craft sailing. It made him more money than he had ever seen before. More important, it established Bernard as one of the elite bluewater sailors of the world, the singlehander, and attracted the attention of many influential people in the yachting world. One of these, besides his publisher, was the well-known naval architect, Jean Knocker, who approached Bernard with a plan to design a new boat incorporating his practical experience. For a year, the two wrangled over details. Then a manufacturer named J. Fracaul, head of a 250-employee metal-working firm and a yachtsman, asked Bernard to come see him. Fracaul had a new technique for building steel boats and wanted to build one for Moitessier for just the cost of the materials.

The result was that Knocker and Moitessier designed 39-foot steel *Joshua*,[8] which was in due time launched and operated out of Marseilles as a sailing school boat for three seasons. During this period, Bernard met again an old childhood sweetheart, Françoise, now grown up and with three children by a former marriage. The two ex-colonials were married and Bernard became the father of a ready-made family.

On October 20, 1963, the children having been sent to boarding schools and relatives, Bernard and Françoise set sail for Tahiti on the first leg of a circumnavigation. The first stop was Casablanca to spend the winter. There Françoise got a job in a hospital to earn a little money. In May, they departed for the Canaries, and their children came down to Las Palma₃ for a long visit. The harbor was crowded with yachts from all over the world. Among the sea gypsies were anchored fifteen yachts with English, American, German, Dutch, Norwegian, and Australian flags. Waiting there were friends like Pierre and Cathy Deshumeurs on *Vencia*, and none other than Bernard's old friend, Henry Wakelam, and his bride, Ann, on their new 55-foot ketch.

On November 9, *Joshua* departed for the West Indies. In Trinidad, the fleet was already there, now including new additions. The boat was careened and repainted here. After the holidays, during which time the news came that the Smeetons had been rolled over and dismasted near the Horn, Bernard and Françoise sailed to Panama, arriving in late Feburary 1957. The passage through the locks was handled easily, and they paused at Balboa for more refitting. It was here that they decided they would not circumnavigate, but return to France from Tahiti via Cape Horn—"the logical route," as Bernard called it. He took advantage of Balboa's worldwide chart service to stock up on everything he would need later.

On March 14, they left for the Galápagos Islands, arriving on March 26. Here they spent a leisurely six weeks visiting remote anchorages, skin diving, lobster fishing, and exploring. They visited with the German, Belgian, Swiss, and American settlers on Santa Cruz, and on June 1 headed out for the long trade wind passage to the Marquesas.

They spent several weeks in the Marquesas, and in August sailed through the Tuamotus for Tahiti, stopping along the way. On August 20, *Joshua* came to anchor in Papeete harbor alongside Fred Debel's *Tereva*. In Tahiti, their little dog, Youki, brought all the way from France, was run over by a car. Bernard met the legendary William Robinson and was invited aboard *Varua*, where Robbie gave a graphic account of his fight with the survival storm near Cape Horn.

When they were ready to depart, *Joshua* looked more like a submarine, with the decks clear and a special enclosed steering station made with a plastic dome reached from inside. The lifeline stanchions were raised, the bow pulpit strengthened, and a steering vane improved.

After only two and a half months in Tahiti, *Joshua* was ready. Supplies and water were aboard to last three months. From Papeete, they sailed to Mooréa for a restful holiday, then on November 23, 1965, they slipped out of Cook Bay for the 15,000 mile nonstop sail to Gibraltar, the hard way. On December 10, they were at 40°32'S— in the Roaring Forties. In the first of many gales, Bernard experimented with various types of drogues, warps for trailing astern, and sea anchors, analyzing the techniques of many who went before him, such as Dumas, Slocum, and Smeeton.

It was during the worst one of these gales, with its monstrous seas, that Bernard conceived a bold technique. After a long weary stretch at the helm, while dragging warps to prevent broaching or pitchpoling, it came to Moitessier that *Joshua* was essentially a trade winds vessel, entirely out of place in these latitudes. He tried to recall what Dumas had said, but could not remember. He called down to Françoise to look it up in the book.[9] The secret was there somewhere. Françoise read aloud to him. Then they came to it. Dumas had followed the Roaring Forties all around the world, not by dragging warps (the Slocum school of thought), but by carrying sail and running with the seas (the Dumas school of thought). His technique was to take the seas at an angle of 15–20° instead of straight on the stern. That was it!

Bernard immediately cut loose all his warps and let *Joshua* run. As a big comber came up roaring behind him, Bernard would put the helm down and present *Joshua's* stern at about a 15° angle. The vessel would heel over sharply but respond perfectly to the rudder, and the comber would break harmlessly alongside.

He had discovered the secret of Dumas, and it had worked! From then on, the passage around the Cape was easy going.[10]

On January 13, they were well past the tip of South America and east of Staten Island. They changed course to the north and beat between the Falklands and Patagonia. On February 22, their noon position put them 50 miles north of the equator, 91 days out of Mooréa. On March 14, a swallow circled the boat and flew off toward Madeira. For two days, they heaved-to in a storm (something they would not dare do in the Southern Ocean), and on March 25 brought up Gibraltar to port at 6:30 A.M. On March 29, they were becalmed off Alicante and were almost run down by a trawler. At 3 A.M., the wind freshened and they put into Alicante, 126 days and 14,216 miles from Mooréa.

Bernard had lost four pounds. Françoise was as fresh as a spring breeze. She took a train to Marseilles to be with the children. Bernard stayed behind to look after the boat, and later joined them for the summer holidays. In the harbor at the time were many fellow yachtsmen, admirers, good friends, and fellow sea birds.

By now, Bernard was a national hero. Like Gerbault, he had become a legend in his time. His book was still selling well. Now he wrote another one, *Cape Horn: The Logical Route*, also an instant success. (See Bibliography.)

Joshua, which had been the epitome of all his dreams and practical experience, had proved to be the ultimate vehicle for a sea gypsy. She was fast, easy to sail, immensely strong, and comfortable. Also, Bernard now had a wife and family, plenty of money to indulge any whims, and a unique status among the yachtsmen of the world. He was in demand for books, articles, and lectures during a period when the round-the-world mania had been stimulated by Chichester and Rose, inflaming a whole new generation of romantics and adventurers.

It was while "Chichester fever" gripped the United Kingdom that the *Sunday Times* Golden Globe Race was conceived and organized. At least ten erstwhile voyagers entered the race immediately, or announced their intentions. Among the possibilities, everyone turned to Bernard Moitessier. What would the legendary Frenchman do?

> *Bernard Moitessier of France, among long-distance sailors, was already a legendary figure. He was regarded as the man to beat. He had already completed the longest nonstop voyage by a small sailing boat . . . A sensitive and literate writer, he had written two classics of the sea . . . Like Crowhurst, Moitessier had a Colonial background. A strong man, wiry, by temperament a romantic . . .*[11]

Under such pressure from the world yachting press, Bernard felt pressed to enter, which he did after his visit in January 1968 to the French Boat Show. He then left for Toulon to complete several months of outfitting, as *Joshua* was now five years old. On August 21, he departed Plymouth. Somewhere between this date and the spring of 1969, after rounding the Horn for the second time in *Joshua*, something happened to him. Within sight of the prize, he suddenly changed his course to the east and started on the second nonstop circumnavigation, having crossed his outbound track.

When word of this came to Françoise, she knew what had happened. The months of solitude, she told reporters, had temporarily unnerved Bernard. He would be all right. Just let him play this one out. But it was not likely that many in the world whom Bernard had left behind would really understand.

"When Bernard hauls in a tuna for food," wrote Barrault, "it is something akin to regret, for the tuna although food was also his friend. Gandhi of the sea? Explorer of the body and the mind seeking the limits of human endurance? Extraordinary sailor and possibly the greatest of all time?" Bernard would deny it.

How can anyone understand when he himself does not. A man of two worlds—East and West—perhaps he can accept only one infinite universal goal: truth and humility. Perhaps it is just that he longs only for those carefree days of *Marie-Thérèse I* and *II*, fishing among the sharks in the underwater world of remote reefs, bull sessions with fellow sea gypsies in exotic ports, long weeks of serene life aboard on passages, to read and think and marvel at the sea of which he feels a part.

"Do not think I am mad," he writes in his log. "But I have the impression that there is something that resembles not the third dimension, but the fourth . . . I am in very good health."

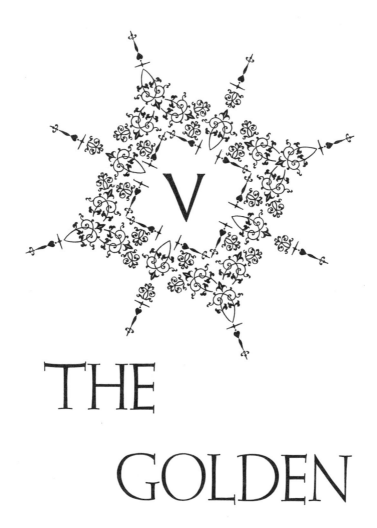

V

THE

GOLDEN

GLOBES

CHAPTER

26

Only Super Heroes
Need Apply

*The salute for Chichester is for achievement,
yes, for tenacity, courage, self-dedication, all
that. But there is something more.*[1]

DURING THE 1960s, THE PLANET EARTH PASSED THROUGH A
cosmical convulsion in science, super-politics, war and peace, and
social upheaval. The most costly and miserable undeclared war in
modern history—in Southeast Asia—touched in some way every living
soul in every corner of the globe, and ground relentlessly and frus-
tratingly upon their hopes, aspirations, goals, and personal liberties.
The news media, now augmented by omnipotent television, brought
instant crises into every home equipped with electric power (even if
only batteries and transistors), until viewers and listeners were surfeited with the extraordinary and the unbelievable. Even when Neil
Armstrong stepped out of the lunar module *Eagle* on July 20, 1969,
and announced to an audience 96 million miles away, "One small
step for man, one giant leap for mankind," effete network commen-
tators remarked sneeringly that Armstrong's epigram writer was
slightly cornball.

People everywhere desperately needed something personal to believe in, and they did not even trust themselves.

Then, in the middle of this decade, appeared the ultimate diversion, the epitome of useless and unproductive effort: the single-

handed around-the-world race in a wind-driven yacht. Because it was so expensive, so exquisitely unnecessary, it appealed to the perverse side of human instinct, not because of the competitive aspects (Damon Runyon once described a yacht race as being as exciting as watching the grass grow), but perhaps because it was merely one man doing his thing and accepting a challenge he did not have to.

But almost no one was prepared for what happened when an aging stunter named Francis Chichester arrived back home at Plymouth, England, after having sailed alone around the world on the old clipper route via the three capes—Good Hope, Leeuwin, and Horn—in his 54-foot, specially-designed *Gipsy Moth IV*. It was estimated that a quarter of a million cheering people were present to watch him finish, including the Queen and her court, there to dub him Sir Francis on the spot. No one was more astonished at the reception than old Chichester himself. In a lifetime of attempting spectacular achievements—mostly in the ancient and lovable old airplane known as the *Gipsy Moth*—no one had taken him very seriously.

This time, there was even less reason for all the fuss. After all, his trip around the world, even with just one stop, was nothing new. Hundreds of yachts had sailed around the world, most of them anonymously, in the three-quarters of a century since Captain Joshua Slocum showed them how. It had been proved time and again that any well-founded small boat could do it safely.

Not that there was not a precedent for the super-hero response to this episode. Down through history, people have (for reasons behaviorists have not yet discovered) inexplicably, spontaneously, and convulsively seized upon the individual of the hour and elevated him to a pedestal of adoration. Charles Lindbergh was one of these, Wrong-Way Corrigan was another, and Sir Edmund Hillary still another of recent times.

Of Chichester's feat, London *Times* staffers Ron Hall and Nicholas Tomalin wrote: "American news magazine essayists, puzzled as always by British reflexes, attempted lengthy explanations of the phenomenon: with the Empire gone and no money to send men to the moon, British reverted to the nobler, uncomplicated heroism of conquering the elements . . . (but) the public's response was scarcely as simple as that."[2]

I have attempted, unsuccessfully, to find the sources of such references in American news magazines. Indeed, *Time* magazine's comment was entirely different: "Sir Francis Chichester has managed to reawaken the world to one man's capacity to seek and to endure. He has served men by living their dreams of acting with tenacity and courage under pressure. And in this he has become a genuine hero— perhaps the greatest of the adventurers of his time."

Although *Time*'s summary of Chichester was more accurate than the gratuitous reference to American essayists made by Hall and Tomalin, there is much evidence that the spontaneous British response was, in fact, psychologically rooted in rebellion to Great Britain's lesser role in the post–World War II world, a fact which Hall and Tomalin tried hard not to recognize.[3]

In any case, Chichester's voyage not only renewed the secret dreams of thousands of people who led lives of quiet desperation, but inspired hundreds to duplicate or surpass his feat; and not only people in England, but in every part of the world, including behind the Iron Curtain.

The *Sunday Times*, which had belatedly become a sponsor of Chichester's stunt, found itself the recipient of one of the greatest newspaper promotional bargains of the century. Now the *Times* had become receptive to future stunts of this kind. This was especially true after Harold Evans, the *Sunday Times* executive who had sensed the importance of Chichester's voyage, became editor of the newspaper.

In January 1968, the well-known press agent George Greenfield, who had managed his client, Francis Chichester, with so much success, was now looking for another bombshell. He thought he had it in a young, clean-cut, refreshingly handsome and easy-going merchant marine officer named Robin Knox-Johnston. Greenfield approached Harold Evans about it, and a month later, Murray Sayle, who had covered the Chichester story, was assigned to background the new proposal, which was a *nonstop* around-the-world contest. After all, this was about the only stunt that had not yet been done.[4]

Sayle, during his investigation, learned to his surprise that literally dozens of erstwhile circumnavigators were already planning trips. These included not only Knox-Johnston, in his "scruffy little ketch," but one who was the favorite of everyone to win if there was a contest—an Australian dentist known as Tahiti Bill Howell, in a catamaran. On Sayle's recommendation, the *Times* set Knox-Johnston aside and began to favor the more colorful Australian.

Next, Ron Hall, one of the authors of the Crowhurst book and Sayle's superior, came up with the idea of holding a *race*, instead of a contest, with the prize going to the one making the fastest circumnavigation. After much discussion and argument, the final form, which was drafted in March 1968, became the *Times* "Golden Globe Race," in which there would be two prizes—one a trophy for the first to finish, and the other a £5,000 cash award to the fastest. The awards were not as incompatible as they appeared at first glance. The start of the race was not to be a "racehorse" getaway. The yachts would be racing against the clock, not each other. A fast boat, starting late, could obviously finish last and still win on fastest time.

By this time, at least a dozen serious contenders were already building or rebuilding boats to enter. To discourage the irresponsible, the *Sunday Times* wisely adopted a plan that was similar to the famous Northcliffe prizes in the age of air pioneering. To get around numerous complications, it was stipulated that anybody was eligible. As one writer described it, "It is rather like a horse setting off for a canter across Epsom Downs and suddenly finding itself taking part in the Derby." Anyone who left alone from any port north of 40°N latitude (to encourage French participation), starting between June 1 and October 31, 1968, and returning to Plymouth, was entered whether he knew it or not.

No route was specified, but since it is possible to sail around nonstop by only one route—the Southern Ocean and Cape Horn—this did not need to be spelled out. The *Sunday Times* publicly announced the race on March 17, 1968. Within a matter of days came the first official entry, Donald Crowhurst, an electronics manufacturer, in a Piver-designed trimaran. The erratic Crowhurst had first attempted to obtain Chichester's *Gipsy Moth IV*, but then turned to the trimaran design. Crowhurst claimed with some justification that he had been the originator of the nonstop race around the world.

Others who were well along in their own plans included an ex-submarine commander, twice winner of the D.S.O., Bill Leslie King, who had teamed up with Colonel H. G. (Blondie) Hasler, inventor of the self-steering vane, and designer Angus Primrose, on a radical design named *Galway Blazer II*, a junk-rigged, submarine-like yacht of extremely light displacement. *Galway Blazer II* was displayed at the London Boat Show in January 1968, at which time it had been announced that King already had two sponsors—the *Daily* and *Sunday Express*.

The previous April, even before Chichester had made his triumphant return, Robin Knox-Johnston had been discussing designs with Colin Mudie, the well-known bluewater sailor and yacht designer.[5] But Robin could not raise the necessary funds or sponsorship, and had to fall back on his home-built Colin Archer type, the 32-foot ketch *Suhaili,* which he had brought around from India. This clumsy vessel was considered by all, including Knox-Johnston, as being the least likely to win.

It was at this point that the young merchant marine had sought out George Greenfield, the literary agent and publicist, in an effort to raise money with an advance on a book to be written about his voyage from India to Britain. Greenfield instantly saw bigger things in store for Knox-Johnston.

As Hall and Tomalin wrote later, "His [Knox-Johnston's] judgment was impeccable always. Throughout the project, he had an uncanny gift for saying and doing the right thing—not the least of which was actually completing the voyage."

Another early entry was the famed French-colonial navigator, Bernard Moitessier, who was already a legend among bluewater yachtsmen, and considered the greatest singlehander of them all. He would be sailing his steel ketch, *Joshua,* in which he had already made a spectacular voyage around Cape Horn. Moitessier had been planning a circumnavigation as early as 1966. In the January 1967 Boat Show in Paris, he announced detailed plans. Then he went to Toulon to begin months of refitting and reconditioning the vessel, now five years old but a tough, proven yacht that had been tested on the wildest oceans in the world.

At the end of 1967, John Ridgway, a captain in the British Special Air Services who had achieved fame of sorts with his sergeant, Chay Blyth, by rowing across the Atlantic, got leave of absence and announced his plans to sail *English Rose IV* nonstop around the world. *English Rose* was only 30 feet overall, but compared to a rowboat, she was a veritable *Queen Mary.*

The *Sunday Times* assembled a prestigious panel of judges to make sure the voyages were properly completed without touching port and without outside assistance (and to use their influence to dissuade the irresponsible from entering, such as the young man in a skiff from the Outer Hebrides who could only be restrained by a court order). Chairman of the panel was none other than Sir Francis Chichester. Other members were: Michel Richey, executive secretary of the Institute of Navigation; M. Alain Gliksman, editor of *Neptune Nautisme,* and a respected French yachtsman; Denis Hamilton, chief executive and editor-in-chief of the *Times* newspaper, and Colonel Blondie Hasler.

Other entries coming in were Loick Fougeron, a well-known French voyager, with a steel-hulled yacht; Commander Nigel Tetley, a South African and British naval officer, in *Victress*, a Piver trimaran, which had been the home of Tetley and his wife for some time; and Chay Blyth, Captain Ridgway's companion on the transatlantic stunt, who entered *Dytiscus*, a 30-footer.

Tahiti Bill Howell did so badly with his catamaran in the *Observer* Singlehanded Transatlantic Race that he withdrew from the Golden Globe.

Crowhurst modified his *Victress*-class trimaran extensively and named it *Teignmouth Electron*.

Another Frenchman, Yves Wallerand, announced plans to enter, but never showed up and no one ever heard from him again.

There were, finally, 10 starters in the *Times* Golden Globe Race. One of them, Alex P. Carrozzo, who was dubbed "Last-Minute Alex," built his 66-foot ketch, *Glancia Americano*, in a record six weeks before the deadline. After starting the race officially, he remained at Plymouth harbor for another week to complete work on the boat. Alex, a big, bearded man, 6 foot 6 inches tall, collapsed with a bleeding ulcer brought on by the pressure, but departed anyway. He later had a relapse, got medical aid by radio, and finally put in at Lisbon with the help of the Portuguese Navy.

Loick Fougeron, in his 30-foot cutter *Capitaine Brown*, encountered a hurricane in the South Atlantic and had to seek shelter at St. Helena, where he anchored at Jamestown harbor on November 28.

Bill Leslie King, caught on the fringes of the same hurricane, was capsized south of the Cape of Good Hope and dismasted. He limped into Cape Town, out of the race.

John Ridgway, after ninety-two days at sea, put into Recife for repairs, and he was out of it.

Chay Blyth sailed nonstop for nine thousand miles, but was defeated by the monstrous waves south of the tip of Africa, and decided to put in at Port Elizabeth. His wife, Maureen, flew out from England and together they sailed *Dytiscus* back home.

Nigel Tetley, on his trimaran, made an almost flawless circumnavigation and crossed his outbound track near the Azores on the way home, to be technically if not legally the first to complete the voyage around (also in the fastest time). But, misled by the false reports sent out by Donald Crowhurst on the other trimaran, Tetley pushed his craft too hard, stove in one of the hulls, and barely had time to get off an S.O.S. before sinking. He was picked up soon after, having lost the race, his yacht, and his home.

Within sight of victory, the unpredictable Frenchman, Bernard

Moitessier, crossed his outbound track and then inexplicably broke off the race and headed eastward on a second nonstop circumnavigation, hoping to find his soul.

The English-colonial and erratic electronic genius, Donald Crowhurst, who had claimed to have originated the Golden Globe Race, and schemed to win it by cheating, continued his aimless wandering around the South Atlantic, putting ashore once at an obscure Argentine village for repairs, for a total of 243 days and an estimated 16,591 miles, sending in false radio messages and position reports according to a pre-planned schedule.

On July 10, 1969, at 7:50 A.M., Captain Richard Box, master of the Royal Mail vessel *Picardy*, bound for London from the Caribbean, was roused from his bunk by lookouts who had sighted a sailing yacht, apparently with no one aboard, ghosting alone at two knots with only the mizzen set. He stopped the ship to investigate, finding the trimaran in good condition, but like another ghost ship, the *Marie Celeste*, mysteriously abandoned. Donald Crowhurst, who had schemed to win the *Times* Golden Globe by fraudulent means, had succeeded only in destroying first his mind and then himself. The whole sordid story was left for others to reconstruct later from his logs and personal journal.

Robin Knox-Johnston, who had not been heard from since November 21, reappeared on Easter morning off the Azores. After 312 days at sea, the bearded but otherwise healthy young merchant seaman sailed into Plymouth the winner of both prizes. The least likely to even finish, in his "scruffy little ketch," Knox-Johnston became a real live bluewater tortoise who had through dogged British determination defeated all the more glamorous hares.

27

The Over-the-Hill Sailor

I stood and stared at that great hump of land. This was it. This was the moment I had dreamed about and planned for. I thought of all the others who had passed this way. Lone sailors as well as those in the great square-riggers. I was just another one, looking with awed respect at this most feared of all capes.[1]

THE LIVELY LADY RAN DOWN CHANNEL FROM LANGSTONE Harbor under mainsail and light genoa, drew near the "starting line" designated by the Royal Albert Yacht Club at their signal station on Southsea Front. The boom of the starting gun came across the way precisely at noon. *Lively Lady* gradually left behind her escort of yachts. The date was July 16, 1967.

The man at the helm waved a last farewell to his wife, Dorothy, who was with friends on an escort vessel. Then he was alone, heading for the English Channel, with 150 days of solo sailing to the next landfall on a two-stop circumnavigation of the world via the old clipper route.

The man was Alec Rose, a florist by trade, a few days past his fifty-ninth birthday, tall, lean, and hard, with a prominent high-bridged nose and soft eyes partly lidded when relaxed, but at an age when most men are reviewing their financial affairs, preparing for retirement, and looking at condominium advertisements. This one was at last completing a boyhood dream of sailing alone around the world in the manner of old Joshua Slocum.

By chance, his round-the-world plans were shared by another over-the-hill yachtsman, Francis Chichester, the flamboyant ex-airplane driver, real estate promoter, author, map publisher, and public figure. Neither knew of the other's plans, however, until Chichester, anxious to attract financial sponsors (and to enhance his own publishing business) announced his intentions in the usual flamboyant style. Publicity earned Chichester not only a brand-new yacht, designed especially for his adventure, but thousands of pounds in cash and material assistance. For Rose, it only sharpened his anticipation and caused him to abandon his usual methodical, stolid, and deliberate preparations in favor of the excitement of a round-the-world race.

Now, perhaps, because of his haste and carelessness, he was making his second start, almost a year behind Chichester. All it was now was a race against the clock to beat Chichester's time.[2] Worse yet, he was now merely following the sea track of his over-the-hill rival.

What kind of a man would contemplate a solo circumnavigation—to say nothing of a race around—at fifty-nine?

Rose was not by nature a competitive or combatant man, unlike Chichester. He was basically a loner who did not like to be beholden to anyone, and he had already become deeply committed to his goal before he became the object of nationwide television and press attention. He had not sought, and did not want, financial assistance or commercial sponsorship. He had viewed the voyage first as the culmination of a lifelong dream, and second as a holiday away from the pressures of his business. The last thing he had anticipated was, upon the completion of his trip around, to be heaped with honors, celebrated internationally, and knighted by the Queen.

Born July 13, 1908, at Canterbury, he was the third child of a family that included one brother and three sisters. His father was an engineer and trucking contractor, engaged mainly in hauling hops to brewers and produce to Covent Garden. Traditionally, the Rose family had been for generations associated with farming and growing things, with no ties at all to the sea.

A delicate child, he was so weak when he started school that he had to be wheeled to class, not able to stand by himself. He gradually overcame this, however, and his handicap—as is often the case—served to harden his inner determination and teach him how to handle adversity. Educated at St. Paul's primary school and the

Simon Langton Grammar School at Canterbury, he took to sports as he outgrew his childhood disabilities, joining the athletic club, taking part in long-distance running and rowing on the Avon. He also liked to read, and spent long hours curled up with adventure and sea stories.

At sixteen, he left school for an insurance broker's office. By now, he had acquired a deep interest in the sea and had worked long months on a three-foot model of a windjammer. He soon learned that a desk job was not for him. He then tried to ship out on a vessel at Gravesend. Unsuccessful, he returned home to join his father in the trucking business, where he learned to overhaul and service engines and equipment. He took up pigeon racing as a hobby, along with his father, who was an enthusiast. But racing pigeons to France and Spain only increased his desire to travel. His brother, Dennis, was in India with the army on the Northwest Frontier. So, at twenty, he bought a one-way ticket to Canada, where he worked on a wilderness farm near Edmonton. It was a hard life, working as a cowhand, logger, road-builder, and the pay was low; but at age twenty it builds muscles and helps release pent-up energies.

Later he returned to England and again worked as a mechanic and truck driver. At twenty-three, he married, and for six years worked with his father in the business. His first two children were born in 1932 and 1934. By 1939, the family had a small farm at Littlebourne near Canterbury, but soon the war broke out and he volunteered for the Royal Navy. Called up in 1940, he served with the minesweepers out of the Thames, and later in a convoy escort on the brutal North Atlantic run. In 1944, he was commissioned and placed in charge of a fleet of landing craft. He suffered a collapse and was invalided out of the service in 1945 with the rank of reserve lieutenant. The long, grueling convoy duty had broken him down.

By now, his family had grown to four children—two boys and two girls. His nursery business began to prosper, and when he was able to devote full time to it, he bought a larger one, raising flowers for the wholesale market. It proved to be a financial failure, however, and he was forced to sell and try to recoup with a retail fruit business on the coast at Herne Bay.

It was during this period that his interest in ships and voyaging reawakened. He subscribed to all the yachting magazines, bought books on small craft voyages, joined a yacht club, and purchased a war surplus German lifeboat and rebuilt it. Rigged as a wishbone ketch, he named it *Neptune's Daughter*. It had taken five years to complete this project, meanwhile studying celestial navigation with the help of one of his sons who was a merchant marine officer.

His marriage of twenty-eight years broke up, and for a while he lived alone on the yacht, sailing occasionally on the Channel and North Sea, using Ramsgate as a base. These voyages gradually lengthened until he was sailing regularly to the Continent. After he met and married his second wife, Dorothy, she joined him on these cruises.

Together they found a business they wanted, a fruit and flower shop at Southsea on the coast. For two years, the business kept them busy, but in the spring of 1963 Rose got the urge to enter the second annual *Observer* Singlehanded Transatlantic Race, which had been originated by Colonel H. G. (Blondie) Hasler, inventor of the famed self-steering vane. Rose sold *Neptune's Daughter* and looked around for a more suitable boat. He found what he wanted in a sturdy teak and padouk cutter called *Lively Lady*, which was then lying at Yarmouth on the Isle of Wight.[3]

He engaged Captain John Illingworth of Illingworth and Primrose to draw a new sail plan, shorten the bowsprit, and add a doghouse to the flush deck. Colonel Hasler himself installed the vane.

The second transatlantic race started from Plymouth on May 23, 1964, with fourteen boats entered, commanded by some of the most famous bluewater sailors—Eric Tabarly, Val Howells, Chichester, and Hasler. The race gave Rose the confidence he needed to attempt greater things—and he did not do badly in his first race, either, coming in fourth. The race had also opened up a new career, that of writing articles for the yachting magazines and lecturing. In the winter of 1965–1966, he and Dorothy began to plan his circumnavigation. While they were engaged in this, Francis Chichester announced his plans to sail around via the old clipper route. Rose thought then that they could make a match of it. His son had married an Australian girl and was living there. It would give him a chance to visit them and see his two grandchildren for the first time.

Rose kept his plans to himself, unlike Chichester, but word got around as it always does, and the yachtsmen and town officials of Portsmouth heard of it. Their civic pride aroused, they wanted to sponsor Rose against Chichester in the faster yacht. But Rose did not want to be sponsored. In the end, he accepted some financial assistance and all of the rousing support of the Portsmouth people. Before getting out of the harbor, *Lively Lady* was damaged by a series of accidents, including falling over at the quay on an ebbing tide.

Bitterly he postponed his departure until the following year, hauled out *Lively Lady* for repairs, and returned to his business at Southsea, commuting back and forth on weekends. The work done, the yacht launched again, the masts stepped, and the stores back aboard, finally, after months of delay, Rose cast off the moorings for the second time.

Accompanying Rose on his long, arduous voyage around was Algy, a large stuffed white rabbit which his grandchildren had given him for the singlehanded race. By now, Algy had become to him what the pilot of the *Pinta* was to Slocum.

His track took him past Ushant, then across the Bay of Biscay to Cape Finisterre, down between the Azores and Canary Islands, to the Cape Verdes and almost to Tristan da Cunha before turning east around the Cape of Good Hope. He was off the Cape on September 14, off St. Paul on November 12, rounded Cape Leeuwin on December 3, and reached Melbourne on January 19, 1968.

Lively Lady proved to be a good seaboat on this passage in the southern latitudes, but the violent seas at times made life almost unbearable, especially with his chronic lumbago which gave him great pain. On shore, lumbago is something to joke about, but on a small vessel with its constant motion, it is a crippling disability. Rose, unlike most bluewater sailors, kept his engine in good repair and ran it at regular intervals to charge batteries. Thus he was able to maintain radio contact almost all the way. There were the usual minor mishaps—a small electrical fire, a flaying halyard that struck him in the eye—but he ate well and enjoyed good health.

In the southern latitudes, he encountered monstrous seas and at one point was nearly dismasted. In between storms, he endured the maddening calms with heavy rolling.

His welcome at Melbourne was just short of tumultuous. He was met by his son and daughter-in-law on a yacht from the Royal Yacht Club, and stepped ashore to be met by a representative of the Governor General of Australia and the state governor. Messages of congratulation were read to him during the ceremonies. There were receptions, parades; then, finally, he retreated to his son's home in Williamstown for a hot meal, a hot bath, and blessed sleep in a real bed.

While he enjoyed Australia's famous hospitality, repairs were made to *Lively Lady*. When it came time to leave again, a large crowd gathered, along with television cameras, and an escort of vessels. On

January 15, he sailed south across Bass Strait, past King Island and Reid Rocks, and down the west coast of Tasmania to Eddystone and Southeast Cape, before heading east toward New Zealand. After a rough passage, he put into Bluff harbor where he was welcomed by another tumultuous crowd of yachtsmen, citizens, television cameras, and public officials. Repairs to the vessel were made, and, on February 6, he departed for Cape Horn—five thousand miles away. On the first night out, a Force 8 gale came up.

On Sunday, February 11, he crossed the International Dateline. He adjusted to the stormy passage down the Roaring Forties. On March 29, while he was trying to contact Punta Arenas on the radio, the British tanker *Wave Chief*, out of the Falklands, which had been sent to the area to look for him, came on the air. Via the *Wave Chief*, he was able to send and receive many messages.[4]

An airplane with television cameramen along with a reporter team from the *Mirror* flew over. He actually rounded the Horn on April Fool's Day, and during a clear spell saw Horn Island outlined sharply against the overcast. This was the moment he had dreamed about all his life. Now he could only stare at it. While he was staring, the *Wave Chief* came up to accompany him for a while. He went below to make a hot drink of lemon, honey, and whiskey to toast his achievement. Then a cloud descended, blotting out the Horn. He changed course to the northeast for the long run uphill and home.

On April 2, he passed through Le Maire Strait. The *Wave Chief* broke off and returned to the Falklands. On April 16, he was off the Rio de la Plata. On May 7, he crossed his outbound track off Trinidade Island. On June 4, he was off the Canary Islands, and on July 4, 1968, he entered Portsmouth harbor, after a circumnavigation that took just under a year and included two stops.

His progress since leaving the Horn had become the object of mounting public interest at home and around the world. As he neared the British Isles, the anticipation became intense, with the news media keeping up a continuous coverage. At home, preparations were made for a royal welcome—one that turned out to be the biggest in the history of small-boat voyaging. The escort that met him was a veritable armada of yachts and official vessels. On the Commander-in-Chief's barge came his wife, Dorothy, guest of Admiral Sir John Frewen and Lady Frewen. Rose was led to a buoy reserved for him off the Royal Albert Yacht Club. As he crossed the finish line, he dipped his ensign and received the finish gun. The crowd on the quay was estimated at more than 250,000. From shoreward came the roaring of cheers, the sound of sirens and factory horns; in the air rockets burst.

Algy came up on deck with Rose to wave a response. On shore, they were driven to the Guildhall where a civic reception was held, followed by a press conference. Another crowd was waiting at home. Meanwhile, the Royal Navy took *Lively Lady* in charge for safe-keeping.

Later, Alec Rose was dubbed Sir Alec by the Queen, after a recommendation by Harold Wilson, and the truck driver, cowboy, logger, ranch hand, florist, mechanic, and sometime yachtsman attained knighthood. He and Lady Rose would dine with the Queen and Prince Phillip and the family in the Royal Palace. *Lively Lady* would go on display as a symbol of the achievement of one low-born, over-the-hill sailor.

For one Rose, it was a fairy story come true.

CHAPTER

⋘ *28* ⋙

On the Wings of a Moth

This is Gipsy Moth IV GAKK
  calling London . . .
GAKK calling London . . .
  Do you read me? Over . . .[1]

At 0500, MARCH 20, 1967, A COLD GRAY MONDAY MORNING, the wind veered to the west again, but the barometer held. Francis Chichester emerged from the cabin, expecting to see nothing but wild ocean. To his surprise—and some annoyance—he saw, not a half mile away, the ice-patrol ship H.M.S. *Protector,* the presence of which was no accident, for all the British commonwealth of nations, to say nothing of the rest of the world, was concerned about this aging, if not ancient mariner.

After establishing contact, Chichester altered course to the north and at 1107 hours, while making good about seven knots speed, he recorded his position as being just off Horn Island, although the overcast weather prevented him from seeing anything but the *Protector,* still standing by.

He was beginning to hate that ship, especially since she looked stable as a billiard table, while on *Gipsy Moth IV* he felt like he was being churned in a cement mixer. On board the *Protector,* a reporter recorded that the translucent bottle-green seas moved like mountains of water, rolling and rearing up, to subside with brutal force as a 50-knot wind slashed off the tops of the foaming crests. The temperature was 43° and the icy wind cut through heavy parkas like a knife.[2]

While Chichester alternately fought the seas and cursed the

Protector, he heard an airplane and looked up in astonishment to see a Piper *Apache* coming in low and bouncing in the turbulence. In the Piper were Murray Sayle of the *Sunday Times,* one of Chichester's sponsors; Clifford Luton and Peter Beggin of BBC; and the pilot, former Chilean air force captain Rodolfo Fuenzalida.[3]

Photos taken from the aircraft and the ship revealed a long slender yacht, with only a tuft of spitfire set on the forestay, wallowing at awkward angles, almost lost in the streaks of foam. Had the lone circumnavigator in the yacht been able to see himself and his ship from the relative safety of the *Protector* or *Apache,* he might have exclaimed in horror: "My God, what is a 66-year-old man doing down there in that!"

But the man down there at the climax point of a spectacular, record-breaking singlehanded circumnavigation was about to reach the pinnacle of achievement and recognition in his long and erratic life as an adventurer, sometime daredevil stuntman, flyer, yacht racer, publisher, author, real estate promoter, and fighter. If all his other notorious endeavors had been mostly failures that were barely tolerated if at all noticed by the British public, this one would make him an immortal in maritime annals, earn him a fortune, worldwide fame, the soul-sweet aura of being a living legend, and knighthood.

In the past, the British public had created national heroes out of Shackleton, Scott, Hillary, and even Roger Bannister, who beat the four-minute mile. In 1967, England desperately needed a new national symbol, and Francis Chichester became a sort of super-hero.

If there was any doubt of this, it was removed a few weeks later, on May 28, when he sailed into Plymouth—from whence he had departed the previous August 27—to find a quarter of a million cheering citizens on the shore to greet him, and an armada of boats disgorging to meet and escort him in. There followed receptions, speeches, television interviews, and a ceremony in which the Queen formally knighted him. The welcome amounted to almost mass hysteria. The book he was to put together hastily would become a world best-seller. His little chart and map business would enjoy a kind of success never before expected. His place in history and financial fortune was suddenly real. Everything that came later would be anticlimactic.

Born in Devon, home of many of England's great seafarers, Francis Chichester's first encounter with notoriety occurred when he was eleven and had been bitten by a viper he had picked up and was tormenting. When his stern clergyman father made him ride nearly five miles to a dispensary for medical attention, the poison very nearly killed him. Only the timely arrival of the serum from London (although not by dog team) saved his life. The episode made all the newspapers, and for days strangers came to the hospital to see the brave little lad.

Rebellious by nature, Chichester had an unhappy childhood, devoid of the usual parental affection and security. Sent to school at age seven, he was constantly in trouble with the other pupils or the headmaster. With no friends and little affection at home, he drifted into a world of his own making, one in which he pursued excitement and adventure. Expelled from school after school, he later recalled only one with any sort of nostalgia—Old Raide, where he had been captain of the cricket team and excelled in military drill.

He attended Marlborough College, with its abominable diet and beatings administered for every kind of offense, including tardiness. He was good at rugby and most other athletics, and became the youngest boy to qualify for officer's training at summer camp.

In 1918, during his last term, the entire college came down with Spanish influenza. The infirmary and the gymnasium were jammed with sick boys, although few deaths occurred. When the Armistice was signed, he quit school. This infuriated his father, who had hoped Francis would stay there and prepare for the Indian Civil Service. It was family tradition that there would be one son for the army, one for the navy, and one for the Church. This one did not fit any of these careers, and now he had thrown off the opportunity for a career in the civil service. But the lad had read too many novels of adventure, especially those with Australian and New Zealand backgrounds. He decided to go there but outbound ships were booked months in advance. Meanwhile, he got a job as a farm boy in Leicestershire, where he worked for seven months at five shillings a week. It was a hard life, and he suffered from ringworm and homesickness. He ran away and tried to bum his way back to Devon. On the way, he was picked up by police as a robbery suspect. At home, he tried to get a job in a garage without success.

Finally, his father secured passage for him to New Zealand, and gave him £18. Francis was now eighteen, and it was to be the last time he saw his father.

Like many a son—and daughter, too—who, because of circumstances and personalities, have been prevented a close association with a parent, Francis had lost the one fleeting chance to break through the cold and distant barrier. One day, before he left home, his father, who was a bird's egg collector, suddenly invited the lad to go for a walk with him. Stopping on a bridge, they saw an egg below in a water wagtail's nest. His father softly offered to let Francis down so he could reach the nest. It was a poignant moment, which caught the lad by surprise, and he hesitated too long to grasp it. He never had another chance.

Francis sailed to New Zealand on the old *Bremen,* a famous German ship that had become a British prize of war. On the way, to supplement his stake, he got a job with the black gang in the boiler room and earned £9 before docking in Wellington. His first job in his new home was on a farm for 10 shillings a week. He was fired soon after, apparently because of his bad eyesight.[4] His next job was at a sheep station.

When he had emigrated to New Zealand, he had set a goal for himself not to return until he had a fortune of £20,000. After sheep farming, he tried coal mining, prospecting for gold, and lumbering. He became a magazine salesman, an auto salesman, a real estate promoter, and got married (and eventually divorced). In those booming years, he made his £20,000 and returned to England to visit the family in Devon, and no doubt to flaunt his success. Always fascinated by airplanes, he had learned to fly in New Zealand. Home again, he bought a De Haviland *Gipsy Moth,* the famous training ship with the Hadley Page wing slots that made it almost impossible to stall.[5] Most of his subsequent adventures involved this airplane, and years later nostalgia inspired him to name all his yachts after it.[6]

This was in 1929, just before the worldwide panic and depression. Unfamiliar with his new toy, Francis cracked up a couple of times, once with his sister on board, and then set off on a flight around Europe, which at the time was a minor air epic in itself, although just two years before the American "Lone Eagle," Charles Lindbergh, had flown nonstop across the Atlantic from New Jersey to Paris. This tour, however, was just a warm-up for what Chichester really had in mind—a solo flight from England to Australia, which had been done only once, by the Australian, Bert Hinkler.

Even then, or especially then, the monumental risks involved in these stunts never seemed to give Chichester even passing apprehension. A contemporary flyer of his, Group Captain E. F. Haylock, once observed that Francis had a genius for doing the right thing at the wrong time, which enabled him to escape death at the last moment.

Back in New Zealand, Chichester decided to fly solo over the

Tasman Sea. He had learned something about navigation and devised a simple method of obtaining latitude. He crashed at least once, and *Gipsy Moth I* sank at her moorings on Lord Howe Island. He raised the wreckage and rebuilt her and flew her to Sydney. Next he attempted a flight around the world singlehanded via England and the East Indies. In Katsuura, Japan, he flew into some telephone wires and crashed into the harbor wall.

Once more returning to New Zealand, he gave the wreckage to a grammar school, it now being beyond repair. During the next five years he fished, tried to write books, and lived by his wits. He persuaded a wealthy sheep rancher named Frank Herrick to buy a *Puss Moth* in which they would fly to England via Siberia. They got as far as Peking where the U.S.S.R. refused them a visa to enter the Soviet Union. They flew back across China and eventually to England.

Chichester again visited his family, and was as unwelcome as usual, especially since he was now broke. While visiting some cousins, he met Sheila Craven, who turned out to be a perfect mate for his impulsive nature. He proposed on a train soon after they met, saying, "I have £100 in money, debts of £14,000, and some trees in New Zealand. Will you marry me?"

She did, and they went to New Zealand by steamer. Sheila did not like colonial life, and they returned to England just before World War II erupted. Francis tried to join the Royal Air Force as a fighter pilot, and was turned down much to his astonishment. He had not considered thirty-seven to be old in view of all his flying experience.

With a friend at the Royal Aero Club, Chichester tried to form a squadron of private pilots who had lost limbs, an eye, or were too old for active duty. The RAF also turned down this proposal. Next he turned to writing navigation articles in aviation journals, which led to a job in the RAF as an instructor, and after the war into business publishing charts, maps, and navigation texts.

By chance, his business office was on the corner of St. James' Place, almost next door to the Royal Ocean Racing Club. Business being slow, Chichester accepted an invitation to go on a yacht cruise with a friend, a jaunt that would take him over the area of *The Riddle of the Sands*, one of his favorite adventure books.

Now bitten by the yachting bug, he took up racing. He and Sheila purchased an old derelict named *Florence Edith*, rebuilt her, and renamed her *Gipsy Moth II*. With his usual zest and competitive spirit (which the modern generation scorns as "combative"), he soon became an accomplished sailor and navigator, crewing on such famous yachts as the American *Figaro* and the South African *Stormvogel*.

Then he commissioned Robert Clark to design a new and fast boat, which he named *Gipsy Moth III*. This was built by Jack Tyrell of Arklow, Ireland, and proved to be most successful.

At this time, he was having financial difficulties, his map business languished, and he had come down with pleurisy diagnosed as cancer of the lung. Doctors told him the only hope was an operation, but Sheila, who was a believer in natural medicine, persisted until the head surgeon made further tests and found the tumor to be benign. There followed more setbacks and illness. Francis finally went to the south of France for rest and recuperation, and gradually got better.

One day, he saw a notice on the board of the RORC announcing Blondie Hasler's proposed singlehanded transatlantic race. Chichester entered, even though still half-sick, with the support and encouragement of Sheila, who knew it was just what he needed. The first race, sponsored by the *Observer*, had five entries, including Hasler and his unique junk-rigged *Folkboat*, *Jester*. Also entered were *Eira*, another *Folkboat*, with Val Howells; a small French yacht, *Cap Horn*, with Jean Lacombe; and David Lewis in *Cardinal Vertue*.[7]

Although Hasler's wind vane was acknowledged as the best in the world, Chichester devised his own. He bought a book on model yacht racing in which he discovered that the principles and techniques were well-established in this hobby. He went out to Kensington Gardens and for hours watched the model yacht races. In the book, he found the formula that a wind vane must be four and a half times the area of the rudder, and from this built his version, which he called *Miranda*.

Chichester won the first *Observer* Singlehanded Transatlantic Race, and placed second in the second race the following year, which was won by the lofty French naval officer, Eric Tabarly. This was the beginning of his fame as an ocean racer. He was cited by such people as President John F. Kennedy and Prince Phillip for his achievements. His business began to prosper. He wrote a best-selling book with the help of J. R. L. Anderson, *The Lonely Sea and the Sky*.[8]

The oldest entry in the first race, he also had the biggest yacht, a 39-foot overall vessel. He crossed the finish line in 40 days, 12 hours, and 30 minutes, beating three of Britain's best yachtsmen. During the race, to pass the time, he wrote a 50,000-word log, which was later published. The originator of the race, Colonel Hasler, came in second, 10 days later.

Chichester thought he could improve on the time, so for the 1964 race he made a number of modifications to *Gipsy Moth III*. There were fourteen starters this time, and Tabarly came in first in his radically new ketch design. Chichester did achieve his goal of crossing in less than thirty days—with only three minutes to spare.

By now, he had raced three times across the Atlantic, and crossed the ocean six times alone (except for one trip when he was accompanied by his son, Giles, as crew). Meanwhile, he had been reading about the great days of the wool and grain clippers that chalked up record runs out to Australia and back in the middle 1800s. His research led him to write another popular book, *Along the Clipper Way*, which revealed his plan to race around the world on the old clipper route and try to beat their time.

Still ailing and getting older, he commissioned Illingworth and Primrose to design a yacht especially for this venture. It was built in the famed yard of Camper & Nicholsons and named *Gipsy Moth IV*. She was a jinx ship from the start. The project cost an enormous amount of money, many times more than estimates, and the construction was delayed months beyond the deadline. On launching, to the dismay of Sheila and Francis, she turned out to be a "rocker." Modifications were made to improve the balance, but many who saw it thought it would be suicide to take her out of the harbor. Meanwhile, Chichester's sponsors were getting restless and financial problems mounted. Just pulling the project together and getting ready to depart proved to be a minor miracle.

Finally, on August 27, 1966, all things behind him, Francis departed Plymouth on the long 107-day and 14,000-mile leg via the South Atlantic and Indian Ocean to Sydney. It was an ordeal in itself just getting to Australia. Sheila and Giles flew out to be there when he arrived. His reception was a huge one, a preview of the one waiting at home for him. It was announced that the Queen had knighted him, but the ceremony would be postponed until his return. In Sydney, changes were made to the keel and to the self-steering vane. Then he was off again.

On the last leg, he suffered a knockdown in the Tasman Sea which nearly ended his voyage. But he was equipped with radio and was able to maintain constant communication with the outside world. Another innovation on his specially-designed yacht was a gimballed pilot chair below deck at the chart table, and within reach of this was a draft beer tap provided by one of his sponsors, Colonel W. H. Whitbread, chairman of a big brewing company.

In the end, his greatest feat was successfully sailing the cranky 53-foot *Gipsy Moth IV*, perhaps one of the worst racing yachts ever built, around the world singlehandedly with only one stop in 226 days at the age of 66.

Home again, not pausing to bask in the new fame as a super-hero, Sir Francis donated his yacht to a maritime museum and commissioned *Gipsy Moth V*, a 60-foot sleek racer designed by Robert Clark, which incorporated a lifetime of experience in flying and sailing small craft. Chichester's purpose was to establish a new ocean speed record for sailing ships. In her he set off to sail across the Atlantic in 20 days, covering 4,000 miles. He failed to do this by two days due to calms.

In May 1971, he showed up at Plymouth for the *Observer* Single-handed Transatlantic Race. By now, however, he had a painful tumor at the base of his spine, this time malignant. To ease the pain, he took drugs. Out at sea, he failed to make scheduled radio contacts, and a search was launched by the Royal Air Force. When located, his son, Giles, was put aboard with a navy crew while Sir Francis was flown to a naval hospital. There he rallied and went home. Not long afterward, he died. The date was August 26, 1971.

Sir Francis had long foreseen his death, and had described it as a "spinnaker run across the Styx from which there is no return."

He was buried with members of his family in the churchyard of the little Devon village of Shirwell, where his father had been rector.

He was given a hero's funeral with a coffin draped with the blue ensign of the Royal Western Yacht Club of which he had been commodore, and members of the club acted as pallbearers. As they buried him, a perfectly-timed flight of Royal Air Force *Hunters* passed low overhead in formation.

Pioneer aviator, gold prospector, adventurer, navigator, real estate promoter, publisher, author, racing enthusiast, few men have ever led a more colorful life despite personal obstacles. What mysterious chromosome in his makeup had snatched this man from a career as a soldier, sailor, or minister—or for that matter, from a life of degradation and dissipation, and at best obscurity—and thrust him into the lofty regions of the super-hero almost at the end of his life? It almost seemed as if it had been preordained from the beginning.

No one will ever know, but with Chichester, the Slocum school of bluewater voyaging came to an end. It never would be the same again.

$\approx$ 29 $\approx$

The Globe-Girdling Gourmet

I cannot say for sure what woke me at midnight. All was quiet insid(the cabin, but a peculiar scraping sound came from forward. The port hull had come loose. Worse yet, in coming off, the bow of it had holed the main hull. I went straight to the radio-telephone and broadcast a May Day call.[1]

LIEUTENANT COMMANDER NIGEL TETLEY, ROYAL NAVY, first learned of the *Sunday Times* Golden Globe Race on a cold Sunday morning in March 1968, while he and his wife, Eve, were relaxing on board their trimaran, *Victress*, at the dock in Plymouth. The newspaper carried the lead story on page one. Together, they read it:

> . . . *The yachts must start and finish at the same port north of 40°, leaving not earlier than June 1 or later than October 31. They must round the three capes— Good Hope, Leeuwin, and Horn. The circumnavigation must be completed without outside physical assistance, and no food, fuel, water, or equipment may be taken aboard after the start.*

Commander Tetley, a South African who had made a career after the war in the British navy, was up for retirement and he was restless. The idea of a round-the-world race in a yacht caught on instantly.

Eve also felt the excitement, and as they talked it over, they agreed that he should enter.

As with most entries, he found himself short of time once he had decided to enter. There were sponsors to round up, money to raise— at least £10,000 to build the 50-foot trimaran he had in mind. He approached a builder. Could the boat be ready by September? It could. He assembled a list of engine manufacturers, oil companies, food and tobacco suppliers—anyone who would be willing to contribute with the hope of getting some publicity. The trouble was that there were at least a dozen other serious entrants, and the gold vein of sponsors that Chichester found so willing was rapidly being mined out. As the responses dribbled in, it became obvious that most British firms regarded the appeals as not worth the drain on their advertising budgets.

In the end, Tetley was left with only one alternative—*Victress*, their family home.

Victress was a 40-foot, Piver-designed, ketch-rigged trimaran, built of plywood and covered with fiberglass. She had been constructed in the winter of 1962, and in her Nigel and Eve had cruised extensively in Holland, Denmark, Sweden, and around the British Isles. The boat was in need of considerable repairs and replacement of gear for such a grueling voyage, on which at least 14,000 miles would be in the Roaring Forties.

After Tetley notified the *Times* that he still needed financial help, the newspaper sent down Michael Moynihan to interview him, along with photographer Bob Salmon. As they sat around in the cabin drinking beer and talking, Tetley demonstrated the yacht's built-in stereo system. This immediately suggested to Moynihan a sponsor—a record company. Subsequently, Music For Pleasure took over as major sponsor, and the *Times* story was headlined,

AROUND THE WORLD IN 80 SYMPHONIES.

The departure of the round-the-world gang was not exactly a race-horse start—they were spread out over the summer months. The *Times* entry, Robin Knox-Johnston, had left on June 14 in his 32-foot ketch, *Suhaili*. Chay Blyth had been dismasted off South Africa, and had been disqualified. Moitessier and Fougeron had started, followed in a few days by Commander Bill King. Tetley got away September 16 amid the usual publicity ceremonies and television cameras, with Music For Pleasure's brass-band records blaring loudly from the wheelhouse speakers.

Outside the breakwater, *Victress* caught a fresh wind and boiled along at nine knots. Tetley had trouble right from the start. The tri was poorly balanced with its load of a year's supply of food and gear. The log speed and distance recorder was defective. To give the plunging bows more buoyancy, he had to turn on the wash-basin tap and drain all fifteen gallons of fresh water from the bow tank, leaving only eighty gallons aboard in tanks, plus thirty-two in plastic containers. Because he was exhausted from weeks of preparations and suffering from a nervous letdown, the heavy weather encountered at the start almost proved disastrous. The first day out, he broke a spar and had to replace it.

But gradually he got things under control and settled into a routine that lasted all around the world, which consisted mainly of eating and listening to stereo music. He and Eve had put up an incredible store of gourmet foods to tempt his appetite on the long, lonely stretches. He started on this by snacking on smoked trout and fresh fruit, working up to a large roast chicken while relaxing to Handel's "Water Music." As the days went by, this routine was interrupted only by sail handling, navigational chores, and keeping regular radio schedules with the news desk at the *Times*.

In between, he would cook a menu such as Chinese-style chicken and beef, with onions, beans, tomatoes, mushrooms, and peppers, washed down with a half bottle of Beaujolais.

Once he lost the line on the Walker log, which left only his spare. He took his mind off this with a lunch of cold chicken, tomatoes, beans, fruit, and smoked cheese, and ghosted along with the genoa listening to Schubert's "Unfinished Symphony." When the wind increased, he took in the genoa and had a supper of rice and curried prawns.

Sometimes in the mornings he felt weak, and attributed this to undernourishment, so he would prepare a special breakfast of eggs, tomatoes, brown bread, cod roe, and a milk shake with yeast added. To aid his digestion, he would put on Sidelius' "First Symphony."

So the days passed, Tetley dining royally, enjoying his favorite symphonies, while the *Victress* sailed south down the Atlantic past Cape Finisterre to the Canaries. On slow days, Tetley would cheer himself with roast duck and a bottle of wine. Nearing the equator, he took sunbaths, read books, and listened to stereo music. To tempt his appetite, he munched on smoked octopus or salmon. He kept his radio schedules, made daily time checks, lunched often on prawns with mushrooms and tomatoes cooked in wine. Breakfast would be varied with fried trout and a quart of milk shake with dried apricots and yeast tablets. At times, supper would be herring roe, olives, beetroot, and nuts. He varied his milk shakes with chocolate and butterscotch flavoring. There was candy to munch on night watches, whisky or wine before dinner. Lunches sometimes would be varied with Hungarian paprika-stuffed pork, with tomatoes, onions, and rice.

Victress was a good self-steerer, which left him much time to read, enjoy music, and to think up new menus. Usually his meals were supplemented with vitamins and yeast.

When he ran out of store bread, he began baking his own. On October 1, he wrote in the log that the day began with music and ended with roast goose, peas, and a half bottle of wine; and in between were chicken and ham rolls, orange juice, mushroom pie, crab, and milk shakes; along with Bach's "B Minor Mass" were stuffed carp, stewed lamb, baked beans, and red currant jelly.

He kept track of the other entries through radio messages. Knox-Johnston was crossing the Indian Ocean. Bernard Moitessier had not been seen nor heard of since September 1. Bill King in *Galway Blazer II* had lost radio contact. Crowhurst, in the other trimaran, was making superb time.[2]

In late October, Tetley felt giddy spells, which he diagnosed as dehydration and salt deficiency. He made up for this with Chinese broiled croaker and rice, consumed with lime juice. Feeling better, he planned a dinner of venison in wine. The next day, he tried out *nasi goreng* with prawns, fried potatoes, and kidneys in wine. Then he relaxed with Hawaiian music. His portable solar still did not work, so he read Coleridge's *Ancient Mariner* and snacked on cockles, prawns, and rice.

In the trade winds, he began to get flying fish aboard. These were fried in butter, and supplemented with Polish sausage, roast duck, smoked salmon, onions, cuttlefish, mushrooms, and stereo music.

Down past St. Paul Rocks, Trinidad, and Martin Vas, he repaired his engine and replaced a broken propeller. In mid-November he passed Tristan da Cunha. Passing the longitude of Cape Town, he ate the last of his apples. His eggs were down to half a dozen. He was in the Roaring Forties.

In two months, he traveled six thousand miles on the old clipper route. The hard going had now begun to show on the hulls. About this time, he found ten gallons of water in the port float and seventy gallons in the starboard one—about eight hundred pounds of surplus weight.

Reading more, he finally finished J. R. R. Tolkien's *Lord of the Rings*. He learned that Bill King was out of the race, and that Knox-Johnston was in trouble. He began to tape silly poems on the recorder.

The weather turned colder and more boisterous. He felt moody and depressed, and suffered from a sore throat and headache. He diagnosed this as poor diet. Studying the food list, he came up with a "tiger milk" mixture of Nestlé's full cream with vitamins A and D, Marvel skimmed milk, yeast, and fruit juice.

The seas began to smoke and roar, building up vicious pyramids of cross waves. There were frequent squalls and heavy rain. Then would come periods of calm with nothing but the endless motion of the swells.

At about Christmas, he was near St. Paul and Amsterdam. He lost contact with South Africa, but picked up Australian radio stations loud and clear. There were numerous whales around him, as well as large fish he could not identify.[3] He learned that Donald Crowhurst was the front-runner, and that Moitessier had been sighted off Tasmania on January 2. On January 11, he was south of Leeuwin and running into gales. *Victress* was damaged by a rogue sea. The wind increased to Force 11. The majestic waves rolling down on him were frightening. He decided to make for Albany, 450 miles to the north, as he did not think he would survive. The next day, the weather moderated slightly. Radio contact was made with Wellington. Pieces of molding were coming off the hulls. He decided to keep on while he could.

On February 1, he skirted south of Stewart Island, crossing Foveaux Strait. Near Dunedin, he encountered a fisherman, Keith Reid, who came alongside and took a plastic package of films and recordings to be forwarded to the press.

Just missing Hurricane Carrie, he continued on, marking his forty-fifth birthday and the date on which his retirement from the Royal Navy became effective. The trimaran was now leaking badly, and he tried to make repairs. He received news that Moitessier had been sighted off the Falklands—there was no chance of catching him now.[4] Nothing was heard of Crowhurst or Knox-Johnston.

Becalmed, he was gripped by intense loneliness. He fought it off with rice, runner beans, mushrooms, crab, and mackerel in tomato sauce. He scribbled poems and sang into the tape recorder. He listened to "Violin Concerto" and the "1812 Overture." Near Cape Horn he could hear South American radio stations. Once he was nearly pitchpoled by a giant wave. A panel in the wheelhouse was broken. The bilge was full of water again, and rice from a broken piece of Tupperware got into the pump. He had near misses with rogue seas. Some of the deck edging came loose.

On March 18, he sighted Horn Island sticking up through the clouds. His navigation had been right on the nose. He celebrated with a supper of rice, fried onions, mushrooms, and a bottle of wine.

On March 24, he cleared the Falklands and began the long climb uphill. By April 27, he was off Recife, and the next day north of the equator again. He learned that Moitessier had dropped out, but that he still had Crowhurst to beat. It was no longer the same though— some of the competitive spirit had gone out of the race. He recalled that Moitessier had told him: "It will be a question of survival. Every-one who goes around will have won."

On April 19, *Victress* was on a course to intercept the outbound track. The next day, the final drama began unfolding. He found a large hole where the port wing was supposed to be. The hull, weakened by six years of use and the grueling ordeal of a nonstop circumnavigation, was breaking up. He made repairs, and had a dinner of steak and kidney on deck. Gradually, he closed the distance until there were only fourteen miles to go, then ten, then five, and finally, at 6 P.M. one night, he reached the point.[5] He toasted *Victress* and decided to continue on.

But next came a series of squalls. The fiberglass had now peeled off to bare wood. There was flooding in the center section. Radio contact was re-established and a complete report made to the *Times*.

On Tuesday, May 20, 245 days out of Plymouth, the wind built up to Force 7. He was 1,100 miles from home. At midnight, something wakened him. The port hull had come adrift. Water was running in. By the time he got to the cabin, there were 6 inches of water in the main hull. He went straight to the radio and broadcast a May Day; he got the life raft and survival equipment on deck, waded through the cabin for the log and warm clothes and camera, and the emer-gency transmitter. Then he was alone on the ocean in the life raft watching *Victress* slowly sink beneath the foaming crests. It was a moonless night. At the first light, he set up the transmitter. He heard an American air-sea rescue plane reporting his position. In the fore-noon, the raft broached and got everything wet. He unpacked the life raft's rations and had a meal of tinned water, bread, and glucose tablets. Studying the instructions, he found that he had improp-erly set up the transmitter's antenna. He corrected this and immediately made contact with another American plane which remained overhead circling. Then came rescue by an Italian ship, the *M. T. Pampero*. Calmly Tetley photographed the U.S. Air Force *Hercules* rescue plane overhead and the approach of the ship. He was taken aboard in a classic example of rescue at sea, along with his log and films which were saved.

Eve flew out to Trinidad and was there when he arrived.

He had not finished the race officially, but unofficially Tetley became the first man to solo a trimaran around the world, and he did it in the record time of 179 days. He also sailed the first trimaran around Cape Leeuwin and Cape Horn, and had he not driven *Victress* so hard, thinking he had Crowhurst to beat, he might have finished those last tantalizing 1,100 miles to Plymouth and won the £5,000 cash prize and the Golden Globe trophy.

But even though he did not officially finish the race, no one—not even those who sail around the world on a luxury cruise ship—could say they enjoyed better cuisine or better music on the way.

❧ 30 ❧

A Tortoise
Among the Hares

*I could not accept that anyone but a Briton
should be the first to do it, and I wanted to be
that Briton. Nevertheless, there was an element
of selfishness in it. I was sailing around the
world simply because I bloody well wanted to—
and I was thoroughly enjoying myself.*[1]

ON THE DAVID FROST TELEVISION TALK SHOW ONE NIGHT
early in 1970, there appeared as one of the guests a young bearded
man of remarkable poise, engaging of personality, with a well-modu-
lated British accent of the kind that seems to fascinate Americans.
Unlike many of the tortured, self-righteous, bearded young dissidents
of the period who populated this production, this one seemed almost
disgustingly "normal" in political views and reaction to social stimuli.

In fact, Mr. Frost had some difficulty keeping his guest's mind off
one of the other guests—a beautiful and voluptuous movie starlet.
What had he missed most, Frost asked, on his 313-day nonstop solo
voyage around the world in *Suhaili?*

The young man leered at the other guest and replied: "What do
you think?"

The bearded young man was, of course, the winner of the *Sunday
Times* Golden Globe round-the-world race of 1968–1969, in which he
had sailed alone in his 32-foot ketch some 30,123 nautical miles at an

average speed of 4.02 knots, without putting into a port, without anchoring, and without any outside assistance.[2]

Many people since Captain Joshua Slocum's time had sailed around the world in small vessels, many of them alone—but none had done it nonstop. This young man, a professional merchant marine officer named Robin Knox-Johnston, had achieved a real first in bluewater annals, a fact which he himself tended to pass off casually, and which was largely unappreciated at the time because the general public had become pretty well surfeited with dudes sailing around the world, which after all had become ruddy commonplace.[3]

After all, three young Americans, also the previous year, had circumnavigated the moon for the first time in the history of man, and returned with a spaceship load of epochal scientific data—a voyage of infinitely more importance than a frivolous yacht race. This may have been partly the reason why Knox-Johnston did not receive his country's official blessing in the form of knightship from Her Majesty, as had both Chichester and Rose for lesser feats of seamanship.

Almost the direct opposite of Sir Francis Chichester, Robin caught the fancy, however, of a large cross-section of the public at the time. He almost perfectly fit the British image of a young, plucky merchant seaman—which, indeed, he was. His boy-next-door charm, outgoing personality, and obvious competence had wide appeal. Moreover, as has been noted by perceptive British journalists, such as Ron Hall and Nicholas Tomalin, "his judgment was impeccable . . . and he had an uncanny gift of saying and doing the right thing at the right time" (not the least of which was winning the Golden Globe).[4]

As Knox-Johnston himself puckishly noted in his own book, he had been sent to a psychiatrist before and after the voyage so that the mental effect of such an ordeal could be assessed. On both occasions, the head-shrinker found him "distressingly normal."

His only eccentricity, for one so young—wrote the young journalists, Hall and Tomalin—was his unfashionable tendency to very right-wing and blimpish views.

Born on St. Patrick's Day, March 17, 1939, in Putney, this "distressingly normal" boy was christened William Robert Patrick Knox-Johnston, which almost at once became Robin Knox-Johnston. He was of mixed Ulster and English stock. Both the Knoxes and the Johnstons were Presbyterian farmers who fled the lowlands of Scotland to Ireland in the early seventeenth century. His ancestry also included at least one East India civil servant who spent many years as a prisoner in Ceylon, but lived to escape and retire as a pensioner from "John Company's" service. His mother was a descendant of a Scottish family of lawyers which had migrated to Kent and thereafter engaged in maritime activities.

When Robin was an infant, World War II was raging. Once, when his father was home on leave, their flat in New Brighton was destroyed by a buzz bomb, the family narrowly escaping disaster. They moved then to Heswall on the Dee estuary where boats and the sea soon were to capture the lad's fancy. When he was four, he built a raft of orange crates. Next came a ten-foot canoe. At seventeen, he decided to join the Royal Navy, but failed the mathematical phase of the examinations. He then shipped out as an apprentice in the Merchant Navy, with the British Indian Steam Navigation Company as an officer cadet.

He spent three years on the cadet ship, learning seamanship, navigation, and other skills, sailing between England and the East African ports. He passed his second mate's examination in 1960, joined the *Dwarka* between India and the Persian Gulf ports, took his first mate's examination, and got married. The couple set up housekeeping in Bombay. The monotony of this life eventually motivated Robin and a fellow officer to build a yacht and sail her back to England. They sent for plans which appeared in a British yachting magazine, but got by mistake those of a modified Colin Archer. Since they wished to catch the monsoons of the following season, they decided to build this model instead.

The vessel, which was named *Suhaili*, the Arab word for the local southeast wind, was built by hand of native teak. The work went slowly, and she was not launched until September 1964, too late to keep their planned schedule. Meanwhile, Robin's marriage broke up and his wife flew home to England.

In December 1966, with the yacht about half-finished (and only half paid for), Robin and his brother, Chris, and a fellow officer, departed Cape Town on Christmas Eve. After a nonstop run of seventy-four days, they tied up at Gravesend. *Suhaili*, although small, proved to be a remarkably seaworthy and easy-to-handle vessel.

The vessel was berthed at the Benfleet Yacht Club, of which Robin was a member, and he reported back to work. While waiting for a ship, he began to write a book about his voyage. Meanwhile, he became interested in the current excitement over bluewater yacht racing. England was buzzing with sea fever over the upcoming *Observer* Singlehanded Transatlantic Race and Chichester's well-publicized escapades at sea. One day, his father remarked casually that Tabarly was building a trimaran, which was reputed to be faster than anything the British could come up with. The idea of a Frenchman beating a Briton on the sea appalled Robin.

Also, Robin suspected that Tabarly was going to attempt a nonstop circumnavigation, a project he had mulled over in his mind for a long time. As he said later, it was something that remained to be done, and he didn't care who achieved it as long as it was a Briton. Now the idea grew on him, until it became an ambition and eventually a crusade, as he confided to close friends and fellow yacht-club members. One of them, David Waterhouse, took him to see the now-famous designer, Colin Mudie. The imaginative and innovative Mudie had several suggestions of revolutionary concept—all of which cost a lot of money. Robin and his friends began to look for sponsors (there always seem to be well-heeled English angels around who don't mind investing a few quid in a ruddy yacht race).

But Robin needed £5,000, and even if he sold *Suhaili*, he would need £2,000 more. Failing to find enough sponsors, he wrote to his company and asked for its help. He was granted an interview at the head office, but the final decision was no. He still owed £2,000 on *Suhaili*, and also he owed the Royal Navy some reserve time. He then joined the H.M.S. *Duncan* in Portsmouth to discharge his obligation, and meanwhile had the good fortune to interest George Greenfield, the literary agent who had handled Sir Francis Chichester, in the book he was writing. Greenfield immediately grasped the potential, and urged Robin to go ahead with his preparations for the circumnavigation and leave the financial worries to George.

Robin went on active duty January 2, 1968, and a few weeks later, Greenfield signed a contract for a book about a nonstop circumnavigation that had not even got to the departure stage yet. This contract was followed by another for the American edition, plus numerous magazine and television commitments in the United Kingdom and the U.S. But also by this time, several of the contestants in the Golden Globe were well along with their projects, including Bill King, Moitessier, Chay Blyth, and Captain John Ridgway.

Completing his reserve training, Robin and his backers, including newly formed fan clubs, flung themselves into final preparations. Robin chose Falmouth as the starting point and finish line. *Suhaili* was reconditioned and fitted out. Finally, on June 14, 1968, Robin cast off amid the usual farewell publicity and official escort vessels. Then, suddenly, he was alone on the Atlantic, the months of tension, preparations, and uncertainties behind him. Ahead were more than 30,000 lonely miles. The moment of truth had come. His reaction was one of extreme let-down and depression.

It was to be a long, plodding voyage, and generally uneventful. Unlike the spectacular and glamorous starters, *Galway Blazer II* and the Piver trimarans, *Suhaili* was a lumbering tortoise in a race against fleet hares.

On June 21, Robin was off Cape Finisterre. On the twenty-eighth, he passed the Azores. On July 12, he left the Azores to port. Wallowing through the doldrums, he reached the latitude of Cape Town on August 23. He encountered a gale that knocked *Suhaili* flat. On September 10, he doubled the Cape. Sailing along on the northern edge of the Roaring Forties, he came up on the rocks called St. Paul and Amsterdam on October 4, after 112 days out. On the 133rd day he was approaching Cape Leeuwin. Passing close in on the Australian bight, he sighted Kooringa on October 25. A few days later, the self-steering mechanism failed. He made contact on shore near Melbourne on November 8, receiving news of home and passing on reports.

Passing to the north of Tasmania, he came up off South Island in the middle of November—and on November 20 he ran aground. Getting off, he headed eastward along the old grain and wool clipper route toward Cape Horn, crossing the International Dateline on November 25.

On January 17, 1969, *Suhaili* passed Cape Horn at 1915 hours, with light westerly winds. Robin wrote in his log: "Yippee!!!"

He passed the Falklands on January 23, and by February 2 was out of the variables. He passed to the east of Trinidade Island after 252 days out of Falmouth. On March 6, he crossed the equator, and on April 5 spoke to the tanker *Mobil Acme*, reporting his position by radio to the *Sunday Mirror*.

From then on, it was smooth sailing, and waiting for him at home were fame and fortune and the assurance that he would not have to worry about drudging through life in a boring career job again. The other nine entrants in the Golden Globe had failed or dropped out. All he had to do was cross that finish line. The press and television build-up had already begun, and by the time he approached England, public interest had reached fever pitch.

On April 22, after 313 days out of Falmouth, he crossed the finish line and was escorted into port to a noisy welcome at 3:25 P.M. First on board *Suhaili*, now rust-streaked and peeling, her bottom foul, and her sails tattered, came the customs men.

"Where from?" asked the senior port officer.

"From Falmouth," replied the now-bearded Robin Knox-Johnston with a puckishly straight face.[5]

After the excitement had settled down, and Robin learned that Donald Crowhurst was supposed to be missing at sea, he generously offered his £5,000 cash prize to the Crowhurst Appeal Fund for the family of the "lost" contestant. Later, at the Golden Globe dinner aboard the *Cutty Sark*, when the real story of Donald Crowhurst had been revealed, Robin stuck to his original intention of donating the cash prize to the Crowhurst family.

"None of us," he said, "should judge Donald Crowhurst too harshly, and the family will need the money now. . . ."

Still later, he announced he would stand for election to Parliament as a Conservative candidate, and immediately embarked on a publicity tour of the U.S.A. and British Isles to promote his books. From this, he drifted into more yachting activities, made several short voyages in *Suhaili*, and found himself pondering what to do now with his young life.

Still in his mind was the thought that had followed him all the way home on the last leg from Cape Horn, after he had listened to radio stations from the southern United States broadcasting recordings from the Apollo 8 crew as they circled the moon.

> *There they were, three men risking their lives to advance scientific knowledge, to expand our frontiers that have so far held us to this planet. I was doing absolutely nothing.*[6]

CHAPTER

31

British Steel Faces the Test

Maureen said, "Well, why not sail around the world the other way?" I had other things to think about, but her words stayed in my mind. Why not?[1]

THE TIME WAS 1950 G.M.T., DECEMBER 24, 1970. FIVE miles to the south of Cape Horn, a long white and sleek ketch with main and jib set, rose and fell slowly in the heave, beating against the prevailing light winds and currents.

On board the 59-foot *British Steel* was not a crew, but just one man—30-year-old Chay Blyth—and he was engaged in the last great individual sailing adventure left on the Seven Seas. He was sailing alone around the world, the "wrong way," east to west in the high southern latitudes—nonstop.[2]

Now on Christmas Eve, not even halfway around, Chay Blyth broke out his "Cape Horn meal," packed for him before leaving by his wife, Maureen, for the occasion—crab, ham, roast potatoes, and wine. It was not so much a celebration as a milestone on his voyage, marking passage from the Atlantic into the Pacific. He still had the Pacific ahead of him, then the Indian, and finally the Atlantic again, before he would see his wife and daughter once more.

But he was not exactly alone. Only the day before, he had rendezvoused with the British H.M.S. *Endurance*, on ice patrol.[3] A boat had been sent off to bring him mail, fresh fruit, bread, and whisky. Moreover, with his modern radio equipment aboard, Blyth had been in contact with shore stations during the entire trip so far. Now, with the *Endurance*, he was able to send out feature material for the newspapers at home as well as still and motion pictures taken thus far, to his agent.

This circumnavigation by Chay Blyth in *British Steel* was the best-planned and equipped voyage of its kind in the history of yachting adventures. All the skill of a century of shipbuilding had gone into the design and construction of this modern steel yacht for the single purpose of providing a vehicle for the last remaining spectacular ocean stunt. To assure success, the state-owned British Steel Corporation had expended about £50,000 or $120,000, of which £20,000 had gone into the design by Robert Clark, and the construction in record time of only four months by Philip & Son of Dartmouth.[4] Launched on August 19, 1970, *British Steel* was the epitome of modern yacht designing and the use of steel in yacht construction. She was also equipped with an expensive array of electronics, and other appliances needed for one man to master this large a vessel with its cloud of 1,300 square feet of sail.

The man himself was no ordinary sailor. In fact, Chay Blyth had a reputation of being a non-yachtsman, somewhat disparagingly, as it were. All of his yachting so far (and including this trip) was regarded as "publicity yachting." Even Blyth thought of himself as an expert in survival, not as a sailor.[5]

Born May 14, 1940, in Hawick, Scotland, he joined a parachute regiment when he was eighteen. At twenty-one, he was already a sergeant with experience in several overseas assignments. He had completed the Arctic Survival School as well as the Desert Survival School, and had become an instructor in the Eskdale Outward Bound School by 1966, when an officer named Captain John Ridgway of the Parachute Regiment at Aldershot called for a volunteer to accompany him on a rowing trip across the Atlantic in an open dory.[6] The stunt was successfully completed in ninety-two days, and for his part, Blyth was awarded the Empire Medal. In 1967, he left the army and the following year entered the *Sunday Times* Golden Globe Race around the world.[7]

Blyth's participation in the race ended off Cape Town when his 30-foot Kingfisher-class *Dytiscus* pitchpoled backward (bow over stern). Making port, Blyth repaired the vessel, and with his wife, Maureen, who had flown to Cape Town, sailed back to England. Home again in civilian life, Blyth took a job as a traveling salesman for a beverage company. But he was restless without a physical challenge, and seriously considered a suggestion by a former buddy in the Parachute Regiment that they cross the Andes and canoe down the Amazon for kicks. He even went to London and talked to the pros on Fleet Street, who advised him the Amazon stunt would probably arouse the most interest, since everything had already been done in the yachting arena. Later, he remembered a chance remark by Maureen, and the idea of a nonstop singlehanded voyage around grew upon him.

In March, 1969, he went to the Birmingham Boat Show, and there met a former newspaperman and public relations practitioner named Terry Bond. Out of this meeting evolved a working partnership and a plan which was presented to the British Steel Corporation, which was casually shopping around for some way to publicize its image.

Next came months of planning, designing, conferences, setbacks, hectic preparations, and inevitable frustrations. For this kind of project, one needs a course in survival to maintain one's health and sanity. Finally, on Sunday, October 18, Blyth went aboard the sleek new yacht from the jetty of the Royal Southern Yacht Club in the Hamble River with Maureen and a party of friends for one last farewell. They motored down to the starting area near the Hook Buoy in Southampton Water. There, Maureen and their friends were taken off by the *Blue Crystal*, and Chay was alone waiting for the starting gun to be fired by Commodore A. R. Lightfoot.

In the melee that followed, as the fleet escorted him out to the Needles, one of the launches rammed his boat and cut a nasty dent in the sleek white topsides. But he was on his way, on the most spectacular adventure of his young life, and the one which would bring him a share of British maritime immortality to say nothing of a small fortune.

His route was to take him south to Cape Horn, west against the Roaring Forties, across the Indian Ocean, around Cape Horn, and back up the Atlantic to England, for the most part against prevailing winds and currents. What else was left to do if one were to record another first in a bluewater yacht? Since Captain Joshua Slocum's voyage, which started it all, hundreds and maybe thousands of yachts had sailed around the world in all directions. As Professor Roger Strout had remarked back in the 1930s on his circumnavigation, everything that came after Magellan was anticlimax. Sir Francis Chichester had beaten the average wool and grain clipper ship time, east-about, when in his late sixties. The young merchant marine officer, Robin Knox-Johnston, had become the first to sail around nonstop, also east-about. Dozens of stunters had rowed across the oceans, even long before the ordeal completed with Captain Ridgway. Circumnavigations had been made by concrete vessels, by catamarans and trimarans, and even by an amphibious Jeep. Until someone came up with a suitable private submarine capable of sailing around the world underwater, the only remaining feat was a wrongway nonstop singlehanded passage.

Physically as well as spiritually, no man was ever better prepared for such an undertaking than Blyth. In robust good health, full of zest for life and adventure, his reactions and coordinations sharpened by years of commando training, even a wrong-way voyage was expected to be an easy cruise.

Sailing down the Atlantic, he had trouble in the northeast trades with the sails. Off the Río de la Plata, he encountered a *pampero* and could not lower his mainsail because of jammed slides, making necessary a hazardous trip up the mast. Off Cape Horn, he was driven south into the ice fields by a Force 9 gale in enormous seas that smashed his self-steering gear beyond repair and caused a serious head injury. From then on, he had nothing but trouble.

In late February, near New Zealand, he suffered a severe knockdown by a graybeard wave which bent the mast and damaged the rigging. When he crossed the southern Indian Ocean, he was battered for five days by the worst storm he had ever experienced, and probably one which he could not have survived had not his steel vessel been built like a submarine. He was driven five hundred miles off course by it.

Rounding the Cape of Good Hope, he was forced to spend as long as twenty hours at a time steering. On June 28, he crossed his outbound track, having technically circumnavigated. On July 19, he celebrated his daughter's birthday with a special pack of goodies, and was spoken west of Ushant by the H.M.S. *Ark Royal*. He sailed through the tunny fleet, and, on July 31, a chartered airplane with a *Sunday Mirror* team flew over to take photos. Navy ships stayed with him the rest of the way while he toasted himself with champagne and prepared himself and the ship for the homecoming.

On August 2, the *Blue Crystal* came out to meet him and to lead him to a mooring at the Royal Southern Yacht Club. The voyage was over, the 292-day passage, Hamble to Hamble, the fastest nonstop on record. His welcome was even bigger than those of Rose, Chichester, and Knox-Johnston; and unlike those homecomings, as the *British Steel* sailed up the Solent, the yacht looked as if it had just come out of the yard, its topsides spotless, its gear in first-class condition. Blyth, himself, clean-shaven and dressed in his best, bounded about the deck ebullient of spirit and in the best of health. The grueling voyage had been carried off in the best British tradition; and with superb timing, Blyth managed to make his appearance in the midst of Cowes Week. And to complete the tableau, he was greeted personally by the Prince of Wales, the Duke of Edinburgh, Princess Anne, and Prime Minister Edward Heath.

Upon his return, the yacht was given to him to keep, and the young national hero went on to share the limelight with Sir Francis Chichester, Sir Alec Rose, Knox-Johnston, and the others.[8]

CHAPTER

✒ 32 ✒

Opogee's Orbit

*I, too, had these dreams, and they burned with
enough fire to realize them. I had dreamed and
saved enough, and the voyage was unusual in
only two respects—Opogee was the first fiberglass boat to sail around the world; and one of
the few yachts that has the very dubious distinction of being attacked by a school of
whales.*[1]

OPOGEE SAILED ALONG BY HERSELF SMARTLY UNDER THE
twin jibs as usual. Alan Eddy had gone below to get a dish towel
to finish drying the dishes which he was doing up in the cockpit.
Suddenly the boat jolted violently. He stumbled and fell against the
bunk. *Opogee* shuddered and trembled from keel to masthead. Had
they struck a reef? Or a floating derelict? Here, in the middle of the
Indian Ocean, seven hundred miles from land?

He rushed up on deck in time to see a dark shape rolling astern in
the wake. A whale! While he watched, the beast turned over, rolling
in an unusual way, as if hurt. Apparently *Opogee* had run up on the
sleeping cetacean. Then there came another shuddering blow, rever-
berating like a drum against the fiberglass hull. Then another and
another. A whole school of whales!

Stiff with fear, Eddy tried desperately to think of an escape. He
had no gun and only a small fish spear which would only antagonize
them. He thought of throwing over dish water, oil, detergent. Futile.

Then, from another direction, he saw steaming toward him another school of a dozen or more whales, until the ocean around
Opogee was filled with fins and blunt noses. He could have reached

over and touched the nearest ones. Once more there came a shuddering blow against the hull. He hoped the then relatively untried fiberglass skin would withstand the beating. But if several of the whales decided to attack at once, nothing could stand up to it.

The tension went on for twenty minutes or more, the whales swimming alongside, seeming to watch him with their pig-like eyes, at times striking the hull. Slightly smaller than *Opogee*, they were identified as false killer whales or pilot whales.

When the whales had broken off the contact and gone, Eddy went below with much relief to assess the damage and was further relieved to find no structural defects.[2]

The whale encounter, which could have been very serious indeed, turned out to be the only flaw in an otherwise pleasant circumnavigation for singlehander Alan Eddy. Leaving Hampton, Virginia, in June 1963, alone in his new 30-foot *Seawind* ketch, *Opogee*, he sailed south to the West Indies, Antilles, Colombia, went through the Panama Canal, on to the Galápagos Islands, and followed the usual track to the Pacific islands and along the trades, around the Cape of Good Hope and back to the West Indies.

Until ten years before he embarked, Eddy had never set foot on a sailboat. He picked up some experience aboard friends' boats and then on two of his own boats before purchasing *Opogee* new from the factory. At the time he left Virginia for the West Indies, he had never been offshore overnight or taken a sight with a sextant. Moreover, his adventure was undertaken in a stock boat, built of fiberglass, which at the time was still a controversial material in some quarters.

Once the voyage began, he gained experience rapidly, and happily chose the most trouble-free route: Panama, Galápagos, Marquesas, Tahiti, Cook Islands, Tonga, Samoa, Fiji, New Zealand, New Hebrides, New Caledonia, Australia, Great Barrier Reef, New Guinea, Christmas Island, Keeling-Cocos, Rodriguez, Mauritius, Réunion, South Africa, St. Helena, and the West Indies.

In almost 40,000 miles across three oceans, Eddy spent 50 percent of his time enjoying a superb Sunday sail, 40 percent in reasonably good sailing conditions, and only 10 percent in what he called hard slogging. During one leg, from the Galápagos to the Marquesas, *Opogee* averaged better than 160 miles a day, a remarkable record for a 24-foot waterline vessel. His highest run, noon to noon, was 179 miles; the longest nonstop passage, 3,880 miles from St. Helena to Grenada, which took 34 days. The second longest run was the 2,990 miles from the Galápagos to Nuku Hiva. Third longest was the

Keeling-Cocos to Rodriguez, a passage of 2,020 miles. In five years, he made 400 ports or anchorages—alone except for the South Africa to West Indies passage, on which he carried a girl companion.

Opogee's route had been deliberately planned to take advantage of the trade winds and to avoid heavy weather passages.

"Different routes are possible," he wrote later, "but less enjoyable. The fastest route is also the poorest—the old wool and grain route in the Roaring Forties. Any small boat which attempts the three capes (Good Hope, Leeuwin, and Horn) has my admiration."

At the time of Eddy's circumnavigation, modern self-steering vanes had not been perfected. It was common then to carry twin headsails of some arrangement suitable to the particular vessel. These had been used successfully on *Trekka* by John Guzzwell; on *Wanderer III* by the Hiscocks; and on *Stornoway* by Al Petersen. On *Opogee*, Eddy used twin jibs, carrying 330 square feet of sail in the trades. On occasion, when the wind was abeam or on a broad reach, he modified this somewhat. His one objection to twin headsails—the same one others have had—is the uncomfortable rolling, which is more noticeable on a narrow beamed hull.

Altogether he carried a set of eight sails, all Dacron—a main, mizzen, two working jibs, a number two genoa, a storm jib, mizzen staysail, and a spinnaker. After his experience, he said he would make only one change, a drifter for a spinnaker under light air conditions.

For auxiliary power, *Opogee* had a small Graymarine gasoline engine, which gave no trouble in the six and a half years he lived aboard, although it required frequent maintenance.[3]

Opogee also carried a startling amount of ground tackle for a vessel of only six and a half tons. This included 50 fathoms of 5/16 inch chain, 50 fathoms of ¾ inch nylon rope, a 75-pound fisherman anchor, a 40-pound and a 22-pound Danforth. The weight of all this served as a large part of the boat's ballast.

He did all his celestial navigation with H. O. 249, the Air Navigation Tables, and the Nautical Almanac. On long voyages, he took sun sights three times a day, weather permitting, and plotted the position at noon local time. He used star sights only near landfalls and on difficult passages, such as through the Tuamotus. In only one instance, a miscalculation and an unknown current on a moonless night put him on a reef near Fiji, where the boat pounded for an hour and a half before he was able to get off unaided. Only minor damage was sustained by the fiberglass hull.

Except for squalls, *Opogee* encountered gale-force winds only four times in the entire circumnavigation. In each of these cases, life aboard was tense and uncomfortable, but there was never any fear the vessel could not handle the situation. On one occasion, *Opogee* was picked up bodily by an enormous swell left over from a hurricane in the Coral Sea, and laid over with the mast almost horizontal to the water. This created chaos below, but there was no hull damage and the episode was never repeated.

Only on the passage around the bight of South Africa was it necessary to man the tiller twenty-four hours a day. This was due to the tremendous ship traffic created by the closing of Suez. At times between Durban and Cape Town, Eddy would sight from thirty to forty steamers in one day. Spending Christmas in Durban, as have most circumnavigators, Eddy found the harbor jammed with yachts on world cruises (this was 1967), a record number due to the closure that year of the Suez Canal.

Eddy's voyage around, aside from the whale encounter and the temporary grounding on a reef near Fiji, turned out to be a singularly unexciting experience in terms of high adventure; but it was carried off so easily by careful planning and on a minimum budget—almost frugally. It was a leisurely journey, never pushing luck or weather, marking time to assure good passages, being satisfied with only the necessities of living while at sea and in port, and having a vessel that required a minimum of maintenance along the way, including only one haul-out.

Of all the circumnavigators, Alan Eddy represents that almost anonymous group who sail on long world voyages without advance publicity, without commercial sponsorship, without contracts for subsequent books or television documentaries; and, most important, without getting themselves into those situations that make hair-raising reading (if they survive), and require super skills, to say nothing of blind luck, to extract themselves from. Because they are so seldom heard of, the anonymous ones never make the headlines and never take the bows, but there are many more Alan Eddys orbiting the globe on safe modern vessels like *Opogee* than there are the Chichesters, the Dumases, and even the Slocums.

> *Should you have the grit and determination to start out on a long voyage, there is no better feeling than to see your very first landfall lying dead ahead. You know that all the planning, hard work, and money invested in the trip is just beginning to pay off.*[4]

~§ 33 §~

Around the World on the Installment Plan

I saw John standing amidships. Incredibly he was standing, because, as I could see now, both masts were gone, and the motion was now so quick that I could not keep my feet on the deck. He was standing with his legs wide apart, his knees bent and his hands on his thighs. I called to him to give me a hand. He came up and knelt down beside me, and said, "This is it, you know, Miles."[1]

FEBRUARY 13, 1957 WAS A DATE THAT JOHN GUZZWELL would not likely forget. He had an impacted tooth, which he had neglected to have removed in Melbourne before leaving on this detour in his planned circumnavigation, to accompany Miles and Beryl Smeeton to England on *Tzu Hang* via Cape Horn. And on this date, while his own little *Trekka* was hauled out in a shed in New Zealand and he was five thousand miles away, in the vicinity of the Horn, he found himself upside down with tools and furniture crashing about his head.

Guzzwell was the third person in the now-famous episode in which *Tzu Hang* was pitchpoled and corkscrewed by a giant wave in a survival storm, and dismasted.[2] By sheer pluck and ingenuity, the damage was repaired, a jury rig fashioned, and the battered vessel brought into Valparaiso, some one thousand miles away. Guzzwell was that type of British mechanic who, in the midst of almost total disaster in which emergency repairs were immediately required, calmly set up a makeshift vice in the dark and cluttered cabin and first sharpened every one of the tools he would need.

As Brigadier Smeeton, who admitted to never sharpening a tool, recalled later, it was this simple act that provided the sense of competence and right thinking that sustained them all through the next terrible three weeks.

His tools keen, Guzzwell set about methodically to patch the hole in the deck, rebuild temporarily the cabin trunk, and fashion a steering oar and a gin pole mast, while being tossed around in thirty-foot swells.

John Guzzwell, perhaps more than most circumnavigators, was born to the oceans. His ancestors had been trawler men, whose red sails were common to the fishing port of Grimsby, England, and the North Sea fishing banks. His father had been born there, son of a trawler owner, but had wandered about the world to mine gold in Alaska and go pearl fishing in the South Seas, only to wind up in Jersey, where John was born and where his memories began.

The family had not been settled long when the elder Guzzwell became restless with shore life. The result was the construction of *Our Boy*, a 52-foot gaff ketch in which the family sailed to South Africa. There John grew up, acquiring a trade and a hobby of motorcycle racing. Recalling his father's many stories about the logging camps on the northwest coast of North America, when John was old enough he emigrated to Canada and settled at Victoria, British Columbia—near where the Smeetons had also settled on a retirement farm.

Arriving at Victoria in March 1953, he soon had a good job and was saving money. In the back of his mind was a plan to sail around the world in his own ship. On days off, he would go down to the Maritime Museum on the waterfront and look at *Tilikum*, Captain John Voss's famous dugout canoe. He did not, however, have any harebrained stunt in mind.

With characteristic good judgment, he wrote to J. Laurent Giles of Laurent Giles & Partners, Lymington. Jack Giles, designer of the famous *Vertues*, in which more long voyages have been made than any other small-boat class, had been the genius behind *Sopranino*, the 19-foot miniature cruiser in which Patrick Elam and Colin Mudie had made their flawless passages.[3] Giles considered *Sopranino* the smallest practical ocean cruiser. For Guzzwell, he produced a slightly larger version, the 21-foot *Trekka*. Because it was necessary to strengthen the hull for the log and debris-filled waters of the Pacific Northwest, the heavier planking resulted in a displacement nearly twice that of *Sopranino*, although *Trekka* was only two feet longer.

With watertight compartments, *Trekka* was unsinkable, an unusual feature of any sailboat, especially one this small. Another innovation was a fin keel that could be unbolted and shipped overland separate from the hull.

With great skill, Guzzwell laminated the keel himself in the basement of the Y.M.C.A. where he lived. The frames and hull planking were assembled in the back of Bell's Fish and Chips in Victoria. In only nine months, working in his spare time, Guzzwell completed the hull. She was a beautiful little ship, and Giles had created an astonishing amount of room below decks by the use of reverse sheer. To minimize the hogged effect of reverse sheer, the topsides were given severe tumblehome, which tended to give the vessel the appearance of great speed. The decks (and later the bottom) were sheathed in fiberglass.

Launched, *Trekka* became to Guzzwell something alive and vital, like woman created from the rib of man. There was something vaguely sacred about her.[4]

Trekka was launched in August 1954. The masts and rigging were added later, in the spring of 1955. Bending on the new sails, John let go the lines. The wind caught the sails for the first time, and John felt the surge of power as the tight little ship came alive in his hands. He knew then that he had done his work well. She was fast, sailed upright in fresh breezes, and steered herself to windward with minor adjustments.

In September 1955, laden with sixty days provisions, and twenty-four gallons of water in plastic bottles, *Trekka* departed Victoria harbor. Beating out past Race Rocks, and up the Strait of Juan de Fuca, he was spoken by a Scandinavian fisherman who wanted to know who he was and where he was going in that "ploddy little pisspot."

When Guzzwell replied that he was headed for Honolulu, the fisherman shook his head and ripped off an oath of disbelief.

Out on the rugged North Pacific, *Trekka* immediately encountered her first test of bad weather. Guzzwell discovered that she would not ride to a sea anchor, so he lashed everything down and lay ahull until the wind veered off to the southwest. He experimented with a twin headsails self-steering arrangement, and soon *Trekka* was boiling along by herself. Off Cape Menocino, *Trekka* encountered the worst gale in her 30,000-mile circumnavigation, with winds up to 70 miles an hour, and seas more than 30 feet high. Guzzwell had time to ask himself, "What the hell am I doing here?"

A landfall was made on Punta Arenas. While in San Francisco, Guzzwell met the Smeetons and their daughter, Clio, with *Tzu Hang*. A warm friendship developed, and they sailed together for Hawaii. *Trekka* beat the larger *Tzu Hang* to the islands, to their surprise. After some time cruising in those waters, the two yachts departed for the south, making Fanning Island first, and then continuing on to Samoa, Tonga, and New Zealand.

There, Clio had to fly back to England and school. The Smeetons did not want to attempt a Horn passage on the old clipper route alone, so Guzzwell volunteered to accompany them. He hauled out *Trekka* and stored her with friends. Then he went aboard *Tzu Hang* and helped prepare and outfit the big ketch for the long hazardous passage through the Roaring Forties to Stanley in the Falklands, where Guzzwell planned to get off and return to New Zealand. The final preparations were made in Melbourne.

Departing on December 22, 1955, they sailed down past the northeast tip of Tasmania, through Bass Strait, thence south of New Zealand between 40° and 50° directly for the Horn. Compared to *Trekka*, *Tzu Hang* was an ocean liner. She was 46 feet overall with an 11-foot 6-inch beam, a double-ender of solid teak, built in Hong Kong in 1938. The Smeetons had bought her from the first owner in 1951, and without any previous sailing experience, had taken her to British Columbia from England, with only their young daughter, Clio, as crew. They were to spend almost 20 years sailing the oceans of the world in *Tzu Hang*.

They were near the 100° meridian on February 14, at the time of the capsizing, almost directly west of the Strait of Magellan. Making from fifty to seventy miles a day under jury rig, they limped into Arauco Bay and the port of Coronel on March 22. With the help of the British consul, the Chilean navy, and many kind people, to say nothing of the skills of John Guzzwell, the ketch was repaired and new masts stepped. John stayed long enough to see the project through, but finally had to leave to live his own dreams.

The Smeetons hated to see him go, not only because of his skills, but because he had become part of the family and much of him was to be seen in the rebuilt *Tzu Hang*. Moreover, they had been through the ultimate adventure together, and they had survived together.

Leaving the Smeetons in Chile, Guzzwell flew to South Africa to visit his mother in Natal. She was preparing to return to the Channel Islands, and had sold her house. There was much work to do, selling the furniture and taking care of the paperwork involved. He accompanied his mother to Jersey, and saw her settled before leaving by ship for Sydney, Australia. From there, he found passage to Auckland, and immediately rushed out to Russell where *Trekka* was stored, with his friends, Francis and Millie Arlidge.

With his ever-present tool box, John went to work. He had been gone from *Trekka* for sixteen months, during which she had waited faithfully for him to return. Now she looked mighty sweet, sitting on the cradle. But there was much to do. First he covered the bottom with a sheath of fiberglass. Then he made some changes based on his experience with the Smeetons. At last, he was ready to sail again.

Crossing the Tasman Sea to Australia, he sailed up through the Barrier Reef, through Torres Strait, and the Arafura Sea to Keeling-Cocos. Unlike most voyagers, he found mild sailing while crossing the Indian Ocean. In one passage, from Keeling-Cocos to Rodriguez, he made 2,000 miles in 17 days for an average of about 111 miles a day—astonishing for a boat of *Trekka*'s 18-foot waterline.

At Middle Island, he encountered another English circumnavigator, Norman Young, in a Falmouth punt, *Diana*. They sailed in company all the way from the Barrier Reef to Thursday Island. The summer and early autumn months were spent crossing to Africa. Off the coast of Madagascar, taking advantage of currents, *Trekka* made one daily run of 155 miles, noon to noon. Guzzwell reached Durban on December 2, and was welcomed with the usual hospitality. He spent the Christmas season here. One day, he met a man who had just returned from British Columbia—a man who had been one of the rubberneckers when *Trekka* was being built behind the fish and chips joint.

On January 15, 1959, Guzzwell departed for Cape Town, immediately encountering steep seas and a southwest gale in which he had to heave to for days. At one point, he was pushed back fifty miles by the Agulhas Current. But he reached Cape Town with no further problem. As he entered the harbor, he saw the "table cloth" being set on Table Mountain, a sure sign of a southeaster. He barely made it to moorings before darkness and the storm descended, but at the last moment a violent williwaw knocked *Trekka* flat.

Taking on stores, he put to sea again on February 14, 1959, exactly two years after the capsizing on *Tzu Hang*. On March 2, he arrived at St. Helena. Another week of sailing brought him to Ascension. On St. Helena, everyone had talked of Napoleon and the old days; on Ascension, the talk was of the Snark guided missile and rocket motors. He crossed the equator on March 30. On April 30, he sighted the light on Ragged Point, Barbados. The port officials seemed impressed not by the arrival of such a small vessel—but by the fact that it had arrived without hoisting the yellow quarantine flag.

After a week, he sailed for Panama, arriving at Cristobal on May 12. He made the canal transit without fuss, tying up to a banana boat and using old auto tires for fenders. He was charged $2.16 for the passage, including the pilot. He thought this was reasonable, in lieu of the alternative, which was to sail around the Horn.

From Balboa, he decided not to attempt an uphill beat. Instead, he sailed for Hawaii, recording one fantastic day's run of 175 miles, aided by the equatorial current. In one week, he recorded 1,101 miles. This fast trade winds passage was made with twin headsails and a small spinnaker set to ease the roll.

On the afternoon of July 22, 1959, he sailed around Diamond Head, and made a board up the Ala Wai Channel. He had now completed his circumnavigation, crossing his outbound track on the twentieth, the smallest vessel in history to have accomplished this feat. The voyage had been made entirely without mishap, a near flawless circumnavigation.

From Hawaii, Guzzwell set off for the 2,600-mile passage to Victoria before the winter gales set in. Three weeks later, he sailed up Victoria harbor, where *Trekka* had been born in the back of a fish and chips joint, exactly four years to the day after John had departed on his adventure.

Guzzwell next wrote a book[5] and edited the movie footage he had taken at sea, including the voyage with the Smeetons. With the money he made, he was able to get married. In 1961, John and his wife, Maureen, sailed *Trekka* to Hawaii and back to California. There they sold her to another couple, Cliff and Marian Cain, who were novices at the game. But with the confidence *Trekka* inspired, the Cains sailed out of Monterey and around the world, repeating Guzzwell's circumnavigation.

A sister ship of *Trekka*, the *Thlaloca*, built by Hein and Siggi Zenker at a cost of $2,800, was sailed around the world from 1962 to

1966 at a running cost of $70 a month from Canada and back to Canada.

John Guzzwell, with his earnings from royalties and the sale of *Trekka*, built another dream ship, another Giles design, but this time a 45-foot, 20-ton ketch, *Treasure*. On it, John and Maureen sailed to New Zealand. There the Guzzwells settled in permanently—or until the oceans again called.[6]

CHAPTER

34

The Schoolboy
Circumnavigator

Home is the sailor, home from the sea
And the hunter home from the hill.[1]

ON HIS SIXTEENTH BIRTHDAY, MARCH 5, 1965, ROBIN LEE
Graham said to his mother and father: "Know what I'd really like—
a boat of my own that I could sail to the South Pacific islands."

Most parents, upon hearing such talk, would dismiss it as impetu-
osity, but four and a half months later Robin stepped aboard his own
24-foot fiberglass sloop, *Dove*, a light displacement craft usually regarded as a day-sailer, and shoved off from Los Angeles for a shakedown cruise to Hawaii, a passage that took 22½ days and was a piece
of cake all the way.

Alone except for a pair of kittens, he entertained himself most of
the way with his guitar and folk tunes, navigating the 2,230 nautical
miles with the aplomb of a veteran topgallant hand. It was so easy, in
fact, that once in the islands, it seemed the most natural thing in the
world just to keep going on around. At first, he hoped to find a
companion to share the adventure, but few schoolboys have parents
as lenient as were Robin's mother and father. Then he made up his
mind to do it alone, just as had Captain Slocum back in 1895–1898.
But where Slocum had made his voyage at the end of a long career at
sea, Robin would be doing it at the beginning of his, and if successful he would become the youngest person ever to sail alone around
the world.[2]

So, at 11 A.M. on Tuesday morning, September 14, 1965, he said his good-byes again to his parents and departed Honolulu's Ala Wai yacht harbor. In spite of its small size, *Dove* was easy to manage and had been modified for ocean voyaging. There was a small inboard engine, supplemented by an outboard with a long shank. A steering vane designed and built by his father had been installed. As for Robin, although a mere callow boy, he was far from inexperienced. During 1962 and 1963, with his mother, father, and older brother, he had helped crew the family 36-foot ketch, *Golden Hind*, all through the Pacific islands. During that cruise, his father had taught him seamanship, celestial navigation, shipboard maintenance, and all the other skills so vital to bluewater voyaging. Robin was a good student, and along with his lessons, he acquired a deep love for the sea and sailing.

This background, then, explains why his parents were so "lenient" and understanding. Moreover, sailing around the world had been a lifelong ambition of Robin's father, but World War II and then raising a family had intervened. Robin had often heard his father talk about this, and perhaps by some psychological osmosis had assumed responsibility for fulfilling the goal.

His family had helped him prepare for the voyage, besides furnishing the boat. They had collected charts and navigation materials, food and supplies, a camera and film for recording his adventures, and a tape recorder with which to make on the spot comments.[3] His father, it seemed, became more obsessed with the voyage than Robin, perhaps seeing it vicariously as his own. He threw himself into the preparations and outfitting, spending most of those last hectic weeks with his son. As Robin recalled later, it was a period when he and his father were the closest in their entire lives. Along with taking care of preparations, Robin's father had also become his manager and agent, and complex arrangements were made to sell the story of his circumnavigation to publications and broadcast media, and set up lecture tours. It was going to be one circumnavigation that made money or else.[4]

The only malfunction on the passage to Hawaii had been the vane steering. This was rebuilt by his father. He had aboard a transistor radio for news and weather and the WWVH time ticks. He later picked up a Gibson Girl war surplus emergency transmitter, which sends out an S.O.S. when cranked. He also had fishing gear, a .22 caliber pistol, and a large supply of recording tapes.[5]

The newspapers prior to his departure, had called him the "Schoolboy Sailor," and he was well aware that his voyage was unique and newsworthy. His frequent long sessions with the tape recorder revealed this adolescent sense of destiny.

Leaving Hawaii with only $75 in cash, he made a perfect landfall fourteen days later at the British-owned Fanning Island,[6] only 12 miles square and 1,050 miles down course. Robin was a competent seaman, and shooting sights with a sextant on a 24-foot cork was child's play for him. When on deck, he always wore a harness with lifeline. He kept the harness on at all times, even when in the bunk below, so that all he had to do when he came up on deck was snap the lifeline to it. The only times he failed to do this on the entire voyage, he fell overboard and narrowly escaped being left behind— once in the Indian Ocean and once in the Atlantic.

The further from Honolulu he got, however, the more lonely and homesick he became. He began talking almost constantly into the tape recorder. Among his stores, Robin had about 500 pieces of secondhand clothing, plus various trinkets for trading among the islands, in the naïve belief that he could exist by bartering among the islands. He spent several days at Fanning, a former cable station, but now a copra plantation, and when he left he took a sack of Her Majesty's mail for posting in Pago Pago.

Only twenty miles from Tutuila, after two weeks of hard sailing, a squall buckled his mast and the lower shrouds parted. Robin felt like crying, but he lashed the wreckage to the deck and set up a jury sail. His engine could not cope with the wind and current. An airplane passed over. Robin showed a bright orange distress flag and fired flares, but was unseen. After anxious hours, he limped into Apia.

In Samoa, he received mail and supplies from home, including a spare sextant and a log spinner to replace one taken by a shark. Reluctant to set out, he decided to wait until April, when the hurricane season was over. This was a fortunate decision. On January 29, a vicious hurricane swept the islands and nearly wrecked *Dove* in the harbor.

On May 1, 1966, he finally departed. His only companion was Joliette, one of the kittens. The other had jumped ship. The passage to Tonga was enjoyable and now he had company in other world cruisers he had encountered, including the *Kelea* from Vancouver, B.C.; *Corsair II* from South Africa; *Morea* from California, *Falcon* from New Zealand. He was to meet the same yachts (and others) again and again at various ports. He reached Suva on Viti Levu, Fiji's main island, on July 1. He had only $23 cash, and since an airline ticket of a $100 bond was required by authorities, he had to prevail upon the American consul for a loan. He enjoyed his stay in the Fijis more than any place he had ever been. In fact, here the voyage was nearly terminated for the first time. He had met through friends a girl named Patti Ratterree from Los Angeles, another restless and curious young American who was traveling around the world on her own, stopping to work at various places and living mainly by her wits.

It was love at first sight, Robin wrote, and after weeks of an idyllic existence sailing among the tropical islands of Fiji, only Robin's firm commitments and his father's pressure could induce him to give it up and go on. So he and Patti split up, but agreed to keep in touch by mail and to meet ten months later in Darwin, or failing that, in Durban.

Leaving the Fijis alone, Robin met his father again in the New Hebrides. They spent the next few weeks together, then Robin sailed for the Solomons and his father took passage on an inter-island schooner, meeting him in Guadalcanal. His father stayed through Christmas, Robin's second so far on the voyage, and they had good times together exploring the islands, many of which had those familiar names from World War II, which his father's generation had come to know so well—Savu, Tulagi, Florida—where many of the natives still remembered the G.I.'s with fondness, never understanding why they did not return. They visited the rusted old hulks of ships and tanks, the weed-grown foxholes, finding bits of bone, pieces of rotted boots, bullet-pierced helmets. Robin was impressed by the sacrifices which his father's generation had made in those dark days. But now, he felt, this was his world.

At Honaira, Robin sold his inboard engine, which was useless. He earned additional money by renting his spare genoa to a local yacht going to New Guinea. On his eighteenth birthday, he wrote his draft board and later received a reply in Australia, telling him to check with them upon his return. He did not know then that it would be another three years before he would be home.

From the Solomons, he encountered calms and sticky hot weather, mixed with squalls and adverse currents. It took twenty-three days to cover the nine hundred miles to Port Moresby, where he spent three weeks on shore. On April 18, he departed for Darwin through Torres Strait and into the Arafura Sea, a heavily traveled shipping route. The many ships passing in the night kept him up until exhaustion drove him below. One night, while lying in the bunk, he heard a loud swish and felt something scrape the hull. He rushed up to see a large black unlighted ship disappearing into the night. He had escaped a collision by the thickness of a coat of paint. He wondered how many lonely navigators—including Captain Slocum himself—had near-misses, for just this reason—unmarked, unlighted ships without lookouts, passing callously in the night.

Robin reached Darwin on May 4, and spent several weeks ashore, including a month working on a power station project, rigging guy wires on towers. The further Robin had sailed on his circumnavigation, the more disenchanted he had become with the idea. He would have quit back in the Fijis had it not been for his father and those firm commitments (the *National Geographic* magazine had already started running a series on his voyage). When his father first heard about Patti, he was somewhat furious—especially when Patti showed up in Darwin. From that point on, Robin's relations with his father were strained at best, and may have contributed to his parents' breaking up their marriage. When his father first met Patti, he obviously considered her something of a tramp and an obstacle to completion of the round-the-world voyage. At Darwin, too, a *National Geographic* photographer showed up with his equipment and some firm instructions to get some usable material for future issues. Apparently, the principal sponsors of the adventure were also having second thoughts.

Before leaving Darwin, Robin and Patti agreed to meet in Durban, and this was probably all that kept the lad going during the next leg of the circumnavigation, across the Indian Ocean via Keeling-Cocos, Mauritius, and Réunion.

On July 6, 1967, he sailed again, his first landfall to be Keeling-Cocos, the family-owned autocracy and fiefdom in the Indian Ocean. It had been from Thursday Island to Cocos that Captain Slocum made his famous run of 2,700 miles in 23 days without touching the helm. Robin made the 1,900 miles from Darwin to Cocos in 18 days—almost exactly the same speed as Slocum had recorded in the *Spray*. This was a pleasant sail, with little to do but fill his hours with sewing sails, making rope belts, taking photos of himself with a tripping line, and dictating into the recorder.

From Cocos to Mauritius, some 2,400 miles, it was usually all downwind, and once you leap off from Cocos there is no turning back. But only 18 hours out, running through a line of Squalls, *Dove* was dismasted again. Rushing out on deck to save what he could, Robin was thrown overboard as the boat lurched. It was the first time he had not worn his lifeline. By sheer fate, another lurch brought the boat within reach. He caught hold of the rail and climbed back aboard. Coming out of the warm water into the cold rainy wind, he was overcome by chills. He went below to wait daylight. He had 2,300 miles to go to reach Mauritius, and no chance to get back to Cocos. When daylight came, he was able to rig a small square sail from a bedsheet and set it on the forestay. This ripped out in the 25-knot winds, so he set an old yellow awning which he had to patch with a tea towel and an extra shirt.

In this manner, he limped along through heavy seas and continued squalls for twenty-four days, averaging almost one hundred miles a day, and reaching his destination almost at his original E.T.A!

At Port Louis, he again met fellow ocean vagabonds—the *Shireen* and *Mother of Pearl* from England; the *Edward Bear* and *Bona Dea* from New Zealand; *Corsair II* from South Africa, and the *Ohra* from Australia. Here Robin stayed to enjoy the local hospitality and to make repairs. The National Geographic Society shipped out a new aluminum mast from California by Quantas.

The next stop was Réunion, a beautiful but expensive place. After a short stay, he left in company with the *Bona Dea* and the *Ohra* for Durban. Three days later came the most violent weather of the entire voyage, with mountainous seas. For seventeen days, *Dove* was battered and pummeled, at times threatening to roll over and at other times to pitchpole. It was too unsafe to be on deck, so Robin spent his time in the bunk reading books and periodically talking into the tape recorder. Anything loose in the cabin soon became a flying missile. Doors were smashed, water ruined his flour and dry provisions, his tape recorder took a soaking. Robin held on and prayed for calmer seas, which came one morning with a gentle northeast breeze. Soon after he saw the coast of Africa and then was caught up in the heavy ship traffic caused by the closing of Suez. Then he reached Durban, crossed the bar, and tied up to the mooring at the Royal Natal Yacht Club.[7]

It was now spring in South Africa, and Robin had completed half his circumnavigation. And Patti was waiting here for him.

They had decided to get married, but Robin was still a minor. He had to get permission from his parents. It finally came, and Patti officially became Mrs. Robin Lee Graham. They bought a motorbike which they named *Elsa*, and took off on a honeymoon to Johannesburg and the Transvaal. They had a wonderful time, one that grew more difficult to end the longer they waited.

Dove had to be almost entirely rebuilt and beefed up. The deck had been coming loose from the hull, several bulkheads were cracked, and there were signs of general deterioration. After much soul searching—and pressure from parents and sponsors—he got underway at last. The difficult passage around the bight of Africa was the worst of the entire voyage. He made it by running close to shore and pulling in frequently at available havens, beset by head winds and adverse currents. This was better, however, than the mountainous seas out beyond the 100-fathom line. With increasing exhaustion, he ducked into East London, Port Elizabeth, Plettenbergbaai, Knysna, Stilbaai, Struisbaai, and Gordon's Bay. At Port Elizabeth, he nearly lost *Dove* when the anchor dragged. The deck pulled away from the hull again, and opened up a seam which leaked. There were signs of rot in the plywood, and the layers of fiberglass were separating.

He confided in his secret journal that he had planned to scuttle the vessel here along this lonely coast and claim an accident, so he could quit this voyage and be with Patti. But something kept him going. At Cape Town, more repairs were necessary. This gave Robin and Patti another two months together, most of which they spent at a delightful old boardinghouse called Thelma's. They made many friends among the older people living there. One couple in particular they became fond of were a man about eighty-five and his bride, seventy-five, who had been married about five years and acted like newlyweds. Their happiness made Robin and Patti feel good and right.

From Cape Town, the next leg would be five thousand nautical miles to Surinam with a stop at Ascension. Robin acquired two more little kittens, Fili and Kili, which he named after the youngest dwarfs in J. R. R. Tolkien's *The Hobbit*. While Robin sailed on *Dove*, Patti would be on an Italian line, the *Europa*, bound for Barcelona. They made arrangements with the captain to keep a radiotelephone schedule, which was only partly successful, but did help Robin's morale.

The loneliness was the worst thing about the Atlantic crossing. When the weather was good, he worked positions, read books, sewed sails, listened to the battery radio, bathed, cooked, played with the kittens, talked into the recorder. In his log, on July 27, 1968, he recorded the third anniversary of his departure.

It began to get to him. One day he found a Japanese float with two crabs and some barnacles clinging to it. Knowing the crabs would die in the open sea, he made a raft of plastic foam and sent them adrift in this. He even put the gooseneck barnacles on the raft so the crabs would have something to eat.

He sighted St. Helena but did not land. On August 23, he dropped anchor at Clarence Bay, Ascension, where he was welcomed by PanAm crews manning the tracking station. He passed Fernando de Noronha on the twenty-first, and picked up the coastal current off South America. On the twenty-fifth, he crossed the equator for the second time. On the thirty-first, he made the lightship at the mouth of the Surinam River, entered and went upstream to Paramaribo.

The Atlantic crossing had been the worst of all, from the standpoint of mental and spiritual exhaustion. Moreover, he had fallen overboard again and this time barely made it back aboard as *Dove* sailed on. The sloop was literally coming apart, and each spell of bad weather increased his apprehension. Finally, Patti was not there when he arrived, and did not show up for several weeks. Meanwhile, Robin toured the back country with local officials and National Geographic Society staffers. When Patti arrived, she was flown in to the jungle to meet him, and they spent three weeks together.

At this point, Graham knew he could not go on. He told the National Geographic people and his parents and other sponsors. The NGS sent a top editor down to talk to him. His mother came out from California to see him and meet Patti for the first time. Robin put *Dove* up for sale in the West Indies.

Finally, a compromise was worked out. *Dove* was replaced by a new 33-foot sloop, manufactured by Allied Boat Company, Inc., of Catskill, New York.[8] There were more advances from articles to be published. The couple found a nice apartment on the leeward shore of the Barbados and settled down to housekeeping for a while. They toured the islands by motorbike, and Robin obtained part-time work.

The sleek new 33-footer was named *The Return of Dove*. It was delivered in Florida. He and Patti picked it up and sailed to the Virgin Islands, where little *Dove* was finally sold. The new boat had a depth sounder, a radiotelephone, a kerosene stove (Robin found alcohol unsuited for ocean cruising—and as Eric Hiscock wrote, it is cheaper to buy bonded whisky in many places, than stove alcohol).

As soon as the hurricane season was over, the new boat was hauled and painted, and refrigeration installed. On November 21, Patti left on the S. S. *Lurline* for Panama. Robin got underway again. At Porvenir, they met again, explored the San Blas Islands, and motored into Cristobal, where they tied up at the yacht club.

Over the Christmas holidays, they visited friends, fixed up *The Return of Dove* a little, and on January 17, the pilot came aboard and the canal transit was made. At the Pacific end, they stopped briefly at Balboa, then sailed for the offshore islands for a couple weeks alone.

On Friday, January 30, Robin headed again to sea, and on February 7, he made San Cristobal in the Galápagos Islands. Patti flew to the airport at Baltra with her father and stepmother, Allan and Ann Ratterree. Another idyllic vacation was spent here.

On March 23, Robin departed on the long run uphill to Los Angeles. He now had 2,600 miles to go against some of the worst conditions of the voyage—adverse winds and currents, coupled with frequent calms. But now, however, he had a working auxiliary engine to get through the calms, he had two-way radio, and even ice cubes.

In spite of this, the little mishaps became major annoyances, and he at times gave himself over to periods of violent frustration, during which he would hurl things against the bulkhead and fuss over his inability to untie a knot in a line. The going was agonizingly slow, sometimes making only thirty miles a day. On April 15, he heard American ships on the radio. The next day, he raised the fishing vessel *Jinita* out of San Diego, which relayed a message to Patti's father in Long Beach. The next day the engine would not start and he had no more electric power.

The trouble was simple. He had forgotten to open the engine exhaust. The *Jinita* called him and reported that she was not able to reach Al Ratterree, while another boat, the *Olympia*, broke in to say she could relay and deliver the message.

Then Kili began to go crazy, alternating between viciousness and limp whining. Everyone on *Dove* was getting channel fever.

The uphill beat was increasingly rough. On the twenty-fifth day, however, he was only 250 miles from Long Beach. On the twenty-eighth, he was about 100 miles away. On the twenty-ninth, he passed San Clemente Island. For the first time, the prospect of actually going home became a reality.[9]

His first impression of the California coastline was the stench of land and civilization. It had a raw, pungent smell of hot asphalt and concrete.

At 7 A.M., on April 30, 1970, Robin sailed in between the breakwaters of Los Angeles harbor, which he had left 1,739 days before in the first *Dove*. He had traveled 30,600 sea miles. He was five years older, now a mature young man, with a wife (pregnant) and his whole life ahead of him.

After the enthusiastic welcome by friends, family, and the television cameras, he set about to settle the draft board problem, and to enter Stanford University in his native state.[10]

When the excitement had subsided, he and Patti enrolled at Stanford. Until they could sell *The Return of Dove*, they had little money, but were able to find a patched-up secondhand mail van and rent a one-room cabin in the hills near the campus. Robin worked at odd jobs around the campus. At one point, they had to live on fruit and vegetables Robin picked up behind a supermarket.

Robin had planned to get an engineering degree with architecture as his goal. But the young couple, after roaming the world, found they had nothing in common with others their age. At the most critical point in their lives, they had acquired experiences and attitudes that the average youth is never exposed to. Robin noted in his journals how sad it seemed to him to see some students coming to college right out of high school, ready to believe anything told them by cynical professors. He remembered one professor in particular, a Maoist, who preached passionately for bloody revolution in class, and was applauded loudly by those students who owned the most expensive Porsches and Jags.

That first semester at Stanford seemed longer to Robin than the first two years at sea. After one particular trying day in which he had to listen to the Maoist professor ranting about his new society in which "everyone would be equal and thieves would be treated in a hospital," Robin and Patti stayed awake all night discussing what to do. The next morning, they decided it was time to move on.

The Return of Dove finally sold, and as soon as the papers were signed and they had the money, they headed their battered mail van toward the northwest. They had discussed going to Canada to settle, but did not really want to lose their American citizenship. The next best thing seemed to be Montana, and it was there that they found what they wanted on a rugged 160-acre timbered homesite in the mountains near Kalispell. The nearest neighbors were three miles away.

In the woods around them, they could find the fresh signs of deer, elk, and bear. They started by building a lean-to cabin from scrap timber. They cleared a garden patch and planted fruit trees. For the next six weeks, they stayed in the village where Robin took lessons in logging and forestry. With a mail order course, they planned to help educate their daughter, Quimby, and themselves, and meanwhile they would build a new and simple life style based on understanding and enjoying the natural world. The neighbors brought them some homemade cheese, wine, and bread. They stocked their cabin for the coming winter. Robin went about learning how to kill a deer or elk for their winter meat supply.

The thought of Patti and Quimby standing in the doorway of the cabin, as he came up the trail with a deer over his shoulders, brought back the words he had copied into his notebook from the gravestone of Robert Louis Stevenson in Samoa:

> *Home is the sailor, home from the sea,*
> *And the hunter home from the hill.*

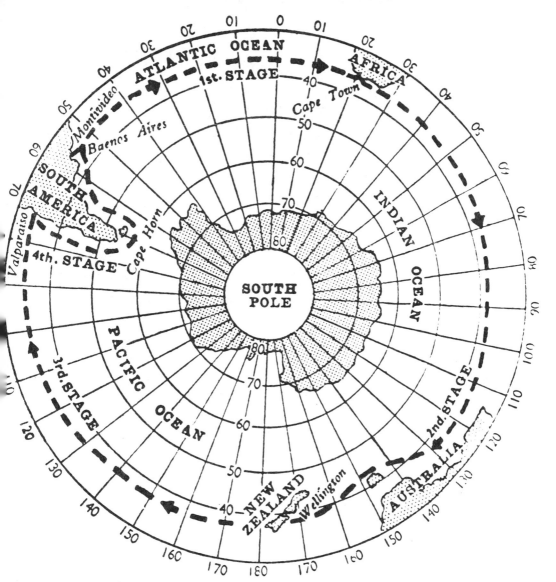

Track of *Legh II* around the world in the Roaring Forties. (The Slocum Society)

Sad ending for *Legh II*, in which Vito Dumas sailed alone around the world in the Roaring Forties in the early part of World War II. She was last seen as a derelict on the beach at Mar del Plata, an Argentine summer resort, by Richard McCloskey, one of the founders of the Slocum Society. In August 1971, she was being sailed to Mar del Plata by students of the National Nautical School when the weather turned bad and *Legh II* was driven ashore. Later efforts were made to salvage the famous yacht and place her in a museum. (The Slocum Society)

A 68-peso postage stamp issued by Argentina in honor of its solo circumnavigator, Vito Dumas, the first man to sail alone around the Roaring Forties. (The Slocum Society)

Lang Syne, the 39-foot Block Island schooner in which the Crowes circumnavigated in the post–World War II period. (William Crowe)

Billy and Bill Crowe aboard their schooner, *Lang Syne*, during their circumnavigation. (William Crowe in *Heaven, Hell and Salt Water*)

Phyllis Crowe aboard *Lang Syne* on a 1971 cruise in Baja California waters off Todo Santos Islands. (William Crowe in *Cruising Club News*)

William Crowe, in 1971, aboard the veteran schooner *Lang Syne*. (William Crowe in *Cruising Club News*)

Marjorie and Al Petersen aboard *Stornoway*, their 33-foot gaff cutter. (Marjorie Petersen)

Tzu Hang at her moorings in Singapore. It is easy to see why the Smeetons fell in love with this ship. (Miles Smeeton)

Miles and Beryl Smeeton as they looked during their first year aboard *Tzu Hang*. (Miles Smeeton)

Brigadier Miles and Beryl Smeeton during their winter in Japan aboard *Tzu Hang*. (Miles Smeeton)

Awahnee shown surrounded by the ice off the south coast of Tierra del Fuego. (*Awahnee* photo)

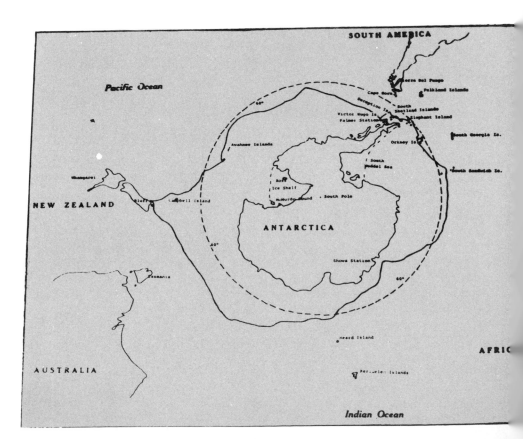

Captain Bob Griffith of *Awahnee*. The photo was taken while he was sailing master aboard the *Westwind*, a training schooner out of Boston. (*Awahnee* photo)

Track of *Awahnee* around the world at Antarctica, beginning and ending at Bluff, New Zealand. The route, indicated by a solid black line, follows a clockwise direction. Courtesy of *Sea Spray* magazine)

Jean Gau watching the ocean and his beloved *Atom*.
The famed Tahiti ketch was ultimately rescued by Good Samaritans
and the Coast Guard. (O.V. Wootten in *National Fisherman*)

Rescue crews trying to get *Atom* off the beach on Assateague Island in
the winter of 1971. (O.V. Wootten in *National Fisherman*)

FIGURE 1

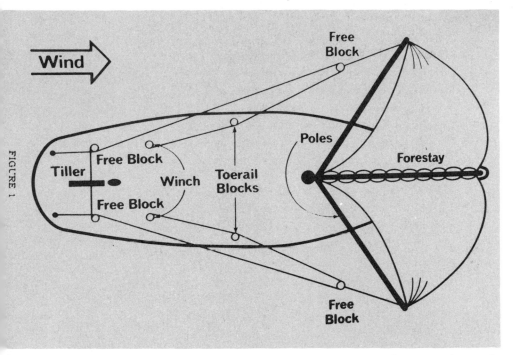

Wind

Free
Block

Poles

Forestay

Tiller

Free Block

Winch

Toerail
Blocks

Free Block

Free
Block

Self-steering system devised by Alan Eddy on *Opogee*, using twin headsails, with the wind astern and abeam. (Allied Boat Co.)

FIGURE 2

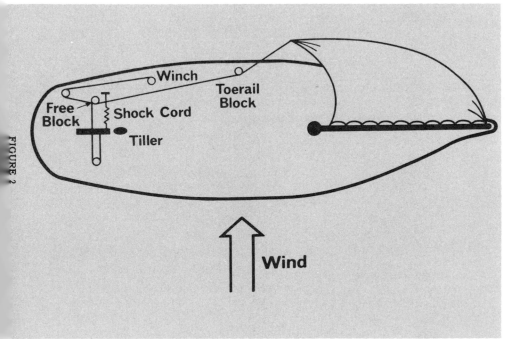

Winch

Toerail
Block

Free
Block

Shock Cord

Tiller

Wind

Opogee leaving Durban, South Africa. She is still sailed by owner Alan Eddy out of Atlantic Yacht Basin in Virginia, showing almost no signs of her age or experience. (Allied Boat Co.)

Opogee running under twin headsails somewhere in the Indian
Ocean. She was the first fiberglass
boat to sail around the world. (Allied Boat Co.)

The Return of Dove, the 33-foot Luders yawl built by Allied Boat Co. of New York, in which Robin Lee Graham completed his interrupted circumnavigation. She is shown here running under twin headsails. (Robin Lee Graham in *Dove*)

Robin Lee Graham, showing the strain of his long passage across the Atlantic on his circumnavigation. He is en route here from the Virgin Islands to the San Blas Islands near Panama. At this point he sold the battered *Dove* and bought a replacement, the 33-foot Luders yawl, *The Return of Dove*, to complete his voyage. (Robin Lee Graham in *Dove*)

The "schoolboy" circumnavigator, Robin Lee Graham, was only sixteen when he began his voyage. He was already an expert navigator, however. (Robin Lee Graham in *Dove*)

The *Luders* 33. This is a sister-ship to the one used by Robin Lee Graham to complete his circumnavigation. It is a fiberglass 33-foot sloop. (Allied Boat Co.)

CHAPTER

❧ 35 ❧

The Impromptu Circumnavigation

I had no intention of sailing TARMIN *around the world when I bought her. She was very run down and I purchased her with the view only of fixing her up as a winter project and then using her as a day-sailer the following summer in Mallorca.*[1]

TARMIN WAS A LITTLE YACHTING WORLD SHIP, A FIVE-tonner, designed by Robert Clark and built by William King & Son at Burnham-on-Crouch, England, in 1948. She was in extremely run-down condition when John M. Sowden found her on the beach at Majorca, Balearic Islands, Spain, in October 1966. A boat's good qualities, like a woman's, often are mainly in the eyes of the beholder, but Sowden thought he saw possibilities in *Tarmin* as a summer coastal cruiser. Besides, he needed a winter project. So he bought her.

She was just under 25 feet length overall, 21 feet on the waterline, with a 7-foot 10-inch beam and a draft of 4 feet 7 inches. A previous owner had changed her from a cutter to a masthead sloop with a short bowsprit.

Once he had her, however, Sowden thought it would be more pleasant to do the work in a milder climate that winter, so with only minimum repairs he left Palma on November 1, 1966, with a friend who accompanied him as far as Gibraltar. Here more repairs were made, and with another companion, a young Englishman who had never been on a yacht before, Sowden sailed to Casablanca, arriving on December 13. His destination had been the Canary Islands, but had been unable to get through the Strait due to currents and head winds.

In Casablanca, where many sea vagabonds spend the winter waiting for better weather to make the trade winds crossing of the Atlantic, he met for the first time the mysterious Pole, Leonid Teliga, a circumnavigator who had built his own dream ship in his backyard, and when he could not get a license to sail out of the Baltic, shipped his yacht *Opty* as deck cargo to Africa.[2] Sowden was to encounter Teliga many times in the coming months.

On December 18, in light and variable winds, Sowden left Casablanca for Las Palmas, arriving December 28. His English companion by then had had enough. He had been seasick most of the passage. Never again, he told Sowden, would he set foot on a yacht of any size.

Las Palmas was a filthy port, infested with harbor thieves, but there was much work to be done on *Tarmin* before she could go anywhere. Leon Teliga arrived and left soon after for parts unknown. The work finally done, Sowden thought it was too early to return to Majorca, so on an impulse one day he decided to go across to the Caribbean before the hurricane season started. For this passage, he installed a Quartermaster self-steering device, which had been airfreighted down from England. He cleared Las Palmas on March 23, 1967, for Barbados. He had never been alone at sea before, but things looked "right," so he left, knowing that once out into the trades he was committed.

It was a slow passage of forty days, much of the time becalmed. He discovered that in light airs there was not enough torque from the wind vane to operate the rudder, and he had to attend the tiller himself. Arriving on May 2, he found Leon Teliga and *Opty* waiting for him. Several weeks were spent cruising the West Indies. He went up to St. Lucia and Martinique, and thought about going down the coast of South America, but changed his mind after reading *Ocean Passages of the World*. This was when he decided to go to Tahiti.

He left for Panama on June 26, stopping along the way at various ports on the leeward route. He found Leon Teliga waiting at Colón to transit the canal. Sowden's two-cylinder, two-cycle engine had already expired, so he had to obtain a tow from a tugboat—and thereupon endured the most harrowing experience of the trip. The tug almost towed *Tarmin* under at ten knots, which was far above the yacht's design hull speed. While at Balboa, he met John Riving, who was circumnavigating in his famous *Sea Egg*.

On September 2, he departed for the Galápagos Islands, without an operative engine, and discovered what hundreds of sailors had learned over the centuries—just getting out of the Gulf of Panama against prevailing currents and winds was an accomplishment. It took twenty-three days of slogging, with a broken roller reefing gear, to make the passage to Wreck Bay, Chatham Island. Here he spent two weeks, during which time he learned that Teliga was at Academy Bay. Before he could rendezvous, however, the harbormaster reported that Leon had already left.

Sowden departed for the Marquesas on October 30 and on the long downwind sail chalked up the best run of the entire voyage, 150 miles on one noon-to-noon observation. He found the anchorage bad at Hiva Oa, so left immediately for Nuku Hiva, arriving on November 27. Three days later, a familiar sail hove in sight. It was Leon Teliga and *Opty*. Leon, now adorned with a heavy black beard, dropped anchor alongside. Sowden remained at Nuku Hiva until the middle of December, loafing and enjoying the company of six other yachts there.

He arrived at Papeete on Christmas Eve and spent the entire hurricane season in the harbor. The time passed easily, as there were usually a couple dozen bluewater yachts in port. Leon came in and moored stern-to alongside him. Still later, another solo navigator, Johann Trauner, arrived with his *Folkboat, Lei Lei Lassen*, from Toronto, Canada. These three singlehanders, who rightly regarded themselves in a class apart from the usual Papeete yachtie crowd, stuck together much of the time while in Tahiti.

"While none of us is young, except at heart, we managed to do our share of dancing at Quinn's," Sowden wrote later.[3]

During his stay here, Sowden had the engine repaired with parts sent out from England, but by now he had become accustomed to sailing without it. He next visited Bora Bora, then headed for American Samoa, arriving at Pago Pago on June 9. Due to the $25 harbor fees, he left as soon as he could take on food and water for Suva.[4]

He was becalmed only fifteen miles from Suva harbor, and his engine was again inoperative. But he was delighted to find Leon Teliga also waiting to sail into port. By now, Sowden had decided on a circumnavigation and two months were spent in Suva, refitting and outfitting *Tarmin*. One night, harbor thieves broke in and stole $300 worth of clothing and equipment. During his time here, his step-mother flew down from the United States for a visit. Teliga applied for an Australian visa, but it was denied him so he took on supplies for a *nonstop* passage from Fiji to Casablanca!

"I may stop en route," Leon told Sowden, "but not unless I have to for repairs or medical reasons."[5]

Sowden cleared Suva on August 29 and sailed to Vila on the island of Efate in the New Hebrides. He spent a week in Port-Vila, then went on to Port Moresby, New Guinea, arriving on September 27. He remained until October 16, hauling out *Tarmin* for hull inspection. Here he applied for a cruising permit for Indonesia, and obtained the necessary inoculations required. He left for Timor and Bali, navigating the Torres Strait without an engine, taking only five days for the passage, and anchoring four nights in the lee of small islands. This anchoring cost him two anchors as a result of coral heads, a fisherman and a Danforth. This led him to pass up Thursday Island, arriving at Dili, Portuguese Timor, on November 3. Here he found his cruising license wanting for him at *poste restante*. He also found the American consul at Djakarta most helpful—a decided contrast to the experiences of early voyagers such as Long, Robinson, and the Fahnestocks.

Tarmin was one of the first yachts to visit Bali in the postwar period, although the Crowes had cruised there in the early 1950s. Sowden stayed in Benoa, Bali, until March 25, 1969, during which time another yacht came in, the trimaran *Cetacean*, from California, also on a circumnavigation.[6]

The crews of the two yachts took turns guarding the vessels, and in this way they were all able to enjoy a leisurely exploration of the island which had long been off the tourist track.

Sowden left for Surabaja to find a slip for bottom painting, and made a difficult passage up the narrow, uncharted, and unlighted straits, taking 11 days to run 250 miles. He spent three weeks trying to get *Tarmin* hauled out and painted, during which the vessel was damaged when a shoring slipped. The work still undone, he left for Singapore to get competent help. While there, he got word of his father's death. Leaving *Tarmin* at the Singapore Yacht Club, he flew to the United States to help with the estate matters. When he returned to Singapore, it was too late to go to the Seychelles.

"As a matter of fact," he told friends, "it was too late to go anywhere."

The southeast monsoon was now well-established, which would

mean beating all the way down Sunda Strait against a 2-knot current. Moreover, there was considerable political turmoil now in the region. In the end, he had to make the 800-mile passage through the strait against the current and often violent head winds. It took twenty-eight days from Singapore, before he entered the Indian Ocean. He then reefed down for the sail to Keeling-Cocos, and six days later encountered the worst gale of the voyage so far. His mainsail ripped out before he could get it down. Knowing he was close to Keeling-Cocos, and could not come back if he overshot, he heaved-to to repair the sail. Then, on September 16, he sailed into the anchorage in the lee of Direction Island.

He spent eight days at Keeling-Cocos, then cleared for Durban, experiencing boisterous seas. He put into Mauritius for fresh fruits and vegetables, which added 2,400 miles to his planned passage. Leaving Mauritius, he was becalmed just outside the harbor—an experience that many voyagers have reported. It is almost as if even the elements do not wish visitors to leave this hospitable island.

He sailed south of Madagascar, enduring four Force 8 gales, which delayed his arrival at Durban until November 7. Once there, he was greeted by Dr. Hamish Campbell of the Slocum Society and assisted through customs.[7] At the time, there were about twenty other world voyagers in the yacht harbor, and that winter the famous Durban hospitality overflowed. And, of course, there was much time for gamming among the bluewater sailors.

On January 21, 1970, Sowden cleared for Cape Town. At about noon on the thirty-first, he rounded the Cape, and at 5 P.M. was within fifteen miles of the harbor. He poured himself a drink to celebrate, and immediately was struck by a Force 10 buster which lasted two days, during which he was blown 130 miles past Cape Town. He did not get back to harbor until February 7. The yacht club was close to a switching terminal, he discovered, with a constant rain of coal dust. The harbor was also badly polluted with oil. But the hospitality was unequaled, so he stayed on for three weeks.

Here he learned of a defunct dealership that had a stock of spare parts for his engine, so he removed it for major overhaul. After that, the engine worked perfectly.

In Cape Town, he met Rollo Gebhard, the German solo circumnavigator, who was there with *Solveig III*. Rollo was also having engine troubles.

On March 27, Sowden left Cape Town under power. "I must say," he wrote, "that I've learned a great deal about sailing by virtue of having been without the use of an engine from Panama to Cape Town. But an engine certainly makes things easier and removes a great deal of anxiety in maneuvering in restricted waters."

He had a fine sail to St. Helena. After a short visit, he went on to Ascension, and, on May 7, left for the long haul uphill to the Azores. He crossed the equator for the fourth time at 25°W and never encountered the doldrums. The wind went from southeast to east and at 30° he was in the northeast trades. He got on the starboard tack and stayed close-hauled most of the time. On May 29, at 20°N and 33°W, he crossed his outbound track between the Canaries and Barbados, completing a singlehanded circumnavigation in three years and forty-nine days.

He stopped in the Azores for a visit, sailed over to Ponta Delgada on San Miguel Island, and on July 13 departed for Gibraltar. On August 14, with a fair wind, he breezed through the Strait. It was so much fun that he kept his genoa on too long and it blew out. With Gibraltar now a lee shore, he put into Algeciras, Spain, then worked back slowly to the Balearics, stopping at Gibraltar and Cartagena. His cruise was coming to an end, and he wanted to make it last.

On September 8, he tied up again at the Club Nàutico in Palma. Thus ended a short holiday cruise that turned into a solo sail around the world, almost completely devoid of incident or accident, in a 25-foot sloop.

CHAPTER

36

The Lone Pole

*Leonid Teliga, the Polish yachtsman who left
Gdynia in the fall of 1966 on his 30-foot yawl
Opty, passed through Panama on his way to
Tahiti, in September 1967.*[1]

LEONID TELIGA CELEBRATED HIS FIFTIETH BIRTHDAY ALONE
at sea on a solo circumnavigation of the world in his home-built
dream ship. This was not only the way he wanted it, but the way he
had planned it for years, ever since his boyhood days when he had
devoured the books of Slocum and Gerbault.

This early fascination with voyaging, in fact, led him to expand his
school studies on his own into more advanced fields to prepare for
the time when he would be captain of his own ship. He soon could
master problems in algebra and geometry far ahead of his class-
mates.[2]

He knew also that boats cost money, so he must have a career that
paid well. In his home town of Gdynia, on the seacoast of the Bay of
Danzig, a few miles north of the city of Danzig, the best-paid profession seemed to be that of a doctor, so he turned his studies this way.
But, in Poland, an intermediate school diploma was not sufficient to
get him admitted to a medical college. He turned then to a maritime
school where he completed the course, and in 1938 shipped on a
fishing schooner.

After Hitler's legions marched into Poland the following year, Teliga found himself stranded in a Caspian fishing port, where he had been employed in the industry. He helped in the evacuation of Rostow, then enlisted in the Polish National Army and became a bomber pilot. By this time, Poland had been overrun and split up between Nazi Germany and the U.S.S.R. In those days of fast-changing alliances, Germany and Russia soon became enemies, and the latter allied with the rest of the Free World—at least until the Axis powers were defeated.

After the war, Teliga returned to Poland, a country now under the red flag but no more subservient than its people had been under Nazi rule. Teliga became a sailing instructor, and to raise money to pursue his dream, he became a freelance translator, a writer, and member of the diplomatic staff. He went to Korea as a staffer with the International Conciliation Commission, and later worked as a correspondent in Rome, and served with the International Commission in Laos.

Meanwhile, he worked on the plans for the boat he wanted. Returning to Warsaw in June 1965, he devoted most of his time to the project. *Opty*, as his dream ship was called—short for "Optimism"—was launched in October 1966, exactly twenty-eight years after he had completed his sailing course in the maritime school. By December, Teliga was ready to depart, but the Polish Sailing Society would not grant him a permit for a lone voyage across the Baltic in December. After much negotiation, Teliga compromised with a permit to ship *Opty* by freighter to Casablanca. Then followed hectic days of scrounging supplies, anchor chain, instruments, canned goods, guns. A farewell dinner was given Captain Teliga.

Then, the next morning, Teliga sailed *Opty* the twenty miles to Gdansk (port of Danzig), and the yacht was hoisted on the deck of the *M/S Slupsk* for the trip to Casablanca, on December 8, 1966.[3] In this North African rendezvous for yachtsmen, he met John Sowden for the first time. Sowden had not planned a circumnavigation, but they talked about it frequently, and this probably put the idea into Sowden's head.

Anyway, there was no doubt in Teliga's mind what he wanted to do. He left on January 25, 1967, for the Canary Islands, reaching there after a 16-day passage during which he encountered a Force 9 storm. The bouncing around opened seams on the coach roof, and from the damp cabin Teliga came down with lumbago. On March 16, he departed for the Barbados, a 2,700-mile passage which took 31 days at an average speed of 3.1 knots. During this passage, he suffered from an aching tooth and had to remove a plastic cap from it. The going was slow and he wrote in his log, "The ocean is so damn big and to cross it one must display as much patience as there is water."

He spent several weeks cruising in the Indies, putting in at Grenada on April 21, and arriving at Panama in August. Because of his Polish flag, Teliga unfortunately experienced red tape and some unpleasantness in the Canal Zone, but finally, with diplomatic connections, he was able to obtain clearance. He reported in his log that the American yachtsmen and local yacht club officials were friendly and helpful, in contrast to the official attitude. He left Balboa on August 17, taking twenty-nine days to reach the Galápagos Islands, where he missed meeting Sowden by just one day. Other yachts at Santa Cruz, he logged, were the U.S. *Renee Tighe, Discovery, Free Flight*; and the *Seafair* from New Zealand.

He departed October 26 for the Marquesas, arriving at Nuku Hiva on November 30, where he found at anchor *Tarmin* and all the boats he had met in the Galápagos. On December 21, he left for Tahiti, passing through the dangerous Tuamotus between Rangiroa and Arutua atolls where navigation is tricky with variable light winds and unreliable currents. He once hit a floating palm tree which scraped off a patch of anti-fouling paint and exposed the planks to worm damage. On December 31, he entered Papeete harbor and moored alongside *Tarmin*. It was New Year's Eve, and the time had come for a celebration—even for a Lone Pole.

He waited out the hurricane season here with Sowden and Johann Trauner, another solo circumnavigator. The time passed pleasantly. Among the other yachts were the *Eryx II*, a large French-owned steel schooner flying the Union Jack, and the well-known Canadian sloop *Driver*, sailed by the Graham family.

On May 5, he crossed to Bora Bora, then sailed directly to Suva where he was cordially welcomed by the British authorities and local yachtsmen. He spent a pleasant two months here, but was unable to get a visa from the Australian immigration office, an episode which aroused a good deal of local opinion when the word got around.

Somewhat embittered, Teliga decided to head for home as directly as possible. For one thing, he was not feeling well—something he kept between himself and his log. He loaded supplies aboard for 180 days, just in case he did not stop anywhere on the west coast of Africa. He had 400 liters of fresh water aboard and enough food to go straight through to the Baltic if necessary. Leaving the Fijis on July 29, 1968, he crossed to the New Hebrides, sailed through the coral-strewn Torres Strait, and entered the Indian Ocean. In mid-October, after a storm, he spotted the English freighter *Egton*, which changed course and hove-to. This was the first vessel Teliga had seen since leaving Torres Strait two months before.

"Some ship masters," he wrote, "are sea gentlemen and really care about yachts."

It was the wrong time to sail around the bight of Africa, but he did not want to have to fight his way into a port and then fight his way out again. It was bad enough out here. Besides, the pains he had been enduring almost constantly were now worse. At first he had thought it was because of an accident in which he had been hit in the abdomen by the boom. The intestinal and bladder troubles persisted, however, with the occasional passage of blood. The passage around the Cape was a trying experience with southwest storms and winds over sixty knots much of the time. On November 3, he was altering course to the north, keeping to the east of the usual sailing route to take advantage of the inshore currents. He also wanted to see a region of the oceans that few yachtsmen visited.[4]

Now he was no longer in a hurry. Perhaps he felt the end coming too soon. He entered Dakar on January 9, 1969, after 165 days at sea, one of the longest solo voyages on record, having sailed 14,263 miles nonstop.

In Dakar, the French navy looked after *Opty*; Polish, French, and Sengalese friends looked after Teliga. It was one of his most enjoyable port visits. Feeling better, he left Dakar on April 5 and crossed his outbound track from Las Palmas to Barbados, thus completing a circumnavigation solo in two years, thirteen days, twenty-one hours, and thirty-five minutes, according to his log.

He stopped in Las Palmas from April 16 to April 20, and then sailed to Casablanca, which he entered on April 29. He could go no further, not even the last final and triumphant leg to the Baltic and home. For some time now, he had been extremely ill. In order to attend the ceremonies waiting for him in Warsaw, as the first Pole to sail alone around the world in a small boat, he flew back on a commercial airliner to attend the official dinners and functions, and to be honored by his country's high decorations. *Opty* was returned later and a Gdynia shipyard took charge to prepare the yacht for the next season free of charge.

Typically, not even Teliga's close friends knew how seriously ill he had been. Only his log knew. The pains, we now know, had been with him during the entire voyage. Later a friend and neighbor, Witold Tobis, wrote:

> *We did not have the slightest idea about the illness and the pains which Teliga had to endure during the whole voyage. It is now supposed that what Teliga took for the ishias was in fact the first attack of cancer. It was during the first part of the voyage. The unfortunate crash of the boom on his abdomen seemingly developed or accelerated this illness. This happened during the Grenada to Cristobal crossing. The next paroxysm of pains and the bigger one was during the passage through the Torres Strait. After passing the Cape of Good Hope, at the horse latitudes, Teliga got a high fever and as now we know from his log book, he lost his mind for some days.*
>
> *And then comes the last leg of the voyage, namely the quick passage from Las Palmas to Casablanca, when Teliga was in such pain he had to bite his blanket.*
>
> *About a week or ten days before his death, Teliga came to my backyard, when I was putting the finishing touches to my self-made yacht. He said then, "Your boat seems to be a mini-Colin Archer type," and we had a little chat, and it was for the last time.*[5]

Teliga's solo circumnavigation on the trim little home-built *Opty* ranks among the best of them. It was made in fast time for such a small vessel, and with a precision that surpassed most voyages. Had it not been for Teliga's log, and occasional letters from faraway places to friends, no one would have ever known about the Lone Pole.

In 1969, the Polish government issued a special 60-gr. postage stamp in honor of Leonid Teliga and his voyage. The stamp shows a map of the world with Teliga's route on *Opty* and an explanatory legend.[6]

CHAPTER

37

The Same Girl in Every Port

My voyage from Cape Town to Helgoland was uneventful, except for the fact that I sailed straight from the Equator to the entrance of the Channel against northeast winds. It was very hard for me and the boat.[1]

ROLLO GEBHARD WAS ALREADY IN HIS LATE FORTIES WHEN he made a singlehanded voyage across the Atlantic in his seventeen-foot *Solveig II*. On his return he put together an 8 mm movie film of the adventure, and through lecturing earned enough to purchase a larger boat and plan a three-year circumnavigation of the world.

In the summer of 1966 he bought *Solveig III*, a Condor-class sloop of fiberglass, twenty-four feet length overall.[2] She was built at Lake Chiemsee in Upper Bavaria, along with forty others from the same mold, but was a day-sailer, not intended for ocean cruising.

On August 3, 1967, *Solveig III* was taken to Italy and launched at Portofino near Genoa. Four days later, Rollo departed on his circumnavigation. The first leg took him to the Mediterranean where he was joined by his girl friend, Birgitta Lundholm, for sightseeing in Spain and Morocco. On this part of the cruise, he experienced the first of a long series of difficulties with the ten-horsepower diesel engine. On the second day out, the exhaust pipe began leaking and the engine compartment filled with water. They put into Minorca for repairs, but the damage had already been done.

"Never again," said Rollo, "shall I go on a long cruise with a new boat. I think something has to go wrong."[3]

Final repairs were completed in Gibraltar, except for the generator which had been ruined by seawater. In late October, the couple reached Las Palmas in the Canary Islands. Here Birgitta left for home. Gebhard stayed until he could complete bottom painting and prepare for the Atlantic crossing. On December 12, he cleared for Barbados, which he reached on January 7, 1968.

He was joined by Birgitta, who obtained a free ride from Sweden to Grenada, and together they cruised the islands from Grenada to Antigua. There, Birgitta left again for home, and Rollo continued on to Bonaire and Curaçao, the Dutch Islands, where he had a pleasant stay among hospitable people. He became ill here with an infected tooth, which had to be extracted.

The passage to Cristobal was a rough one. In Panama, he had to enlist a crew to get through the canal. Returning to the yacht club at about noon one Sunday, he was attacked from behind in broad daylight, mugged, beaten severely, and robbed. He lost his watch and all the money he had on him to the robbers, and was sick for several days after.

He transited the canal on July 6, and in Balboa outfitted for the Pacific voyage. On July 17, he left for the Galápagos, taking extra fuel along in deck containers. But the exhaust pipe began leaking again, and he had to sail the entire distance in fluky winds. It took twenty-one days to make the nine hundred miles—fairly good time under the circumstances. After cruising among the islands for six weeks, he departed directly for Tahiti.

"After Panama," he wrote, "I was a bit tired; and after visiting a dozen uninhabited islands with some dangerous anchorages, I made the great mistake of not stopping in the Marquesas and the Tuamotus."

His girl friend, Birgitta, again flew down to be with him, and they spent two months in Papeete and two more in Mooréa. On the way to Fiji, they stopped at Huahine, Raïatéa, Bora Bora, Aitutkaki, Suwarrow, Apia, and Suva. At Suwarrow, they spent two weeks with the legendary New Zealander, Tom Neal, who had lived alone on this atoll for ten years. Neal, in his little dinghy, took them on trips to other tiny motus of the atoll, showing them how to live off the land and sea.

"It was really hard to leave him, and I shall never forget seeing his figure on the beach getting smaller and smaller as we sailed away."

Birgitta returned to Europe on a cruise ship from Suva. Rollo continued his circumnavigation, departing for the New Hebrides and New Guinea. He paused long enough to explore these island groups, and at one point made a roundtrip by air over New Guinea to Port Moresby.

It was a great pity, he commented later, that so many yachtsmen who pass through Port Moresby never see this most interesting part of New Guinea. Most of them are traveling on a tight budget and cannot afford the luxury of side trips.

From Port Moresby to Bramble Bay and through Torres Strait, he encountered bad weather and tricky navigational hazards. He departed from Thursday Island for Durban, South Africa, on September 12, via Christmas Island, Keeling-Cocos, and Mauritius. Approaching the latter after the long Indian Ocean crossing, the weather was so favorable that he decided to go straight on to Durban.

In the Mozambique Channel, he ran into Force 11 storms, but on November 30 saw the lighthouse at Durban. He used most of his remaining fresh water to clean up, with the anticipation of going right into port. Within the hour, however, the north wind increased to Force 11 again and he had to lower sails and heave to. He drifted to leeward for twenty miles by morning, and had to sail back against the four-knot Agulhas Current, and the wind from the north. The next day, he was hit by a southerly gale and drifted seventy miles the other way. The second time, he made it to within ten miles of Durban, only to have the wind drop to a dead calm. Only five miles from the harbor entrance, he was caught by a tidal current and was sent southward again. The next day, he was thirty miles from Durban. Once more he tried to sail in, but the wind dropped to a calm, then came on from the north.

"It was dangerous and pointless to fool around any more, trying to reach Durban," he wrote. "So I decided to sail around the Cape."

At this time, he had almost no water, his batteries were dead, he had no gasoline left for the little Honda generator, and the diesel engine had not worked since Thursday Island. One sail had been damaged off Madagascar, the bottom was a floating garden, and one hatch leaked—all things he had planned to remedy in Durban before attempting the Cape.

He sailed through the heavy ship traffic around the Cape in this condition, without navigation lights, enduring three more gales. He arrived at Cape Town on December 17 to learn he had been listed as missing by German news services.

He started at once to get repairs completed, but again was incapacitated by pain with an infected tooth. All the dentists in town were on holiday until January 15, he learned, and even then were booked up weeks in advance. The tooth would have to wait their pleasure—and he was not free of pain until late February.

He stopped at St. Helena, then went on to Madeira where he had friends, crossing his outbound track to complete the circumnavigation. He had sailed from Cape Town on February 25, and arrived at Funchal May 5, only one hour before a prearranged date with Birgitta, who had flown down. Her plane was one hour late, otherwise the rendezvous would have been kept precisely on time after 5,500 miles of sailing, 2,500 of which were beating against head winds.

He and Birgitta enjoyed two weeks of vacationing with friends from home. After their departure, a movie company came on board for two weeks of shooting. Then the yacht was hauled, and the bottom scraped and repainted.

On June 17, he left Funchal and sailed north, meeting light winds and averaging only twenty-five miles a day. In the Bay of Biscay, he encountered calms, but in the channel the winds freshened to Force 6 and he arrived at Portsmouth on July 10, three days after his forty-ninth birthday.

He spent a week in London with his brother, then departed on the last leg of the voyage July 17. He found hard going in the Straits of Dover and North Sea, where he was also greeted by fog and much ship traffic. He took extra care not to have a mishap on the final leg of the journey. He was convinced by now that the best way to sail from Cape Town would be first to Rio, then to the West Indies, and from there to Bermuda and New York and across.

The German television and newspaper people wanted to shoot pictures of *Solveig III* from the air, and a meeting was arranged by telephone from England at a point fifty miles from Helgoland. Rollo was there at the appointed time, to the minute, at 1400 hours on July 22. A seaplane from the German navy with six reporters on board flew over him at an altitude of from seven hundred to one thousand feet at 1403 hours and came back ten minutes later for another pass—and failed to see him.[4]

So, after a leisurely three-year circumnavigation, Rollo Gebhard returned home to Garmisch and an enthusiastic reception from the

German television and news media. He spent the rest of the year editing and recording sound on the films he had taken, and looked forward to settling down with a modest income as a minor celebrity and the girl he had had waiting for him in every port.

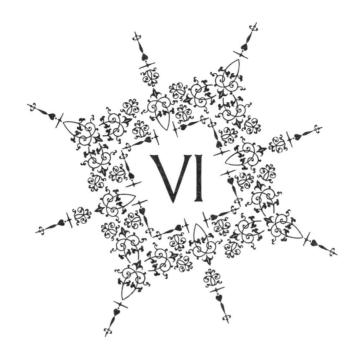

VI

THE
MULTI-HULLS

CHAPTER

ᵒᶳ 38 ᶢᵌ

A Whale's Tale and Others

Lodestar departed Wairoa December 9, 1962, for the trip through the Roaring Forties. Although the vessel was sailed south to the forty-second parallel, the only heavy weather was an hour-long squall, during which Lodestar maintained a speed of twenty-five knots, with that day's run totalling 250 miles.[1]

IN THE 1950s AND 1960s, THE ANCIENT AND HONORABLE profession of yacht designing and building began to feel the undermining of its traditional prerogatives and customs by modernized versions of the Polynesian and Melanesian multi-hulled sailing craft. All of the early circumnavigators had written with awe of these speedy craft—usually a pair of canoes lashed together—and sailing enthusiasts had begun to experiment with them long before World War II.[2]

After the war, especially in Hawaii and Southern California, the "cat craze" swept the young (and not so young) generation. In the islands, brilliant natural designers such as Rudy Choy, Woody Brown, Alfred Kumalae, and others, were developing large ocean-going multi-hulled racers. In the 1955 TransPac (open only to mono-hulls), the Choy-designed *Waikiki Surf*, entered unofficially, and in one of the stormiest TransPacs on record, came in ahead of forty-nine others in an elapsed time of ten days and fifteen hours, beaten only by the famous *Ticonderoga*, *Stormvogel*, and *Morning Star*. At times, *Surf* would be leading the pack at speeds up to twenty-five knots.

Another catamaran, the *Aikane*, sailed unofficially in the 1957 and 1959 races and was first to finish both times, setting a still unbeaten record of nine days, twenty-two hours, and thirty-three minutes for a multi-hull.

Meanwhile, in Sausalito, California, across from San Francisco, a former World War II pilot, print-shop operator, and small boat sailor named Arthur Piver, who had been one of the first to build and sail modern catamarans, began experimenting with a three-hulled version which he dubbed the trimaran. Piver's tris, in a half-dozen different sizes, began to appear in all parts of the world—built mostly in backyards from plans sold by Piver. Many advantages were claimed for the ungainly-looking trimaran, and to prove them, Piver himself sailed one of his Lodestar models across the Atlantic, and another across the Pacific.[3]

As the trimaran craze surfed along at high speed, two of Piver's *Victress*-class models—Donald Crowhurst's *Teignmouth Electron* and Nigel Tetley's *Victress*—were entered in the *Sunday Times* Golden Globe Race. Tetley became the first person to sail around the world nonstop singlehanded in a trimaran, and probably the first to circumnavigate in a multi-hull.[4]

This naturally inspired dozens of similar attempts, and not a few disasters. Piver himself was lost without a trace off the California coast while testing a new trimaran. At this writing, word has come of two trimaran disasters to young amateur voyagers who left the Columbia River port of Portland, Oregon, on world cruises, only to soon become disasters. One of them capsized, and drifted for more than two months almost across the Pacific Ocean before being rescued by a passing ship. Of the three aboard, only one survived.

The more popular the multi-hulls become, the more numerous they are—even respectable yacht designers have turned their talents in this direction—and the more controversial they become. While the arguments rage pro and con over their seaworthiness, speed, and sometimes outrageous claims of superiority, literally hundreds are being built and dozens are venturing out onto the Seven Seas on long, often astonishing voyages.

One of the lesser-known circumnavigations was the voyage around the world of *Cetacean*, a 37-foot Piver-designed trimaran, built at Port Hueneme on the southern California coast by Clark Barthol, his partner, Dennis Fontany, and Clark's wife, Meta.

Leaving in March 1967, the three of them sailed down the Baja coast to Acapulco, and then crossed to the Marquesas in June. From there, they went to Penrhyn in the Cook Islands, a then-popular stop for voyagers, and on to Samoa to wait out the hurricane season.

In Samoa, they met John Sowden and his sloop, *Tarmin*. Sowden was only there four days, but the *Cetacean* crew remained ten months. They would meet again many times along the way around.

In Suvan, they spent two months on a major refit. Sowden was there also, as was Leon Teliga with *Opty*. From Fiji, they cruised part-way with *Tarmin* to Port-Vila, New Hebrides, Port Moresby, New Guinea, Dili, and Timor.

In company with *Tarmin*, the next major lay-over was in Bali, an East Indian paradise in which postponement of departure time comes easy. They stayed here from November 1968 to June 1969. In Samoa, the *Cetacean* crew had been increased by Patricia Ahlson, an American schoolteacher. Miss Ahlson left the ship at Bali to return to her home in Chicago. For five months, *Tarmin* and *Cetacean* were the only yachts in the tiny picturesque Balinese harbor of Benoa.

In June, they sailed for Christmas Island, and then on to Keeling-Cocos. Next came the Seychelles, seldom visited by yachts, where they arrived on July 31 at Port Victoria. From here, they went on to Mozambique, arriving September 1, and then sailed down the channel to Lourenço Marques. On October 2, they put in at Durban, where they were welcomed by Dr. Hamish Campbell, the unofficial greeter of world voyagers and the local yachtsmen.

They sailed for Cape Town on December 20 and encountered two stiff gales en route, taking one week for the passage. At the end of January, they sailed nonstop for St. Helena, took on water and stores, and then embarked on the longest passage of the trip—4,900 miles to Colón, Panama, arriving March 31, 1970.

Here, Meta, who was pregnant, flew home and Miss Ahlson flew down from Chicago to join the trimaran for the last leg through the canal and uphill to Los Angeles.

They did not go directly north from Balboa, but as usual with most voyagers, sailed out to the Galápagos Islands, taking fifteen days from Las Perlas Islands. They spent ten days at Barrington and Santa Cruz, then with one hundred gallons of water and food for six weeks, set off toward home.

The passage uphill was made with less than twenty-four hours of calms, making good an average of one hundred miles a day, taking forty-three days, most of the time sailing to weather. This passage over this route certainly is one of the fastest on record. Most vessels, large or small, are not as fortunate in capturing the right wind.

Cetacean arrived at Oxnard, sixty miles north of Los Angeles, without any untoward incident, thus completing a successful circumnavigation. The Barthols and Dennis Fontany then swallowed the anchor, sold the trimaran, and adjusted to a more domestic life inland. They had got the bug out of their systems.

THE PRAIRIE SAILOR

LIKE RAY KAUFFMAN AND GERRY MEFFERD, WHO ACQUIRED their love of the sea and yen for bluewater voyaging in Des Moines, Iowa (to say nothing of Harry Pidgeon long before), Quentin Cultra grew up on a farm in the Corn Belt, ninety miles from the nearest water deep enough to float the kind of ship he dreamed about.

A farm boy in the rich, black dirt country of southern Illinois, he had never seen an ocean or been near any water that even looked like it, except Lake Michigan, when he taught school briefly in Chicago. In the mid-1960s, when Piver-fever was spreading rapidly, he was fascinated by the 35-foot trimaran designed by Arthur Piver for home-building. It was of simple construction with a plywood skin covered with fiberglass cloth, and with spars of laminated fir. Out on the farm, he had plenty of room for construction (a trimaran needs a lot of room, not only for construction but for docking). But as the work progressed, he found he needed help for moving or rolling over hulls, so he would go into the village, and pass the word around the local taverns that there was free beer at the Cultra farm. Soon he would have twenty or thirty helpers, often including the bartenders of said taverns.

Putting together the framework and applying the plywood skin was fairly easy. Cultra, like most farmers, was handy with tools. Applying the fiberglass, however, presented new problems. The work required a constant temperature of 70° or better, and since this phase of the job came during the winter months, he had to surround the hulls with a tent-like cover, heated with electric elements, and breath the semi-toxic fumes while he worked.

Finally, the hulls were finished and bolted together. The next step was getting the 20-foot-wide craft into some water, which meant moving it over Illinois highways. At the state capital, officials laughed at his requests for a permit. Then he called a house-mover, who hung up on him. A helicopter company offered to do the job, but did not have a machine big enough to airlift 4,500 pounds of boat.

In the end, Cultra, being a young man of direct action, simply loaded the trimaran on a trailer, covered it with a sheet of black plastic, and started down the country roads at dawn one morning, over a route he had previously scouted and measured. On several occasions, the local constables stopped him.

"What have we got here, son?"

"Oh, why it's an experimental asparagus picker."

In rural areas, people can understand an experimental asparagus picker whereas they might be highly suspicious of a 35-foot trimaran.

The *Queequeg*—for that was her name, after the character in *Moby Dick*—reached water on New Year's Eve in 1967, when she was christened by Cultra's girl friend, Judy, with a bottle of frozen champagne, and launched into the Illinois River. The temperature dropped to minus 18° that night and *Queequeg* was frozen solid in the ice. Later, Cultra chopped her loose with an ax and lifted her out with a crane to await spring.

In March, with a crew that included Jack Downs, a Chicago social worker (who had never seen an ocean, either), Cultra started off down the Illinois, entered the Mississippi, and motored southward toward the Gulf of Mexico propelled by a 25-horsepower outboard motor. During the winter, Cultra had taken a course in celestial navigation at the Adler Planetarium in Chicago, but had yet to set his first sail.

Into the gulf and around to Port Isabel, Texas, went the *Queequeg*. There, with the help of members of the "Confederate Navy," the sailors from the Corn Belt learned how to handle the boat under sail at sea.

By October 1968, they were ready to challenge that sea, and the first leg was a nice sail to the beautiful tropical island of Cozumel off the Yucatán Peninsula—except for the first crisis, which turned out to be an encounter with the edges of Hurricane Gladys, in which they learned seamanship almost overnight. Passing through the Yucatán Channel, they visited Costa Rica, Panama, transited the Canal, then headed for the enchanted islands of Galápagos.

From here, they took the traditional yacht route to the Marquesas, 3,100 miles in 26 days, mostly using the self-steering mechanism with the rudder working off the jib. It was hands-off almost all the way.

The two lads were disappointed with Tahiti, which by now had become a crowded tourist trap, and nothing like the island paradise reported by Robinson, Gerbault, Nordhoff and Hall, and Kauffman and Mefferd.

But they had to stay four months to wait out the hurricane season. Here they were joined by Don Travers, a navy lieutenant looking for a ride home and willing to go the long way around. They sailed to Western Samoa, then to Tonga and the New Hebrides. After some adventuring with headhunters in the Malekula country, they sailed to Australia, then up Queensland inside the Great Barrier Reef, through Torres Strait to Indonesia. They stopped frequently at such places as Bali, Komodo, where the twelve-foot dragons lived (described by Robinson and Long).

From Bali, they shaped course to Mauritius, then sailed on to Madagascar. After three days on which sightings could not be taken, currents swept them off-course and piled the *Queequeg* up on a reef. Downs was swept overboard. When Cultra tried to launch the dinghy to save him, he lost the dinghy and found himself in the water fighting for his life. Only Travers remained on board. Cultra finally caught a life ring thrown to him, and made the beach where he found Jack waiting. They could hear Travers calling to them over the roar of the surf, but it was now impossible to swim back, so they buried themselves in the sand to keep warm until daylight came.

At first light, they saw *Queequeg* still there. Travers had trailed some lines ashore attached to plastic jugs, but they could not reach them. Downs volunteered to go for help and departed down the beach. Had he waited a few more minutes, it would have been unnecessary, as some friendly natives came along and helped Cultra get hold of one of the lines and get aboard. He and Travers then got the sails up and on the tide, floated off the reef.

They sailed alongshore trying to spot Downs, but did not see him. For thirty-six hours, they sailed on and off the beach, waiting for Downs to reappear. During this period, while in their bunks, Travers and Cultra were suddenly thrown violently about. They rushed outside in time to see a huge ship looming overhead. One of the outboard hulls was crushed and both masts torn off. The main mast weighed four hundred pounds, and could not be handled alone. The ship had passed on without stopping. They quickly sent up a flare and flashed an S.O.S. with a flashlight. The ship then slowed down, made a long circle and came back, the maneuver taking about two hours. The captain apologized and offered to tow them to Mauritius. From the ship, a radiogram was sent to the American consul in Madagascar explaining what happened and asking for help in locating Downs.

As it happened, Downs was already in jail—he had been taken into custody as a spy. Finally released, he flew to Mauritius. A month was spent repairing *Queequeg.*

Leaving this hospitable island, they sailed to Durban, and thence around Cape of Good Hope to Cape Town, encountering some monstrous storms, the most violent of the entire trip. Next came St. Helena and Ascension, then the bulge of Brazil. Their route took them up to Grenada, the Virgin Islands, and to Bermuda. From here they sailed direct to New York, then into the Hudson Waterway and up to the Great Lakes, and finally home to Chicago to complete the circumnavigation.

The adventure took the farm boys two and a half years and covered about forty thousand miles. Aside from the Madagascar episode, it was a remarkably easy voyage, free of serious accident. At home, the Corn Belt sailor married his Judy, and settled down to raise a family.

DOCTOR OF THE WINDS

In the summer of 1963, an odd-looking yacht rounded the Lizard and stood up Plymouth Sound with passing vessels and villagers on shore doing double takes. Not only was the yacht unusual, for it was a twin-hulled catamaran, but along the guard rails and flying in the rigging were dozens of diapers drying in the wind.

British yachtsmen, accustomed to seeing vessels dressed for entering harbor with strings of signal flags, may have dropped monocles at the sight, but not for long. The skipper was a well-known London physician, Dr. David Lewis, and a yachtsman who had made a number of unusual voyages in small craft, including one singlehanded race to America. With him this time were his wife, Fiona, and their two daughters, Susan, one and a half, and Vicky, three months. They had just come from the Orkneys, through the North Channel and across the Irish Sea, with no problems even in the boisterous weather encountered—except that they ran out of baby food, and also out of Nappies, which meant the emergency of washing and drying non-throwables for recycling.

This voyage had been a short leg, part of a trip to Iceland that Dr. Lewis had made to test the new catamaran, with three experienced crewmen. In the Orkneys, on the return, the family had come aboard for the home stretch to test their reactions. It was, in fact, Dr. Lewis's intention to sail around the world in *Rehu Moana,* and this had all been a dress rehearsal.[5]

In any case, the family was already committed. He had given up his medical practice in London. They had sold their home. All their money was tied up in the new yacht. A New Zealander of Welsh extraction, David Lewis had been a general practitioner in East Ham, London, for seventeen years in the post–World War II period. By a previous marriage, he had a fifteen-year-old son, Barry, and a twenty-year-old married daughter, Anna. His present wife, Fiona, was in her late twenties, some eighteen years the doctor's junior. She was a South African, tall and feminine, but also athletic and keen on the outdoors and mountain climbing, as was Dr. Lewis. She was skilled in many things, such as cooking, making clothes, party-giving, and graphic arts. She had taught dancing and physical education. She was, unfortunately, also susceptible to seasickness.

Dr. Lewis had entered the 1960 Transatlantic Singlehanded Race in his first yacht, *Cardinal Vertue*, a J. Laurent Giles sloop, 25 feet 3 inches length over all.[6] His book about this voyage (*My Ship Would Not Sail Due West*) and his sailing background became a popular best-seller in the United Kingdom, and helped convince the doctor that he could quit his practice and voyage the oceans and still make a living.

In the winter of 1962–1963, he commissioned Colin Mudie, the inventive and imaginative English yacht designer, to come up with a catamaran based on the Polynesian double-canoes. Dr. Lewis was a student of the South Pacific and her peoples, and secretly longed to return to New Zealand. Built of plywood, *Rehu Moana* had many experimental features, including flaring bows, a wishbone rig, covered steering position, and two heavily-weighted centerboards. The shakedown voyage to Iceland was made with three mountain-climbing and yachting friends. Severe gales that were encountered, a couple of dismastings, and a few other incidents that generally can be expected with a new boat, convinced Lewis that the design and construction were sound.[7]

Entered in the 1964 Transatlantic Race, Lewis was again up against some formidable competition: Francis Chichester, Blondie Hasler, the two Frenchmen, Tabarly and Lacombe. Because the rules specified only one person aboard, Fiona and the children had to take passage on a freighter to America. The race was a terrible ordeal for all boats, but in spite of this, Dr. Lewis made it in thirty-eight days and twelve hours from Plymouth to Newport, most of the time in emergency conditions. He came in seventh after Chichester, Tabarly, Val Howells, Alec Rose, Hasler, and Tahiti Bill Howell. Both of the multi-hulls in the race—*Folâtre* and *Rehu Moana*—were damaged in the crossing.

In America waited Fiona and the two restless girls, staying with John Pfleiger, the genial commodore of the Slocum Society, who himself later went missing at sea. The family had crossed on the M/V *Sunset* from Hamburg, landing at Richmond, Virginia, where they rented a car and drove over the unfamiliar keep-to-the-right freeways through New York to Newport

The race over, now the serious voyaging was to begin with the family aboard. This meant re-outfitting for the second Atlantic cross-ing to Cape Verdes and then down to Rio. The twin hulls became jammed with toys, bikini pants and brassieres, suitcases, dresses on hangers, children's books, feminine toiletry, all of which over-whelmed the basic bachelor disorder of the first crossing.

Before leaving, Dr. Lewis was given the title of Honorary Citizen of Newport, and had gone to one of his race competitors, Tahiti Bill Howell, who was a dentist, to have an abscessed tooth removed. What with all the partying at the end of the race, the irrepressible Howell managed to remove the wrong tooth by the hurricane lamp in the salon aboard *Stardrift*. By the time they had discovered the error, a local disturbance had brought the local gendarmes and Howell disappeared. Lewis had to find another dentist to extract the ab-scessed tooth.

The children developed a passion for ice cream in America, and a reluctance to leave. Fiona, too, had become reluctant without know-ing why. Once at sea, her problem was magnified by seasickness, claustrophobia, and the constant motion. Dr. Lewis, who kept an almost clinical daily log of the voyage, noted that her condition became progressively worse until it threatened to abort the voyage. Once Fiona recognized it as anxiety and fear, she was able to control the condition. The children at first had suffered pitifully from the close quarters, the constant stench of vomit, the constant motion, and the anxieties of the parents. But gradually, as the gales subsided and shipboard life became more routine, they all got over it.

After a stay in the Cape Verdes, they departed on the third Atlantic crossing to Brazil. Several weeks were spent in Rio, outfitting and repairing, and making modifications for the coming trip around Cape Horn. This leg of the circumnavigation was one of the most interesting ever recorded, in my opinion.

The Lewises on *Rehu Moana* thrashed down into Cape Horn

latitudes and spent several months exploring the wild and remote channels of Patagonia, seldom seen by yachtsmen, and even then only passing through.[8] It was a paradise for Dr. Lewis, the amateur naturalist, and a busy time for Dr. Lewis, the physician, for he was much in demand among local residents to treat their ailments. The days were filled with navigation and ship handling, dispensing medicine, studying flora and fauna, taking care of the children, making notes on anthropology. For weeks, they cruised among the channels, often in the vicinity of the Horn, recording everything, including the antics and cute sayings of the two girls. At Punta Arenas, at 3:30 on the morning of Christmas Eve, they heard on the radio that Bill Nance, one of the most brilliant and daring of all singlehanders, who had purchased the old *Cardinal Vertue,* had just rounded Cape Horn, some two hundred miles to the south, on his solo circumnavigation.

Leaving the Patagonia channels, they cruised up the remote waterways of the Chilean coast, stopping frequently at settlements and Indian camps. Dr. Lewis was especially interested in the remnants of the Alacalufe or Canoe Indians, a native people who had been decimated by disease and civilization in one of the most remote parts of the world. His studies indicated to him that because they were a hunting society, they had survived and adapted and had every chance of rebuilding, given time and modern medical help.

The stay in Valparaiso was a delightful one, filled with hospitality. The girls, who had been thriving on shipboard life, had grown astonishingly, and their antics, wherever they went, were a constant source of amusement, trial and tribulation, keeping Dr. and Mrs. Lewis constantly on their toes. Here they cabled to England for a friend, Priscilla Cairns, an experienced sailor and navigator, to join them. She would be a helpful crewmate, but also could relieve Lewis of navigational chores so that he could make a study of the Polynesian methods as explained by Harold Gatty in *The Raft Book,* during the Pacific crossing.

The route took them in a rough passage to Easter Island (Rapa Nui), visiting Juan Fernández on the way. *Rehu Moana* was apparently the first multi-hull to visit this remote island since prehistoric days, and the natives regarded them as reincarnates of the old legends.[9] The children were especially popular. The family next sailed to Mangareva via Pitcairn, then to Papeete, Rarotonga, and down to New Zealand.

In his native country, Dr. Lewis and the family were idolized. He was named the New Zealand yachtsman of the year for 1965. He made a television film, edited from his footage taken on the voyage so far, wrote another book, and with the help of the local multi-hull clubs, put the catamaran in condition for the second half of the circumnavigation.

From New Zealand, they sailed to Tonga, Fiji, the New Hebrides, and Port Moresby; then through Torres Strait to Thursday Island and Darwin. Breaking loose from the hospitality of Darwin, they sailed across the Indian Ocean via the Keeling-Cocos to Durban. This was Fiona's native land, and the hospitality was again overwhelming.

Rounding the Cape of Good Hope, they stopped at Walvis Bay in South West Africa where a tug broke loose in a blow and crashed against *Rehu Moana*, nearly ending the voyage there. Repairs were made with the help of local residents, and the girls got their first close-up experience with ostriches, jackals, gemsbok, and baboons. The next stop was Lobito in Angola. Then came the Congo River and the frontier town of Banana, visited last by the Crowes on *Lang Syne*.

At the end of March, they set off on the final leg, arriving at Plymouth, after three years of excitement and adventure during which the children had grown into young ladies and had associated with peoples of all races, nationalities, and social status. The deck of the *Rehu Moana* had been their playground; climbing the rigging was their exercise. They had attended kindergarten in New Zealand and again in Walvis Bay, and spoke or understood several languages. Lewis was awarded an honorary degree from Leeds University, and a research fellowship by the Australian National University to study surviving fragments of Polynesian navigation.

Rehu Moana was sold, and a heavy 39-foot, gaff-rigged ketch, *Isbjorn*, purchased. The family left Plymouth on March 7, 1968, made Antigua in twenty-three days, cruised among the West Indies, on the way to the South Pacific. Aboard now was Lewis's son, Barry, who obtained his master's ticket and later took over the *Isbjorn* for trading and chartering after a spell in the merchant marine.

Dr. Lewis' research in Micronesia and Polynesia completed, he went back to Canberra to a desk and a library to complete the writing. The girls started regular school, and the family settled down to life ashore.

Dr. Lewis, however, could never fully accept this. On October 19, 1972, at one P.M., aboard the 32-foot, steel-hulled sloop *Ice Bird*, built especially for Antarctic waters, he departed Sydney Heads on an attempted solo circumnavigation of the Antarctic Continent. Waving good-bye from the pilot vessel were his two daughters, eleven-year-old Susie and ten-year-old Vicky.

His route took him down to the Screaming Sixties and around the icebergs to Palmer Station, during which he capsized twice and suffered some incredible physical and mental ordeals. At Palmer, lying against the rock pier when he arrived, was Jacques Costeau's *Calypso*. His vessel badly damaged, there was doubt he could continue his planned circumnavigation of the Antarctic. His would not have been the first anyway, as Dr. Griffith and family had already achieved this on *Awahnee*. Besides, he was not sure that it could be achieved by a singlehanded yacht. But he had accomplished one thing—he had been the first singlehander to touch the Antarctic continent. It was something of a first, and no one could take that away from him.[10]

VII

THE
PERMANENT
ITCH

⋘ 39 ⋙

From Adams to Zantzinger

> *People who are unhappy here and go some-*
> *where else are usually unhappy there, too. It's*
> *a thing from within. I don't think anybody can*
> *escape from themselves. People who complain*
> *about dragging off to the office every day, would*
> *complain somewhere else about the heat.*[1]

JEAN-CHARLES TAUPIN, FORMER HONORABLE SECRETARY OF
the esoteric Slocum Society, and perennially frustrated editor of its
infrequent publication, *The Spray*, once gently chided the stoic
small-boat adventurers of the world for the maddening lack of news
of their whereabouts.

> *Now, there are two kinds of sailors who hose the deck*
> *with a sense of relief when land drops behind the horizon*
> *—the* Loners *and the* Sharers. *Some singlehanders are*
> Sharers *and some families are* Loners. *Born and brought*
> *up to a world they have not created, they have turned in-*
> *ward and out to a new world of their own, a world*
> *which had to be and which each one alone recognized.*
> *Physically they appear here, reappear there, and disappear*
> *for long periods of time. They do not know, nor care,*
> *who follows in their wake. The Sharers have remained*
> *open to the world of their fellow men. They have found*
> *a measure of peace and want to share their discovery*
> *with kindred minds.*

> *But both are headaches to the editor of* The Spray.
> *The* Loners *can only be caught by accident—and what a*
> *tale they usually have! The* Sharers *are all ready to share,*
> *but preferably over a bottle of rum in some quiet harbor,*
> *not over a typewriter, pounding out a written message*
> *to a distant and somewhat anonymous organization.*[2]

In the closing years of the nineteenth century, when Captain
Joshua Slocum, "born in the breezes, and cast up from old ocean,"
hewed the new *Spray* out of solid New England pasture oak, and
sailed into immortality, the world had not yet experienced the two
"world wars," nuclear power, or even air travel, to say nothing of a
man walking on the surface of the moon and sending back via television such poignant messages as, "One small step for man, one giant
leap for mankind."

Although Slocum's circumnavigation alone in *Spray* is regarded as
the first small step for the anonymous seagoing rebels of the world, it
was also a giant leap toward acceptance of world cruising in small
boats. Everywhere that Slocum went, he was welcomed warmly, not
only because of his own innate Yankee charm and intelligence, but
because he became a symbol of all the restless urgings of all men
everywhere.

The hundreds and perhaps thousands who have circumnavigated
since Slocum profited by this acceptance, whether they meant to or not,
and not a few exploited it to their own advantage. It is significant
that, where Slocum was received cordially, more recent circumnavigators such as Richard Zantzinger on the *Molly Brown*, seventy-five
years later, found the welcome mat ripped up and shredded. Zantzinger reported how, arriving at the gentle family autocracy of
Keeling-Cocos, he was warned by a cable station attendant, who
rowed out to meet him, not to anchor over in the family lagoon. In
Slocum's time, the good captain noted in his log how he was held
there from departing by the *kpeting*, the legendary crab of the children's tales. Even in Durban, that fantastically hospitable port for
world wanderers, harbor restrictions and red tape have taken over,
and even that long-time local greeter, Dr. Hamish Campbell, in a
recent letter, told how he no longer could find time to keep track of
visitors.

In Slocum's day—and for years after—one could wander the seas
and put into exotic places almost at will (except possibly at the
Galápagos Islands, where local petty officialdom often made life

miserable for unsuspecting yachtsmen). In many cases, not even a visa was needed, to say nothing of a passport. Earlier voyagers frequently mention the arsenal of arms and ammo they had with them for sport and self-defense (Slocum had several adventures in which only his faithful Martini-Henry repeating rifle helped assert his independence). Today's more effete generation of voyagers not only eschew such "crudity," but also report the crushing burden of suspicion and red tape that everywhere results from declaring any firearms aboard.

In short, the world today, after a half century of war, subversion, hostilities, crusades, and revolution all in the name of freedom from fear and want, has gained none of the freedom and lost little of the want, that characterized Slocum's world.

Yet, each decade finds more and more voyagers setting out upon the oceans, many of them never to be heard of again, but most of them doing their thing, with or without publicity. Indeed, some of the more able and adventurous of them seem almost anonymous, such as Sir Percy Wynn Harris.

SIR PERCY WYNN HARRIS

In 1963, SIR PERCY, AGE SIXTY AND ANOTHER MOUNTAIN climber turned voyager, began a circumnavigation from England. He sailed through the Mediterranean and the Suez Canal, then down the west coast of Africa to Gambria, where, as a former governor of this colony, he had been invited to attend the independence celebrations.

From there, Sir Percy sailed to the West Indies, went through the Panama Canal, and on to Tahiti. With his son aboard, he detoured to New Zealand for a six-month visit. Then he sailed to Australia and up inside the Great Barrier Reef, through Torres Strait, and across the Indian Ocean, reaching Durban in time for Christmas, 1968. His last stop before returning to England to complete the circumnavigation was in Bermuda in July 1969.

His circumnavigation was completed thirty-five years after he had failed in two attempts to climb Mount Everest in the days before portable oxygen was available.

BILL NANCE

CARDINAL VERTUE, A J. LAURENT GILES SLOOP OF 25.3 FEET length overall, had been built for Dr. David Lewis, a London physi-

cian of New Zealand birth, who sailed her in the first *Observer* Singlehanded Transatlantic Race. She was purchased from Dr. Lewis
by Bill Nance of Wallaby Creek, Australia, and in September 1962
Nance departed England alone for Melbourne via Buenos Aires.[3]
The 6,800-mile passage, west-about, took 75 days. He arrived in
Freemantle with the main mast broken 16 feet above the deck, under
a jury rig.

Leaving Auckland on December 1, 1964, he sailed along the high
southern latitudes, around Cape Horn and up to Argentina, mostly
under a working staysail and main, well-reefed, steered by a wind
vane. On December 30, at 51°S, running before a gale under bare
poles with thirty fathoms of warp astern, he reported "a sea bigger
than any I have ever seen before," which crashed aboard, broke the
tiller and rudder head, and forced him to lie ahull.

"I have no great faith in lying ahull," he said later, "and probably
only survived because the weather eased and by the following day I
was able to fit the spare tiller."

Near Cape Horn, the barometer dropped to 28.73. On January 7, a
landfall was made on Diégo Ramirez, and later the same day he ran
close to the Horn in a rain squall, 38 days and 5,000 miles from New
Zealand. He still had 1,600 miles to go to Buenos Aires, and a long
struggle through the tide rips of Estrecho de la Maire. His circumnavigation was completed in Argentina, and his was the smallest
vessel at that time to sail around the world—and he had done it the
hard way, most of it in the Roaring Forties. He averaged 121 miles a
day for 6,500 miles on the last leg.

From Buenos Aires, he made another fast run to the West Indies,
averaging 123 miles a day. From Antigua to Nassau, en route to
Florida, he logged 180 miles from noon to noon on one occasion, the
best day's run of the entire circumnavigation, and an astonishing
record for a vessel of only 21 feet 6 inches waterline length.

In 1968, he was reported married and living on the Oregon coast,
building a larger vessel for his next circumnavigation, this time an
east-to-west Horn passage.

DIDIER DEPRET

Not until didier depret promised his sweetheart,
Bernadette, that he would take her to the ends of the world, would
she say yes. He meant it literally. Their honeymoon trip started in
the fall of 1960 and lasted seven years.

After leaving Cannes, they spent most of 1961 cruising the Medi-terranean, before crossing the Atlantic to the West Indies, and then on to New York for Christmas. Leaving New York after the holidays, they sailed to the West Indies, and nearly lost their ship, the *Saint Briac*, in a winter storm. From there, they followed the usual route through the Panama Canal, across the Pacific to Australia, and up in-side the Great Barrier Reef, and returned to France via India, the Red Sea, and the Suez Canal.

At home, the *Saint Briac* was put up for sale, and Didier Depret had found a life-long career at home—building dream ships for erstwhile voyagers.

WILLIAM MURNAN

WILLIAM MURNAN WAS A TRUE SEA WANDERER IN THE Slocum and Pidgeon tradition. As a lad, he spent six years, from 1911 to 1917, on a windjammer whaler in the Arctic, where he learned about small boats as a chaser in a 32-foot whaleboat.[4]

After World War II, living in Los Angeles then, he built by hand in his backyard a stainless steel version of Thomas Fleming Day's famed *Sea Bird* yawl. As a former shipyard welder during the war, he was able to do all the work himself. He modified the original plans somewhat, eliminating the cockpit and bringing the trunk cabin aft, leaving only a tiny hole after of the mizzen mast for steering.

With a 25-horsepower Universal engine as an auxiliary, he loaded aboard 120 gallons of fresh water and 150 gallons of fuel in the hollow keel tanks, and six years' supply of dehydrated foods, plus a stock of canned foods, meats, vegetables, and fruits. His vessel, the *Seven Seas II*, floated eight inches below her load waterline.

Sailing from San Pedro with his wife, Ceice, they visited Hawaii, Tahiti, and Samoa. Ceice became ill and had to return to a cooler climate. Bill waited until the hurricane season was over, then sailed alone to the Fijis, New Hebrides, Solomon Islands, New Guinea, Australia, and through the Arafura Sea to Timor.

At Christmas Island, he was caught by a hurricane in the exposed harbor. Weak from a local bug, he put to sea and rode out the storm, using an automotive tire with a cable bridle as a sea anchor. He could not put in at Keeling-Cocos or Rodriguez because it was the season of the year with frequent gales. He sailed about a hundred miles a day under bare poles, the 5,100 miles direct to Africa. In Mozambique

Channel, a gale drove him toward Durban, and he arrived after 53 days passage from Christmas Island.

In Durban, again loaded below the waterlines and again at Port Elizabeth, he upset the local gamblers by getting around the Cape in the wrong season. He carried, in addition to his supplies, two Northill anchors of twenty-five pounds each, an enormous amount of ground tackle, with spares for everything, plus much gear of a survival nature. For fourteen days, he logged less than four hundred miles, and passing Cape Agulhas, he was hit by a northwest storm off Danger Point, and had to heave-to for five days. At Cape Town, he was reported missing, but Bill's wife, waiting for him, insisted he would show up.

"Bill knows the ocean," she told reporters, "and he knows his boat. He'll make it."

When he showed up between the breakwaters, the whole city turned out to welcome him. Horns and sirens announced his arrival. A case of champagne was donated by two Australians, one of whom had lost a £10 note on a bet.

One of his many innovations on *Seven Seas II* was the seven-to-one worm gear steering, which held a positive course on any point of sailing. During fair weather, he used spinnakers mostly, rigged to hollow stainless-steel poles attached to goosenecks on the mast and hanked to jackstays. With this rig, he sailed thousands of miles hands-off the wheel.

Completing his circumnavigation in 1952, he became the first to do it in a stainless-steel vessel.

DR. WILLIAM F. HOLCOMB

CRUISING CLUB OF AMERICA MEMBER, DR. WILLIAM F. Holcomb, set off in 1953, with Mrs. Holcomb and miscellaneous crew members on a voyage around the world aboard the 46-foot schooner, *Landfall II*. Official departure was from San Francisco on September 18. During the first ten months, they visited Panama, Ecuador, the Galápagos Islands, Pitcairn, Gambier, the Marquesas, and Tahiti.

Later, after a rough passage of the Tasman Sea, *Landfall II* was badly damaged by a hurricane that struck while in port at Brisbane.

The next leg took them up inside the Great Barrier Reef to Thursday Island and then to the island of Bali. At Benoa, the yacht was swept up on a reef, but refloated and powered into Surabaja for repairs.

Next came Singapore, Penang, and Colombo. On the passage to Aden, a giant swordfish rammed the hull below the engine bed and made an inaccessible hole in the plank. Due to bad sea conditions, repairs had to wait four days, until they reached harbor at Cochin, India, with the pump manned one hour out of four. For the emergency repairs, Dr. Holcomb was forced to pay excessive charges.

The passage up the Red Sea, in December 1955, was unusually mild, with temperatures almost cold. Visits were made at Port Said and Suez. The Middle East weather also was unusually cold and stormy, but they stayed in the Mediterranean until spring, then departed Gibraltar for England.

After two months in the United Kingdom, *Landfall II* crossed the Atlantic via the Canaries and Barbados.[5] The passage from Las Palmas to Bridgetown took a casual thirty-three days.

After cruising the West Indies, *Landfall II* sailed to Miami via Cuba, then up the coast to New York, back down to Bermuda and Great Inagua in the Bahamas; then on to Jamaica, Panama, and through the canal.

A fast passage was made uphill to San Francisco, with a stop at Acapulco, completing a circumnavigation in just three days short of four years. For the voyage, Dr. Holcomb was awarded the coveted Blue Water Medal of the cca for 1957.

During the voyage around, as a dentist, Dr. Holcomb was much in demand everywhere he went. On one remote South Pacific island, with the assistance of Mrs. Holcomb, he extracted free more than one hundred teeth from the mouths of long-suffering natives.[6]

THE HOLMDAHLS

ONE OF THE MORE UNSUNG CIRCUMNAVIGATIONS WAS THAT made by the Swedish couple, Sten and Brita Holmdahl, on *Viking*, an ancient revenue cutter and fishing boat, which the couple purchased in November 1951 and rebuilt. Sten was a boatbuilder by trade and his wife, Brita, a seamstress.

Being frugal and hard-working people, the Holmdahls, were able to do most of the work themselves. The basic hull was of sturdy oak. They rebuilt it into a beautiful ocean-cruising yacht rigged as a ketch. There was no motor, except an outboard for the skiff, and a small gasoline-powered generator to charge batteries for the lights.[7] Everything except the rigging screws and a pair of doors was made by hand. They had a sextant and a radio aboard, but no chronometer (the radio was used for getting time ticks). A good compass and set of charts and pilot books completed their list.

In June 1952, the couple left Gothenburg for Marstrand with a friend aboard, during which the only accident on the circumnavigation occurred—someone dropped a sugar jar on the cabin floor. Sten was not only a skilled sailor, but never took a risk unnecessarily.

Leaving Marstrand alone, the Holmdahls sailed to Denmark, thence to Dover, Falmouth, Douarnenez in France; then on to Cascais in Portugal, down to Madeira and La Palma (not Las Palmas). They crossed the Atlantic in thirty-four days to Barbados, cruised the West Indies, spent Christmas in Antigua. Passing through the Panama Canal, they sailed directly to the Marquesas in fifty days, then went on to Tahiti, Fiji, New Hebrides, Port Moresby, Darwin, Christmas Island, the Keeling-Cocos Islands, Mauritius, and Cape Town.

They spent Christmas in South Africa, then started out from Cape Town on a passage to Falmouth, which took seventy-eight days. They saw land at St. Helena and the Azores, but did not stop. From Falmouth, they went on to Dover for a brief stop, and then to Denmark, and finally home to Gothenburg, arriving June 22, 1954.

For the voyage they were awarded the cca Blue Water Medal for 1954.

THE WIDOW ADAMS

At thirty-seven, suttie adams was a widow and housewife with a brood of growing kids. No one would have suspected that she aspired to be a circumnavigator. But late in 1961, she departed San Francisco with as crew: Rick, seventeen; Jon, sixteen; Sue, eleven; Patrick, seven, and two friends. They sailed their 58-foot gaff schooner, *Fairweather*, to the Marquesas, Tahiti, Samoa, and Fiji. Then they spent five months in New Zealand, where a bottom job was done, before departing for Nouméa, New Caledonia. A hurricane was encountered on the way, but port was made with minimum damage. Six weeks were spent in Nouméa before sailing on to New Guinea, the Torres Strait via Thursday Island and Darwin; then across the Timor Sea to Bali, Java, and Singapore.

They spent seven months in Singapore while work was done on the schooner by Chinese craftsmen, who carved panels, doors, and chests of teak. On May 13, they departed for the Nicobars, through boisterous seas and adverse currents. They were chased by pirates when leaving Great Nicobar, and with the auxiliary inoperative, the boys crowded on all the canvas they could and slowly pulled away. They then sailed on to the Chagos and Seychelles, on down to Zanzibar and Mombasa, Kenya, where they spent a month.

Rich was married there to Melanie, who had joined the crew in New Zealand, and the honeymoon was spent on safari to the Tsava Big Game Reserve.

It took a month to sail from Aden to Suez. A five-month stay was spent in Rhodes, Greece, and there Suttie became a grandmother with the birth of a daughter to Rick and Melanie.

They leisurely cruised the Corsica coast, stopped in Italy, sailed on to Las Palmas, crossed the Atlantic to Barbados, cruised the West Indies, passed through the canal, and sailed up the coast of Central America and Mexico, arriving at San Francisco on May 18, 1965.

During the entire voyage, there were no complaints—not even from experienced hands—about the lady skipper. As for the children, they developed into real sailors on the voyage, in addition to growing up into young adults and teen-agers. Strict study hours were maintained aboard during passages for the youngsters, and during long stays in New Zealand, Singapore, and Rhodes, they went to school on shore. Patrick, who was only seven when they left, quickly learned not only how to hand, reef, and steer, but became a whiz at taking noon sights and plotting positions with H. O. 214.

THE KITTREDGES

Often mentioned by other world voyagers, the Kittredges, who circumnavigated in their *Svea*, were another almost anonymous couple. Robert Y. Kittredge started early on his lifetime of adventuring, with a 3,000-mile trip down the Danube in 1928, at the age of 18, in a folding canoe. The voyage took him from Rosenheim on the Inn to the Delta. For 15 years prior to World War II, he was a sculptor and architect, designing among other things a housing development in Oak Creek Canyon, Arizona.

In the spring of 1960, Kittredge and his wife, Mary, bought a 38-foot Danish double-ended ketch, *Svea*, and sailed to the Marquesas. After a visit, they sailed on through the Pacific islands, across the Indian Ocean, spent two years in the Mediterranean, then crossed the Atlantic via the southern route to the Caribbean and Florida to complete a five-year circumnavigation.

At last report, the Kittredges were living aboard *Svea* at Fort Lauderdale, where Bob conducts a school in celestial navigation.

THE VAN DE WIELES

ANNIE AND LOUIS VAN DE WIELE WERE IN THEIR TEENS when World War II broke out and the German Blitzkrieg rolled over Belgium and France. Both were of staid, respectable bourgeois families—Louis, slender, sensitive, close-mouthed, with an engineering bent; Annie, short, vivacious, somewhat tomboyish, and game for anything. Both shared a longing to be sailors and go to sea on long voyages—which was what brought them together during the Occupation.

The war meant five years of miserable oppression for Belgians living in the homeland, although the colonies prospered during it all. Courtrai is a small town thirty-five miles from the sea, through which the Lys River meanders, lined with Flemish houses, where the citizens ate well, dressed well, drank copiously, and thought only of business—until the Germans came.

At sixteen, Louis applied for navigation school, but was rejected for nearsightedness. He then took a dreary job in an office, but soon resigned to enroll at the University of Ghent. Here he did so well that he became an assistant professor and met Annie, who was also a student. Later he joined the Resistance and went underground. When the Allies liberated Belgium, he joined the British navy. After the war, he was demobilized and returned to Ghent to find his parents both dead. Now he and Annie became engaged and set about designing, building and outfitting their dream ship.

The name had already been selected—*Omoo*. This was a Polynesian word meaning "one who wanders from island to island"—at least that's what Herman Melville said in his book of the same name. *Omoo* was designed by Louis and naval architect Fritz Mulder, and built of steel by the firm of M. Meyntjens in Antwerp. She was 46 feet overall, 37 feet 10 inches on the waterline, 12 feet 4 inches of beam, drawing 6 feet 4 inches, and displacing 18 tons. Ketch-rigged, she had a total sail area of about 200 meters, plus a twin staysail system for self-steering. Auxiliary power was a Kermath-Hercules diesel of 27 horsepower, plus a small 12-volt lighting plant. Her lines were conventional, with long keel and fairly easy bilges. Similar, in fact, to the famed Alden schooners.

After the usual problems of postwar shortages, delays, and frustrations, *Omoo* was launched and the initial bugs worked out. With Fred, a family friend and ironmonger, Annie and Louis (who had been married meanwhile) made trial runs. Then on August 5, 1949, the young couple departed Ostend, sailed to Dunkirk, then over to Dover and Cowes. Fred, on leave, joined the ship for the passage across the Bay of Biscay to La Coruña, Vigo, Lisbon, and Gibraltar. Months were spent cruising the Mediterranean, and in re-outfitting at Nice for a round-the-world voyage.

There they were invited to sail to Tahiti with Robert Argod aboard *Fleur d'Océan*, a large ketch. *Omoo* was left with a friend at Nice, while the Van de Wieles made the voyage to Tahiti and returned to Europe on a freighter. They found *Omoo* waiting for them, and lost no time getting her ready for a circumnavigation.

With Fred as crew member, they departed on July 7, 1951. The first passage was Nice to Gibraltar, thence to Alicante for slipping and bottom painting. They were to haul *Omoo* many times during the circumnavigation for repainting, for the metal hull and postwar paints were not compatible.

At Las Palmas in the Canaries, they found a veritable fleet of yachts waiting to cross the Atlantic. Among their owners were a couple of Texans on the little cutter *Festina*, and the Smeetons on *Tzu Hang*. The Smeetons had just purchased the yacht and were on their way home to British Columbia with their young daughter, Clio. This was the very start of their long career of voyaging that took them around the world, and Annie Van de Wiele's perceptive observations were the first published accounts of this remarkable couple.

"Astonishing people, these Smeetons," Annie wrote in *The West in My Eyes*. "Miles Smeeton was a retired brigadier-general of the Indian army. They lived on a farm on an island in British Columbia. They had crossed the Argentine on horseback, climbed in the Himalayas, explored North Africa in a jeep, and Central Europe on a bicycle, not to mention other adventures of smaller caliber. They had just returned from climbing to the top of Teyde. On mule back."

Annie also recorded the best description of the Smeetons. "The crew of *Tzu Hang* was composed of Mr., Mrs., Miss and a friend, all well over six feet tall. Alongside them, my two men seemed only average in height, and as for me—I looked as if I was standing in a hole in the deck."

"Mrs. Tzu Hang," as Beryl Smeeton was known, also was noted for her massive voice, which could be heard all over the harbor when she called for Clio—the latter usually being found in the engine room, covered with grease, in the dinghy under the counter, or perched in the crosstrees.

"It was undoubtedly the most energetic family I have ever met," said the almost nonplussed Annie.

Omoo and *Tzu Hang* traveled together or nearly so all the way to the West Indies and through the Panama Canal. In the Canal Zone, the Belgians had their first contact with Americans and it was almost overwhelming for Annie—especially the American women. Her descriptions of the canal, the passage through, and the people she encountered are among the best recorded by literary voyagers.

They were unable to get a visa for the Galápagos due to the perfidy of the local Ecuadorean consul, and so they bypassed these islands. They had already visited them aboard the *Fleur d'Océan* anyway. They sailed directly to the Marquesas, next through the Tuamotus to Tahiti, and then to Bora Bora and Fiji. Of all the places in the world they visited, the one they most wanted to come back to was Mooréa, the enchanting island near Tahiti—and to which they eventually did return.

From Fiji, the voyage took them to Port Moresby, New Guinea, Torres Strait, and across the Indian Ocean to the Keeling-Cocos Islands. They arrived about the time an Australian transport with a load of soldiers was in the harbor, and the stay there was a long series of parties. They also managed to anchor at the exact point where the transoceanic cables crossed, much to the consternation of the cable company crew. When they left, the wireless boys cabled ahead to Mauritius of the impending arrival of *Omoo*, and warned them to watch their cables.

It is interesting to note the recent visit, in 1973, of the California yacht *Skylark* to the Keeling-Cocos. Owner Bob Hanelt reported there were thirteen yachts anchored at Direction Island, bound for the Seychelles or Mauritius, including four in the flotilla which Hanelt had joined. These tiny coral specks in the middle of the Indian Ocean have become a busy waystation for the bluewater yachts of the world.

With stops at Port Louis, and a long stay in Durban and Cape Town, the *Omoo* sailed on to St. Helena, Ascension, then uphill to the Azores, on to England, then on to Ghent for a joyous family reunion, and finally to Zeebrugge, arriving on August 2, 1953.[8]

WALTER KOENIG

THE VOYAGE OF THE GERMAN SAILOR, WALTER KOENIG, around the world alone in *Zarathustra*, a converted 27-foot fiberglass lifeboat rigged as a sloop, ranks among the most harrowing and little-known circumnavigations—one that ended in death—a story as depressing as Friedrich Wilhelm Nietzsche's philosopher character.

Koenig left Hamburg in 1965 on his circumnavigation, and the next word of him came from the Red Sea. There he was sighted by the crew of an oceanographic research vessel, which was conducting a geophysical survey. Aboard was a member of the Slocum Society, Sidney Shaw, who filed this report with the Secretary:[9]

> *Early in March 1969, the oceanographic research vessel on which I was sailing, sighted what we thought at first to be an Arab dhow. Closer inspection revealed the boat to be a Marconi-rigged sloop with the upper one third of its mast broken off. It was the* Zarathustra *of Hamburg. We went alongside and offered assistance. It was the singlehander, Walter Koenig. We decided to take the yacht in tow, so we could visit at greater length with Koenig while we went on with our survey. After a hot shower and a hearty lunch, I was able to get Koenig's story of his struggle against the sea and the Arab world.*
>
> *He had left Hamburg in early 1965, crossing the Atlantic from the Canaries to Barbados that winter. From Panama to Tahiti he sailed first on the 87-foot schooner* Dante Deo.[10] *He then returned to Panama to sail this route the second time on* Zarathustra. *After a lengthy stay in New Guinea, he met and married a New Zealand girl, and pushed on to complete the circumnavigation.*
>
> *When we met, he had been at sea six weeks since leaving Djibouti. His plan had been to sail north to Eilat, Israel, on the Gulf of Akiba, then to truck his boat to the Mediterranean and continue on from there to Hamburg, with a stop in Cyprus to pick up his wife.*
>
> *Walter had been ill in Djibouti with what the doctors thought was abdominal infection, requiring an operation which they were unable to perform, but which they said he could get in Israel. So with a supply of medication to keep the infection in check, he set out for Israel. Un-*

fortunately, Zarathustra's engine, a Wankel, was out of commission and the winds in the Red Sea at the time were either flat calm or Force 6 down from the north.

In spite of this he managed to beat his way to within a couple hundred miles of Eilat, only to be blown back by a northerly gale. Seeking shelter, he anchored in the lee of a reef along the Egyptian coast. The following morning he was spotted and a boat put out from shore. Seeking to avoid problems, he weighed anchor. This action was met by gunfire from the Egyptian boat. Zarathustra took several hits, but the damage was superficial, and Walter escaped unhurt.

Fearing that the attackers might radio for a patrol boat, Walter ran off under full sail. Several hours later, still in a panic, he accidentally jibed, breaking off the upper third of the mast. He managed to jury-rig the sail on the remainder of the mast, but was limited to being able to point only 70° into the wind. Since nearly all the winds were headwinds, this made progress almost impossible.

Several days later, he accepted a tow from a merchant ship bound for Jeddah, Saudi Arabia, where he hoped to affect repairs. There, however, the authorities searched Zarathustra and on finding a single tin of food packed in Israel, decided to confiscate the boat and jail Walter. He managed to sail off before this threat could be carried out.

He drifted and sailed almost aimlessly until we spotted him days later. Walter later said that he had seen us the day before we picked him up, but he had made no effort to signal us since he feared we were an Arab vessel. As a fact, we were the first U.S. vessel in those waters since the Six Day War in 1967.[11]

We offered to tow Zarathustra back to Port Sudan, from which we were operating, and to assist him in repairing the mast. He declined this offer, since he wanted to avoid any further contact with any and all Arab countries. He also declined my offer to mail letters for him. He said that he was already several weeks late, and that if he wrote now it would only cause his wife even greater concern; a bit of logic I never really followed. Anyway, that night after topping off his water tanks, larder and

*library, and supplying him with some medication and
flares and smoke markers, for use in attracting ships,
Walter left. He felt intimidated by the Red Sea, which
he had considered a petty lake compared to the oceans
he had conquered and was annoyed by the difficulties it
was causing him.*

*At this point, he had given up hope of sailing all the
way to Eilat and was hoping instead to signal a ship
bound for Eilat or Akaba and get a tow.*

*After bidding farewell and wishing him luck, we cast
off Zarathustra. We drifted through the night while
Walter tried to sail north, yet at dawn he was one and
a half miles south of us. That was the last I knew of
Walter until June 1969, when I visited Eilat and inquired about him. I couldn't get much information, but
I did learn that he had arrived in April, after getting a
tow and had shipped Zarathustra to the Mediterranean.*

*More recently, I learned from his widow, Sheila, that
she rejoined him in Messina, Sicily. At this time Walter
flew to Germany where his disease was finally properly
diagnosed as lukemia and he was given only three to
six months to live. Courageously, he returned to Zarathustra and with his wife he completed his voyage, arriving in Hamburg in October 1969. He was taken to
a hospital immediately upon his arrival. He died there
on December 30, 1969. Sheila returned to New Zealand
and Zarathustra was given to a museum in Bremen.*

ANNE BRITTAIN

AT THE ADVANCED AGE OF 21, ANNE BRITTAIN, THE AUS-
tralian, decided to buy a 61-foot ketch and sail her around the world.
Six years after leaving Australia, she reached Gibraltar. During the
interim, she had earned a living as a photographer for the government of Papua, New Guinea, as a laborer in a pineapple canning
factory, and at various other endeavors.

The long voyage took her from Sydney to Papua, inside the Great
Barrier Reef, then through Torres Strait, across the Indian Ocean to
Kenya, with stops at Keeling-Cocos, Diégo Garcia, and the Seychelles.
She sailed down the east coast of Africa and up the Atlantic to

Gibraltar to Europe, before planning the final leg to complete the circumnavigation.

She met with no disasters and had no problems with the ship nor any of her crew. But as a female skipper in her early twenties, her arrival in various ports usually raised eyebrows. In a letter, she wrote:

> *For example, during one stretch when I happened to have an all-male crew, almost everyone I met seemed to think that I was either trying to set up a female version of Haroun al-Raschid's harem, or that instead of dealing with the many problems of a yacht at sea, I was spending all my time being chased around the decks by a lecherous crew.*
>
> *Nothing could be further from the truth. What I was really doing was trying to prevent my motherly-minded crew from adopting every stray goat from the hundreds of islands in the Australian Great Barrier Reef.*
>
> *Of course, with the publicity about Women's Lib in recent months, the newest theory about women skippers is that they hate men and want to prove they are as good or better. This isn't true either, as I think men are lovely —in their place, of course, which is one in every port.*[12]

FRANK CASPER

IN 1959, FRANK CASPER, AN ENGINEER LOOKING FORWARD TO retirement, bought the 30-foot Norwegian-type cutter *Elsie*, built for North Seas fisheries research and formerly owned by Hannes Lindeman.[13]

He and his wife sailed to the Bahamas in 1960, to Bermuda in 1961, and the Azores in 1962. In December of the following year, after his wife had died, Casper departed home port at Melbourne Beach, Florida, and sailed to Tahiti via the Panama Canal. After a two-month visit, he sailed to Bora Bora and Rarotonga, then on to Pago Pago and the Cook Islands, and to Auckland, New Zealand.

Late in 1964, Casper departed on the circumnavigation via Timor, the Indian Ocean, South Africa, and the West Indies, completing the world voyage in 1967.

Known by ocean vagabonds everywhere as a quiet and friendly man who is always willing to share his knowledge and his company, he was awarded the CCA Blue Water Medal in 1969 in recognition of nearly a decade of flawless seamanship. Subsequent years have been spent cruising between the West Indies and the Mediterranean.

THE UBIQUITOUS TAHITIS

DESIGNED IN THE 1920s BY THE DUNEDIN, FLORIDA, GENIUS, John G. Hanna, the 30-foot *Tahiti* ketch arrived on the scene just in time for the Depression Thirties, when restless and frustrated would-be sea vagabonds everywhere were dreaming of escape to those languorous South Sea islands, where living was easy and native girls willing.

A solid little ship, salty as a seagull, double-ended for seaworthiness, with wide decks, high bulwarks, snug cockpit, generous living quarters below, and rugged in construction, *Tahiti* was a dream ship come true. By the time the plans were released for publication (with Hanna's salty comments) by W. H. (Buzz) Fawcett, Jr., in *Modern Mechanix*, and later in *How To Build 20 Boats*, the design had been proved by the construction of several oceangoing versions.[14]

Tahiti was not an easy boat to build, but the plans were cheap and Hanna's instructions so inspiring that literally thousands of erstwhile voyagers were hooked (including this writer who was then completing high school on the snow-drifted prairies of North Dakota, two thousand miles from the nearest ocean). But with a little skill and a lot of careful and patient work, one could build a *Tahiti* out of locally obtained materials, and outfit it for about $1,000. Today, the wood version of *Tahiti* (the plans are still available from John's widow, Dorothy Hanna) would cost a minimum of $15,000, and probably more. A 32-foot fiberglass version is offered by a Carpenteria, California, firm in kit form for home completion which would cost at least $20,000 to build and outfit.

But in the 1930s and 1940s, literally hundreds of *Tahitis* were built all over the world, and dozens of them went on long bluewater voyages, many of them around the world. At least two *Tahiti* owners have circumnavigated twice—Jean Gau in his *Atom*; and Tom Steele in his *Adios*.

The tales and confirmed reports of *Tahiti's* performance in weather that would, and did, disable large ships while the owners were snug in the cabin below, would fill a book. But, would-be voyagers should know that both *Adios* and *Atom* (and perhaps others) were on occasion capsized and rolled over completely. This is not due to any fault of the design—merely that owners tend to take

Tahiti into water and weather in which it is possible to be over-whelmed, no matter what size the vessel be.

Southern California was an early hotbed of *Tahiti aficionados*, and dozens were built there by amateurs and professional craftsmen. One of these was purchased after World War II by Tom Steele, who departed San Diego on a circumnavigation via the trade winds route and the Cape of Good Hope with various companions. Off the tip of South Africa, with an inexperienced hand, Ray Cruickshank, aboard, *Adios* encountered what was later called the worst storm in years. *Adios* was knocked down several times, rolled over, and badly dam-aged. Trying to make Port Elizabeth, they were again struck by an eighty-mile-an-hour gale with mountainous seas and freezing weather. They lost the mizzen mast, the main boom, the dinghy, and the rudder, and suffered severe damage internally.

Steele later managed to get the auxiliary running and they motored into port. Ashore, friendly South Africans took up a collection to help rebuild *Adios*. But Steele refused to accept such generosity, and found a job and financed all the work himself. Moving on months later, Steele completed the circumnavigation successfully. Only on his return did it occur to him that this was as good a way as any to live his life.

He did not live it alone, however. Along the way, he picked up a bride, Janet, and together they made a second circumnavigation via the two canals. A well-known meeting of sea vagabonds was recorded in Aden on the way up the Red Sea, when the Steeles encountered the Eric Hiscocks, who were also on a second circumnavigation with *Wanderer III*.

The Steeles, on the second circumnavigation, showed other voy-agers what an experienced couple can do with a 30-foot boat. They had a washing machine in the forepeak for hooking up to freshwater facilities ashore. They carried a small motorcycle on deck for use in port. For example, while at anchor off the Club Nàutico in Algeciras, Spain, they used the motorcycle for touring to Málaga and Granada, the first time in four years they had spent a night off *Adios*.

On long passages, with moderate winds, Janet would bake large supplies of fresh bread in their pressure cooker. In the trades, they would commonly hoist a squaresail on the mainmast.

Completing the second leisurely circumnavigation at San Diego in 1964, this *Tahiti* chalked up 55,472 sea miles and visited 286 ports and anchorages in seven years.

Steele was awarded the cca Blue Water Medal for 1964. The

award was presented to the Steeles in Panama during the uprisings there, where Tom was temporarily employed as an operator of one of the canal "mules."[15]

In 1974, Tom and Janet were on a *third* circumnavigation.

MICHEL MERMOD

ALTHOUGH THERE HAVE BEEN INNUMERABLE JOKES ABOUT the Swiss "navy," this landlocked mountain country has produced many good sailors, including at least one singlehanded circumnavigator.

He was Michel Mermod, who set off in 1960 in a 24-foot converted lifeboat, *Geneve*. He followed the popular route via Panama, the Galápagos Islands—with a detour to Ecuador where he was arrested as a Peruvian spy—then on to the Marquesas, Tahiti, the Cook Islands, Samoa, Tonga, and Fiji.

From there, instead of going through Torres Strait, he sailed north from New Caledonia to the New Hebrides, the Carolines, and the Philippines; then he headed across the China Sea to Singapore and the Strait of Malacca. He visited Ceylon, the Chagos Islands, Seychelles, Madagascar, and South Africa.

Crossing the Atlantic, he touched South America at Natal, Brazil, and then returned via the Balearic Islands (capsizing once in the Gulf of Lion). The only known Swiss circumnavigator, he was alone all the way except for the last few miles in the Gulf of Lion.[16]

THE STURDY ONE

FEW, IF ANY, CIRCUMNAVIGATORS ATTEMPTED THE EAST-about route via the Mediterranean Sea and the Suez Canal, until the Smeetons did it in the 1960s on *Tzu Hang*. Slocum had started out that way, but was warned at Gibraltar by British naval officers about pirates, and thereafter went the other way. Robinson, Long, Petersen, the Hiscocks, and the Griffiths had taken the westbound Suez Canal and Red Sea route before the canal was closed in the 1967 war, and all of them reported varying degrees of discomfort, shipwreck, or harassment.

The first recorded yacht circumnavigation east-about was by the solo navigator, Edward Miles, who left New York on August 29, 1928 in the little schooner *Sturdy*, which he had built himself. It took forty-nine days to reach Gibraltar, after which he sailed through the Med, touching at Tangier, Algiers, Tunis, and Malta, with a detour to Constantinople and the Greek islands. At Alexandria he laid up *Sturdy* and returned to the United States via steamship for a visit. Nine months later, he returned to Egypt and started through the canal. During the passage, in the blistering heat of the desert, there was an accident in which spilled gasoline was ignited. The *Sturdy* burned to the water's edge and Miles lost everything.

He made his way back to Alexandria and thence by steamship to New York. Immediately he began work on *Sturdy II*, somewhat larger than her predecessor, being 36 feet overall with a beam of 10 feet 10 inches and a draft of just under 5 feet. Instead of a gasoline auxiliary, this time he installed a 20-horsepower diesel with a fuel tank holding 500 gallons, giving him a range of more than 4,000 miles under power alone.

He shipped *Sturdy II* to Egypt on a steamer and launched her there in September, 1930, a year after the destruction of *Sturdy I*. Passing through the canal again, he took a month to sail through the Red Sea. From there he went to Ceylon, Singapore, Manila, Hong Kong, and Yokohama.

On July 14, 1931, he departed Yokohama for Hawaii, which he reached after fifty days. From Honolulu, he made the Pacific crossing in only eighteen days—somewhat of a record—arriving September 30. Coasting downhill past Mexico and Central America, he went through the Panama Canal, and then on up to New York.

The elapsed time was just under four years, but about two years of this was spent rebuilding his dream ship, following detours, and enjoying "time off."

To date, no one has duplicated his route east-about around the world, and no one is likely to until the Suez Canal is reopened.

THE CHALDEAN GODDESS

Anahita was the name of a favorite childhood character, the Chaldean goddess, and Commander Louis Bernicot thought she fitted his idea of a retirement ship perfectly. Born and raised in L'Abervrac'h, on the Brittany coast, he owned his first sailboat at the age of ten, and spent all of his life by the sea or sailing over it. He earned his master's ticket in the tall sailing ships, and in later years was an officer or agent for steamship lines. At one time he was stationed at Houston, Texas.

In 1934 Bernicot retired to a farm at Dordogne, but he was a sailor and out of his element. Like Slocum, he felt cast up on the beach by

Old Ocean. Then it came to him: Why not sail around the world as had Captain Slocum? Perhaps this would cleanse his soul of the dreary November.

Anahita was built in 1936 at Moguérou. Rigged as a sloop, she was 41 feet long with a beam of 11 feet 6 inches and a draft of 5 feet 7 inches. The ballast was all in the keel, and a novel arrangement of the tiller allowed one man to handle the vessel while lying down. Other features included roller reefing and self-tacking jib. Supplies included 90 gallons of fuel for a small motor, and 90 gallons of fresh water.

Leaving on August 22, 1936, Bernicot conducted the shakedown tests on the first leg—during which everything that could go wrong, did go wrong, including a broken rudder. Without steering, he had to put into Funchal, Madeira, for repairs. With everything shipshape again, he sailed down past the Cape Verdes to South America, touching at Argentina, where he refitted and took on stores. On December 22, he departed. In early January he encountered a bad storm, and a severe knockdown—most likely a partial capsizing—which made a mess of the cabin, but caused no structural damage, except to the rail stanchions. Later he thought that *Anahita* must have rolled past 180 degrees and pitchpoled at the same time.

At Cape Virgins Bernicot entered the Strait of Magellan, with its enormous tides, williwaws, and vicious currents. He had little trouble passing through, however, and thirteen days later sailed out past the Evangelistas and Cape Pilar into the Pacific. Then he encountered the same kind of a storm which had driven Slocum back toward the Horn. Suffering from a kidney infection, and almost incapacitated, Commander Bernicot hove to on a starboard tack and managed to make some offing. Once reaching the edge of the trade belt, he sailed westward to Easter Island, where he was unable to land or to anchor, and then went on to Gambier and Tahiti.

From there he sailed across the Coral Sea and through Torres Strait to Thursday Island. He crossed the Arafura and Timor seas, stopped at Keeling-Cocos, Mauritius, and Réunion. On November 6 he reached Durban.

Next came Cape Town and the west coast of Africa, with calls at Pointe-Noire and the Azores. On May 30, 1938, he rounded the buoy and entered the Gironde and anchored under the point of Graves in the early evening.

In later years, he sailed *Anahita* on many short voyages, and in the fall of 1952, while he was working atop the mast, a stay snapped and knocked him to the deck, killing him.

THE FRANÇOIS VIRGINIE

ALTHOUGH BORN AND RAISED AWAY FROM THE SEA, ROGER Plisson was a Breton and Bretons are the last descendants of the old Celts, who as everyone knows are creatures of the sea. In Malestroit, where he was regarded as a local wit and character by the bistro bunch, he painted houses for a living and stubbornly preserved his bachelorhood.

But somehow, at times, he would get the feeling that he was missing something in this good life. He did not find out what until one day his friend, Christian Bothua, invited him to come along on a voyage to England. During the crossing, Roger learned how to handle the tiller and to trim the sails. It was his first time on a sailboat, but as he felt the power of the wind filling the canvas and the salt spray on his face, the age-old stirrings of his ancestors came to him strongly. Before they returned to France he had already made up his mind that he would build a boat and sail around the world.

Build her he did, and named her *François Virginie,* and trucked her from his backyard to the nearest water. There he outfitted, loaded aboard food and water, and sailed out from the Isle of Houat on November 12, 1967 for Cape Horn—an ambitious start for a 24-foot sloop.

Two days later he encountered a typical Bay of Biscay buster. He was dismasted and had to put back to La Corogne under jury rig. Replacing the mast, Roger started out again, even though it was very late in the season. This time his destination was Cayenne in French Guiana. Without any actual experience or technical knowledge of navigation, he had to rely on only his Breton tenacity. Somehow he made it. The details of this fantastic voyage, he glosses over.

From Cayenne, he sailed to Martinique, thence to Panama and through the canal. Down through the islands to the South Seas and Australia sailed the *François Virginie;* then up inside the Great Barrier Reef, through Torres Strait. Here he damaged the rudder, but made it as far as Réunion, where he stopped for repairs.

Off the Cape of Good Hope he lost the mast again in a blow. He limped into Cape Town for repairs and a new mast. Sailing once more, he called at St. Helena, then clawed uphill to the Cape Verdes, the Canaries, and finally the Isle of Houat, 18 months after his departure.

When reporters interviewed him, they asked him why he did it.

"If you really want to know," he said. "Try it yourself."

He had, after all, a reputation to maintain as a local character in the provincial town of Malestroit on the Oust in Morbihan, Brittany.

THE ZANTZINGER STORY

MOST READERS WOULD FIND IT DIFFICULT TO SYMPATHIZE with the problems of Richard Zantzinger, who could probably be the first and last of the beat-to-windward generation to circumnavigate the world in a small boat. A middle-aged swinger, with an ex-wife, a girl friend, a pad on Spa Creek in Tidewater, Maryland, a bankrupt contracting business, and a $20,000 commitment to the Internal Revenue Service for back taxes, he somehow was able to buy for cash a $16,000, 35-foot fiberglass sloop, outfit it and set off on a circumnavigation to cleanse his soul of its wintry November, and prepare himself for life's future tribulations. Yet, his experience is a lighthearted and refreshing departure from the usual contrived motivations of blundering paupers seeking escape by sea.

His is the story of how a real swinger does it.

Born of an old family in southern Maryland, the Chesapeake Bay had been his playground, and sailing boats his passion. His was the usual pattern of school, college, war service, fast company, freewheeling life, marriage, children, divorce, business failure, and then in middle age trying to start life over again.

It all began in late 1968 and early 1969, when his firm, R. C. Zantzinger, Jr., Inc., Concrete Contractor, after a particularly bad setback on a school contract, went belly up about the same time his marriage ended finally in divorce and the Internal Revenue Service began pressing for $20,000 in back taxes.

The idea of a circumnavigation, suggested by his girl friend, Connie, came during the depths of his personal depression. He immediately began searching for a proper ship, and after the usual futile encounters with brokers who did not know any more about it than he did, he found the 35-foot sloop only ten miles from his apartment and bought her on Christmas Eve. He had already crewed on a sister ship of this particular model and was familiar with its performance. When he broke the news to Connie, she told him she thought he had lost his mind, even though she had been the one to suggest the adventure.

The next few months were spent remodeling and outfitting, and taking a correspondence course in celestial navigation, and dodging creditors. In between times, with the aid of pilot charts, he plotted a course around the world in the middle latitudes that would give the most ideal conditions.

He renamed the yacht *Molly Brown* after the unsinkable lady of American folklore.

He had hoped to get permission from his ex-wife to take his children—Kyle, seven, and Richard, five—along on the first easy leg to Key West, when school was out. When he finally departed, he had aboard Kyle and the oldest son of a family friend, and Connie's brother, Robert, and another friend, Howard Jennings, both graduates of the University of Virginia, who would go as far as Panama.

Leaving Annapolis on June 9, 1969, they had a picnic all the way to Morehead City, North Carolina, along the Intercoastal Waterway. Then, going outside for the 500-mile leg to Fort Lauderdale, they encountered a gale with mountainous seas, and for several days were "lost," unable to take a sight or get a radio bearing. They made it 6 days later, after missing their landfall by 400 miles.

A week was spent ashore while repairs were made. The family friend flew home, and his place was taken by John Tucker, who wanted some sailing experience.

Sailing leisurely down the Keys, they reached Key West on June 29. His daughter, Kyle, left here in a tearful good-bye and flew home.

Heading south, Zantzinger awoke at dawn one morning to find the mountains of Cuba just off the port side, only three miles away. Frantically starting the engine, he used up most of their gasoline supply getting clear. The next stop was Grand Cayman, where some local hoodlums came aboard pretending to be customs officials. Zantzinger loaded the shotgun and they split. After some pub crawling in Georgetown—which, in Georgetown, isn't easy—they departed for Panama.

His girl friend, Connie, flew down to join him for the stay in the Canal Zone, and some wild parties were enjoyed in the local yacht clubs and nearby fun cities. At Balboa, the *Molly Brown* underwent some repairs to further assure an unsinkable status, sightseeing trips were made about the Panamanian countryside, and after some encounters with trigger-happy Panamanian cops, Zantzinger drank one last bottle of wine with Connie, waved good-bye, and headed for the Galápagos.

At Wreck Bay the local port officer proved friendly and co-operative, and once ashore they quickly found the local pub. After having dinner with the local immigration officer, Zantzinger discovered that his visa had been validated for ten years instead of ten days.

In the village of El Progreso, Zantzinger met Maryrose Monnier, twenty-four, a Swiss female soldier of fortune who had been stranded in the Galápagos, where she had gone as a tourist guide. When the *Molly Brown* left, Maryrose was aboard, and from Tahiti to Cape Town she was Zantzinger's only permanent crew member and companion. After visiting the Marquesas and sampling its alcoholic delights, they sailed through the Tuamotus and called at Makatéa, before entering Papeete. In French Polynesia, every encounter with a petty official resulted in a violent argument between the fiery Maryrose and the unfortunate chap in French, which Zantzinger could not understand. All he could gather was that Maryrose had a violent distaste for petty officialdom.

John Tucker left the ship in Tahiti, where he had found a girl friend who owned a motorbike. Completing a thorough job of research on the drinking establishments of Papeete, now a tourist-ridden hub of commercialized fun, and rehabilitating the *Molly Brown*, departure was made—but not before getting into a loud hassle with a stranger who turned out to be Marlon Brando—for Nuku Alofa, Nouméa, and Queensland. Sailing up inside the Great Barrier Reef, they stopped at Townsville, Cairns, Cooktown, and Thursday Island. On Thanksgiving Day, Zantzinger called home to talk to his son, Richard. He learned that Kyle was in the hospital, but only for a barbed-wire cut. At Townsville, also, he had waiting for him a $1,000 check from his brother, which arrived in time to save the voyage from an untimely end.

A young Australian joined the ship for the trip to Darwin, which they reached after much pub crawling ashore and reef crawling at sea, meeting crews of other yachts for impromptu parties, and meeting new drinking companions at every stop.

From Darwin, the odyssey led through the Arafura Sea to Timor, Bali, and way points, one of thich was Kupang, a remote exotic fishing village where families lived and died on boats. From a small greasy trading vessel tied up to the quay, a loudspeaker system was blaring out, "You Ain't Nothin' But a Hound Dog," by Elvis Presley.

They sampled Bali via a Honda, and with new-found friends from the Quantas Airlines local staff took in a Balinese cremation ceremony, various local festivities, and impromptu parties with others in the European colony, while Zantzinger waited for more money from home, his bankroll having shrunk to less than $30. While waiting, they also took an excursion into the mountains with a group of hippies from New Zealand and Australia, went to cock fights, at one of which Maryrose got into another wild argument over a bet, and finally were saved at the last moment by the arrival of $250 from home. After replenishing fuel, groceries, and paying local bills, they departed with $1 remaining.

Crossing the Indian Ocean in February, they encountered much bad weather. At the Keeling-Cocos Islands, a young Australian on the cable station staff rowed out to tell them that visiting yachtsmen had worn out their welcome at the plantation, and showed them where to anchor near the airfield. Recent visits by yachts, such as one from Denmark which had been wrecked on the reef after which the crew sponged off the islanders for six months, and a grubby 28-footer with a penniless American aboard who was still there, had helped create the current state of inhospitality.

The next stop was Mauritius, where the *Molly Brown* was robbed and vandalized by a young local hood who stole Zantzinger's chronometer, sextant, cameras, and $1,600 in traveler's checks from home. The local Criminal Investigation Department soon caught the culprit, who turned out to be a frightened sixteen-year-old Indian boy.

From Réunion, they sailed to Durban, then Port Elizabeth, and Cape Town. In South Africa, the hospitality was, as usual, overwhelming. At one of the many parties, Maryrose took up with a handsome young Frenchman, and Zantzinger met Gail, a British schoolteacher.

After an expedition to Zululand with Gail and two new friends, Zantzinger asked her to join his crew. He had already anticipated that Maryrose would be leaving. Maryrose had other ideas, however, and it was necessary to use all his salesmanship, tact, and maneuvering skill—along with some implied threats and a cash pay-off—to get her to leave the *Molly Brown*.

While visiting with a local family with children, Zantzinger thought how much fun it would be to have children aboard again, so he called his brother in Maryland and suggested that Willie, his eight-year-old nephew, join the ship. His brother called back later to say that Willie was flying to Johannesburg, and with him was another family friend, Cathy Hartman. When they arrived, Zantzinger was shocked to see that Cathy was no longer a scrawny twelve-year-old, but a wholesome young lady.

After hectic sightseeing, shopping, and last-minute partying, the voyage began again on June 1. The sail to St. Helena was a picnic all the way. At Jamestown, they managed with the help of the crew of a visiting ship to find more exciting things to do than a whole generation of circumnavigators before them. By coincidence, also in port was the Danish yacht *Sawankhaloke*—and aboard her was Zantzinger's former crew-mistress, Maryrose. A good time was had by all.

From St. Helena, stops were made at Ascension, Paramaribo, and several ports in the West Indies. There they were met by his children, Richard and Kyle, for the final leg to Miami, where the *Molly Brown* was moored at the same marina she had left a year before, completing the circumnavigation.

On the passage back to Annapolis, Zantzinger nearly sank the *Molly Brown* in the Intercoastal Waterway after a series of misadventures, including an encounter with a closed bridge. At last, the *Molly Brown* was moored again at Spa Creek, where Zantzinger and Gail put up with friends. The morning after arrival, a Coast Guard boat moved up the creek and tied up alongside the *Molly Brown*. With the Coast Guard was a middle-aged man with close-cropped hair and wearing civilian clothes. His name was "Mr. Green," and he was from the Internal Revenue Service. He was seizing the boat for nonpayment of $19,300 in back taxes. He gave Zantzinger one hour to raise the money. At that moment, he could not even raise $20.[17]

This did not, however, faze the unsinkable Richard Zantzinger, who now presumably was ready for another assault on the citadels of the financial establishment.[18]

APPENDICES

The Blue Water Medal

THE MOST COVETED HONOR AMONG SMALL-BOAT VOYAGERS of the world, the Blue Water Medal of the Cruising Club of America has been awarded annually since 1923 to individuals and man-wife crews who through outstanding seamanship have exemplified the goals of the club. It is awarded to a recipient selected from all amateur yachtsmen of the world, whether or not they are members of the club. Indeed, most recipients have not been members.

The medal itself is a five-inch diameter bronze circular medallion with a wooden base, depicting a stylized hemispherical map with inscriptions. It was designed by member Arthur Sturgis Hildebrand, one of the crew of the yacht *Leiv Eiriksson* which was lost in the Arctic with all hands in September 1924.

The *Leiv Eiriksson* was a 42-foot Colin Archer cutter purchased in Norway by William Nutting and some fellow members of the CCA for a daring voyage along the great Viking way to Iceland, Greenland, and down along the North American continent. Nutting was in command, and the crew included John O. Todahl of New York, and Bj. Fleischer, a Norwegian yachtsman. They sailed on July 4, touched in at the Faroes, and arrived in Iceland on July 25. The last word of the ship was from Julianahaab in southwest Greenland. She was never seen again, despite an extensive search order by the President of the United States, which included navy ships, the famous Captain Bob Bartlett in the Arctic schooner *Effie M. Morrisey*, as well as Canadian, Danish, and Norwegian rescue expeditions.

The Hudson's Bay Company even broadcast on Christmas Eve to all its posts a notice of a $5,000 reward for information, which indicates the prestige, esteem, and influence this private cruising club generated even in its early years.

The club was the brain-child of William Washburn Nutting, a midwesterner of great personal charm and energies, with no yachting experience whatever when he arrived in New York in about 1907 to begin a career as a writer and later editor of various yachting magazines, including *Motor Boat*. He subsequently was commissioned in the U.S. Navy and served on the famed 110-foot sub chasers of

World War I. In fact, many of the charter members of CCA were veterans of this service.

In the fall of 1920, on a duck hunting trip to the Bras d'Or Lakes aboard Gilbert Grosvenor's 54-foot *Elsie*, Nutting and some pals conceived the idea of sailing a William Atkin gaff-ketch, *Typhoon*, across the Atlantic to England in time for the Cowes races and the Harmsworth Cup Races. During the Cowes festivities, Nutting's engaging personality created a warm welcome from British yachtsmen, and many friendships were begun with members of the Royal Cruising Club, including the famed Claud Worth, Tom Ratsey, and the Earl of Dunraven, owner of the America's Cup challenger, *Valkyries*.

Members of the British cruising club, who had been awarded its coveted Seamanship Award, were Lieutenant G. H. P. Mulhauser of *Amaryllis* and Conor O'Brien of *Saoirse*.

On August 31, Nutting sailed *Typhoon* back to the United States with a crew that included a young Sea Scout master named Uffa Fox, who was to become a renowned British naval architect. The return trip was made via the Azores and the West Indies, and a boisterous one it was. The *Typhoon* was a shambles of wreckage and out of food and water by the time it reached Gravesend Bay.

During the winter of 1921–1922, Nutting and a group of yachting cronies, who gathered frequently at a cellar café known as Beefsteak John's on Grove Street, Greenwich Village, to talk yachts and cruising, formed the nucleus of the club which was formalized at a dinner meeting on February 9, 1922. A second meeting at the Harvard Club on March 22 was held to establish the original rules. The new CCA was patterned after the RCA.

The thirty-six charter members included such well-known yachtsmen as John Alden, Frederic Fenger, Gilbert Grosvenor, Herbert L. Stone, Thomas Fleming Day, and W. P. Stephens.

From the first, the club concerned itself with both ocean racing and cruising at a time when the public and most newspapers regarded both as foolhardy antics of the wealthy sportsman. The revival of the Bermuda Race and the establishment of rules for both racing and cruising events are credited to the club.

The idea of the Blue Water Medal was put forth by Henry A. Wise Wood in a committee report of February 27, 1923, "to be awarded annually for the year's most meritorious example of seamanship, the recipient to be selected from among the amateurs of all the nations. The medal itself was the work of Hildebrand, a freelance writer and early member, who was to lose his life the same year the first award was made.

According to the late John Parkinson, Jr., it was ironic that the first one should go to Alain Gerbault, the French iconoclast, who bumbled across the Atlantic in *Firecrest*.

"Today," wrote Parkinson in *Nowhere Is Too Far* (New York: Cruising Club of America, 1960), "well-executed ocean crossings in small vessels are quite frequent, and Gerbault would not even be considered for a Blue Water Medal."

1923   *Firecrest*   Alain J. Gerbault   France

Left Gibraltar on June 7, 1923, and arrived at Fort Totten, L.I., exactly 100 days later. Nonstop. Dixon Kemp-designed British cutter, 39 feet oa. Singlehanded.

1924   *Shanghai*   Axel Ingwersen   Denmark

Departed Shanghai on February 20, 1923, and arrived in Denmark via Cape of Good Hope in May 1924. Double-ended ketch, 47 feet oa, built by native laborers. Crew of three.

1925   *Islander*   Harry Pidgeon   U.S.A.

First circumnavigation. From Los Angeles to Los Angeles via Cape of Good Hope and Panama Canal, November 18, 1921–October 31, 1925. Home-built 34-foot-oa yawl of the *Sea Bird* type. Singlehanded.

1926   *Jolie Brise*   E. G. Martin   England

Double transatlantic crossing, including Bermuda Race. Le Havre pilot cutter, 56 feet oa. April 3, 1926, from Falmouth, arrived July 27 at Plymouth.

1927   *Primrose IV*   Frederick L. Ames   U.S.A.

This 50-foot-oa Alden schooner had been sailed to England for the 1926 Fastnet. Medal was awarded for her return passage, from Portsmouth, north-about, Iceland, Labrador, Cape Breton Island, 58 days to Newport, R.I.

1928   *Seven Bells*   Thomas F. Cooke   U.S.A.

An eastbound transatlantic passage, Branford, Conn., to Falmouth, July 5–July 31, 1928. Roue-designed 56-foot-oa ketch.

1929   *Postscript*   F. Slade Dale   U.S.A.

A 4,000-mile cruise in the West Indies with a crew of two, from and to Barnegat Bay, N.J. The 23-foot-oa cutter, designed by the owner, was subsequently lost with all hands under different ownership.

1930   *Carlsark*   Carl Weagent   U.S.A.

A 13,000-mile cruise of this 46-foot-oa ketch from Ithaca, N.Y., to Ithaca, Greece, and return to New York City. Started June 20, 1929, completed May 30, 1930.

1931   *Svaap*   William A. Robinson   U.S.A.

This 32-foot 6-inch oa Alden ketch departed New London on June 23, 1928, in the Bermuda Race of that year, and circumnavigated via Panama and Suez Canals with crew of two, except for a period of race. Arrived New York on September 24, 1931.

Without   *Jolie Brise*   Robert Somerset   England
Date

Award for remarkable feat of seamanship and courage in rescuing all but one of a 11-man crew of burning schooner *Adriana* in the 1932 Bermuda Race.

1933   *Dorade*   Roderick Stephens, Jr.   U.S.A.

A three-month, 8,000-mile transatlantic crossing from New York to Norway and return, including victory in the Fastnet Race. The 52-foot 3-inch oa Stephens-designed yawl returned home from England by the northern route in the remarkable time of 26 days.

1934   *May L*   W. B. Reese   England

A singlehanded passage in a small double-ended ketch from England in the fall of 1933 to Nassau in January 1934.

1935   Charles F. Tillinghast   U.S.A.

"For his seamanship in the effort to save three members of the crew of the *Hamrah* who were overboard in the North Atlantic, and in bringing the disabled and shorthanded ketch safely into Sydney, N.S."

1936   *Arielle*   Marin-Marie   France

A singlehanded transatlantic passage in a 42-foot 7-inch oa motorboat (July 23–August 10, 1936) with two self-steering devices. Marie had sailed on the cutter *Winnibelle II* (without power) from Brest to New York in 1933.

1937   *Duckling*   Charles W. Atwater   **U.S.A.**

A voyage from New York to Reykjavik, Iceland, and return to Newport via Trepassey, Newfoundland, June 19–August 26, 1937. A 37½-foot oa Mower cutter.

Without   *Igdrasil*   Roger S. Strout   **U.S.A.**
Date

Circumnavigation in a *Spray*-type cutter (eventually rigged as a yawl) designed and built by owner. He and his wife circumnavigated via Panama and Cape between June 1934 and May 1937.

1938   *Caplin*   Cdr. Robert D. Graham, Royal Navy   England

Bantry Bay, Ireland, to Funchal and Bermuda between April 20 and June 27, 1938, and then to West Indies. Graham's daughter completed the crew of two in 35-foot-oa yawl.

1939   *Iris*   John Martucci   **U.S.A.**

An 11,000-mile cruise from New York to Naples and return in a 36-foot-oa MacGregor yawl. The return home including a nonstop, 35-day run from Tangiers to Bermuda, was made after outbreak of World War II.

1940   British Yachtsmen at Dunkerque   England

Awarded to British yachtsmen, living and dead, who had helped in the evacuation of the British Expeditionary Force in June 1940.

1941   *Orion*   Robert Neilson   **U.S.A.**

Orion was a 30-foot auxiliary ketch of 10-foot beam and 4½ foot draft designed by John G. Hanna. On June 5, 1941, Neilson and one companion sailed from Honolulu and arrived San Pedro, Calif., on July 15. The medal was awarded for this passage, and *Orion* subsequently carried on through the Panama Canal to Tampa, Florida—a total distance of 7,978 miles.

1947   *Gaucho*   Ernesto C. Uriburu   Argentina

A cruise in a 50-foot ketch from Buenos Aires through the Mediterranean and to the Suez Canal and then to New York, following Columbus's route from Palos, Spain, to San Salvador.

1950   *Lang Syne*   William P. and Phyllis Crowe   U.S.A.

From Honolulu around the Cape to New England, from Easter Sunday, 1948, to the spring of 1950. After the award, the 39-foot-oa, home-built Block Island-type double-ended schooner completed her circumnavigation to Hawaii.

1952   *Stornoway*   Alfred Petersen   U.S.A.

A circumnavigation from and to New York via the two major canals in a 33-foot double-ended cutter. Single-handed, June 1948–August 18, 1952.

1953   *Omoo*   L. G. Van de Wiele   Belgium

A circumnavigation by owner, wife, and one other, plus dog, from Nice, France, to Zeebrugge, Belgium, July 7, 1951–August 2, 1953, via Canal and Cape of Good Hope. Steel 45-foot-oa gaff-rigged ketch. Said to be first steel yacht and first dog to circumnavigate.

1954   *Viking*   Sten and Brita Holmdahl   Sweden

A circumnavigation by Canal and Cape of Good Hope by owner and wife from Marstrand to Gothenburg, Sweden, between June 17, 1952, and June 22, 1954. A double-ended 33-foot ketch converted by owner and wife from a fishing boat.

1955   *Wanderer III*   Eric and Susan Hiscock   England

Circumnavigation by Canal and Cape of Good Hope by owner and wife, July 24, 1952–July 13, 1955, in a 30-foot Giles-designed cutter.

1956   *Mischief*   H. W. Tilman   England

A 20,000-mile voyage of the 50-year-old Bristol pilot cutter from England through Strait of Magellan, up west coast of South America, through Panama Canal and return to England, July 6, 1955–July 10, 1956.

Without   Carleton Mitchell   U.S.A.
Date

"For his meritorious ocean passages, his sterling seaman-ship and his advancement of the sport by counsel and example."

1957   *Landfall II*   Dr. William F. Holcomb   U.S.A.

Circumnavigation west-about from San Francisco of Schock-designed 46-foot 6-inch oa schooner via the Suez and Panama canals, with side trips to South America, England, North Africa, and New York. September 18, 1953–September 15, 1957.

1958   *Les Quatre Vents*   Marcel Bardiaux   France

Singlehanded circumnavigation west-about around Cape Horn and the Cape of Good Hope in home-built sloop, 30-foot 9-inches oa. From Ouistreham, France, May 24, 1950 to Arcachon, France, July 25, 1958.

1959   *Trekka*   John Guzzwell   Canada

Singlehanded circumnavigation in home-built yawl 20-foot 10-inches oa via the Cape of Good Hope and the Panama Canal. From Victoria, B.C., to Victoria, September 10, 1955–September 10, 1959.

Without   *Legh I, Legh II, Sirio*   Vito Dumas   Argentine
Date

Global circumnavigation in *Legh II*, 1942–1943. Other phenomenal singlehanded voyages in *Legh I*, 1931–1932; *Legh II*, 1945–1947; *Sirio*, 1955.

1960   *Gipsy Moth III*   Francis Chichester   England

Winner of the first Singlehanded Race across the Atlantic in 1960, from east to west across the Atlantic.

Without   *Seacrest*   Dr. Paul B. Sheldon   U.S.A.
Date

Extended cruises along the coasts of Nova Scotia, Newfoundland, and Labrador.

1962   *Adios*   Thomas S. Steele   U.S.A.

Two circumnavigations in a 32-foot ketch; one in 1950–1955, the other in 1957–1963.

1964   *Pen-Duick III*   Eric Tabarly   France

Winner of the second Singlehanded Race across the Atlantic from Plymouth, England, to Newport, R.I., in 27 days, 1 hour, 56 minutes.

1965   *Delight*   Wright Britton   U.S.A.

From New York to Greenland and return with his wife, Patricia, as sole crew.

1966   *Joshua*   Bernard Moitessier   France

From Mooréa, west to east, around Cape Horn to Alicante, Spain. His wife, Françoise, was sole crew.

1967   *Gipsy Moth IV*   Sir Francis Chichester   England

Singlehanded passage around the world via the Cape of Good Hope and Cape Horn. Stopping only at Sydney, Australia, the distance was 29,630 miles for the whole voyage.

1968   *Lively Lady*   Sir Alec Rose   England

Singlehanded circumnavigation of the world with stops only at Melbourne, Australia, and Bluff, New Zealand. He departed Portsmouth, England, July 16, 1967, and returned to that port on July 4, 1968.

1969   No award was made.

1970   *Elsie*   Frank Casper   U.S.A.

Extended singlehanded cruising, including one circumnavigation and numerous transatlantic passages.

1970   *Carina*   Richard S. Nye   U.S.A.

For meritorious cruising and ocean racing.

1971   *Whisper*   Hal Roth   U.S.A.

For an 18,538-mile voyage around the Pacific basin in the Spencer 35 fiberglass sloop, with his wife, Margaret, as crew. The 19-month cruise started at San Francisco and covered a route never before taken by a cruising sailboat, arriving back in San Francisco in October 1970.

1972	*Awahnee II*	Robert Lyle Griffith	U.S.A

For his three circumnavigations with his wife, Nancy, and son, Reid, the first in the Uffa Fox-designed cutter, *Awahnee I*, which was lost on a reef in the Tuamotus while engaged in a rescue mission for a missing American yacht; and the second and third in their home-built ferro-cement cutter, a modified version of *Awahnee I*. The first circumnavigation was east to west around the Horn and Cape of Good Hope; the second was east-about via the Capes and Japan; and the third, a 12,800-mile voyage in the high southern latitudes around the Antarctic continent from Bluff, New Zealand, with time spent in port at American, Russian, English, Chilean, and Argentine scientific stations.

1973	*Tzu Hang*	Miles and Beryl Smeeton	Canada

For outstanding performance in cruising and for meritorious seamanship. The Smectons cruised to almost every area of the globe in the period from 1955 to 1970 in their 45-foot ketch, *Tzu Hang*.

Of the Blue Water Medals awarded to date, twelve have been for singlehanded voyages. There have been sixteen ketches, eleven cutters, six yawls, three sloops, three schooners, and one motorboat named in the citations. Recipients have included twenty-four Americans, nine Britons, two Canadians, six Frenchmen, one Dane, one Swede, one Belgian and two Argentines. Two of the awards have been for heroism: the British Yachtsmen at Dunkerque; and the rescue of the crew of *Adriana* by the *Jolie Brise*. One man, Francis Chichester, received the award twice. One boat, the *Jolie Brise*, was cited twice. In five instances, the award was made without date. Although the award was originally intended to be given annually, no award was made in 1942, 1943, 1944, 1945, 1946, 1948, 1949, 1951, 1963, 1969. Two awards were made in 1970. Beginning in 1950, a series of awards were made jointly to man-wife crews before reverting back to the single recipient award.

Of all the awards, fourteen have included circumnavigations via the Cape of Good Hope, seven via Cape Horn, three via Suez Canal; seven have been for Atlantic crossings, two westbound and four eastbound; five for Atlantic cruises, three for a Pacific cruise, one for a China to Copenhagen voyage.

In two cases, the award named the recipient instead of a vessel, Charles F. Tillinghast in 1935 for heroism; and the famed bluewater sailor, Carleton Mitchell, between 1956 and 1957, just on general principles, as he had been a nominee many times, but always lost out to something more spectacular that year. Two of the awards were made to persons and vessels, the Hiscocks on *Wanderer III* and Tom Steele on *Adios*, who had circumnavigated twice (although Jean Gau, the Frenchman-American in *Atom*, the sister ship to *Adios*, also circumnavigated twice and was never a recipient). In at least one instance, Dr. Robert Griffith, three circumnavigations were made. *Trekka* was the smallest vessel to receive the award and the first Canadian vessel to circumnavigate.

There have been some curious omissions in the naming of the awards, for reasons best-known to the CCA committee and board. Dwight Long, who completed a circumnavigation just prior to World War II, and at the time was the youngest to do so, did not get the coveted citation, which was given to what seem today lesser voyages such as those of the *Tahiti*-ketch *Orion*, and the yawl *Iris*, or the *Caplin*, or *Duckling*. But obviously the judges had good reasons, as they had in passing up the sixteen-year-old solo circumnavigator Robin Lee Graham.

In one instance, the Argentinian solo sailor, Vito Dumas, probably one of the most deserving, caught up with the awards posthumously in 1960 (without date) for his multiple voyages in three different vessels. He was, however, beat out of the honor of being the first Argentinian to receive it by Uriburu on *Gaucho*, a later and lesser achievement.

Miles and Beryl Smeeton of *Tzu Hang* fame finally were honored by the awards committee, their voyages having covered 15 postwar years on all oceans, and having included one circumnavigation and three attempts at Cape Horn, two of which resulted in the incredible capsizings which they survived through rare displays of courage and seamanship.

The competition for the prestigious award has become in the 1970s as keen as any, including the Nobel, Pulitzer, and Oscar all rolled into one. Bluewater voyaging has come a long way since Alain Gerbault blundered across the Atlantic in one hundred days, and the number of modern yachts happily voyaging to all parts of the world has proliferated like cars on the Hollywood Freeway. It has become increasingly difficult to find new worlds to challenge. The British captured the solo singlehanded circumnavigation feats, including the difficult west-about route. The route along the Roaring Forties south of the three capes has long since been done. Dr. Robert Griffith in

Awahnee II grabbed off the circumnavigation of the Antarctic via Captain James Cook's route. He was followed by Dr. David Lewis, who at this writing was attempting it alone. The Pacific Rim route, clockwise, was done by both *Stornoway* and Al and Marjorie Petersen; and *Whisper*, with Hal and Margaret Roth.

About the only spectacular challenges left to amateur voyagers are a circumnagivation of the North American continent—and the as yet unexplored realm of private yachting in submarines.

Moby Dick and
Other Hazards

On June 15, 1972, a British ex-farmer named Dougal Robertson, turned bluewater sailor, and his family, including his wife, Linda; his son Douglas, 17; the twins, Sandy and Neil, 12; and a student friend, Robin Williams, 22, were about 200 miles from the Galápagos Islands on the downhill run to the Marquesas, aboard the old 39-foot schooner *Lucette*.

Robertson was below, working out a sextant sight. Suddenly the *Lucette* shuddered under a wrenching blow. He first thought they must have struck a submerged reef or a heavy floating object, perhaps a derelict. Then, to his horror, Robertson saw the head of a killer whale poking through the bottom strake, almost where he was standing at the chart table.

The *Lucette* had been savagely attacked by a pod of at least four killer whales, one of which was believed to have killed itself by smashing its head against the lead keel.

Robertson quickly set up emergency procedures. The fiberglass dinghy was cut loose (it had been built by students at Miramar High School in Fort Lauderdale, Florida, in 1970 as a class project). Only nine feet long, it could not function as a lifeboat, but they also had aboard two rafts, and a three-day survival pack. Within sixty seconds, the *Lucette* sank, so there was no time to save the sextant and chart, or to take more food and water.

Distracted by the death of their comrade, the other killer whales paid no attention as the family scrambled into the dinghy and rafts and paddled around the scene trying to collect a few items from the flotsam, anything that would help them survive.

For the next thirty-seven days, the castaways survived through raw courage, incredible ingenuity, and unfailing hope, until they were picked up by the Japanese trawler *Toka Maru*, seven hundred miles to the north off the coast of Costa Rica, and within one hundred miles of Robertson's estimated position. They, of course, would never have been able to make it back against the prevailing winds to the Galápagos Islands, nor could they have hoped to survive a drift down the three thousand miles to the Marquesas.

During their ordeal, they caught small fish, dolphins, sharks, and turtles with fishhooks from the survival kit. Some of the fish was eaten raw, the rest sun dried. Moisture was obtained from the eyes of the fish and the blood of a seventy-pound turtle. To help prevent dehydration, they gave themselves enemas with brackish water, which would have induced vomiting if taken by mouth.

Seven days after the sinking, they sighted a ship about three miles away, but the vessel steamed on without stopping.

When finally picked up, Robertson estimated that they had sufficient supplies for fourteen more days.

This region of the world's oceans has a long record of whale attacks or intimidations, whether by true whales or killer whales. The first recorded instance was the sinking of the ship *Essex* by a huge ferocious whale on November 20, 1819, which assaulted it again and again as it went down. This episode, and another related in *Mocha-Dick: or the White Whale of the Pacific*, by J. N. Reynolds, which appeared in the May 1839 issue of the *Knickerbocker Magazine*, formed the basis for Herman Melville's immortal *Moby Dick*. In the latter case, the creature was described as being more than 70 feet long, and that "the scars of his old wounds were near his new." It could have been a right or a sperm whale, probably it was the latter.

Although there is no space to relate it here, the escape of some of the crew of the *Essex* in a whaleboat, and their subsequent adventures until they reached South America, is one of the great untold sea stories of all time.

Another early recorded case was the ramming and sinking of the *Ann Alexander* by a whale in August 1851, the news of which provided a lucky coincidence for the sale of *Moby Dick*, which had just been published.

In more recent times, Ray Kauffman wrote in *Hurricane's Wake*, while he was in that area in the mid-1930s, of encountering a pod of four menacing whales, which appeared about to attack until something changed their minds and they swam off.

Gerald Spiess, in a letter dated April 16, 1971, told of how, on a six-day passage on *Yankee Doodle*, a 17-foot sloop, from Panama to Esmeraldas, Ecuador, he was constantly harassed by whales:

"There were about a dozen, some of which were jumping completely out of water. We tried to avoid them, but as we passed them, one came charging directly for us. He came at us until he was about 200 feet away, then followed alongside for about five minutes before jumping completely out of water, crashing down, and rejoining the pack."

On March 8, 1973, four hundred miles off the coast of Mexico, just to the north of where the Robertsons were rescued, another Briton, Maurice Bailey and his wife, Marily, on a circumnavigation aboard their 31-foot sloop, *Aurelyn*, were attacked by or collided with a whale (this one probably a gray whale), and began taking on water. They had just an hour to get their Avon raft over, collect supplies, and get away from the sinking derelict.

For the next incredible 118 days they drifted about on the Pacific, sighting many ships and yachts, but unable to attract their attention. Drifting slowly southward, they fished with bent safety pins, catching at least six small sharks, and ate about thirty turtles and eight seagulls.

They were finally picked up by the Korean ship *Weol-Mi* off Guatemala on July 4, 1973, in a semi-conscious condition. Given emergency treatment, they recovered to the point where they decided to go on with the ship to Korea, instead of getting off at Honolulu, and then return to England to build another boat to continue their circumnavigation.

Just before leaving on the world cruise, Bailey, a printer by trade, ironically had published a book called, *Safety and Survival at Sea.*

The famed trimaran designer and sailer, Arthur Piver, who was later lost at sea, reported that on his passage from Wairoa, New Zealand, to Rarotonga on *Lodestar*, a group of twenty killer whales surrounded and paced them close astern for twenty minutes, while the crew remained rigid with fear and suspense, wishing their ten-knot speed could be doubled.

In 1971, during the Cape Town to Rio race, the South African yacht *Pioneer* was at about the halfway point in the South Atlantic when she was rammed by a whale and sank within fifteen minutes, shortly after midnight. The crew barely had time to launch a life raft.

Before the yacht sank, it turned over enabling them to see where the spade keel had been torn out of the fiberglass hull, leaving a gaping hole. The five crew members were miraculously picked up a few hours later by a passing American freighter. Race officials later said that it would have been three weeks before anyone could have determined the yacht was in trouble, and their chances of making land or being sighted by another vessel were perhaps one in a million.

In the summer of 1967, the 30-foot fiberglass *Seawind*-ketch *Opogee*, the first of its kind to circumnavigate, was running down the trades under twin jibs in the Indian Ocean, more than 700 miles from the nearest land, when it was attacked by a school of whales.

Skipper Alan Eddy had just gone below to get a dish towel to dry the dishes he had washed in the cockpit, when he heard and felt a tremendous crash. *Opogee* shuddered from keel to truck. Thinking he had struck a tree or some other large floating object, he rushed up on deck to see a dark shape moving alongside the vessels. There was another shuddering crash, which echoed from the fiberglass hull like a drum. To his horror, Eddy saw three or four more whales swimming abreast of *Opogee*, their fins and blunt noses out of water, and their small beady eyes trained on him. He could have reached over and touched the closest one.

Again there was a drum-like sound of a collision and *Opogee* shuddered. Off in the distance, there appeared a dozen or more whales, attracted by the action. Now they came rushing over to join in. Eddy knew that if they all made a concerted attack, he would never survive. Already his cabin flooring had been knocked loose.

But after about thirty minutes of this, during which Eddy dared not show any movement, the whales tired of the play and went away.

These creatures were about thirty feet in length—or about the same size as the yacht. They were black with white markings and high dorsal fins. From Eddy's description, they appeared to be false killer whales, sometimes called pilot whales.

In the twenty-fourth Sydney-Hobart yacht race on Boxing Day, December 26, 1968, a usually boisterous one of 640 miles across the Tasman Sea, there were 67 entries. One of these, the 45-foot *Matuka*, was attacked and sunk by a whale. The crew was able to take to the life raft, which had been obtained for the race just before leaving New Zealand in order to comply with the race rules for safety. The crew members endured five days on the raft before being sighted and rescued by the steamer *Whoolara*.

In 1970, three German bachelors set out from Hamburg on their 31-foot sloop *Beachcomber* for a leisurely circumnavigation. Aboard were Erich Neidhardt, Wolfgang Stolling, and Sigfried Schweighofer. They visited the West Indies, went through the Panama Canal, sailed down to the Galápagos Islands.

After a pleasant interlude in the islands, they set out once more on the classic run down the trades to the Marquesas. About 1,900 miles southwest of the Galápagos, they were attacked by two whales and the *Beachcomber* sank almost immediately. For twenty-four days, the three Germans drifted with a dinghy and a life raft, sustaining themselves on a half cup of water and some oats a day. They were rescued by a Russian ship on a passenger charter from Australia and New Zealand to the United Kingdom.

Commander Bill King, after his capsize and abortive attempt at a nonstop circumnavigation during the 1968 Golden Globe Race, set out again in 1970 on *Galway Blazer II*. Forced by health and need for hull repairs, he put in at Western Australia, and on December 12, 1971, left again from Freemantle. About 400 miles to the southwest, he was suddenly attacked by a killer whale and the yacht badly stove in. Only his skill and heroic efforts were able to keep the vessel afloat until jury repairs could be made, including a patch over the hole. He managed to limp back to port.

After the attack, Captain King reported, the killer whale came up astern and leered at him, but did not attempt a second charge.

D. M. R. Guthrie, in the summer of 1969, on a passage from Antigua to Bermuda on his 30-foot *Widgee*, which he had sailed for 30,000 miles on his circumnavigation with his Welsh dog, Cider, heard and felt a crashing thud. The vessel rolled down on her beam ends, although the weather was mild at the time. He thought at first that he had hit a tree or an uncharted reef. Then came another jolting crash from astern. He rushed up on deck to see a large swirl of water. Then an enormous black fluke rose ten feet in the air, thrashing angrily. Guthrie said later that he thought it was a blue whale. More likely it was a finback.

The next morning, when it was light, he found a lump of skin and torn blubber caught in the rigging. It took two days to fix the rudder where it had been jammed before completing the fourteen-day voyage to Bermuda.

The Cruising Club of America book *Far Horizons* recorded this episode from a report by Dr. Hendrik M. Rozendaal:

> *During an early morning watch, Bill Hartman, the first mate, ran into a solid object with such force that we below all fell out of our bunks. We ran for the companionway. Just behind the stern of* Katrina *we saw a 30-foot sperm whale sticking his head up above the water. After a long and ugly look at us, he disappeared under the water. For a few moments we lived in lively fear that he might give us a whipping with his flukes. We hastened*

to check the bilge. Fortunately there was no evidence that Katrina *had been damaged. I had never thought about this hazard of ocean sailing, and I am sure it must be a rare occurrence.*

There is a growing body of evidence, however, that whale attacks or at least encounters are not as rare as most sailors hope. This mounting evidence may be because of the increasing number of small vessels sailing the oceans of the world, which leaves a higher percentage of surviving Ishmaels to tell the story; or it may be, as the more imaginative speculate, that the oceans' large mammals, hunted ruthlessly into the farthest corners of the globe and decimated by man to the point of near extinction, have begun to fight back, attacking any target that comes into range. It may also be that the more frequent episodes are the result of more vessels accidentally colliding with the huge mammals, and becoming damaged in the encounter.

In the March 1973 issue of *Sail* magazine, the editorial writer pointed out:

> *The attacks (by whales) have made sailors speculate on the risks they run, and what actually causes an attack. Is it the shape of the hull, the color of the anti-fouling, the accidental intrusion into a whale ceremony of some kind?*
>
> *Dr. Peter Beamish of the Marine Ecology Laboratory in Dartmouth, Nova Scotia, talked with us recently about his research on whales in the Gulf of St. Lawrence. For his work he found it necessary to use a sailboat and he moved among the schools of whales—not killer whales —without fear.*
>
> *"Occasionally they would come straight at our boat, but they always would dive before reaching us," he said.*
>
> *The attacks on* Lucette *and* Galway Blazer II, *are of course, immensely interesting to anyone who sails offshore. They add a new dimension, just as the cluttering up of our oceans with massive and potentially dangerous pieces of debris does for small boat sailors. But surely the lesson of the* Lucette *is that of the attitude of her skipper and survivors.*

During the pre–World War II days, while sailing among the islands of Southeast Alaska, I often encountered whales in the passages. They seemed to be leaping and playing—we thought to shake off barnacles. They would frequently come up alongside the boat or dive underneath, or even follow astern. Always, however, they would avoid actual contact with us. At first it was frightening, especially when we could smell their foul breath—they were that close aboard at times. But after becoming accustomed to the encounters, we came to be amused, and even to look forward to meeting them. Needless to say, this youthful naïveté tends to give me cold chills today when I think of it.

In more recent years, cruising the west coast of Baja California, we have encountered the gray whales, which migrate from the Bering to some of these remote tidal lagoons to breed each year. They seem to offer no danger, unless you happen to get between a female gray and her youngster.

Practically every voyager in small vessels who has written about his experiences has reported encounters of some kind with whales, including Captain Joshua Slocum. He relates how, on the long run from Juan Fernández to Samoa, he had at least one hair-raising experience and near miss with a great whale that was "absent-mindedly plowing the ocean at night while I was below." The noise of the whale's startled snort and the commotion of the sea brought Slocum up on deck in time to take a wetting from the water thrown up by the mammal's flukes. The monster was apparently just as frightened as was Slocum, for it quickly headed east, while the *Spray* continued west. Not long after, another whale was sighted, following in the wake of the first.

Vito Dumas, on his epic circumnavigation in the Roaring Forties, reported many whale encounters. Once, off Tasmania, he awoke to find two huge cacholots (sperm whales) swimming alongside. As soon as he made a movement, they disappeared. On another occasion, he reported a baby whale playing off to port, while the mother cruised alongside, keeping a baleful eye on the vessel.

In the Indian Ocean, Dumas saw many whales, often all around him, so close he could smell their breath and hear their breathing, which sounded to him like a far-off naval bombardment "punctuated by the splash of projectiles."

Off Cape Leeuwin, a cacholot nearly 50 feet long made two passes at *Legh II*, but did not make contact. Another time, during a dark night, Dumas spotted a whale dead ahead. It swerved off and swam around to the stern, probably out of curiosity. But Dumas did not like such a "dangerous neighbor" and flashed his electric torch to scare it off. This was followed some time later by an incident when an enormous whale cut across his bows and nearly collided. Just as the vessel was about to touch him, the whale dived.

Marjorie Petersen relates in *Stornoway, East and West,* how, in the Mediterranean, they encountered a huge whale which circled while huffing and puffing, but eventually swam away without attacking.

Chay Blyth, who sailed nonstop around the world "the wrong way," from east to west in the high southern latitudes, related how in the vicinity of Cape Horn he encountered whales close aboard and for a few tense moments pondered whether or not to use the explosive charges he had brought along just for this purpose. He finally decided it might anger them into attacking his 57-foot steel yacht.

Eric Hiscock, in *Around the World in Wanderer III,* wrote:

> We had previously regarded whales as benign and harmless creatures, as indeed they generally are; but now that we know more about them and their habits, it seems to us that when we are sailing through a pod, especially at night, there is some risk of a yacht striking, while approaching in the blind sector, and the result might then be serious. We kept a more careful lookout than usual on our way home and saw a large number of whales.

Bill and Phyllis Crowe, who also won the Blue Water Medal, on their circumnavigation had an almost identical experience to the Hiscocks in the same general location:

> One evening while in the galley fixing coffee, there was a sudden crash that shook the ship from stem to stern. My knees came up and I had to hold on to keep from falling. Lang Syne *was clipping along about eight knots with the mate at the wheel . . . so my first thought was that the mainmast had broken, and I ran to the hatch. The mate was holding her side and pointing to a commotion in the wake astern of us.* "A whale," *she gasped.* "He threw me clean off the seat!" *Several sleeping whales had been seen on the surface and I had always wondered if they would hear us coming if we got close. This one was evidently a sound sleeper . . . The bobstay was slack and the seven-eighths inch diameter bronze eyebolt had been bent and the stem split.*

Whale attacks—or at least recorded legend—goes back to Jonah, son of Amittai, who, in fleeing the presence of the Lord, went down to Joppa and found a ship bound for Tarshish. He paid the fare and went aboard. During the voyage, the Lord caused a great tempest, during which the captain and the crew threw Jonah overboard to appease the evil spirits. The Lord then appointed a "great fish" to swallow up Jonah, and he remained in the belly of the whale for three days and three nights, before the whale vomited Jonah up on dry land.

Few of the reports of encounters identify the large ocean mammals by species, but generally lump them all into the term "whales." Actually there are many families of whales—baleens, finbacks, narwhals, sperms, and beaked whales, as well as the large dolphin family which includes the so-called killer whales. Of the true whales, the finback, sperm, and gray have been regarded as the most dangerous, especially during the mating and calving season. Charles Nordhoff (uncle of the co-author of *Mutiny on the Bounty*), in his rare book, *Whaling and Fishing*, wrote that sperm whales were known among whalemen as the ones which fed upon the giant squid from the bottom of the sea. The sperms would make incredible dives of up to a mile deep to find and do battle with the enormous cuttle fish which some believed to be larger than the largest whale. This was undoubtedly the "kraken" of ancient tales.

Hunted commercially for at least 500 years, whales are believed to have once numbered more than five million. During the past fifty years, more than two million have been ruthlessly slaughtered, mostly by the killer fleets of Japan and Russia, until at this writing eight of the fourteen species over twenty feet long are on the brink of extinction. The largest of the fourteen, the blue whale, which is believed to be the largest animal that ever lived on earth, reaching a length of more than one hundred feet, numbers only about a hundred remaining in all the oceans. This may be too few for the survivors to find each other for mating purposes.

The finback, once estimated at half a million, now numbers less than 80,000 and is a prime target of the Japanese gunners. The Pacific right and the gray whale border on the endangered zone. The sei, sperm, humpbacked, and Baird's beaked whale are also in deep trouble.

The other species over twenty feet long include the Pacific blackfish, little piked whale, killer whale, false killer whale, goose beaked whale, and Stejneger's beaked whale.

The United States banned all whaling in 1971 and now even prohibits the imports of whale products. Canada followed in 1973 with a similar ban. Neither country, however, had much of a whaling industry left, the economics of it being prohibitive. The net result was that Japan and Russia continued their intense whaling efforts just outside the twelve-mile limit off the North American continent— waters which U.S. and Canadian whalers had abandoned. In 1973, the total Japanese and Russian take of whales in the North Pacific alone was about ten thousand.

If any species or family of species on earth has had reason to turn upon man, it is the whale.

Many of the encounters have not been with whales, but killer whales. This species (*Grampus orca*) has long had a reputation of being a ruthless and ferocious hunter, compared to the more docile whale. Killer whales are found in all oceans and seas, tropical and polar, from the Arctic to the Antarctic. They are distinguished by the distinctive white patches on an otherwise black skin, and large conical teeth. They often travel in packs, hunting like wolves. In fact, they are sometimes called the "Wolves of the Sea."

Rogert Strout, who built and circumnagivated in a reproduction of Slocum's *Spray*, from 1934 to 1937, reported how he and his wife witnessed an attack of a pack of killer whales on a blue whale in the Tasman Sea. The killers circled the whale, repeatedly darting in to slash the victim until it died.

Once, while salmon fishing from a small boat in the waters off Vancouver Island, I witnessed a blood-curdling episode. A large pack of about twenty killer whales appeared, almost in military formation, their high scimitar dorsal fins cutting precise wakes, the largest in front, the smaller ones or juveniles behind. They were pacing a large school of salmon, which was migrating through the strait on the way to the Fraser River. Suddenly the killer whale formation broke off into two circles, each going a different way around the school of salmon. As the circles drew smaller, the salmon were driven to the surface in a boiling frantic mass of confusion and panic. Then, when the salmon were bunched up and disoriented, the killer whales broke formation and slashed in for the kill. Few of the salmon escaped.

Killer whales, according to Dr. Bruce W. Halstead in *Dangerous Marine Animals* (Cornell Maritime Press, 1959), are fast swimmers and will attack anything that moves. They have been known to come up through the ice in polar regions and to knock people and seals into the water. They are extremely intelligent animals, and a number of them have been caught, trained, and kept as pets in the Puget Sound area.

Among other recorded whale encounters are the following:

The 42-foot plywood *Matuku* was sunk by a whale in December 1968 between New Zealand and Australia.

The 32-foot fiberglass fin-keel *Pioneer* was sunk by a whale in January 1971, during the Cape Town to Rio Race.

The yacht *Rage* hit what was reported to be a 30-foot sperm whale in the 1971–1972 Sydney-Hobart Race.

The *Phayet* hit a whale during the 1972 Bermuda Race and injured the whale.

The 57-foot slooper *Aries* was hit three times by a whale 180 miles from Tahiti during the 1972 Tahiti Race.

Flame and *Sargasso II* both reported hitting whales in the 1972 Victoria-Maui Race.

One of the crewmen on the *Sargasso II* told me that the yacht had run up on the back of the whale, and for some time was in danger of being capsized.

Not all encounters have been with whales or killer whales. In *Desperate Voyage* (New York: Ballantine Books, 1949), John Caldwell tells of a giant devilfish:

> *Slightly abaft the beam and about 100 yards out, the sea surface rippled, then it rippled again. I stood up and watched, expecting to see a school of porpoises. The splashes and eddies drew near. Then, breaking the water and gliding smoothly beneath the keel, came a giant devilfish. He approached Pagan as though he hadn't seen her, and when he passed, he turned and slipped deliberately back, coming close enough to touch the planking, eyeing me with black protruding eyes . . . remorseless in his power; confident as a peacock; more arrogant than a shark.*

In one of his fine books on voyaging, Eric Hiscock related how *Wanderer III* was attacked in the South Atlantic by what appeared to be a giant swordfish.

In a similar episode, Dr. Holcomb reported that on his circumnavigation, while in the vicinity of Madagascar, his yacht was rammed by a giant swordfish, its sword holing a plank below the engine bed, which was inaccessible from inside the hull. The pumps had to be manned for four days, until they reached Cochin where repairs were made.

Alain Gerbault also reported an attack by a giant swordfish in New Guinea waters.

The most dangerous sea creatures, however, are not the large mammals. Dr. Halstead, in *Dangerous Marine Animals,* lists dozens of marine denizens that bite, sting, or are poisonous to eat—a large percentage of which are usually fatal to man. Sharks are a serious hazard to swimmers and divers. So are groupers, rays, barracuda, morays, tridacna clams (the kind that Slocum filled *Spray* with in the Keeling-Cocos), sea wasps and anemones, a number of species of sea worms and urchins, ratfishes, catfishes, scorpionfishes, stonefishes, and poisonous molluscs. The seas are swarming with such hazards.

But by far the most serious are the many species of man-attacking sharks. Since antiquity, when man first entered or sailed upon the seas, the shark has been regarded as a mortal enemy, and with good reason. One of the early references to this comes from Pliny the Elder, during the first century A.D., who wrote about the encounters of sponge fishermen with dogfish (a species of shark).

During World War II, when thousands of men were thrown into the sea by ship sinkings, and the chance of finding one's self in the salt chuck among the maneaters was very good indeed at times, the Navy published a good deal of nonsense designed to reassure sailors and soldiers, and a number of so-called shark repellent devices were invented and issued. Today we know that most of the advice on how to handle sharks was hogwash, and most of the repellents do not work.

Not all marine creatures are enemies of man, however. For more than twenty years, until the spring of 1912, mariners crossing Cook Strait between the main islands of New Zealand reported being piloted by a dolphin. This was Peloris Jack, probably a Risso's dolphin (*Grampus griseus*), and his appearance was always regarded as a good omen. Peloris Jack disappeared in the spring of 1912, and was believed to have died of old age.

MEDICAL HAZARDS

ALTHOUGH SLOCUM, PIDGEON ET AL. DWELLED MUCH UPON how good was their health when making passages, the incidence of sickness, deaths, and emergencies requiring operations is far larger than most voyagers would like to think. Medical disasters probably account for the unexplained disappearance of as many, if not more, small-boat voyagers than marine mammals. Not many—especially not many singlehanders—leave detailed clinical journals of their problems, as did Donald Crowhurst, who lost his mind and committed suicide in the 1968 Golden Globe Race.

In this age of vitamins, concentrated minerals, and health fads, the idea of the ancient disease of the sea—scurvy—seems as far-fetched as a *kraken*. Wasn't this cured and wiped out as far back as Captain James Cook's voyages?

Not so. The disease, often unnoticed or undiagnosed, has struck even some of the transatlantic solo racers, even those on a daily diet of vitamins. Undoubtedly, many of Vito Dumas's medical problems during his solo circumnavigation in the Roaring Forties can be attributed to the early stages of scurvy. On a passage from Bermuda to England, Captain J. H. Illingworth, the famed British yachtsman and naval officer, began to feel the symptoms only a week out, although he was taking vitamins and had fresh fruit aboard.

Conor O'Brien, who suffered from blindness on his homeward passage from Pernambuco to the Cape Verde Islands, was without doubt a scurvy victim, and by the time he got to port his Tongan mate was also incapacitated by some unknown illness.

Ann Davison, who singlehanded across the Atlantic to New York in 1952 aboard the 23-foot *Felicity Ann* after her husband died, reported the effects of what surely was the early stages of scurvy.

In no less than half of the hundred or so voyages analyzed for this book, symptoms of this mariner's disease cropped up here and there, usually undetected by the victims. Symptoms begin with a depressed mental outlook, then progress to boils, abscessed teeth, great weakness of limbs, loss of hair, and skin rash. Even in mild cases, loss of some teeth is common. Nutritionists say that the disease is not uncommon today, even among those on land who follow "normal" diets, especially if they are limited to dehydrated milk and juices.

The food lists and diets published in the appendices of many accounts of small boat voyages vary from the incredible to the bizarre, and are guaranteed to shock any conscientious dietitian. They are, in fact, dietetic time bombs which can create not only loss of good judgment on long passages, but also a physical condition that cannot cope with unusual sea conditions.

The cure for scurvy, of course, is simple and spectacular, and has not changed since Cook's day. Raw vegetable and fruit juices, and raw potatoes, especially those which have not been washed of the earth from which they were dug are recommended. One of the best, if not the best, anti-scorbutics, is the lemon. Fresh bread, made from flour, yeast, or sourdough, is believed helpful. Any kind of raw vegetable and most fruits are also good. In any case, voyagers should consult a physician who is also a nutritionist (many doctors know little or nothing of dietary matters), before departing. NASA research for space travel, when released, should be invaluable.

If one needs any incentive to do so, a reading of Anson's circumnavigation in the early eighteenth century should convince anyone. In one of the most horrible continuing episodes of scurvy in maritime history, 626 men out of the combined crews of the *Centurion, Tryall,* and *Gloucester,* totaling 961, died from the disease.

William Robinson, who had not been sick a day in his life, even during his first voyage when he lived for months on native fare in the remote islands of Melanesia and Micronesia, including disease-ridden New Guinea, described in living color his experience with a ruptured appendix in the Galápagos Islands on a second voyage aboard *Svaap.* The spectacular rescue by ships and planes of the U.S. Army and Navy from Panama in the nick of time, and his recovery, has been told elsewhere in this volume.

The Galápagos area of the Pacific, in fact, has been the scene of an astonishing number of appendectomies. Perhaps it is the water or the food. After leaving one appendix in a hospital in Balboa, the Irving Johnsons on *Yankee* had a second such emergency, which required a detour into a mainland Ecuador port to get air transportation back to Panama. Later, on the same voyage, another appendix case occurred as they approached South America from the Atlantic side, this one requiring an emergency operation.

Robin Lee Graham, the youngest person to sail around the world alone, suffered an attack of appendicitis during an earlier voyage with his family on the 36-foot *Golden Hind.* The attack occurred while in the doldrums, and again when 120 miles from Tahiti. He spent three weeks in a primitive hospital infested by giant cockroaches.

On their last voyage, around Cape Horn and up to the Hawaiian Islands, the Smeetons nearly ran out of luck. Beryl Smeeton was then developing a serious intestinal problem which erupted soon after they reached Hawaii, and required major surgery. Had it happened a little sooner, she probably would not have survived.

Sicknesses have been common. Jack and Charmian London had to abort their circumnavigation on the *Snark* in New Guinea because

Jack picked up a serious tropical bug. The fun-loving Ray Kauffman was decked in New Guinea waters by recurring tropical fevers, which required a detour to medical facilities in Australia. The Fahnestocks had to abandon their circumnavigation and sell *Director* in the Philippines for the same reason. Both Peter Tangvald and his girl friend suffered what he reported as heart attacks on his circumnavigation.

Leonid Teliga and Walter Koenig sailed around the world with terminal illnesses that took them soon after completing the voyages.

Commander George Fairley, who had been invalided out of the Royal Navy for diabetes, required daily injections of insulin on his voyages. This often became a matter of life and death when the seas were too rough to boil a needle, to say nothing of administering to himself. Once or twice he ran out of insulin before reaching port, arriving just in time to be taken ashore in a coma. His dream ship was a 23-foot sloop, *Dawn Star*.

The Reverend Frederick Watts was 82, and he had loved the sea and sailed over it all his life. He had just survived another heart attack and major surgery for cancer. He knew his time was about up. He left Suva, Fiji Islands, in April 1969, without a destination, on *Jessie W.*, his trimaran. In July, his vessel was found dismasted and sinking. The last entry in the log, dated May 29, just a routine note, was beside the body. The captain of the ship which found him decided to sink the *Jessie W.* with the body aboard. The seacocks were opened, and he was buried at sea with his ship.

Steve Dolby discovered in 1964 that he was going blind, at age 26. Before this happened, he wanted to see more of the world. He outfitted his 24-foot fiberglass sloop, installed a self-steering vane, named the ship *Ghost Rider*, and departed Sydney, Australia in July 1971 on a circumnavigation. His first leg was to Mauritius. Encountering a gale in the Indian Ocean, he broke the top of the mast, and made port under a jury rig for repairs. Leaving there, he headed for South Africa, again alone. By this time, he could not take a star sight because of blurred vision, and could only read a chart by holding his face a few inches away from it.

No one will ever know how many erstwhile circumnavigators succumbed to the loneliness of weeks and months at sea. Even Slocum, who had sailed the oceans all his life, including five circumnavigations, reported how on several occasions he gave way to his feelings and broke down.

Dumas reported many fits of melancholy, especially during his Atlantic crossing to South Africa in 1941. It was during this voyage that an arm became so badly infected that he had decided to amputate it himself. Fortunately, the septic wound broke open and drained itself in his sleep, before he had to attempt a self-operation.

Fits of loneliness have affected even the most extroverted of voyagers, such as Tahiti Bill Howell, who at times broke down and cried with frustration when things went wrong. The case of Donald Crowhurst has been well-documented, and the authors of the clinical book on this tragic subject offered the rather sobering reminder that would-be voyagers ought to consider what happened to Crowhurst when contemplating long singlehanded passages. The records of even the popular Transatlantic Singlehanded Race, a relatively short passage with plenty of assistance available if needed, show a high incidence of mental and emotional breakdowns. Dr. David Lewis, who with his family circumnavigated in their catamaran, recorded almost clinically the mental and emotional strains of sea life, and how unreasonable fears and anxieties nearly aborted their voyage at the start. Such unflappable sailors as Eric Hiscock admitted to these mental pressures. Hiscock wrote that at sea on a long passage, especially during rough weather, anxiety almost always was present, sometimes bordering on panic.

This ever-present subconscious fear of the sea, in fact, may be the psychological reason for its great fascination for many voyagers, although few of them have really understood this, and fewer yet have admitted it.

F. DeWitt Wells, the aging middle-class New Yorker who purchased the famous teak ketch *Shanghai* from its owners upon its arrival in Denmark from the Orient in 1924 to fulfill a life-long ambition to make an ocean voyage, realized this and candidly wrote of it in his book, *The Last Cruise of the Shanghai*, in which he related the causes of dissension on the rough two-month passage across the North Atlantic with an amateur crew:

"Chapman had told the truth, and like all truths it hurt; for I realized for the first time that I was afraid nearly the whole of the way, but I did not know that I had shown it. I began to question whether after all I was not a coward and I decided that I was. It was a curious psychology that probably the reason I had taken the trip was because I managed to get such a tremendous pleasure out of being afraid of the sea. The sea is an enemy to everyone."

The effects of such mental and emotional pressures often resulted in hallucinations, especially when accompanied by a physical problem—such as when Slocum ate purple plums and white cheese, and rolled on the floor semi-consciously as *Spray* sailed on through the night. It was during this attack when the pilot of the *Pinta* appeared to take charge, and thereby became the patron saint of all single-handers.

Slocum also reported hallucinations in the high southern latitudes near the Falklands, when seagulls appeared on the horizon as big as ships, and the next instant everything appeared microscopic, like some latter-day Gulliver's travels.

No one will ever know how many vessels have disappeared without a trace (including Slocum's *Spray* and the first copy of it, *Pandora*), because of judgments influenced by mental aberrations. None other than the founder of the Slocum Society himself, John Pflieger, went this way. On a voyage from Bermuda to Antigua in the spring of 1966, aboard his *Stella Maris*, he disappeared. The last entry was July 10, 1966, when he spoke a large tanker overtaking him at 20°26′N and 61°18′W.

When the *Stella Maris* was found, everything was in order, and Pflieger's pipe was on the seat.

William Wallin left Kalmor, Sweden, aboard his sloop *Vagabond* on May 1, 1969, headed for the Azores via Kiel and Plymouth. His vessel was found abandoned with everything in order on July 6, by the Swedish ship *Goler*, 600 miles short of the Azores. His disappearance is a mystery.

One of the most poignant medical disasters happened to Commander George Fairley, who started on a four-year circumnavigation in July 1968 with a companion, Mrs. Jean Oatley, who was also a diabetic (see above), aboard *Dawn Star*. On June 25, 1969, they sailed from Las Perlas bound for the Galápagos Islands. Four days out, Mrs. Oatley complained of illness but continued to stand watches and cook meals. The next day she was in much pain, localized in the abdomen.

Fairley turned the vessel around and with both sail and power, tried to find help. On July 1, Mrs. Oatley died. The *Dawn Star*'s log for that date reads:

"Stopped at 1800. Gave service and wrapped her in a blanket and with two shackles round her legs, committed her to the deep at 1015, five miles west of Cabo Mala."

OTHER HAZARDS OF THE SEA

THE LOGS OF MOST VOYAGERS ARE FILLED WITH ENTRIES that should be given consideration by any would-be circumnavigator. These include such things as harassment by customs and port officials, harbor thievery, lack of supplies and repair facilities, and outright piracy.

Such incidents are as common today as they were when Slocum spread tacks on his deck and loaded the old Martini-Henry, or outran the pirate fellucas. Richard Zantzinger recorded in *The Log of the Molly Brown* how he was boarded by phony port officials at George-town, who left only at the point of a shotgun; and of being robbed by a sixteen-year-old hoodlum in Mauritius.

Captain Ted Falcon-Baker, an Australian ex-commando, was attacked one night aboard his 30-foot sloop off Haiti, near a place appropriately called Massacre Bay. The three persons aboard were at the time suffering from fish poisoning when the attackers came out in a canoe. One of Falcon-Baker's crew was killed by a knife wound, but not before two of the attackers were killed by shotgun.

A similar encounter occurred to another voyager, Francis Brenton, off the Dominican Republic.

But of all the non-medical emergencies that can occur at sea, the most frequent are man-overboard, collision, fire at sea, hull failure, and weather—in that order, with weather far down on the list.

Falling overboard is a far more frequent happening than most people, even sailors, realize. It does happen often, and in the case of a singlehander, can be a harrowing experience. Robin Lee Graham went over the side twice during his circumnavigation, both times without the safety line attached.

It has occurred even to such careful and experienced sailors as Dr. and Mrs. Bob Griffith. On one passage, Nancy was caught by a bellying mainsail during an accidental jibe and thrown up six feet and over the rail into the ocean. At the time, they were making a good eight knots. It took a half hour of expert ship handling to get her back aboard.

Beryl Smeeton was thrown into the sea during their first capsize after her safety line snapped on their attempt to round Cape Horn, and was miraculously rescued by John Guzzwell and Miles Smeeton, although she had a dislocated arm and the vessel was in imminent danger of sinking.

Chris Loehr, on a singlehanded transatlantic passage aboard his yacht *Frilo*, was swept overboard and lost. The last log entry aboard was dated January 31, 1971, made during a storm. The yacht was taken aboard the British ship *Port Vinoles* in good condition.

Aake Mattson, on a singlehanded passage from Sweden in 1971, was swept overboard from his wrecked yacht off Brazil and swam for two days before being rescued by a passing trawler.

Rudi Wagner left England aboard his new 35-foot catamaran with his wife and son, Rudi. They had a rough passage, and in the Bay of Biscay, Rudi was washed overboard by a following sea which swept the decks clean. He was saved by his lifeline, which held, and his wife pulled him back aboard.

Probably the most harrowing of all was the experience of single-hander Fred Wood, who was swept off the deck of his *Windsong* in an accidental jibe during a passage from Tahiti to Hawaii. At the time, fortunately, he was only five miles from Christmas Island. He swam for seven hours before reaching a reef.

He managed to stay clear of the surf breaking by listening to the sounds in the dark, and made his way on the coral to a place where he could fashion a raft and cross the lagoon. He reached the settlement 15 days after the accident, surviving on coconut meat and land crabs. He never saw *Windsong* again, nor has the vessel ever turned up.

The most controversial case of man-overboard, of course, was the disappearance of Captain John Voss's mate, Louis Begent, on the passage from Fiji to Australia. Voss's former mate, Norman Luxton, later accused Voss of murdering Begent.

The incidence of collision, too, is far higher than most sailors like to think about. As the oceans of the world become increasingly crowded with vessels of all kinds, the problem is bound to get much worse. But it has always been a problem, and it is entirely likely that many missing voyagers have been run down unnoticed by passing ships, even in the most remote parts of the oceans. Both Slocum and his successors on the *Pandora* are believed to have disappeared this way. Captain Harry Pidgeon was nearly dismasted by a freighter in the South Atlantic. Robin Lee Graham missed being run down by a freighter one dark night in the Solomon Sea by the thickness of a coat of paint.

Even if they see a yacht on a collision course, modern ships, especially the big tankers, cannot be stopped or even turned in less than about a mile. Some of them are so huge that the people on the bridge cannot see anything on the water less than eight miles away. Radar is of questionable help. The officers on the bridge glance at the screen only occasionally. Lookouts are notoriously lax in keeping a sharp eye out for other vessels or obstructions. Many ships, especially those of marginal operations, are undermanned and criminally careless even during periods of fog and limited visibility in crowded ship channels.

For the small-boat voyager, in addition to the very real danger of being run down by a larger vessel, there is also the hazard of colliding with the increasing amount of flotsam on the oceans of the world—derelicts, logs and trees, partly submerged tanks, lumber, and trash of all kinds.

The waters of the North Pacific, where I cruise, are filled with floating and half-submerged logs which are called "deadheads," with good reason, and are extremely difficult to see. On the ocean, I have found the best indicator to be seagulls. Every floating log will usually have a few birds perched on it.

On one voyage off the coast of Baja, in 1969, we struck at night what turned out to be a large wooden cable reel. It damaged the prop, bent the rudder, and nearly holed the vessel.

Clearly, the oceans of the world are inherently hazardous and unforgiving to those who would sail upon them, especially in small yachts. This, however, has not in the past and never will in the future deter those blithe souls who take to the sea in small boats. There are hazards and things to worry about everywhere in life, including the home, office, and city streets.

If the circumnavigators have had anything in common, it is that they do not worry much about things that might happen.

Around the Three Capes

Cape Agulhas	34° 50′ South	20° 01′ East
Cape Leeuwin	34° 22′ South	115° 08′ East
Cape Horn	55° 59′ South	67° 16′ West

During the first part of this day (Wednesday) the wind was light, but after noon it came on fresh, and we furled the royals. We still kept the studding-sails out, and the captain said he should go around with them, if he could. Just before eight o'clock (then about sun-down, in that latitude), the cry of "All hands ahoy!" was sounded down the fore scuttle and the after hatchway, and hurrying upon deck, we found a large black cloud rolling on toward us from the south-west, and blackening the whole heavens.

"Here comes Cape Horn!" said the chief mate; and we had hardly time to haul down and clew up, before it was upon us.

In a few moments, a heavier sea was raised than I had ever seen before, and as it was directly ahead, the little brig, which was no better than a bathing machine, plunged into it, and all the forward part of her was under water; the sea pouring in through the bow ports and hawse-hole and over the knight-heads, threatening to wash everything overboard. In the lee scuppers it was up to a man's waist.

This incident, described by Richard Henry Dana, Jr., in *Two Years Before the Mast*, on a voyage aboard the small brig *Pilgrim* in the 1830s, communicates the awe and reverence sailors had for "Cape Stiff" in the days when iron men in wooden ships had few choices of routes if they wanted to sail from one ocean to another.

Slocum originally intended to sail east from Gibraltar through the

Mediterranean, and the 92-mile long Suez Canal which was in operation; but when he was warned against pirates (and was actually chased by them off Morocco), he turned downhill, across the Atlantic again to Brazil, then south and through Magellan Strait. Old newspaper files in Buenos Aires indicate that he had also intended to sail around Cape Horn. Whether this was just interview talk for the benefit of reporters, or he changed his mind again to take the strait route, is unknown. He had a difficult time in the strait, due to violent winds and currents and harassment by a native band of renegades led by a half-breed outlaw; and the first time he attempted to make an offing into the Pacific, he was blown back down toward the Horn on the outside and nearly wrecked in the Milky Way.

The rest of Slocum's voyage, however, generally followed the trade route, with a loop down around the Cape of Good Hope (the southernmost tip of Africa being actually Cape Agulhas). Voss started from the west coast of North America and, while he doubled Hope, too, he didn't complete his circumnavigation in *Tilikum*, and thus was not faced with the Horn.

The later circumnavigators, with the new Panama Canal opened, established the pattern that became pretty much standard for voyages around the world in small vessels, and remains so today. This route is via the Panama Canal, then slanting down into the northeast trades to the Marquesas, often with a detour to the Galápagos Islands on the way. The Marquesas are the first taste of the true South Sea atmosphere that most voyagers experience. From here, most of them sail down through the Tuamotus to Tahiti for a long stop.

From Tahiti, the route lies westward to Bora Bora, or up to Samoa and the Fijis, thence to New Guinea, through Torres Strait and the Arafura Sea, across the Indian Ocean via Keeling-Cocos, Rodriguez, Mauritius, and Réunion, to Africa. Robinson, Long, and many others made the long, hot beat up the Red Sea to Suez and through the canal into the Mediterranean. Others sailed to the hospitable port of Durban, South Africa, to get prepared for the hard 900 miles around Hope to Cape Town; after which they made the long passage across the Atlantic via St. Helena, Ascension, and the West Indies. This southern route could only be made in the summer months, usually November and December. In winter, the voyagers usually took the Suez Canal.

With the closing of the Suez Canal in 1967, all voyagers had to go around Cape of Good Hope. There was no other choice, unless one wanted to ship one's yacht overland from a Persian Gulf port.

The route then became strictly a trade wind route west-about, except for the unpleasantness at the tip of Africa. Hundreds of yachts have made this circumnavigation. From Europe, they would sail to Gibraltar or to Vigo, then down to the Canaries where dozens of yachts might be rendezvoused at the same time to wait out the hurricane season in the Caribbean; then came the easy Atlantic passage, the leisurely weeks in the West Indies, and on to Panama. After the canal transit, a minor ordeal, they then followed the classic route to the South Pacific, and so on around.

By this route, it was reaching or running all the way, and few passages were longer than thirty days. Moreover, most of the world's bad weather could thus be avoided.

It was Conor O'Brien, the Irish rebel, who circumnavigated first from east to west, *south* of the three principal capes—Leeuwin, Horn, and Agulhas or Good Hope. He sailed down the Atlantic to Cape Town, then to Durban, and down into the Roaring Forties, past the remote rocks of Amsterdam and St. Paul, down past Cape Leeuwin on the southwest horn of Australia, across the Australian bight to Melbourne; thence across the Tasman Sea to New Zealand.

Too late for his mountain-climbing appointment in New Zealand, he wandered a bit about the islands, then took off for home via Cape Horn, the Falkland Islands—from which he made a detour to the Antarctic aboard a supply vessel—and up the Atlantic, stopping once in Brazil and again in the Azores.

What O'Brien had actually done was sail the old wool and grain clipper route from the British Isles to Australia and return. In his day, some of these old clippers were still in use. In fact, a few remained in service up to the outbreak of World War II. Anticipating Chichester by half a century, O'Brien had made a thorough study of old clipper ship logs.

It was a rough passage, most of the way in the high southern latitudes, subjected to frequent storms and to enormous seas which often overwhelmed even the largest and sturdiest ships. From Europe, a ship sailed from 50°N to 50°S and back again, while also going from 0° longitude to 180° and back again. A stop was usually made at Cape Town, which had been a strategic port for commerce between the East and the West for 300 years or more.

Leaving Cape Town, an offing was made to pick up the westerlies, after which the tall ships roared on down across the Indian Ocean to Australia. Amsterdam and St. Paul were about halfway across. These

French-owned rocks were a haven for whalers and sealers and for shipwrecked sailors.

Cape Leeuwin is actually not the southernmost tip of Australia. West Cape Howe is in a higher latitude. But Leeuwin was usually the first landfall after the long Indian Ocean passage. Ships went into Perth, or on around to Adelaide or Melbourne, passing through Bass Strait. From Australia, the fast ships sailed across the Tasman Sea, south of New Zealand's South Island, and thence eastward just north of the Antarctic ice, and around the Horn to the Falklands.

Actually an island, called "Horn Island," Cape Horn is like the broken tip of a spear thrust at the solid ice of the Antarctic. It is one of a maze of islands in the Tierra del Fuego region. Between the Horn and Palmerland, there is a wild bit of water called Drake Passage, where the ocean is relatively shallow and subject to sudden changes; where enormous swells rolling eastward with a fetch of thousands of miles meet opposing currents and build up into vicious confused seas. Even in the summer season of November, December, and January, it is a cold forbidding place with fog, rain, snow, and changeable winds. In the winter season, as the old sailors knew, it was sheer hell. In these months, few ships tried to go from east to west around.

A Dutch ship, the *Eendracht*, which sailed from Hoorn, Holland in 1615, with a supporting vessel, the *Hoorn*, was the first recorded ship to sail from the Atlantic to the Pacific below Horn Island. The two ships belonged to a company which hoped to compete with the Dutch East India Company by finding a new route.

The *Hoorn* was accidentally lost on the Patagonia coast, but the *Eendracht*, carrying the whole party, continued down and around, passing through the strait they named for the head of the company, Isaac Le Maire, sailing from the latitude of the Strait of Magellan to the opposite entrance, in twenty-seven days. The ship continued on to Juan Fernández and then to the Dutch East Indies where the ship was confiscated by authorities. The Smeetons, centuries later, made the same passage in twenty-six days.

Sir Francis Drake, on his foray into the Pacific a quarter century earlier, had seen this passage, but had not doubled the Horn. He had gone through the strait, then been blown east in a storm, before recovering and continuing up the Pacific—an episode repeated by Captain Joshua Slocum on the *Spray* centuries later. But it was Drake who determined there was a passage here.

During the next 350 years, the Horn passage became the standard route of the sailing ships of all maritime nations bound on expeditions of exploration, commerce, privateering, and whaling. Among the earliest were the sealers who poked into Antarctic waters, including the 17-year-old master of the 47-foot *Hero* out of Stonington, Connecticut, Nat Palmer, who in November 1820 claimed to have discovered the Antarctic continent. This was the route of the Yankee whalers, the China clippers, and the scientific ships such as H. M. S. *Beagle,* which carried the young naturalist, Charles Darwin. The first trading ships to California and the Northwest coast for hides, tallow, and furs took this route, as did the earliest gold seekers. When steam propelled vessels became practical, they invariably took the Magellan Strait passage, instead of rounding the Horn.

Slocum, during his passage through the strait in the middle 1890s, reported on the frequent steamer traffic, and on graffiti left on the rock cliffs along the way by passing ships that had to anchor frequently on account of adverse currents and violent williwaws.

With the settlement of Australia, New Zealand, and the Pacific Islands came the great wool and grain windjammers from England down the Atlantic, around Good Hope, roaring across the Indian Ocean and south of Leeuwin to Sydney and Melbourne. Other tall ships, such as the one Irving Johnson sailed on as a boy, departed Hamburg, sailed down and around the Horn and up to Chile and Peru for cargoes of nitrates.

All this activity in the Roaring Forties nearly came to an end with the opening of the Suez Canal, and later the Panama Canal, along with the modern steam and motorship. Only a few windjammers continued to haul grain, wool, and nitrates. For years these southern waters were left to the anonymous whaling and scientific voyages, and the occasional unrecorded lone adventurer such as J. M. Crenston, who sailed the 40-foot cutter *Tocca* from New Bedford to San Francisco in 1849, a voyage of 13,000 miles in 226 days. After Slocum, who did not double the Horn, came George Blyth and Peter Arapakis of Australia on *Pandora,* a copy of the *Spray.* Sailing east-about, they rounded the Horn on January 16, 1911, in a violent storm that rolled them over and dismasted the vessel.

The first known yachtsman to circumnavigate via all three capes was the puckish Irishman, Conor O'Brien, on *Saoirse* in 1923–1925, east-about, making the whole adventure sound like a piece of cake.

Al Hansen, on the 36-foot Norwegian *Mary Jane,* called at Buenos

Aires in the early 1930s, visited with Vito Dumas, and then departed in midwinter to double the Horn, alone except for a cat and dog. They reached Ancud, Chile, safely in 100 days, but later were wrecked and lost.

In the early part of World War II, Vito Dumas, a restless middle-aged Argentine of Italian ancestry, departed on *Legh II* for a circumnavigation via the three capes in the Roaring Forties, becoming the first to do so singlehanded and in these high latitudes.

He was followed by the great Australian singlehander, Bill Nance, one of the boldest and most competent, but least-known circumnavigators, on the tiny 25-foot *Cardinal Vertue*, in 1963–1965.

The 1960s saw a spurt of sailing voyages along the old clipper route, including Bernard Moitessier's dual circumnavigation and the ventures of Francis Chichester and Alec Rose, all climaxed by the *Sunday Times* Golden Globe Race which saw Robin Knox-Johnston make the first solo nonstop circumnavigation south of the capes, and the first trimaran circumnavigation, by Commander Tetley. It also saw Bill King capsize off Good Hope. (On a later voyage he was to be attacked by a whale off Leeuwin.)

In 1966, the Griffiths on the 52-foot ferro-cement *Awahnee II*, did it on their second circumnavigation (and on a third circumnavigation in 1971, circled the Antarctic in the Screaming Sixties).

Since 1967, all circumnavigations have had to double the Cape of Good Hope (Agulhas), with the Suez Canal closed. There would seem to be no good reason remaining for challenging the violent and unfriendly tip of South America. But this region has always held a fascination for yachtsmen and explorers. The famed artist, Rockwell Kent, with a companion bought a converted lifeboat in Punta Arenas and sailed among the islands and passages for weeks in the 1920s. The Griffiths, after rounding the Horn in a snow squall, turned into Beagle Channel and passed Edward Allcard's *Sea Wanderer* on the way. The Smeetons made two attempts at the Horn in the 1950s and capsized both times. A third attempt in the 1960s, west-about, was successful. The three Australians, Des Kearns, Andy Whall, and Bill Nance's brother, Bob (who was also with the Smeetons on their last voyage) did it from west to east, by ducking into the channels at times for safety. Bill Watson, on a voyage with *Freedom* from New Zealand, driven into the Horn by a southwest gale, took refuge in a cove in the lee of Horn Island, after having all but abandoned himself and his 40-foot vessel to the gods. The following year, he explored Horn Island in a canoe.

Warwick Tompkins sailed with his family in the 85-foot pilot schooner *Wanderbird* from 50°S to 50°S in 28 days back in 1936. Major H. W. Tilman, the mountain climber and explorer, in the cutter *Mischief*, explored all the Patagonia channels, and even sailed down to the Shetlands and Antarctica, wherever his curiosity drove him. In the early 1950s, Marcel Bardiaux doubled the Horn in midwinter, after twice capsizing, then found shelter inside before continuing on up the Chilean coast. In the middle 1960s, Dr. David Lewis and his family, aboard the catamaran *Rehu Moana*, spent six weeks among the channels of Patagonia, then followed Bardiaux's route up the Chilean coast. It was Lewis's former yacht, *Cardinal Vertue*, incidentally, that carried Bill Nance on his solo circumnavigation via the capes.

Even the famed South Africa racing yacht, *Stormvogel*, a light-displacement 73-footer, on her way to a race in 1967, on New Year's Eve rounded the Horn from west to east and landed on Horn Island for some sunbathing. She then rounded it from east to west, in order to claim she had doubled the Horn twice. The second time, she ran into a violent southwest gale and had to fight her way to safety in the channels.

Nowadays, the region is a busy place. Punta Arenas is a city of 25,000 or more. Even remote Ushuaia has three or four thousand people, as does Port William. The Argentine and Chilean navies have charted and patrol these waters regularly. There is much traffic between the mainland and the Antarctic Peninsula where permanent scientific stations are located. The islands of Patagonia are also well-settled with sheep and cattle raisers of many nationalities. Fishing fleets, which now range the world's oceans for their catches, frequent the region. The giant super-tankers which cannot use the canals, must now take the southern routes again.

Like Leeuwin and Good Hope, civilization has come to Cape Horn, and instead of the terror of the sailing vessel and the circumnavigator, it has become just another yachting region.

John and Maureen Guzzwell aboard *Trekka*. (John Guzzwell)

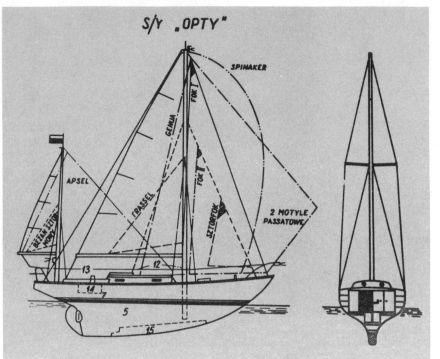

Opty's profile and sail plan. (The Slocum Society)

Leonid Teliga aboard *Opty* in Poland before departing on his circumnavigation. (The Slocum Society)

One of the few stamps issued in honor of a circumnavigator, this one for Leonid Teliga. (The Slocum Society)

Dr. David Lewis in *Icebird* at the start of his circumnavigation around Antarctica from Sydney, Australia, and return. (By courtesy of the Sydney *Morning Herald*)

Dr. David Lewis prior to his attempted circumnavigation of the Antarctic continent in *Icebird*. (*The Australian*, Nationwide News Pty. Ltd.)

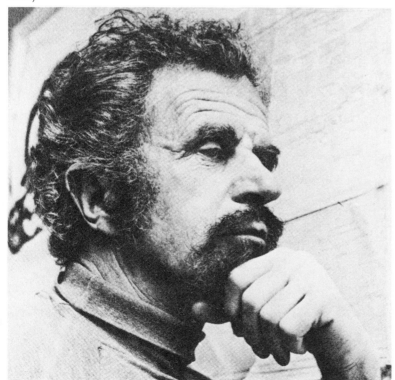

A meeting of famous bluewater voyagers on Rollo Gebhard's arrival at Cuxhaven. Left to right, John Adam, Gebhard, Hannes Lindeman, Claus Hehner. (The Slocum Society)

Rollo Gebhard aboard *Solveig III* on his circumnavigation. (The Slocum Society)

The crude but effective sea anchor used by Bill Murnan on *Seven Seas*. (The Slocum Society)

The crew of the *Cetacean*: Clark and Meta Bathol (left), and Dennis Fontany. (The Slocum Society)

Skipper Quen Cultra shoots the sun with his $15 plastic sexton aboard the *Queequeg*. (Quen Cultra, courtesy of *Popular Mechanics*)

Annie and Louis Van de Wiele aboard *Omoo*. (Annie Van de Wiele, *The West in My Eyes*)

Omoo hauled out at Cape Town at the Royal Cape Yacht Club for bottom painting. (Annie Van de Wiele, *The West in My Eyes*)

Omoo under sail. (Annie Van de Wiele)

Around the world in a 12-foot sloop! Shown here is the *Sea Egg* leaving San Diego on another leg of a circumnavigation by Englishman John Riving. In the summer of 1973, the 33-year-old Riving was reported missing somewhere between Auckland, New Zealand, and Sydney, Australia. He failed to appear after a planned 66-day passage. (Vern Griffin, in *American Boating*)

Six-foot, four-inch John Riving, the English circumnavigator, aboard his 12-foot sloop, the *Sea Egg*, off Point Loma, California, beginning the Pacific leg of his voyage. The tiny craft makes between two and three knots under sail. (Vern Griffin, San Diego *Tribune*)

A most unusual gathering of circumnavigators, on the occasion of the publication of the French edition of Chichester's *Gipsy Moth Circles the Earth*. Seated (left to right): Marcel Bardiaux; Guy Tabarly (father of Eric); Sir Francis and Lady Chichester; and Françoise Moitessier, the first woman to round Cape Horn on a yacht. Standing (left to right): Alain Gliksman, editor of *Neptune Nautisme* and singlehanded sailor; Alain Hervé and Madame Hervé; Pierre Auboiroux, who made a singlehanded circumnavigation in 1965–1966; Louis Bourdens and Madame Bourdens; Bernard Moitessier; Annie Van de Wiele; Joan de Kat; Jean Michel Barrault; publisher Jacques Arthaud; Louis Van de Wiele; Alain Bombard; Dr. Stern-Veyrin; Madame le Serrec. Also present but not in photo: Maria Marie and Pierre Rombach. (The Slocum Society)

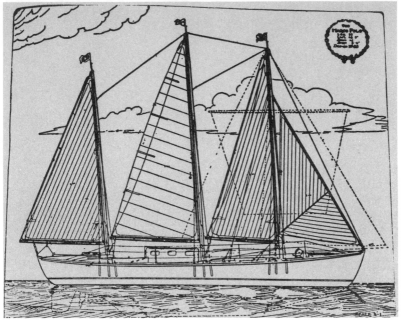

L. Francis Herreshoff's famed *Marco Polo*, a 55-foot three-masted schooner designed expressly for round-the-world voyages with small crews. The ingenious sail plan can be handled by one man on watch. The lifeboat hull model is non-capsizable and unsinkable. Note the squaresail arrangement on the foremast for running in the trade belt. Designed in 1946 and published in *Rudder*, for some reason it did not catch on. (Reprinted with permission of *Rudder* magazine, copyright, Fawcett Publications, 1946)

A practical and efficient sea anchor designed by Harry Newton Scott. It consists of (for a 56-foot boat) a 7-foot by 7-foot piece of strong canvas, with a 6-inch hole in the center, attached to a wood spar on top and an iron pipe below. For a 42-foot boat, a 4-foot square canvas with a 4-inch hole would suffice. (The Slocum Society)

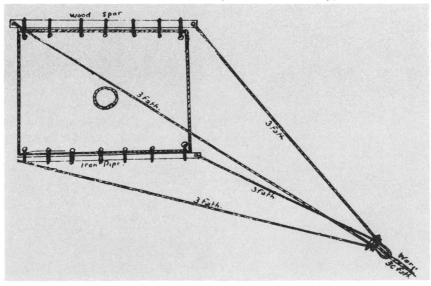

SUHAILI

JOSHUA

CAPTAIN BROWNE

GALWAY BLAZER II

VICTRESS

ELECTRON V

Examples of different boats entered in the Golden Globe Round the
World Race. (The Slocum Society)

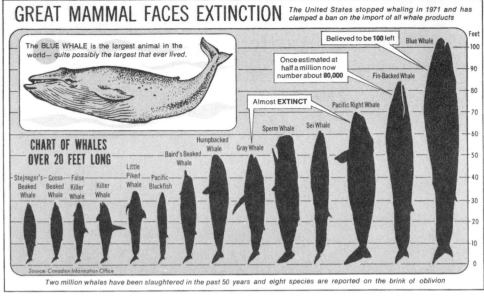

Chart of present status of world's whale population. (Canadian Information Office)

The *Tahiti* ketch, showing her salty lines and trim, well-balanced sail plan. (The Slocum Society)

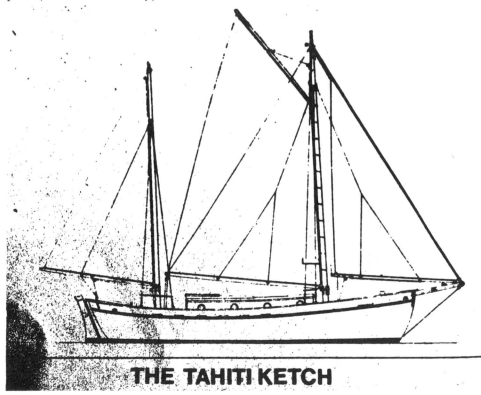

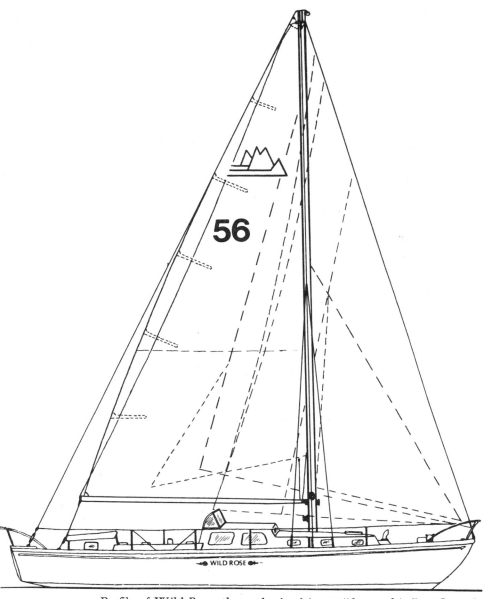

Profile of *Wild Rose*, the author's ultimate "dream ship," a Cascade 42 sloop, designed by Robert A. Smith of Portland, Oregon, and manufactured as a kit by Yacht Constructors Inc., Portland, Oregon. (Art by Don Holm)

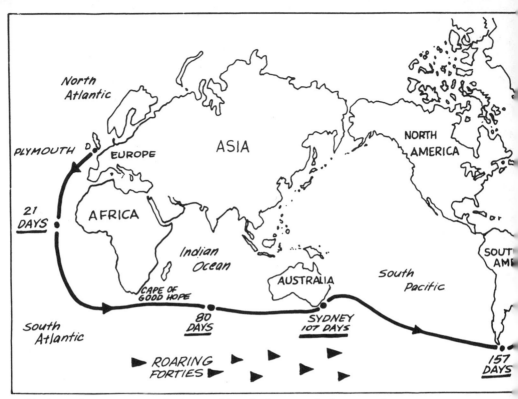

Chichester's route around the world, which started the east-about races along the old wool and grain clipper route. (Art by E. Bruce Dauner)

The southernmost tip of the South American continent. From an H. O. navigation chart, showing Cape Horn, the Strait of Magellan, and adjacent areas. Depths are in fathoms, land elevations in feet. (U.S. Naval Oceanographic Office)

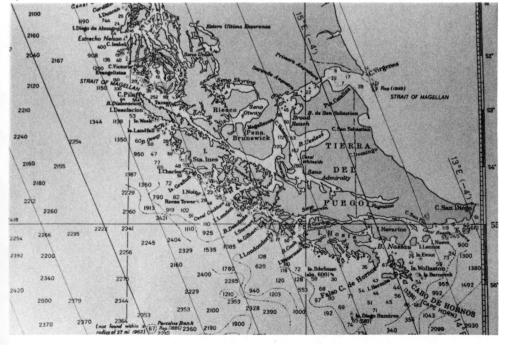

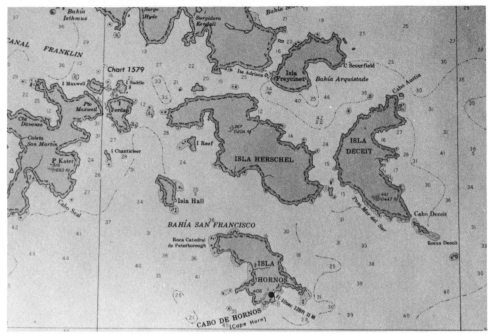

Navigation chart of the fabled Cape Horn, which is in reality an island—*Isla Hornos* or Horn Island. Depths shown are in fathoms, elevation of land areas in feet. (U.S. Naval Oceanographic Office)

The tricky Torres Strait area passage between Australia and New Guinea. Note the reef-studded waters and shallow depths. This was the route of Captain Slocum, Pidgeon, and many circumnavigators who followed them. (U.S. Naval Oceanographic Office)

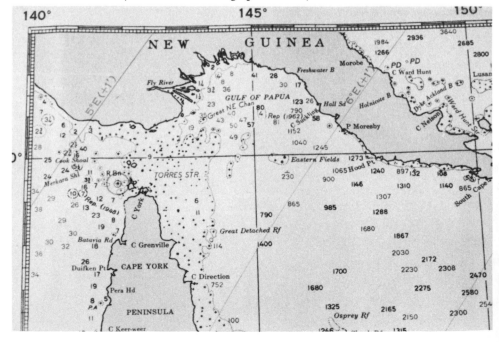

The Anatomy

of a Dream Boat

To face the elements is, to be sure, no light
matter when the sea is in its grandest mood.
You must then know the sea, and know that
you know it, and not forget that it was made
to be sailed over.

CAPTAIN JOSHUA SLOCUM

WHAT IS THE IDEAL YACHT IN WHICH TO MAKE LONG passages on the oceans of the world in comfort and safety, with speed and economy, within the reach of serious dreamers?

In this book we have seen that almost every possible size and type of floating device has not only crossed oceans, but also circumnavigated the globe. They have ranged from canoes and rafts to amphibious Jeeps; from lovely little 20-foot sloops to luxurious 100-foot brigantines. They have been motorless sailboats and sailless motorboats; and auxiliary-rigged craft of every description. They have been cutters, sloops, ketches, yawls, wishbone ketches, square-riggers and morphodite brigs. They have been monohulled, catamaran, and trimaran. They have been deep-displacement, light-displacement, and planing hulls. They have had long keels, short keels, fin keels, and centerboard keels. They have been built of wood, fiberglass, steel, aluminum, and even concrete. One at least was hollowed out of a giant cedar log. They have been, when they began their voyage, a century old, and a few weeks old. They have been manned by one person, and as many as twenty-five. Their cost has ranged from as little as $500 to more than a quarter million dollars.

In short, one can only conclude—even at the risk of being a male chauvinist—that a boat is truly like a woman. And what is one man's wine, woman, or bluewater yacht, is another man's poison, bitch, or derelict.

The first consideration, of course, is seaworthiness. Howard I. Chapelle in *American Small Sailing Craft* (New York: W. W. Norton & Co., Inc., 1951), summed it up masterfully:

"No known boat (of less than 40 feet on deck), can be considered *wholly* safe in heavy weather, for there are conditions of sea and wind that will overwhelm even the best surfboats and lifeboats. Fortunately, such conditions are relatively rare and, with forethought, can usually be avoided by small-boat sailors. (Also) a good boat is no more seaworthy than her crew—in other words, skill of handling is a part of seaworthiness in small craft . . .

"For the beginner, or relatively inexperienced sailor, to venture out into a heavy sea and wind in any small boat is folly that invites disaster."

Chapelle's advice has been proved sound time after time in the hundred or more voyages that were analyzed for this book, and in the dozens more that were researched but not used.

Conor O'Brien wrote that his ideal vessel would be 48 feet on the waterline and 12 feet in beam, with proportions for beam to length decreasing to about 33 percent for a 38-foot waterline vessel. Below that size, he said, he would keep to short passages of not more than a week or so.

Patrick Elam and Colin Mudie, who sailed *Sopranino*, which was only 17 feet 6 inches on the waterline, on some astonishing ocean passages, considered her an extremely efficient sea boat in every way—in fact, "one of the safest vessels of any kind that has ever floated on the ocean."

Elam hastened to add, in *Two Against the Western Ocean*, "I would not pretend that *Sopranino* is the optimum size. At sea she is near perfect, but could with advantage be a few inches longer to give a slightly bigger cockpit and a separate stowage for wet oilskins below. In harbor, she is too small (for comfort). In harbor she is too delicate and vulnerable."

He recommended a larger *Sopranino*, about four feet longer. It will be remembered that when John Guzzwell asked Jack Giles for the smallest practical yacht to sail around the world, Giles came up with *Trekka*, which was about two feet longer—and it circumnavigated *twice*. Colin Mudie, incidentally, a Giles associate, went on to become a famed yacht designer and innovator in his own right.

It was Bernard Moitessier, who was more a sea creature than alien man who sailed over the seas, in his first book recommended a 30-footer as ideal, but when it came to building his own dream ship, it had stretched to 38 feet. He noted later than even the most salty bluewater sailors seldom make passages of more than a few weeks. The rest of the time is spent in harbor or anchored. In a world cruise of four or five years even, seldom more than 10 to 12 months are spent at sea.

"The majority of long-cruise sailors will agree that at sea a boat can never be too big."

The idea that size has handling limits has been disproved many times. Bernicot sailed alone in his 42-foot *Anahita*. The Van de Wieles circumnavigated in *Omoo*, which could easily be handled by one person and was unattended much of the time. Chay Blyth raced around the world alone the "wrong way" in *British Steel*, a sleek modern 59-foot yawl.

Even the Hiscocks, who preferred small ships and twice circumnavigated in the 30-foot *Wanderer III*, in the end grew tired of cramped conditions and the vicious roll of a narrow hull, and settled upon the 48-foot *Wanderer IV* for a permanent home.

On the other hand, among modern bluewater voyagers, Hal Roth and his wife, Margaret, summed up their grand design nicely in a 35-foot John Brandlmayr designed Canadian-built Spencer-class fiberglass sloop.

Cost, of course, is a vital factor in making a dream ship come true. Most voyagers are maddeningly vague about how they financed their projects. Many of them professed to having been pushed into dropping out of society and into the ideal nomadic life because of financial disaster. Yet somehow out of this major disaster, they would have us believe, a genie appeared out of a bottle with the bread needed for their escape ship. A casual glance at the boat ads in the yachting magazines indicates that it takes a minimum of $15,000 to even talk bluewater boat.

Slocum was probably responsible for the image of a cheap boat. When he was "cast up from old ocean," he was given a ship by his friend, Captain Eben Pierce. It turned out to be an old derelict oysterman which he rebuilt himself for a cash outlay of $553.62 in thirteen months. Harry Pidgeon perpetuated this myth with his *Islander*, which took eighteen months of his labor and a thousand dollars cash. Robinson's *Svaap*, a beautiful little Alden ketch, cost him about $2,000 even in the booming 1920s. Dwight Long, on the opposite coast, acquired *Idle Hour*, which was similar in size and design, for about the same amount at the beginning of the Depression. *Suhaili*, the 32-foot ketch which was first to circumnavigate nonstop singlehanded, cost Robin Knox-Johnston about $12,000 built by native labor in India in the 1950s. Jack London's *Snark* cost $30,000 in 1906. Ray Kauffman's *Hurricane* was built by the Gulf Coast character, Sidoine Krebs, for $2,000, during the depths of the Depression. Chay Blyth's *British Steel* cost that corporation about $100,000, which was charged off to advertising. The debt-ridden contractor, Richard Zantzinger, spent about $20,000 buying and outfitting the *Molly Brown*, a 35-foot modern fiberglass racer-cruiser. The Roths' *Spencer*, about the same size and rig, cost them about $35,000 ultimately. The record so far probably is Eric Tabarly's latest *Pen Duick*. His entry in the Whitbread round-the-world race cost the French navy more than a million and a half dollars. On the other hand, Bardiaux and Le Toumelin both built their dream ships under the noses of the Boche in occupied France during World War II, from materials mostly scrounged.

Anyone seriously planning a dream ship has probably already read everything on the subject he can find. But for anything he has missed, I would recommend the following: the books of Bernard Moitessier, which go into minute detail on the practical aspects; the books of Eric Hiscock, which are precise and accurate and carefully thought out; the aforementioned *American Small Sailing Craft*; the books of William A. Robinson, a man whose experience and skill in small craft is matched by his mental capacity: those of Slocum, Pidgeon, and the Crowes; the books of Conor O'Brien (especially the later ones); Frank Wightman's *The Wind Is Free*; Voss's *Voyages*; London's *Snark*; Donald M. Street, Jr.'s *The Ocean Sailing Yacht*; Richard Henderson's books on cruising and sailing; *The Good Little Ship* by Vincent Gilpin; *Sea Quest* by Charles Borden; L. Francis Herreshoff's books on yacht design and cruising; and Alan Eddy's little booklet on sailing around the world in the first fiberglass yacht to do so.

Very few bluewater yachts have been built expressly for that purpose. In most cases, the owner took what he could get, or the most he could afford, and went on from there. This usually resulted in at best a compromise, and at worst a suicidal impulse. It is interesting to note, however, that Frank Wightman, who built the sister ship to Pidgeon's *Islander* from *Rudder* plans (the enlarged *Sea Bird*, also made famous by Thomas Fleming Day and Captain Voss), at a cost of about $1,000, regarded it as a no-compromise boat. A man who refused to compromise his personal principles in order to join the Establishment noted that "you do not compromise with the sea in small yachts. You triumph or you are extinguished. The verities of the sea are few, simple, and austere. *Wylo's* characteristics were buoyancy, and speed before the wind."

There was much nonsense about "comfort" at sea, Wightman also noted. Any small yacht is acutely uncomfortable in heavy weather, and even in mild weather there is no such thing as "ease of motion." Jack London also pointed this out after his experience in *Snark*, which was built to sail around the world in comfort.

In all such research leading up to making a major lifetime decision such as buying or building a dream ship, one should keep in mind that no single source, no one authority, no matter how prestigious, should be regarded as the ultimate—not even the saltiest of the bluewater sailors.

As Don Street pointed out: "Seamanship is seldom really well-learned unless a person has sailed on various boats with various people. Many singlehanders have done all their sailing on their own boats, with no one to point out their errors, and with no exposure to other people's methods. As a result, they have often been doing the same thing wrong—or the hard way—for many years. They drift, as it were, around the world. They think they know how to sail, but often really do not."

The same can be said for yacht designers, yacht builders, yacht brokers, and yachting writers.

When it comes to beating one's own drums, however, there are no more vigorous wielders of the drumsticks than yacht designers themselves. They frequently become so convoluted by their own creative enthusiasm that their opinions are unreliable and often dangerous. It is a natural thing, of course, for a man to praise best his own creations and his own acquisitions, whether it be a design, a piece of creative writing, or a newly acquired wife or automobile. How much of this praise is justifiable pride, and how much of it is justification of argument is difficult to separate.

For example, a more controversial boat has never existed than Slocum's *Spray*. For three-quarters of a century, sailors and designers have been arguing over its merits. The controversy started on the day Slocum disappeared, and burst into flame with the well-known classic analysis of *Spray's* lines in *Rudder* magazine by Cipriano Andrade, Jr., who was first praised and then condemned by none other than John Hanna, who himself had designed a modified *Spray*. Although most thoughtful students today consider Andrade's analysis a little too pat, it is true that most *Spray* detractors today have never even read Slocum's book, and therefore are immediately suspected of not knowing what they are talking about.

On the other hand, no one could rightly say that Howard I. Chapelle knew not what he was talking about. As a young draftsman, he worked for Charles Mower, the great yacht designer who first put *Spray*'s lines on paper for *Rudder*. In a letter to me, he wrote:

> *Slocum's letters are like those of a 4th grader—rather backward at that. He was 60 per cent fine seaman, 10 per cent liar, and 30 per cent showman, I would say. Had a lot of guts. He was going nowhere in no hurry so I suppose he sailed as the boat wanted to go.*
>
> *As I said, no lines were actually taken off* Spray, *so that poor Andrade was victimized by the old fraud, Tom Day, with Charley Mower the fall guy. Had Mower taken off the lines we would have had something to work on— now we have no reliable plans as a basis for analysis. But the whole story of the wonderful abilities of* Spray *is now highly questionable.*

The legendary John Hanna, who in 1923 created perhaps the most famous dream ship that has ever existed—the 30-foot *Tahiti* ketch— called it a vessel suitable for "all oceans and all conditions of sea . . . one that would take you anywhere you wanted to go" in comfort and safety. His choice of a name for his creation was part showmanship, part genius, and self-suggestive—for *Tahiti* was everyman's inspiration and Valhalla in those days. In fact, Hanna's construction notes accompanying the first publication of the lines in the old *Modern Mechanix* were prefaced with:

> *Poke her nose to the mornin' sun.*
> *On a tide that's ebbin' speedy—*
> *Start her sheets to the breeze fresh run*
> *On a slant for old Tahiti.*

What romantic dreamboat dropout could resist an appeal like that?

As John Stephen Doherty wrote of the 30-year old dream boat in the March 1967 issue of *Modern Mechanix*'s successor, *Mechanix*

Illustrated, "In the history of small-boat ocean voyages, no single design ever logged more miles at sea."

Hundreds of *Tahiti*s were built or started, and dozens of them made world cruises—some making dual circumnavigations. But yet, *Tahiti* is not for amateur builders. Skill and patience are needed. In time, figure three to five years depending upon skill and resources. In Hanna's day, the cost of home-building was estimated at about $1,000. Today, $15,000 would be minimum for home-building; $30,000 for a custom job. In early 1974, a 20-year-old *Tahiti* was advertised in a Seattle newspaper for $25,000.

At 20,000 pounds displacement, she is no ocean gazelle. It takes half a gale to drive her, as some had noted. Yet she was not built for speed, but for ocean passages in the Slocum tradition. This was my impression the first time I actually set foot on the deck of a *Tahiti* in San Pedro harbor in 1937. It was like stepping on the deck of a real ship. Even the heavy wakes of passing ferries scarcely ruffled her skirts. One sensed instantly that if any ship could take you to the South Seas, *Tahiti* was the one.

Perhaps when all is said and done, and the current generation of "Tupperware yachts" has passed on, *Tahiti* will still remain the one and only true dream ship.

In the same year that Jack Hanna was creating *Tahiti*, the Irish rebel, Conor O'Brien, was scouring the secondhand bookshops in seaport towns for cruising books and the logs of old sailing vessels from Colonial passage days and the wool and grain trade. As he noted, the cult of the sailing ship had been reborn again then, just as it had every decade or so, and which it has every decade since. The result of his research and personal inclination was *Saoirse*, a ship with a waterline length of 37.5 feet, modeled after an Arklow fishing boat, with a design speed of seven knots, and an average passage-making speed of about five knots. In her, O'Brien became the first to circumnavigate east-about south of the three capes. And he did it with such ease and understatement that it could have misled many who undertook the same passage and failed.

Most world cruisers are designed, of course, for the trade wind belt, circumnavigating from east to west, making use of the canals, running or broad reaching most of the time. O'Brien's reason for going the "wrong way," he said, was because he did not have an engine and was too impatient to wallow in calms frequently found in the middle latitudes.

Besides, he said, "Every passage is in a sense a race, a race against the consumption of stores; and even if one had unlimited stores, it would still be a race against boredom."

"On the whole," he added, "it was worthwhile; there are not so many adventures offering nowadays that one can afford to miss even a modest one." This is 1923!

It will please dream ship *aficionados* to no end to know that as of this writing, *Saoirse* is alive and well and still sailing.

Summed all up, one has to go back to basics: What is the yacht going to be used for? What is the biggest one can afford? Where will it be taken? How much time will be spent at sea, and how much in port or sheltered waters? How many people will live on it?

Today, prospective boat buyers are really in luck, in spite of high costs and material shortages. Largely because of the unprecedented boom in world cruising in the preceding twenty years, and the even greater boom in ocean racing, there have been more advances in boat design than in the previous two thousand years. Up until say a decade ago, the average speed of a boat—as Conor O'Brien pointed out a half century earlier—was only four or five knots on an ocean passage. Today, with a modern hull, you can count on six to eight, and some of the fast ocean racers are now approaching the speed of the old clipper ships which reeled off twenty knots day in and day out. Modern materials have all but eliminated the nagging old problem that voyagers used to have in remote out-of-the-way places where regular bottom maintenance could not be done. Fiberglass, steel, and aluminum, along with greatly improved paints, have simplified routine maintenance.

The same can be said for modern yacht equipment and accessories: light small diesel auxiliaries, dependable electrical sources, transistorized electronics, aluminum spars, synthetic ropes and sails, compact refrigeration units, and even such things as low-cost radar, loran, and automatic direction finders. Today, with a $50 transistor radio you can hold in your hand, you can get the time ticks from WWV and a dozen other signal sources, eliminating the need for an expensive chronometer that needs frequent rating.

As Robinson said in *To the Great Southern Sea*, in spite of the few hardheaded hold-outs, "Sentimentality about sailing without an engine may be left to a few diehards. The question today is what form the auxiliary power should take." Today, a lightweight diesel engine costs little more than a gasoline engine, and if properly maintained, is more dependable and economical to run, with a lower fuel consumption, and infinitely safer to use.

In the December 1973 issues of *Sail* magazine and *Yachting World* the latest study made by the Ocean Cruising Club was released. Membership in occ is worldwide, and is restricted to amateurs who have made passages of a thousand miles or more in vessels of less than 75 feet overall. The study was based on a comprehensive questionnaire returned by 300 members, who were asked to give their opinion on what they considered an ideal ocean cruiser, if they had the opportunity and the resources to build their own dream ship for a typical world voyage which would take them into northern and tropical waters (excluding the high southern latitudes and Arctic waters).

When the questionnaires were analyzed and a composite yacht drawn up by Colin Mudie, the results revealed a significant trend that is still going on, and a decisive departure from previous concepts, during the past decade from 1964 to 1974—the period during which ocean voyaging in small craft has shown the most growth.

The trend shows a swing away from the ketch and yawl and toward the sloop or cutter. A decade ago, occ members dreamed of a 35-foot loa vessel; today they consider the 40-foot range as the ideal (58 percent chose a length of from 29 feet to 40 feet loa). A surprising number—41 percent—chose 40 feet and over as the ideal.

Another surprise was the fuel for cooking. Unlike the old days, modern bluewater yachters chose propane or butane, 52 percent over 31 percent for kerosene (paraffin), and 11 percent for the highly touted alcohol.

Ninety-five percent wanted a single hull vessel, over the catamaran or trimaran. Eighty percent said the draft should be between 5 and 7 feet. Twenty-four percent chose wood for hull construction; 15 percent wanted fiberglass (G.R.P.); 13 percent, foam sandwich; 15 percent, welded steel; 10 percent, welded aluminum; and only 4 percent, ferro-cement.

Ninety-eight percent wanted Terylene (Dacron) sails. Sixty-three percent chose the wheel steering over the tiller. About 76 percent wanted some kind of vane self-steering. Seventy-two percent chose the aft cockpit arrangement. Ninety-four percent wanted a single auxiliary engine on the centerline; and 93 percent wanted it to be diesel. None wanted a motorless sailboat. Most of them, or 70 percent, wanted an auxiliary with a range of from 200 to 800 miles. The greatest percentage wanted electric starting, 12-volt d.c. ship's electrical system, electric refrigeration, electric running lights and navigation systems, and their battery preferences jumped from a single

12-volt battery to a bank of four. The British CQR plow anchor won hands down over the Danforth (the choice of anchors is mainly a nationalistic, political, and emotional one, it seems, for some strange reason). The 360° compass card was chosen over other types. The choice of dinghy changed from the rigid to the inflatable. Sixty percent chose the dry chemical fire extinguisher over the more dangerous CO_2.

Ninety-five percent would take an inflatable dinghy; 91 percent an RDF; 96 percent a depth sounder; 49 percent a high frequency radiophone; 72 percent a spinner log; 49 percent taped stereo music; 26 percent a pressure water system; 67 percent sleeping bags over bedding; and 68 percent a diaphragm type bilge pump over other kinds.

For an earlier definitive study of trends in auxiliary cruisers see the article by Pete Smyth in the October 1972 issue of *Motor Boating & Sailing.*

By happy (and at times unhappy) coincidence, my own dream ship became a reality at about the same time this long book project was drawing to an end; and *before* the results of the occ survey were made public. Compare my final choices (compromises) with the results of the survey:

Yacht *Wild Rose.* Documented No. 546703, 11 net tons.

Length overall	42 feet
Load waterline	34 feet
Beam	11 feet 2 inches
Draft	5 feet 6 inches
Displacement	19,000 pounds

The hull design (by Robert A. Smith of Portland, Oregon), is modern semi-displacement, with a large fin ballast keel, large skeg and rudder, and the modified counter preferred by most occ members. It is sloop-rigged, without bowsprit, with center cockpit and after cabin trunk. Hull construction is of hand-laid fiberglass cloth and woven roving (no mat), marine plywood bulkheads and deck, covered with fiberglass cloth.

The engine is a 4-107 Westerbeke of 37 horsepower, with a Paragon hydraulic reverse gear, a monel shaft and two-bladed fixed prop. Diesel fuel capacity is 184 gallons, giving a theoretical range under power of between 1,000 and 2,000 miles. Cooking is with a modern gimballed propane gas range, with deck storage for the fuel, and flexible high-pressure fuel lines. The engine has two alternators, one for engine use only with its own bank of two high-capacity marine batteries; and an auxiliary 85-amp alternator feeding a bank of three batteries for ship's service. Separate shore-power converters take over the battery load automatically when moored. In addition, there is an alternator-run 115-volt AC unit that will provide 3,600 watts either moored or at sea.

Electronics include a VHF/FM twelve-channel transceiver, a SSB high frequency transceiver, and a battery-portable Zenith Trans-Oceanic all-band receiver. A hand-held Vec/Trak RDF is used for coastal navigation (an amazingly simple and accurate unit). And, because I have been an amateur radio "ham" since high school days, I have the ship equipped with portable VHF/FM in the ham bands; and transistorized SSB all-band transceiver capability in the medium and high frequency ranges, which gives me a theoretical worldwide communications systems. By "patching" in with other hams, I can reach almost any country in the world, from almost any place in the world. Incidentally, yachts equipped with the regular marine VHF/FM units can, through the telephone company marine operators, also reach practically any landline telephone in the world, and of course any other yacht similarly equipped.

Few yachtsmen to date really understand how practical, inexpensive, and effective the new VHF channels are.

Other details of *Wild Rose* include electric refrigeration and a small portable freezer; stainless steel rigging; fiberglass water tanks with filtered supply lines, pressure water system with hot water by dual electric and exhaust-driven elements; electric anchor windlass; a modern solution to the toilet controversy—an electric macerator-chlorinator head with provision for a holding tank later; dual fresh-water and seawater galley supplies; shower bath; hydraulic center cockpit wheel steering; compact vented charcoal and Pres-To-Log fireplaces in main and after cabins; teak trim; and a vinyl enclosed cockpit winter weather shelter. The dinghy is an Avon inflatable.

As can be seen, the essence of my own independent accumulation of experience, research, analysis, personal preferences, expediency, and advice of those better qualified, pretty much followed the general trend—a coincidence that might interest the perceptive market analyst today.

I departed from the general trend in some things, however, for example in the choice of a hollow wooden mast, instead of the popular aluminum spars; and in going back to the old-fashioned slab reefing in preference to modern roller reefing. The main reason was financial. The aluminum job would have cost $2,000 more. For less than $500, I built my own laminated hollow wood stick, which is just as light and has the advantage of being tapered for better weight distribution. Moreover, it has a little give in the way of stress, and simplifies the attachment of cleats, winches, and other accessories. It requires more maintenance, but on the other hand, modern synthetic glues, wood preservatives, and new type paints reduce this to a minimum.

As for roller reefing, it takes two people to properly reef this kind of sail, and the additional mechanism requires special boom and fittings, adding not only to the cost but also to the probability of failure. Slab reefing is not only simpler, and cheaper, but results in a better airfoil. Besides, the new "jiffy reefing" technique makes furling even easier.

With a little thought and planning, I was able to reduce the need for so many hand winches, which have become the most costly part of a boat. Why these should be so expensive, I have never been able to understand. On some racers the cost of the winches comes to more than that of the bare hull itself. The use of carefully selected blocks in strategic places eliminates the need for many winches, as well as the "winch apes" for running them. After all, old Slocum and his contemporaries handled much heavier gaff-sail gear alone without these chrome-plated goodies.

Sharp-eyed readers will be quick to ask, then why the extensive use of electronic gadgets? Isn't the purpose of an escape machine to sever communications with the complexities of society? True, but number one, electronics has been a personal hobby of mine since high school days; and number two, since those nostalgic years when I first met *Tahiti*, and especially after the war was over, I never had the urge to "escape," whatever that is. Somewhere down the years, early attitudes changed and with maturity came different perspectives. As Edward Allcard noted, anyone who can't come to grips with society, can't adjust to the world around him no matter where he is. The human is a herd animal by nature, not a lone wolf. Dropping out is little more than passing the buck of collective responsibility onto someone else, while still sharing the accrued benefits of society. The exception, of course, is the retiree, who has spent his life working and saving, with his rewards to accumulate for later enjoyment—if he lives to enjoy them.

The story of *Wild Rose*, then, really began in the middle 1930s on the blizzard-swept prairies of North Dakota, about as far from salt water as you can get. And it began with Hanna's *Tahiti*, published in the 1935 edition of *How To Build 20 Boats* (New York: Fawcett Publications, Inc.), as it did for thousands of the restless kids of the period. I still have the original plans, and in the intervening years they were carried all through the war and all over the world. Faded and brittle now, with little pieces torn from them and faded pencil notes here and there, they are in a safe place, as a nostalgic keepsake of a generation that was unique in all its aspects, and will never happen again.

Along with these plans, there is a crumbling old catalogue from Bay City Boats of Bay City, Michigan, which sold prefabricated dream boats, one of which was *Tahiti*. In those days you could buy the frame and planking kit for about $1,000, all ready for reassembly. As noted, *Tahiti* was not really a boat for amateur building, in spite of Hanna's inspiring prose. In the late 1930s, then in Juneau, Alaska, I had worked up through several boats to a *Tahiti*, and saved enough money from gold mining and commercial fishing to buy the kit. I had rented space in a waterfront shop and engaged a boatbuilder to help put the parts together. Then came World War II.

After the war came readjustments, college, family, career, and all the pressures and crises of a more sophisticated and changing world. Not until I was within sight of retirement age did the opportunities and possibilities of fulfilling an old dream put new spice into what had tended to become a lusterless life of quiet desperation. At the same time had come more maturity, changes in objectives, different tastes and requirements. I had never had any special desire to sail around the world *per se*; but had always held the view that any yacht in which one invested so much money should be *capable* of going anywhere.

And, since those first dreamy wintry days in 1935, I had never had any desire to sail off to romantic South Sea islands—even before the war in which millions of us got a free ride to many of these same places. The islands left me for years with the impression of being pest-holes full of insects, tainted food, alcoholics, and a general slothfulness that perhaps offended my Anglo-Saxon origins.

Down through the years, my old dream faded away, only to reappear from time to time. There was a succession of lesser boats, and a continuing interest in the sea and in developments in cruising and racing. It became a relaxing diversion in times of stress, and as the files of research grew, I also acquired building plans and specifications for a number of what I considered ideal dream ships.

These included, as a matter of interest to others, Slocum's *Spray* model, the *Rudder*'s enlarged *Sea Bird* or *Islander*, Hanna's *Tahiti* and the larger *Carol* ketch, a design or two from the prestigious Sparkman & Stephens, a Tom Colvin junk-rigged cruiser, and L. Francis Herreshoff's famous *Marco Polo*. The latter I consider the finest world cruiser ever designed. Unfortunately, most of the yachts built from these plans were altered by the builders for aesthetic reasons and thereby the original concept was destroyed. In conversations with the old master himself at "The Castle" prior to his death, I gathered that *Marco Polo* was one of his favorite "babies," and it disappointed him that it had not achieved more acceptance.

Appearing in a *Rudder* series in 1945, *Marco Polo* embodied almost everything that our by-now war-weary and disillusioned generation longed for, in a world cruiser. Fifty-five feet in overall length, with a lean 10-foot beam and a 5-foot draft, she was based on the whaleboat model. Rigged as a three-masted schooner, one man on watch could easily handle all the sails. On the foremast, she carried a square sail for running down the trades. For the doldrums, and for running up exotic rivers, she was diesel-engine powered and capable of making up to 12 knots, with a fuel capacity for runs up to 4,000 miles under auxiliary alone. The extra fuel capacity also provided for possible oil burning cooking and heating facilities, as well as the ability to purchase oil in bulk quantities for as little as 10 cents a gallon then.

She was cut-away forward and aft in just the proper proportions for heaving-to, running before a gale, or fetching up to a sea anchor or drogue. She also incorporated the spade rudder with a 150° one for maneuverability and for lashing down to take the strain off the blade when making leeway. Everything about *Marco Polo* showed the genius of Herreshoff in distinctive relief. In a dozen different ways she was far ahead of her time.

She was then, and still is, the one bluewater displacement yacht that can consistently make 200-mile-plus noon-to-noon runs in all but the worst weather. Considering that most ocean voyagers seldom average more than five knots, this is indeed remarkable.

Unfortunately, *Marco Polo* was a little too "radical" for the fickle consumer market. Average blokes reacted nervously to the three masts, even though they simplified the overall rig; they did not like the narrow 10-foot beam, although the length gave the vessel an unusual roominess; they were afraid of the spade rudder, although this is now almost standard on racing craft; and perhaps the double-ended whaleboat model was not as aesthetically pleasing as the modern yacht club type reverse-canted transoms, even though the vessel was designed to be incapable of capsizing or being over-whelmed when running or lying ahull.

Marco Polo was my first choice, and still is; however, I had neither the time nor the space convenient for building her, and with wood becoming more difficult, it was not practical in my circumstances. For reasons of financing, convenience, and ultimate maintenance, I finally selected fiberglass or G.R.P. as the basic mode, after long consideration of sandblasted and zinced steel, aluminum, and even ferro-cement. Once this was decided, I began a search for a hull I could live with, in kit form, which I could complete myself in a convenient place, either in or near the water.

During this time, a fascinating correspondence with veteran de-signer Weston Farmer, who entertained secret ambitions of building John Hanna's version of Slocum's *Spray* out of aluminum, led me to buying a set of *Foam II* plans from Hanna's widow, Dorothy, in Dunedin, Florida. I also had some interesting correspondence and long distance telephone conversations with Tom Colvin, whose steel junk-rigged 42-footer I admired much and almost went for. Joe Koelbel, consulting designer for *Rudder* magazine, also offered some valuable comments during this period on building Herreshoff's *Marco Polo*. At one point, I even considered having my friend and Portland boatbuilder, Jim Staley, a wizard with plywood, build me a copy of *Rudder's Seagoer*, the 34-foot version of *Sea Bird*, designed by Frederick W. Goeller, Jr., which became Harry Pidgeon's *Islander*.

All of which shows the mental gymnastics and the sweet sensual pleasures (and agonizing conception) that one goes through getting married to a dream boat. At one point, it all led me to buying an armload of one-dollar offset tables from Howard Chapelle's collection at the Smithsonian, in a short-lived impulse to find my dream in the traditional old Atlantic fishing boats. In the end, I often wished for the simplicity of Erskine Childer's *Dulcibella*, in the *Riddle of the Sands*.

I was later to understand that the fun is in the search, the anticipa-tion, the exquisite expectation, not in the finding. It is like being on the prowl for a mate, on the stalk for a prey. Everything that comes later is anti-climactic. I inspected dozens of brands and types, trav-eled hundreds of miles, covered the yacht harbors of half a dozen centers. California is a major fiberglass boatbuilding region. One of the largest firms in Southern Cal offered several models I liked, at what seemed the lowest prices. Investigation, however, showed the hulls to be of marginal construction. But what really turned me off were the company's terms, printed on the order blank, which offered "15 minutes of consultation time" with each hull purchase. It took less than 15 minutes to decide they could keep their hull along with their consultation.

But one model intrigued me—the 32-foot fiberglass version of the *Tahiti*, custom-molded in Carpenteria, a pleasant little seacoast town south of Santa Barbara. I went down there, looked over the sample, and was greatly impressed. Workmanship was excellent, and the mold was said to have come off Tom Steele's *Adios*, which had twice circumnavigated the world. Even the relief of the original planking was molded into the outer skin, with salty, pleasing effect.

In the end, for several reasons, I reluctantly passed this up. Ultimately, I chose a *Cascade 42* sloop, designed by Robert A. Smith and built within thirty miles of my home. This was also one of the first possibilities I had looked into, so now I had come a full circle, arriving back home.

About 250 *Cascades*, in the 29-foot, 36-foot, and 42-foot lengths, had been molded and sold by this time. They were well-built, by hand, of stout construction that used no mat in the lay-up. They were sailing in all parts of the world. Jerry Cartwright had sailed a 29-footer in the Singlehanded Trans-Pacific Race sponsored by the Slocum Society; a number of them had been entered in the Victoria–Maui and the Los Angeles–Honolulu races with fair showings. Still others had been proved on long ocean voyages, including several that had sailed around the world.

The *Cascades* were the second generation of yacht designs produced by a partnership of three local yachtsmen. Back in the 1950s, five yacht club members had pooled their resources and commissioned Robert A. Smith to design for them a 34-foot fiberglass auxiliary. They then incorporated, built a temporary shop and a mold, and pitched in to turn out five hulls. After all five hulls were completed, they drew lots to see who got which ones. It was a successful venture, and all five *Chinooks* are still sailing.

After the project was completed, it seemed a shame to dispose of the facilities, so three of the five went together and formed a company to produce more hulls for sale. Several hundred *Chinooks* were sold before the design was replaced by the more modern *Cascade* line. Of the three original incorporators, one of them worked full-time and ran the shop. The other two kept their regular jobs and worked part-time. I will call them Tom, Dick, and Harry. Tom ran the shop, Dick taught at a nearby university, and Harry was an executive in a manufacturing plant building heavy equipment. All of them were easy-going, cooperative, and took a personal interest in their customers. But of the three, Harry was hands down the workhorse, and over the years, since their shares depended upon how much they put into the firm individually, Harry wound up with a controlling interest and became president.

After the customary deliberation, consultation, and cross-examination of the partners on commitments and prices, I put down an initial $100 for a set of plans for the 42-foot model. At that time I was still undecided between the 42 and the 36, a more popular selling model. I was scheduled to take a long trip to Alaska, the Aleutians and Bering Sea, and down to the Hawaiian Islands, so I took the plans along with the idea of reviewing the whole thing en route and making a decision when I returned.

The decision was that the 42 was the minimum size I could get by with, and so I made a $500 deposit and got on the list for the first available hull, which I anticipated would be ready sometime in January the coming year. The full price for the hull alone, with chain plates molded in, shaft log and deck stringers, was $4,950. For a nominal amount I could also order the floors, keelson, main bulkheads, deck beams, molded freshwater tank, and molded shower and toilet room installed. Altogether, I estimated very carefully, the hull could be completed ready for engine and equipment, for about $12,000, a figure which I could easily afford.

It was at that point, after I was committed too far to back out, that the trap was sprung—a story as old as unrequited love itself.

Not even such experienced and level-headed voyagers as Eric Hiscock and Miles Smeeton have escaped the ecstasy, frustration, depression, elation, disillusionment, and financial difficulties involved in acquiring the ultimate retirement boat. In Miles and Beryl Smeeton's case, it was a matter of a robust adventurous couple, retired from the wars on a stump farm in Canada with all their money tied up in England during the sterling freeze. They had previously owned a small outboard boat in which they commuted from Salt Spring Island to the mainland, and had gotten to know some of the yachties in the area. Thus they conceived the plan of going to England, using their impounded funds for buying a yacht, sailing it back to British Columbia and selling it for a profit. How they did this, and their subsequent acquisition of *Tzu Hang* and their misadventures learning to sail her, were finally related in Smeeton's last book, *The Sea Was Our Village*, a tale that will startle Smeeton fans who perhaps had the impression that this famous couple had been born to the breezes like Slocum. The Smeetons, incidentally, were the prototypes of Nevil Shute's couple in *Trustee From the Tool Room*, who tried to smuggle their savings out in the form of diamonds imbedded in the cement ballast.

In the case of the Hiscocks, perhaps history's most famous voyaging couple, who had behind them decades of experience in world cruising and had written several books that became standard texts, it would seem that when they ordered built *Wanderer IV*, their retirement boat, everything would progress smoothly. Not so. The aches and pains, disappointments, builder deceits and poor workmanship, misfit equipment, cruddy accessories, overcharges and broken promises so paralleled my own experiences, that comparing notes later I could shake my head ruefully and laugh with tears streaming down my cheeks. And it really ain't that funny.

Readers who like to suffer vicariously can follow the Hiscocks' thorny wake to Holland during the building of *Wanderer IV*, from there to England for refitting, and then on to America and New Zealand, in their last and one of their most charming books, *Sou'-West in Wanderer IV*.

Their experiences, and mine, proved to me once more that the only way to beat the system is to be your own builder, or to do it at the taxpayers' expense, or to write it off as a business venture. Looking back over years of research, I find very few besides Slocum, Pidgeon, Trobridge, and Colvin who have done it. One of the few also would be William A. Robinson, who owned a shipyard when World War II broke out. With the help of the legendary Starling Burgess and L. Francis Herreshoff, he worked out the design of *Varua*, possibly the most beautiful and efficient yacht ever built, and put it together in a back corner of his yard with professional artisans as expansion began for defense work, presumably charging it off to research and engineering. When the war ended, he was ready to drop the tools, close the yard, and retire to Tahiti with his well-earned millions.

It has been only recently that I have reread Jack London's *Cruise of the Snark*, and his experiences with boatbuilding sharpies. I had forgotten how similar our lives were, although we lived in different periods. London earned his living, after a harsh boyhood struggle, by writing; so did I. He had done much of his early sailing in Alaskan and Bering Sea waters; so had I. Our marital histories were similar, as were our basic personalities. In later years he made the decision to build his dream ship, before it was too late; so did I. His method of financing it, like mine, was by spending most of the time one would normally devote to home-building, in writing to raise extra money to pay professionals to do the hard part. Like London, I also worked on the boat doing less exacting jobs in my "spare" time, and undertook to do all the finishing myself.

London had estimated his probable cost at $7,000 in 1906; the *Snark* cost more than $30,000 and was uncompleted inside when they departed San Francisco for the South Pacific. I had estimated $12,000 in 1972; the project ultimately came closer to $50,000 with still plenty of work to do inside. Of the difference, I would estimate that $10,000 was labor padding and inflated charges on equipment. The rest was the result of my own inexperience, misjudgment, and inability to estimate costs realistically. Afterwards, I knew that it would have been cheaper to have purchased a stock boat from a production builder. Or I could have saved half the cost by shopping carefully for a used vessel at one of the many yachting centers in Florida, California, the Eastern Seaboard, Panama, or Hawaii.

But I didn't.

Walter Magnes Teller, Slocum's principal biographer, claimed London built *Snark* at a cost of $30,000 by "cheating contractors," a statement which does Teller no credit. There is not the slightest evidence that London cheated his builders. Indeed, he himself was the victim of perfidious contractors and associates. London later explained the excessive costs. He had contracted to write 30,000 words about the proposed voyage for a magazine at the going rate. As soon as the contract was signed, the magazine began promoting the forthcoming series widely. The publicity created the public impression that the magazine was underwriting the venture, prompting all his contractors and suppliers to inflate their charges as much as 300 percent. Actually, London himself financed the project out of his writings, a commitment that forced him to turn out a thousand words a day, every day before, during, and after the voyage, even at sea during gales and emergency situations and when decked with blackwater fever in New Guinea.

London laid the keel for *Snark* on the morning of the San Francisco Earthquake. The genesis of *Wild Rose* was not quite so earth-shaking. As I learned later, another customer had backed out of his deal for a *Cascade 42*, sloop, leaving the firm with the hull still in the

mold. I had originally wanted a ketch, but was talked out of it in
favor of a sloop. The reason was obvious later. The chain plates have
to be molded into the hull, and differ between the ketch and sloop
configuration. This was the first in a number of subsequent "compromises" that came about primarily for the convenience of the
builders, rather than through the judgment of the owner. Thus, I was
informed to my surprise in October, that "my" hull was already out of
the mold and on the floor, three months ahead of schedule. This
moved up my financial plans to my inconvenience.

But a payment of $3,500 around Christmas brought me up to date
with progress on the hull. I was in good shape and determined to
keep it that way. It was a pleasure doing business with the firm. The
partners and crew were easy to get along with, personally interested
in my boat. My funds had nearly run out, so I asked for a monthly
accounting as long as the boat was in the shop, and ordered no work
done unless I specifically ordered it. It was not, however, until the
following March that I received the next statement, a "partial" one
for $12,000. This was when the bubble burst with a sickening splat-
ter. The established catalog prices for standard parts and equipment
installed had given way to custom labor charges which impressed me
as being miscalculated or padded. For example, there was one labor
charge of $5,000 to which I could relate only the construction of two
bunks in the main cabin.

I thought of all the things I could buy with five grand, besides two
wooden slat bunks with less than $25 worth of materials, which I
could have built myself in less than a week's time.

From then on, I followed the example of another customer, who
refused to pay for any work done when he was not there personally to
supervise it. He camped on the job, sleeping in his trailer, while
working on the boat himself. I decided to do the same thing, but was
told the crew objected to owners working on their boats. I questioned
the crew individually and they denied it. I then threatened to remove
the boat from the shop, and suddenly the objection was removed. It
was the slack period, and mine was the only hull on the floor.

More personal supervision revealed an old and established tradition
in custom shops where craftsmen are paid by the hour, with the
customer charged double the worker's rate to take care of the
overhead and profit. Workers kept record of their time in a ruled
notebook in the shop. Checking entries against my own daily journal,
I found that everyone apparently put down from 30 to 50 percent

more time than actually worked against my hull. This accounted for the high labor costs.

Obviously, the sooner I got my boat out of the shop, the more I would save. I tried to hurry things along, but the work went agonizingly slow, interrupted by other jobs that came in, and delayed by growing material and parts shortages. Instead of a March launching, it now began to look like late May.

Meanwhile, I felt that one reason for the delay was that my hull was being used as a floor demonstrator to sell other prospects. For weeks my boat was subjected to a daily procession of dreamers, curiosity-seekers, cigar-chomping executives, dentists and doctors, bearded hippies, and erstwhile yachties, crawling over, under, and into every compartment, getting in the way, impeding the work of the crew, distracting me with silly or personal questions and insipid remarks. Even more frustrating was the knowledge that the expense of all this was subsidized by me. I felt like a drowning man, gasping his last and reaching out for rescue, which could come only when I finally got the boat out of the shop and away from the vultures.

There were some advantages to the arrangement: The shop had a ready stock of screws, bolts, small parts, and tools, only a few steps away. Moreover, the management and crew were unfailingly ready to show me an easier way of doing a job, based on long experience. I was not charged shop rent, and the plant was open nights and weekends. Not the least advantage was the availability of equipment and gear at reduced prices, sometimes even at wholesale prices, and of quality British equipment imported in large quantities at competitive prices.

At other times, I had to battle for my own choice in the matter of some items of equipment that I felt were better suited to my needs. Sometimes the shop went ahead and installed things their way, presenting me with a *fait accompli*, which I would have to tear out at my own expense. I have some definite and unswerving opinions on many things, and among these is that I will not permit copper tubing for propane and engine fuel systems on any ship of mine. These were installed over my protestations, and I promptly ripped them out and reinstalled flexible high pressure hoses at extra expense.

Their idea of a 12-volt electrical system was truly pre–World War I. I redesigned and installed all the wiring myself. No provision was made for removing the engine shaft in case of a break. I had a battle over this one, and there was another flap over my insistence on installation of a flexible shaft coupling. I had requested a three-bladed prop to use the first year, when I would be motoring until the mast and sails were installed. Instead they installed a two-bladed one they had in stock. Later I went to the expense of buying the proper propeller and hiring a diver to change the blades. Another controversy arose over my insistence on an automatic bilge pump before launching. I was told I only needed a vacuum cleaner for the bilges. Although I ordered bronze through-hull seacocks on all hull penetrations, brass gate valves were installed in about half of them.

And so it went, week after week, month after month.

Much of the frustration was due to the current shortages, high cost, and poor quality of much marine equipment and parts. Often I would wait weeks for delivery of an order, only to find some of the vital parts missing, requiring more delays and correspondence. Pride and dependability seem to have been two qualities abandoned by manufacturers these days. Much marine equipment is of poor design, even worse quality, and incredibly over-priced. For example, a $600 marine head arrived without a single piece of instruction for installing its complex mechanism, and without a necessary high-amp solenoid switch. The navigation sidelights, designed for recessing into the side of the trunk cabin, did not have enough overlapping lip to cover the hole necessary for recessing them. The horn turned out to be made of pot metal, which fell apart during the installation. The plexiglass windows were covered with a protective paper with a glue so tenacious that the paper could not be removed without scratching the plexiglass. I tried every solvent known to science without success. The glue remains on the windows to this day.

The fuel and water pumps, without exception, burned out impellers during initial tests. I paid $80 for a stainless steel sink that I later saw advertised for $30 in a Montgomery Ward catalogue. Many of the standard items of rigging called for had been discontinued by original manufacturers, and substitutes could not be found. Other standard parts, such as bronze turnbuckles, were inflated beyond reason. The ten required turnbuckles for the standing rigging were priced at $40 apiece, plus the toggles at $12 each. Quite a markup for an item that costs no more than $2 to manufacture. It was impossible to find the proper size sheaves for the running gear. Not manufactured any longer. The expensive gimballed propane stove was engineered with the hose attachment at the rear, which is impossible to inspect for gas leaks once installed. Marine type cabin light fixtures were costly beyond belief, but I solved this by shopping in trailer parts stores where similar fixtures can be obtained for a fraction of the marine prices. The expensive marine diesel engine came without the proper filter and hoses, and with a parts and operating manual I'm sure was put together by a not too bright grade school pupil, with most of the instructions applicable only to other models, not the one I bought.

Like Hiscock, I found that nothing ever fit the first time, nothing ever worked the first time, and nothing ordered ever arrived complete or on time.

On launching day, I again checked to see if the bilge pump was working, and also rigged up an anchor and line in case of engine failure, much to the amusement of the management and crew. The crane lowered *Wild Rose* gently to the water. As the rain poured down in a late spring deluge, I toasted the occasion with a few friends and a couple of bottles of champagne. Then, light-headed and gay, I started the engine and maneuvered out into the channel. The engine quit cold. Air in the fuel lines. We tied up again and bled the lines. The second departure got us a little farther into the channel. The engine quit again. Air in the lines. Fortunately, I had the anchor ready, which saved us from drifting aground. We bled the lines once more, started up, and headed out again. After a few preliminary maneuvers to check the steering, I put into the dock to let off some guests. At the dock the shaft pulled out of the engine coupling. Someone had forgotten the set screws and safety wiring. The shaft slipped back until the prop rested against the skeg. Water gushed into the engine compartment.

That's when my foresight in demanding an automatic bilge pump saved us from sinking.

Getting a tow back to the crane, we hauled *Wild Rose* out and reinstalled the shaft. Then we had a second launching, this time without champagne.

A half hour later, we ran aground on a mud bank on the way to the marina. I was able to back off. At the marina, we no sooner docked than the engine quit again. Air in the fuel lines.

For the next three months, I fought that "Red Devil" in the engine room, bleeding lines repeatedly and reinstalling fuel filters, lines, and fittings. Nothing worked. The engine would run for about an hour, then quit. I changed filters. This did not help. I appealed to the factory and received an asinine form letter that was of no help whatever. Obviously, I was going to have to fight for my warranty rights.

At last, after a frustrating summer during which all my spare time was spent trying to get the engine and fuel system working, I accidentally discovered the source of the problem: The machine screws holding down the top of the fuel pump had never been tightened at the factory. The engine had gone through final assembly and testing this way, with a heavy coat of paint hiding the defect.

Lost were three months of my time, a couple of hundred dollars in spare parts and hired help, and all the good weather for the year.

Meanwhile, dozens of other defects showed up: The pressure water pump was defective and had to be replaced; the main line came off the combination hot water heater and engine cooling system and flooded the engine room; the rudder tube leaked and filled the rear cabin bilge; the hinges came off the six hatch covers; the propane storage proved inadequate and inaccessible and I had to redesign and reinstall new tanks on deck; the main engine shaft developed a warble at certain speeds; the bow pulpit, which was to have been installed at the shop, wasn't, and it didn't fit; the custom-made drawers did not fit—if closed, they could not be opened, and if opened could not be closed; my five thousand dollar bunks proved not very practical; the fiberglass water tank had not been steamed and I was stuck with a resin-tasting water supply; the engine instruments worked only sporadically; the genoa track kit was minus some parts which could not be replaced. . . .

One of the few bright spots in this endless tale of frustration was the discovery of the mobile home and trailer parts industry. Unlike marine suppliers, this industry is a healthy one, which carries a wide variety of parts and equipment that can be substituted easily for standard marine items, at a fraction of the cost. I made a few fortuitous purchases. I found an anchor capstan in a war surplus catalogue for $190 that works just as well as a $900 marine model of the same capacity.

The last blow was yet to fall, however. When the final bill arrived, it came to more than $21,000 in addition to the $18,000 I had already paid, plus another $4,000 I had spent outside the shop in parts and equipment. Because the builders were essentially honest people and reasonable of heart, and because I was able to find a number of errors in their chaotic bookkeeping system, we eventually negotiated a settlement acceptable to both sides.

But the experience was a traumatic one, with little comfort in the knowledge that it happens to most dream ship addicts sooner or later, and that not even such cautious and experiened hands as Eric Hiscock have been able to avoid it.

Once your decision is made and you are hooked, and it's too late to turn back, you have no choice but to sail on and make the best of the bad weather. Sooner or later, you learn to be philosophical about the whole thing, and even to take fierce pride in the result, as did Slocum, Pidgeon, O'Brien, and even Gerbault, none of whom could boast of having a finer vessel than *Wild Rose*.

We have come to know that she is a basically good ship, and her performance has been all we had expected. Out of all the misery has come a more intimate knowledge of her advantages and disadvantages, which is indispensable in any ocean-going yacht.

As with any expensive mistress, you either have to live with her or kick her out. We plan to live with her for some time to come.

AUTHOR'S NOTES

Chapter One

1.   The *Spray*'s dimensions were, in the words of its captain, 36 feet 9 inches overall, 14 feet 2 inches wide, and 4 feet 2 inches deep in the hold. Her net tonnage was 9, and her gross, 12.71 tons.

2.   Robinson & Stephenson, 189?. An 1894 edition was published in Boston by Roberts Brothers, who also acted as Slocum's literary agents during his circumnavigation.

3.   Slocum's eldest son, Victor, considered his father's dollar-and-a-half chronometer merely one of his sly jokes. The captain, although he had no formal education, was an expert navigator with long experience. In point of fact, a chronometer is not absolutely necessary. Both latitude and longitude can be found with sextant and dead reckoning, and the captain had all his instruments with him.

After forty-three days from the island of Juan Fernández to Nuku Hiva, the *Spray* was found to be exactly on course. The high and beautiful island in the Marquesas, said Victor, was used merely to check on her longitude.

At this point, Slocum wrote: "I hope I am making it clear that I do not lay claim to cleverness or to slavish calculations in my reckonings. I think I have already stated that I kept my longitude, at least, mostly by intuition. A rotator log always towed astern, but so much has to be allowed for currents and for drift, which the log never shows, that it is only an approximation."

Slocum made lunar observations for his own satisfaction, finding errors in the tables he carried.

"The tables being corrected, I sailed on with self-reliance unshaken, and with my tin clock fast asleep. I was *en rapport* with my surroundings, and was carried on a vast stream where I felt the buoyancy of His hand who made all the worlds. I realized the mathematical truth of their motions, so well known that astronomers compile tables of their positions through the years and the days, and the minutes of the days, with such precision that one coming along over the sea five years later, may by their aid, find the standard time of any given meridian on earth."

4.   "Looking out of the companionway," Slocum wrote, "to my amazement I saw a tall man at the helm. His rig was that of a foreign sailor, and the large red cap he wore was cockbilled over his left ear, and all was set off with shaggy black whiskers. 'Señor,' said he, doffing his hat, 'I have come to do you no harm. I am one of Columbus's crew. I am the pilot of the *Pinta* come to aid you. Lie quiet, Señor Captain, and I will guide your ship tonight.' "

With this little bit of whimsy, Slocum started a tradition that still delights voyagers today. The pilot of the *Pinta* has become the patron saint of all solo circumnavigators.

5.   Slocum cannot even bring himself to mention Virginia in his book. He does tell how Captain Howard, when he learned of the pilot of the *Pinta*, refused to return aboard the *Spray*.

6.   Enormous waves, the culmination of several joined together on the long fetches of the southern oceans, have been encountered by all voyagers in those waters, including Vito Dumas, Dwight Long, Harry Pidgeon, Alain Gerbault, William Albert Robinson, and the Smeetons. Another phenomenon which Slocum alluded to, but which others failed to record, was mirages and illusions, which at times made seagulls appear as giant birds one moment and as tiny specks the next.

7.   During this storm, in which he was blown down toward the Horn by a northwest gale, Slocum kept his ship under control and running before the tempest by towing large warps astern. He was the first to report on this technique which is now standard practice among small-boat voyagers.

8.   The Keeling-Cocos Islands were discovered in 1608 by Captain William Keeling, in the service of the East India Company, and settled by Captain John Clunies-Ross in 1814, who brought in Malay natives to colonize them. Later a cable station and now an airways communication link, they are under Australian protection although still held by the Clunies-Ross family. This is a popular landfall on the long run across the Indian Ocean, and almost every yacht calls in here for a rest before tackling the usually boisterous ocean to Mauritius.

9.   Clark was still there when Harry Pidgeon arrived in the *Islander*, almost a quarter century later, and got the goat story firsthand.

10.   The document was later turned over to the Treasury Department as a record of the voyage.

11.   *The Voyages of Joshua Slocum* (New Brunswick, N.J.: Rutgers University Press, 1958).

12.   Ironically, the first copy of the *Spray* to attempt a circumnavigation, the Australian *Pandora*, went missing in the same general area in 1911 after surviving a capsize and dismasting while rounding the Horn. The *Pandora* was the first to attempt the Cape Horn route, and was an almost exact copy of the *Spray*.

13.   Slocum was described by a reporter on the day he left Boston for his circumnavigation as a man 5 feet 9½ inches tall, weighing 146 pounds, and "as spry as a kitten and nimble as a monkey."

As a matter of further historical interest, during World War II, a Liberty ship, the *Joshua Slocum*, was launched at a Portland shipyard, in honor of the old gent who as a youth had designed and built Columbia River gillnet boats, and who fished and hunted in this area for some months. After the war, the Joshua Slocum was tied up for years in the Moth Ball Fleet at Tongue Point, near Astoria, within sight of his old fishing grounds.

Chapter Two

1.   *The Venturesome Voyages of Captain Voss*, by John Claus Voss, Charles E. Lauriat Company, Boston, 1913. First published in Yokohama in 1913, a second edition appeared in London in 1926, followed by a "cheap edition" in 1930. A Mariners Library edition appeared in the 1960s, but the book is long out of print and scarce, especially in the original printings.

The most controversial, misquoted, misread, and misunderstood book on small-craft voyaging ever published, it is also one of the most literate and fascinating. It is so well-written that I am inclined to believe that Voss never wrote it. The style suggests that it was at least rewritten from Voss's original manuscript by a professional, and my guess would be none other than Weston Martyr, who first met Voss at Cape Town and later came to know him well in Yokohama (and who, in fact, wrote the introduction to the original). It is far superior as a literary account of voyaging in the early 1900s than Luxton's posthumous account, published in 1972, almost sixty years later.

In spite of detractors (who seem not to have read *Venturesome Voyages*), the techniques of heavy weather sailing in small vessels, related in detail by Voss, remain among the best and most authentic ever published, and were certainly the first. They are as valid today as they were when Voss experimented with them. Many of the popular voyaging books that came later relate versions of Voss's techniques without credit, or at least unknowingly. Those who have deprecated Voss's use of the sea anchor, for example, apparently never really studied his technique, for their versions differ in important details from Voss.

For more than half a century, Voss's book has been underrated and too often casually dismissed. It deserves a fresh appraisal and evaluation, especially for its sea lore.

2.　　　　Although later writers claim Voss's beginnings are shrouded in mystery, the old gentleman himself once gave his birthday as August 6, 1858, and related that he shipped on his first voyage to sea at Hamburg, Germany, in 1877, on a 300-ton bark bound for Guayaquil, Ecuador.

3.　　　　*British Columbia Directory* for 1895.

4.　　　　This was confirmed by none other than Weston Martyr, who met Voss in Cape Town and later in Japan.

5.　　　　Luxton's book, edited and published after his death from his private letters to his family, appears to be mostly casual memoirs of an old man, not intended for readers outside the family circle. The fact that he made no effort to publish his account during his lifetime, although he owned and operated a printing business, is strong evidence that he was afraid to do so. An opportunist, if nothing else, Luxton probably saw in Voss an opportunity to cash in on the contemporary Slocum fever, but found in Voss a stronger and more mature personality.

6.　　　　Luxton's version of how they raided the Indian burial grounds does not follow Voss's. The latter wrote that they acquired the trinkets while on the west coast of Vancouver Island waiting for the weather to improve—which is probably the actual case since not enough time had elapsed between acquiring and outfitting the *Tilikum* and their departure to have done all the things Luxton said they did.

7.　　　　There is neither an authentic record of these charges nor of registering the *Tilikum* as the *Pelican*.

8.　　　　Voss and Luxton differ in their accounts of the stay on the west coast of the island. Also, Voss said he accompanied the Indian whaling expedition, and gave his own version of it.

9.　　　　Luxton and Voss are invariably a day or so apart in their accounts of arrival and departure, indicating that either or both of them had dropped or lost a day in his log. Most likely Voss was correct, since he was the navigator and knew their actual position in respect to the International Dateline.

10.　　　　Voss makes no mention, of course, of the episode involving the use of the gun, and in fact it is probably not true.

11.　　　　Voss dismisses the entire Samoan interlude as follows:

"The Samoan Islands, the natives and their habits, have been so often described that I omit that part, and proceed with my voyage." It is probable that Luxton did try to make some trouble for Voss here, but the latter chose to ignore it.

12.　　　　Luxton's account of the shipwreck and Voss's alleged attempt to abandon him does not hold water, and in fact the time element precludes that it ever happened.

13.　　　　*The Venturesome Voyages of Captain Voss*, by John Claus Voss, Charles E. Lauriat Company, Boston, 1913.

14.　　　　Voss devotes an entire chapter to this trial and the dramatic demonstrations which he put on to convince the jury that the defendants were at fault. This has an air of being highly overdramatized, almost like a Perry Mason courtroom drama. But it is a fact that everywhere Voss went he was feted and lionized as a hero and an outstanding seaman. In Australia, New Zealand, South Africa, and England, he took every opportunity to have the *Tilikum* hauled out and transported sometimes hundreds of miles overland to exhibit at his lectures.

15.   In Dunedin, New Zealand, Voss had his name changed to McVoss and the ladies of the town sponsored *Tilikum* in a floral parade, decorating it with flowers from keel to tops of masts.

During Voss's stay in New Zealand, he became friends with Harold Buck-ridge, who had just returned from Captain Scott's South Pole expedition on the relief ship *Morning*, and who joined the *Tilikum* as a crew member for a time, participating with Voss in the surf-running exhibitions at Sumno. During one of Voss's lectures, Buckridge jumped up and related some episodes of his South Pole expedition at great length, not knowing that also in the audience was Lieutenant Ernest (later Sir Ernest) Shackleton, his superior, who later became famous for his own South Pole adventures.

Sailing to Nelson via French Pass, Voss comments at length on the local legend of Peloris Jack, the only circumnavigator to make direct reference to this unique mammal. He reports, however, that Peloris Jack failed to show up to accompany him, although Voss waited on the west side of the strait for slack water as all vessels had to do. Conor O'Brien later also commented on Peloris Jack.

Peloris Jack was more than a legend. He was a Risso's dolphin (*Grampus griseus*), a beakless species of the Tasman Sea. This dolphin met and accom-panied ships that crossed the Cook Strait, between the North and South islands for more than twenty years. In the spring of 1912, the dolphin disappeared and was believed to have died of old age. The complete story can be found in *Dol-phins, the Myth and the Mammal* by Antony Alpers (Cambridge, Mass.: The Riverside Press, 1961).

16.   The *Tilikum*'s figurehead was kicked by a horse.

17.   Voss had first visited Pernambuco in 1877 as a young seaman. It was here that the British consul made him remove the Canadian flag which he had used up to now, and replace it with the British ensign.

18.   Voss claims to have been elected to membership, but the Society's records do not list him as such.

19.   The account of the *Sea Queen*'s voyage, during which Voss cele-brated his fifty-fourth birthday and was twice interrupted, is one of the best of the small-boat adventures. The first departure was aborted about six hundred miles at sea due to a bad leak; the second attempt was met with the worst typhoon in memory, in which many ships foundered. The *Sea Queen*, although capsized twice, made it safely back to Yokohama under jury rig—probably the most severe test ever given to Thomas Fleming Day's famous design.

20.   After Voss's adventures with the *Tilikum*, he spent about five years as master of sealing schooners in the North Pacific. The 1911 treaty between the U.S., Russia, and Japan, which prohibited sealing, put an end to this, and his share in the compensation paid to sealers was slow in coming. Most likely he returned to Victoria and the hotel business, during which time he went through a divorce from his wife, and the family scattered.

21.   He was, in fact, only sixty-four at the time of his death.

Chapter Three

1.   *The Cruise of the Dream Ship* by Ralph Stock (London: William Heinemann, 1921, 1922, 1923, 1927, and 1950). Ralph's sister, "Peter," also wrote a book of their cruise, *The Log of a Woman Wanderer* (London: William Heinemann, 1923). Peter was an early women's libber, but a petite and delightful one (and her real name was Mabel).

2.   It is a detail, in fact, that stands in the way of most dreams of this kind, but those who are really serious and determined will somehow find a way. Unfortunately, most chroniclers of escape via bluewater boats are aggravatingly vague about the details of how they managed to finance their dreams. This can be exceedingly frustrating to a working slob, stuck on a boring job and keeping one jump ahead of the bankruptcy referee. A parallel to Ralph Stock, however, was Gerry Trobridge, the South African who carried his battered plans for a John Hanna ketch through World War II with him, and finally made it home to build his own in his backyard.

3.   Then, as now, small-boat sailors mind the old ditty:
June, too soon
July, stand by
August, if you must
September, remember
October, all over.

4.   "Swizzling," of course, referred to swizzle sticks in highballs. Most other travelers to the West Indies have made a point of mentioning the insolence and arrogance of the local natives.

5.   Most voyagers spoke of the harrowing experience in the locks. Robinson was the first to suggest a practical method of handling a small craft in the turbulence, but not until Marjorie Petersen of *Stornoway*, did any of them write a complete and graphic account of a typical Panama Canal yacht passage. See *Stornoway, East and West* (New York: Van Nostrand, 1966). Local lock tenders tell me, however, that there is no excuse for giving yachts the treatment they get at Panama. They say the water intake can be controlled by the lock tender to avoid the turbulence. Also see *Boating* magazine, March 1971, p. 62.

6.   The Union Club.

7.   Balboa is also known as the used-yacht graveyard of the Pacific, where broken dreams of hundreds of erstwhile voyagers have ended for many reasons, mostly financial. At this writing, Balboa is considered a happy hunting ground for purchasers of "previously owned" dream boats.

8.   Muhlhauser, a year later, described this treasure-hunting fever in detail.

9.   Muhlhauser got fresh water here in the same manner.

10.   Stock did not mention the legendary host of Nuku Hiva, Bob McKittrick, a former sailor who jumped ship to become a trader and who, for decades, served as a greeter of visiting yachts. Muhlhauser, however, did mention McKittrick, but the trader had been there in the Marquesas for several years already.

11.   Stock did not mention two other famous ex-World War I refugees, Charles Nordhoff and James Norman Hall, who were to produce *Mutiny on the Bounty, Hurricane,* and many other South Seas classics.

Chapter Four

1.   *The Cruise of the Amaryllis* by G. H. P. Muhlhauser (Boston: Small, Maynard & Company, 1925).

2.   "She struck me as a sound, well-built, and powerful little ship, snugly rigged, and fit to go anywhere. Nevertheless, she is not my ideal cruiser, as she has a counter 10 feet long, is yawl rigged, and steered with a tiller, whereas my preference is for a very short counter, or canoe stern, ketch rig, and wheel steering. Moreover, her draft of 10 feet was rather too much for knocking around amongst coral reefs, though a very good feature from the point of view of keeping the sea." It should be noted that this analysis was made *after* Muhlhauser returned from his voyage around the world, with practical experience to back it up.

3.   *Amaryllis* was the shepherdess in Virgil's *Ecologues*; it is also any of the genus *Amaryllis* of the bulbous African herbs with showy umbellate flowers, a type of lily.

4.   By coincidence, Plymouth was celebrating the three-hundredth anniversary of the sailing of the *Mayflower*, which accounted for the full-dress uniform of the deputy assistant harbormaster.

5.   *Small Craft*, published by the Bodley Head.

6.   Not counting Ralph Stock's *Dream Ship*, which did not actually complete a circumnavigation.

7.   Muhlhauser meant North America, not the United States especially.

8.   This was the piano that belonged to Peter Stock, and had been aboard the *Dream Ship* when Ralph Stock unwittingly sold her on their visit to this port.

9.   Muhlhauser probably had an incurable cancer.

10.   As Muhlhauser was returning from his long voyage, another erstwhile circumnavigator named Conor O'Brien was leaving Dublin on *Saoirse*. And it is interesting to note that the famous Claud Worth, considered the father of British yachting, wrote the introduction to the accounts of both these intrepid bluewater yachtsmen.

Chapter Five

1.   *Sea Tracks of the Speejacks* by Dale Collins (Garden City, N.Y.: Doubleday, Page & Co., 1923).

2.   "Speejacks" was the college nickname of Albert Y. Gowen. He was educated at St. Paul's School and at Harvard. His primary business was cement, in which he had made a wartime fortune, but he also had other substantial business interests. He· was a well-liked man, not the least pompous or imperious, who enjoyed life and wanted to get the most out of it.

3.   Most bluewater voyagers in smaller sailing yachts have found that a half gallon a day per person adequately supplies crew needs.

4.   Tin Can Island was a famous tourist attraction. Here, passing ships delivered the mail by placing it in sealed cookie cans, which the natives would swim out and retrieve. They got to keep the cookies, while the mail was delivered to the addresses.

5.   The circumnavigation of the *Snark*, while ill-conceived and executed, would have become one of the most famous in history had not the

famous author and his wife become ill. On this voyage, the crew included a young man named Martin Johnson, who later became the famous explorer, with his wife, Osa. Years later, young Dwight Long, in *Idle Hour*, met the Johnsons in the East Indies while on his circumnavigation.

6.   William Albert Robinson, on his circumnavigation, put into Hollandia desperate for supplies and funds from home. He found the port almost deserted. Most G.I.s will remember it as a huge supply port and staging area in World War II.

7.   These were prophetic and surprisingly perceptive words. Later events dramatized the changing social and economic order—but not until a quarter century and World War II had come and gone.

8.   Gowen was a large stockholder in Standard Oil Company, which simplified his fuel problems considerably.

9.   A speed of 175 miles a day for a twin-screw motor boat of 98 feet length cannot be considered even average. Most well-founded sailing yachts of much smaller waterline length can equal or surpass this.

Chapter Six

1.   *Around the World Singlehanded* by Harry Pidgeon (New York: Appleton, 1932). Pidgeon, who took four years to write his book, obviously had Slocum's *Sailing Alone Around the World* before him as a model during this unfamiliar business. There are many similarities of organization and style, but unfortunately Pidgeon did not have a talented *Century Magazine* editor to give his work the professional touch as did Slocum.

2.   Douglas fir, often called Oregon pine, is the tree which forms the backbone of the timber industry in the Pacific Northwest. At that time, huge straight-grained timbers of almost any size were readily available, as were extra long planks for full-length strakes. Circumnavigator William Crowe used such one-piece planks in building his 39-foot *Lang Syne* in 1936.

3.   Before the famous and glamorous Klondike Gold Rush, the center of interest in gold mining was at Circle City in Alaska. Gold was discovered later on Klondike Creek in the Yukon Territory, and sparked the mad rush that led to Dawson and other gold fields.

4.   This plans book is still available from *Rudder*. Probably more vessels have been built from *Sea Bird* plans than any other yacht ever designed. Styled for easy homebuilding, it used the then-advanced hard-chine technique. The original was sailed to Rome, Italy, by Day and two companions.

5.   Pidgeon helps to solve the mystery of when McKittrick arrived in the Marquesas. Although Stock does not mention the trader, Muhlhauser did. Since McKittrick told Pidgeon about meeting the *Amaryllis* and the *Dream Ship*, he must have arrived there before 1919.

6.   Early voyagers, from Slocum on, all reported the warm welcome received at Keeling-Cocos. In 1973, however, visiting yachtsmen discovered that their welcome had long since been worn out by sea tramps who have sponged on the Clunies-Ross family. Visitors are no longer welcome at Home Island, although the cable station and air field personnel are still glad to see them.

7.   See *Nowhere Is Too Far*, edited by John Parkinson, Jr. (New York: Cruising Club of America, 1960).

8.   His bride, Margaret, had been an experienced sailor in her own right before marrying Captain Pidgeon. Born at sea on her father's square-rigger,

she early learned the arts of the sailor and of handling small boats. The *Islander* was the couple's home. In 1947, they sailed her to Hawaii from Los Angeles. In November, they departed Honolulu for Torres Strait, encountering rough weather during the 66-day passage to the New Hebrides, and a broken main boom. To make the repair, they put into Hog Island where an unseasonable hurricane caught them.

Returning to California, they began work on a *Sea Bird*, the 25-foot version of *Islander*. Harry was then seventy-nine. He died in 1955.

Chapter Seven

1.   *Across Three Oceans* by Conor O'Brien (London: Edward Arnold & Co., 1926). Like many voyagers since, O'Brien was an enthusiastic mountaineer as well as yachtsman.

2.   The three stormy capes of the old sailing ship route were Cape of Good Hope, Cape Leeuwin (off the southwest tip of Australia), and Cape Horn. The usual yacht route around the world is west-about in the trades via the Panama Canal, the South Pacific islands, Torres Strait, and either Cape Town or Suez (before the canal was closed).

3.   O'Brien and his sister served under the super-patriot, Erskine Childers, whose book, *The Riddle of the Sands*, is considered to be the best yachting novel ever written, and one of the all-time classic spy stories. Childers, a clerk in Parliament and a yachting enthusiast as well as idealistic intellectual, took the side of the Irish in the Civil War, mostly smuggling guns to the rebels. He was ultimately executed by the I.R.A. which had turned against him after using him.

4.   O'Brien filled his water tanks with whatever was available, wherever he stopped, without bothering with chlorine, on the theory that if the water had not yet killed the local inhabitants, it must be all right—a very dangerous practice, to say the least, and certainly not recommended today.

5.   O'Brien was a half century ahead of Sir Francis Chichester in seeking out and analyzing the old sailing-ship logs.

6.   None other than L. Francis Herreshoff said of him: "I consider O'Brien's books the most masterly analysis of seagoing conditions perhaps ever written, and even if he and I do not see eye to eye in all matters pertaining to rig and rigging—well, no progress would be made if we all thought alike; but under no circumstances would I contradict Conor O'Brien for he has had actual experience."—Quoted from the old master's instructions on how to build *Marco Polo*, which ran in *Rudder* magazine, 1946.

7.   When the cloud cover forms over Table Mountain, it is said that the "table cloth is set," which signals the coming of a southeast gale.

8.   *New York Times*, July 20, 1943.

Chapter Eight

1.   *The Fight of the Firecrest* by Alain Gerbault (New York: Appleton, 1926). First of Gerbault's three highly successful voyaging books, and one of eight he wrote during his lifetime.

2.   Stock, who had lived in France for a time following the publication of his successful book, *The Cruise of the Dream Ship*, now had a replacement. He and Gerbault were good friends.

3.   Down through the years to World War II, the Korean War, and
the conflict in Southeast Asia, only the labels have been changed. The motives
and substance of each new generation are remarkably similar.
4.   So he said, but he was an avid reader and well-known to him
were the voyages of Slocum, Voss, and others.
5.   In this statement, Gerbault, I suspect, was merely rationalizing
for the benefit of the reading public.
6.   According to Jean Merrien, the well-known French yachtsman and
maritime writer.
7.   Those few included Slocum, Voss, Stock, Muhlhauser, and perhaps many others whose adventures went unheralded.
8.   *The Fight of the Firecrest*, by Alain Gerbault (New York: Appleton, 1926).
9.   He has been credited with winning the Davis Cup of that year by
some starry-eyed writers. This is a team competition, however, and no French
team won it until 1927.
10.   He was, in fact, the first winner of the coveted Blue Water Medal
of the cca, for the year 1923, and without doubt it was his friendship with
William Nutting, founder of cca, which influenced the board.
   The medal was designed by Arthur Sturgis Hildebrand, a freelance writer
and cca member, who lost his life at sea the same year the first award was made.
   "Today, well-executed ocean crossings in small vessels are quite frequent, and
Gerbault would not even be considered for a Blue Water Medal." So commented John Parkinson, Jr., the late cca historian, in *Nowhere Is Too Far*.
11.   Cobos will be remembered as the gracious host who told his story
to every voyager who came that way during the 1920s and 1930s. He married
the beautiful Norwegian girl with whom Robinson gamboled over the mountains
on horseback in the moonlight during his idyllic stay with *Svaap*. For the most
authentic account of the Norwegians and the Cobos family, see *To the South
Seas*, by Gifford Pinchot (Philadelphia: John C. Winston Co., 1930).
12.   Actually, all those he mentioned had visited the Dangerous
Archipelago, as have numerous other yachtsmen since.
13.   Friday the thirteenth was Gerbault's unlucky day, in spite of
his protestations that he was not superstitious. It was on a Friday the thirteenth,
that his sails were torn away during the first Atlantic crossing, when he suffered severe damage. Again, it was Friday the thirteenth when he suffered
damage on the passage to Bermuda.
14.   See Chapter 16 for another clue to the mystery of how Gerbault
died.

Chapter Nine

1.   *Deep Water and Shoal* by William A. Robinson (London: Rupert Hart-Davis, 1957). One of the many editions which includes the original
10,000 Leagues Over the Sea was published by Harcourt, Brace & Co., Inc., New
York, 1932.
2.   Robinson came in a poor third in his class and was out-sailed by
none other than Captain Harry Pidgeon in *Islander*. *Svaap* took twelve days;
Islander, seven days.
3.   Robbie's experiences in the locks can be contrasted with Gerbault's. By official order from Washington, on request of Paris, the locktender
gently raised *Firecrest*.

4.   Karin was the daughter of a Norwegian family, the last remnants of an ill-fated colony begun in 1926. She married the Paris-educated Manuel Augusto Cobos, whose father had been in charge of a penal colony on San Cristóbal, where the prisoners provided free labor for a coffee plantation. When the elder Cobos was murdered by the convicts, the Ecuadorean government gave the island to Manuel and his sister as compensation. At the time Robinson visited them in 1945, Karin had six children, and a brand-new eleven-day-old baby. The family was down to living on bare essentials, their backs to the wall—all of which depressed Robinson so much that he cut short his visit.

5.   *10,000 Leagues Over the Sea*, by William A. Robinson (New York: Harcourt, Brace & Co., Inc., 1932).

6.   On New Year's Eve, while *Svaap* was making a landfall after crossing the Pacific, Robinson's contemporary, Alain Gerbault, was celebrating the incoming of 1929 at a big party in the Cape Verdes, on the last leg of his circumnavigation. Both adventurers were lucky enough to escape the Great Depression in the most idyllic way; and, of course, Robinson's star guided him into making a fortune in a wartime shipyard, instead of adventuring in exotic places as a member of the armed forces.

7.   *10,000 Leagues Over the Sea*.

8.   Robinson's sense of timing seldom failed him. During his voyages, he kept many a rendezvous, often arranged months in advance and subject to many unpredictable factors such as weather, navigation errors, and man-made circumstances.

9.   *10,000 Leagues Over the Sea*.

10.   It was not until Robinson's third visit to the Galápagos, in 1945, that he learned the details from an eyewitness of what happened to *Svaap*. When he did learn, he was so incensed and outraged at the behavior of the corrupt and greedy officials at Wreck Bay during the 1930s that he picked up his informant and threw him off the ship.

11.   *To the Great Southern Sea* (Tuckahoe, N.Y.: John de Graff, Inc., 1966; first published by Harcourt, Brace & Co., Inc., 1956).

Varua, which means "spirit" or "soul" in Tahitian, is considered by many *aficionados* to be the most beautiful and functionally perfect sailing yacht ever built. Based on his years of experience sailing the oceans of the world, the lines were worked up to Robinson's specifications by W. Starling Burgess, famous designer of the America's cup defender, *Ranger*, and numerous other fine ships. The model was tested and refined by tank tests at the Stevens Institute, and the hull was constructed of the (then) advanced composite steel frame and wood-planking technique. She was launched March 19, 1942, just after the U.S. was plunged into war with Japan and Germany. During the war, Robbie and his wife lived aboard and made plans for the future. One weekend in 1943 they had as a guest aboard, the famed circumnavigator Conor O'Brien, whom Robbie found to be exceptionally charming and entertaining.

Varua's dimensions are: 66.2 feet overall, 60 feet on the waterline, 16.2 feet in beam, with a draft of 6.6 feet, a net tonnage of 37, and a gross tonnage of 43. Her A.B.S. rating is *A I Y S.

The rig was designed with the assistance of Robbie's friend, the late L. Francis Herreshoff, whose *Ticonderoga* is in the same class and closely resembles *Varua*. It is a unique brigantine rig with a foremast and a mainmast, square courses, and fore and aft mainsails, staysails, and flying jibs. The total sail area is 2,700 square feet. Herreshoff originally designed his fine 44-foot *Ocean Cruiser* for Robinson, but Robbie finally chose *Varua*.

The auxiliary is a 47-horsepower Deutz, swinging a two-bladed feathering prop off center and giving a speed of about 7 knots.

She carries 625 gallons of water and 800 gallons of diesel fuel.

The counterclockwise trip made around the South Pacific in the 1950s, into the Roaring Forties and up the west coast of South America, then back to Tahiti, proved *Varua* to be a superb vessel in every respect, easily handled by two men, and roomy enough for a large family to live aboard in comfort.

Robinson's account of his encounter with the ultimate survival storm is a classic of seamanship.

Richard Maury, who also visited Tagus Cove aboard *Cimba* in July and August, was probably the last person to see *Svaap* before Robinson's famous vessel was confiscated and wrecked by Ecuadorean officials. Tagus Cove resembled a Norwegian fjord, Maury wrote, with sheer rock cliffs on which were painted the calling cards of many famous vessels—the schooner *Zaca, Yankee, Pilgrim, White Shadow,* and others, some of which were dated as early as 1833. Entering the old crater and anchoring in ten fathoms, they found *Svaap* "rolling abandoned amid the silences of Tagus Cove." Assembling their folding dinghy, Maury and his companion rowed over and boarded the ketch.

"Leaving Dombey in the cabin, I went on deck and eased myself into the steering well. What sights can be seen from the helm of a single craft guided by resourceful hands!" Maury wrote in *The Saga of Cimba* (Harcourt, Brace and Co., 1939).

In the cabin, by the light of matches, they found signs of hurried leave-taking, emptied sail lockers and chart racks, remnants of clothing, rusted tins of food scattered on the floorboards. During their stay in Tagus Cove, they borrowed *Svaap*'s cuyucka to replace their dinghy. Before they left, they overhauled the ground tackle, pumped out the bilges, tied up the rigging, paid out more chain scope, made sure the cabin was ventilated to prevent dry rot. They then helped themselves to some of the rusty cans of food and pumped over some of *Svaap*'s remaining fresh water for their use.

"For a moment we stood upon the dry deck, feeling the air of faithfulness, of loyalty pervading all good and hard-tried ships."

They then departed for the Marquesas and the Pacific islands, where *Cimba*, herself a jinxed ship, was lost.

11.   *Return to the Sea* (New York: John de Graff, Inc., 1972).

  – 12.   *Return to the Sea.*

13.   In a wartime edition of *Ten Thousand Leagues Over the Sea,* published by Harcourt, Brace thirteen years after the original edition, Robinson told in the foreword what had happened to Etera. Now building landing ships, he noted patriotically that some of these would be storming South Pacific beaches he had visited in *Svaap.*

One of Robinson's little-known adventures involved the purchase in Colombo, Ceylon, of the *Annapooranyamal,* an Indian copy of a full-rigged New England clipper in miniature, which he had first seen on his circumnavigation in *Svaap.* Returning to India later, he found the vessel, bought her, outfitted her at Colombo, and with an all-Indian crew, he and his first wife, Florence, sailed her back to Gloucester. There, the *Florence C. Robinson,* as the *Annapooranyamal* had been renamed, startled the natives when the Hindu crew flew kites from the deck to celebrate the safe passage. The clipper was used as a rigging model for the sailing ships Robinson's firm was then building, along with working fishing boats. The unique qualities of the square rig, including that of being able to sail backward while maneuvering in crowded waters, were noted by Robbie and some of them were incorporated in *Varua.*

In a personal letter from Mr. Robinson in March 1974, he said most of his time has been spent on a research project on his island, Tairo, now a scientific reserve.

"The three older girls have become practically international characters, what with dance tours, modelling, etc. Formerly they were known and introduced as the daughters of Robbie Robinson. Now I am introduced as the father of the Robinson Sisters."

Chapter Ten

1.   *Seven Seas on a Shoestring* by Dwight Long (New York and London: Harper and Brothers, Publishers, 1938; also published in England as *Sailing All Seas*).
2.   *Idle Hour*'s vital statistics were: 32 feet 6 inches overall, 29 feet 6 inches on the water line, 11 feet of beam, and drawing 5 feet 6 inches light and 6 feet loaded. She was rigged as a gaff-headed ketch, originally carrying 722 square feet of sail. When he remodeled her, Long equipped her for chartering, a sideline that earned him money along the way.

Built in 1921 in Tacoma, Washington, she cost $2,500 completely outfitted. About $3,000 was spent by Long during the voyage for all expenses. Even then, Long remarked, to make a circumnavigation for less than $6,000 was not easy and much scrimping was necessary. When he started out, he did not even have a camera. It should be remembered, however, that from childhood days, Long had been brought up and thoroughly grounded in the principles of good business practices. He knew how to earn and how to hang onto a buck. Moreover, young as he was, he never allowed himself to be intimidated or exploited by land sharks or petty officialdom wherever he put in.

"What I could not afford, I did not buy," he wrote. "I never would risk having my floating home sold out from under me."
3.   An inveterate seeker of the famous and the influential, Rotarian Long bagged an impressive list of names for dropping later, including: ex-President Herbert Hoover, Will Rogers, Mack Sennett, Harry Pidgeon, Alain Gerbault, W. A. Robinson, Alan Villiers, the Fahnestocks, Charles Nordhoff and James Norman Hall, Rear Admiral Yarnell, Zane Grey, Martin and Osa Johnson, and numerous others.
4.   'Tis a pity that San Francisco folks so neglected Amundsen's ship that Norway repossessed her and took her home to stay.
5.   Captain Pidgeon took young Long under his wing and taught him not only celestial navigation but some secrets of successful small-boat voyaging.
6.   Grey, one of the world's foremost pioneer big-game anglers, in addition to being a highly successful author of Western novels, made four expeditions to Tahiti, usually on his own yacht. On one trip, he caught the world's largest marlin, and the world's largest mako shark. He later purchased acreage on Tahiti, which was still in the family as late as 1972. Dr. Loren Grey, his youngest son, told me at that time that he and his sister planned to sell the now immensely valuable waterfront property if a proper price could be obtained.
7.   See Robinson's wartime edition of *10,000 Leagues Over the Sea* for what had happened to Etera in the post-*Svaap* years.
8.   Penrhyn was a mecca for many voyagers, including Voss and Luxton, who had most of their fun there. Flying Venus Reef, eight miles from Penrhyn, has the unique distinction of being the resting place of the *Derby Park*, a four-masted lumber carrier from Vancouver, and the *Flying Cloud*, a vessel

chartered to bring a replacement order of lumber to Melbourne. By coincidence, they were both wrecked on the same reef. As far as is known, the lumber order was not placed the third time.

9.   *Cimba,* one of the most beautiful sailing yachts ever built, was also one of the unluckiest. Maury, a great-grandson of the founder of the Navy's Hydrographic Office, was also a gifted writer. *The Saga of the Cimba,* the story of his ill-fated expedition, has been re-issued at this writing. Maury later became a merchant ship captain.

10.   Captain Tommy Drake remains a controversial character, and probably the rapscallion some claim he was. Dwight sheds some light here on what happened to Drake during those long periods he disappeared, purporting to be sailing alone on his home-built schooners. Because Long was from Seattle, scene of many of Drake's earlier tales, the old fraud probably took this opportunity to talk to someone from "home."

11.   Martin Johnson, as a lad younger than Long, had volunteered for the position of cook on Jack London's *Snark,* and been accepted. This adventure led him into a lifetime of adventures, later with his wife, Osa.

12.   Robinson had seen this ship on his circumnavigation and could not get her out of his mind, like the memory of an exotic woman. He returned later, found her, bought her for 20,000 rupees ($9,000), and outfitted her for a world cruise.

13.   The *Idle Hour* that was operated out of Orcas Island for years by my friend, the late Captain Chris Wilkins, was a different vessel.

14.   Dwight Long told the author that it was his articles—sometimes as many as six a month—in the old *Seattle Star* newspaper that paid most of his expenses. They were also responsible for widespread publicity. The staff on the *Star* had taken a liking to the young circumnavigator and had turned his rough copy, which he mailed in periodically, into more professional prose. His later book was mostly a condensation of these articles, he said.

In 1974 he was living on the waterfront at Venice, California, where he operated a string of gift shops, one of which is on the *Queen Mary,* now a land-bound Long Beach tourist and convention center.

During the war, as a Navy officer in the photographic section, he had charge of putting together the well-known war-time film, *Fighting Lady,* the story of the U.S.S. *Hornet,* which was narrated by Robert Taylor. He also produced another official film on fighting submarines, which was never released because the war ended in the meantime.

In 1974 he was also operating a lecture series called "Armchair Cruises," which used his own films along with others, and traveled frequently overseas.

As for the *Idle Hour,* she was sailed to Honolulu before the war by Dwight and his brother, Philip. In 1944, Philip sold her on behalf of Dwight, and the *Idle Hour* has been at the Honolulu yacht harbor ever since, having passed through several ownerships.

In 1974, *Idle Hour,* the aging old girl that began life in the early 1930s as a Bering Sea trading vessel, and subsequently sailed around the world, survived World War II, and the postwar world, finally sank one day off Oahu Island, just too tired to go on anymore.

Long had planned to buy back the boat and have her restored in the Seattle Maritime Museum, but was too late. He recently acquired a new motor sailer from England and has named her *Idle Hour,* to keep the name alive. He sails her almost daily from his waterfront headquarters at Venice.

Still the ebullient businessman, Long was planning a voyage with the Irving Johnsons aboard *Yankee* through the European canals, to make a travel movie and write an article for *The Reader's Digest*. He was scheduling for his lecture series, his old friend, Alan Villiers.

One of his saddest memories of his cruising days, he told me, was having to help bury his old friend, Harry Pidgeon, in the 1950s. Until the day before the old gentleman died, Pidgeon refused to leave the yacht on which he and his wife, Margaret, lived. Long helped get him to the hospital and assisted Margaret with the funeral details.

Chapter Eleven

1.   *Yachting*, September 1937. Also see *National Geographic Magazine*, July 1939. Vol. LXXVI, No. 1.

2.   See *In the Wake of the Spray* by Kenneth E. Slack (New Brunswick, N.J.: Rutgers University Press, 1966) for the true story of Slocum's model, Mower's lines, and Howard I. Chapelle's explanation of *Rudder's* version.

Strout's version of *Spray* was not an exact copy, being 37 feet overall, 14 feet 6 inches in beam, and 5 feet of draft. Also, Strout's version had an unbroken deckhouse and a different cabin arrangement. *Igradasil* was constructed of pitch pine and white oak, and had originally a four-cylinder Miller gasoline engine. The *Spray*, of course, did not have an auxiliary engine. Of the many copies of the *Spray*, John Hanna's version, *Foam II*, probably comes closest to being the best. The plans for this and other Hanna dream boats are still available at this writing from his widow, Dorothy, at 636 Wilkie Street, Dunedin, Florida 33528.

The *Basilisk* was almost an exact copy, and was built at the same yard in Maryland as at least one other, the so-called Oxford *Spray* of Captain R. D. Culler. *Basilisk* was rigged as the original and owner Gilbert C. Klingel reported her performance, even in the bad storm he encountered, to be comfortable and seaworthy. She was wrecked through a miscalculation on Great Inagua in the Bahamas, but the sails were salvaged and purchased by Roger Strout. See Klingel's book *Inagua*, for the complete story.

4.   Cipriano Andrade's famous analysis of the *Spray's* lines appeared in *Rudder Magazine*, June 1909. In a letter to me, Howard I. Chapelle, now curator, Division of Transportation, Smithsonian Institution, wrote: "Slocum's letters are like those of a 4th grader—rather backward at that. He was 60 per cent fine seaman, 10 per cent liar, and 30 per cent showman, I would say. Had a lot of guts. He was going nowhere in no hurry so I suppose he sailed as the boat wanted to go. As I said, no lines were actually taken off *Spray*, so that poor Andrade was victimized by the old fraud, Tom Day, with Charley Mower the fall guy. Had Mower taken off the lines we would have had something to work on —now we have no reliable plans as a basis for analysis. But the whole story of the wonderful abilities of *Spray* is now highly questionable."

It might be added, that as a young draftsman, Chapelle was an assistant of Charles Mower, and heard the story firsthand of taking the lines off the model.

5.   Strout later said that he bought *Basilisk's* sails not only because they were a bargain, but because he wanted to test out some of Slocum's statements about how the *Spray* handled under various conditions.

6.   This reason or "excuse" is vaguely familiar. One is reminded that Conor O'Brien said he had not intended on sailing around the world; he just wanted to go mountain climbing in the New Zealand Alps, and sailing there in his own boat seemed the most convenient way. The New Zealand Tourist Bureau assures me, however, that public transportation in the form of jet airliners and cruise ships is now available.

7.   See William A. Robinson's *To the Great Southern Sea* for his explanation of the Penguin Village. On his second voyage with *Svaap*, Robinson and his wife, Florence, and cousin Dan West, built a miniature "village" of stone for the purpose of filming an "animal story" using live penguins. When Robinson was stricken with a burst appendix, *Svaap* and the project were abandoned. Later visitors have marveled at the "village," not knowing it was built by human hands.

8.   There have been dozens of variations of the events on Santa Maria. Edith Strout said Mrs. Witmer, with her husband and two sons, settled there, or on Charles Island, in 1931. They were preceded by Dr. Friedrich Ritter and Frau Dore Koerwin, who had sought an idyllic tropical paradise. The tranquillity of the island was shattered with the later appearance of the Baroness Eloise de Wagner Wehrborn and two male consorts. After years of strife, the Baroness and one of her consorts disappeared and have never been heard of since. The other, Alfred Lorenz, died of thirst and hunger on an island to the north. Dr. Ritter died and Frau Koerwin returned to Germany.

9.   The incidence of whale encounters and attacks in this area of the oceans is a hair-raising phenomenon. See Appendix for a discussion of this.

10.   The well-known habit of Samoans of "harassing" visiting yachts is explained by Edith in her *National Geographic* account. She pointed out that for generations the Samoans had developed a tribal attitude of communal ownership, and unlike other places where natives respect other's rights and property, the Samoans thought nothing of swarming aboard a yacht without asking permission, and staying indefinitely without invitation.

11.   Modern circumnavigators have found the Clunies-Ross descendants on Home Island somewhat less than hospitable. The yacht traffic, even in this remote Indian Ocean waystation, has become so heavy, and the visitors perhaps so calloused, that they are no longer welcome. Moreover, the governors of this feudal patriarchy perhaps do not want the population becoming restless with imported ideas about the outside world.

12.   Durban or Port Natal is another place where voyagers have worn out their welcome. For decades, visitors found Durban to be one of the most hospitable places on earth. That this is no longer true was indicated in a letter to me from Dr. Hamish Campbell of Durban, who had given up greeting visiting yachts for personal reasons.

13.   St. Helena was not only the site of Napoleon's exile and death. The British used it for years as a political prison. During the Boer War, several thousand prisoners captured by the British were held there. Several Zulu chieftans, including a Sultan of Zanzibar, were also among the inmates over the years. This stopping place was first described by Captain Slocum, who had an enjoyable stay and was given a live goat by the American consul, R. A. Clark.

14.   *The Spray*, Volume XV, 1971 publication of the Slocum Society.

15.   *In the Wake of the Spray*, by Kenneth E. Slack (New Brunswick, N.J.: Rutgers University Press, 1966), p. 211.

Chapter Twelve

1.   *Hurricane's Wake* by Ray F. Kauffman (New York: Macmillan, 1940).

2.   Another famous Iowa sailor was Captain Harry Pidgeon, who twice sailed around the world alone on *Islander*.

3.   *Hurricane's Wake*.

4.   *Hurricane's Wake.*

5.   *The Cruising Manual* by Gerry Mefferd (New York: Whittlesey House, 1941).

6.   Hector, like Robinson's Etera, was paid a small salary, in this case $5 a month, which was usually blown in one extended drunk at every port of call. But, unlike Etera, he never had to be bailed out of jail.

7.   *Nowhere Is Too Far*, ed., John Parkinson, Jr. (New York: The Cruising Club of America, 1960).

8.   On Robinson's second voyage on *Svaap*, he had a similar experience up the Sambu River in Darien, where it took weeks to salvage the stranded yacht.

9.   They had departed from the States with *Hurricane* still unfinished in many respects. Work continued on the vessel all around the world.

10.   Neither Kauffman nor Mefferd make mention of *Svaap*, which left New York on June 11, 1933, with William A. Robinson, his wife, Florence, and cousin, Daniel West, on an expedition to Central America and the Galápagos Islands. Only months before *Hurricane* reached the Galápagos occurred the famous race to save Robinson's life when his appendix burst, which made headlines all over the world. Also while *Hurricane* was there, Robinson's *Svaap* was confiscated and wrecked by some petty officials.

11.   *Director's* crew included Bruce and Sheridan Fahnestock; Dennis Puleston, the English voyager (see Bibliography); Ned Dair, an artist; and a Panamanian Negro prize fighter, Hey Hey, who was cook. The Fahnestocks' equally irrepressible mother also joined them here.

12.   *Hurricane's Wake.*

13.   Aboard *Yankee* on her second circumnavigation were Irving and Electa Johnson (see Bibliography), their two-year-old son, a paid cook, and about twenty paying guests ranging in age from sixteen to twenty-five, two of whom were girls. "If I owned her," Ray commented, "I would sign on a crew of ten-bob-a-month Pauans and fish trochu shells out of the Coral Sea, and I'd never go ashore except twice a year in Sydney."

14.   In this same area, the Hiscocks on *Wanderer III* and the Crowes on *Lang Syne* also reported near-disastrous encounters with whales.

15.   As it turned out, they never saw *Director* again—the Fahnestocks sold her in the Philippines—but they did meet Bruce and Sheridan in New York two years later and held a reunion. While in the East Indies they also received word of the disappearance of aviatrix Amelia Earhart and her navigator, on their flight over Japanese-controlled islands—a mystery that has never been solved.

16.   They were the first voyagers to report on the character of Jamestown, where they found a mixture of races that could be traced to Portuguese, English, French, Dutch, Chinese, Indian, Malayan, and African—St. Helena for centuries being a waystation for ships before Suez Canal was built. They found it one of the most promiscuous islands on earth, the streets filled with children who did not know who their fathers were, and the town overrun with prostitutes, the most persistent one being an African they called "Midnight Molly," whose pleadings could be warded off only by physical violence.

17.   *Hurricane's Wake.*

18.   As a final note to the story of *Hurricane*, bluewater *aficionados* will be glad to know that she is still sailing somewhere in the Caribbean. Ray Kauffman told me, in March 1974, that he had sold the ketch after their return from the world cruise just before World War II. From 1945 to 1950, *Hurricane*

was used by the U.S. Navy for a recreation vessel at Quantánamo Bay, Cuba. Wrecked once, she was later salvaged by the navy and sold. Since then she has been owned by at least two different parties, and been restored to her original condition. Kauffman said it was his understanding that the name had been changed, but she was just as sound as the day she was launched at Sidoine Krebs's bayou shipyard—and the owners were just as proud of her as were Kauffman and Mefferd.

Kauffman, incidentally, is now retired and living in Williamsburg, Virginia, where he keeps a 49-foot *Alaskan* diesel motor cruiser, and makes periodic trips offshore and to southern waters.

Chapter Thirteen

1.   *The Voyage of the Cap Pilar* by Adrian Seligman (New York: E. P. Dutton & Co., 1947). The book first appeared in 1939 in London under a British imprint.

2.   The Seligman family has a large number of American relatives, including a family of New York bankers.

3.   Bequests, expected or unexpected, were responsible for a surprising number of circumnavigations, or at least long voyages. Another well-known inheritance was that of the fun-loving Fahnestocks, who used the money to buy *Director* and start a world cruise.

4.   The *Cap Pilar* measured 118 feet between perpendiculars, 27 feet beam, 13 feet deep in the hold, with a gross tonnage of 295. The main truck was 103 feet above the deck. The foreyard was 50 feet across. Hardly the type of vessel for a crew of amateurs on a world cruise, but at least it made possible the signing on of a larger paying crew. A better choice would have been a North Sea pilot schooner, such as Warwick Tompkins and the Irving Johnsons chose, although the cost would have been considerably more.

5.   Trader Bob McKittrick was probably the most familiar and yet mysterious character encountered by voyagers in the 1920s, 1930s, and 1940s. He was mentioned as early as Voss and Muhlhauser. Most of the information on him is derived from tales he told visiting yachtsmen. Apparently, he was an old Liverpool shellback, who spent his early years at sea, and was put ashore ill on Tahiti about 1912 or 1913. Subsequently, he turned up as a beachcomber and trader at Nuku Hiva. His establishment still exists at this writing, run by his son, also a local character.

6.   *Voyage of the Cap Pilar.*

7.   This area of the world appears to be the Appendicitis Belt. It was here that Robinson went through his dramatic rescue after a burst appendix, and where the Irving Johnson crew suffered two similar emergencies. After passing through this area on the way to Honolulu on the last voyage of the *Tzu Hang*, Beryl Smeeton also was stricken with a similar emergency, fortunately after they had reached port. There have been numerous other similar episodes.

8.   As reported by practically every visitor to Wreck Bay, beginning with William A. Robinson who had a crush on her, Karin Cobos had married the son of the governor of the penal colony, who had been murdered by inmates. At the time of the *Cap Pilar* visit, she now had four children. On Robinson's last visit in the 1950s, the brood had grown to ten. She was the last of a party of three hundred Norwegians who had founded a colony in 1926.

Chapter Fourteen

1.   *Yankee's Wander-World* by Irving and Electa Johnson (New York: W. W. Norton & Company, Inc., 1949).

2.   *Shamrock V's Wild Voyage Home* by Irving Johnson (Springfield, Mass.: Milton Bradley Co., 1933).

3.   For other episodes of appendectomies in this part of the world, see the voyages of William Robinson and the *Cap Pilar*.

4.   See other accounts, including Robinson, the *Cap Pilar*, Kauffman and Mefferd, the Strouts, and others. Practically every voyager who visited the Galápagos mentioned Señora Cobos and her life story.

5.   Of all the accounts of the eccentric colonists in the Galápagos, that of Electa's in *Westward Bound in the Schooner Yankee* is the most sympathetic and accurate.

6.   One of the Johnsons' sons was named after a Pitcairn leader, Parkin Christian.

7.   Mangareva, in the Gambiers, will be remembered as the scene of the tragic and sinister story of the mad priest Père Laval, who destroyed most of the native population with his grandiose schemes of a feudal Popian empire.

8.   Aboard the *Patria* when it was wrecked was none other than James Norman Hall, co-author of *Mutiny on the Bounty*.

9.   Among the many shipboard romances that flowered on *Yankee* voyages was that of Steve Johnson and Mary Booth, who were married subsequently.

Chapter Fifteen

1.   *Alone Through the Roaring Forties* by Vito Dumas; first published in English by Adlard Coles, Ltd., 1960, in association with George G. Harrap & Co., Ltd., London; and John de Graff, Inc., New York. Translation by Captain Raymond Townes.

2.   Most voyagers chose either the strait or sneaked through the passages behind Horn Island; see Griffith, Bernicot, Slocum, Bardiaux, Tilman, Lewis, and others.

3.   Campos also designed and built *Gaucho* for Ernesto Uriburo, which made one of the first yacht voyages after World War II.

4.   *Alone Through the Roaring Forties.*

5.   *Solo Rumbo a la Cruz del Sur.* Long out of print and rare; publisher unknown.

6.   Dumas was not the first voyager to be enchanted by South Africa and almost overcome with temptation to end his voyage there. See Slocum, Pidgeon, Gerbault, Moitessier, and others.

7.   This psychic phenomenon is apparently very common among long-distant solo sailors. Slocum had his pilot of the *Pinta*, Alec Rose had his talking doll; many have reported hearing voices, some of which they attempted to answer. The tragic Donald Crowhurst episode was a classic and clinical case of a man's mind decaying over a long period alone at sea.

8.   *Alone Through the Roaring Forties.*

9.   Conor O'Brien, on his voyage, expressed almost the identical sentiment, which borders on the unsporting. These two lonely rocks, however, in

the 1960s and 1970s, have become the mecca for ham radio operators on "DX Expeditions."

10.   In this same general area, Bill King, on *Galway Blazer II*, was rammed and stove in by a whale. He was barely able to limp back to Perth.

11.   Moitessier and Bardiaux had other ideas about this region. In their view, the shallow depths here created vicious seas, which they considered much worse than those on the open oceans.

12.   *Alone Through the Roaring Forties.*

13.   Reported by Richard McCloskey, founding father and first secretary of the Slocum Society, in *The Spray*, Vol. XV, 1971.

Chapter Sixteen

1.   *Heaven, Hell and Salt Water* by Bill and Phyllis Crowe (London: Rupert Hart-Davis, 1957).

2.   One of the entries was the *Arcturus*, the black-hulled yacht of General George Patton, the controversial leader of the Third Army in World War II.

3.   How times have changed. In 1973, when I tried to cash a small check in Honolulu, I was regarded as a member of an international smuggling ring. I had to produce three credit cards, leave my thumb print, and pose for a mug shot before my request would be considered.

4.   The Crowes used this system for the entire voyage around the world. Tests in the Stevens Institute tank, however, have more recently shown that there is less drag when the prop is not rotating.

5.   With his disarming manner, Bill Crowe, who spoke Spanish fairly fluently, had little trouble talking himself out of such situations. The Miles Smeetons, about a decade later, also visited the island illegally and barely escaped a boat sent out to intercept them.

6.   The Belgian couple was probably the L. G. Van de Wieles of *Omoo* fame.

7.   Hospitality in French Oceania has become a thing of the past, current voyagers report.

8.   The Crowes were among the first bluewater voyagers to use the cheap and efficient propane for cooking. Their two tanks lasted them all the way around the world. Properly installed and used, butane has proved to be safe, clean, and entirely practical aboard yachts.

9.   This little-known pearl of information seems to authenticate Gerbault's internment as a war prisoner, and his death from a tropical disease. Unfortunately, Crowe does not give the name of the doctor.

Chapter Seventeen

1.   From a letter by Edward Poett of the cutter *Kefaya*.

2.   By coincidence, *Stornoway*'s home port in New York was also for some years the moorage of Harry Pidgeon's *Islander*.

3.   See "Transit Through the Funnel of the World" by Marjorie Petersen in the March 1971 issue of *Boating* for the best account of a yacht passage through the Panama Canal. On Al's first transit, *Stornoway* was nearly wrecked in the turbulent locks.

4.   Petersen's adventures on the Red Sea and encounters with Arabs match those of William Robinson, who was captured by pirates, and of Dr. Robert Griffith, whose first *Awahnee* also went aground on a reef in the same locality.

5.   There have been many garbled version of Al's good deeds, but this one is the most authentic, originating with the Petersens.

6.   See *Stornoway, East and West* by Marjorie Petersen (New York: Van Nostrand, 1966).

7.   "Lewis" was the second dinghy smashed in by a curling wave coming over the cabin. This also happened to them on the rough passage of the coast of Venezuela en route to the Pacific.

8.   From a letter to Eleanor Borden, in *The Spray*, Vol. XIV, 1970.

9.   From a letter to the author dated April 29, 1973. The new book referred to was then being published by Van Nostrand, now Litton Educational Publications.

In a later letter, from *Stornoway* at Zea Marina, Piraeus, Greece, Marjorie reported a stormy passage after crossing the Atlantic, via Haiti, Bermuda, Fayal, San Miguel, and on to Algeciras. In the Mediterranean, they suffered a knock-down one night in the Strait of Sicily in a sirocco.

"We will be here for awhile, waiting for winter to subside. Not too bad—39 degrees the lowest so far—but frightening southerly gales that have us right on a leed shore. And Piraeus is not the greatest—mud-colored high-rises taking the place of balconied shuttered gracious old houses; this senseless twirling of worry beads, the dirty-windowed coffee houses looking like the lobbies of old men's homes. We need to go sailing!"

Chapter Eighteen

1.   From a BBC newscast, quoted in *Around the World in Wanderer III* by Eric C. Hiscock (New York and London: Oxford University Press, 1956).

2.   The *America* was designed by George Steers after the fast pilot schooners of the time for a syndicate headed by John Cox Stevens, founder of the New York Yacht Club. The *America* was finished in June 1851 and sailed across the Atlantic for the race around Wight. She easily defeated the fourteen other vessels in the Royal Yacht Squadron Race. In 1857, the owners deeded the Cup to the New York Yacht Club with the condition that it be forever placed in international competition, open to any foreign yacht club with a vessel of thirty to three hundred tons. Over the years, English, Scottish, Canadian, Irish, and Australian yachts have tried to win it, but as of this writing, the Auld Mug remains at the NYYC.

3.   The Hiscocks, who thought *Wanderer II* too small, were taken aback when the new owner, "Tahiti Bill" Howell, and another Australian, Frank McNulty, sailed her from the United Kingdom to the Society Islands in good time with no difficulty; and when Bill later sailed her alone to Hawaii and then to Seattle, where he sold her. The Hiscocks met up with *Wanderer II* later in Hawaii, where they found her in good condition, but mounting a large outboard motor on the transom.

4.   See Bibliography for a list of Hiscock books.

5.   Erstwhile voyagers who dream of financing their ships with free-lance writing should take note that the Hiscocks were the only couple in yachting history to do so successfully. They succeeded, not only because of proper timing at the proper point in history, but because they were industrious, level-headed,

thrifty, and simple-living to an extreme seldom found in dreamers. They were also good business people, and started with a sound financial footing. It also helped to be able and articulate writers, and competent photographers. Even if one could sell regularly to the yachting publications and Sunday supplements in the face of the competition, the rates paid are so low that no one could finance a voyage outside the harbor from this source alone, especially at today's costs. The most successful sea wanderers have some sort of profession or trade that is in demand wherever they go, such as that of machinist, welder, doctor, dentist, cabinetmaker, rigger, with which temporary employment can be obtained. Today, the ports of the world frown darkly on penniless wanderers.

Incidentally, the Hiscocks purchased *Wanderer III* for only £3,300 in 1950. Their annual expenses on the first circumnavigation amounted to about £700 a year.

6.   Without doubt, the Hiscocks obtained *Wanderer IV* at considerable discount in return for the subsequent worldwide publicity and implied endorsement, which is one of the fringe benefits of becoming rich and famous.

Chapter Nineteen

1.   Paraphrased from Nevil Shute's introduction to Miles Smeeton's *Once Is Enough* (New York: John de Graff, Inc., 1960).

The Smeetons, incidentally, were the prototypes for John and Jo Dermott in Nevil Shute's *Trustee From the Toolroom*. Unlike the Dermotts who tried to get out of England with their funds converted to diamonds imbedded in the concrete ballast of their yacht, the *Shearwater*, the Smeetons planned to use their impounded savings to buy a yacht, sail it to British Columbia, and sell it there. See Smeeton's last book, *The Sea Was Our Village* (Sidney, B.C.: Gray's Publishing Ltd.).

2.   John Guzzwell was also in Victoria at the time, building his tiny Giles-designed *Trekka*.

3.   *Tzu Hang* was designed by H. S. Rouse and built by Hop Kee at Hong Kong in 1939. She was 46.2 feet overall, 36 feet on the waterline, with a beam of 11.7 feet and a draft of 7 feet. A double-ender, she was originally fitted with a Gray gasoline engine.

4.   In 1951, William A. Robinson, with a crew of Tahitians, sailed his 70-foot brigantine *Varua* over the same route and survived the ultimate storm.

5.   *Tzu Hang*'s first capsize and dismasting was in the same general area where Robinson encountered the ultimate storm in 1951. Robinson later reported that he believed this was an uncharted shoal area.

6.   Like many a sailing man, the Smeetons were hung-up on engines. Not liking them, they gave them little attention—except in an emergency, when, because of neglect, they usually didn't function. Nevil Shute chided them mildly for this. At the first opportunity, the Smeetons replaced the old engine with a modern lightweight marine diesel.

7.   *The West in My Eyes.* See Bibliography.

8.   The Smeetons were miffed over this legal entanglement which spoiled their stay in Alaska, but had no one but themselves to blame for it. It is surprising that old travelers and experienced hands at dealing with customs would fall into this trap. They did not enter Alaska properly, but even so they would have gotten away with it had it not been for the over-officious part-time agent in Cold Bay. Moreover, the fact that a port of entry is maintained at Sand Point in the lonely Shumagins for the express purpose of serving Canadian fishing

vessels suggests that there is a continuing customs problem here with Canadians (and the Smeetons flew the Canadian flag). It is a standard joke in the Aleutians and Westward Alaska that the Canadians think they own Alaska. Most Alaskans overlook it, but to some it is a continuing galling irritation.

9.   The Smeetons were awarded the Blue Water Medal for 1973 by the Cruising Club of America.

10.   During the preparation of this book, I saw the *Tzu Hang* from the deck of an Anacortes-Sydney ferryboat, tied to a mooring in the San Juans, looking peaceful and content to stay home. Later I made a special trip back by private boat but could not find her.

11.   Trying to locate the Smeetons, I was told by their present publisher, Tim Campbell of Gray's Publishing, Ltd., in Sidney, B.C., that I could track them down in Alberta. "They are presently raising two moose on their own game farm near Cochrane, Alberta (about forty miles west of Calgary). They sold their boat to Bob Nance, but come back to the coast now and then to check up on her."

When I found the Smeetons in Cochrane, Alberta, Miles Smeeton confirmed that, indeed, they were really raising moose, and that they were working on their next book, *Moose Magic*. Clio and her husband were also living in Canada. At the time I contacted the Smeetons, they had just entertained Annie Wiele, who was on a visit to Canada.

Chapter Twenty

1.   Suggested by Kipling's children's story of the white seal. See also *Conversation with a World Voyager* by Gerry Trobridge (New York: Seven Seas Press, 1971).

2.   Plans for *Tahiti* and many other Hanna designs are still available from his widow, Dorothy, at Dunedin, Florida.

3.   *Conversation with a World Voyager* (see Note 1).

4.   *Tahiti*'s vitals are: length overall, 30 feet; load waterline, 26 feet; beam, 10 feet; draft, 4 feet; displacement, 18,100 pounds. *Carol*'s are: 36 feet 8 inches, 32 feet 10 inches, 12 feet, 4 feet, and 29,300 pounds, respectively.

5.   *White Seal* had a steel trough of ¾ inch plate for a keel. Bottom plating was a ³⁄₁₆ inch steel plate. Topsides and cabin were ⅛ inch. Frames were 4 inches by ½ inch steel, with six longitudinals of 1½ by ¼ inch steel let into the frames. The chine and sheer strake were bolstered with 1½ inch pipe.

6.   While in the Great Lakes area, the president of the Le Roi company heard about *White Seal*, came down to see the engine, and later had it torn down and rebuilt at no charge.

7.   For one thing, the old belief held by the Boers that the world was flat, not round, still persists in some quarters. See Slocum for an amusing account of this.

8.   Since the closing of the Suez Canal, the heavy tanker and steamship traffic makes the offshore passage hazardous. See Robin Graham for his experiences in *Dove*, trying to get around close to shore.

9.   Although they had hurried to get to Brisbane in time, they needn't have, Gerry said later. The baby didn't come for a full three weeks. They were to learn later that their daughter was never on time for anything, said Gerry.

10.   In a recent letter, Hamish Campbell, now a physician who took over his father's practice, said he had to confine his sailing to inland waters on a day sailer.

Chapter Twenty-one

1.   From *Awahnee Newsletter* #14, in *The Spray*, Volume XVI, 1972.

2.   Soon after the Griffiths' voyage, Dr. David Lewis, another well-known circumnavigator, departed on an attempt to circle the globe at 60° S, nonstop and solo, on the small *Icebird*.

3.   See also *Sea Spray* magazine published at Wellington, for June, July, and August 1971.

4.   The nearest charted land was the Nimrod Island group, three hundred miles to the north. The U.S. Hydrographic Office reported the islands were discovered in 1828 and not sighted again. In 1952, they were removed from all charts as nonexistent. The Griffiths applied to have them named the Awahnee Islands.

5.   Named for the legendary Nathaniel Palmer, who, in his teens, skippered a whaling supply vessel and purportedly was the first to discover or actually sight the Antarctic continent.

6.   See also *National Geographic* magazine, November 1971, Vol. 140, No. 5, pp. 635.

7.   Man-overboard is one of the most harrowing things that can happen to voyagers, and it happens all too frequently. Another notable incident was when Beryl Smeeton was thrown into the sea as *Tzu Hang* pitchpoled near Cape Horn.

8.   In a letter from Bob Griffith, early in 1974, from Hawaii, he indicated *Awahnee* was still alive and well after 13 years of world voyaging, making frequent passages to and from the mainland.

Chapter Twenty-two

1.   *Kurun Around the World* by Jacques-Yves Le Toumelin (New York: E. P. Dutton & Company, Inc., 1955). First published in France as *Kurun Autour du Monde*.

2.   Later it was claimed that they had joined the *Maquis* (French underground group during WW II).

3.   This is possibly the original root of the present word America.

4.   *Kurun*'s dimensions were: length overall, 33 feet; waterline, 27 feet 10 inches; beam, 11 feet 10 inches; draft, 5 feet 4 inches; displacement, 8.5 tons. She was of the Norwegian double-ender design.

5.   Also aboard were the Belgian couple, the Van de Wieles, who later became famous for their voyage in *Omoo*.

6.   Lee was the prototype for Jack Donelly in Nevil Shute's *Trustee From the Toolroom*.

7.   Peter Pye, the somewhat haughty Englishman who called here later on his well-publicized voyage, also wanted to meet Robinson and was snubbed to his dismay.

8.   Such a sail is similar to the "Swedish mainsail," a heavy weather sail designed to be used unreefed.

9.   See Slocum's account of this delightful interlude.

Chapter Twenty-three

1.   Bernard Moitessier, on the occasion of the meeting of the four French sailors in Durban.
2.   Quoted from an interview with Tom Hutch of the *Washington Post*.
3.   From *The National Fisherman*, Vol. 52, No. 9.
4.   See the story of John Hanna in the *Designs of John Hanna* (New York: Seven Seas Press, 1971).
5.   See *Sailing to the Reefs* by Bernard Moitessier for the fascinating and salty—and sometimes acrimonious—bull sessions held by these four legendary French seamen. Also in Durban at the time were Henry Wakelam on *Wanda*, and Raymond Cruikshank on *Vagabond*, among other sea wanderers.
6.   *Aficionados* of John Hanna and *Tahiti* should note also that Tom Steele in *Adios*, a 32-foot version of *Tahiti*, was capsized and dismasted off Cape Horn in almost the same spot. Although Steele also made two circumnavigations in his *Tahiti* ketch, he would be the first to point out that there is no such thing as a "non-capsizable" boat.
7.   *The Spray*, Vol. XVI, 1972.
8.   From *The National Fisherman*, Jan. 1972, Vol. 52, No. 9. In the fall of 1972, the John Swain boat shop in Cambridge, Maryland was selected to repair and refasten *Atom's* hull. Swain removed a defective plank from the yacht's garboard strake, which now hangs proudly in his office to "remind him of his friendship with M. Gau." Swain, at the time only 28, was already well-known for his boat designs.
   A final note on the aging circumnavigator and his aging *Atom*: After his boat was repaired and re-outfitted, Jean Gau sailed again across the Atlantic. When he had not been heard from for five months, the French government launched an extensive search, unsuccessfully. Months later, in 1973, Gau turned up in France —alone, penniless, and without *Atom*. His beloved ketch had been blown up on the beach of North Africa and this time had been wrecked beyond salvage.

Chapter Twenty-four

1.   Advice given to Marcel Bardiaux on navigating the Patagonian channels. From *4 Winds of Adventure* by Marcel Bardiaux (London: Adlard Coles, Ltd., 1961). Originally published by Flammarion, 1958.
2.   Henri Dervin also designed Le Toumelin's *Kurun*. The completed vessel was 30 feet 8 inches overall, with a beam of 8 feet 10 inches, a draft of 5 feet 9 inches, a displacement of 4 tons. The Marconi rig normally set 435 square feet of canvas. A spanker was fitted at Buenos Aires, much in the same manner that Slocum added a jigger before attempting the Horn.
3.   Such bureaucratic red tape has finally reached the United States. Current proposals will give the Coast Guard unlimited power to prevent a yacht from leaving port if, in the opinion of an officer, the vessel is "unsound."
4.   This book was even then out of print. Not even Bernicot had a copy of it. The inscription Bernicot wrote on the flyleaf was: "To M. Bardiaux, in expression of my fellow-feeling with most sincere good wishes for the success

which he deserves. I have no doubt he will make one of our best sailors. La Rochelle, 26.6.50, L. Bernicot."

5.   Such bureaucratic logic can be found in the military of every country in the world.

6.   A Brazilian buddy in my navy outfit during World War II never went anywhere without his bag of pills, which included a hypodermic needle for frequent self-inflicted shots.

7.   Among others who explored the Patagonian channels in the same period were the Griffiths on *Awahnee,* Dr. David Lewis, Edward Allcard, and Major Tilman.

Chapter Twenty-five

1.   From Bernard Moitessier's logbook, on his decision to drop out of the Golden Globe race, quoted by Nicholas Tomalin and Ron Hall in *The Strange Last Voyage of Donald Crowhurst.* See Bibliography.

2.   By a quirk of fate, another colonial, Donald Crowhurst, was in the same area at the same time, trying to win the Golden Globe Race fraudulently.

3.   In a letter to his publishers, Flammarion, Paris, explaining why he was dropping out of the race.

4.   *The Spray,* Vol. XIII, No. 1, Spring, 1969.

5.   At the same time, Crowhurst, another colonial, was growing up in nearby India.

6.   See *Sailing to the Reefs* (London: Hollis & Carter, 1971), by Moitessier for the further details of these bull sessions on the *Korrigan.* Among other subjects, that of sea anchors came in for a most stimulating analysis by these experts.

7.   Flammarion, Paris, 1960.

8.   *Joshua's* specifications were: 39 feet 6 inches, loa; 33 feet 9 inches, lwl; 12 feet beam; 5 feet 3 inches draft; ballast 6,615 pounds; displacement 13 tons; sail area 1,100 square feet.

9.   *Alone Through the Roaring Forties* by Vito Dumas. See Bibliography.

10.   In spite of Moitessier's bold experiment, the Dumas school of thought on running before the seas of the Southern Ocean is considered foolhardy by many deepwater sailors, including Robinson, Hiscock, and the Smeetons. It definitely is not for amateurs without adequate life insurance.

11.   See *The Strange Last Voyage of Donald Crowhurst.*

Chapter Twenty-six

1.   J. R. L. Anderson in the epilogue to Sir Francis Chichester's *The Lonely Sea and the Sky* (New York: Coward-McCann, 1964).

2.   *The Strange Last Voyage of Donald Crowhurst* by Nicholas Tomalin and Ron Hall (New York: Stein and Day Publishers, 1970).

3.   In his book, Robin Knox-Johnston remarks, "If I was not to be first, then it must be a Briton." Another stunter, John Fairfax, who rowed across both the Atlantic and the Pacific in an Uffa Fox designed rowboat, remarked at the completion of the voyage that he would donate his boat to anyone, as long as it was a Briton. That nationalistic pride motivated most of the entrants is pretty obvious.

4.   Later, one of the Golden Globe entrants, Chay Blyth, conceived the idea for a "wrong way" nonstop circumnavigation, west-about against prevailing winds of the southern latitudes.

5.   See *Two Against the Western Ocean* by Patrick Elam and Colin Mudie.

Chapter Twenty-seven

1.   On passing Cape Horn, from *My Lively Lady* by Sir Alec Rose. See Bibliography.

2.   In this turn of the card lay the seed that led to the interest in a round-the-world race and the *Sunday Times* Golden Globe competition.

3.   *Lively Lady's* vital statistics were: 36 feet loa; 31 feet lwl; 9.2 feet beam; 6.6 feet draft; displacement 13.75 tons. The boat was designed by the first owner, S. J. P. Cambridge, O.B.E., and F. Shepherd, and built by the owner in Calcutta in 1948. It was originally a cutter rig, changed to a yawl by Rose, although mizzen was only used normally for a staysail. The engine was a Morris paraffin (kerosene) model originally. See the Appendix of Rose's book for a discussion of Cape Horn, and a comparison of the vessels of Slocum, Gerbault, Rose, and Pidgeon.

4.   The personal interest and paternal attitude of the Royal Navy toward its yachting nationals never fails to astound and awe American yachtsmen who are too frequently regarded as damn fools at best, if not completely ignored, by the U.S. Navy and Coast Guard. Certainly the Navy Department would not be likely to station a ship off the Horn to watch out for lonely American yachts, as England did for Chichester and Rose. Unofficially, to be fair, however, Navy and Coast Guard personnel are individually hospitable and helpful when the occasion arises.

Chapter Twenty-eight

1.   A radio signal used by Chichester on his record-breaking circumnavigation during which he maintained constant communications with shore stations.

2.   Reported by Michael Hayes, Reuters staff writer.

3.   Sayle's story appeared in the *Sunday Times*, March 21, 1967, to scoop the world press.

4.   Chichester had a defect of vision from childhood days, but this was corrected by glasses. It was not a progressive disease and it never interfered with his flying or sailing.

5.   Pilots affectionately refer to the old *Gipsy Moth* as a ship that "takes off at 40, flies at 40, and lands at 40." It is the British equivalent of the Piper *Cub*.

6.   *Gipsy Moth II* was the derelict *Florence Edith*, rebuilt by Chichester. *Gipsy Moth III*, designed by Robert Clark, was built at Arklow, Eire, by Jack Tyrrell. It was 39.6 feet overall; 29 feet on the waterline, 10 foot beam, and had a draft of 6.4 feet. *Gipsy Moth IV*, designed by Illingworth & Primrose, was built of laminated wood by Camper & Nicholsons, Gosport, Hants in 1966. Length overall was 53 feet; lwl, 38.5 feet; beam, 10.5 feet; draft, 7.7 feet, displacement, 11.5 tons. She was equipped with a Perkins 4–107 diesel engine.

Gipsy Moth V, designed by Robert Clark, was 60 feet in overall length, a staysail ketch (without mainsail), long, lean, and steady for ocean racing.

7.   *Cardinal Vertue* was later sailed around the world via Cape Horn singlehandedly by the Australian, Bill Nance, brother of Bob, who accompanied the Smeetons on their third and successful attempt at the Horn.

8.   The title comes from John Masefield's *Sea Fever,* the passage being, "I must go down to the sea again, the lonely sea and the sky."

Chapter Twenty-nine

1.   *Trimaran Solo* by Nigel Tetley (Lymington: Nautical Publishing Company, 1970).

2.   Actually, Crowhurst was loafing along aimlessly at about sixty miles per day in the Atlantic, which he never left, sending false position reports.

3.   In this area, on a second attempt to sail around the world, Bill King was attacked by a whale or killer whale, his vessel stove in, and he was barely able to limp into port.

4.   Tetley did not learn until weeks later that Moitessier had dropped out of the race after passing the Falklands.

5.   Although Tetley was technically the first to circumnavigate solo in a trimaran—having crossed his outbound track before he sank—the first *successful* circumnavigation in a tri probably was made by Mike Kane of California, on *Carousin II.* (See *The Spray,* Fall, 1968, for details.)

In a letter to me dated February 15, 1974, Commander Errol Bruce, well-known deep-water sailor, author, and director of Nautical Publishing Co., Ltd., wrote:

"Sadly enough, Nigel Tetley died a year or so after his circumnavigation. . . . Bill King is now in good health, but he certainly looked very frail on completion of his circumnavigation. [See Chapter 31.] Of course Alec Rose arrived back in the best of good health and settled down with us here in Lymington to write his book very soon after his arrival in England."

Chapter Thirty

1.   *A World of My Own* by Robin Knox-Johnston (New York: William Morrow & Co., 1970).

2.   *Suhaili's* vital statistics were: 32 feet 5 inches loa, 28 feet lwl, 11 feet 1 inch beam, 5 feet 6 inches draft. The plain sail area was 666 square feet, Thames measurement, 14 tons; gross tonnage, 9.72, net 6.29. The keel was cast iron of 2¼ tons.

3.   The spectacular voyages of Francis Chichester and Alec Rose, both of whom were of retirement age, had so captured the public's imagination, that it obscured Robin's greater achievement.

4.   See *The Strange Last Voyage of Donald Crowhurst,* cited elsewhere. See Bibliography.

5.   Ironically, Robin almost missed crossing the finish line, which had been changed by the *Sunday Times* committee after he had departed.

6.   *A World of My Own.*

Chapter Thirty-one

1.   *The Impossible Voyage* by Chay Blyth (New York: G. P. Putnam's Sons, 1972).
2.   The *only* way one can sail nonstop around the world is via the sailing ship passages south of the capes.
3.   The *Endurance* was on ice patrol at least *officially*. It is noteworthy that the British navy takes such an interest in its yachtsmen. Chichester, Rose, and Robin Knox-Johnston were also the object of navy interest in the vicinity of the Horn. One reason may be that the United Kingdom would like to draw attention to its role in those waters and to its presence in the disputed Falklands.
4.   *British Steel's* dimensions were: 59 feet loa; lwl, 43 feet 6 inches; beam 12 feet 10 inches; draft, 8 feet. The sails by Ratsey & Lapthorn included a main of 408 square feet, a mizzen of 150 square feet, a main jib of 693 square feet, plus a boomed foresail of 208 square feet. The hull was built of mild steel plate to Lloyds Grade A specification. The deck was of half-inch marine plywood, covered by two layers of fiberglass with epoxy resin.
5.   Blyth later built a 77-foot ocean racer, *Great Britain II*, at Ramsgate, and trained a crew of 13 paratroopers for the Whitbread round-the-world race to start and finish at Portsmouth. This 34-ton new yacht was designed by Alan Gurney, designer of *Windward Passage*, called the fastest racing yacht in the world after winning several ocean races, including the 1971 TransPac.
6.   Another rowing team was not so successful. The boat used by David Johnston and John Hoare was found months later, overturned and barnacle-encrusted.
7.   Captain Ridgway was also entered in the Golden Globe, but dropped out early.
8.   Chay Blyth says he carried with him the rope doll, "Winston," a lion, given him by Sir Alec Rose, for whom it brought good luck—thus giving Winston a second circumnavigation. Winston, however, was not mentioned by Rose in his book. Instead, he mentions being given a leprechaun by Irish actor Ray McAnally, a friend of his son David. It was claimed the leprechaun would undo all the snarled ropes. "Algy" was a large stuffed white rabbit which David and Baba loaned their father as a mascot, and was carried around the world. Mrs. Rose wrote later that Algy and the leprechaun "did not get on" together, so Alec decided not to take the latter.
   Early in 1974, Blyth and *Great Britain II* were on the last leg of Whitbread round-the-world race, and leading the surviving fleet of contestants by several hundred miles.

Chapter Thirty-two

1.   *So You Want To Sail Around the World* by Alan Eddy; published without date by the Allied Boat Company, Inc., Catskill, New York; with cover painting by marine artist James Mitchell.
2.   See Appendix for other encounters with whales, one of the most serious hazards of ocean voyaging in small boats today.
3.   *Opogee* was a Luders-designed *Seawind* model, built of fiberglass by Allied Boat Company of Catskill, New York, one of the pioneers in fiberglass

sailing yachts. Another Allied Luders was the 33-footer in which Robin Graham finished his tedious circumnavigation.

4.   From *So You Want To Sail Around the World*.

In a letter to me, dated February 19, 1974, Albert F. Smith, Jr., sales manager of Allied Boat Co., Inc., reported *Opogee* still being sailed by Eddy, and still in excellent condition. He also noted that Robin Lee Graham (see Chapter 36) finished his circumnavigation with an Allied *Luders* 33, one of the company's stock fiberglass yachts.

Chapter Thirty-three

1.   *Once Is Enough* by Miles Smeeton (London: Rupert Hart-Davis, 1960).

2.   W. A. Robinson in *Varua* encountered the ultimate storm in the same general area a few years earlier.

3.   See *Two Against the Western Ocean* by Patrick Elam and Colin Mudie. Mudie, a young Giles associate, later became a well-known designer in his own right.

4.   *Trekka* was 20.8 feet loa; 18.5 feet lwl; 6.5 feet beam; 4.5 feet draft. She was built of plywood bulkheads tied to bunks and internal parts, with a laminated keel and steam bent timbers of oak. The skin planking was $\frac{9}{16}$ red cedar, edge-glued. The hull and plywood deck were covered with fiberglass, and later in New Zealand, the bottom also was sheathed with fiberglass. The fin keel and skeg were of $\frac{3}{8}$ inch steel plate. She was ketch rigged, with a total of 340 square feet of sail.

"Trekka" comes from the Boer, "Voortrekkers," who trekked up into the Transvaal and Natal in the 1860s.

5.   *Trekka Around the World* by John Guzzwell. See Bibliography. Guzzwell was awarded the Blue Water Medal of the Cruising Club of America for his circumnavigation.

6.   In March 1974, however, I found him aboard *Treasure* at Honolulu's yacht harbor.

What's John doing now? In a letter to the author he wrote:

"After building *Treasure* in England we voyaged to the South Pacific, to Australia and New Zealand, staying some fours years in New Zealand where I built a couple of yachts. We circumnavigated New Zealand in 1970, then came to Hawaii where I built a 47-foot ketch for a local man and am now halfway through building a sister ship of my *Treasure* for another man. In 1972 we took *Treasure* to Alaskan waters, Kodiak, Prince William Sound and the Inside Passage, then returned to Hawaii. We plan to continue cruising after I've finished building this present yacht. My sons are now 12 years old and although we'd like to be cruising now, I also have to earn our living like the rest of the world— however, we escape once in a while!"

Chapter Thirty-four

1.   From the epitaph on the gravestone memorial of Robert Louis Stevenson, written by himself before his death on Samoa.

2.   Robin was the youngest to circumnavigate, but *Dove* was not the smallest. John Guzzwell in *Trekka* had already established this.

3.   Many voyagers, particularly those who sail alone, now carry tape recorders. If nothing else, it provides the morale-booster of having something to "talk to." Behaviorists have found in recorded tapes a gold mine of research into how the human mind behaves under conditions of extreme tension and long periods of loneliness.

4.   See *Dove* by Robin Lee Graham with Derek L. T. Gill (New York: Harper & Row, Publishers, 1972). Also the *National Geographic* magazine, October 1968; April 1969; and October 1970. At this writing, Gregory Peck has announced that he will produce a movie based upon Robin and Patti's life, including the circumnavigation. A yacht like *Dove* sold for between $6,000 and $10,000 at the time. Another $5,000 would be required to outfit and prepare for ocean cruising.

5.   A better selection of a firearm would have been a .22 rifle or a combination .22/.20 gauge double-barreled survival gun. In most parts of the world today, any kind of a handgun is regarded with suspicion, a completely irrational and emotion-charged viewpoint, but a fact of life. The most recent voyagers have reported *any* kind of a firearm is now treated with suspicion and official red tape in most popular ports of call. They recommend none be carried —which shows how much the world has become "civilized" since Captain Slocum's day. Three-quarters of a century ago, every sailing yacht carried a sizable arsenal of weapons, and no one ever questioned it. Significantly, there was less violence at that time than there is now, when private firearms are illegal almost everywhere.

6.   The Fanning Island group includes Palmyra and Kingman which are U.S. controlled; and Christmas and Washington, both Commonwealth administered. They lie directly south of Hawaii and about halfway to Tahiti.

7.   The *Ohra*, a 25-foot cutter with an Australian skipper and Canadian mate, had left Darwin on a global voyage, but off Madagascar broke the rudder in a storm. A Japanese freighter came alongside to help, but damaged the boat. The two men had to abandon her. A day later the *Ohra* washed up ashore near Durban. She was salvaged with the help of a bulldozer.

8.   This is the same firm that built *Opogee*, the first fiberglass boat to sail around the world.

9.   By comparison, it took Captain Harry Pidgeon almost eighty days to cover the same route.

10.   One reason for Robin's unexpected welcome was that he entered harbor as the fleet entered in the annual Ensenada Race was leaving. All the boats saluted him riproariously as they passed. He was also met by Al Ratterree with Patti and the family yacht at 6 A.M. with a basket of sweet rolls, melon, and champagne, before the customs and immigration officials and the press reached them. Robin remembered the babble of American voices seemed strange to his ears.

Chapter Thirty-five

1.   From a letter by john H. Sowden, *The Spray*, Vol. XIII, No. 1, Spring 1969.

2.   See Chapter 36 on Leonid Teliga and *Opty*.

3.   *The Spray*, Vol. XIII, Spring 1969. From Papeete, the three single-handers, Sowden, Teliga, and Trauner, wrote a long letter to the Slocum Society about this. Among other things, they asked that a list be compiled of all solo

circumnavigations—a list that remains to be compiled, and probably would be impossible.

4.   Complaints about foreign harbor fees and red tape are common among American voyagers. Few of them realize that other aliens have similar problems at times in U.S. ports.

5.   No one suspected at this time that Teliga was already suffering from terminal cancer.

6.   For the story of *Cetacean*, see Chapter 38. As of this writing, partly due to the post–World War II "pioneers," Bali is again becoming a yachtsmen's mecca, and a tropical, exotic Far East paradise, replacing such places as Tahiti as a romantic waypoint.

7.   In a recent letter, Dr. Campbell told me that voyagers no longer will find Durban a haven of hospitality. The welcome mat is no longer out. Dr. Campbell, himself a sailor and a long-time host, found his medical practice too demanding, and any spare time was spent sailing a Solent on inland waters.

Chapter Thirty-six

1.   From a notice published by the Slocum Society for members, Autumn 1967.

2.   From a story in a Polish periodical, translated by Michael Chelchowsky.

3.   *Opty* was a neat and trim yawl with underwater lines similar to the John Alden yachts, and a small but pleasing transom and overhang. She was 32 feet loa, and registered as a five-ton vessel. She was built by Teliga in his backyard and fitted out mainly by his own hands. Existing photos attest to the good workmanship that went into the construction. No one will ever know the whole story of the legal red tape and complications that had to be overcome to make his dream come true in an Iron Curtain country.

4.   For another voyage in this area, see the account of Bill and Phyllis Crowe on *Lang Syne*.

5.   From a letter dated April 4, 1971.

6.   Teliga was one of the few voyagers to be so honored; not even Captain Joshua Slocum achieved this. Commodore John Pfleiger of the Slocum Society tried in vain to get the U.S. postal officials to issue a commemorative stamp on the fiftieth anniversary of Slocum's circumnavigation. A 68-peso stamp was issued by Argentina in 1968 to mark the twenty-fifth anniversary of Vito Dumas's solo voyage during the early years of World War II. He was first to do it in the Roaring Forties, his track having been followed later by Bill Nance, Chichester, Alec Rose, Nigel Tetley, Robin Knox-Johnston, Moitessier, the Smeetons, the Griffiths, Dr. David Lewis, Marcel Bardiaux, and others.

Chapter Thirty-seven

1.   From a notice published by the Slocum Society in the club bulletin, Summer 1970.

2.   The Condor-class sloop is 24 feet loa, 8 feet beam, and 5 feet draft, with a sail area of 280 square feet.

3.   For all the things that can and do go wrong with a new boat, even with veteran circumnavigators, see *Sou'West in Wanderer IV* by Eric Hiscock (London: Oxford University Press, 1973).

4.   This once more illustrates how difficult it is to spot a small boat in a running sea. Once, not long ago, I accompanied a search and rescue mission for a 40-foot boat disabled in the Gulf of Alaska. Although we had constant radio communications and had the vessel on the radar screen with perfectly clear weather and only a moderate sea, the vessel was not spotted until we closed in to only a few hundred yards.

Chapter Thirty-eight

1.   *Trans-Pacific Trimaran* by Arthur Piver (Mill Valley: Pi-Craft, 1963).

2.   In the mid-1930s, Eric de Bisschop sailed his *Kaimiloa* from Hawaii to France by way of the Cape, and, in 1967, Dr. David Lewis and his family completed a circumnavigation in *Rehu Moana*.

3.   Comparing Piver's time with those of early conventional voyagers, however, is revealing: Slocum's passage to the Azores and Gibraltar, for example, was much faster than Piver's, in spite of the speed claimed for the trimaran.

4.   In *The Spray*, Vol. XV, 1971, Michael Kane claims his *Carousin II* was the first trimaran to sail around the world. He and an Australian designer Jock Crother were at the time building a 57-foot trimaran for an attempt at a nonstop circumnavigation averaging 200 miles a day. By early 1974, it had not yet started.

5.   *Rehu Moana* means "ocean spray." Design by Colin Mudie, she was built by Prout Brothers at Canvey Island, Essex, in 1963. The length overall was 40 feet; lwl, 35 feet; beam, 17 feet; draft, 3 feet and 5 feet with centerboard down; displacement, 8 tons; sail area 700 square feet; power, British Seagull 4-horsepower outboard. The skin was ⅜-inch plywood on laminated frames and knees. A half ton of lead was used for ballast. Behind watertight bulkheads were foam floatation compartments designed to float the vessel even if both hulls were stove in.

6.   *Cardinal Vertue* was purchased by Bill Nance, the Australian, who circumnavigated singlehanded east-about via the three capes, from September 1963 to August 1968, ending in Florida.

7.   One of the crew on the shakedown cruise was Axel Pedersen, who later circumnavigated in *Marco Polo*.

8.   Others in the same general area at the time included Bill Nance on *Cardinal Vertue*, the Griffiths on *Awahnee*, and no doubt others.

9.   Hoto Matur'a was reputed to be the first of the ancient voyagers to visit Easter Island and to people it. Since the Lewises arrived on a twin-hulled vessel, they were regarded by some superstitious natives as the second coming of Hoto Matur'a.

10.   For a clinical report of life aboard a catamaran, while circumnavigating with a wife and two small daughters, see *Daughters of the Wind* by David Lewis. His attempt at circumnavigating the Antarctic was carried by *National Geographic* magazine, December 1973.

Chapter Thirty-nine

1. Edward Allcard, *The Spray*, 1970, Vol. XIV.
2. Jean-Charles Taupin, *The Spray*, Autumn 1969, Vol. XIII, No. 3.
3. Bill Nance is the brother of Bob, who accompanied the Smeetons on the third and successful attempt at the Horn, and who purchased *Tzu Hang* when the Smeetons retired to an Alberta ranch.
4. See *The Spray*, Spring 1969, Vol. XIII, No. 1, for Murnan's discussion of his novel sea anchor.
5. For this passage, Dr. Holcomb received the CCA John Parkinson Memorial Trophy Award.
6. Dr. Holcomb was also a well-known TransPac competitor.
7. *Viking* was 35 feet 6 inches loa, 30 feet lwl, 12 feet beam, and 6 feet 6 inches draft. Under new ownership, *Viking* was lost in the Galápagos Islands on a subsequent voyage. In a recent letter from the modest couple, it was learned they are operating a charter service on their new yacht in the Virgin Islands, with home port at St. Thomas.
8. In a letter received at the last minute before publication, Louis Van de Wiele wrote that he and Annie had purchased, and were living in, the Château de Madaillan, a castle in Par Laugnac, France:
    "My wife has gone to Canada for a month [to visit the Smeetons]. . . . She must be fairly close to you right now. . . . We sold *Omoo* in Mombasa in 1955, after sailing her from Belgium via the Red Sea. We lived up country in Kenya for five years. Back to Belgium in 1960, where I took up yacht designing, which is now my profession and livelihood. In 1968 we bought a 13th–14th Century feudal castle, or what remains of it, in the southwest of France, where we came to live permanently in 1970. I still design boats, but do little sailing, my wife rather more, when she gets the chance."
9. *The Spray*, Autumn 1969, Vol. XIII, No. 3.
10. By coincidence, Shaw was later aboard the *Dante Deo* when she was wrecked in the China Sea.
11. The Suez Canal has been closed since that war, forcing all yachts to go around the Cape of Good Hope or transport overland.
12. *The Spray*, 1971, Vol. XV.
13. Hannes Lindeman had gained fame by crossing the Atlantic in a folding canoe. *Elsie* was formerly the *Liberia IV*, her actual measurements being 29 feet 6 inches loa. She was built in Hamburg in 1958. Dr. Lindeman sailed her from Germany to the Congo via the Bahamas.
14. *Tahiti's* original dimensions were: 30 feet loa; lwl, 26 feet; beam, 10 feet; draft, 4 feet. The ocean sailing rig totaled 422 square feet, the coastwise rig, 470 square feet. Displacement was 18,100 pounds—more than most modern ocean-racing 40-footers. Later builders increased the sail area to 500 square feet for better performance. *Tahiti's* prototype was named *Orca*, and appeared in 1923. *Carol*, the 37-foot version, appeared in 1924.
    John G. Hanna was born on October 14, 1889, in Galveston, Texas. Deaf since a scarlet fever attack at age seven, he was largely a self-taught engineer and designer, writer, and inventor. During World War I, he was an aeronautical engineer, designing propellers for Glenn Curtis. In a letter to Weston Farmer in 1930, Hanna related that Wilbur Wright himself had told him that his control patent was up to that time the only one that was not an infringement of the original Wright patent.

He married a schoolteacher from South Dakota named Dorothy Trask, whom he met aboard ship on a voyage between Galveston and New York. They settled permanently in Dunedin, Florida, in 1921, and had four children. He was a long-time contributor to *Rudder, Motor Boat,* and other yachting publications, and was widely known as the Sage of Dunedin because of his sharp and pithy comments.

15.   *Adios* was a 32-foot version of *Tahiti* and was the "plug" for the fiberglass model now molded by a Carpenteria, California, firm, I was told.

16.   Technically, Mermod did not complete his circumnavigation because he did not cross his outbound track.

17.   Readers will find all the raw and irrepressible clinical details in Zantzinger's book, *The Log of the Molly Brown* (Richmond, Va.: Westover Publishing Company, 1973).

18.   Readers will also be delighted to know that Zantzinger came through his financial and tax difficulties in reasonably good shape. In March 1974, he told me that he had finally gotten the *Molly Brown* back and was still sailing her on weekends. He was then living in a Washington, D.C., suburb with his parents, and working in a job that required traveling around the Eastern Seaboard.

Although the *Molly Brown,* and Zantzinger himself, proved unsinkable, the publishing firm that printed and marketed his book did not. In 1974, the firm went out of business, and the book went out of print.

Bibliography

THE LITERATURE OF THE SEA HAS GROWN RICH IN BOOKS OF bluewater adventuring, especially since the publication of Captain Slocum's best-selling classic (still in print), *Sailing Alone Around the World*. The insatiable appetite of readers who long for escape from their humdrum lives of quiet desperation and find it vicariously in the books of others is only whetted by each new one that gets published. The post–World War II boom in ocean voyaging, which leaped into a vigorous new generation of bluewater sailing in the 1960s with the Chichesters and the Roses, has become the phenomenon of the 1970s. And there seems to be no limit in sight, as long as the oceans remain free to the voyages, the voyagers, and their literature.

Another phenomenon of the 1970s has been the boom in book collecting, usually in specialized fields of interest—voyaging, for example. This has resulted in the rebirth and reprinting of many old classics, and a haunting of old book stores by *aficionados*. Many a rare edition has turned up, such as Tom Drake's *The Log of the Lone Sea Rover*, for lucky finders.

This bibliography is as complete as I could make it, yet still remains within shouting distance of the central theme of *The Circumnavigators*. It includes volumes which are available in English, either in print or in libraries—or in the possession of collectors, wherever they may be. Many of these books include not only narratives of high adventure, but also practical information on bluewater boats, heavy weather sailing, provisioning, and other fascinating details. Some of them are abominable examples of amateur writing, but are valuable for other reasons. In a couple of instances, even novels were included, such as the all-time classic of yachting, Erskine Childers' *The Riddle of the Sands*, not only for their literary excellence, but because they are based on real events and people.

During my own research for *The Circumnavigators*, I made an interesting discovery: Many of the voyagers reported encounters with others at various times in various parts of the world. By cross-checking these references, it was possible to get a more accurate perspective and more insight into the unwritten motives in many instances.

These are the books (and the list is in no way complete) I believe would be of interest to would-be voyagers, to collectors, to ordinary readers, and to all those home-bound souls seeking a vicarious passport to adventure on the oceans of the world.

ALLCARD, Edward, *Single-Handed Passage* (New York: W. W. Norton & Co., Inc., 1950).
———, *Temptress Returns* (New York: W. W. Norton & Co., Inc., 1953).
———, *Voyage Alone* (New York: Dodd, Mead, 1964).
An English naval architect and marine surveyor, Edward C. Allcard ran away to sea and abandoned his career in 1947 to become the dean of the loners who live the lives of sea birds that wander the oceans of the world. He is the British edition of that French iconoclast, Alain Gerbault. Literate and worth reading.

ANSON, Lord George, *A Voyage Around the World* (London and New York: J. M. Dent & Sons, Ltd., and E. P. Dutton & Co., 1911).
Worth reading, along with the accounts of circumnavigations by Dampier and Woodes Rodgers during the golden age of sea exploration when England, France, Portugal, Spain, and the Dutch fought for trade routes and dominance over the oceans. Most of their ships were not much larger than present-day yachts, and all of them were less seaworthy and less well-equipped. Anson's account of his voyage in the years 1740–1744 is valuable not only for details of the sea routes and encounters with foreigners in such places as Macao and Canton, but the introduction by John Masefield to this edition is a superb description of the British sailor and his life at sea in those times. No wonder they called them "iron men in wooden ships."

ANTHONY, Irvin, *Voyagers Unafraid* (Philadelphia: Macrae Smith Co., 1930).

BARDIAUX, Marcel, *4 Winds of Adventure* (New York and London: Adlard Coles, Ltd. and John de Graff, Inc., 1961; originally published in France by Flammarion in 1958).
The rambling narrative of one of France's greatest singlehanders, including the incredible account of building *Les Quatre Vents* under the noses of the Germans during the Occupation, and the author's subsequent daring and often hilarious adventures on his ultimate circumnavigation, although this volume takes you only as far as Tahiti (and maybe that's as far as you want to go).

BARTON, Humphrey D. E., *The Sea and Me* (London: Ross, 1952).
———, *Vertue XXXV* (New York: John de Graff, Inc., 1951).
Popular works by the venerable, salt-encrusted, irrepressible grand old man of British yachting.

BAUM, Richard, *By the Wind* (New York: Van Nostrand, 1962).

BELLOC, Hilaire, *The Cruise of the Nona* (Boston: Houghton-Mifflin Co., 1925).

————, *On Sailing the Sea* (New York: John de Graff, Inc., 1951).
Delightful books by one of the most literate of all writers of the sea and small boats.

BERNICOT, Louis, *The Voyage of the Anahita* (London: Rupert Hart-Davis, 1953).
This account of a singlehanded voyage around the world is one of the best by one of the least-celebrated of all the solo circumnavigators. Probably the best-loved of the French voyagers, Bernicot ironically predicted his own death—a fall from the mast of the *Anahita*.

BLYTH, Chay, *The Impossible Voyage* (New York: G. P. Putnam's Sons, 1972).
The hastily tossed together hodgepodge of this British stunter's life and solo circumnavigation in the *British Steel*, sponsored by the British steel industry and various others in England. If nothing else, it is a graphic account of how badly Britain wants to excel on the seas again, as in the days of the old empire.

BOMBARD, Alain, *The Voyage of the Hérétique* (New York: Simon & Schuster, 1954).
One of the stunters, Bombard, as a 27-year-old medical student, crossed the Atlantic alone in a 15-foot rubber dinghy without stores or water. Valuable as a clinical account of survival at sea.

BORDEN, Charles, *Sea Quest* (Philadelphia: Macrae Smith Co., 1967).
A personalized narrative of selected voyages and voyagers by an experienced sailorman and talented writer, with some interesting observations on types of craft, dangers encountered, and personalities involved. The late author had a career as colorful as any of his subjects, and had sailed the Pacific in his own 17-foot sloop.

BRADFIELD, S. E., *Road to the Sea* (London: Temple Press, 1964).

BRADFORD, Ernle, *Ulysses Found.* (New York: Harcourt, Brace, 1964).

BRASSEY, Mrs., *Around the World in the Yacht Sunbeam* (New York: Henry Holt and Co., 1879).
The housewifely account of a Victorian voyage around the later 1870s on the brigantine *Sunbeam*, with eleven passengers and a crew of thirty-two, including nurse, ladies' maid, and stewardess, by the wife of Thomas Brassey, Esq., M. P., millionaire liberal member of Parliament. Those days are gone forever, and almost forgotten.

BRUCE, Erroll, *Challenge to Poseidon* (New York: Van Nostrand, 1956).
A collection of adventures at sea.

CALDWELL, John, *Desperate Voyage* (New York: Ballantine Books, 1949).
The incredible account of an ex-merchant seaman who bought a 29-foot cutter in Panama and blundered across the Pacific to the ultimate end on a reef in order to be reunited with his sweetheart, Mary, in Australia in the hectic months following World War II.

Even if only half true, this is surely one of the most harrowing adventure (and love) stories ever written. What Caldwell lacked in literacy, he made up for in the sheer vigor, raw manhood, and resourcefulness of a young man against the unforgiving sea.

Caldwell eventually made it to Australia, was reunited with his Mary, and with the fortune he must have made off this book, built a Hanna *Carol* and a Herreshoff ketch, and with his wife and kiddies embarked on further and more sedate voyages. At last report he was managing a resort hotel in the West Indies.

CARLIN, Ben, *Half-Safe* (New York: Morrow, 1955).
The account of an amphibious trip around the world in the war surplus landing craft, *Half-Safe*, an optimistic name even at best, by the Australian, Ben Carlin. As a flack for an oil company in the 1960s, I had the duty of waving him on his way as he blundered his way through the Pacific Northwest of North America.

CHAPELLE, Howard I., *American Small Sailing Craft* (New York: W. W. Norton & Co., Inc., 1951).
A classic, still in print and going strong, this one is more than just what the title suggests. It is a brilliant history of the development of the best of American sailing craft under 40 feet, most of which were work boats, by a veteran naval architect, author, and head of the Department of Transportation of the Smithsonian Institution. The discussion on building boats and seaworthiness of small craft alone, makes it worth the price of admission.

CHAPMAN, Walker, *The Loneliest Continent* (Greenwich, Conn.; New York: Graphic Society Publishers, Ltd., 1964).
Résumés of some of the explorations of the southern continent. Interesting ones include that of Captain James Cook, and that of young Nat Palmer, who captained a supply ship while still in his teens, and made some important discoveries. At least two modern yachtsmen, Drs. David Lewis and Bob Griffith, have attempted Cook's circumnavigation of the continent in modern times.

CHATTERTON, E. Keble, *Ships and Ways of Other Days* (London: Sidgwick & Jackson, Ltd., 1913).
Chatterton was one of Britain's best-known yachtsmen and maritime writers in the early part of the century.

CHICHESTER, Sir Francis, *Gipsy Moth Circles the World* (New York: Coward McCann, 1968; London, Hodder and Stoughton, 1967).
————, *Alone Across the Atlantic* (New York: Doubleday, 1961).
————, *Atlantic Adventure* (New York: John de Graff, 1963).
————, *Along the Clipper Way* (London: Hodder & Stoughton, 1966.
————, *The Lonely Sea and the Sky* (New York: Coward-McCann, 1964).
The best-known works of that prolific writer of the sea and ocean voyages, and one of Britain's most astonishing sailors, who started out as a dare-devil airplane pilot. They reveal some of the inner workings of a born rebel who never let anything stop him from doing anything he felt like, and who was a master of getting himself out of the jams he got himself into.

CHILDERS, Erskine, *The Riddle of the Sands* (London: Rupert Hart-Davis, 1969).
One of the many editions of this classic sea-spy novel. It is considered not only first-rate fiction, but the greatest yachting story ever written. As a tale of espio-

nage, it was accurate and prophetic of later events. The author, a clerk in Parliament, became a leader in the Irish Rebellion, and a smuggler of arms (two of his co-conspirators were none other than Conor O'Brien and his sister). Childers was eventually executed by the I.R.A.

CLEMENTS, Rex, *A Gipsy of the Horn* (London: Ruper Hart-Davis, 1951).
Narrative of a voyage around the world in a three-masted bark, and how good it was (and wasn't) in the old windjammer days. Good reading and lots of on-board information about ports of call, sea conditions, and routes along the old clipper track, which is now becoming popular with yachtsmen.

CLIFFORD, Brian, *The Voyage of the Golden Lotus* (New York: John de Graff, Inc., 1963).

COLE, Jean, *Trimaran Against the Trades* (Tuckahoe, N.Y.: John de Graff, Inc., 1970). (First published in 1968 by A. H. & A. W. Reed, Wellington, N.Z.).
The voyage of the Piver trimaran *Galinule*, from Mobasa, Africa, to Wellington, N.Z., by the Cole family when their farm in Kenya was "confiscated" by the new government. On a trimaran they built themselves, the family found a new life in a new land. On the voyage were George and Jean Cole; their son, Charles, and daughter, Jane; and Granny Emie, who was ninety years old at the start of the voyage.

COLES, Kaines Adlard, *Heavy Weather Sailing* (New York: John de Graff, Inc., 1968).
A sobering, sensible, and painstakingly accurate analysis of storms at sea and the handling of small craft therein, especially under conditions of ultimate survival. Mandatory reading for any serious bluewater voyager, by a veteran yachtsman and writer.
———, *Close-Hauled* (London: Seeley, Service & Co.).
———, *North Atlantic* (New York: Norton, 1950).
———, *In Broken Water* (London: Seeley, Service & Co., 1925).
———, *In Finnish Waters* (London: Edward Arnold & Co., 1932).
Other fine books of cruising by the same author, accompanied by his wife.

COLLINS, Dale, *Sea Tracks of the Speejacks* (Garden City, N.Y.: Doubleday Page & Co., 1923).
A rare volume, the narrative of the voyage of the *Speejacks*, a 98-foot motor yacht, around the world in the Roaring Twenties, with the owner, a wealthy young midwest sportsman, his wife, and a crew of twelve. This is how they did it, when they had money, in the days of bathtub gin, Stutz Bearcats, and the Charleston dance. Worth reading, if only for the nostalgia, and the contrast to other circumnavigations.

COLVIN, Thomas, *Coastwise and Offshore Cruising Wrinkles* (New York: Seven Seas Press, 1972).
Some design ideas and philosophies by a self-taught naval architect, and some practical suggestions for outfitting and sailing small boats on long voyages. Includes some excellent charts for sea-wind conditions, when to reef and when to heave-to. Colvin is best-known for his shoal draft vessels and his modern version of the Chinese junk rig.

CONRAD, Joseph, *Sea Stories* (London: Rupert Hart-Davis, 1969).
A recent edition of an old classic. Somewhat tedious reading today, but the feel of the sea by this master of both fiction and ships is ageless.

COOK, Captain James, *The Explorations of Captain James Cook: As told by Selections of His Own Journals*, 1768–1779 (New York: Dover Publications, Inc., 1970).
One of the many reprints of the journals of this great pathfinder and sea explorer. Valuable to anyone voyaging around the Pacific.

CREALOCK, W. I. B., *Cloud of Islands* (New York: Hastings, 1955).

CROCKER, Templeton, *Cruise of the Zaca* (New York: Harper, 1923).
Another product of the 1920s, this time a voyage to the South Seas in utter luxury.

CROWE, Bill and Phyllis, *Heaven, Hell and Salt Water* (New York: John de Graff, Inc., 1957).
A rather wild title for an otherwise delightful book about how one American couple dropped out of the rat race in the late 1930s, and took to the sea in their own yacht, eventually sailing around the world in *Lang Syne*, a Block Island schooner, which they built themselves on the beach at Waikiki in the halcyon days just before Pearl Harbor.
What they lack in writing ability is made up for generously in their never-failing good humor, thorough competence and ability to handle easily any situation, including diplomatic as well as nautical and mechanical.
At this writing, the Crowes were still cruising in *Lang Syne,* in out-of-the-way places such as Baja, with the same quiet enthusiasm.

DAMPIER, William, *A New Voyage Around the World* (New York: Dover Publications, Inc., 1968).
A paperback version of the original published in 1967, by one of the most remarkable adventurers and travel writers who ever lived; in a period of discovery and exploration, political intrigue, buccaneers and privateers, and the stirrings of modern science and inquiry.

DARWIN, Charles, *The Voyage of the Beagle* (New York: Bantam Books, 1958).
A recent paperback edition of this classic, which is as good reading today as when written by the young scientist who sailed on a five-year voyage, while still in his twenties—a voyage that provided him with a lifetime career, plus his famous theory of evolution. A fascinating and remarkable journal by a gifted naturalist and writer, and one of the great minds of the nineteenth century. His accounts of explorations in the Magellan and Chilean straits will interest all small boat voyagers. His theory of how atolls were formed has been confirmed by modern test drilling through coral on South Pacific expeditions.

DAVENPORT, Philip, *The Voyage of Waltzing Matilda* (London: Hutchinson, 1953; New York: Dodd, Mead, 1954).
Voyage of the 46-foot Australian cutter to England, by way of the Strait of Magellan in the 1950s. The vessel was eventually lost at sea under new ownership.

DAVISON, Ann, *Last Voyage* (New York: Sloan, 1952).
——, *My Ship Is So Small* (New York: Sloan, 1956).
The writings of a famous lady singlehander who went on sailing after her husband died at sea, although obviously in a perpetual state of semi-terror. More the conquering of one's fears and the seeking of peace of mind, than of voyaging.

DAY, Beth, *Joshua Slocum, Sailor* (Boston: Houghton-Mifflin Co., 1953).
A little-known version of the famed captain's life and voyages, from information taken by the author from Slocum's daughter, Jessie Slocum Joyce. It is written on the juvenile level, but contains some previously unpublished details of the family, although it avoids some of the more unpleasant details such as the birth and death of the twins on the schooner in the Bering sea and some of Josh's other trials and tribulations.

DAY, Thomas Fleming, *The Voyage of the Detroit* (New York: Rudder Publishing Co., 1929).
——, *Across the Atlantic in Sea Bird* (Huntington, L.I.: Fore and Aft, 1926).
Rare today, but two of the best-known works of Day, veteran editor of *Rudder*, the father of American yachting and "day" sailing, who designed and built the famous *Sea Bird* and sailed her to Gibraltar and Italy in 1911. The first practical, home-built type sailing yacht capable of ocean voyages, *Sea Bird* was the basis for Pidgeon's *Islander*, Wightman's *Wylo*, Voss's *Sea Queen*, and hundreds of others. In 1912, with a crew of three, he took the 35-foot motor boat *Detroit* across the North Atlantic to Russia, where it was confiscated. The plans of *Sea Bird* are still available from *Rudder* after all these years.

DE BISSCHOP, Eric, *The Voyage of the Kamiloa* (London: G. Bell & Sons, Ltd., 1940).
An unusual book by a good writer on a unique voyage that was generally overlooked in the confusion of war when it first appeared. A student of oceanography, de Bisschop sailed from Hawaii to France in a Polynesian contraption consisting of two canoes lashed together with a platform. More than just a stunt.

DEVINE, Eric, *Midget Magellans* (New York: Harrison Smith & Robert Haas, 1935).
Some brief accounts of earlier bluewater voyages, but out of date and incomplete today.

DIBBERN, George, *Quest* (New York: Norton, 1941).
Rare but good.

DODD, Edward H., Jr., *Great Dipper to Southern Cross* (New York: Dodd, Mead, 1930).
Voyage of the 72-foot *Chance* from New England to Australia in the late 1920s.

DRAKE, Thomas, *The Log of the Lone Sea Rover* (Stanwood, Wash. Privately printed. Date unknown).
Very rare, this is the somewhat questionable narrative of the adventures of the Baron Munchausen of voyagers, Captain Tommy Drake, who was shipwrecked in every boat he sailed on, including the last one, in which he went missing. Most

of the information about him comes from the "morgue" files of the Seattle newspapers.

DUMAS, Vito, *Alone Through the Roaring Forties* (New York: John de Graff, Inc., 1960; also, Adlard Coles, Ltd.).
Dumas, a middle-aged Argentinian of Italian descent, became the first man to sail alone around the world east-about and in the high southern latitudes and completed the longest nonstop passages until Francis Chichester's day, in what was a personal adventure of incredible hardships and personal courage to the point of being almost masochistic. His seven-year itch became a two-year circumnavigation under the worst possible weather and sea conditions. The book suffers from poor translation from the original, which was neglected and overlooked during World War II.

EDDY, Alan, *So You Want to Sail Around the World* (Catskill, N.Y.: Allied Boat Co., no date).
A rare sleeper, long out of print, this was originally a promotion publication by the company that built the first fiberglass boat to sail around the world. Tantalizingly sketchy, it contains much valuable information for the aspiring bluewater voyager, including costs, dangers involved, and weather. Included also is a chilling account of an attack by a school of whales on his tiny vessel.

ELAM, Patrick and MUDIE, Colin, *Sopranino* (New York: John de Graff, Inc., 1958).
The story of *Sopranino*, designed by the brilliant Jack Giles, which at 20 feet overall length, became the first practical small vessel capable of safe ocean passages, and was a prototype for others to come, such as *Trekka*. With great wit and charm, it narrates also *Sopranino*'s first great test, across the Atlantic to the West Indies and the United States, with two carefree and adventurous lads. Mudie went on to become one of England's most imaginative and best-known small-boat designers. In a way, his career was similar to that of the late Uffa Fox, who was a crew member on Nutting's *Typhoon*, in the early 1920s, a voyage which resulted in the organization of the prestigious Cruising Club of America.

FAHNESTOCK, Bruce and Sheridan, *Stars to Windward* (New York: Harcourt, Brace, 1930).
Narrative of the voyage of the 60-foot schooner *Director*, on a circumnavigation from New York that ended in the Orient because of illness. With a crew of six, the voyage was for the most part a gay and often hilarious one, led by two members of a notoriously irrepressible Washington, D.C., family.

FAHNESTOCK, Mary Sheridan, *I Ran Away to Sea at Fifty* (New York: Harcourt, Brace, 1939).
Another account of the voyage of the *Director*, by the madcap mother of the Fahnestock boys, who joined the vessel for part of the cruise after her husband died of pneumonia.

FENGER, Frederic A., *The Cruise of the Diablesse* (New York: Yachting, Inc., 1926).
————, *Alone in the Caribbean* (New York: George H. Doran Co., 1917).
Two sea yarns by a charter member of the CCA, both with displays of right good seamanship, with a dash of adventurism. The latter is the log of the seventeen-foot sailing canoe, *Yakaboo*, on a six-month voyage through the Lesser Antilles.

FOX, Uffa, *Sailing, Seamanship, and Yacht Construction* (London: P. Davies, Ltd., 1934).
A classic by the famed British sailor and designer, who made his first ocean voyage in Nutting's *Typoon.*

FREEMAN, Ira Henry, *White Sails Shaking* (New York: Macmillan, 1948).
Some superficial excerpts from a few well-known voyages.

GARRETT, Alastair (ed.), *Roving Commissions* (London: RCC Press, Royal Cruising Club of London, no date).
Annual collection of cruising logs by members of the most prestigious cruising club in the world, with the possible exception of America's own CCA.

GATTY, Harold, *The Raft Book* (New York: George Grady Press, 1943).
This little jewel is now extremely rare, although hundreds of thousands of copies were printed during World War II in various editions. It was designed as a handbook for survival in the days when American ships and airplanes were being sunk and shot down by the hundreds. Gatty, who gained fame in the 1930s as navigator on the Post-Gatty round-the-world flight, was a student of oceanography as well as a navigator, with particular interest in the ways of the ancient Polynesian seafarers. He compressed into one pocket-sized volume an astonishing amount of lore of the sea, sky, and island life, and how to find one's way across trackless oceans with only the tools used by the Polynesians. The book contains (at least my edition does, which I acquired while in the navy during the war) fold-out star charts, wind and current charts, and the materials for making navigation tools.
Bombard, in his raft voyage across the Atlantic, cursed Gatty for what he called "inaccuracies." Sir Francis Chichester, who was staunchly naïve about anything American in spite of his worldliness in other areas of thought, claimed Gatty had told him that the book had been privately printed, and some 400,000 copies sold, which would have made the author a millionaire, which may have been true, but the Army-Navy editions alone would have exceeded this.

GERBAULT, Alain, *The Fight of the Firecrest* (New York: Appleton [John de Graff, Inc.], originally published in 1926).
———, *In Quest of the Sun* (New York: Doubleday [John de Graff, Inc.], 1955).
———, *The Gospel of the Sun* (London: Hodder & Stoughton, 1933).
The principal writings of the most famous of the French circumnavigators, which at times become rather tedious when he lapses into his noble savage themes.

GILPIN, Vincent, *The Good Little Ship* (Narbeth, Pa.: Livingston Publishing Co., 1961).
A valuable little book with some startling concepts of seaworthy small-boat design, first published in 1952 with an introduction by the late L. Francis Herreshoff. It is primarily a discussion of the seakindliness and sailing qualities of the *Presto* class offshore boats designed more than seventy years ago by Commodore R. N. Munroe of Coconut Grove, Florida.

GRAHAM, Robert D., *Rough Passage* (New York: John de Graff, 1952; also, Rupert Hart-Davis).
A classic of small-boat voyaging, but not a circumnavigation.

GRAHAM, Robin Lee (with Derek L. T. Gill), *Dove* (New York: Harper & Row, Publishers, 1972).
At last, the book version of the remarkable circumnavigation by a sixteen-year-old California lad in a 24-foot sloop (later replaced by a 33-foot Allied sloop). The original defanged and sanforized version appeared in a series of articles in the National Geographic Society magazine. The book gives Robin's version of how he was almost literally "pushed" from port to port by his ambitious father and the contractual commitments made in his behalf, when all he wanted to do was be with the girl he found in the Fijis. Not a writer himself, Graham had the book "ghosted" by another from transcripts of rambling tape recordings made on the passages, and from the logs. The book suffers from this treatment.

GUZZWELL, John, *Trekka Around the World* (New York: John de Graff, Inc., 1963). (Adlard Coles, Ltd).
An uncommonly good narrative by an uncommonly engaging young Briton, the first Englishman to sail alone around the world, and at the time, in the smallest vessel. His version of the side trip, with the Smeetons on *Tzu Hang*, when they capsized near Cape Horn, is better than the Smeetons', although Guzzwell had the benefit of that version when he wrote his own. Guzzwell, for his age, was an extremely competent and level-minded person, who got on well with everyone, and only lapsed once into the Briton's inevitable snide *non sequitur* about Americans and things American—and in this instance, it probably was a bit of gratuitous revision by some obscure little editor. *Trekka* is one of the best of the modern narratives of circumnavigation, and a pity that it went out of print so soon.

HEATON, Peter, *The Sea Gets Bluer* (London: Black, 1965).
Selections of voyages from some of the author's favorite writer-sailors.

HENDERSON, Richard, *Sea Sense* (Camden, Maine: International Marine Publishing Co., 1972).
Some good advice for those who would venture offshore in small boats, backed up by logic and examples.

HERRESHOFF, L. Francis, *Sensible Cruising Designs* (Camden, Maine: International Marine Publishing Company, 1973).
A collection of some of the old master's finest designs, including the famed *Marco Polo*, *H-28*, *Ticonderoga*, and *Nereia*. Included also, is the unbuilt (as yet) *Ocean Cruiser*, a 49-foot salty ketch, designed originally for William Albert Robinson as the ultimate world cruiser. Robbie later selected the design of *Varua*, by W. Starling Burgess, in which Herreshoff also had a hand.
This was Herreshoff's final literary effort, edited by Roger C. Taylor, and contains the master's last words, which are just as vigorous and pithy as always.

HISCOCK, Eric, *Around the World in Wanderer III* (New York and London: Oxford University Press, 1956).
———, *Voyaging Under Sail*. 1959.
———, *Cruising Under Sail*. 1950.
———, *Beyond the Western Horizon*. 1963.
The earlier books from this prolific writer, who has made a profession of cruising the world's oceans with his wife as first mate, and writing about it. The unquestionable dean of British bluewater yachtsmen, Hiscock is noted for his accuracy and good common sense. Mandatory reading for anyone contemplating cruises off-soundings.

————, *Sou'West in Wanderer IV* (London: Oxford University Press, 1973).

The latest book by this famous authority on world voyaging, and also one of the best. It tells of the trials and tribulations suffered by him and Susan: having their "retirement boat" built in Holland; the latent poor workmanship, inflated prices, and low quality of marine parts and equipment they had to put up with; and the problems they had getting the yacht outfitted and shaken down. The new yacht owner will find a sense of relief in this book, knowing that it happens even to the best of them.

The book also takes the Hiscocks from England, across the Atlantic, to winter in Southern California, next to Hawaii, and then on to New Zealand.

HOLDRIDGE, Desmond, *Northern Lights* (New York: Viking, 1939).

Not a circumnavigation, or even a bluewater voyage, but a gripping narrative of a winter voyage off Labrador in a small boat with a feuding crew. A little-known classic.

HOWARD, Sydney, *Thames to Tahiti* (London: G. Bell & Sons, 1933; also, Rupert Hart-Davis).

A good account of a 12,000-mile, 13-month voyage by the narrator and a friend from London to the Marquesas via Panama in the *Pacific Moon*.

HOWELL, William, *White Cliffs to Coral Reefs* (London: Odhams, 1957).

The often ribald narrative of that irrepressible seagoing dentist, "Tahiti Bill" Howell, on his first bluewater voyage in the Hiscocks' old *Wanderer II*.

HOWELLS, Valentine, *Sailing into Solitude* (New York: Dodd, Mead, 1966).

Often confused with Bill Howell, Howells is a different type of sailor, and a different kind of personality, whose speciality is the transatlantic race.

JOHNSON, Irving and Electra, *Yankee's Wander-World* (New York: W. W. Norton & Co., Inc., 1949).

————, *Westward Bound in the Schooner Yankee*.

————, *Sailing To See*.

————, *Yankee's People and Places*.

Readers of the *National Geographic* magazine will have been exposed to most of this material over the past thirty years or so, and fans will be glad to know that this durable couple is still cruising at this writing in European waters on another *Yankee*.

JOHNSON, Irving, *Shamrock V's Wild Voyage Home* (Springfield, Mass.: Milton Bradley, 1933).

Not so well known, indeed rather rare, is an earlier book by Irving, of ferrying the *Shamrock V* home to England in pre-*Yankee* days, when Johnson was a professional yacht crewman, after this J-boat's unsuccesful try for America's Cup.

JOHNSON, Peter, *Ocean Racing & Offshore Yachts* (New York: Dodd, Mead & Company, 1972).

In spite of the title, anyone contemplating going offshore, or building an offshore cruiser, should have this one. It is filled with details, hard to find elsewhere, on rig, crew selection, gear, life aboard, first aid, and emergency procedures.

KAUFFMAN, Ray E., *Hurricane's Wake* (New York: Macmillan, 1940).
A scarce volume, uncommonly well-written, of one of the most hilarious and ribald circumnavigations ever made by small boat.

KENT, Rockwell, *N by E* (New York: Harcourt, Brace, 193?).
The voyage in the 33-foot cutter *Direction* from Halifax to Greenland, where it was wrecked. A fair account of an amateur voyage to Arctic regions that turned out tragic, but no way as good as that of Major Tilman in *Mischief*. This one, like Kent's other literary efforts, suffers from too much poetical syntax, a common affliction of artist-writers.

KING, Bill, *Capsize* (Lymington: Nautical Publishing Co., 1969).
The story of this British naval hero's adventures in yachting after his retirement from submarine duty in World War II, and especially the design and construction of *Galway Blazer II*, which was an unsuccessful entry in the *Times* Golden Globe Race.

KIRKPATRICK, J. B., *Little Ship Wanderings* (London: Edward Arnold & Co., 1933).
Offshore voyages in small vessels and racing craft.

KLEIN, David and JOHNSON, Mary Louise, *They Took to the Sea: Great Adventures in Small Boats* (New Brunswick, N.J.: Rutgers University Press, 1948; also, Collier Books).
A very good selection of excerpts from bluewater voyagers, with some witty comments and perceptive editorializing. Unfortunately, it is somewhat out of date, as the 1950s and 1960s were yet to come.

KLINGEL, Gilbert C., *Inagua* (London: Readers Union/Robert Hale, 1944).
An obscure account of a voyage to the West Indies on a scientific expedition in an exact copy of Captain Slocum's *Spray*, and the subsequent shipwreck. A valuable source of information for Slocum buffs. The sails, incidentally, were salvaged and sold to Professor Strout, who made the first successful circumnavigation in a *Spray* copy, *Igdrasil*.

KNIGHT, Edward F., *The Falcon on the Baltic* (New York: John de Graff, Inc., 1952).

KNOX-JOHNSTON, Robin, *A World of My Own* (New York: William Morrow & Co., 1970).
The hastily put together account of the first solo, nonstop circumnavigation east-about, by the indefatigable young British merchant seaman in the *Times* Golden Globe Race.

KORIE, Kenichi, *Kodoku: Alone Across the Pacific* (Rutland, Vt.: Tuttle, 1964).
The adventures of a young Japanese singlehander who sailed alone to the United States against incredible odds, including official red tape. He was sort of a Japanese Wrong-Way Corrigan of the sea.

LA BORDE, Harold, *An Ocean to Ourselves* (New York: John de Graff, Inc., 1962).

LESLIE, Anita, *Love in a Nutshell* (London: Hutchinson, 1952).

LE TOUMELIN, Jacques-Yves, *Kurun Around the World* (New York: E. P. Dutton & Co., 1955).

———, *Kurun in the Caribbean* (New York: John de Graff, Inc., 1963).

The principal works of this somewhat starchy French singlehander, which have been translated into English, with, apparently, some liberties taken by the translator.

LEWIS, David, *The Ship Would Not Sail Due West* (New York: St. Martin's, 1961).

———, *Dreamers of the Day* (London: Gollancz, 1964).

———, *Daughters of the Wind* (London: Gollancz, 1966).

———, *We, the Navigators: The Ancient Art of Landfinding in the Pacific* (New York: The Dolphin Book Club, 1973).

The books of the New Zealand-born London doctor, who gave up his practice for bluewater cruising, including a circumnavigation in a catamaran with his second wife and two small daughters, which is the best of them (*Daughters of the Wind*). At this writing, Dr. Lewis was trying to make a solo circumnavigation of the globe at 60° South.

LONDON, Charmian, *The Log of the Snark* (New York: Macmillan, 1916).

LONDON, Jack, *Cruise of the Snark* (New York: Macmillan, 1911).

Accounts of the ill-fated attempts to circumnavigate in one of the worst yachts ever built, by the famous writer and his wife.

LONG, Dwight, *Seven Seas on a Shoestring* (New York: Harper, 1939).

Long was the youngest person to circumnavigate at the time, and his book was a hurriedly written effort to capitalize on it. In spite of its almost painful prose at times, it is a fascinating account by an amateur at both writing and sailing, especially because Long was an incurable tourist and seeker-out of famous people, and gives the reader valuable historical reports on brazen visits (unannounced) to President Herbert Hoover, Martin and Osa Johnson, Zane Grey, Captain Harry Pidgeon, Professor Strout, William Robinson, and Alain Gerbault, and even the legendary Count Luckner, and Alan Villiers. Long was nothing if not a Rotarian.

LOOMIS, Alfred, *The Cruise of the Hippocampus* (New York: The Century Co., 1922).

LUXTON, Norman Kenny (ed. by his daughter), *Luxton's Pacific Crossing* (Sidney, B.C.: Gray's Publishing, Ltd., 1971).

A valuable addition to the Voss legend, compiled from the journals of the "other man" on the famous voyage of the *Tilikum*, by Norman Luxton's daughter, Eleanor Georgina Luxton. Luxton was the young adventurous newspaperman who financed the attempt to outdo Captain Slocum in an Indian dugout canoe, the *Tilikum*. The book purports to be Luxton's "true version" of what happened, and accuses Voss of murdering a later shipmate. A careful analysis of both Luxton's and Voss's accounts sheds little light on what really happened, as both men were disposed to self-exultation and questionable veracity.

Luxton went on to become a local character, businessman, and tourist promoter in Banff, and in later years would not discuss the voyage even with family members, although the journal was preserved obviously for posthumous publication.

MANRY, Robert, *Tinkerbelle* (New York: Harper, 1966).
The story of the Ohio newspaperman who crossed the Atlantic in the 13-foot *Tinkerbelle*, and somehow made it seem like a normal, legitimate voyage, instead of a stunt.

MARIN-MARIE, *Wind Aloft, Wind Alow* (London: Davies, 1947; also, New York: Scribner's, 1947).
A classic from the famous French artist, writer, and iconoclast, whose real name is Marin-Marie Paul Durand-Coupel de Saint-Front, of solo Atlantic voyages in the cutter *Winnibelle* and the motor launch *Arielle*.

MARTYR, Weston, *The Southseaman* (London: Rupert Hart-Davis, 1969).
The tale of two landsick Britishers, working in New York, who go to Nova Scotia, have a 45-foot schooner built for the $6,000 they have saved, and go sailing, winding up in Bermuda where the ship is sold to a rum-runner.
A delightful tale by a widely known yachtsman-writer.

MAURY, Richard, *The Saga of Cimba* (New York: Harcourt, Brace, 1939).
The ill-fated voyage of the 25-foot schooner on a circumnavigation that ended in Suva, by the great grandson of the man who founded the Navy's Hydrographic Office, and one of the most gifted of sea writers. He later became master of steamships.

McMULLEN, R. T., *Down Channel* (London: H. Cox, 1893).
An enduring classic by a British yachtsman of the old school.

MEFFERD, Gerry, *The Cruising Manual* (New York: Whittlesey House, 1941).
The product of Ray Kauffman's partner and mate on the voyage of *Hurricane*, and a scarce item.

MELVILLE, Herman, *Typee* (New York: Wiley & Putnam, 1846).
Few voyagers call at the Marquesas without a copy of this classic as a guide to the islands.

MERRIEN, Jean, *Lonely Voyagers* (London: Hutchinson, 1954). (Also New York: G. P. Putnam's Sons; originally published in France as *Les Navigateurs Solitaires*.)
Stories of Slocum, Voss, Gerbault, Wightman, Ahto Walter, and some of the early stunters, as well as later voyagers like Long, Le Toumelin, and Bardiaux.

MIDDLETON, Empson E., *The Cruise of the Kate* (New York: John de Graff, Inc., 1951).
A recent edition of this famous cruising book.

MOITESSIER, Bernard, *Sailing to the Reefs* (London: Hollis & Carter, 1971). French original version, *Un Vagabond des Mers du Sud* (Paris: Flammarion, 1960).
————, *Cape Horn: The Logical Route* (London: Adlard Coles, Ltd., 1969). French version, *Cap Horn à la Voile* (Paris: B. Arthaud 1957).
————, *The First Voyage of the Joshua* (New York: The Dolphin Book Club, 1973). American version of *The Logical Route*.
The works of France's most famous living sailor, and one of the greatest of all

bluewater voyagers in small boats. Moitessier is also a gifted, if not always accurate writer, and a talented and tireless innovator.

MULHAUSER, G. H. P., *The Cruise of the Amaryllis* (Boston: Small, Maynard & Co., 1925).
Mulhauser died before he finished his book on his return from circling the globe, but it was published anyway by family and friends who filled out the missing chapters with excerpts from Mulhauser's log which were more revealing of his character than his own revised narrative. There are several editions of this book, at least one of which is still in print.

NICOLSON, Ian, *Sea-Saint* (London: Davies, 1957).

NOSSITER, Harold, *Northward Ho!* (New York: Charles E. Lauriat Co., 1937).
A voyage of a 35-foot schooner from Australia to England, one of the first of its kind over this route, with a valuable appendix for any serious bluewater sailor.

NUTTING, William, *The Track of the Typhoon* (New York: Motor Boat, 1922).
The account by the charming, but often bumbling sailor from the Midwest, who became a well-known yachting editor and founder of the Cruising Club of America. On a second voyage, he was lost with all hands off Greenland. Uffa Fox was a member of the crew of the *Typhoon*, which was an apt name considering the weather encountered on this crossing.

O'BRIEN, Conor, *Across Three Oceans* (London: Edward Arnold & Co., 1927).
————, *Deep Water Yacht Rig* (New York: Oxford University Press, 1948).
Two of several books written by this puckish, caustic, and pugnacious Irish sailor and mountain climber. The best one is his *Across Three Oceans*, an account of his voyage to New Zealand to go mountain climbing, which turned out to be a circumnavigation around the three capes, the first time it had been done. A constant experimenter with rigs, some of the conclusions he gave as gospel in his first book were later revised in the second, in the light of later experience.

Crusty and a little arrogant, he did not suffer fools gladly nor unbend his stiff back easily. During the Irish Rebellion he was an arms smuggler with his sister and Erskine Childers, and in World War II was a sub-lieutenant in the British merchant ship service, who made many trips to New York in convoy, and on at least one occasion spent a weekend in Connecticut with William Robinson, who was operating a small shipyard with war contracts—and, incidentally, building his beautiful *Varua* for postwar use.

OFAIRE, Cilette, *The San Luca* (New York: Simon & Schuster, 1935).
A little-known but charming boat of cruising European waters by the author under the pseudonym of Cilette Hofer.

PARKINSON, John Jr. (ed.), *Nowhere Is Too Far* (New York: Cruising Club of America, 1960).
A collection of voyages and other club news, including Blue Water Medal winners to that date.

PETERSEN, E. Allen, *Hummel Hummel* (New York: Vantage Books, 1952).

PETERSEN, Marjorie, *Stornoway, East and West* (New York: Van Nostrand, 1966).
The charming story of Marjorie and Al Petersen's voyages on *Stornoway*, to the Mediterranean and back, after Al's singlehanded circumnavigation and their subsequent marriage.
A letter from them as this is written, dated at Cristobal, Canal Zone, also informed me of another book, *Trade Winds and Monsoons*, also published by Van Nostrand, due to be released, which tells the story of their three-and-a-half-year cruise of the Pacific islands and the Orient.

PIDGEON, Harry, *Around the World Single-Handed* (New York: John de Graff, Inc., 1955). (Originally published by Appleton, 1932).
The account by the most famous singlehander, next to Slocum, in his home-built *Islander*. Pidgeon subsequently made another circumnavigation, and on his third attempt at age seventy-six, was shipwrecked in the New Hebrides.

PINCHOT, Gifford, *To The South Seas* (Philadelphia: The John C. Winston Company, 1930).
The wealthy retired governor, and Secretary of the Interior under Teddy Roosevelt, who is best remembered as an early day conservationist, environmentalist, and ecologist, made his college-days dream come true with a 148-foot three-masted schooner, a large professional crew, and a gang of scientists, on an expedition to the South Pacific. A sort of an early-day Jacques Cousteau, Pinchot was a keen observer, a tireless investigator, and a good writer. His account of the Galápagos Islands, and especially the real story of the ill-fated European settlers, is the best of the lot.

PIVER, Arthur, *Trans-Atlantic Trimaran* (San Francisco: Underwriters Press, 1961).
―――, *Trans-Pacific Trimaran* (Mill Valley: Pi-Craft, 1963).
―――, *Trimaran Third Book* (Mill Valley: Pi-Craft, 1965).
The principal works of the ex-flight instructor and printer who developed the trimaran into a worldwide craze. Although the tri is regarded as the fastest ocean-sailing vessel, Piver's voyages were made no faster than the average conventional hull. He himself went missing off the California coast on a solo cruise on one of his own creations.

PULESTON, Dennis, *Blue Water Vagabond* (New York: Doubleday, 1943).
Wartime publication of the adventures of the English lad who sailed his 30-foot yawl *Uldra* to the United States and then joined the irrepressible Fahnestocks on the *Director* as a crew member.

PYE, Peter, *Red Mains'ls* (New York: John de Graff, Inc., 1961).
―――, *A Sail in a Forest* (London: Rupert Hart-Davis, 1961).
―――, *The Sea Is for Sailing* (New York: John de Graff, Inc., 1961).
The well-known British yachtsman who, with his wife and an occasional crew member, has done a bit of sailing about in an ancient converted cutter.

RANSOME, Arthur, *Racundra's First Cruise* (New York: John de Graff, Inc., 1958). (Originally published by B. W. Huebsch, London, 1923.)
The Baltic cruise by one of the finest of all seafaring writers.

REBELL, Fred, *Escape to the Sea* (London: Murray, 1951).

REISENBERG, Felix, *Shipmates* (New York: Harcourt, Brace & Co., Inc., 1928).

REYNOLDS, Earle, *The Forbidden Voyage* (New York: McKay, 1961).

———— (with Barbara Reynolds), *All in the Same Boat* (1962).

RIGG, Philip, *Southern Crossing* (New York: E. P. Dutton & Co., 1936).
Voyage from Greece to Florida in the 54-foot North Sea pilot boat, *Stortebeker*.

ROBINSON, William A., *10,000 Leagues Over the Sea* (British edition, *Deep Water and Shoal*) (New York: Harcourt, Brace, 1932).
————, *A Voyage to the Galápagos* (London: Jonathan Cape, Ltd., 1936).
Early books by one of the greatest bluewater sailors of all time, and his adventures on *Svaap*, the Alden ketch which was the smallest vessel to sail around the world in those days and was lost finally in the Galápagos Islands after Robinson's ruptured appendix and his subsequent melodramatic rescue by the air and sea forces of the United States, with a running account on the network radio of that day.
————, *To the Great Southern Ocean* (New York: John de Graff, Inc., 1966). (First published by Harcourt, Brace, 1956).
————, *Return to the Sea* (New York: John de Graff, Inc., 1972).
The later books of a mature Robinson on his beautiful yacht *Varua*, first on a eleven-month voyage east from Tahiti along the clipper route to Chile, then north to Panama and back to the Society Islands, during which he encountered his famous survival storm; then subsequent cruises through Polynesia and Melanesia and up to Southeast Asia on semi-scientific expeditions.
His last book is sort of a summing up of the career of this legendary voyager, whose life was a struggle between his staid New England commercial inclinations and his beloved Tahiti, with the latter winning; and how he channeled his tremendous energies and no doubt considerable financial resources into tropical medical research and improvement of the native islander's lot.

ROGERS, Captain Woodes, *A Cruising Voyage Around the World* (New York: Dover, 1970).
A paperback reprint of the most successful British privateering circumnavigation ever made, from 1708 to 1711, during the golden age of discovery and piracy, by one of England's greatest leaders. The voyage is of interest for many reasons, including the fact that William Dampier, who had already made two circumnavigations, was an honored crew member and pilot, and because it was during this voyage that Alexander Selkirk was rescued from Juan Fernández to become a prototype for Defoe's *Robinson Crusoe*. The account of shipboard life, courses sailed, and landfalls made are good reading even today, and shows that times have not changed much after all.

ROSE, Sir Alec, *My Lively Lady* (New York: McKay, 1968).
The account of the second Briton to circumnavigate via the three capes as a senior citizen, and the second to be knighted for doing it.

ROTH, Hal, *Two on a Big Ocean* (New York: Macmillan, 1972).
A professional writer and photographer and his wife, Margaret, purchased a 35-foot fiberglass sloop in British Columbia, outfitted it themselves at a cost of about $25,000 in the late 1960s, and sailed it from San Francisco clockwise around the

Pacific rim, a distance of about 19,000 miles, to win the coveted Blue Water Medal of the cca, and write a profitable book.

The route taken was novel and well-conceived, and they proved themselves competent seamen most of the time, but the narrative has the somewhat contrived and superficial treatment of the effete travel folder, and the photographs distract from the narrative because they have no captions.

The author's comments on selecting, building, and outfitting a yacht for blue-water sailing are well-taken and based upon personal experience—and in a tone that suggests this is the final word.

Considering the route taken, the places visited (i.e., from Polynesia to the Aleutians), and the potential for riproaring adventure, it comes off pretty bland much of the time.

SELIGMAN, Adrian, *The Voyage of the Cap Pilar* (New York: E. P. Dutton & Co., Inc., 1947).
The author, his financée, and her brother buy an old French barkentine at St. Malo, recondition it, and with a crew mostly of amateurs and young adventurers like themselves sail around the world in 1936–1938, arriving back in Plymouth during the days when World War II is brewing, and thus their tale of high adventure and romance becomes lost for the duration. A little-known circumnavigation, one of the last of its kind ever attempted.

SHERWOOD, Martyn, *Voyage of the Tai-Mo-Shan* (London: Geoffrey Bles., 1935).
The story of a voyage from China to England by five naval officers.

SHUTE, Nevil, *Trustee From the Toolroom* (New York: Ballantine Books, 1967).
A novel by the famed British author whose real name was Nevil Shute Norway, an experienced yachtsman who based his fiction on real characters and episodes. Of interest because of the extensive yachting episodes.

SINCLAIR, W. E., *The Cruise of the Quartette* (London: Edward Arnold & Co., 1937).
A voyage in a 60-foot ketch from England to Africa and South America.

SLACK, Kenneth E. *In the Wake of the Spray* (New Brunswick, N.J.: Rutgers University Press, 1966).
An excellent compilation and analysis of all known copies of Captain Slocum's famous sloop, by an Australian Slocumphile who spent years searching the world for clues. The search also turned up much unpublished insight into Slocum and his times. An engineer and amateur yacht designer, Slack painstakingly worked out a new and refined set of the original lines and offsets of *Spray*, as well as many technical charts on aspects of the design. The book also reprints Cipriano Andrade, Jr.'s classic analysis of *Spray* done for *Rudder* in June 1909. Slack's book offers final proof that no lines were actually ever taken from *Spray*, only from the model which had been carved by eye, except for some topwater measurements made by Mower.

SLOCUM, Joshua, *Sailing Alone Around the World* (New York: Century, 1900).
This is the one that started them all. An immortal classic of a middle-aged has-been who refused to knuckle under. It is a true literary masterpiece, an inspiring adventure of personal achievement, and a superb example of understatement.

Many editions have been brought out, and there are usually one or two in print, now that the copyrights have expired.

————, *Voyage of the Liberdade* (Boston: Roberts Brothers, 1894).

An earlier adventure by Joshua, published at his own expense, and little-known except to Slocum buffs, it narrates the building of a 35-foot junk-rigged dory in Brazil and sailing it back to the United States with his family after a shipwreck stranded them.

SLOCUM, Victor, *Capt. Joshua Slocum* (New York: Sheridan House, 1950).

The fascinating life and voyages of Captain Joshua Slocum, written by his oldest son, Victor, shortly before his death, which contains much unpublished material about the old gentleman and the family (and carefully avoids some episodes such as the birth and death of the twins to Virginia while in the Bering). The cover jacket illustration of Josh at the wheel of the *Spray*, running before a fresh wind, is a masterpiece and a collector's item.

SMEETON, Miles, *Once Is Enough* (New York: John de Graff, Inc., 1960).

————, *Sunrise To Windward* (London: Rupert Hart-Davis, 1966).

————, *The Misty Islands* (Lymington: Coles, 1969; New York: John de Graff).

————, *Because The Horn Is There* (Sidney, B.C.: Gray's Pub., Ltd., 1970).

These works of the globe-girdling Brigadier and Beryl Smeeton cover about twenty years of post-World War II voyaging on *Tzu Hang*, including the story of the two capsizings off Cape Horn, and a third successful attempt to double it. Certainly the most remarkable husband-wife team of voyagers in maritime history, who finally gave it up and retired to a moose "ranch" in Alberta. The books are well-written, but at times tend to become stream of thought ramblings that leave out more than is revealed.

————, *The Sea Was Our Village* (Sidney, B.C.: Gray's Publishing Ltd., 1973).

The last and best voyaging book by Miles Smeeton, and how he and his wife, Beryl, came to leave a British Columbia stump ranch, after his retirement from the British army as a brigadier, go to London and, although they had never sailed a boat before, buy the famed *Tzu Hang* and start a 15-year career of world cruising.

In this book, Smeeton reveals much of their motivation (as well as a taciturn Britisher can), and the hilarious account of trying to learn how to handle the big yacht before they started on their first long voyage to British Columbia. Sharp readers will also spot the Smeetons as the prototype for a similar couple in Nevil Shute's last book, *Trustee From the Toolroom*.

SMITH, Stanley and VIOLET, Charles, *The Wind Calls the Tune* (New York: Van Nostrand, 1953). Good salty reading.

STOCK, Mabel, *The Log of a Woman Wanderer* (London: William Heinemann, 1923).

Ralph Stock's sister, "Peter," gives her version of the escapades of the *Dream Ship*.

STOCK, Ralph, *The Cruise of the Dream Ship* (London: William Heineman, 1921, 1922, 1923, 1927, 1950).
First of the post–World War I escape voyages, intended to be a circumnavigation, until a wealthy planter bought out from under the owner, his sister, and their friend. Up until then, it is a delightful account of a couple of war-weary veterans and a girl named "Peter," who were trying to get as far from the sound of guns as possible. Not very factual, but the author, who was a professional writer, shows flashes of deep perception at times, and at no time did the three take themselves seriously.

It was upon Stock's return and purchase of a new dream ship, that Alain Gerbault, while visiting aboard, spotted the *Firecrest* nearby, bought it, and began his legendary career.

STREET, Donald M., Jr., *The Ocean Sailing Yacht* (New York: W. W. Norton & Company, Inc., 1973).
A complete and fascinating compendium on how to rig, outfit, and handle a bluewater sailer, by an experienced and competent professional. A bit imperious at times, and has an occasional obvious error in editing, but a salty and useful reference to have around.

TABARLY, Eric, *Lonely Victory* (New York: Clarkson Potter, Inc., 1966). (First published in France as *Victoire en Solitaire*).
France's most aloof lone-hander, who has been called by some the world's best solo sailor, tells how he won the Singlehanded Transatlantic in *Pen-Duick*, first of a series of revolutionary trimarans.

TAMBS, Erling, *The Cruise of the Teddy* (New York: Harcourt, Brace, 1934).
The old favorite of bluewater buffs, by a professional writer who blundered around the globe in the early 1930s, acquiring a family and experience on the way. His first Colin Archer was wrecked on the coast of New Zealand; his second pitchpoled in the Atlantic with the loss of one man.

TANGVALD, Peter *The Sea Gypsy* (New York: John de Graff, 1966.)
A little Norwegian with a big ego tells how he did it.

TATE, Michael, *Blue Water Cruising* (New York: John de Graff, Inc., 1964).

TELLER, Walter Magnes, *The Search for Captain Slocum: A Biography* (New York: Scribner's, 1956).
———, *The Voyages of Joshua Slocum* (New Brunswick, N.J.: Rutgers University Press, 1958).
The principal works of Slocum's best biographer to date, with much new material for the Slocum buff, including some of the captain's earlier adventures, and recently discovered correspondence.

TILMAN, H. W. *Mischief in Patagonia* (New York and London: Cambridge, 1957).
———, *Mischief Among the Penguins* (Chester Springs, Pa.: Dufur, 1961).
———, *Mischief in Greenland* (New York: John de Graff, Inc., 1964).
———, *Mostly Mischief* (London: Hollis & Carter, 1966).

————, *Mischief Goes South* (London: Hollis & Carter, 1968).
————, *In Mischief's Wake* (London: Hollis & Carter, 1971).
The nautical works of Major Tilman, a prolific writer and famed mountain
climber, who got interested in yachting and continued his adventures on the
bluewater. His are the best adventure books in the English language.

TOMALIN, Nicholas and HALL, Ron, *The Strange Last Voyage
of Donald Crowhurst* (New York: Stein and Day Publishers, 1970).
A thoroughly documented and clinical analysis of the rise and fall of a brilliant
young man who sought to win fame and fortune in the *Times* Golden Globe
Race by cheating, and ended by committing suicide. Ironically, the 243 days that
Crowhurst tooled around the Atlantic in his trimaran until his mind and spirit
broke, would have won him the prize had he spent the time legitimately compet-
ing with the others. Also ironically, it was Crowhurst's false position reports
that prompted Nigel Tetley to push his trimaran beyond endurance and sink
her almost within sight of victory.
Anyone contemplating long ocean passages alone should read this book first.

TOMPKINS, Warwick M., *Two Sailors, and Their Voyage Around
Cape Horn* (New York: The Viking Press, 1939).
Best-known narrative of bluewater sailing by this famous yachtsman of the 1930s,
who also wrote *Fifty South to Fifty South, Coastwise Navigator,* and *Offshore
Navigator.* Tompkins was the first of the share-the-expense sailing ship operators,
and the model for the Irving Johnsons and their seven circumnavigations. In fact,
the Johnsons met on *Wander Bird,* when Irving was a professional crewman, and
Electa was a guest. The two sailors in the book, which was written as a juvenile,
were, of course, Tompkins' two children. One of them, "Commodore," told me
in a recent letter that they had never actually made a circumnavigation, although
their voyages took them to many parts of the world. The *Wander Bird* was the
Tompkins' home, as well as cruise ship, for years.

TROBRIDGE, Gerry, *Conversation With a World Traveler* (New
York: Seven Seas Press, 1971).
A brief outline story told in third person by the man who bought Trobridge's
White Seal, the story of a six-year circumnavigation beginning in South Africa
in a homemade steel version of John Hanna's *Carol* ketch.

URIBURU, Ernesto, *Seagoing Gaucho* (New York: Dodd, Mead,
1951).
The story of an Argentinian diplomat stationed in the U.S. during World War
II, who longed for a ship of his own, and finally got home to Buenos Aires where
Manuel Campos (who had built Dumas's *Legh II*), designed for him a Colin
Archer-type 50-foot ketch, in which with three fellow *bon vivants,* he sailed
around the rim of the Atlantic. It is written in a rather spontaneous "me" style,
that is tedious at times (probably by a tipsy ghost), but the appendix is extensive and informative for outfitting a boat of this size on a long voyage.

VILLIERS, Alan, *Monsoon Seas: The Story of the Indian Ocean*
(New York: McGraw-Hill, Inc., 1952).
A narrative history of the Indian Ocean and its people and ships from before
Marco Polo to present time, written in a fascinating way by the well-known square-
rigger sailor and sea writer. Other books by Villiers, such as *Cape Horn* and
Sons of Sinbad, would be valuable to any voyager's library.

VOGEL, Karl Max, *Aloha Around the World* (New York: Putnam, 1922).
The story of a circumnavigation in the 130-foot bark *Aloha*, which is dull reading at times, but is a classic example of how they did it before the days of income taxes.

VOSS, John C., *The Venturesome Voyages of Captain Voss* (New York: C. E. Lauriat Co., 1926 [also de Graff]).
A rare and valuable book, especially in the early editions, it is a classic of small-boat seamanship and heavy weather sailing by an undisputed expert whose veracity has long been unfairly questioned. Regardless of whatever else he was, Voss was a real man and a superb seaman. He and Luxton were the second ones to attempt a circumnavigation, after Slocum, in the Indian dugout *Tilikum*. Now, almost three quarters of a century after it happened, one can compare this book with Luxton's version (see *Luxton's Pacific Crossing*).
The book also narrates some of Voss's other voyages, and his comments on the use of sea anchors and other techniques are as good as anything available today. Most modern writers who deprecate Voss never actually tried his methods, or at least gave them an honest test.

WALTER, Ahto and OLSEN, Tom, *Racing the Sea* (New York: Farrar & Rinehart, 1935).
Mostly the story of Ahto Walter, one of the least-known and most resourceful of bluewater sailors, and his many crossings of the Atlantic.

WEINS, Herold J., *Pacific Island Bastions of the United States* (New York: Van Nostrand, 1962).
An excellent outline history and political discussion of the Trust Territories administered (often badly) by the United States since World War II. Anyone visiting this part of the world would find this the best and quickest briefing possible.

WELLS, De Witt F., *The Last Cruise of the Shanghai* (New York: Minton, Balch & Co., 1925).
The elusive *Shanghai* keeps cropping up in many of the voyaging books of the 1930s. This book tells the story of the 41-foot yacht after it was sailed from China to Denmark, and purchased by Wells for a voyage along the Viking track, only to be wrecked in Nova Scotia.

WHARRAM, James, *People of the Sea* (Harrow, Middlesex: Sun & Health, 1965).
The catamaran and its voyages, by the well-known designer and multi-hull sailor.

WHELPLEY, Donald A., *Weather, Water, and Boating* (Cambridge, Md.: Cornell Maritime Press, Inc., 1961).
One of the best books on the subject available, by a veteran Navy meteorologist, it gives one a good understanding of the workings of wind and waves at sea.

WIBBERLEY, Leonard, *Toward a Distant Island* (New York: Ives Washburn, 1966).

WIELE, Annie Van de, *The West in My Eyes* (New York: Dodd, Mead, 1956).
Good account of *Omoo* and her circumnavigation by the most famous Dutch couple.

WIGHTMAN, Frank A. *The Wind Is Free* (New York: John de Graff, Inc., 1955). (Rupert Hart-Davis, 1949).

————, *Wylo Sails Again* (New York: John de Graff, Inc., 1955). Engaging accounts of the voyages in *Wylo*, which Wightman built on the lines of Pidgeon's *Islander* (neé *Seabird*) in South Africa. A rebel and iconoclast, Wightman's personal philosophies get a little tedious at times, but his experiences with this type vessel are informative and interesting.

WILLIS, William, *The Gods Were Kind* (New York: E. P. Dutton & Co., 1955).

————, *An Angel on Each Shoulder* (New York: Meredith, 1967). Books of the well-known senior citizen stunter who finally went missing.

ZANTZINGER, Richard, *Log of the Molly Brown* (Richmond: Westover Publishing Company, 1973).
A recent circumnavigation by a middle-aged swinger who is lots of fun, although a bit tipsy at times. This is how it was done in the seventies.

Tzu Hang, 185–93, 289, 292, 294, 349–50, 357, 377, 378, 423–24, 448n, 452n–54n, 464n

Uriburu, Ernesto C., 374, 449n

Vagabond, 396
Valkyries, 370
Van der Meer, S. M., 184
Van de Wiele, Annie, 348–50, 409, 450n, 454n, 464n
Van de Wiele, Louis, 348–50, 374, 409, 450n, 454n, 464n
Varian, George, 10
Varua, 74, 88, 96–98, 231, 238, 441n, 452n, 460n
Vencia, 238
Viator, 164
Victress, 250, 267–73, 326
Viking, 181, 345–46, 374, 464n
Villiers, Alain, 106, 113, 136, 445n
Vincent, S. A., 24
Viva, 124
Vivid, 40
Voss, John Claus, 15–26, 48, 61, 78–79, 398, 401, 410, 433n–35n, 443n, 448n

Wagnalls, Adam, 9
Wagnalls, Mabel, 9
Wagner, Rudi, 398
Wahlen, Rudolph, 52
Waikiki Surf, 325
Wakelam, Ann, 238
Wakelam, Henry, 236, 238
Walker, Virginia, 12–13
Wallerand, Yves, 250
Wallin, William, 396
Wanda, 236
Wanderbird, 140–43, 406
Wanderer, 179–84 287, 356, 374, 387, 390, 424, 447n, 451n–52n
Washington, 12
Waterhouse, Colin, 277
Watson, Bill, 405
Watts, Frederick, 394
Watts, J. Murray, 195
Wave Chief, 257
Weagent, Carl, 372
Weld, Bill, 99, 104–5

Wells, F. DeWitt, 395
Wells, Jim, 148
Wentzel, Roland, 144
Weol-Mi, 382
West, Daniel T., 94, 446n, 447n
Westwind, 206
Whall, Andy, 192, 405
Whisper, 376, 379
White, Sallie, 96
White Seal, 195–200, 216, 452n
Whoolara, 383
Widgee, 384
Wightman, Frank, 410–11
Wild Rose, 417–18, 425, 429–31
Wilful, 40
Williams, Art, 147
Williams, Roger, 200
Williamson, Dan, 58–59
Winchester, Capt. Joe, 19, 61
Windsong, 398
Windward Passage, 459n
Winnibelle II, 373
Wolman, Eric, 148
Wood, Fred, 398
Wood, Henry A. Wise, 370
Worth, Claud, 73, 370, 437n
Wright, George, 191
Wright, John, 148
Wright, Willoughby, 90–91
Wylo, 411
Wyoming, 64

Xora, 17, 23

Yankee, 124, 127, 142–50, 167–69, 214, 220, 393, 444n, 447n, 449n
Yankee Doodle, 381
Yarnell, Rear Adm., 104
Yeomans, Bill, 142
Young, Norman, 293
Young, Terry, 149

Zantzinger, Richard, 340, 361–65, 397, 410, 465n
Zarathustra, 351–53
Zarefah, 40
Zelee, 105
Zenker, Hein, 294–95
Zenker, Siggi, 294–95